D1272999

80°

U S S R

60°

ENGLAND

GER-
MANY

40°

FRANCE ITALY

Azores
(PORTUGAL)

A T L A N T I C

Norfolk · Bermuda(Br.)

Canaries
(SPAIN)

20°

Bahamas
(Br.)

Guatanamo Bay

Virgin Is.

maica
(Br.)

Puerto
Rico

Cape Verde Is.
(PORTUGAL)

Castries
(Br.)

I N D I A N

nal

LIBERIA

Equator

60°       30°       0°       30°       60°       90°

O C E A N

O C E A N

20°

40°

60°

80°

INSTITUTE OF INTERNATIONAL STUDIES
YALE UNIVERSITY


The Far Eastern Policy of the United States

*The Yale Institute of International Studies was organized in 1935 for the purpose of promoting research and post-graduate training in the field of international relations. Although concerned with all aspects of this broad field, its research program is devoted primarily to studies designed to clarify contemporary problems in the foreign policy of the United States.*

*Nicholas J. Spykman,* Director

# The
# Far Eastern Policy
# of the United States

BY A. WHITNEY GRISWOLD

ASSISTANT PROFESSOR OF GOV-
ERNMENT AND INTERNATIONAL
RELATIONS, YALE UNIVERSITY

Harcourt, Brace and Company, New York

COPYRIGHT, 1938, BY

HARCOURT, BRACE AND COMPANY, INC.

*Designed by Robert Josephy*

PRINTED IN THE UNITED STATES OF AMERICA

# ACKNOWLEDGMENTS

I wish to acknowledge with thanks the many courtesies for which I am indebted to Tyler Dennett, Philip C. Jessup, Henry F. Pringle, Thomas LaFargue, Charles N. Spinks, T. A. Bailey, Cyril Wynne, Alfred E. Hippisley, S. Dillon Ripley, Major General Preston Brown, Major General William S. Graves, Arnold Wolfers, Frederick S. Dunn, Edwin Borchard, Kenneth S. Latourette, George Vernadsky, Russell G. Shiman, Timothy T. G. Mar, and the staffs of the Sterling Memorial and Sterling Law Libraries at Yale, of the Division of Manuscripts of the Library of Congress and of the Library of the Department of State. The editors of the *Yale Review* kindly permitted me to incorporate material that had appeared in the *Review*. I am also indebted to the following publishers for permission to quote from books of their imprint: Doubleday, Doran, for *Woodrow Wilson and World Settlement* by Ray Stannard Baker and *An American Diplomat in China* by Paul S. Reinsch; Harper Brothers, for *The Far Eastern Crisis* by Henry L. Stimson; Little, Brown, for *The Interest of America in Sea Power, Present and Future* by A. T. Mahan; The Macmillan Company, for *A Life of Joseph Chamberlain* by J. L. Garvin and *Willard Straight* by Herbert Croly; Frederick A. Stokes Company, for *Powerful America* by E. J. Young. I am particularly grateful to my wife for helping me with the proofs; to Mrs. W. W. Rockhill for placing her husband's papers at my disposal; to Samuel F. Bemis for his instruction; to Nicholas J. Spykman for his criticism; and to the Yale Institute of International Studies for the opportunity to write this book.

A. WHITNEY GRISWOLD

# CONTENTS

# CONTENTS

The Far Eastern Policy of the United States

# I. New Frontiers in Asia

THE year 1898 was a dramatic turning point in American history. To contemporaries of a prophetic turn of mind it was evident that the War with Spain had opened new vistas of national achievement not to be realized in their lifetime. No one expressed this *fin de siècle* mood more poignantly than the sensitive Henry Adams. From England, where he had smelt the battle distastefully from afar—where, aloof from the martial passions of his countrymen, he had beguiled the summer with lawn parties and fine conversation in the company of Ambassador John Hay—Adams wrote his friend William Rockhill in October, 1898, that "the task of converting our old Mississippi-raft of a confederate government into a bran-new [sic] ten-thousand ton, triple-screw, armored, line-of-battle ship, is the work of a hundred years. I do not care to open a chapter that I cannot close, or to assist, or to resist, a movement which concerns only another generation. They are old enough and eager enough to manage their own affairs." [1] Truly, in 1898, American diplomacy departed from the traditions of one century and assumed the obligations of another.

Had the War with Spain gone no further than the crusade to liberate Cuba the change would not have been so momentous. But it did go further. It was carried beyond those continental boundaries envisioned in Washington's Farewell Address, beyond the popular conception of the Monroe Doctrine and Manifest Destiny; beyond, even, the seemingly inevitable assertion of American supremacy in the Caribbean, and the long-pending annexation of Hawaii. Amid the clash of arms the Philippine Archipelago became an American colony. These islands, lying some six hundred miles

[1] Adams to Rockhill, October 31, 1898. Rockhill papers.

3

off the Chinese coast, bore no conceivable relation to American
supremacy in the Caribbean, much less to the continental security
of the United States. With their annexation the United States
emerged from its habitual, self-sufficient abode in the Western
Hemisphere and entered the limitless realm of world politics,
naval rivalry, and imperial dominion. A step so unprecedented
could not have failed to influence the character of American diplomacy in every quarter of the globe, and nowhere more profoundly than in that which included the Philippines.

For a hundred years the United States had conducted its relations with the countries of the Far East according to rules and
principles that were mainly the product of nature. The excessive
remoteness of Eastern Asia as well as the vast dimensions of that
region made for perpetual competition among its Western exploiters. China, the principal object of their interest, was too far away,
too huge and too amorphous to be brought under the domination
of any single Western power. If Siam and Korea were to a certain
extent exceptions to this rule, they were also of minor importance
in the political history of the Far East. The insularity of Japan
had much the same effect as the bulk of China. The racial and
cultural strangeness of the peoples of Eastern Asia combined with
the geographical situation of their countries to make that region
a remote and dangerous frontier of Western enterprise. But only
when native uprisings compelled the Westerners to choose between
hanging separately and hanging together was there any real co-
operation among them.

Into this competition the United States had been drawn by its
traders and missionaries. New England merchantmen had found
their way to Chinese ports late in the eighteenth century. In 1853
Commodore Perry, advance agent for American commerce, had
introduced Japan to the modern world. Missionaries had not been
long in following traders to both countries. Diplomatic rules and
precedents conceived in the interests of these two groups had
slowly accumulated, to form, in 1898, a well-defined Far Eastern

policy. The United States extended the same diplomatic protection to its citizens in the Far East as it did in every country in the world. Only the protective measures were peculiar to the region. American gunboats patrolled Chinese rivers and coastal waters as a deterrent to anti-foreign outbreaks; and, in common with other Western powers, the United States enjoyed extraterritorial rights in each of the Far Eastern countries.[1] Because their proselytizing made them the most frequent victims of native violence, missionaries were among the principal advocates of these forms of protection. Even so, evidence is not lacking to show that the American Government made use of them with reluctance. There are not a few cases on record in which an American carried the Gospel into hostile native areas against the express warnings of American consular and diplomatic officials.[2] When the American Legation in Japan was burned the United States participated half-heartedly in the famous allied punitive expedition that bombarded Shimonoseki (1864), accepted its share of the indemnity in bad conscience and ultimately remitted it to Japan.[3]

The large majority of Americans in Eastern Asia, however, had gone out there to make money rather than to preach the gospel. It was for the means by which their interests were safeguarded that America's Far Eastern policy was chiefly significant. Since the first Oregon fur was bartered in Canton, American business men in the Far East had sought the same equality of opportunity, the same protection against unfair competition as they demanded at home. The Department of State had early adopted the practice

[1] By a series of treaties of 1894 the powers relinquished this right in Japan; but the treaties were not to take effect until 1899.

[2] For example, the Chiang Pei Ting mission riot, March 15, 1898, and settlement, *Papers Relating to the Foreign Relations of the United States, 1896-1922* (hereafter referred to as *For. Rel.*), 1898, 191-199. The American Minister to China, Mr. Denby, had warned missionaries not to take up property in the vicinity in which the riot occurred. Almost any volume of *Foreign Relations* from 1861-1900 recounts similar episodes.

[3] Dennett, Tyler, *Americans in Eastern Asia*, 400-401; Treat, Payson J., *Diplomatic Relations between the United States and Japan*, I, 220-238; II, 174.

of insisting on unqualified most-favored-nation treatment for American commerce in and with each Far Eastern nation. This meant simply that American traders should enjoy rights and privileges equal to those embodied in the most favorable terms granted to any of their competitors. Here again was a universal axiom of American diplomacy. Only the phrase by which it was to become identified in the Far East—the open door policy—made it peculiar to that region. The open door meant, from the very beginning, the open door to equal commercial opportunity *via* the most-favored-nation clause. It first became the rule of America's Far Eastern policy, at the instance of the Chinese themselves, in 1842, when Commodore Kearny negotiated a most-favored-nation agreement with the governor of Canton. The Chinese felt that to grant equal terms to all foreign nations would prevent exclusive exploitation by any one. Two years after the conclusion of Kearny's agreement the American diplomat Caleb Cushing formalized this policy in the Treaty of Whanghia.[1] Thenceforward the open door to equal commercial opportunity was the cardinal principle of America's Far Eastern policy.

The open door was the chief objective of American diplomacy in the Far East in 1898. The chief means to that end was respect for the territorial integrity of the Far Eastern nations and detachment from their politics. Not being able to afford fleets and naval bases in Far Eastern waters, the United States sought to win by propitiation what Europe extorted by force. To be sure, the most-favored-nation clause and the right of extraterritoriality permitted the United States to share and defend the commercial privileges Great Britain and France had had to achieve by the bayonet. But whereas the European nations carved out spheres of influence and territorial concessions on the continent, and would have liked to do the same in Japan, the United States denied itself this type of concession in either country (as in Siam and Korea) and fostered

[1] Dennett, 108 ff.

the progress of both towards autonomy and power.[1] Thus it enjoyed the confidence of each and in each, for a long time, a moral
ascendancy over all other nations. It should be noted that up to
1898—indeed to 1900—the American policy of respect for the
territorial integrity of the Far Eastern nations had the effect of a
purely self-denying ordinance. It did not enjoin on the United
States the obligation of defending this territorial integrity from
others. The United States was thus able to keep free of serious
involvement in the politics of Eastern Asia.

It should be observed, however, that the character of the treaty
rights enjoyed by American citizens in China necessarily placed
American diplomacy in that country on a different basis from
American diplomacy in European countries. In Germany, for example, there was no such irregular competition for special privileges as China's weakness and lack of complete autonomy invited.
Foreigners in Germany, Americans among them, were subject to
the jurisdiction of German courts. Such claims to political or economic advantages as their governments sought to establish were
adjusted according to the sovereign discretion of the German Government. Thus a great deal of the international jockeying and
bickering that was the rule in China was eliminated, or confined
within formal limits; and, in consequence, the chances of political
involvement growing out of the routine diplomatic protection of
American nationals in that country were fewer than was the case
in China. The principles observed by the United States in extending this protection to its nationals and treaty rights in China were
the same as those which governed its relations with other countries.
It sought no more than commercial—not political—opportunities
equal to those enjoyed by most other governments in China.

[1] Already the established rule of American diplomacy in the Far East, the principle of respect for the territorial integrity of China was expressed in treaty form
in the Burlingame Treaty of 1868. Cf. Dennett, 378 ff. American adherence to
this principle in Japan was an important factor in that country's rise to power
without the alienation of any of its territory. See Treat, *op. cit.*, esp. Vol. II,
*passim.*

Nevertheless, in the implementation of these principles it entered into, in spite of itself, political relationships that it eschewed in other parts of the world.

The restriction of Oriental immigration had become an American objective by 1898. Chinese coolies had been imported in considerable numbers to help build the transcontinental railways and to supply the demands of the Pacific coast for cheap labor. With the passing of the labor shortage Congress had suspended the immigration of Chinese laborers for ten years (1882), a restriction renewed for another ten years by a treaty with China in 1894. Similar difficulties with Japan were shortly to follow. Immigration was not a major issue between the United States and the Far Eastern nations in 1898, but restricting it was definitely a principle of American diplomacy.

By 1898, then, the modern Far Eastern policy of the United States had all but crystallized. Its fundamental aim was commercial, not political. Equal commercial opportunity for Americans; no territorial concessions for the United States; a strong Eastern Asia to resist a designing Europe; restriction of Oriental immigration into the United States; peace, amity, trade—these were its objectives. Let us now consider, first, to what extent they entered the calculations of the men who planned and executed the annexation of the Philippines and, second, how they were affected by that annexation.

Manifestly the War with Spain was not undertaken in the interest of America's diplomatic stakes in Eastern Asia. Business groups were for the most part strongly opposed to the war,[1] and it is safe to say that the handful of Americans engaged in commerce with the Far East at first saw no connection between *Cuba Libre* and the open door in China. Neither did the American people as a whole. On the other hand, the imperialist currents so strong in

[1] Cf. Pratt, Julius W., "American Business and the Spanish-American War," *American Historical Review*, XIV, 162-201; same author, *Expansionists of 1898,* Ch. VII.

Europe at the time had begun to be felt in the United States ten years before the sinking of the *Maine*. A protracted dispute with Great Britain and Germany over the partitioning of Samoa, which had begun in the 'seventies, had taken on new importance. So had the possible annexation of Hawaii, contemplated with increasing seriousness since 1854, and now a prominent issue in party politics. "Our nation," proclaimed the New York *Commercial Advertiser* in 1893, "stands on the threshold of a new policy as surely as it did in 1803, when Jefferson annexed Louisiana and the United States realized that it must govern it." [1] From about 1890 until the outbreak of hostilities with Spain similar expressions were not uncommon in the pages of the press and in the halls of Congress.

Not only were such thoughts stirring, but they had found a native prophet. In 1890 Captain Mahan of the United States Navy had published *The Influence of Sea Power upon History*, the first of a long series of books that were to earn him the reputation of foremost naval strategist of the world. By the time of the Spanish War he had been lionized by Queen Victoria and the British Cabinet, the Kaiser and Admiral Togo were among his disciples, and he had been thrust into the oracular role expected of such persons by the American public.[2]

The books of this pedantic sailor did not start the race for naval supremacy and colonial empire or propel the United States into taking part in it. Like most popular oracles, Mahan merely rationalized what he saw already in progress around him. He hastened, rather than molded, the future; he helped prepare the minds of his countrymen for an adventure that many of them already ap-

[1] Pratt, "The 'Large Policy' of 1898," *Mississippi Valley Historical Review*, XIX, 229.
[2] For estimates of Mahan and his work see Taylor, Charles, *The Life of Admiral Mahan*; Langer, W. H., *The Diplomacy of Imperialism*, II, 418 ff.; Pratt, *Expansionists*; Millis, Walter, *The Future of Sea Power in the Pacific*; Beard, Charles, *The Idea of National Interest* and *The Open Door at Home*; Dennett, Tyler, "Mahan's 'The Problem of Asia,'" *Foreign Affairs*, Vol. XIII, 464-472; and the forthcoming study of Mahan by Capt. W. D. Puleston, U.S.N.

peared to be vaguely anticipating. By preaching the glories of the British navy, naval bases and colonial dominion he whetted American appetites that were suddenly, and unexpectedly, to be satisfied under cover of a humanitarian crusade in Cuba.

"Comparative religion teaches that creeds which reject missionary enterprise are foredoomed to decay," he had written in 1893. "May it not be so with nations? Certainly the glorious record of England is consequent mainly upon the spirit, and traceable to the time, when she launched out into the deep—without formulated policy, it is true, or foreseeing the future to which her star was leading, but obeying the instinct which in the infancy of nations anticipates the more reasoned impulses of experience. Let us, too, learn from her experience. Not all at once did England become the great sea power which she is, but step by step, as opportunity offered, she has moved on to the world-wide pre-eminence now held by English speech, and by institutions sprung from English germs. How much poorer would the world have been, had England heeded the cautious hesitancy that now bids us reject every advance beyond our shores!" [1]

A few Americans—and these in high places—were ready to play for larger stakes than *Cuba Libre* or supremacy in the Caribbean when war with Spain broke out in 1898.

Perhaps the two most articulate and influential political leaders of this new imperialism were Theodore Roosevelt and Henry Cabot Lodge. Senator Beveridge drummed up popular enthusiasm for their schemes.[2] Various other individuals had a share in their work. But, although neither was a member of the State Department, nor in any official way connected with the diplomatic service, the foreign affairs of the United States in general, and American diplomacy in the Far East in particular would, for the next fifty years, bear the stamp of these two personalities.

[1] Mahan, *The Interest of America in Sea Power, Present and Future*, 50.

[2] Beveridge, like Mahan, drew his inspiration from Great Britain. "Fate has written our policy for us," he told a Boston audience in April, 1898; "the trade of the world must and shall be ours. And we will get it as our mother [England] has showed us how." Bowers, C., *Beveridge and the Progressive Era*, 69.

Life-long friends, and leaders of the Republican Party for a generation, each freely acknowledged his debt to Mahan. "You probably don't know how much your letter has really helped me clearly to formulate certain things which I had only vaguely in mind," Roosevelt wrote the Captain in March 1898. "I think I have studied your books to pretty good purpose." [1] After the War, when Lodge was preparing some articles on certain of its battles and learned that Mahan was doing the same thing, he wrote the latter that he did not think their efforts were "likely to clash in any way, although I think it highly probable that my general conception may accord with your views, for I venture to hope that I have not studied your teachings upon this subject wholly in vain." [2] These men were the authors of what Lodge termed the "large policy," [3]—a policy that included, among other things, the conquest and annexation of the Philippine Islands.

When Roosevelt first conceived the idea of taking the Philippines is not entirely clear. Until 1898 few Americans had ever heard of the islands. Though Mahan had advocated (in *The Interest of America in Sea Power, Present and Future*) the annexation of Hawaii, construction of the Nicaraguan canal, and the acquisition of Caribbean bases, prior to that year, he does not seem to have mentioned the Philippines. The desire for a more spirited competition with Germany, Russia and Great Britain for the markets of the Orient was voiced by Beveridge as early as 1890, but it did not suggest the Philippines to him. [4] Lodge seems likewise to have followed Roosevelt's lead, as did the rest of the country. [5]

Whoever first thought of it, Roosevelt took the initial action that led to annexation.

[1] Roosevelt to Mahan, March 21, 1898. Taylor, *Life of Admiral Mahan*, 174.

[2] Lodge to Mahan, Oct. 19, 1898. *Ibid.*, 117.

[3] Lodge to Roosevelt, May 24, 1898. Lodge, H. C., *Selections from the Correspondence of Theodore Roosevelt and Henry Cabot Lodge*, I, 300; Pratt, *The "Large Policy" of 1898*, and *Expansionists*, Ch. IX.

[4] Bowers, C., *op. cit.*, 57, 67 ff.

[5] Cf. Lodge, *op. cit.*, I, 299; Pratt, *Expansionists*, 231; Pringle, H. F., *Theodore Roosevelt*, 178.

He had held office as Assistant Secretary of the Navy only a short while before he began to press his views on the administration. His friend Lodge had had to pull wires to get him the appointment. Roosevelt, discouraged by McKinley's faint enthusiasm, had at one time abandoned hope of receiving it, for McKinley had hesitated in suspicion of his jingoism. "I hope he has no preconceived plans which he would wish to drive through the moment he got in," the President-elect said to Lodge. Whereat Lodge reassured him, and added, "I have no right to ask a personal favor of you, but I do ask for Roosevelt as the one personal favor."[1] This had transpired at McKinley's home in Canton soon after the election. Within a year, the new Assistant Secretary had justified McKinley's worst fears. By September, 1897, he was urging both the President and Secretary of the Navy Long to launch a naval attack on the Philippines the instant war broke out.[2] He continued to agitate this plan all through the fall.[3]

The White House and Department of State, normally the two executive agents responsible for the formulation of all foreign policy, were too slow and cautious for the Assistant Secretary of the Navy. He proceeded to take matters in his own hands. Roosevelt selected Commodore George Dewey for his instrument, encouraged him to seek political favors, and saw him, as a result, ordered (on the twenty-first of October, 1897) to sail for Nagasaki, Japan, there to assume command of the American Asiatic Squadron.[4] What happened next is an old story. Tension rapidly developed between Roosevelt and his chief over the conduct of affairs in the Navy Department. On Friday, February 25, exhausted by the strain of trying to stave off the war that his sub-

[1] Lodge, *Selections, etc.*, I, 241-242.

[2] Pratt, *Expansionists*, 222, note. Millis, Walter, *The Martial Spirit*, 81; Lodge, *op. cit.*, I, 278.

[3] Pringle, *Theodore Roosevelt*, 178.

[4] Millis, *The Martial Spirit*, 86; Olcott, C. S., *The Life of William McKinley*, II, 39.

ordinate was doing everything in his power to promote, Secretary Long took the afternoon off. In his absence Senator Lodge, by a remarkable coincidence, called at the Navy Department to find Roosevelt in charge. The entry in Mr. Long's diary for the next day records that "the very devil had seemed to possess" the Assistant Secretary. "I find that Roosevelt, in his precipitate way, has come very near causing more of an explosion than happened to the *Maine*. . . . Having authority for that time of Acting Secretary, he immediately began to launch peremptory orders . . . He has gone at things like a bull in a china shop . . ." [1] One of the "peremptory orders" ran as follows:

DEWEY, Hong Kong:
  Secret and confidential. Order the squadron, except Monocacy, to Hong Kong. Keep full of coal. In the event of declaration of war with Spain, your duty will be to see that the Spanish squadron does not leave the Asiatic coast, and then offensive operations in Philippine Islands. Keep Olympia until further orders.
                                                                ROOSEVELT.

Mr. Long promptly rebuked his Assistant for taking "any such step affecting the policy of the Administration without consulting the President" or himself, reminding Roosevelt that he had been intended only "to look after the routine of the office while I got a quiet day off." [2] But the authors of the "large policy" had already started fighting.

Their plans were still dubious. They may have wished at first only to destroy the Spanish fleet in Manila Bay. But it was not long before they were insisting on the retention of the entire archipelago. Hastening away from the Navy Department to lead his Rough Riders to Cuba, Roosevelt left Lodge to watch over their joint enterprise. The two kept in close touch throughout the war. Four days after Dewey's victory Lodge wrote Henry White (May 4) that "we must on no account let the islands go . . . they

---

[1] Pringle, *Theodore Roosevelt*, 178; Millis, *The Martial Spirit*, 111-112.
[2] Millis, *The Martial Spirit*, 112.

must be ours under the treaty of peace . . . the American flag is up and it must stay. . . . We hold the other side of the Pacific and the value to this country is almost beyond imagination." [1] Here was one of the earliest references, characteristically vague, to the possible relation of the islands to American interests in the Far East. Lodge redoubled his efforts and kept Roosevelt posted. By May 24 the Senator thought it safe to say "in confidence but in absolute certainty, that the Administration is grasping the whole policy at last," that unless he was "utterly and profoundly mistaken" it was "now fully committed to the large policy that we both desire." [2] From the army transport that was carrying his command to Cuba, Roosevelt wrote back: "You must get Manila and Hawaii; you must prevent any talk of peace until we get Porto Rico *and the Philippines* as well as secure the independence of Cuba." [3]

As the summer progressed so did the "large policy." President McKinley and Secretary of State Day, as yet undecided about the Philippines, found it impossible to escape the importunities of Lodge. "The whole policy of annexation is growing rapidly under the irresistible pressure of events," the latter exulted on June 15. "You may judge a little of the change when I tell you that Judge Day [the Secretary of State] said to me two or three days ago, 'there is of course no question about Porto Rico, everyone is agreed on that, the only question for us to consider is how much we should do in the Philippines.'" [4] A few days later the Secretary of State dined with the Senator and Captain Mahan. What transpired was duly retailed to Roosevelt: ". . . Mahan and I talked the Philippines with him for two hours. He said at the end that he thought we could not escape our destiny there. The feeling of the country is overwhelming against giving the Philip-

[1] Nevins, Allan, *Henry White*, 136; Pratt, *Expansionists*, 231.
[2] Lodge, *Selections, etc.*, I, 299-300.
[3] Roosevelt to Lodge, June 12, 1898. Lodge, I, 309. Italics inserted.
[4] Lodge to Roosevelt, June 15, 1898. Lodge, I, 311.

pines back to Spain." [1] Nevertheless, both the President and his
Secretary of State remained lukewarm toward annexation. The
most Lodge could report by the middle of July was that McKinley was "worrying over the Philippines—he wants to hold them
evidently but is a little timid about it"; while "Day is very weak
about the Philippines but I am hoping for the best." [2]

The difficulties of overcoming McKinley's caution, enhanced,
apparently, by the State Department, increased rather than dimin-
ished. By August, Lodge had pulled in his horns to the extent of
hoping the Administration "will at least keep Manila, which is the
great prize, and the thing which will give us the Eastern trade,"
and had turned his attention to the personnel of the Peace Commission on which, he said, "everything will depend." [3]

Meanwhile the "irresistible pressure of events" that Lodge had
found of influence on the Administration came more strongly to
his assistance. Dewey's dramatic victory over the Spanish fleet in
Manila Bay (May 1, 1898) seemed to have converted the nation
overnight to the design of taking possession of the islands. Until
the Battle of Manila, Roosevelt, Mahan and Lodge had been far
in advance not only of public opinion, but also of the President
and the State Department. Scarcely had the smoke of the battle
cleared than business, hitherto hostile, or apathetic toward the war,
began to take an interest in the markets of the Far East, and to
petition the President to retain the islands. Memorials poured in
upon the State Department from business groups and chambers of
commerce all over the country, urging the value of the archipelago to the United States especially as the key to the markets of

[1] *Ibid.*, 313. Mahan was then serving on the board of naval strategy in which
capacity it may be supposed he advanced his views on the Philippines subsequently
outlined in *The Problem of Asia*.

[2] Lodge to Roosevelt, July 12, 1898. Lodge, *Selections*, I, 323-324.

[3] Lodge to Roosevelt, August 15, 1898. *Ibid.*, 337. The same idea is expressed
to Roosevelt in *ibid.*, 330, and to Henry White in a letter of August 12, in which
Lodge hoped for the retention of Manila and Luzon. "The other islands are not
so important." Nevins, *Henry White*, 136.

Eastern Asia.[1] It was with cries of "Bridge the Pacific!"[2] ringing
in their ears that the President's peace commissioners departed
for Paris.

The church was likewise inspired. Dewey's triumph created the
inviting prospect of new mission fields in the islands of the southwestern Pacific. American missionaries had long been active in
China and Japan. In China especially their political significance
was great. For nearly a century they had been virtually the sole
interpreters of the Far East to their own countrymen.[3] Almost
without exception, the publications of churches of all denomina-
tions maintaining missions in the Far East came out strongly in
favor of Philippine annexation. There were few discordant voices.
Most of them agreed with the author of *God's Hand in Recent
American History* who wrote: "We have been morally compelled
to become an Asiatic power. . . . Every American missionary in
Asia from whom I have heard in recent months, has thanked God
that the American flag has entered the Far East."[4] On the
strength of this growing public sentiment in favor of annexation,
Lodge and Roosevelt had easier going. It was gradually becoming

[1] Pratt, *Expansionists*, Ch. VII, esp. 266 ff. and 273. In this chapter is incorporated most of his previous essay, *American Business and the Spanish American
War, loc. cit.* Pratt's conclusion, based on an exhaustive study of commercial publications, is that "American business had yielded reluctantly to the necessity of a
war with Spain, forced upon the United States by popular reaction to the dis-
tressing situation in Cuba. It had not foreseen, or if it foresaw it feared, the
colonial responsibilities to which such a war might lead. But when Dewey's dramatic victory on the first of May offered a Far Eastern base from which the
threatened markets of China might be defended, it had gladly accepted the result,
and long before the conclusion of peace with Spain, it was building high hopes
upon the supposed opportunities for trade and exploitation in a string of de-
pendencies stretching from the Philippines to Puerto Rico." *Expansionists*, 278.
Cf. also McKinley papers, Vol. 16, and the interesting unpublished study of
A. A. Greenberg, *Public Opinion and the Acquisition of the Philippine Islands.*
[2] Philadelphia *Press* quoted by New York *Commercial*, May 13, 1898; Pratt,
*Expansionists*, 274.
[3] Cf. Dennett, Tyler, *Americans in Eastern Asia*, Ch. XXIX.
[4] Pratt, *Expansionists*, 298 and Ch. VIII, *passim.*

evident that they could count on wide Congressional support backed by millions of votes.[1]

Still other forces impelled McKinley toward the fateful decision. Not the least of these was the attitude of the powers with which the United States was now associated in the Far East, especially Great Britain, Germany and Japan. From the devious complexity of the relations of these three nations with the United States at the time, a few simple facts emerge. The pivot of their diplomacy was Anglo-German colonial rivalry. Each of these two nations was determined that the Philippines should not go to the other. England made positive efforts to persuade the United States to retain the islands; while Germany's dubious intentions, at various times appearing to contemplate dislodging the Americans, contesting their claim, or attempting to partition the fruits of their victory, contributed to the same end. Japan gave to American ownership her official encouragement, having first served the annexationists as a potential "menace." Undoubtedly these facts counted heavily in the calculations of official Washington.[2]

Great Britain's position at the outbreak of the war was doubtful. She was still involved with the United States over the Venezuela

[1] In this connection it is interesting to recall McKinley's famous explanation (to a delegation of clergymen visiting the White House after the war) as to how he made up his mind to keep the Philippines. He had, he said, "walked the floor of the White House night after night . . . and prayed Almighty God for light and guidance more than one night, and one night late it came to me this way—I don't know how it was, but it came: (1) that we could not give them back to Spain—that would be cowardly and dishonorable; (2) that we could not turn them over to France *sic* or Germany—our commercial rivals in the Orient—that would be bad business and discreditable; (3) that we could not leave them to themselves—they were unfit for self-government—and they would soon have anarchy and misrule over there worse than Spain's was; and (4) that there was nothing left for us to do but to take them all, and to educate the Filipinos, and uplift and civilize and Christianize them, and by God's grace do the very best we could by them, as our fellowmen for whom Christ also died, and then I went to bed, and went to sleep, and slept soundly. . . ." Olcott, *McKinley*, II, 108-111.

[2] In the Senate debates on various resolutions disposing of the Philippines there are frequent references to the dangers of allowing the islands to fall a prey to other interested powers. Cf. *Congressional Record*, 55th Cong., 3rd Session.

boundary. The question of American control of the isthmian canal was plainly upon the diplomatic agenda of the two nations. On these two points, particularly, they were at cross purposes. On the other hand, the increasing pressure of Germany's ambitions, French designs on the Nile Valley, and the Russian menace to the Indian frontier tended to drive England into America's arms. As we shall see in the next chapter, feelers for an understanding with the United States had already been extended. In view of these facts it might seem a foregone conclusion that England would support the United States in the war with Spain from the beginning. But such was not the case. Sir Julian Pauncefote, British Ambassador and dean of the diplomatic corps at Washington, perhaps under the influence of a queen who sympathized with her dynastic relatives in Spain, perhaps yielding to pleas from Austria-Hungary, joined with the representatives of the other European powers in an eleventh hour appeal to President McKinley to avert the war. When this availed nothing, Sir Julian took the initiative in summoning a conference of ambassadors who proceeded to urge their foreign offices by telegraph to join in a moral protest against the war. Balfour, then in charge of the British Foreign Office, was favorably inclined, but the dogged opposition of the Colonial Secretary, Joseph Chamberlain, killed the project so far as England was concerned.[1]

An immediate revision of British policy followed. During the war, through the press [2] as through official acts and assurances, Great Britain left no doubt of her enthusiasm for an American victory and especially for American annexation of the Philippines. Chamberlain campaigned actively for Anglo-American friendship

[1] Garvin, *The Life of Joseph Chamberlain*, III, 296 ff.; Dugdale, Blanche E. C., *Arthur James Balfour*, I, 262 ff.; Rippy, J. F., *The European Powers and the Spanish-American War*, James Sprunt Historical Studies, Vol. 19, No. 2, 22 ff.

[2] The New York *Times* called the British press "unanimous in favor of the United States." Such, with one or two minor exceptions, was actually the case. Reuter, Bertha A., *Anglo-American Relations During the Spanish-American War*, 128-129 and 130-149.

and (he hoped) a political entente. He had the news of the Battle of Manila before McKinley, and was glad of the opportunity to "render a pleasant little service to the United States" by passing it on to Hay, from whom it first reached Washington.[1] After several unmistakable intimations to the same effect, Hay wired the State Department July 28, 1898, "that the British Government prefer [to have us] retain [the] Philippine Islands, or failing that, insist on option in case of future sale." [2] Spring-Rice later admitted acting as the secret emissary of Chamberlain and Balfour to give Hay their approval of American annexation.[3] And finally, the somewhat legendary moral support given Dewey by a British squadron anchored near him in Manila Bay was exploited to the full by the protagonists of Anglo-American solidarity.[4]

Much credit for the improvement in Anglo-American relations during the war undoubtedly belongs to Dewey himself. Besides awakening his own countrymen to their supposed destiny in the

[1] Garvin, *Chamberlain*, III, 301.

[2] Dennett, Tyler, *John Hay*, 191.

[3] *Ibid.*, 280. See also Dennis, A. L. P., *Adventures in American Diplomacy*, 77-88.

[4] After defeating the Spanish fleet, on May 1, Dewey remained in the harbor to blockade Manila while Filipino insurrectionists under Aguinaldo and American troops under General Merritt invested the city from the land. Meanwhile various neutral "observers" had anchored in the harbor, including a British and a German squadron under Captain Chichester and Admiral von Diederichs respectively. Dennett, *Americans in Eastern Asia*, 620; Dennis, *Adventures*, 77 ff. Diederichs allegedly caused Dewey much annoyance by violating the blockade, threatening the insurgents, and communicating with the besieged Spaniards. On August 13, as Dewey was moving up to shell the Spanish forts in conjunction with the assault of troops under Aguinaldo and Merritt, the German commander was alleged to have placed his squadron directly across Dewey's line of fire, from which position he was dislodged by an ostentatious maneuver of Chichester who steamed in between the two fleets. Cf. Dennett, *Americans in Eastern Asia*, 620; Dennis, *Adventures*, 77 ff. A careful study of German and British admiralty records, including the logs of both Diederichs and Chichester has convinced T. A. Bailey that the activities of both were grossly distorted for propaganda purposes. Bailey to author, March 22, 1938, including abstract of the former's article, "New Light on Dewey, von Diederichs, and Chichester at Manila Bay, 1898."

Far East, it is not improbable that his victory suddenly revealed to Great Britain an unexpected way out of an awkward predicament. Nothing short of outright appropriation of the Philippines would have prevented Germany from securing at least a naval base there. Had Britain been forced to make the seizure herself, the effect on her already strained relations with Germany might have proved disastrous. In any event, Great Britain did not relax her efforts to persuade the United States to retain the Philippines and take an active part in the politics of Eastern Asia.

Germany's attitude toward the Spanish-American War, and especially toward American annexation of the Philippines, was far more enigmatical. Alarmed at the outset for the future of the monarchical principle as well as by the increasing cordiality of Anglo-American relations, and the potentialities of American commercial rivalry, Germany was strongly tempted to take part in any joint intervention that held reasonable promise of averting the war.[1] She would not take the lead in this, however. Bülow opposed German participation in Sir Julian Pauncefote's scheme to put moral pressure on McKinley.[2] Throughout the hostilities Germany's official position as a neutral was circumspect. Nevertheless, it was known in the United States that German public opinion favored Spain, while her actions in the western Pacific excited American suspicions.[3]

[1] Cf. *Die Grosse Politik*, XV, esp. 5-24.
[2] Bülow to Kaiser, Apr. 15, 1898, *Die Grosse Politik*, XV, 23-24.
[3] *Die Grosse Politik*, XV, 1-113, has provided the basis for two penetrating studies of this subject, Rippy, J. F., *The European Powers and the Spanish-American War, loc. cit.*, and Shippee, L. B., "Germany and the Spanish-American War," *American Historical Review*, XXX, 754-777. Vagts' version in his *Deutschland und die Vereinigten Staaten in der Weltpolitik*, 1307-1410, overlooks both of these articles, and though infinitely more voluminous, is not so complete as they, particularly on the events in Manila harbor. Dennis, *Adventures*, 76 ff., bases his account primarily on American archives material. See also Langer, *The Diplomacy of Imperialism*, II, 519 ff., who ascribes much of the "almost pathological suspicion of Germany" to the deliberate insinuations of British diplomats "like Spring-Rice."

On May 3, two days after the Battle of Manila, Hay telegraphed Secretary Day from London, warning him on "excellent authority" of German intentions toward the islands, and urging prompt action to forestall them.[1] Hay's strong Anglophile tendencies made him particularly susceptible to British insinuations calculated to deepen American distrust of Britain's great rival. "I have been under great obligation the last few months to Spring-Rice," Hay wrote Lodge toward the end of July, "who knows Germany as few men do and has kept me wonderfully au courant of facts and opinions there. *Voilà l'ennemi* in the present crisis." [2] In October, while the peace conference was in session at Paris, Henry White spent four days golfing with Balfour, who never lost an opportunity to urge American retention of the entire archipelago, and to harp on Germany's "perfect craze" for colonial expansion.[3] The American press made sensations of German activities in the Philippines, provoking journalistic recriminations in Germany and so adding fuel to the fire.[4] It should be remembered that the United States did not make known its intentions regarding the Philippines until several months after Dewey had vanquished the Spanish fleet. During this time the islands remained in the possession of Spain, fair prize or purchase for all comers. The German Foreign Office, influenced as much by its desire to observe a correct neutrality as by the despatches of its diplomatic and consular agents in Hongkong and Manila urging a German protectorate for the islands, finally ordered Admiral von Diederichs to Manila to observe and report developments.[5] His mere presence there was used by both the American and the British press to stir up anti-German feeling in the United States.

The official correctness of German neutrality is therefore somewhat beside the point. By defeating the Spanish fleet in Manila

[1] Dennis, *Adventures*, 76.
[2] Hay to Lodge, July 27, 1898. Dennis, *op. cit.*, 78.
[3] Nevins, *Henry White*, 140.
[4] Shippee, *op. cit.*, 766 ff.; Rippy, *op. cit.*, 31.
[5] Shippee, *op. cit.*, 764-767.

Bay, the United States had staked out a psychological claim to the islands. It had thrust itself into the arena of world politics where it was bound to feel the heat of the Kaiser's aggressive foreign policy in company with Germany's other rivals. If Germany was not neutral toward American annexation of the Philippines, neither was the United States neutral toward German annexation. Consequently it was easy for the United States to discern a lack of neutrality in German motives. Germany's diplomatic attempts to partition the islands, to neutralize them, to obtain "maritime fulcra" in them, were well known to Washington.[1] The long dispute over Samoa (still hanging fire) had revealed the difficulties of partitioning groups of islands so as to leave the United States and Germany close, yet friendly, neighbors. So it was that Germany's designs appeared evil to Americans, for the most part blind to the larger aspects of the situation. They did not see it as the clash of an American imperialism with a German imperialism. They did not realize that the United States was being sucked into the vortex of Anglo-German *Realpolitik*, to the brink of which its own imperialistic ambitions had brought it. Because Germany seemed to want the Philippines, the United States wanted them also. While Great Britain encouraged this desire, Germany's challenge to it was scarcely less influential in crystallizing it into determination.

Japan weighed but lightly in the calculations of Washington. It is true that Roosevelt took up the Kaiser's talk of the Yellow Peril and used it for what it was worth. But Japan was just emerging from the backward nation class herself. Concentrating on preparations for a war with Russia, she was ill disposed, even had she been able to do so, to prevent American annexation of the Philippines. For nearly half a century Japanese-American relations had been cordial. So, although Japan favored sharing in a protectorate over the Philippines in the event that the United States should give them up, she approved American annexation once it

[1] Cf. Shippee, 770-777.

was announced. In fact, Japanese diplomats had freely urged the decision on the United States, preferring that country to any other as a neighbor in the south Pacific.[1] Thus, indirectly as a "Yellow Peril," and directly as a circumspect friend, Japan added her slight influence to that of Great Britain and Germany.

Apart from the vague prophecies of the authors of the "large policy," there was no identification of the Philippines with the Far Eastern policy of the United States prior to, or even immediately after, the Battle of Manila. Just before Dewey's descent upon the luckless Spaniards, the principal European competitors of the United States in China had indulged in a frantic scramble for territorial concessions. Germany had taken Kiaochow on March 6; Russia, Port Arthur and Talienwan March 27; Great Britain, Weihaiwei April 2; France, Kwangchau Bay April 22. The State Department had kept close watch of these events, which seemed to presage the downfall of the Chinese Empire, but which did not prompt the Department to recommend the annexation of the Philippines as a counterstroke.[2] In response to a British suggestion of March 8 that the United States engage with England in the defense of China's territorial integrity, President McKinley declared that he was yet unable to see in the concessions-scramble any jeopardy to American trade.[3] "The public all along the Yangtse are excited over the rumors which reach them that China is to be partitioned . . ." the American Minister to China wrote Secretary

[1] Dennett, Tyler, *Americans in Eastern Asia*, 638; Dennis, *Adventures*, 81, 86; Lowe, James T., "Japan's Offer to Guarantee American Possession of the Philippines," *Far Eastern Review*, April, 1936, 153 ff., publishing despatches from Department of State Archives.

[2] *For. Rel.*, 1898, 182-191. Great Britain later (June 9) extended her holdings at Hongkong to include Deep Bay and Mirs Bay. Dates given are those of the actual signing of leases. Kiaochow was occupied by the Germans November 14, 1897. A Russian fleet was ordered to Port Arthur December 14, though the port was not actually taken over by Russian forces until March 16, 1898. See Gooch and Temperley, *British Documents Relating to the Origins of the World War*, I, 1-3, 22.

[3] Dennett. *Hay.* 285.

Sherman on April 2.[1] But Mr. Sherman on several occasions expressed his indifference to the partitioning of China.[2] He could see in it no reason why American interests should suffer; and he confined his representations to the concession-hunters to inquiries as to what commercial regulations they would establish in their new leaseholds.[3]

Sherman's attitude was not surprising. The combined import and export trade of the United States with China in 1898 amounted to only 2 per cent of its total foreign trade. American finance and industry paid almost no attention to the Chinese market or to the European groups exploiting it.[4] Despite the enthusiasm of business groups engendered by Dewey's victory, the fundamental fact remained that China was a remote and relatively insignificant province of American economic enterprise. Three months after the Battle of Manila a member of the American Legation at Peking wrote that the Chinese "would give us anything, from a loan to a cession of a port if we asked for it; *but our people do not seem to realize the splendid opportunities which are offered.* We now have two of the most important railroad concessions in China. . . . But in both cases it is very doubtful if we will be able to raise the necessary funds. . . ."[5]

In the minds of the framers of the "large policy" themselves

[1] *For. Rel.*, 1898, 194.

[2] Pratt, *Expansionists*, 263 and footnote.

[3] Cf. despatches between Sherman and Hitchcock in the Rockhill papers, discussed in the next chapter.

[4] Since 1860 American trade with China had slowly declined from 3 per cent to 2 per cent of the total American foreign trade, while that with Japan had risen from zero to 2 per cent. Dennett, *Americans*, Ch. XXX.

[5] Squiers to White, August 9, 1898. Vagts, Alfred, *Deutschland und die Vereinigten Staaten in der Weltpolitik*, II, 1038 ff. Italics inserted. Vagts' methodical examination of the economic factors influencing American diplomacy in the Far East at this time (*Ibid.*, 950-1058) has led him to conclude that so far as the United States was concerned capital did not actuate a more aggressive diplomacy, but, on the contrary, diplomacy strove to create an expansion of capital investment.

the wish to take the Philippines appears to have fathered the thought that their annexation was vital to America's Far Eastern policy. Mahan did not begin to "talk the Philippines" in earnest until, as a member of the Board of Naval Strategy, he had become absorbed in planning the strategy of the War with Spain. Even then he seems to have sensed that the burden of proof rested with him, that his doctrines were a radical departure from tradition rather than a fulfillment of it. His writings at the time were filled with deprecations of anti-imperialists "clinging to certain maxims of a century ago." [1] The American "impulse toward expansion which has recently taken so decisive a stride" was to him "but one phase of a sentiment that has swept over the whole civilized European world within the last few decades." [2] Under the impact of this sentiment a conflict had been precipitated within the United States between the old, continental view of foreign policy and a new "long view, raising its vision gradually above the Antilles and the Isthmus" to include "the Pacific, Hawaii, and the beginning of the momentous issues in China and Japan."

It was to such a state of mind that the war with Spain came; and the result has the special interest of showing the almost instantaneous readiness with which a seed of thought germinates when it falls upon mental soil prepared already to receive it. . . . *Though staggered for an instant by a proposition so entirely unexpected and novel as Asiatic dominion*, the long view had done its work of preparation; and the short view, the action necessary at the minute, imposed primarily and inevitably by the circumstances of the instant, found no serious difficulty of acceptance, so far as concerned the annexation of the Philippines— the widest sweep, in space, of our national extension. [3]

It has been said that the annexation of the Philippines was "a continuance of traditional American policy in Asia, for it was exerted in the interest of the open door and of sustaining China,

[1] Mahan, *Lessons of the War with Spain*, 293. Cf. also *Ibid.*, 277-320.
[2] Mahan, *The Problem of Asia*, 4.
[3] *Ibid.*, 7-9. Italics inserted.

yes, sustaining Asia against the aggressions of Europe." [1] To Mahan (and who could speak on the subject with greater authority?) it was a "proposition . . . entirely unexpected and novel." It would seem more reasonable to conclude that the annexation of the Philippines and the desire for a more spirited defense of American rights and interests in China were co-products of the same thing—the "impulse toward expansion which has lately taken so decisive a stride"—rather than that one resulted from the other.

The more the plan to retain the entire Philippine archipelago gathered momentum the brighter the prospects of American supremacy in the markets of Asia held forth by its proponents.[2] These, together with British persuasion, German rivalry, the machinations of Lodge and Roosevelt, the doctrines of Mahan and the growing imperialist sentiments of the voters, gradually convinced the McKinley Administration. The President and his Secretary of State Judge Day (who had succeeded Mr. Sherman April 28) had yielded to the "irresistible pressure of events" to the extent of telegraphing Ambassador Hay in London on June 14 that not all of the islands might be returned to Spain; that no disposition of them was yet possible.[3] However, Lodge's reports to Roosevelt continued unsatisfactory. On September 8 the Senator did not think it was imperative to demand all of the Philippines though he wished to "leave the door open for that if necessary, and certainly take ground against returning to Spain any people whom we have freed, or Manila which was the prize of Dewey's great victory." [4]

[1] Dennett, *Americans*, 631-632.

[2] Cf. Pratt, *Expansionists*, Chs. VII and VIII.

[3] *Ibid.*, 327; Dennett, *John Hay*, 191. Secretary Day had wired Hay June 3 that only "a port and necessary appurtenances" would be retained. *Ibid.*, 190, and Pratt, *Expansionists*, 327.

[4] Lodge urged Roosevelt to incorporate these points in the platform on which he was running for Governor of New York for the good effect he thought it would have "on national opinion and on the action of the Peace Commission." Lodge, *Selections*, I, 343.

Meanwhile the President, with his Cabinet divided, was still unable to make up his mind.[1] He was plainly reluctant to take such a radical step. On July 22 the Spanish Government through the French Ambassador, Cambon, requested his peace terms, and he was forced to reply. The Cabinet Meeting occasioned by this communication lasted several days and resulted in a draft protocol, submitted by Secretary Day, proposing to return all of the Philippine Islands to Spain "except sufficient ground for a naval station." After further debate, in which the cabinet "was about equally divided," and during which "all of the arguments with which the country subsequently became familiar were brought forth in favor of abandoning the islands and restoring them to Spain," the protocol was revised so as to read (Article 3): "The United States will occupy and hold the city, bay, and harbor of Manila pending the conclusion of a treaty of peace which shall determine the control, disposition, and government of the Philippines."[2] The document was signed August 12, the cessation of hostilities immediately proclaimed, and the United States had at last published its formal, however vague, intentions toward the islands. The President's revulsion against acquiring possessions in the Far East had been balanced by his feeling that the people would never be content to give the islands back to Spain. Secretary Wilson (Agriculture) had wanted to keep the entire archipelago for evangelical reasons as did Secretary Bliss (Interior) and Attorney-General Griggs for commercial reasons. Secretaries Long (Navy), Day (State) and Gage (Treasury) had held out for a naval base only. The President had twitted his Secretary of State for only desiring "a hitching post."[3] They had made their compromise purposely ambiguous to see what could be done with it at Paris.

[1] Mr. McKinley is said to have admitted, on hearing of Dewey's victory, that he "could not have told where those darned islands were within 2,000 miles." Pratt, *Expansionists*, 326. Certainly neither he nor Judge Day was a student of the Far East.

[2] Olcott, *McKinley*, II, 61 ff., 73.

[3] Olcott, *op. cit.*, 63.

The American peace commission was overwhelmingly expansionist. Whitelaw Reid was one of the earliest and most outspoken advocates of Philippine annexation. In this he was supported by Senators Davis of Minnesota and Frye of Maine. Secretary Day, who resigned his office to serve on the commission, was a middle-grounder; while Senator Gray was the only uncompromising anti-annexationist of the five.[1] Ambassador Hay was summoned from London August 15 to take Day's place as Secretary of State,[2] and a month later the commissioners embarked for Paris. For a moment the course as well as the conduct of foreign affairs in the United States was in confusion. Anything was possible. "Hay started yesterday for Washington," wrote Henry Adams to Rockhill on September 15. "I went to see him off, and to see whether he had any last words for me. As far as I can see, he goes home without the faintest idea of his position. What sort of control or direction is exercised by anyone at Washington is a mystery. Here is the future Secretary of State crossing the late Secretary and his Peace Commissioners in the middle of the ocean, as though they had agreed to have nothing in common."[3] It is possible that the President saw in Hay a more dependable instrument of annexation than his predecessor. Or it may have been that the new Secretary helped his chief to make up his mind. In any case the despatches from the expansionist peace commissioners, particularly Whitelaw Reid's, added to the various other influences already noted, finally swayed McKinley to demand the cession of the entire archipelago. After a stiff fight, that lasted from October 1, when the conference assembled, to November 28, the Spaniards finally accepted these terms.[4] Senator

[1] Pratt, *Expansionists*, 331-332.

[2] Dennett, *John Hay*, 195. Hay accepted the appointment reluctantly.

[3] Adams to Rockhill, September 15, 1898. Rockhill papers.

[4] Pratt, *Expansionists*, 332-341. Olcott, *op. cit.*, II, Ch. XXVIII. The despatches of the peace commissioners are published in Senate Document 148, 56th Congress, 2nd Session, *Papers Relating to the Treaty with Spain*. The United States agreed to pay Spain $20,000,000 in return and the cession included Guam.

Gray had opposed annexation "in whole or in part" to the bitter end. Day with an equally dogged consistency had favored retaining only Luzon and a few neighboring islands. But the President had listened to Reid, Davis and Frye, reaching his decision on October 26 when Hay's famous wire instructed the commissioners that, "The cession must be of the whole archipelago or none." [1]

From that moment on, the annexation of the Philippines was a major objective of American foreign policy. The decision had been made. It had yet to survive the opposition of the Spanish commissioners, who contested every inch of ground with all the legal and emotional arguments at their disposal. It had yet to pass the Senate. But with the executive branch of the government committed to it, and a clamorous public opinion behind it, its consummation was all but a foregone conclusion. However repulsive the idea of distant colonies may originally have been to the President, he had been rapidly converted. Well before the peace conference assembled he had accepted in principle the cession of at least part of the Philippines, leaving to the conference only the rather academic problem of how much of them to demand. To have taken Luzon, or even Manila, and nothing more, would have been as great a departure from the continental policy of the fathers as was the ultimate decision. [2]

That the American stake in Eastern Asia had entered the final calculations of the President is evident from his instructions to the peace commissioners, issued September 16, 1898. Much may be read between the lines dealing with the Philippines. Having justified the expulsion of Spain from the Western Hemi-

[1] Pratt, *Expansionists*, 338. *Sen. Doc.* No. 148, 35. On October 3, Dewey, who had just returned from Manila, urged McKinley that it was his duty "to keep the islands permanently." Olcott, *op. cit.*, II, 96.

[2] Cf. *Sen. Doc.* No. 148, *passim*. Davis, Frye and Reid, in a wire to Hay of October 25, stated that inasmuch as their instructions called for "retention of at least Luzon, we do not consider question of remaining in Philippine Islands at all as now properly before us." *Ibid.*, 32.

sphere in terms that would have been perfectly familiar to President Monroe, he declared:

The Philippines stand upon a different basis. It is none the less true, however, that, without any original thought of complete or even partial acquisition, the presence and success of our arms at Manila imposes upon us obligations which we cannot disregard. The march of events rules and overrules human action. Avowing unreservedly the purpose which has animated all our effort, and still solicitous to adhere to it, we cannot be unmindful that without any desire or design on our part the war has brought us new duties and responsibilities which we must meet and discharge as becomes a great nation on whose growth and career from the beginning the Ruler of Nations has plainly written the high command and pledge of civilization.

*Incidental to our tenure in the Philippines is the commercial opportunity to which American statesmanship cannot be indifferent.* It is just to use every legitimate means for the enlargement of American trade; but we seek no advantages in the Orient which are not common to all. Asking only the open door for ourselves, we are ready to accord the open door to others. *The commercial opportunity which is naturally and inevitably associated with this new opening depends less on large territorial possessions than upon an adequate commercial basis and upon broad and equal privileges.*

It is believed that in *the practical application of* these guiding principles the *present interests* of our country and the proper measure of its duty, its *welfare in the future,* and the consideration of its exemption from unknown perils will be found in full accord with the just, moral, and humane purpose which was invoked as our justification in accepting the war.

In view of what has been stated, the United States cannot accept less than the cession in full right and sovereignty of the island of Luzon.[1]

---

[1] *Sen. Doc.* No. 148, 7. Dennett, *Americans in Eastern Asia,* 622, points out that McKinley's reference to the "open door" constitutes the first use of that phrase in an American document. He also holds that the first paragraph quoted above was "obviously a reference to the alarming international situation in the Far East"; and that the reference to the open door "establishes the connection

The President was rationalizing a deed already done. Dewey had fought and won the Battle of Manila. After that the open door in China provided McKinley with a convenient frame of tradition for the radical undertaking into which he had been propelled by forces beyond his understanding or control, by Lodge, Roosevelt and Mahan, or, as he chose to call it, by "the march of events." [1]

Two more factors may finally be noticed as of influence in drawing the United States into the Philippines. First was the initial objection of the Spaniards to including the Philippines in the protocol and their subsequent resistance to the American peace terms. This tended to increase the national *hauteur* of the United States,

between McKinley's Chinese and Philippine policies." *Ibid.*, 621-622. Italics inserted.

[1] One reason, perhaps the most important, why the entire archipelago was ultimately demanded was the fear of hostile naval bases in the immediate vicinity, largely inspired by the experience in Samoa, not to mention German activities in the Philippines. There are allusions to this danger in the despatches of the commissioners. Cf. *Sen. Doc.*, No. 148, 34-35, 46. On October 14 occurred the following colloquy between Senator Frye and Commander R. N. Bradford, U.S.N. Frye: Q.: "If we should adopt your line of demarcation what do you think Spain would do with the balance of those islands?" A.: "Sell them to Germany." Q.: "Is not Germany about as troublesome a neighbor as we could get?" A.: "The most so, in my opinion." Dennett, *Americans in Eastern Asia*, 623 n. McKinley himself stressed this factor: "The interdependency of the several islands, their close relations with Luzon, the very grave problem of what will become of the part we do not take, are receiving the thoughtful consideration of the people and it is *my judgment* that the well-considered opinion of the majority would be that *duty* requires we should take the archipelago." McKinley to Day, October 25. McKinley Papers. This advice was typical of that given by the numerous military and naval experts advising the peace commissioners. General Merritt came to Paris from the Philippines for that purpose. His testimony, compiled from his own and Dewey's observations as well as those of numerous residents of the islands, emphasized the value of their natural resources, especially tobacco, hemp, wood, coffee and cane sugar; also cheap labor. Cf. *Sen. Doc.*, No. 148, 18-21, 26-27. These constituted the second reason for demanding the entire archipelago. Third in importance was the missionary propaganda which contemplated great opportunities among the Filipinos, and which Pratt thinks had considerable influence on McKinley. Cf. *Expansionists*, 316-334.

and to blur the issue by merging it with the many other fruits of victory. Second, and of even greater importance, was the Filipino insurrection that at last broke out on February 4, 1899, just two days before the treaty of peace was ratified. The treaty had met with unexpectedly determined opposition from the anti-imperialists of the Senate, led by Hoar of Massachusetts, whose fight against annexation has become a parliamentary classic. Lodge called it the "closest, hardest fight I have ever known." [1] The opposition centered on the Philippines. Though the debate on the treaty itself was in executive session, secret and unreported, various resolutions pertaining to the right to acquire colonies were openly debated. Page after page of the *Congressional Record* is filled with legalistic pedantry, spread-eagle orations and humanitarian appeals for and against annexation, with hardly a mention of American interests in the Far East.[2] A motion to promise the Filipinos ultimate independence was defeated only by the casting vote of the Vice President.[3] When the final count was taken, on February 6, ratification was secured by the narrow margin of one vote more than the required two-thirds majority.[4] Unquestionably the challenge to American pride flung down by the *insurrectos* stiffened the determination of the annexationists and contributed to their victory.[5]

While the character of the Senate's executive session remains a secret, so consistent was the strategy of the anti-imperialists in all open debate, both in Congress and in the press, that it is diffi-

[1] Lodge to Roosevelt, Feb. 9, 1899. Lodge, *Selections*, I, 391.

[2] *Cong. Rec.*, 55th Cong., 3rd Sess., *passim*. Pratt, *Expansionists*, Ch. IX.

[3] Pratt, *Expansionists*, 358-359.

[4] It was 57-27. *Ibid.*, 345. The treaty had been signed in Paris December 10, 1898, and went to the Senate January 4, 1899.

[5] Roosevelt thanked "the Philippinos" for having "pulled the treaty through for us." Lodge, impressed by the opposition, discounted their assistance. Lodge, *Selections*, I, 390-391. Dennett believes that the situation in the Philippines "had the effect of coercing the Senate." *Americans in Eastern Asia*, 631. Indeed he asserts the situation was deliberately created for that express purpose. *Ibid.*, 627 f., 630-631.

cult not to infer that it remained the same behind closed doors. This strategy was to object to the annexation of the Philippines first on Constitutional and second on humanitarian grounds.[1] Save for the most casual references, the problem of American interests in the Far East was ignored. The anti-imperialists carried the fight to their opponents, forcing them to rebut their argument in kind. It was no longer a partisan conflict. Expansionism had so far carried the day that Bryan advised Democratic Senators to vote for the treaty, perceiving its inevitable acceptance, and wishing to get it out of the way.[2] For the most part only one side of the expansionist argument was heard, Mahan's, and it was practically never answered except by a constitutionalism so captious as to be beside the point. The only opposition in the field overlooked almost entirely the question of foreign policy.

The few warnings that were sounded on policy were ineffectual. Senator Caffery challenged the economic value of a Far Eastern outpost. "Do we want it as an avenue of trade?" he demanded.

Sir, the idea is absurd. We are capturing the markets of civilized man. Five-sixths of the enormous exports of the United States go to Great Britain. The statistics show that not one-tenth of the exports of the United States go to Asia, Africa, and South America combined.

[1] Cf. *Cong. Rec.*, 55th Cong., 3rd Sess., *passim*; Harrington, F. H., "The Anti-Imperialist Movement in the United States," *Miss. Valley Hist. Rev.*, 22, 211-212; Gillett, *Hoar*, 211-266; Pratt, *Expansionists*, 345-360; Dennett, *Americans in Eastern Asia*, 624-632; Holt, W. S., *Treaties Defeated by the Senate*, 165-177.

[2] Bryan's tactics were not the result of a change of heart on imperialism. He wanted to bring the war to an end, and to dispose of the issue of imperialism so as to return to what he considered the more vital matters of trusts and free silver. He may also have believed it wise to allow the Republicans to pass the treaty so as to make a campaign issue of it in 1900. Instead of opposing the treaty he therefore counseled its acceptance and urged his followers to concentrate on bringing about Philippine independence as quickly as possible. Cf. Harrington, *Anti-Imperialist Movement*, loc. cit., 222 ff.; Pratt, *Expansionists*, 357 n. Bryan wired Carnegie, December 30, 1898, that he hoped "to see the question disposed of before 1900, so the fight against trusts and for free silver may be continued." Curti, Merle E., *Bryan and World Peace*, Smith College Studies in History, XVI, Pts. 3 and 4, 128.

Nine-tenths of our exports go to our neighbors in Western Europe, and, Sir, it is manifest that if we want markets for our surplus manufactures, our surplus cereals, all that we cannot consume, we must send them to the people who will consume them.[1]

Senators Chilton, Spooner and Hoar feared the political entanglements into which the United States might be drawn by the Philippines.[2] But facts and figures and warnings for the future lacked the appeal of the "large policy" and its disciples. "The Philippines not contiguous?" challenged Beveridge. "Our navy will make them contiguous!" And his hearers applauded his oratorical depiction of the United States marketing industrial and financial surpluses, at enormous profits, in the Philippines.[3] Actually the United States was still a debtor nation, its principal exports agricultural. Industrial or financial surpluses were things of the future. Capital and labor were still being imported from abroad. The surface of the country's natural resources had scarcely been scraped. The trade of the United States with all of Eastern Asia amounted to a small fraction of its total foreign trade. American capital for the exploitation of China was being raised with difficulty. Beveridge, like the rest of the annexationists, was animated by great expectations rather than existing needs.

It was in this manner that the Philippine Islands became American territory. A small, rather self-conscious, politically effective group of expansionists, led by Captain Mahan, Theodore Roosevelt and Henry Cabot Lodge, had become inspired to follow the example of Great Britain and take up the scepter of sea power and colonial empire. Chance supplied them with the Philippines. Under cover of a war to liberate Cuba and complete the American hegemony of the Caribbean, they schemed the annexation of colonies in the China Sea. American interests in the Far East were an afterthought. Roosevelt had selected and groomed Dewey for his

[1] *Cong. Rec.*, 55th Cong., 3rd Sess., 438.
[2] Pratt, *Expansionists*, 350.
[3] Bowers, *Beveridge and the Progressive Era*, 76.

mission before either he or Mahan—or the American people—
identified the Philippines with the Far Eastern policy. First came
the Battle of Manila, then the predictions and rationalizations as
to the value of the islands to American interests in the Far East.
Within eight years' time Theodore Roosevelt himself, foremost
of the annexationists, was wishing he could be rid of the islands.[1]
"The Philippine Islands form our heel of Achilles," he wrote his
Secretary of War in August, 1907. "They are all that makes the
present situation with Japan dangerous. . . . I think that to have
some pretty clear avowal of our intention not to permanently
keep them and to give them independence would remove a temp-
tation from Japan's way and would render our task easier."[2]
Clearly annexation of the Philippines had spelled the end of the
old detachment and committed the United States, now a land-
owner, to an anxious watch over political developments in the
Far East.

[1] According to his friend, German Ambassador Speck von Sternburg, Roosevelt
freely expressed the wish to give up the islands if he could only hit on some
honorable means of doing it. Sternburg to Foreign Office, January 20, 1906.
Vagts, *Deutschland und die Vereinigten Staaten in der Weltpolitik*, II, 1232 n.

[2] Roosevelt to Taft, August 21, 1907. Pringle, *Roosevelt*, 408-409.

# II. Writing the Open Door Notes

THE Philippines had been called the key to the markets of Asia. Now the key had to be fitted to the lock, and turned. Would the United States emulate Great Britain and turn Manila into a *bona fide* Hongkong, from which by displays of naval power to challenge its competitors in China? Or would the precarious situation of the new colony dictate a more cautious decision? First answers to these questions came in the two great declarations of policy embodied in the open door notes of September 6, 1899, and the Hay circular of July 3, 1900.

Like the annexation of the Philippines, the famous notes were to a large extent influenced by forces extraneous to both the United States and the Far East. Chief among these were Great Britain's attempts to restore the balance of world power recently upset by her three great rivals. In Europe, Germany was building alliances and a fleet with which to assert her own continental supremacy and break down the British colonial monopoly. In Africa, German colonies were being founded, and diplomatic fences erected against British conquest of the Boers. The Anglo-French struggle for the Nile Valley nearly resulted in the outbreak of war at Fashoda in 1898. All Asia was feeling the impact of Russian imperialism which threatened to overrun British spheres of influence in China and perhaps even the Indian frontier itself. In America the Venezuela boundary crisis of 1895-1896 had shown that the determination of the United States to resist any European intrusions into the affairs of the Western Hemisphere was stronger than ever. For a moment England stood alone, friendless, amid the ruins of her once "splendid" isolation. Then, in a characteristically pragmatic fashion, her diplomats began a search for allies on three continents, and a systematic effort to re-establish the balance of power wherever British interests demanded it. One by one overtures for alliances or understandings were made to Russia, the United States, Japan, Germany and France, ultimately resulting in the Anglo-Japanese Alliance of 1902 and the *Entente Cordiale* with France in 1904.[1]

An early intimation of the way in which Britain's attempts to extricate herself from her predicament would affect the United States is to be found in a letter from Joseph Chamberlain to Lord Salisbury of January 4, 1896. Only the day before, the Kaiser's telegram to President Kruger of the Boer Republic congratulating the latter on his interception of the Jameson raiders had exploded in England like a bombshell. The times called for an "Act of Vigor," wrote Chamberlain. Germany should be warned against any interference in South Africa. There should be "an ostentatious order to commission more ships of war." The colonies should be petitioned to co-operate in the military defense of the empire. Finally—and this Chamberlain submitted as a "Query"—the government should make "a serious effort to come to terms with America" on the Venezuela boundary issue.[2] In other words, circumstances of European, rather than American origin, were to incline British diplomacy toward a *rapprochement* and, if possible, a working agreement with the United States.

Great Britain straightway accepted President Cleveland's demands for the arbitration of the dispute over the Venezuela boundary. As negotiations progressed, it became evident that the United States itself was not wholly unsympathetic toward the idea of a general Anglo-American *rapprochement*. Secretary Olney was so gratified by the British agreement in principle to the terms of the Venezuela settlement that, although he had won his point, he offered to pay a bonus for it. When Chamberlain casually asked

[1] Langer's *The Diplomacy of Imperialism*, 2 vols., covers the circumstances of the British quest for allies in detail.
[2] Garvin, *Chamberlain*, III, 95-96.

him if the United States would co-operate with England in putting a stop to the Armenian massacres then rife in Turkey,[1] an affair seemingly beyond the pale of American national interest, Olney replied:

. . . because of our inborn and instinctive English sympathies, proclivities, modes of thought and standards of right and wrong nothing would more gratify the mass of the American people than to stand side by side and shoulder to shoulder with England in support of a great cause—in a necessary struggle for the defense of human rights and the advancement of Christian civilization. That a great cause of this sort is now presented by unhappy Armenia I cannot doubt. . . .

If, therefore, England should now seriously set about putting the Armenian charnel-house in order, there can be little doubt that the United States would consider the moment opportune for vigorous exertion on behalf of American citizens and interests in Turkey. It would feel itself entitled to demand full indemnity for past injuries to them as well as adequate security against the like injuries in the future. It would support such demands by all the physical force at its disposal—with the necessary result, I think, that its attitude would both morally and materially strengthen the hands of England.[2]

[1] Cf. Langer, op. cit., Chs. VII, IX, XI. The massacres were an incident in the struggle among England, Germany and Russia for mastery of the Near East. Chamberlain had written Olney a very brief note (September 19, 1896) concluding: "Meanwhile, I venture to ask whether you would care to express a confidential opinion as to the reception which would be given by the American Government to any proposition from our side tending to co-operation in regard to Turkey?

"If you do not care to say anything, please do not bother to acknowledge this note." Dennis, Adventures, 59.

[2] Olney to Chamberlain, September 28, 1896. Garvin, op. cit., III, 167. Dennis, Adventures, 59-60. Caution is needed in the interpretation of this note. Garvin prints only the small portion of it quoted above, Dennis the entire text. Dennis makes no comment on the Armenian proposals. Olney carefully prefaced his assurances with a reminder of the American taboo on foreign alliances in any form. "But," says Garvin, "there might be a common cause with England after all." He thereupon takes the Olney note as foreshadowing Anglo-American co-operation during the World War, but does not suggest its possible significance with respect to the Far East.

Further evidence of the new dispensation in Anglo-American relations was offered in 1897 by the negotiation of a general arbitration convention between the two countries, signed by Secretary Olney and Sir Julian Pauncefote on January 11. Although defeated by the Senate, the treaty had been warmly sponsored by Salisbury, and its failure caused much disappointment in the Foreign Office and the State Department alike.[1] Mr. Olney afterwards termed it "more important than the Venezuela affair," and indeed it marked a turning point in the American attitude toward arbitration treaties.[2] Pauncefote was much pleased by the favorable reception of the treaty in England, while the Senate's action was interpreted by diplomats on both sides of the Atlantic as not truly representative of American opinion.[3]

Meanwhile, conditions in the Far East called for immediate attention. England could not afford to bank on American cooperation alone. The United States was but one of the international weights that would have to be shifted to bring the scales of world power into balance.

Since 1840 England had played the leading part in the economic exploitation of China. Now her trade with China amounted to 65 per cent of China's total foreign trade, 85 per cent of which was carried in British vessels.[4] To protect her lucrative Chinese markets from the closing pincers of France in the south and Russia in the north (allies since 1894), England took a new interest in the territorial integrity of China. She opposed any further economic or territorial concessions to France in the south, and as against Russia, actively supported Chinese suzerainty over Korea. The two policies proved complete failures. China was powerless to halt the extension of the French sphere of influence; while Chinese claims to sovereignty over Korea merely ran afoul of Japa-

[1] Holt, W. S., *Treaties Defeated by the Senate*, 154-162; Nevins, *Henry White*, 112-113, 124 ff.

[2] Holt, *op. cit.*, 154.

[3] *Ibid.*, 155, 159-161.

[4] Langer, *Diplomacy of Imperialism*, I, 167. Figures are for 1894.

nese ambitions, precipitating the Sino-Japanese War (1894-1895). As part of her winnings Japan secured Formosa and the Liaotung Peninsula, a long-coveted foothold on the continent. But Russia, assisted by her ally, France, and her erstwhile partner, Germany, intervened to compel the retrocession of the Liaotung Peninsula to China. The net result of the war, therefore, was to remove the last barrier to Russia's penetration from the north, leaving her free to overrun Korea, as she speedily attempted to do.[1] England was thus surrounded in the Far East, as elsewhere, by political rivals and economic competitors.

British diplomacy thereupon underwent a speedy reorientation. With Japan, whether by chance or by design, the way had already been paved for an understanding. Since 1890 Britain had profited as much by the ineptitude of Secretary Blaine's diplomacy as by her own preponderant share of Japanese trade to build up a growing influence over that country.[2] By shrewdly abstaining from the triple intervention she had earned rich dividends of Japanese gratitude.[3]

A period of watchful waiting followed during 1896 and 1897. The cabinet was agreed that British interests in China must be

[1] Cf. Langer, *op. cit.*, Chs. VI, XII; Dennett, *Americans in Eastern Asia*, 482-503; Treat, *Diplomatic Relations between the U. S. and Japan*, II, 445-534.

[2] From 1872 to 1889 England had blocked every move for revision of the unequal treaties with Japan, while the United States supported revision with equal consistency. Suddenly reversing her position in 1889, England took the lead in negotiating the independent treaties of 1894 which terminated extraterritorial rights in Japan and, incidentally, wrecked the co-operative policy of the treaty powers. That she was able thus to steal American thunder appears to have been due in no small degree to the race prejudice of the American minister John F. Swift. Cf. Treat, *Diplomatic Relations between the U. S. and Japan*, II, 321-418; Vagts, *op. cit.*, II, 950 ff.; Dennett, *Americans in Eastern Asia*, 530 ff.

[3] Another reversal of policy. England had twice approached the United States with the project of intervening in the interests of China, first to prevent the war, and then to bring it to an end. So angry was China at the British *volte face* that she forthwith ceded to France a portion of Indo-China that she had promised Britain never to alienate. Another result was to drive China into the arms of

defended,[1] but seemed to have lost faith in attempting single-handed to uphold the integrity of China as a means to that end. It was determined, as Curzon put it, "to pounce the moment any-one else pounces." [2] When, at length, news arrived that a Russian squadron had occupied Port Arthur, Lord Salisbury opined to Chamberlain "that 'the public' will require some territorial or cartographic consolation in China. It will not be useful and will be expensive; but as a matter of pure sentiment, we shall have to do it." [3] No further evidence is needed to show that England per-fectly realized the true relation of China to Europe as that of a pawn to the kings, castles and bishops nearer home. Her only motives were to stay the advance of Russia and protect her own economic stake in the Far East by whatever means seemed most practicable, and in company with whatever nation might be in-duced to come to her assistance.

As the situation now reduced itself, "cartographic consolation" —which meant joining in the scramble for concessions—could not accomplish England's purpose. Further territorial concessions would be costly to defend and of dubious value in checking eco-nomic competition. Of the vast British sphere of interest in the Yangtse Valley, approximately one-third of China proper, neither Britain herself nor any other power could hope to make an exclu-sive territorial concession.[4] To maintain her advantageous position

Russia, with which she secretly concluded the offensive-defensive Li-Lobanov Treaty in 1896. Cf. Treat, *op. cit.*, 492-543; Dennett, *Americans, etc.*, 496-499; McCordock, R. S., *British Far Eastern Policy, 1894-1900*, 76-141; Vagts, *op. cit.*, II, 953-955; Yakhontoff, Victor A., *Russia and the Soviet Union in the Far East*, 30, 365-366.

[1] Cf. the speeches of Balfour at Manchester, Jan. 10, 1898, and Hicks Beach at Swansea, Jan. 17. Reuter, *op. cit.*, 116; Langer, *op. cit.*, II, 465. Balfour claimed for England 80 per cent of China's trade. Each declared British motives were wholly commercial, while, according to Hicks Beach, the government was resolved to defend the open door "if necessary, at the cost of war."

[2] Langer, *op. cit.*, II, 460.

[3] Salisbury to Chamberlain, December 30, 1897. Garvin, *Chamberlain*, III, 249.

[4] As a speaker in the Commons put it (June 19, 1899), "We cannot make the Yangtze Valley a province like Shantung or Manchuria, first, because it is in-

there and to guard against exclusion from other parts of China scarcely less important to her commerce, Great Britain was casting about for a new and more efficacious method of upholding China's territorial integrity. The alternatives that presented themselves were an alliance or, in keeping with balance of power tactics, an international stalemate that would have the same result. Still another faint possibility was that her competitors might be persuaded to open their spheres and leaseholds to British commerce on the most-favored-nation, or open door principle. But even this meager benefit could not be secured without the help of some other nation to weight the scales in England's favor.[1] The problem, which preoccupied the British cabinet during the winter and spring of 1898, was solved at last by cautious moves toward each of the suggested objectives. While the cabinet secretly discussed taking part in the dismemberment of China, its members publicly frowned on that policy and proclaimed their faith in the open door, their determination to defend British interests in China, and, on January 17, extended the first feeler for an alliance—with Russia.[2] When this failed to produce results, they turned to the United States.

As we have seen, a dramatic improvement in Anglo-American relations during the War with Spain resulted. It began early in the year. American traditions against foreign alliances were well known to Downing Street, but the United States seemed to be undergoing a change of heart. Mahan was widely read in England. The enthusiasm of Roosevelt, Lodge, Hay, Whitelaw Reid

finitely larger, and secondly, we are not prepared to undertake the immense responsibility of governing what is practically a third of China." Langer, II, 684.

[1] For the way in which these points were considered, see British Documents, I, 1-18, especially 16-18.

[2] The date of Salisbury's despatch to Sir Nicholas O'Conor instructing him to sound Witte on an understanding. Brit. Docs., I, 5. Thereafter overtures were made to the United States, Japan, Germany, and ultimately France, in that order. Langer, op. cit., II, 491-494.

and Henry White for closer Anglo-American co-operation was remarkable. Then there was Mr. Olney's communication on the subject of the Armenian atrocities, which Chamberlain could scarcely have forgotten.[1] It was not surprising, therefore, that while England dickered for understandings with Russia, and later with Japan and Germany, all kinds of overtures, official and unofficial, were made to the United States for any arrangement that would bring the United States to England's aid in the region of the Far East.[2]

In the process, Chamberlain played a persuasive role. Of all the cabinet he appears to have been the most sanguine of obtaining an alliance with the United States. In any case, he was directly responsible for the first official step toward it. On February 3, 1898, he addressed the following memorandum to the Acting Foreign Secretary:

*Secret*

Highbury,
Birmingham.
Feb. 3. 98.

MY DEAR BALFOUR,

I wish that you read all the papers just now. If you did, you would, I think, agree with me that grave trouble is impending upon the Govt. if we do not adopt a more decided attitude in regard to China.

What are the facts? We have a permanent interest in the trade, and

[1] Langer seems to have missed the point of this. In his *Diplomacy of Imperialism*, II, 490, he says that Chamberlain "had harbored the phantastic notion that the great Republic might be induced to co-operate with England in the Near Eastern crisis. . . ." As Olney's despatch proves, the notion was far from "phantastic."

[2] Cf. 31-35; also Reuter, *op. cit.*, 70-160; Langer, *op. cit.*, II, 465-472, 488-494; Dennett, *John Hay*, 189, 285, 220; Dennis, *Adventures in American Diplomacy*, 122 ff., 183-186; McCordock, *op. cit.*, Chs. IV, V; Dugdale, *Balfour*, I, Ch. XII; Garvin, *Chamberlain*, III, Chs. LVII, LX. While Gooch and Temperley's *Brit. Docs.* cover the negotiations with Russia in considerable detail (Vol. I, 1-42), they are otherwise badly truncated, omitting entirely any reference to the efforts, recorded above, to secure the co-operation of the United States in the Far East.

have gained much credit both at home and in America by insisting that while we do not intend to oppose the occupation by Germany and Russia, we are determined that their ports shall be Treaty Ports, or subject to regulations, and that our influence shall be maintained.

The Germans appear to have accepted our terms, although we have not got, as we ought to get, a definite assurance that Kiao Chau will be a Treaty Port. But the Russians have done us at every point.

They have induced us to let our ships leave Port Arthur, while they have reciprocated our friendly attitude by opposing our loan proposals.[1] They have forced us to withdraw our proposals to make Talien Wan a Free Port.

They are placing Russian officers in control of railways, &c., to the exclusion of English.

They are ousting us from influence in Corea.

They pretend that their occupation is temporary and not in restraint of trade. We all believe that this is false, and that they will transform the occupation into a permanent one, and will exclude us altogether from the Liao Tung peninsula.

We pretend to rely on our treaty rights; but if they declare an annexation these rights disappear, and in any case they will know how to make the position intolerable for our merchants. All this is known to our friends and to our enemies. If matters remain as they are, our prestige will be gone and our trade will follow. I would not give a year's life to the Government under such conditions.

The question is, what can we do, and it is most difficult of course for any of us outsiders to frame a policy. If only Lord Salisbury sees the peril and is prepared to meet it I would rather leave to him the methods than rush in with what may be impossible suggestions. But, as the matter now appears to me, I should propose:

1. To approach the United States officially, and to ask an imme-

---

[1] To pay off the indemnity accorded to Japan by the Treaty of Shimonoseki, China was compelled to borrow from the western powers, causing several disputes among them as to their precise shares in the loans. As a condition to the last English loan of £16,000,000, negotiations for which were still pending, England demanded the opening of Talienwan as a treaty port to foreign trade. To this the Russians objected, would offer nothing in return, and so the loan negotiations fell flat. *Brit. Docs.*, I, 1-2.

diate reply from them to the question—Will you stand in with us in our Chinese policy?

2. To approach Germany at the same time with the same definite questions.

3. Our Chinese policy to be a declaration that any port occupied by a foreign nation shall be, *ipso facto*, a Treaty Port open to all on precisely similar conditions.

That this applies to Talien Wan, Port Arthur and Kiao Chau, and to any other further acquisition of land or ports by any European nation, or by the Japanese.

Further that they should join with us in putting pressure on the Chinese—loan or no loan—to open Nanking and other Ports suggested by us and to give freedom of internal navigation.

That if Russia refuses these terms, we should summon her fleet to leave Port Arthur and make her go if necessary.

I dare say this line is much too strong for the Cabinet, but if we do not do something and that quickly we shall have a bad quarter of an hour when Parliament meets.

yours very truly,<br>J. CHAMBERLAIN.[1]

This document is remarkable, not only because it shows Anglo-Russian antagonism to have been the very axis of Far Eastern politics. It also reveals that eighteen months before the despatch of the Hay notes, and well over a year before the idea of collective action to guarantee the open door appears to have entered the head of an American diplomat, it had been introduced into practical diplomacy by the Colonial Secretary of Great Britain.

The approach to the United States followed soon afterwards. On March 8 Pauncefote addressed a "very confidential" inquiry to Secretary of State Sherman. "There are two methods," Sir

---

[1] Dugdale, *Balfour*, 252-253. Garvin also prints this memorandum in *Chamberlain*, III, 251-252, though not in complete form. Notice the strongly anti-Russian tone. Throughout Russia, rather than Germany, was England's *bête noire* in the Far East.

Julian wrote, "by which foreign Powers may restrict the opening of China to the commerce of all nations, either by procuring the lease of portions of the Chinese coast under conditions which would ensure preferential treatment to the Power acquiring such lease, or by obtaining the actual cession of the Chinese littoral. Her Majesty's Government are anxious to know whether they could count on the co-operation of the United States in opposing such action by foreign Powers and whether the United States would be prepared to join with Great Britain in opposing such measures should the contingency arise." [1]

Sherman and McKinley, preoccupied with the imminent hostilities with Spain, rejected the proposal with the blunt statement that, although they were "not . . . unmindful of the situation in China and its possible effect upon American trade interests" all their "advices up to the present time indicate no foreign occupation which interferes with that trade or aims at exclusive commercial privileges." They could see no reason, therefore, of departing from "our traditional policy of [sic] respecting foreign alliances and so far as practicable avoiding interference or connection with European complications." [2] But in this first British overture (that may very well have been encouraged by Ambassador Hay) was the kernel of a doctrine to which the Department of State was soon to be converted. Vague as was Sir Julian's note, its implications were plain enough. How were foreign powers to be prevented from securing cessions or leaseholds save by defending, in some way, the feeble object of their depredations? For such a venture, in March, 1898, the United States was not prepared. The

---

[1] Vagts, op. cit., II, 1029. See also Dennis, Adventures, 170-171; Dennett, John Hay, 285; Langer, op. cit., II, 472; Nevins, White, 163. Only Vagts prints the complete memorandum, as above.

[2] The text of this undated reply to Pauncefote is given by Vagts, II, 1030. Dennis, 170-171, prints the text of a despatch from Sherman to White of March 17 retailing the substance of the reply to Pauncefote in language almost identical to that of the original.

Battle of Manila had yet to be fought, the national conversion to imperialism yet to be accomplished.[1]

Rebuffed by Russia and the United States, England next approached Japan, then Germany, with like results. Meantime Weihaiwei was taken as "consolation" for Port Arthur.[2] As matters stood when the United States went to war with Spain, British policy had failed of its first and second objectives in the Far East, and had been forced to content itself with a poor third. Neither a collective guarantee of the territorial integrity of China nor an alliance had been secured. The lease of Weihaiwei was more of a stimulus than a deterrent to the partitioning of China. That it would have the desired effect of halting Russia few Englishmen appear to have believed. Its value to England was to be measured in the abstract terms of *amour propre*.

Accordingly, British attention veered back to the United States. Efforts were renewed to promote Anglo-American friendship and, in spite of Pauncefote's early failure, to devise some means whereby the United States might be brought into the Far Eastern balance. Systematic encouragement was given to American retention of the Philippines. The press in England and in the Dominions outspokenly expressed its sympathy for the United States,

[1] This was not England's first attempt to obtain formal American joint action in the Far East. In 1857 she proposed an Anglo-Franco-American political and naval entente which was rejected by President Buchanan. The Cleveland Administration rejected a similar project brought forward by the British Chargé in Washington (October 6, 1894) for joint intervention in the Sino-Japanese War. Dennett, *Americans in Eastern Asia*, 298-304, 498 ff. Treat, *op. cit.*, 492-3. See also Dennett, "Seward's Far Eastern Policy," *Am. Hist. Rev.*, Vol. 28, 45-62, October, 1932.

[2] Japan was approached March 17. The decision to lease Weihaiwei was made March 25; and on the same day the first Anglo-German conversation on the subject of an understanding was held between Chamberlain and Hatzfeldt. Langer, II, 472-474, 494-500. Garvin, III, 254-278 (which reveals the Chamberlain memoranda for the first time); *Die Grosse Politik*, XIV, I, 193-226. For the overture to Japan see Pooley, A. M., *The Secret Memoirs of Count Tadasu Hayashi*, 89; Ito Masanori, *Kato Takaaki* (Memoirs of Baron Kato), I, 292 ff. —both cited by Langer.

and its approval of closer Anglo-American co-operation.[1] Chamberlain virtually took the stump for an Anglo-American alliance.[2] Anglo-American leagues and committees were organized in London and New York to promote the idea which, impractical though it may have been, symbolized the unprecedented friendliness of Anglo-American relations. Concurrently the open door policy was proclaimed so loudly and so consistently by cabinet officers, members of Parliament and journalists as to suggest the desire to impress it on other countries than England.[3] During the winter of 1898-1899, Lord Charles Beresford made his celebrated barnstorming tour of China and Japan, returning to England *via* the United States. It was one long after-dinner speech in favor of the open door. He consulted Hay before leaving London, wrote him letters reporting the enthusiasm of Americans in the Orient for closer co-operation with England, and called on him at the State Department on the way home. As Hay was advised in advance, Beresford had "based all his hopes of keeping the open door by

[1] Reuter, *op. cit.*, 74, 85-116.

[2] In a speech at Birmingham, his own constituency, on May 13, 1898, he cited the common bonds uniting the two nations, and boldly declared in favor of an alliance with the United States. He returned to this theme in speeches in the House of Commons, June 10, and at Manchester, November 15. The speeches received wide publicity and attention in both countries. Though Chamberlain seems to have been in advance of his colleagues in this matter, there is little doubt that they would readily have accepted whatever fruits his efforts might have borne. Cf. Garvin, III, 301-306; Reuter, 20-21, 153-157; Langer, II, 506-518; Dennis, 122-123.

[3] It was expounded and endorsed by Balfour at Manchester, January 10, 1898; by Salisbury in the House of Lords, February 8; by Curzon in the Commons, March 1; by Lord Charles Beresford, April 5; by Sir Charles Dilke, June 20. On November 16, Chamberlain, who had by this time abandoned the idea of underwriting China's integrity, pinned his faith in the open door policy. On December 9, he advocated joint action to defend the open door, and again hinted at an Anglo-American alliance. Reuter, 116-117; Dennis, 122, 183 ff.; Langer, II, 681-682. Hicks Beach told Hatzfeldt in January, 1898, that England was "determined, at any cost, and if necessary by force, to keep the Chinese market entirely open to world trade." Hatzfeldt to Foreign Office, Jan. 22, 1898. *Die Grosse Politik*, XIV, I, 147.

enlisting the sympathies of America during his trip across the Continent." [1] Soon after his return, Beresford published *The Break-up of China*, written as much for Americans as for Englishmen, and further exploiting the theme he had so pointedly advertised in his travels.[2]

Before Beresford reached America, England had made two more efforts to secure the co-operation of the United States in the Far East. In the fall of 1898 the French decided to extend their concession at Shanghai. The plan was immediately opposed by the British, whose minister approached Mr. Conger, the American Minister at Peking, on December 22 with the idea of entering a joint protest against it. Conger wired Hay for instructions, receiving the ambiguous reply: "Protest French extension if against American interest." Mr. Conger protested, though independently rather than in company with the British. He was persuaded to do so, he explained, by the "protests of the American landowners, merchants, and missionaries at Shanghai against having their property included in the extension" and not by the importunities of the British minister. He himself could "see no good reason for this objection to the extension of the French settlement." He thought the British opposition was "mainly political, that it came principally from London" and that it was "directed against any increase of French power or holdings in the Yangtse Valley." [3]

In Washington, meanwhile, acting under instructions from Lon-

---

[1] By Rounsevelle Wildman, American Consul-General at Hongkong in a letter dated Jan. 6, 1899. Dennett, *Hay*, 286-287.

[2] Rockhill prepared for Hay an elaborate memorandum on *The Break-up of China*. See p. 74, below. Obviously kite-flying, Beresford was out for what he could get. He suggested including both Germany and Japan in his *entente*. But his first concern was what he described to Hay as a "Commercial Alliance between Great Britain and America with reference to the 'open door' in China." Dennett, *Hay*, 286. See also Dennett, *Americans in Eastern Asia*, 641-642; Vagts, II, 1050-1051; Dennis, 185-186.

[3] Cf. despatches and telegrams, Conger to Hay, December 22, 1898; Hay to Conger, December 23, 1898; Conger to Hay, January 5, 1899, and March 24, 1899. *Foreign Relations*, 1899, 143-145.

don, Pauncefote again attempted to secure from the President a formal undertaking to co-operate with England in the Far East. "I am aware," he wrote (January 8, 1899), "that it would be a departure from the usual practice of your government . . . who, I believe, adopt the form of identic representations in preference to conjoint action, but the departure in the present instance might be justified by the special community of interest arising out of the new condition of affairs in China." [1] Again the British Ambassador was turned down.

By the summer of 1899 the most England had to show for her troubles was Weihaiwei, an extension of her holdings at Hong-kong, and a railway agreement with Russia. By the terms of the latter (concluded April 28) the great wall of China was mutually recognized as the southern boundary of the Russian sphere of railway construction and the northern boundary of the English. The agreement did not mention the open door for commerce. [2] The dismemberment of China now seemed more likely than ever as, indeed, the decision to take Weihaiwei and the agreement with Russia implied. The Boer War was only a few months off. [3] Un-remitting pressure on America had elicited nothing more definite than expressions of esteem and a few independent and rather non-committal statements in favor of the open door. As Paunce-fote made clear, his country desired something more than sym-pathy and identic action. It wanted a formal understanding—a deposit of American political support in Eastern Asia on which England could draw, whenever necessary, to protect her interests there.

---

[1] Dennett, *Hay*, 288. Dennett suggests that Hay would have liked to accept the proposition as a means of expediting the ratification of the Hay-Pauncefote treaty, the draft of which was then awaiting British approval. Hay did communicate the substances of Conger's despatches "informally" to Pauncefote, presumably to in-dicate that while no joint action was possible, Conger's independent, "identic" protest to a certain extent served the same purpose. Cf. Hay to Conger, March 21, 1899. *For. Rel.*, 1899, 145.

[2] Langer, II, 682 ff.

[3] It began in November, 1899.

The influence on the United States of nations other than Great Britain was less direct. For the most part, it was brought to bear through British diplomacy. Russia and Germany played their parts in calling forth the open door notes as catalytic agents whose hostile *Weltpolitik* and whose overt acts in the Far East spurred Britain to seek American aid. To a lesser degree, so did France. Japan's influence must be counted as relatively negligible, while China's, though considerable, was of a negative character. To perceive the working of these various international forces it is necessary to turn back for a moment and consider the parallel development of an American Far Eastern policy which ultimately met the British halfway.

The United States was far from being an unwilling recipient of British attention. If Chamberlain made speeches in favor of an Anglo-American alliance, so did John Hay.[1] An ardent Anglophile, he did all in his power as Ambassador to abet the British quest for American assistance. "Chamberlain's startling speech," [2] he wrote Lodge, "was partly due to a conversation I had with him, in which I hoped he would not let the opposition have a monopoly of expressions of good-will to America." [3] In a personal letter to President McKinley in June he re-opened the subject of Pauncefote's unsuccessful proposal of the previous March.[4] When Hay became Secretary of State he had lost none of his sympathy for his many friends and his *beau ideal* in England. It was a mood shared by many of Hay's American acquaintances as

---

[1] His famous "Partnership in Beneficence" speech at the Lord Mayor's Eastern dinner, April 21, 1898, was an exposition of the cultural affinities that made the two nations allies automatically. Dennett, *Hay*, 189. The speech suggests that Hay did not take McKinley's refusal of Pauncefote's first proposal any too seriously.

[2] At Birmingham, May 13, in which he came out for an alliance.

[3] Hay to Lodge, May 25, 1898. *Ibid.*, 220.

[4] To which Secretary Day replied that the moment was still inopportune, but that, "The outcome of our struggle with Spain may develop the need of extending and strengthening our interests in the Asiatic Continent." Day to Hay, July 14, 1898. *Ibid.*, 285-6.

well. "If I had my way," Lodge had written him early in 1898, "I should be glad to have the United States say to England that we would stand by her in her declaration that the ports of China must be opened to all nations equally or to none, and if England takes that attitude firmly I am in hopes this may come about, although our foreign policy is always more haphazard than I like to see it." [1] The American press reciprocated the sentiments emanating from British and Dominion pens. Small wonder Downing Street was encouraged to keep trying for an Anglo-American accord, no matter how many failures beset its efforts.

What gave the British policy still greater pertinency was the growing American apprehension of England's enemies in Eastern Asia. Here were four great European nations at daggers drawn over the moribund Chinese Empire. The French, constantly expanding northward from Indo-China into the southern Chinese provinces of Yunnan, Kwangsi and Kwangtung, extorted railway and mining concessions from Peking at the point of the sword. The British were similarly exploiting the enormous Yangtse Valley, as the Germans were Shantung and the Russians Manchuria and Korea. The tendency of the businessmen and diplomats of each nation was, quite naturally, to seek exclusive commercial and financial privileges within their respective spheres. This was as true of the British as it was of all the others, especially in the field of capital investment. Lord Salisbury himself defined a sphere of influence as "a sort of an 'ear mark' upon territory which in case of a break up England did not wish any other power to have." [2] There could be little doubt that the collapse of China would mean the pre-emption of most of its vast territories by England, France, Germany and Russia.

Since the two nations first came on the scene, commercial rivalry between England and the United States had been sharp, and often

[1] Nevins, *White*, 166.
[2] Choate to Hay, June 20, 1900. Dennis, 220; Vagts, II, 1050.

acrimonious.[1] Now England was as determined to preserve the Yangtse Valley for her own bankers and railroad builders as Russia was Manchuria.[2] It is difficult to discern in England's Far Eastern policy any motive essentially different from those of her rivals. "In spite of the immense amount of sentimentality that England and the U. S. have been engaged recently in expressing," Mr. Denby wrote from Peking (April 2, 1897), "the stern fact remains that in the Far East, and I believe elsewhere, England looks on all questions in the light of her own interest. Here in China her people are our rivals in every branch of trade and commerce and industry. Our worst antagonists in the building of railroads or furnishing supplies therefore are the English. I venture to state that there is not an English railroad man in China who does not attack, denounce and belittle American locomotives and the American railroad system." [3] The American Minister's appraisal of the situation was entirely accurate. Nevertheless, compared to her rivals, England was a sated nation, more anxious to keep what she had in China than to acquire more. Her unique

[1] Cf. Dennett, *Americans in Eastern Asia*, and Treat, *op. cit., passim*. Caleb Cushing in 1840 denounced the "base cupidity" of the British in China, Dennett, 104. American traders in China frequently suspected the British of trying to secure tariff discriminations against them, and to stake off spheres of influence on the quiet. *Ibid.*, 157, 198-9. When the British negotiated their revised treaty convention with Japan in 1890 they dictated the tariff schedule which imposed an average of 6½-7 per cent *ad valorem* duties on British imports and 12½-13½ per cent on American. Treat, II, 333.

[2] The determination of the British cabinet to fight for this if necessary has already been discussed, p. 41, above. In February, 1898, England exacted a pledge from the Chinese Government not to alienate any portion of the Yangtse Valley to another power. A year later the Anglo-Russian railroad agreement (April, 1899) further demarcated the British and Russian spheres. England was currently trying for a similar agreement with Germany which she ultimately obtained (October, 1900). Langer, II, 464, 682, 702 ff. France and Japan had also obtained non-alienation agreements from China.

[3] Denby to Sherman, April 2, 1897. Vagts, II, 995-6. Denby had previously reported the failure of an American contingent to float a railroad loan covering the construction of the Peking-Hankow line as due chiefly to British opposition. Denby to Olney, January 10, 1897. *For. Rel.*, 1897, 57-58.

position as money-lender and exporter to the world enabled her to profit more by the application of the free-trade—or open door —principle to China than by preferential tariffs and trade wars. For these reasons, rather than because of any supposed tendency to welcome American commerce and capital to her concessions and sphere of influence, her policy seemed more congenial to the United States than did the policies of Germany, France and Russia. Her sedulous courting of American favor during the War with Spain strengthened the belief that British and American interests in the Far East were identical, Germany and Russia their common enemies.

The French sphere was so far south that it escaped the direct line of American competition. Insofar as France affected American policy at all it was *via* her alliance with Russia and opposition to England, as in the case of the Shanghai extension. Germany's open hostility to the United States in South and Central America, her part in the Samoan controversy and the alleged activities of Diederichs in Manila Bay had, as we have seen, thoroughly aroused American suspicions of the Kaiser's *Realpolitik*. These were only intensified by the seizure of Kiaochow. British insinuations to the too susceptible Hay and Henry White must be held partially to account for the poor state of German-American relations; but a material foundation made the propaganda of Chamberlain and Salisbury all the more effective. To the United States Germany was a suspicious character.[1]

The case of Russia is less clear. Russo-American relations had been extremely cordial since the days of the American Civil War. In 1870 the Russian Empress had actually led one of her ministers to believe that a Russo-American Alliance against England was in the making.[2] Even after the Sino-Japanese War, and the launching of the Czar's ambitious program of absorbing Manchuria and Korea, the two nations remained on excellent terms.

[1] Cf. Vagts, II, esp. 1015-1029.
[2] *Krasnyi Arkhiv*, LII, 126.

In the same despatch that impugned British intentions toward American commerce in the Far East, Denby had concluded that "in the interests of our manufacturers, our friendly relations with Russia should be enhanced."[1] The Russians, on their part, made heroic efforts to cultivate American good will and to prevent England from drawing the United States into her anti-Russian orbit. They held out prospects of large purchases of American raw materials and industrial products essential to the railway building and general economic development of Manchuria.

The American ambassadors to Russia, Hitchcock and Tower, were convinced of Russia's good faith. They repeatedly urged the Department of State not to adopt any policy that would jeopardize American trade with Russia or Manchuria. Hitchcock was a man of considerable influence in Republican circles (he eventually became Secretary of the Interior) and for a while it is safe to say his advice carried more weight than Denby's and Conger's, from Peking. On the very eve of the despatch of the Hay notes an imperial ukase (August 15, 1899) opened Talienwan as a free port, an act hailed by Ambassador Tower as being, "insofar as Russia is concerned . . . the open door to China . . . a great step forward in the progress of the world," one that opened the way "to the future development of American trade and the certain increase of American mercantile prosperity."[2] William W. Rockhill, Hay's closest adviser on the Far East, was more alarmed by France and Germany than he was by Russia. But John Hay's mistrust of Russia was deep. Nor was it unfounded. The whole world knew that in spite of his gestures of amity the Czar's ultimate goal was to extend his empire over as much of Eastern Asia as his armies and diplomats could hold in their grasp.[3]

[1] Denby to Sherman, April 2, 1897. Vagts, II, 995.

[2] Tower to Hay, August 23, 1899. Dennis, 199; Vagts, II, 1048.

[3] The most careful study of Russo-American relations at this period is to be found in Vagts, II, Ch. XI, esp. 1006-1058. It is based almost entirely on the despatches of Messrs. Denby, Conger, Hitchcock, Tower, A. D. White, Peirce, Henry White, Sherman and Hay, taken from the State Department archives and

Japan, while resentful of all parties to the triple intervention of 1895, singled out Russia as her obvious antagonist. Already Japanese statesmen were preparing for the inevitable war for mastery of Korea and Manchuria. In the interim any project that hampered the Russians, or helped to keep them north of the great wall, served Japan well. She could not take the initiative in such schemes, or allow them to infringe upon the sphere which she, too, had staked out for herself in China. Her plans for the future differed from Russia's only in their immaturity. At the time, her power was not great enough to inspire much trepidation in Washington or much hope in London. In the chain of circumstances that produced the open door notes, Japanese links were few and far between.[1]

In the United States itself the "large policy" of 1898 had its commercial counterpart. The annual report of the Department of State's Bureau of Foreign Commerce for 1896-1897 had spoken hopefully of "what may be termed an American invasion of the markets of the world," of which it considered China "one of the most promising." For the United States to secure equality of opportunity in that vast Empire "would doubtless result in immense gains to our manufacturers in the demand, sure to follow, for lines

quoted by the author *in extenso*. Many of these were previously cited, though not nearly so fully quoted, by Dennis, Ch. VIII, esp. 196-208. For the Russian side of the picture, see Romanov, B. A., *Rossia v Manchzhuriia*, 148-212, and *Krasnyi Arkhiv*, LII, 126 ff. and 131-140. These reveal the Russian belief that England was stirring up American enmity toward all the continental powers, as well as the apprehensions of Russian diplomats at the advent of the United States as an imperialist rival in the Far East. Cf. also Bülow's comments to Rudowitz (March 17, 1898) on Britain's hand in American diplomacy. *Die Grosse Politik*, XV, 12-14, and Hippisley and Rockhill Memoranda in appendix.

[1] Cf. Langer, Chs. VI, XII, XIV; Dennis, Ch. VIII; Vagts, Ch. XI. Also despatch No. 25, Hitchcock to Sherman, Jan. 19, 1898, reporting conversation with Baron Hayashi on the German seizure of Kiaochow, copy of which is to be found in the Rockhill papers, and Rockhill Memorandum, August 28, 1899. Also Hippisley to Rockhill, Jan. 4, 1900, a detailed and authoritative estimate of the subject, concluding that Japan desired a strong China as an opposition to Russia.

of supplies and goods of various descriptions that we are pre-eminently fitted to provide." [1] The seizures of Kiaochow and Port Arthur started the first memorials to Washington from apprehensive boards of trade and chambers of commerce. Under their pressure, Secretary Sherman promptly inquired the intentions of the German and Russian governments toward American trade and treaty rights in the neighborhood of the new leaseholds. [2] The replies he received apparently allayed the Secretary's own apprehensions and, for the time being, undoubtedly blunted the point of the intermittent British overtures to the McKinley Administration. [3]

German assurances (if such they may be called) were oral, and somewhat evasive in character. Russia's were hardly more definite. Each consisted in perfunctory statements of respect for existing treaty rights in China, and of the intention to admit foreign commerce to Kiaochow and Talienwan, respectively. That they satisfied Sherman indicates nothing so much as the plain lack of national interest impelling him to seek more binding commitments. Moreover, Sherman appears to have discerned political motives

[1] U. S. Department of State, *Commercial Relations of the United States with Foreign Countries, 1896-1897*, 21-22.

[2] The New York Chamber of Commerce petitioned McKinley to take steps "for the prompt and energetic defense of the existing treaty rights of our citizens in China, and for the preservation and protection of their important commercial interests in that Empire." February 3, 1898. Sherman replied to the Chamber February 11 that he was giving the matter his most careful consideration. Vagts, II, 1017. The same day he instructed Ambassador A. D. White to sound Bülow "as to the intention of the German Government with respect to the foreign commerce of Kiao-chau." Sherman to White, February 11, 1898. Copy in Rockhill papers.

[3] All of the assurances, or statements taken for assurances, received by the State Department from the German and Russian Governments, *up to the date of the despatch of the Hay notes*, are itemized in a handwritten memorandum submitted to William W. Rockhill, September 6, 1899, by Assistant Secretary of State Adee. The latter's initialed note, covering the memorandum, reads: "Dear Rockhill— Here are Mr. Martin's notes of the assurances given by Russia and Germany. I have modified your drafts accordingly. A. A. A." For complete text of memorandum, see appendix.

in England's overtures to the United States, and to have feared the involvement in European rivalries into which they might lead. He could see no reason why the United States should "view with any jealousy the southward movement of Russia," he wrote, the year after his retirement. "Russia is our very good friend and has been so for many years. England would like to enlist us in all the controversies that she has on her hands in Eastern Asia. She would then make sure of us as an ally. But it is not to our interest to act in that manner." [1]

During the summer and autumn of 1898 the McKinley Administration was too preoccupied with the Spanish War to give much further attention to events in the Far East. Twice the President expressed concern for the open door; in his instructions to the peace commissioners (September 16)[2] and in his annual message to Congress (December 5).

"The United States has not been an indifferent spectator of the extraordinary events transpiring in the Chinese Empire," he declared on the latter occasion, "whereby portions of its maritime provinces are passing under the control of various European powers; *but the prospect that the vast commerce which the energy of our citizens and the necessity of our staple productions for Chinese uses has built up in those regions may not be prejudiced through any exclusive treatment by the new occupants has obviated the need of our country becoming an actor in the scene.* Our position among nations, having a large Pacific coast and a constantly expanding direct trade with the farther Orient, gives us the equitable claim to consideration and friendly treatment in this regard, and it will be my aim to subserve our large interests in that quarter by all means appropriate to the constant policy of our Government. The territories of Kiao-Chow, of Wei-hai-wai, and of Port Arthur and Talienwan, leased to Germany, Great Britain, and Russia respectively for terms of years, *will,* it is announced, *be open to international commerce during such alien occupation; and if no discriminating treatment of American citizens and their trade be found to exist, or*

[1] Vagts, II, 1042 n.
[2] Cf. pp. 29-30, above.

*be hereafter developed, the desire of this Government would appear to be realized."* [1]

The President, apparently, was no less willing to accept the German and Russian assurances at face value than Secretary Sherman had been. He was determined to avoid any commitment that might make the United States "an actor in the scene" of European intrigue and aggression then being enacted in China. A month later (January 8, 1899) he proved his determination with a second rebuff to Pauncefote.

With Dewey's victory, the McKinley Administration underwent a change of heart. The first impulse of Mr. Conger (who succeeded Mr. Denby at Peking July 11, 1898) was to combat the concessions-scramble by taking part in it. He deplored his countrymen's lack of interest in the great financial and commercial opportunities in China, an interest which he took it upon himself to promote by urging, first the retention of Manila, then a more agressive American competition for railway contracts, and finally the acquisition of a port in China itself.

"It is true," he wrote Hay (November 3, 1898), "the integrity of China can easily be preserved by an alliance of a few of the great powers. But to what end? If simply it preserve the old China without possibility of material development or trade progress, then it is not worth while. But if real progress is to be made, mines opened, railways constructed, resources developed, markets created, and business established, Orientalism must effectually give way to Occidentalism. In my judgment this is bound to occur. It may and it may not be soon, but the sooner it comes, the better for China, as well as for those who seek her development and the trade which will follow. In that event, we should see to it that as many doors are left open for us as possible *and we ought to be ready, either by negotiation or by actual possession, to own and control at least one good port from which we can potently assert our rights and effectively wield our influence."* [2]

[1] *For. Rel.*, 1898, xxii. Italics inserted.
[2] Conger to Hay, November 3, 1898. Vagts, II, 1040 n. Italics inserted.

A few months later he asked Hay outright if he might not seek for the United States a "strong foothold" in China from which it would be possible "to keep permanently open doors for our commerce." [1]

During the winter of 1899 the pressure of business groups for a more spirited Far Eastern policy increased. American industries (especially the textile) were becoming engrossed in the markets of Northern China and Manchuria, the very regions most affected by German and Russian imperialism.[2] The diplomats of these two nations duly noted the "new and brilliantly successful imperialism" of the United States, which they took for granted would direct its energies toward Eastern Asia. "The United States," wrote Cassini, the Russian ambassador in Washington, soon after the Battle of Manila, "has definitely started on a policy . . . whose horizons are much broader than the traditional ones held heretofore." Mouravieff, the Russian Foreign Minister, spoke of the United States as having "acquired a new view of its mission in this world." [3] It was true: American politicians and diplomats, the statesmen of the expansionist school, had turned promoters on a large scale, and were doing what they could to push American commerce and capital into the Far East. The few business groups already active there were encouraged to seek the support of Washington. Hay responded to their petitions with further soundings of Mouravieff, the reassuring results of which did not mitigate the Secretary's British-fed mistrust of all things Russian.[4]

---

[1] Conger to Hay, March 16, 1899. Vagts, II, 1040.

[2] Cf. Vagts, II, 1038-1058. This was especially true of the newly established southern branch of the industry. In 1899 the millowners of South Carolina formally resolved that "The prosperity of the cotton mill business in South Carolina depends in our opinion on the China trade." *Ibid.*, 1046.

[3] *Krasnyi Arkhiv*, L, 95; LII, 125, 131.

[4] In response to a petition of the Pepperell Manufacturing Co. of Boston, dated January 3, 1899, signed by many influential businessmen, endorsed by Lodge, and expressing the fear of being "shut out from the markets of that portion of North China which is already occupied or threatened by Russia," Hay instructed Peirce (American Chargé d'Affaires at St. Petersburg) to sound Mouravieff as to

Business and diplomacy were not the only forces impelling Hay toward his fateful decision. American missionaries in the Far East had also been thrilled by the conquest of the Philippines. In 1899 there were between one thousand and fifteen hundred of them in China where they, and their predecessors, had early assumed a political importance out of all proportion to their numbers.[1] Now their situation was very comparable to that of American businessmen in China. Just as they were rejoicing in the annexation of the Philippines for the aid and comfort they thought it would give their cause, they found themselves confronted by an anti-foreign movement stirred up partly by the concessions-scramble, partly by their own proselytizing, that was to culminate in the Boxer Rebellion. In 1899 they, too, wished the United States to show a strong hand in China.

So far the McKinley Administration had adhered strictly to precedent in the Far East. It had kept free of alliances or understandings with foreign powers. It had called the attention of Europe to the long-established interest of the United States in the open door and the preservation of existing treaty rights. From the two particular nations that caused it most alarm it had obtained assurances. The President had declared himself satisfied with these, and proved it by rejecting Pauncefote for the second time

his intentions toward foreign trade and treaty rights in these regions. When Charlemagne Tower succeeded Hitchcock (who vacated his post February 5, 1899) he carried out the same instructions. Peirce's and Tower's advices, dated February 25 and April 26 respectively, brought the usual statements of respect for all treaty rights in China, and glowing prospects for American trade with Russia, especially in heavy industries. Peirce and Tower, like Hitchcock, were more impressed by the opportunities for large sales of American industrial products to Russia than by the latter's threat to America's China trade. See their despatches in Vagts, II, 1046-1047. Also in *Foreign Relations*, 1899, Hitchcock to Hay, January 21; Hitchcock to Mouravieff, January 8; Peirce to Hay, February 13, October 11, 594-599.

[1] Denby estimated the number of American missionaries in China in 1898 as 1500. Remer, C. F., in his *Foreign Investments in China*, 259, places the figure for 1900 at "about 1,000 missionaries representing about 30 societies," an increase from 210 in 1875.

within a year. In spite of the concessions-scramble, American trade with China, small though it was, was actually increasing. If it appeared likely to certain business groups that Russia would some day close them out of Northern China, others contemplated great profit in the sale of products essential to Russia in the development of that region. As yet Germany had been no less hospitable to American trade and capital in Shantung than England had been in the Yangtse Valley. American fears of exclusion, like American hopes of gain, were all in the future. Up to the summer of 1899 neither had been strong enough to cause a departure from the diplomatic traditions and precedents of the past hundred years.

Then, in July and August, through informal, personal channels, the British influence was once more turned on Hay, this time with success.

Like most Secretaries of State, John Hay had only a superficial knowledge of conditions in the Far East. To advise him on this complicated subject he had chosen a friend and, as it happened, one of the best-informed authorities on China of his generation, William W. Rockhill. Born in Philadelphia in 1854, Rockhill's early youth was spent in France, where he completed his education at the military school at Saint Cyr, and where he acquired an interest in the Chinese language and literature. After three years of service as lieutenant in the French Foreign Legion in Algeria, he returned to the United States, and in 1884 procured an appointment as Second Secretary of the Peking Legation. The next year he was promoted to First Secretary. During the winter of 1886-1887 he served as Chargé d'Affaires at Seoul, Korea. He had entered the diplomatic service as a means of pursuing his Chinese studies. He resigned because of personal incompatibility with Denby. After two famous journeys of exploration through Mongolia and Tibet (1888-1889 and 1891-1892) he returned to the diplomatic service as Chief Clerk of the State Department in 1893. From February 14, 1896, to May 10, 1897, he served as Assistant Secretary of State under Olney, during part of which period (March 4 to May 10, 1897) he filled the gap between Olney and Sherman as Acting Secretary.

By this time Rockhill's scholarly writings and explorations had brought him membership in learned Oriental societies and scientific institutes all over the world. His wide experience in the Far East and in the Department of State had established his reputation as an expert on China and earned him the friendship and admiration of influential Republicans including Roosevelt, Lodge and Hay.[1] When it became evident that Denby was to be replaced, Rockhill's friends urged McKinley to appoint him Minister to China, a post his training pre-eminently qualified him to fill. They were disappointed. Rockhill was sent to Athens as Minister to Greece, Roumania and Servia. It was from this post that Adee and Hay rescued him in April, 1899, by helping to secure his appointment as Director of the Bureau of American Republics in Washington, presumably in order to have the benefit of his counsel on affairs in Eastern Asia.[2] In any event, Rockhill had no sooner assumed his new office (May 22) than the Secretary of State began to solicit his advice.[3]

Rockhill, too, had his confidential adviser in Alfred E. Hippisley, a British subject and a member of the Chinese Imperial Maritime Customs Service. Hippisley was an old China hand. It should be recalled that the Chinese customs service was super-

[1] Cf. White to Rockhill, March 12, 1898. Rockhill papers.

[2] Telegram, Adee to Rockhill, April 4, 1899. Rockhill was miserable at Athens, where he lost his first wife, and from which post he besought his friends to rescue him. The latter, especially Roosevelt and Adams, urged his appointment as Librarian of Congress. Disappointed again, they were successful in obtaining for him the Pan-American Directorship, which he accepted with alacrity. In the whole transaction, Adee appears to have had as much influence as Hay, perhaps more. See Adee to Rockhill, February 3, 1899; Adams to Rockhill, February 16; Roosevelt to McCauley, March 9. "You will find Hay needing you badly," Adams wrote April 6. "Whether he will be allowed to gratify his needs, I know not." Adams to Rockhill, April 6. Rockhill papers. Could Adams have been alluding to Hay's need for assistance in overcoming the President's opposition to co-operating with the British? Cf. also Dennett, Hay, 298 ff.

[3] Hay to Rockhill, June 1. Rockhill papers.

intended by the British, a privilege ultimately sanctioned by treaty in 1898 for as long as England's share of China's foreign trade should exceed that of any other nation. A member of this service since 1867,[1] Hippisley had long followed political affairs in China with a sharp, intelligent eye. His acquaintance with Rockhill dated from the autumn of 1884 when the latter first joined the staff of the American legation in Peking. "In a small community such as that of Peking," wrote Hippisley many years later, "acquaintance quickly ripens into intimacy between persons who have similar tastes, and both Rockhill and I were deeply interested in China and Chinese politics, and in my case the intimacy was made the closer by my marriage in the following year with Miss Howard, a friend of long standing of Mrs. Rockhill's, who had accompanied the latter and her husband from Baltimore." [2] What Rockhill was to Hay, Hippisley was to Rockhill: an old friend and trusted adviser on the Far East.[3]

Mutual friendship—and fate—drew the three men together in the early summer of 1899. Simultaneously with Rockhill's inauguration as Director General of the Bureau of American Republics, a periodic leave of absence brought Hippisley to the United States on his way home to England. From about the middle of June to the end of July the Englishman visited his wife's family in Baltimore. He was pleased to renew his acquaintance with Rockhill, whom he had not seen for over ten years. "Naturally," he remembers, "I went over as frequently as I could to Washington to discuss the conditions in China with him and especially what could be done to maintain the 'open door' or

[1] Cf. China, Imperial Maritime Customs Service List, 1879-1890, also Hippisley to Harris, May 31, 1921. Rockhill papers.

[2] Hippisley memorandum enclosed in Hippisley to Dennett, August 22, 1935.

[3] During Rockhill's previous service in the State Department he had exchanged much confidential information and criticism on China with Hippisley. Cf. Rockhill to Hippisley, October 30, 1894; Hippisley to Rockhill, January 26 and November 25, 1895, February 28, 1897. Rockhill papers. Hippisley's letters are discerning chronicles of affairs in China and possess considerable literary charm.

equality of opportunity for all nations in that country." [1] On one of these occasions Rockhill, deeply impressed by his friend's ideas, introduced him to the Secretary of State. Hay heard him expound, in outline, the scheme ultimately comprehended by the open door notes.[2]

Throughout the informal negotiations of that summer, Hippisley was clearly the prime mover. Hay, though disposed to cooperate with England, was waiting for Rockhill to find a way to do it. Rockhill, who had been absent from China for seven years, was rusty on China. Hippisley came fresh from the scene, his mind brimming with images and theories of the concessions-scramble and how to deal with it. It was he who took the initiative, who supplied the concrete plans; nor did he lack encouragement. "China is, and will remain, the one absorbing subject," Rockhill told him, "so I am awfully anxious to have all the data you can give me on the subject, that I may not make any mistake, and that my conclusions shall be practicable." [3]

When, about August first, Hay left Washington for his summer home in New Hampshire, and Hippisley departed Baltimore on a leisurely journey, *via* Lenox and Bar Harbor to Quebec (whence he would sail for England September seventh), Hippisley opened an active correspondence with Rockhill. "As I shall not now have an opportunity of seeing you before we start for Europe," he wrote July 25, "I write these lines to ask you to use your influence towards, if possible, inducing the govt. to do what it can to maintain the open door for ordinary commerce in China."

[1] Hippisley memorandum in Hippisley to Dennett, August 22, 1935. Cf. Hippisley to Harris, May 31, 1921; Hippisley to Rockhill, July 25, 1899. Rockhill papers.

[2] Hippisley to Rockhill, July 25, 1899; Rockhill to Hay, August 3, 1899. Rockhill papers. The meeting must have occurred about the middle of July, as Hippisley refers to it in his letter of the twenty-fifth as having taken place "the other day," and Rockhill, on August third as "a few weeks ago."

[3] Rockhill to Hippisley, August 26, 1899. Rockhill papers. On another occasion Rockhill gratefully assured Hippisley that he was but the latter's "mouthpiece." Rockhill to Hippisley, August 29, 1899. Hippisley papers.

Spheres of interest—euphemistically termed "the economic & geographical gravitation of certain portions of the Chinese Empire"—have now been recognized and must be treated as existing facts. So far, however, the special rights and privileges claimed by each Power in its own sphere, consist only of preferential or exclusive rights to construct railroads & exploit mines in it. They have not as yet been extended to a claim to impose a differential tariff on merchandise consumed in or passing through it; but how soon such a claim may be advanced no one can say. I venture therefore to suggest that the U. S. loses no time in calling the attention of all the Powers to the changes now taking place in China, and—while disclaiming any desire on her own part to annex territory—in expressing her determination not to sacrifice for her annually increasing trade any of the rights or privileges she has secured by treaty with China; and, to assure this end, that she should obtain an undertaking from each European Power that a) the Chinese treaty tariff shall without discrimination apply to all merchandise entering its spheres of influence; and that b) any treaty ports in them shall not be interfered with.

This is, I think, all that can be attempted now that events have reached the length they have; but it would do much. It would protect the interests already vested in the open ports and would secure equality of opportunity for commerce proper. It would not, it is true, secure equality of opportunity for mining or railroad building; but such equality has scarcely existed in the past except in name, for such concessions have usually been granted to those who were most liberal in greasing the palms of the middlemen. Merchants in England, too, are gradually coming round to this view, which I ventured to lay before Mr. Hay (as I mentioned to you) when I saw him the other day. But I should like to see the U. S. take the lead in securing such an agreement, partly because I think action by her would be viewed with less suspicion than that of any other Power would be, and partly because, if telegrams published in the newspapers can be relied on, she has already asked for assurances, of which such an agreement would be the logical completion. . . . As things are now, I do not believe any Power would hesitate to agree to such an undertaking; but events move rapidly in China, and what is possible now might easily not be possible later on.[1]

[1] Hippisley to Rockhill, July 25, 1899. Rockhill papers.

Rockhill passed Hippisley's recommendations on to Hay after adding to their weight his own authoritative *imprimatur*.[1] The same day he replied to Hippisley:

You know what my views are about the position the United States should take in China; I would like to see it make a declaration in some form or other, which would be understood by China as a pledge on our part to assist in maintaining the integrity of the Empire. I fear, however, that home politics and next year's elections will interfere with this, for it might be interpreted by a large part of the voting population of the United States, especially the Irish and the Germans, as an adoption of the policy advocated by England, and any leaning towards England on the part of the administration would, at this time and for the next year to come, be dangerous, and might lose the President his nomination. I consequently fear that he will do absolutely nothing either on the lines you indicate, and which are clearly those most beneficial to our interests in China, or in any other which will commit us. We will simply continue drifting along.[2]

Hay confirmed these doubts. "I thank you for your letter inclosing Mr. Hippisley's," he wrote, August 7. "I am fully awake to the great importance of what you say, and am more than ready to act. But the senseless prejudices in certain sections of the 'Senate and people' compel us to move with great caution." [3]

Hippisley did not give up hope. His reason for "urging *prompt* action" along the lines of his last note was, he explained, "precisely to forestall any suggestion likely to prove injurious to the Administration that it was following the lead of or leaning towards England by inducing it to take the initiative itself; then if England took similar action, she would follow America's lead." The Englishman had developed a remarkable solicitude for the welfare of the United States.[4] "I think it would be suicidal for America to drift and do nothing for another year," he warned.

[1] Rockhill to Hay, August 3, 1899. Rockhill papers.
[2] Rockhill to Hippisley, August 3, 1899. Rockhill papers.
[3] Hay to Rockhill, August 7, 1899. Rockhill papers.
[4] On the twenty-first Hippisley wrote that "if my staying longer in this country

My latest advices from Peking say: "the activity of the Russians in Manchuria is simply wonderful. . . . The Russification of Peking and of North China will proceed as rapidly as has that of Manchuria." These are precisely the districts which are the great consumers of American textile fabrics, and I don't for a moment believe that American manufacturers will sit by with folded hands and see these districts closed without making an effort to retain them. Pressure will therefore be brought to bear upon the Administration and it may then have no option but to take such action as I have suggested, with possibly however the difference of following instead of leading England.[1]

This time Rockhill's response was more encouraging. He had received "today," he wrote on the eighteenth, "pretty clear assurances from the State Department that it may take some action sooner than could be anticipated from the position it held until within a few weeks and which I gave you in my last letter." But Rockhill was not over-sanguine. Once more he showed himself to be in advance of Hippisley: he favored securing "tangible" assurances from the powers "as to their desire to maintain and insure the integrity of the Chinese Empire. . . ." This, he still believed the Administration was unwilling to consider; the best he and Hippisley could do was to "keep pegging away at it."[2] The next day he submitted to Adee long extracts from Hippisley's last two letters.[3]

Meanwhile two things had come to Hippisley's support. Almost simultaneously came the news of the return to the United States of Dr. Jacob Gould Schurman, Chairman of the President's Philippine Commission, and the Czar's ukase of August 15 declaring Talienwan a free port. All that restrained Hay from embarking on the policy advocated by Hippisley, apparently, was the opposition to it of the President himself. Whatever the true

would serve any useful purpose, I would willingly defer my sailing." Hippisley to Rockhill, August 21, 1899. Rockhill papers.

[1] Hippisley to Rockhill, August 16, 1899. Rockhill papers.

[2] Rockhill to Hippisley, August 18, 1899.

[3] Rockhill to Adee, August 19, 1899.

source of this opposition—respect for tradition, the lingering influence of Sherman, sincere conviction or mere partisan expediency —it had tied the Secretary's hands since his assumption of office. Undoubtedly Hay had been converted as early as June, 1898, when he had written McKinley a personal letter from the London embassy, urging him to reconsider the first Pauncefote overture. More lately he had professed to be "more than ready to act" and lamented the "senseless prejudices" that restrained him. It is probable that, for the past year, whenever the occasion had offered, he had urged on the President some such policy as that now in the making. Dr. Schurman and the Czar seem to have knocked the last props from under McKinley's resistance.

To post himself on the mysterious Philippines, McKinley had appointed a Commission which sailed for Manila early in February, 1899, under the leadership of Dr. Jacob Gould Schurman, President of Cornell University, to investigate and report exhaustively on conditions in the islands. Academic duties brought Schurman home in advance of his colleagues. He arrived in San Francisco August 14, the day before the Czar issued his ukase. The President had reposed great trust in Schurman, his personal representative, to whom he looked for advice on the Far East as Hay looked to Rockhill. There could be no doubt that Schurman's opinions would carry weight with the White House.[1] It was

[1] Schurman's own account of his selection as chairman of the commission advances the view that until January, 1899, the President had arrived at no definite Philippine policy, and intimates that had the Commission brought an unfavorable report, the islands might still have been relinquished. Schurman, J. G., *Philippine Affairs, A Retrospect and Outlook*, 1-4. Rockhill and Hippisley referred to Schurman's arrival and the influence his views would have on McKinley. "You have no doubt seen the published interview with Dr. Schurman at Chicago on his way back from the Philippines. Enlightened by the Japanese he appears to realize almost as fully as we do the present serious condition of affairs in China and the effect it will have on American and British trade there. His views . . . must exercise considerable influence. . . ." H. to R., August 16. "I have no doubt that Dr. Schurman's views, as expressed in an interview published the day before yesterday in the papers, will exercise very great influence on the decisions of the Administration." R. to H., August 18. Rockhill papers.

therefore much to the satisfaction of Rockhill and Hippisley that the chief Philippine commissioner told reporters:

As I said . . . to one of the great statesmen of Japan, after I had seen something of the Orient, it seems to me that the great question there is not Formosa nor the Philippines, but China. . . . It is feared, now that Russia has taken Manchuria, it will try to encroach gradually on some or all of the other eighteen provinces of China, and when it gets them it will do as that country has done hitherto—put a duty on all foreign goods. . . . Englishmen and Japan [sic] feel that America should stand with them in preventing the dismemberment of China. . . . Everywhere and at all times . . . it was recognized that the future of China was the one overshadowing question. China, it was agreed, should maintain its independent position, but its doors should be kept open. It means much to England and Japan and not less to America.[1]

While apparently belying Schurman's fears of Russia (and substantiating the judgment of Hitchcock and Tower) the Czar's ukase nevertheless had the same effect as Schurman's interview. Hippisley describes it vividly:

"I received last night your interesting letter of the 18th," he wrote Rockhill, August 21. "I am so encouraged by the possibility of the govt. taking action with regard to China that I send you a memo. on the 'open door' I drew up so soon as I read the Czar's ukase declaring Talien-wan an open port *for the whole period of the treaty*, i.e., for the next 23 years. This is most satisfactory. It gives a natural opportunity for opening negotiations to settle the conditions that are to hold in China for, at least, the immediate future, & it seems to promise co-operation on Russia's part in the direction we hope for. Let the Admin. then act at once, say I, and so forestall any advance on the part of Gt. Britain; and if it does, I foretell success. Proposals from England would be viewed with suspicion; proposals from the U. S. would not— on the contrary, they would be received in a friendly spirit. And I

---

[1] Schurman as quoted by New York *Times*, August 16, 1899.

would earnestly suggest that negotiations be opened before Beresford arrives, for, bluff, garrulous, and unrestrained by any sense of responsibility as he is, and already committed to impossible proposals, he will, I fear, do much more harm than good by his speeches.

"Of course, if the independence & integrity of China can be safeguarded, too, let that be accomplished. I entirely agree with you as to the value and importance of such a step; but I had not broached it because it seemed to me the Admin. was very lukewarm about taking any action & hence I cut my proposals down to an irreducible minimum. But the ukase changes everything, for it seems to show that whatever Russia's ulterior objects may be, the Czar desires to move very slowly, realizing that haste may prove the spark to cause an explosion by which the Chinese Empire may be shattered, the pieces being picked up by those who would prove but unwelcome neighbors. And the article in the N. A. Review inspired by Prince Oukhtomsky states distinctly that 'the independence & integrity of China is a fundamental principle of Russian policy in Asia, because her consolidation means our own consolidation.' Exactly how much influence Oukhtomsky possesses, I do not know; but as his relations with the Czar for the past 10 years have been intimate, it must, I presume, be considerable: and as he here invites the U. S. to join Russia in taking steps to insure China's independence and integrity, any proposition put forward to that end by the U. S. seems assured in advance of more than respectful consideration at St. Petersburg. The public need know nothing of the steps taken by the Sec. of State till the negotiations have been consummated, and the announcement then that the U. S. had secured China's independence and so served the cause of peace & civilization would be a trump card for the Admin. and crush all the life out of the anti-imperialism agitation of Bryan, Croker & Co. France is the only Power, in my opinion, from which any opposition is to be anticipated, because wherever she gains a foothold she claims territorial jurisdiction and it has long been well known that she is casting greedy eyes on an extension of her Indo-China Empire through Yunnan to embrace Szechuan, and her claims for indemnification for the anti-missionary outbreak in the latter province have been carefully framed to further that policy. But if Russia adopts the American proposals, France will speedily fall into line. The prospect seems to me therefore bright beyond hope: but the iron being hot, it ought to be struck now. . . ."[1]

This crucial letter was accompanied by a "Memorandum on the 'Open Door' in China," drawn up by Hippisley on August 17, the substance of which was to be incorporated in the open door notes.[2] Hippisley had fired his last telling shot. Though his letters continued, both frequent and hortatory, long after he had returned to England, the writing of the open door notes was now in the hands of Rockhill.[3]

At first Rockhill, still without further hint of action by the State Department, considered incorporating Hippisley's memorandum in a magazine article. For this project on August 26 he sought his friend's approval: "I thought it was better that the article should appear over my name than over that of an English-

[1] Hippisley to Rockhill, August 21, 1899. Both correspondents discounted Beresford's influence, Rockhill on one occasion referring to him as a "bag of wind," R. to H., Oct. 13, 1899. Beresford returned to the United States in October to continue his propaganda, the prospect of which is referred to by Hippisley above. The article in the *North American Review* was submitted to Hippisley by Rockhill August 18, and his criticism invited. The difference between the ukase and the assurances in regard to Talienwan received by Sherman March 28, 1898 (cf. p. 55 ff., above), was that the ukase declared Talienwan a free port, i.e., without tariffs, while the assurances merely declared it an open port—i.e., that foreign commerce would be admitted, subject to the Russian tariff.

[2] The memorandum, together with Rockhill's adaptation of it, is printed in the appendix. It will be seen that the portions of Hippisley's writings quoted or cited by Dennett (*John Hay*, 290-291) are those retailed by Rockhill to Hay from Hippisley's letters of July 25 and August 16, not from the final memorandum, the original of which is in the Rockhill papers.

[3] On August 26 Hippisley wrote a voluminous "continuation" of his communication of the 21st, which, however, did not reach Rockhill until the latter had completed his memorandum for Hay. See R. to H., August 28. Hippisley's postscript amplifies but does not alter the conclusions of his August 21 letter and is of interest chiefly for the mistrust of Russia it reveals. Hippisley was afraid that Russia would try to seize control of the Chinese customs service and was anxious to prevent it. H. to R., August 26, Rockhill papers. Hippisley wrote two more letters before sailing for England, one from Bar Harbor (August 28) and one from Quebec (Sept. 7, the morning of his departure). From England he continued to correspond regularly with Rockhill all through the fall.

man in the Chinese service, for obvious reasons." [1] Hippisley
agreed, but he cautioned Rockhill not to "steal the Admin.'s
thunder" or to alarm France and Russia prematurely by revealing his stratagem in too great detail. He thought it would be
better first to prepare public opinion for the general plan and for
Rockhill "to prime the Sec. of State on the details." [2]

The magazine article was never published. For the day after
Rockhill broached the idea to Hippisley he received the long-
awaited word from Hay:

*Confidential*
Newbury, N. H.<br>
Aug. 24, 99.

DEAR ROCKHILL:

Adee has sent me your note with extracts from Mr. H's letters. I
have already received, from the representatives of the powers concerned, assurances that the recent extension of spheres of influence &c.,
will not result in restricting our commercial freedom of action in China.
But I agree with you that some more formal engagement of that sort
would be desirable. If you have time between now and next Wednesday to set down your views on this question—in the form of a draft
instruction to Mr. Choate, Mr. White, Mr. Tower and Gen. Porter—
I would be greatly obliged. I hope to be in Washington Wednesday
morning the 30th. for a few days' stay.

I am taking a good deal for granted—your presence in Washington,
your leisure, and your inclination to give us a *coup d'epaule*. But if it
should not be convenient, all right.

Yours sincerely,<br>
J. H. [3]

Rockhill was elated. "My project of publishing our views on
the policy of the United States in China has been nipped in the
bud," he wrote Hippisley on the twenty-eighth,

---

[1] Rockhill to Hippisley, August 26, 1899. Rockhill papers.
[2] Hippisley to Rockhill, August 28, 1899. Rockhill papers.
[3] Rockhill papers.

as I have been requested by the Secretary of State, to submit the project to him on the steps which should be taken by the United States at once to insure our commercial interest. I have embodied the substance of all your remarks in it. Colonel Hay will be here tomorrow, and I shall have a talk with him on the matter. . . . I think things are in a fair way to go according to our views.[1]

Rockhill followed this the next day with an even more specific acknowledgment. The memorandum, he explained to Hippisley, embodied "all your views," but was phrased to convey the impression "that the policy suggested was not a British one—that the Britishers had sinned against the 'Open-door Policy' as much if not more than the others. . . . As the memo. will have to be submitted to the President, I thought it better that it should seem as if coming from me alone. He knows me. If coming from you, it would require additional explanation. I have, and shall again whenever I can, show that I am but your mouthpiece. The question seems now in very good shape. Hay's interest is awakened and I think we will do something."[2]

The Rockhill memorandum (dated August 28, 1899) appears to have been the final instrument of McKinley's conversion. For, on September 5, Rockhill composed the actual drafts of the open door notes themselves, which, after a few corrections by Adee, were despatched the following day, over the signature of the Secretary of State, to the American ambassadors in London, Berlin and St. Petersburg.[3] The notes, like the memoranda from

[1] Rockhill to Hippisley, August 28, 1899. Rockhill papers.

[2] Rockhill to Hippisley, August 29, 1899. Hippisley papers. Hippisley was pleased that the "memo. instead of taking the shape of a magazine article went direct to the President, because I believe much more good will result." H. to R., Sept. 7, 1899. Rockhill papers.

[3] This modifies, somewhat, Dennett's statement (*John Hay*, 291) that on August 28 "Rockhill forwarded to Newbury a memorandum from which the notes were written, with slight verbal changes." There was one more step in the transaction. Rockhill not only submitted to Hay the memorandum of August 28, but actually wrote the open door notes of September 6. These do not even seem to have been corrected by Hay but by Adee. Cf. Adee to Rockhill, Sept. 6, 1899,

which they were written, and as their authors had privately agreed, eschewed the subject of China's territorial integrity. This Rockhill felt to be "still such a complex question that I do not think we have it in anything like a shape to discuss it advantageously . . ."[1] so awfully big, that I think for the time being we had better not broach it over here."[2] But, he believed, the notes would have the desired effect of giving China breathing space, of promoting "a general line of policy which may be favorable to the maintenance and the strengthening of the Peking Government."[3]

The notes were carefully worded. Their authors were aware of the exigencies of American politics that restrained their own personal desires. Accordingly they recognized the spheres of influence as existing facts, omitted any reference to mining and railway concessions, and the whole perplexing problem of capital investment, and specifically asked only for equal commercial opportunity within each sphere.[4] Each power addressed was requested to give its formal assurances that it would observe the regulations presented by the notes *mutatis mutandis*. But that is not all the notes requested. In addition to its own assurances, each power was urged to co-operate with the United States in obtaining the assurances of all the other powers concerned. Thus the notes invoked not only the time-honored American principle of the open door, but also the so-called "co-operative policy." The combination of the two, applied to the current situation in China, made the notes something more than a mere iteration of the traditional Far Eastern policy of the United States. It made

p. 57, n. 3, above. Rockhill's memorandum, his draft of the open door notes and the final draft as despatched abroad are printed in the appendix.

[1] Rockhill to Hippisley, August 29, 1899. Hippisley papers.

[2] Same to same, September 14, 1899. Rockhill papers.

[3] *Ibid.*

[4] See text of notes, appendix. To their identical formula Germany, Russia and England were invited to adhere September 6, Japan, November 13, Italy, November 17 and France, November 21. Cf. *For. Rel.*, 1899, 128-143.

them a foray into World politics, an attempt to influence the foreign policies of the European powers in such a way as to establish free commercial competition in the region of Eastern Asia. It was an unusual thing for the United States to seek to influence the dispensations of international politics in regions outside its own hemisphere.

Rockhill continued to play a pivotal role in the open door negotiations until they were concluded.[1] His letters to Hippisley during the fall of 1899 conveyed the optimistic belief that the "Hay" notes had brought a halt to the partitioning of China. He was convinced, he wrote Edwin Denby in January, that the assurances of the powers had "only been granted on account of the strength and position of the United States in the East.

Of course, there is another side to the question, and that is that none of the European Powers interested in China would care, at the present moment at least, to openly oppose such a seemingly very moderate request as that this Government has made, as it would put them in a very awkward position not only as regards each other, but as regards China. There is no doubt, however, that by these assurances, or rather by the acceptance by each of the European Powers of the declarations sought to be obtained from them by the United States, *this country holds the balance of power in China.* I hope sincerely that we may make good use of it, *not only for our trade,* but for strengthening the Peking Government so that it can find no means of escaping the performance of all its obligations to the Treaty Powers. *What we have*

[1] Many of the instructions to White, Choate and Tower were drafted by Rockhill, as well as numerous memoranda for Hay. He personally conducted many—perhaps most—of the "conversations" with Cassini, memoranda of which are among his papers. All of which indicates (as does his subsequent appointment as special commissioner to China) that the whole proceeding was submitted to his scrutiny, and nothing decided without his approval. Cf. Rockhill correspondence, September, 1899, to July, 1900, esp. Rockhill to Hippisley, Oct. 13, 1899. Memorandum for Hay, Nov. 24, 1899; memorandum for Hay, Dec. 1, 1899. Draft Instruction to United States Ambassador in Paris, Dec. 12, 1899; Cassini to Rockhill, Dec. 19, 1899; memorandum for Hay, same date; Rockhill to Hippisley, January 16, 1900. Hay to Rockhill, Feb. 10, 1900; Adee to Rockhill, Feb. 21, 1900.

*obtained will undoubtedly help to insure, for the time being, the integrity of the Chinese Empire,* but, on its side, China can and must discharge its international obligations." [1]

A careful perusal of the replies to the open door notes shows Rockhill's assumptions, both as to the influence of the United States in the Far East and the effectiveness of the notes themselves, to have been unfounded. The replies to the notes were uniformly evasive and non-committal. The first and most satisfactory reply was the British, but even this left much to be desired. Though Lord Salisbury professed his enthusiasm for the open door principle, he was loath to apply it either to Kowloon or to Weihaiwei, contending that the former was a colony, the latter a leased territory, and opposing the application of the principle to areas in either of these categories. [2]

The Prime Minister's attitude was "rather disappointing in view of his first reception of your proposition," Ambassador Choate wrote Hay. [3] Moreover, Salisbury was of the opinion that "we are a little too sanguine in our expectations of obtaining Declarations from the other Powers." [4] Nearly three months elapsed before Salisbury was willing to compromise, which he did grudgingly. Great Britain agreed to the application of the open door principle to Weihaiwei, and to all British leased territory and spheres of interest in China, present or future; the United States acquiesced in the exemption of Kowloon from this rule. The entire British declaration was then emasculated by the proviso that it was "to be considered as dependent on similar assent by the other Powers in like circumstances." [5]

[1] Rockhill to Denby, January 13, 1900. Italics inserted.

[2] Department of State Archives. From London, 1899-1900. Choate to Hay, September 22, 1899; same to same, October 2; Salisbury to Choate, October 14; Choate to Hay, October 21.

[3] Archives, *loc. cit.*, Choate to Hay, October 21.

[4] *Ibid.*, same to same, November 3.

[5] *Ibid.*, same to same, December 1; Salisbury to Choate, November 30; Choate to Salisbury, November 15; Bertie to Choate, December 10; Choate to Hay, De-

The replies of the other powers were full of loopholes, Russia's amounting to a thinly disguised rejection of the whole proposition.[1] Each of them, like the British, made its acceptance contingent upon the acceptance of all the others, which reduced every one to the least common denominator, the Russian. Rockhill and Hay realized the situation perfectly and tried to meet it with bluff. Rockhill privately admitted to Hippisley that the Russian reply "has what we call in America a string attached to it"; but he thought it "prudent" to accept it none the less.[2] "Our object," Hay wrote Tower, "is now to give the widest significance to the Russian reply of which it is capable. Without running the risk of bringing upon ourselves a contradiction of our assumptions, we want to take it for granted that Russia has acceded to our proposals without much qualification." [3] At length, on March 20, the Secretary of State cavalierly announced that he had received satisfactory assurances from all the powers addressed, and that he regarded each as "final and definitive." [4]

Hay had not long to wait to discover just how "final and definitive" they were. In June, not three months after his expression of satisfaction, a Chinese patriotic society known to the West as the "Boxers" stirred up an armed rebellion against foreign missionaries and concession-hunters and the Manchu Government that had truckled with them. Ripping up portions of the Tientsin-Peking Railway and destroying telegraph lines, the rebels cut off Peking from the outside world, murdered the secretary of the Japanese

cember 11. The quoted passage is from Bertie to Choate, December 10. See also *For. Rel.*, 1899, 128-143.

[1] For text of replies see *For. Rel.*, 1899, 128-143. Russia avoided a categorical commitment on either her own leased territories or spheres of influence. Both Mouraviev, the Russian Foreign Minister, and Cassini, Russian Ambassador in Washington, openly resented Hay's attempt to pin them down to a declaration on the open door. See Hay to Tower, January 22, 1900, and Tower to Hay, February 12, 1900, Dennett, *Hay*, 293-294.

[2] Rockhill to Hippisley, January 16, 1900. Rockhill papers.

[3] Hay to Tower, January 22, 1900. Dennett, *Hay*, 293.

[4] Dennett, *Hay*, 293; *For. Rel.*, 1899, 142.

legation, and the German minister, and besieged the foreign legations in the city. An allied military force was hastily despatched to the relief of the legations. From June 20 until August 14, the day the siege was lifted, the foreigners in Peking lived under fire in the legation compound, menaced by starvation and disease, their fate unknown either to their governments or to the troops marching to their rescue.[1]

It was apparent to Hay from the outset that the disorders had provided certain of the powers not unwelcome pretexts for enlarging their spheres and extending their influence in China. Russia and Germany were on the march. Hay sensed the need—or opportunity—for more extensive measures than mere participation in the allied relief expedition. "We have no policy in China except to protect with energy American interests, and especially American citizens, and the legation," he had wired Conger, June 10. "There must be nothing done which would commit us to future action inconsistent with your standing instructions. There must be no alliances." [2] When the Boxers moved on Peking he showed his hand more fully. On July 3, with the approval of McKinley,

[1] The allied relief force, estimated to have numbered from 17,000 to 19,000, was placed under the command of the German Count von Waldersee after it had reached Peking. The American contingent, starting at 1,700, and increased to 2,500 was exceeded by the Japanese (8,000), Russian (4,800) and British (3,000). Prolonged negotiations following the relief of the legations resulted in the Boxer Protocol of September 7, 1901, which imposed terms of punishment and indemnification on China. The United States accepted its share of the indemnity in bad conscience and by two remissions (1907 and 1924) ultimately returned most of it to China. For detailed accounts of the Rebellion, its origins and settlement, see Steiger, G. N., *China and the Occident, passim;* Langer, *op. cit.,* Ch. XXI; Dennett, *Hay,* Chs. XXV, XXVI; Dennis, 215-248; Vagts, II, 1058-1122. Collectively these works exhaust the material contained in *Foreign Relations, British Documents* and *Die Grosse Politik.* See also *Krasnyi Arkhiv,* XIV, 1-49.

[2] *For. Rel.,* 1900, 143; Dennett, *Hay,* 299. The telegram, which Dennett calls "obviously political" was probably intended as much for the edification of the forthcoming Republican National Nominating Convention as for the instruction of the American Minister in Peking.

he despatched to the powers another circular defining American policy. Unlike the notes of the previous September, this circular asked for no assurances and, indeed, elicited none; it was merely submitted to the consideration of each of the powers addressed. Taking cognizance of the "virtual anarchy" existing in China it set forth the purpose of the United States to "act concurrently with the other powers" in restoring order and protecting the lives and property of its nationals and "all legitimate American interests." In its concluding sentence, however, it added to this purpose a momentous new objective, namely, "to seek a solution which may bring about permanent safety and peace to China, *preserve Chinese territorial and administrative entity*, protect all rights guaranteed to friendly powers by treaty and international law, and safeguard for the world the principle of equal and impartial trade with all parts of the Chinese Empire." [1]

The United States had always stood for the "territorial and administrative entity" of China but in a purely subjective way. It had observed the principle itself; it had not assumed the function of persuading others to observe it. The notes of September 6, as we have seen, had accepted the impairment of China's territorial integrity as a *fait accompli*. They had taken it for granted that foreign spheres of influence and territorial concessions in China would continue to exist, and even to expand, as is proved by the fact that the notes asked for most-favored-nation treatment for American commerce in all future as well as present spheres and leased territories. But the circumstances attending the Boxer Rebellion, following the unfavorable reception of the September notes, led Hay to the conclusion that the maintenance of the open door in China depended on the maintenance of China's complete sovereignty over her own territories. In his circular of July 3, 1900, therefore, he went further than reiterating America's traditional policy of respect for China's integrity, further than asking the powers to observe the principle of equal commercial oppor-

[1] For full text of circular, see appendix. Italics inserted.

tunity. He suggested a collective guarantee of both these conditions. To "preserve" Chinese integrity was something different
from merely respecting it. Assuming, as did Hay himself, that
the chief end of America's Far Eastern policy remained commercial, the circular of July 3 and the subsequent adherence of the
United States to the principles it contained, appreciably altered the
means to that end. He had committed the United States to the
policy of striving to deter its competitors for the Chinese market
from violating the territorial and administrative integrity of the
Chinese nation.

Only Great Britain made response to Hay's circular, and this
in the most casual manner.[1] The other powers proceeded with
their independent plans for obtaining satisfaction from, or taking
advantage of, China. Russia continued to pour troops into Manchuria. That England had no faith in the Hay policy, and had
decided to rely on means other than American note-writing to
defend her interests in China, seems obvious. She had never
banked wholly on American co-operation in the Far East, but
had used this only as one of three instruments, the other two being
outright participation in the concessions-scramble, and bilateral
agreements with her rivals.

Hay need not have been puzzled (as he was) by Pauncefote's
uncommunicative attitude during the summer of 1900; by Salisbury's intrigues with the other powers to permit Japan to send an
expeditionary force into northern China; [2] by the Anglo-German
declaration of October 16, 1900, in favor of the open door and
the territorial integrity of China.[3] What these signs indicated was

[1] Dennett, *Hay*, 303.
[2] Dennett, *Hay*, 301-303. Choate telegraphed Hay from London that Salisbury had told him that "Great Britain had asked Japan to send troops, and had
offered to pay part of her expenses in money." Department of State Archives.
From London, 1899-1900. Choate to Hay, July 17, 1900.
[3] In which each declared in favor of the open door and the territorial integrity of China. At first Hay considered this a tribute to his policy; then, after
studying it, as a great "joke" on England. For on the face of it, the agreement

that Great Britain had turned to Japan as her partner in the Far East, her ally against Russia, and had resorted to bilateral negotiations to stay the advance of Germany.

It was in this manner that the partitioning of China was halted, temporarily, in 1900. The Boer War, the German navy, the maneuverings of the hostile European coalitions, the Czar, the Kaiser, Delcassé and Salisbury—these were the factors and agents that called the halt, not the diplomacy of John Hay. It was a case of political stalemate rather than conversion to principle. No power dared move further for fear of precipitating the universal *débâcle* that was destined to come a decade later, and so China was granted a brief respite.

Experience was disillusioning to the authors of the open door notes, as it was to Roosevelt in the case of the Philippines. No sooner had the rescue of the legations been effected than McKinley began to press for the withdrawal of the American troops from China. He feared their continued residence there as a political liability at home.[1] Rockhill, who had done so much to launch the United States on its new policy, and who, in July, 1900, was sent to China as special commissioner to investigate the rebellion and represent his country at the peace settlement,[2] readily confessed his discouragement. So did Hippisley. The excessive indemnities demanded of China, the latter wrote, after a long silence, in March, 1901, would have to be "liquidated by territorial concessions leading to partition and so ultimately to war among the Powers.

appeared to pledge England to the greater sacrifice, since her sphere in the Yangtse was far larger than Germany's in Shantung, and therefore if both powers gave each other open door treatment England would be giving the more. Nor was Germany required to offer support against Russia. Cf. Dennett, *Hay*, 319 ff.; Langer, II, 702 ff.

[1] See his correspondence with Hay on this point, Dennett, *Hay*, 314-315; Dennis, Ch. IX, esp. 233.

[2] Rockhill received his appointment July 19, 1900; reached China late the following month, and returned to Washington October 25, 1901. In his papers are despatches from China and letters to Hippisley that supplement the correspondence printed in his official Report, published as an appendix to *Foreign Relations*, 1901.

The soldiers have committed atrocities horrible beyond description, and the Ministers of their nationals are all engaged in looting. While [*sic*] Russia working independently on her own account places Manchuria, Mongolia and Turkestan under a protectorate, and throws the treaty rights of other nations into the dustbin. Right and reason disappear, and we return to the ethics of the Dark Ages. To an outsider it is all very sad and shows utter demoralisation." [1]

Rockhill replied in the same gloomy vein. He was, he said, "sick and tired of the whole business and heartily glad to get away from it.

I have been able to do something for commercial interests, and in a number of points have been able to carry out the Secretary's views, but have been practically alone in the negotiations. England has her agreement with Germany, Russia has her alliance with France, the Triple Alliance comes in here, and every other combination you know of is working here just as it is in Europe. I trust it may be a long time before the United States gets into another muddle of this description." [2]

Hay's disillusionment, though less outspoken, was if anything more complete. For in November, 1900, under pressure from the War and Navy Departments, he executed the surprising *volte face* of instructing Conger to endeavor to obtain for the United States a naval base and territorial concession at Samsah Bay in the Chinese maritime province of Fukien. The erstwhile champion of Chinese integrity, still outwardly loyal to the policy of his notes, had actually forsaken that policy and tried to enter the concessions-scramble. As it happened Fukien had already been pre-empted as a sphere of influence by Japan, whose treaty rights in the province would be infringed by the American venture. Japan had to be consulted. It must have been embarrassing for Hay to read the Japanese reply, reminding him of his own admonitions against using the Boxer Rebellion as the opportunity for territorial ag-

[1] Hippisley to Rockhill, March 1, 1901. Answered by Rockhill, April 12, 1901. See also Hippisley to Rockhill, June 25, 1901; R. to H., July 6, 1901; H. to R., July 22 and December 9, 1901. Rockhill papers.

[2] Rockhill to Hippisley, July 6, 1901.

grandizement, and reaffirming the Imperial Government's adherence to that principle.[1]

Thereafter the Secretary of State trimmed the sails of his Far Eastern policy ever more closely to the wind. As Russia strengthened her hold on Manchuria, he gradually retreated to the position of his first open door notes, accepting the fact that Manchuria was no longer an integral part of the Chinese Empire, but rather a Russian province, in which open door treatment was to be bargained for with the Czar.[2] "I take it for granted," he told Roosevelt in April, 1903, "that Russia knows as we do that we will not fight over Manchuria, for the simple reason that we cannot. . . . If our rights and interests in opposition to Russia in the Far East were as clear as noonday, we could never get a treaty through the Senate, the object of which was to check Russian aggression."[3] To all intents and purposes Hay had abandoned the doctrine of the territorial integrity of China, at least to the extent of recognizing Manchuria as beyond the Chinese pale.

What, then, had the open door notes accomplished? They had not invented, or even promoted, a "co-operative" policy. There never had been a co-operative policy in Eastern Asia that

[1] Kept secret until 1924, when it was first published in *Foreign Relations*, 1915, 114-115, this self-contradiction of Hay's is not mentioned by either Dennis or, more strangely, Dennett. It is briefly mentioned by Morse and McNair, *Far Eastern International Relations*, 443; and Williams, E. T., *China Yesterday and Today*, 491. Vagts, *op. cit.*, II, 1096-1097, reveals the specific instructions to Conger, as given above. Twice more, in December, 1901, and May, 1902, the Navy Department urged this project on Hay. Cf. Long to Hay, December 2, 1901, Hay to Long, December 9, 1901, Moody to Hay, May 12, 1902. Vagts, II, 1134-1135. Rockhill favored a Korean port, which he thought could be "much more readily secured" than a Chinese one. Rockhill to Hay, July 3, 1902. Rockhill papers.

[2] As early as March, 1901, Rockhill had advised him that the Manchurian provinces seemed "irretrievably lost" to China. Rockhill to Hay, March 28, 1901. Vagts, II, 1112 n.

[3] Hay to Roosevelt, April 28, 1903. Dennett, *Hay*, 405. A few months later Hay paraphrased his attitude as "What's the use? Russia is too big, too crafty, too cruel for us to fight. She will conquer in the end. Why not give up now and be friendly?" *Ibid.*, 406.

rose above joint military expeditions, such as the Shimonoseki and Boxer, or identic notes of protest at anti-foreign riots. Only in common defense of their nationals did the powers stand together. As for co-operating among themselves, in the interest of collective security, fair play, free competition, equal opportunity, there was none of that; there never had been any. Japanese, Russian, British, German, French and American soldiers could all march together to Peking. But once the siege was raised and the diplomats had taken charge, every semblance of co-operation vanished.

It has been suggested that the Hay notes were part of a diplomatic trade by which the United States gained supremacy in the Caribbean, in return for co-operating with England in the Far East.[1] But, in spite of intensive search, no evidence has been discovered that would remove the idea from the realm of conjecture. Chronology alone makes it plausible. By the Hay-Pauncefote Treaty of 1900 [2] the United States gained from England the right to construct and maintain a canal across the Isthmus of Panama. At approximately the same time, America came to England's assistance in China. History abounds, however, with examples of the *post hoc* fallacy. Rockhill and Hippisley, at pains to exhaust every possible argument that might further their designs, never mentioned the connection between the Caribbean and the Far East, which Hippisley has since called "the product of lively but ill-balanced imagination." [3]

England was scarcely in a position to exact any such price as that supposed to have been paid by Hay for her strategic retreat from the Caribbean. The Boer War, the growing power of the United States, not to recapitulate more of the many international factors already reviewed, were sufficient to account for that. Months be-

[1] Cf. Reuter, *op. cit.*, 187; Dennett, *Hay*, 296; also "The Open Door Policy as Intervention," *American Academy of Political and Social Science Annals*, Vol. 168, 78-83, and elsewhere. Dennett has given wide currency to the conception.

[2] Signed but never ratified. The final treaty of this name was ratified February 21, 1902.

[3] Hippisley to author, February 18, 1937.

fore the open door notes were written, Salisbury had informed Hay (through Henry White) in so many words that he realized the United States would build the canal, that he approved, and that "the canal is of comparatively little importance to England now that they have the Suez Canal. . . ." [1] Pauncefote and Salis- bury did not receive the open door notes or the circular on China's territorial integrity as if they were collecting payment for value received.

Hay's claim that he had "accomplished a good deal in the East, but thus far without the expense of a single commitment or promise" [2] is no less difficult to validate. Hay was technically correct: nothing had been "put in writing." Legally the United States was no more bound to pursue the policy of the notes than the powers which had, in varying degrees, evaded their demands. It was the style of the notes, the fact that they were promulgated in a manner deliberately contrived to mobilize public opinion and create the impression of an international commitment, and most important of all, the way Hay's successors practiced what he preached that molded American policy. It may be conceded that the Secretaries of State who followed John Hay did not adhere to the principles of the open door and the preservation of China's territorial integrity solely because he had done so, and at the same time, that tradition and precedent exert a powerful influence on foreign policy.

One thing is clear: Hay had not secured anything approaching an international guarantee of the open door or the "territorial and administrative entity" of China. He had merely oriented American policy toward a more active participation in Far Eastern politics in support of those principles. In so doing he had kept pace with the expansionist forces (of which he was as much product as cause) that had propelled the United States into the conquest and annexation of the Philippines.

[1] White to Hay, December 23, 1898. Nevins, *White*, 145.
[2] Hay to Roosevelt, August 2, 1903. Dennett, *Hay*, 406.

# III. Theodore Roosevelt Tries World Politics

THE history of American diplomacy in the Far East from 1903 to 1938 recapitulates in a series of cycles the experience of John Hay. One after another, with variations only in manner and emphasis, the Presidents and Secretaries of State who followed McKinley and Hay have moved toward identical objectives, with identical results. First in the succession was Theodore Roosevelt. What Hay had been unable to accomplish in the Far East by note-writing and voluntary international co-operation, Roosevelt set out to accomplish by more active participation in Far Eastern and European politics. In the end, like Hay, he was compelled to retrench—to accept, if not to admit, a tactical defeat.

During his first administration, President Roosevelt concentrated his energies on the Caribbean and left the Far Eastern policy to John Hay. As we have seen, the Secretary of State had beat a strategic retreat from the position of the July third circular to that of the first open door notes. He had accepted the fact that Manchuria was no longer an integral part of the Chinese Empire, and shaped his policy accordingly. To the Japanese Government he had explained, as early as February, 1901, that the United States was "not at present prepared to attempt singly, or in concert with other Powers, to enforce these views in the east [as to China's integrity] by any demonstration which could present a character of hostility to any other power." [1] His aim now was, he told the President in the spring of 1902, only to assure that "no matter what happens eventually in North China and Manchuria, the United States shall not be placed in any worse posi-

[1] Dennis, *op. cit.*, 242.

tion than while the country was under the unquestioned domination of China." [1]

While alliances affecting the Far Eastern balance of power closed about him, Hay assailed St. Petersburg with independent and unavailing protests on the score of the open door in Manchuria. To strengthen his hand he and Rockhill negotiated a commercial treaty with China (October 8, 1903) guaranteeing observance of the open door principle in all Chinese-American trade, and opening to such trade the Manchurian cities of Mukden and Antung. But that was as far as he would go. When the Russians broke their promise to evacuate the province, he warned the President against falling into the same difficulty he himself had experienced three years earlier. "I am sure you will think it is out of the question," he wrote, "that we should adopt any scheme of concerted action with England and Japan. Public opinion in this country would not support such a course, nor do I think it would be to our permanent advantage. . . ." [2]

The doom of the "co-operative" policy had been sealed by the conclusion (January 30, 1902) of the first Anglo-Japanese Treaty of Alliance. The treaty was England's first material success in the effort to end her isolation, first link in the chain to be forged around Germany and the Triple Alliance. The regional agreements with Russia and Germany (discussed in the last two chapters) had by no means satisfied the needs of Downing Street. Neither had the seizure of Weihaiwei nor the unfruitful overtures to America. The Boxer Rebellion had left Russia in virtual possession of Manchuria. The Anglo-German agreement of 1900 had failed to enlist the Kaiser's support against Russia. France was Russia's ally; no help could be expected from Paris. The Japanese Government was divided between the exponents of an alliance with Russia based on the partition of Korea, Manchuria

[1] Dennett, *Hay*, 404.

[2] Hay to Roosevelt, April 25, 1903. Dennett, *Hay*, 404. Cf. also *Krasnyi Arkhiv*, II, 108; Romanov, 473.

and northern China, and an alliance with Great Britain. A Russo-Japanese entente, automatically including France, and perhaps Germany as well, would have made England's position in China untenable, menaced the security of India, and made her isolation in Europe more complete than it was. The times called for more efficacious measures than the "co-operative" policy. As for Japan, the new alliance cleared the way for the war with Russia, and became, in the words of a modern Japanese historian, "the corner stone of Japanese diplomacy for the next twenty years." [1]

Underlying the diplomacy of Hay and Roosevelt was the assumption that British and American interests in the Far East were identical. The terms of the Anglo-Japanese Alliance provide an excellent means of testing this assumption. The two cardinal interests in the United States were the defense of its new Far Eastern possessions, the Philippines, and equality of commercial opportunity in China. A third primary interest was beginning to emerge, namely, the exclusion from the United States of Oriental immigrants. Subordinate to these was the territorial integrity of China. The principal Far Eastern interests of the United States, though trifling in comparison with American interests in other spheres, were nevertheless indigenous to that region.

Great Britain's, on the other hand, though large were incidental to her interests in Europe and India. Early in the negotiation of the Alliance, which both parties understood to be directed primarily against Russia, the British tried to persuade Germany to join. But the Kaiser refused, partly because of his obligations to and sympathies for the Czar, partly because he demanded more substantial concessions than any the British had to offer him. Thereupon, at least in British minds, the project assumed an anti-German as well as an anti-Russian orientation. Great Britain's immediate concern was to protect herself from a hostile coalition of European powers led by Germany. Her second concern was the defense of India. The British Government was anxious to

[1] Takeuchi, T., *War and Diplomacy in the Japanese Empire*, 128.

secure the application of the alliance to India, and Lansdowne
tried to write this into its provisions. Here the Japanese balked.
Meanwhile Prince Ito, former Prime Minister of Japan, most
influential of the *genro,* and ardent champion of an alliance with
Russia, had proceeded to St. Petersburg, and with the full knowledge and approval of the Japanese Cabinet had nearly come to
terms with the Russian Government. Apprehension of his success
undoubtedly spurred the British to accept the Japanese draft, that
is, to yield on India in order to stave off the all-too-real threat
of a Franco-Russo-Japanese Alliance, with Germany a silent partner. Nor was India the only point on which the British yielded.

The crux of the treaty was its first article which, after a mutual
disclaimer of "aggressive tendencies," recognized the special interests of both countries in China, and those of Japan "politically
as well as commercially and industrially" in Korea. The alliance
was designed to safeguard these interests "if threatened either by
the aggressive action of any other power, or by disturbances arising in China or Corea, and necessitating the intervention of either
of the High Contracting Parties for the protection of the lives
and property of its subjects." Its remaining articles pledged each
signatory to maintain strict neutrality in case either should become
involved in war with another power; to come to the other's assistance in the event that it should be attacked by more than one
other power; to refrain from entering into "separate arrangements with another Power to the prejudice of the interests above
described" without mutual consultation, and to communicate with
each other "fully and frankly" whenever the "above-mentioned
interests" seemed in jeopardy. Its duration was to be five years.

A preamble dedicated the instrument to "the *status quo* and
general peace in the Extreme East," the "independence and territorial integrity of the Empire of China and the Empire of
Corea" and to the open door "in those countries for the commerce
and industry of all nations." But the true meaning of the treaty
was contained in the clause recognizing the special interests of

both countries in China and of Japan in Korea. England had abandoned Korea to Japan. By recognizing Japan's special interests in China she had helped to lay the foundation of Japan's future expansion, and through the loophole of protection for the "lives and property" of British and Japanese subjects in case of disturbances "arising in" China and Korea, she had sanctioned a type of intervention in Chinese politics that the authors of the open door notes had tried expressly to prevent. In return, Britain had obtained a Japanese guaranty of British interests in China, and assured herself of a diminution of the Russian menace to the Indian frontier as well as to the peace of Europe.[1]

The treaty took Hay by surprise. Poorly informed, he had had no advance notice of its signature, and of all his ambassadors and ministers abroad, only those in Peking and Tokyo seem to have understood its warlike meaning.[2] Even these do not seem to have grasped its significance to Japan's future policy in China. France and Russia at once issued a counterblast, couched in the same general terms, and the Far East was divided into two armed camps.[3] Hay euphemistically hailed both agreements as "renewed confirmation" of the assurances he had already received from the four governments concerned "in respect to the conservation of the independence and integrity of the Chinese Empire as well as of Korea," and the open door.[4]

The stage was now set for Theodore Roosevelt. His cue was the outbreak of hostilities between Japan and Russia (February 8, 1904) followed, two days later, by a declaration of war. The

[1] For the negotiation of the alliance see Langer, II, Ch. XXIII, the most comprehensive account, based on Japanese and Russian as well as the standard British, French and German sources. Cf. also, Dennis, A. L. P., *The Anglo-Japanese Alliance*, University of California, Publications in International Relations, I, 8-18; Chang Chung-Fu, *The Anglo-Japanese Alliance*, 112 ff. *British Docs.*, II, 89-138. For text, *Ibid.*, 115-120. Ishii, Viscount K., *Diplomatic Commentaries*, 34-53.

[2] Dennis, *Adventures*, 352.

[3] *Krasnyi Arkhiv*, XXVIII, 183.

[4] *For. Rel.*, 1902, 931.

President immediately turned his attention to the Far East. "As soon as this war broke out," he told his friend Spring-Rice in 1905, "I notified Germany and France in the most polite and discreet fashion that in the event of a combination against Japan to try to do what Russia, Germany and France did to her in 1894 [*sic*], I should promptly side with Japan and proceed to whatever length was necessary on her behalf. I, of course, knew that your government would act in the same way, and thought it best that I should have no consultation with your people before announcing my own purpose." [1] Actually the President did no such thing, or if he did, the most diligent research has failed to uncover a trace of it, even among the archives of the governments he claimed to have addressed.[2]

Both France and Germany had made clear their intentions to remain neutral, for all too obvious reasons. Neither could afford to take part in a Far Eastern adventure that would impair the security of its European frontiers, and involve it in war with England. The Kaiser had instigated the Czar to fight Japan with the deliberate intention of miring Russia in the Far East and so easing the pressure on Germany's own eastern boundary.[3] Roosevelt's warning, like his subsequently disproved threat to Germany during the Venezuela debt controversy of 1902,[4] appears to have been a product of his own imagination. But it is none the less revealing of his character and his diplomacy.

From November, 1904, to the end of his second term in office, Theodore Roosevelt was to all intents and purposes his own Secretary of State. "The President is certainly introducing a new

[1] Roosevelt to Spring-Rice, July 24, 1905. Dennett, *Roosevelt and the Russo-Japanese War*, 2; Gwynn, Stephen, *The Letters and Friendships of Sir Cecil Spring-Rice*, I, 478. Cf. *Krasnyi Arkhiv*, XXVIII, 184; Romanov, 473.

[2] Vagts, II, 1178-1179.

[3] The Kaiser had written the Czar January 3, 1904, telling him that "everybody here" understood Russia's need for an ice-free port and that it was a "foregone conclusion" that he would win both Manchuria and Korea. Dennett, *Roosevelt*, 67-68.

[4] Cf. Pringle, Henry F., *Theodore Roosevelt*, 282-287.

school of diplomacy," the American Minister to Japan commented *à propos* the Portsmouth Peace Conference.

I believe he has written with his own hand every instruction Meyer and I have received on the subject, and I do not believe he really consulted anybody. Of course, in dealing directly with the foreign Ambassadors and Governments he goes against all traditions and lays himself open to a hard knock some day—a knock which the Secretary of State was intended to take. Let us hope that his extraordinary ability will bring things through all right.[1]

Few Presidents have exerted such an arbitrary control of foreign policy as Theodore Roosevelt.

For partners in his adventures in world politics Roosevelt chose two European diplomats, Sir Cecil Spring-Rice and Baron Speck von Sternburg. "Springy" and "Specky," as he called them, were old friends, charter members of the President's "Tennis Cabinet." Their friendship dated from the early days in Washington before the three had risen to fame, and it was characteristic of the President that he chose to preserve the old terms of intimacy. In 1902 he intervened personally to secure Sternburg's appointment as Ambassador to the United States and later tried to do the same for Spring-Rice.[2] With these two men and to a lesser extent, with Jusserand, the French Ambassador, the President shared a greater measure of his confidence than with any of his own diplomats. He seems never to have questioned their personal loyalty to him, nor to have been restrained by the fact that they were the official representatives of foreign governments before they were his friends. With them as his confidants, and the Russo-Japanese War for his background, he proceeded to trample down the last confining barriers of the continental policy.

His first act, on the day war was declared (February 10, 1904) was not the apocryphal warning to Germany and France, but a

---

[1] Griscom to Rockhill, July 15, 1905. Rockhill papers.
[2] Gwynn, *op. cit.*, Chs. II, III; Pringle, 289; Dennett, *Roosevelt*, 37; Dennis, *Adventures*, 348.

reaffirmation of the Hay policy in its pristine form. The Department of State despatched a circular very like that of 1900 to the two belligerents calling on them to respect "the neutrality of China and in all practicable ways her administrative entity" for the duration of hostilities, and soliciting the co-operation of the neutral powers. As in the case of the open door notes, Japan and Russia each made its response conditional upon the other's, and since Russia would not accept the neutralization of Manchuria, the result was a flat failure. Once more the United States met frustration with bluff. Roosevelt and Hay accepted the Russian reply as "responsive," the Japanese as "adherence" to their proposal, and notified all the neutrals of this interpretation.[1]

What led Roosevelt thus to turn Hay's retreat into a new advance? The answer lies both in the *Realpolitik* of Europe and in the impulsive nature of the President himself. We have observed that both England and Germany favored the war, for one reason or another. England hoped to see Russia driven from Korea and Manchuria. France, Russia's ally, was obligated to the moral and financial support of the Czar, who fought the war almost entirely on French loans calculated to redeem the savings of thousands of French *petits rentiers* already invested in Russia's Manchurian development schemes.[2] The Kaiser's motives, as usual, were more complex. His immediate desire was to unburden his eastern frontier. Once Russia was bogged down in the Far Eastern morass, so that she could no longer threaten Germany in Europe, he hoped to make a treaty with her and by this means hamstring the Franco-Russian Alliance.[3] More than that: it was his secret design to help the Czar win Manchuria, and ultimately to share with him in the partitioning of north China in return for Russian concessions, in Middle Europe and the Near East, to the Berlin-to-Bagdad

[1] Dennett, *Roosevelt*, 69 ff.; *Hay*, 407-408; Dennis, 363; *For. Rel.*, 1904, 2-3. Vagts, II, 1182.

[2] Dennett, *Roosevelt*, 43.

[3] Cf. *Krasnyi Arkhiv*, V, 9, 18-19.

policy and the *Drang nach Osten*. To pave the way toward this
goal he conceived the project of neutralizing China in such terms
as to detach Manchuria from China proper, and open portions of
north China to Russian conquest. The Kaiser knew well enough
that any such proposal coming independently from Berlin would
neither convince nor deceive those to whom it was directed. He
therefore turned to his American admirer, President Roosevelt,
for a more impeccable leadership in the scheme. On the eve of
hostilities he appealed to the President through Sternburg to
summon the belligerents to observe the neutrality of China "outside the sphere of military operations," that is, outside Manchuria and north China. Hay perceived the implications of the
phrase, which was revised in the American circular to "the neutrality of China and in all practicable ways her administrative
entity," a diluted version of the integrity of China, inclusive of
Manchuria.[1]

The circular had no visible effect on the ultimate outcome of the
war. No amount of circulars could have availed against the armies
and alliances that now governed the affairs of Eastern Asia. But
its significance to the Far Eastern policy of the United States, still
in a formative stage, was tremendous. "Yes," confided Roosevelt
six days after its despatch, "it was on the suggestion of 'Bill the
Kaiser' that we sent out the note on the neutrality of China.

But the insertion of the word 'entity' was ours. His suggestion
originally was in untenable form; that is, he wanted us to guarantee
the integrity of China south of the latitude of the Great Wall, which
would have left Russia free to gobble up what she really wanted. We
changed the proposal by striking out the limitation, and Germany cheer-
fully acceded. It is a good thing to give Germany all credit for making
the suggestion. As a matter of fact, in this instance Germany behaved
better than any other power, for England drove us half crazy with

---

[1] Dennett, *Hay*, 407-409. Hay deliberately used the ambiguous phrase "administrative entity" because, as he told Choate "if we attempt the specifications of
metes and bounds we should never get the powers to agree." Hay to Choate,
Feb. 13, 1904, Vagts, II, 1182.

thick-headed inquiries and requests about our making more specific exactly what was highly inexpedient to make specific at all." [1]

Thus the conception of *de jure* Chinese sovereignty over Manchuria was restored to American diplomacy, and the moral obligation to persuade other powers to uphold that conception was reassumed. For Roosevelt to have imagined that he had German co-operation, that "in this instance Germany behaved better than any other power" shows how little he appears to have understood the Kaiser's real motives. Russia immediately complained to Germany about her participation in the affair. Whereupon Bülow informed St. Petersburg that it was not a German idea; that it had been suggested by the French(!) and that whatever the American note said, Germany still considered Manchuria outside its application. [2] It was for this duplicity that the Kaiser earned Roosevelt's thanks for his "generous initiative and powerful co-operation on the matter of Chinese neutrality." [3]

That the President could have taken such a momentous step solely "on the suggestion of 'Bill the Kaiser' " is unlikely. The long wrangle over the Russian occupation of Manchuria had enlisted American sympathies—and none more strongly than the President's—on the side of Japan. Roosevelt was predisposed to favor any plan that might weaken Russia's hold on Manchuria. Already both Hay and Rockhill (still serving the State Department as unofficial expert on China) had resigned themselves to Japanese rule in Korea. The American Minister to Korea himself had written (January 4) that although he was "no pro-Japanese enthusiast" he thought "Korea should belong to Japan by right of ancient conquest and tradition. I think our Government will make a mistake if it tries to have Japan simply continue this fiction

---

[1] Dennis, 363. Roosevelt to Root, Feb. 16, 1904.

[2] *Die Grosse Politik*, XIX, i, 102-109. Cf. Bülow's later declarations to Sternburg, Jan. 20, and March 7, 1905, that the neutrality plan was originated by Germany. *Ibid.*, 2, 564, 580.

[3] Tower to Richthofen, Feb. 16, 1904. *Ibid.*, 109.

of independence." [1] Rockhill agreed with him; he thought the annexation of Korea to be "absolutely indicated as the one great and final step westward of the Japanese Empire" and that it would be "better for the Korean people and also for the peace in the Far East" when it finally happened.[2] On February 8, two days before the despatch of the circular, Griscom had sent Hay identical advice from Tokyo.[3] In the last analysis the Anglo-Japanese Alliance made any course other than acquiescence in Japanese annexation difficult if not impossible. So, although the United States had been the first to open Korea to Western trade, and had consistently given its diplomatic support to Korean independence, it was now prepared to follow Great Britain's example and abandon the country to its Japanese fate.

Russia immediately raised the question as to why the American circular omitted any reference to Korea. The two warring nations had long considered Manchuria and Korea in the same category. The United States had become reconciled to China's "irretrievable loss" of Manchuria. Why, then, Cassini asked Hay, should the United States wish to deprive Russia of Manchuria and not Japan of Korea? The Russian Foreign Minister complained that American intentions were "not clear." [4] Nor were they. Roosevelt could scarcely have foreseen the consequences of his action. He had executed a diplomatic maneuver against Russia without considering the possibility that consistent adherence to the precedent so established would later turn it against Japan.

The next nation to incur the displeasure of Washington on the score of Chinese territorial integrity was neither Japan nor Russia, but England. Once more our inquiry leads us into the tortuous maze of European politics which, it cannot be too often repeated,

[1] Allen to Rockhill, January 4, 1904. Rockhill papers.
[2] Rockhill to Allen, Feb. 20, 1904. Rockhill papers.
[3] Griscom to Hay, Feb. 8, 1904. Vagts, II, 1177 n.
[4] Cf. The German Ambassador to St. Petersburg, Count von Alvensleben, to the Foreign Office, February 12, 1904. *Die Grosse Politik*, XIX, i, 106-7.

was the real source of political developments in Eastern Asia. Once more an opportunity is afforded to test the assumption that British and American interests in the Far East were identical.

Great Britain's unceasing quest for allies met with its second notable success on April 8, 1904, when the *Entente Cordiale* was signed with France. All the outstanding issues that had vexed the diplomatic relations between the two countries, in every quarter of the globe, were liquidated in the most realistic fashion. France gave England a free hand in Egypt; England gave France a free hand in Morocco. In secret articles each country promised its diplomatic support to the other should either wish to extend its control over Egypt or Morocco respectively.[1] France was now definitely within the British orbit. Russia was soon to follow. Instead of the expansion of the anti-British coalition led by Germany, an anti-German coalition led by England was taking shape. It was above everything their mutual fear of Germany that had induced France and England to compromise so many historical issues.

In a cabinet memorandum of December 29, 1903, charting the course of British diplomacy for the duration of hostilities, Balfour had carefully measured the possible advantages to be gained by England from the Russo-Japanese War. In the main they were Russia's disadvantages.

"Even if we assume Russia to get the best of it," he wrote, "we can by no means assume that she will come out of the fight stronger than she went in. Stronger in the Far East for many purposes she may perhaps be. But we have to fear her chiefly as a) the ally of France; b) the invader of India; c) the dominating influence in Persia; and d) the possible disturber of European peace. For these purposes she will not be stronger but weaker after over-running Corea—bound to the East by the necessity of watching Japan, she will be unable freely to take part in strategical combinations against Britain in the West.

[1] For text of *entente*, *Brit. Docs.*, II, 402 ff. For negotiation, *Ibid.*, 285-400; *Documents Diplomatiques Français*, Second Series, Vol. IV.

Though her value to France in a war with Germany might thereby be little affected, her value to France in a war with us would be greatly reduced and her whole diplomacy, from the Black Sea to the Oxus, might be weakened into something distantly resembling sweet reasonableness." [1]

The *Entente Cordiale* had removed England's principal fear of Russia as "the ally of France" and cleared the way for England to deal with her as "the invader of India." The Prime Minister's memorandum had made it abundantly clear where England's first interests lay, and that was assuredly not in the Far East. He had determined on a neutrality benevolent toward Japan. "Every demand made on us beyond this," he had concluded, "should be considered solely in the light of British interests, present and future." [2] The lines already closed against John Hay's co-operative policy by the Anglo-Japanese Alliance of 1902 were tightened by the Balfour memorandum and the *Entente Cordiale*. From now on the dispensation of political fortunes in Eastern Asia would become more and more the private affair of Britain and her allies, and American influence there would decrease proportionately.

Nothing illustrates the trend more vividly than the episode of the Younghusband expedition to Tibet in 1904. Since 1880 Tibet had been the object of both Russian and British intrigue. The Indian Government was apprehensive lest Russia take possession of the exotic country, nominally under the suzerainty of China, and from there penetrate into northeastern India. Border incidents were frequent. In the fall of 1903 the fears of Lord Curzon, then Viceroy of India, were enhanced by Russia's preparations for the Japanese War, and her apparent intention to take Tibet in her stride. On the pretext that the Tibetans had failed to discharge certain treaty obligations, a British military expedition under Sir Francis Younghusband was despatched to Tibet, largely on Curzon's responsibility, and, after several skirmishes with the

[1] Dugdale, *Balfour*, I, 285.
[2] *Ibid.*, 284.

Tibetans, the capital city was seized (August 3, 1904). A treaty was then negotiated which established a virtual British protectorate over Tibet (September 7, 1904).

No sooner had the Younghusband expedition left India than Russian protests began to reach London, where negotiations were far advanced toward the conclusion of the *Entente Cordiale*. A diplomatic triangle at once developed in which France was thrust into the unwelcome role of intermediary between her old ally and her new friend. Russia demanded positive assurances that the British would withdraw from Tibet. England wanted Russia's adherence to Article I of the new *Entente* with France (determining the status of the Egyptian debt). At length, early in June, 1904, France was able to secure an exchange on the two points. Russia gave the desired adherence; Lansdowne promised to withdraw from Tibet as soon as "satisfaction" had been obtained from the Tibetans. The terms of the promise were sufficiently ambiguous, however, to permit the conclusion of the Tibetan Treaty of September 7. Although this was subsequently moderated (to the chagrin of Lord Curzon) England continued to exercise political control over Tibet, in spite of Russian opposition and the legal fiction of Chinese sovereignty.[1]

Into this pre-war diplomatic tangle that hinged on factors unknown to Washington, the United States was led to intrude by its newly refurbished Far Eastern policy. On June 3 Ambassador Choate was instructed to acquaint the British Foreign Office with the State Department's views on the Younghusband expedition. Mr. Choate's instructions took strong exception to the official references of the Indian Government to Chinese sovereignty over Tibet as a "constitutional fiction" and a "political affectation."

[1] For the diplomacy of the Tibetan expedition, see *Documents Diplomatiques Français*, Second Series, Vol. IV, No. 388; Vol. V, Nos. 41, 45, 50, 61, 65, 73, 86, 89, 107, 113, 114, 120, 123, 124, 139, 145, 155, 214, esp. the last three; *Brit. Docs.*, IV. 186-190, 305-326. Cf. also Williams, E. T., *Tibet and Her Neighbors, passim.*

Great Britain had three times (in 1876, 1886 and 1890) recognized Chinese sovereignty "by negotiating with the Chinese Government on questions relating to Tibet." Since then the Chinese Government had waived none of its rights. Great Britain well knew that it was the policy of the United States to promote the "absolute integrity and independence" of the Chinese Empire. It would therefore "greatly tend to relieve our anxiety to receive assurances that no steps will be taken by the British Government which might tend to disturb the present Government of Tibet, or lessen Chinese control over it, whereby serious troubles, which we together with Great Britain are so anxious to prevent, might be caused in other portions of the Empire."[1] Choate made his formal representations to Lansdowne on June 29, receiving from the Foreign Secretary a most evasive reply that referred him, for England's Tibetan policy, back to the very Blue Book to which the Department of State had taken so much exception.

"The American Ambassador said a few words to me today on the subject of the situation which had arisen in Thibet," recorded Lansdowne. "He assumed that we still regarded Thibet as a part of the Chinese Dominions, and that we did not desire to alter the status of the country in that respect. I said that His Excellency's supposition was correct, and that we had indeed from the first endeavored to work through the Chinese Government, although unfortunately without much success—The conduct of the Thibetans had, as His Excellency was aware, obliged us to advance to Lhassa, and I could not take upon myself to say what terms it would be necessary for us to impose upon the Thibetans or how soon it would be possible for us to withdraw the Mission."[2]

The United States was perfectly consistent in the matter. Its contentions were anything if not logical. A British violation of

[1] Dept. of State Archives. Great Britain Instructions. Hay to Choate, June 3, 1904. Copy in Rockhill papers dated April 20.
[2] Lansdowne to Durand, June 29, 1904. *Brit. Docs.*, IV, 313. See also Choate to Hay, June 30, 1904, with appended note Hay to Rockhill. Rockhill papers.

Chinese integrity in one part of the Empire could scarcely fail to encourage Russian or Japanese violations of it in other parts. Nevertheless, the American protest proved futile. It asked for Lansdowne's assurances that Great Britain would not alter the status of the Government of Tibet. No such assurances were given. Great Britain did alter the status of that government. Lansdowne seems to have taken the attitude that the affair was none of Washington's business to begin with and whether he did or not, he paid no attention to the United States in settling it. The security of India, and to a lesser degree, Russia's adherence to the *Entente Cordiale* were his objectives, regardless of what happened to China.

The point was that the British were quite willing to violate Chinese integrity, and to countenance its violation by others, if that happened to serve British interests nearer home: the defense of India, the balance of power in Europe. Because it was unwilling to stomach this unpalatable truth, American diplomacy in the Far East had yet to suffer not a few still more unpalatable rebuffs and disappointments.

Twice more, during the Russo-Japanese War, the United States formally invoked the doctrine of the territorial integrity of China. On January 13, 1905, again at the Kaiser's suggestion, Roosevelt circularized the neutral powers in terms very similar to those of the previous year. Their responses were prompt and favorable. But the effect of the circular was only to precipitate a fresh altercation between Cassini and Hay. Russia had ignored the first circular. In August, 1904, the Russian Minister to Peking had informed Conger that Japanese activities made necessary the extension of the hostile zone "anywhere in China, and that Russia will no longer consider China neutral."[1] Now, though Hay pleaded that both China and Japan had been scrupulous in their

[1] Hay to Roosevelt, August 27, 1904. Dennis, *Adventures*, 366. *For. Rel.*, 1904, 2-3. *Die Grosse Politik*, XIX, 2, 550-568.

observance of it, Russia announced that it would consider Chinese neutrality "from the standpoint of its own interest."[1]

The Kaiser's motives had not changed. This time, to frighten his American colleague into action, he fabricated from whole cloth a French plot to partition China. The way to forestall the nefarious plan, he advised, was for Roosevelt to issue another appeal to the powers to observe Chinese territorial integrity, with the exception of "a grant of a certain portion of territory to both belligerents eventually in North China."[2] The Kaiser was still trying manfully to save Manchuria for the Czar and with it his own chance for a share in the partitioning of north China. Once more Hay carefully drew the poison from the German proposal; the American note made no exception of Manchuria. But neither Hay nor the President was yet able to comprehend the Kaiser's game. "It is a most singular incident," the Secretary of State confided to his diary. "What the whole performance meant to the Kaiser it is difficult to see."[3]

The doctrine of the territorial integrity of China was finally invoked as a condition to the arbitration of peace. Before he would consent to act as mediator, the President demanded and received the assurance of the Japanese Government "that Japan adheres to the position of maintaining Open Door in Manchuria and of restoring that province to China."[4] The phrase "adheres to the position" was by no means a binding commitment for the future. It was a mere declaration of the Komura Government's current policy. The word "restore" signified that Japan considered Manchuria as having once been detached from China. The reason why she now favored returning it to China was to keep it from Russia. To *de facto* Russian domination Japan preferred *de jure*

---

[1] Dennis, *op. cit.*, 393.

[2] Bülow to Sternburg, Jan. 4, 1905. *Die Grosse Politik*, XIX, 2, 556-557.

[3] Dennis, *op. cit.*, 393.

[4] Roosevelt to Taft, April 20, 1905; Barnes to Loeb, April 25, quoting telegram from Komura to Takahira received by the latter April 25 in reply to Roosevelt's demand. Dennett, *Roosevelt*, 178-180.

Chinese sovereignty—at least, for the moment. This was as near as Roosevelt came to securing an international pledge of respect for the territorial integrity of the Chinese Empire through the means of appeals, circulars and identic notes, the instruments of the co-operative policy. But the President had more than one string to his bow.

During the first months of the war, American opinion was strongly pro-Japanese and indeed remained so until the peace conference, when it gave way to sympathy for the Russians. Sentiment alone did not cause the change of heart. The President, who had been quick to applaud the elimination of Russian tyranny from the Far East was no less quick to perceive in victorious Japan a menace to the Philippines. Immigration troubles had arisen to embitter Japanese-American relations. From the intimacy of 1904 Japan and the United States were thrust apart by the events of the war, by immigration problems and by the diplomacy of Theodore Roosevelt, to the estrangement of 1906. The two years stand out as milestones. The first marked the conclusion of the epochal friendship that had begun soon after Perry's visit, under the consulship of Townsend Harris. The second ushered in an epoch of conflict, often bordering on the actual resort to arms. The transition was accelerated, recognized, and then most keenly regretted by Theodore Roosevelt.

When the Russo-Japanese War began, the President dashed into the fray, as it were, with the diplomatic stratagem of a neutrality benevolent toward Japan. His object was to co-operate as much as possible in forcing Russia out of Manchuria, the scene of small but highly vocal American commercial interests. He had not been able to accomplish this by diplomatic negotiations with either China or Russia, so he decided to lend Japan whatever support he could, short of an alliance. Japan would fight his battle. The President's mood was shared by most of his countrymen. American bankers worked hand in glove with their British colleagues to finance the victories of General Nogi and Admiral Togo. While

Russia fought the war on French loans, Japan fought on British and American.[1] But the President, like most of the world, had not counted on such an overwhelming defeat as that administered to the forces of the Czar. He had looked to the temporary exhaustion of Russia; now he feared her complete collapse. As the cataclysmic outcome began to appear inevitable, the President's stratagem underwent two progressive changes. From the mere elimination of Russia from Manchuria he turned to the re-establishment of the balance of power between Russia and Japan, and from that, to the prevention of further territorial expansion by the latter. His means toward both these ends was to attempt to persuade the two great rival European alliances to join the United States not only in bringing the war to a close, but also, as it finally transpired, in effecting a peace settlement favorable to Russia.

This was the co-operative policy on a grander scale than John Hay had ever imagined. Roosevelt had concluded that the powers, especially Germany and England, could be led to co-operate in the Far East without bridging the abyss that separated them in Europe. In this he was to be disappointed. All of his efforts in behalf of peace and the balance of power in Eastern Asia were hampered by the great world-governing political fact of his generation, Anglo-German rivalry.

There is little doubt that at the beginning of the war, the President leaned toward Germany rather than England. He was never the Anglophile that John Hay was. He admired the British Empire but not the British people. "The average Englishman," he remarked in December, 1904, "is not a being whom I find congenial or with whom I care to associate. I wish him well, but I wish him well at a good distance." [2] The remark was indicative

---

[1] Cf. Vagts, II, 1189-1193, 1209 ff. Jacob Schiff, President of Kuhn, Loeb & Co., was decorated after the war by King Edward for his co-operation with the Anglo-Japanese alliance. *Ibid.*, 1209. Cf. Romanov, *op. cit.*, 529-547. Jewish bankers used war loans to Japan as a means of retaliating for Russia's barbaric anti-Semitism.

[2] Roosevelt to Finley Peter Dunne, Dec. 3, 1904. *Pringle,* 281.

only of a passing mood, but it was a mood that possessed the mercurial President during the war. He could not gain the confidence of the cold and formal Sir Mortimer Durand, the British Ambassador in Washington. On the other hand his old friend Speck von Sternburg, the German Ambassador, was there, ready and eager to share his trust.

"England has not a man I can deal with," the President complained to Speck (not long after the Tibet affair). "I do not think much of Balfour and less of Lansdowne. Chamberlain is quite unreliable and might jump into the Yangtse valley at any moment. And how am I to deal with this creature of an ambassador (Durand)? If I had Spring-Rice here things might be different. With France I am in the same position. The only man I understood and who understands me is the Kaiser." [1]

"*Sehr schmeichelhaft*" (very flattering) was the Kaiser's comment at this effusion. [2]

While the President unburdened himself to "Specky" and upheld the virtues of Germany's Far Eastern policy in what manner we have observed, the Kaiser (in the marginal sarcasms for which he is famous) expressed his scorn for Roosevelt's amateurish diplomacy, and with the Czar connived at the German domination of Europe and the Russo-German hegemony of the Far East. It was all a mystery to Roosevelt. To the end he remained, as he himself confessed, "a little puzzled" at the Kaiser's intentions, unable to comprehend his actions "excepting on disinterested grounds." [3] Twice he followed the German Emperor's suggestions with circulars on Chinese neutrality, each time thanking him for his disinterested co-operation. He went out of his way to allay the Kaiser's fears of anti-German machinations, personally

[1] Sternburg to Foreign Office, September 27, 1904. See also Bülow to Kaiser, August 31, 1904. *Die Grosse Politik*, XIX, 2, 542, 535.

[2] *Ibid.*, 537; Vagts, II, 1196 n., gives a slightly different version.

[3] Dennett, *Roosevelt*, 209.

sounding the French Ambassador in order to reassure him.[1] When Sir Mortimer Durand voiced the apprehension of his Government that the Kaiser was plotting a coalition against England, Roosevelt gave him "a pledge that Germany has no such intentions." "And what is that pledge?" Durand inquired. "Sternburg's word," answered the President.[2] In August, 1904, Roosevelt proposed to the Kaiser that they should unite, at the end of the war, in sanctioning a Japanese protectorate over Korea, in placing Manchuria under the rule of a Chinese viceroy "to be appointed by Germany, *not* England," and in coming to a "clear understanding" between themselves "on all East Asiatic questions." [3] "The noble gentleman seems to intend to horn in on world politics" was the Kaiser's private comment.[4] "Very interesting!" he scribbled of another Roosevelt proposition. "But remember, that Teddy is quite a dilettante in his opinions and conclusions. His countrymen are for the most part of another point of view." [5]

The German Emperor appears to have understood the fundamental weakness in Roosevelt's diplomacy, its subjectiveness. "The President is a great admirer of Your Majesty," Bülow had once told him, "and would like to rule the world hand in hand with Your Majesty, regarding himself something in the nature of an American counterpart to Your Majesty." [6] Bülow was flattering the Kaiser, but he had given him a valuable clue. An egotist himself, Wilhelm II knew how to address others of the same failing. Nor was the President wholly true to his German friend. "It al-

---

[1] Bussche to Foreign Office, January 18, 1905. *Die Grosse Politik*, XIX, 2, 563.

[2] Dennis, *Adventures*, 395.

[3] Bülow to Kaiser, August 31, 1904. *Ibid.*, 390. *Die Grosse Politik*, XIX, 2, 535 ff.

[4] "*Der Hohe Herr scheint ja in der Welt schon recht sans façon mitzureden zu beabsichtigen.*" *Die Grosse Politik, loc. cit.*, 537.

[5] "*Sehr interessant! Aber beweist, dass Teddy recht dilettantisch in seinen Anschauungen und Folgerungen ist. Seine Landsleute sind grosstenteils anderer Ansicht!!!!*" Vagts, II, 1234.

[6] Bülow to Kaiser, August 31, 1904. *Die Grosse Politik*, 536 ff. Dennis, 390.

ways amuses me to find that the English think that I am under the influence of the Kaiser," he wrote to Lodge during the Morocco crisis. "The heavy-witted creatures do not understand that nothing would persuade me to follow the lead of or enter into close alliance with a man who is so jumpy—" [1]

Though deprecating his faith in the Kaiser, Roosevelt followed him far enough afield to excite the acute suspicions of Great Britain, and so defeat his own purpose of promoting Anglo-German co-operation in the Far East. The climax of these wanderings was his intervention in the Morocco Crisis of 1905.

With Russia prostrated by the Japanese war, Bülow and Holstein determined on a bold move to break up the *Entente Cordiale* between France and England. This was to be followed by the disruption of the Franco-Russian Alliance. Russia was to be brought to Germany's side, and after her France. England would be isolated. The Kaiser and the Czar would rule the world as the "Admiral of the Atlantic" and the "Admiral of the Pacific" respectively. Spring-Rice had frequently warned Roosevelt of these under-cover designs but the President, always ready to accept the assurances of von Sternburg, disparaged Springy's fears. At length, on March 31, the Kaiser disembarked at Tangier, made his famous speech addressing the Sultan as "an independent sovereign" and expressing the hope that Morocco would "remain open to the peaceful rivalry of all nations, without monopoly or annexation, on the basis of absolute equality." [2] Germany then demanded an international conference to fix the status of foreign rights in Morocco, which, of course, France refused. This was Bülow's challenge to the secret article of the *Entente Cordiale* by which England pledged her diplomatic support to France in making Morocco an exclusive French sphere of influence. Would England fulfill her promise in the face of such formidable opposition from Germany, or would she counsel the French to yield?

[1] Roosevelt to Lodge, May 15, 1905. Lodge, *Selections*, II, 123. Dennis, 399.
[2] Dennett, *Roosevelt*, 84.

Lansdowne's anxiety was exceeded only by his dismay at the blow to the *Entente's* prestige. Moderation finally prevailed in Paris. Not yet ready for war, France agreed to a conference. Having forced Delcassé out of office, Bülow and Holstein pocketed an ephemeral diplomatic victory and another milestone on the way to Sarajevo was passed. The whole episode cemented Anglo-French solidarity and further exacerbated the relations of both nations with Germany. But what had Roosevelt to do with it? [1]

Before he embarked for Tangier the Kaiser invited Roosevelt to join him in advising the Sultan of Morocco to reform his Government and thus earn the diplomatic support of Germany and the United States against France. This brash proposal was too much even for the world-wandering American President, but his refusal of it was so friendly in tone that it may even have encouraged the Kaiser to proceed alone. In any case, Roosevelt supported Germany's demand for a conference, and put pressure on France to accept it. He could not believe that Germany was actually plotting against England and France, and accepted the Kaiser's argument that constancy to the principle of the open door and a "co-operative" policy in Morocco might further the same in China. Moreover, he believed this a practical way to relieve the tension in Europe and obtain a more whole-hearted European support for his peace efforts. "Of course," he wrote Spring-Rice on May 13, "in a way I suppose it is natural that my English friends generally, from the King down, should think I was under the influence of the Kaiser, but you ought to know better, old man." He was "exasperated" he said, at the Kaiser's "sudden vagaries" and his "wholly irrational zigzags." He could never take him seriously.

But I don't see why you should be afraid of him. You have told me that he would like to make a continental coalition against England. He may now and then have dreamed of such a coalition; and only last

[1] Cf. Fay, Sidney B., *Origins of the World War*, I, 168-192; Vagts, II, Ch. XVII.

December your people were fully convinced he intended to make immediate war on them. But it is perfectly obvious that he had no such thought, or he would never have mortally insulted France by his attitude about Morocco. If ever the Kaiser causes trouble it will be from jumpiness and not because of long-thought-out and deliberate purpose.[1]

In the Morocco affair the President had thrust himself unwittingly into the very hotbed of pre-war European intrigue. For a year the Kaiser had been dickering with the Czar for a secret treaty of alliance, egging him on to send more troops and vessels to the Far East, addressing him as the "Admiral of the Pacific"—all, of course, unsuspected by Roosevelt. Finally, on July 24, 1905, the two Emperors met on their yachts at Björkö and amid fumes of anathema for King Edward VII (whom they pronounced "the greatest mischief-maker and the most dangerous and deceptive intriguer in the world") actually signed the treaty. It was never ratified. Had it been, the Kaiser's second objective, the disruption of the Franco-Russian Alliance, might have followed the attack on the *Entente Cordiale.*[2] On this thin ice Roosevelt skated, innocent of the bottomless *Realpolitik* beneath him. He gave nothing away to the Kaiser—but he squandered his last chance of securing Great Britain's co-operation at Portsmouth.

Roosevelt's relations with Great Britain were no less personal. He addressed the British Government not through the formal channels of diplomacy, but through Spring-Rice who, in spite of the President's wishes for his appointment to Washington had become Secretary of the British Embassy in St. Petersburg. The correspondence between the two friends has become a classic. Youthful, ebullient, it reveals as much in its tone as in its pages of detail. Its authors disposed of the complicated pre-war mechanisms of Europe with the uninhibited gusto of undergraduates discussing the merits of rival football teams. By Roosevelt's express arrangement Spring-Rice acted as American Ambassador to the

[1] Roosevelt to Spring-Rice, May 13, 1905. Dennett, *Roosevelt*, 88-91.
[2] Fay, *op. cit.*, 171-177.

Court of St. James, relaying the President's letters to the Foreign Office. What was written to "Springy" was intended for Balfour and Lansdowne, and Springy was faithful to his mission; what was written to "My dear Theodore" was the response of the Prime Minister and Foreign Secretary of Great Britain to the President of the United States. Never were the foreign affairs of a great power conducted on such an informal plane. The President unbosomed himself to Spring-Rice who, like the government he so faithfully represented, withheld to the end his complete confidence from Roosevelt. Valentine Chirol complained to Spring-Rice who had arranged for him to meet the President, that the latter's conversation was lacking in coherence. Spring-Rice's reply was condescending: "If you took an impetuous small boy on to a beach strewn with a great many exciting pebbles, you would not expect him to remain interested for long in one pebble. You must always remember that the President is about six." [1] There is in the comment much that explains the attitude of the British Government toward the impresario of the Portsmouth Peace Conference.

If the correspondence between Sir Cecil Spring-Rice and Theodore Roosevelt proves anything it is that by his ventures in European politics the President lost rather than gained the co-operation of the two mortal enemies, Great Britain and Germany. Even if he had seen all of what was going on behind his back it is probable that he would have failed; for in that case, the chances are he never would have intervened at all. The letters from St. Petersburg never failed to express the apprehensions of their author's government of Germany's dark plot, as well as of the President's intimacy with the Kaiser. So anxious were the British on both scores that Spring-Rice wrote long letters to Hay, detailing the machinations of Berlin, and King Edward himself wrote the President contrasting the fickle nature of Germany's friendship

[1] Gwynn, I, 437.

with the constancy of England.[1] Such deep-rooted fears were not to be put at rest by the scoffing of Theodore to Springy.

When he undertook specifically to persuade the British Government to back up his peace efforts, Roosevelt met a blank wall. He could not seem to appreciate the fact that Great Britain had no intention of putting any suasion on Japan to terminate a war that was going entirely in her favor. Here was another commentary on the identity of British and American interests in the Far East, on which Roosevelt predicated his foreign policy. Germany was for peace, he told Spring-Rice, and so was France.

But I wholly fail to understand the difference in position which makes it proper for France, the ally of Russia, to urge Russia in her own interest (that is, in Russia's interest) to make peace, and which yet makes it improper for England, the ally of Japan, to urge Japan in her own interest (that is, in Japan's interest) to make peace. My feeling is that it is not to Japan's real interest to spend another year of bloody and costly war in securing eastern Siberia, which her people assure me she does not want. . . .[2]

Spring-Rice forwarded this letter to Lansdowne with the comment:

He evidently has not yet grasped the point of view that our alliance is a specific one relating to the Far East, while France's alliance with Russia is of a more general character and does not include the Far East at all.[3]

Balfour himself made the most categorical reply to Roosevelt. In a long memorandum he took up the President's contentions item by item. The Prime Minister had intended giving the memorandum to Spring-Rice to take to the President when at the latter's

[1] Roosevelt forwarded the letter to Hay with the comment: "Dear John: This letter may amuse you. Uncle Edward evidently has his eye on Nephew William and sings a variant on the old song that Codlin is our friend and not Short." Roosevelt to Hay, February 27, 1905. Roosevelt papers.

[2] Roosevelt to Spring-Rice, July 24, 1905. Gwynn, I, 478-479.

[3] *Ibid.*, 480.

urgent request, Spring-Rice made a flying trip to Washington in February, 1905. In deference to etiquette, it was finally withheld. This was unfortunate. No doubt Spring-Rice conveyed the substance of Balfour's observations to Roosevelt, but that could not have been so convincing as it might have been had it come directly from the Prime Minister himself. No document has ever been of greater significance to American diplomacy in the Far East in general and Anglo-American co-operation in particular, not only in 1905, but for all time.

In his letter that prompted Spring-Rice's visit to Washington,[1] the President had talked "Yellow Peril" as a reason for Anglo-American co-operation. Balfour made this his first point. He was "completely skeptical about the 'Yellow Peril.' The idea of Japan heading an Eastern crusade on Western civilization seems to me altogether chimerical." Should it develop it would provoke an automatic combination of Western navies that would prove Japan's undoing. The "real danger" was "not the remote and fantastic dream of a victory of East over West, but the very near and imminent peril of important fragments of China being dominated by more warlike and aggressive powers." The words that followed showed an acute understanding of one of the oldest problems in American foreign policy, and a constant factor in American diplomacy in the Far East.

If America and ourselves were to enter into a Treaty, binding us jointly to resist such aggression, it would never, I believe, be attempted. Together we are too strong for any combination of powers to fight us. I believe there would be no difficulty on this side of the Atlantic in the way of such a Treaty. The difficulty, I imagine, would be rather with the United States, whose traditions and whose Constitution conspire to make such arrangements hard to conclude.

I ought perhaps to add that there is a genuine difficulty connected

[1] "I wish to Heaven you could come over, if only for a week or two, and I think it would be very important for your Government that you should come over." Roosevelt to Spring-Rice, Dec. 27, 1904. Gwynn, 441 ff.

with the strict maintenance of the integrity of China of which we have had some experience. It arises out of the necessity, which, with a power like China, cannot always be avoided, of having to use force to compel either her, or States which are under her nominal suzerainty, to carry out their plain obligations. The Government at Peking is a master of obstructive tactics, and there is a point at which no foreign nation can submit any longer to have its just demands ignored. What, in such an event, is to be the machinery of coercion? It is hard to find any which does not involve at least the threat of a temporary occupation of Chinese territory. If the Chinese know that the threat cannot be carried out it will be made in vain. If it *is* carried out we must face the fact that a temporary occupation has a dangerous tendency to grow into a permanent one. Were it possible that coercion, when it became necessary, could be made international in its character, this danger would doubtless be avoided. But such a scheme seems to involve an international machinery which it would be difficult to create and—in view of international jealousies in that part of the world—still more difficult to work.

The Prime Minister then went on to deal with the President's anxieties about a possible Russo-Japanese alliance, and the danger of Japan's being forced to conclude peace terms inimical to British and American interests. While he did not think either a likely eventuality, he noted that on account of the Anglo-Japanese Alliance "until peace is arranged no material pressure can be put upon Japan by any foreign Power, other than Russia, without bringing us into the field." Meanwhile he thought it to the best interests of both Great Britain and the United States to consider "how they can best prevent Russia indemnifying herself for the moral and material cost of the war by appropriating a large slice of Chinese territory." [1]

There was another, a subtler, reason why Balfour could not co-operate with Roosevelt in 1905. In January, five months before Togo annihilated the Russian fleet at Tsushima, on the initiative of the British Government, negotiations had been instituted for

[1] Dugdale, *Balfour*, I, 288-290.

the renewal of the Anglo-Japanese Alliance.[1] Assured of a Japanese victory uncertain only as to its degree, with Japan confident but worried at the approach of the Russian Baltic Fleet, Great Britain had chosen the psychological moment to persuade her ally to extend the application of the alliance to India, and to insure against a Russo-Japanese *rapprochement* under German auspices at the end of the war.[2] By March the negotiations were definitely under way; the treaty was signed August 12 (before peace was concluded), and published September 27. Roosevelt was not informed of this delicate business until August, when it was all but concluded. Had he known of it, or even had wind of it from his ambassadors, he might have understood why London was deaf to his harangues.[3] In addition to the common interests of both countries in China, Japan recognized England's "special interest in all that concerns the security of the Indian frontier" and "her right to take such measures in the proximity of that frontier as she may find necessary for safeguarding her Indian possessions." England recognized Japan's "paramount political, military and economic interests" in Korea and her right to establish a protectorate over that country. The terms of the original alliance were revised so as to bring either signatory to the immediate assistance of the other in case any of its interests, as defined in the treaty, were attacked by a third power. The instrument was equipped

[1] Dugdale, *op. cit.*, I, 291-292. *Brit. Docs.*, IV, 120-183.

[2] Cf. MacDonald to Lansdowne, May 25, 1905, suggesting reasons for the "alacrity" of Japan's acceptance of the British proposals. *Brit. Docs.*, IV, 126-128. Japanese adherence to the Indian clause was likewise the *quid pro quo* for British recognition of Japan's position in Korea.

[3] The President was told of the negotiations by Durand on a visit to Oyster Bay during the Portsmouth Conference. He was not notified of the conclusion of the treaty until September 5. Durand to Roosevelt, September 5, 1905, Dennett, *Roosevelt*, 258 n. Cf. in this regard the interesting despatch from Cambon to Delcassé, May 4, 1903, in which the French ambassador analyzes Lansdowne's unwillingness to press Japan for peace and guesses the correct reason: the pending renewal of the Japanese Alliance. *Documents Diplomatiques Français*, Second Series, Vol. VI, No. 396.

with a hair trigger in Article II, which specified that the attack or threat to these interests need not originate in the Far East but "wherever arising" would bring the alliance into operation.

The new alliance was to last for ten years. Like its predecessor it was dedicated to peace, the open door and the territorial integrity of China.[1] But its real meaning, as subsequent events would prove, was that the two allies had become partners in Asiatic imperialism. Japan was insured against a Russian war of revenge or a repetition of the experience of 1895.[2] England had her long-sought guaranty of the Indian frontier and a powerful sanction for her activities in Tibet. In a letter officially explaining the new alliance to the British Ambassadors in St. Petersburg and Paris, Lansdowne emphasized its recognition of the principle that propinquity creates special rights. On this, he said, the articles dealing with Korea and India were based.[3] It was an elastic principle, readily stretched. Already Great Britain had carried it two steps beyond her own national frontiers: to India, an imperial possession, and thence to Tibet, the defensive outworks of an imperial possession. Japan had carried it only one step beyond her national frontiers, to Korea. If ever she too, like England, should require defensive outworks to protect Korea, nothing could be more logical than to extend the principle to Manchuria. While America proposed, England disposed: the co-operative policy had received another setback. Nor was the alliance with Japan all that restrained Great Britain from following Roosevelt's lead.

By the spring of 1905 the move toward an Anglo-Russian *rapprochement* was well under way. Actively fostered by France, it culminated in the Anglo-Russian Convention of 1907, very similar in character to the *Entente Cordiale*.[4] In the same year, under

---

[1] For text of treaty see *Brit. Docs.*, IV, 165 ff.

[2] When France, Germany and Russia had forced her to return the Liaotung peninsula to China; cf. p. 40, above.

[3] Dennis, *The Anglo-Japanese Alliance*, 24; Dennett, *Roosevelt*, 111 f.; Ishii, 53-54.

[4] Cf. *Brit. Docs.*, IV, 183, 304.

the friendly influence of Great Britain, Japan signed treaties with both France and Russia, further liquidating regional antagonisms, and bringing all three powers into a solid British concert of power. British diplomacy had accomplished wonders since the friendless, Kaiser-haunted days of 1899. It had progressed steadily and successfully toward its major objectives, protection from Germany, security for India. To England, such an amazing diplomatic triumph was well worth the price of giving ground on the integrity of China. Indeed, had she not been willing to subsidize the Far Eastern *rapprochements* with portions of Chinese territory they might never have been possible.

In the end, President Roosevelt was compelled to organize the peace conference by himself. Impersonal forces beyond his control and national rivalries that he did not understand had conspired to welcome his mediation. The war ended: he did not end it. Such pressure as the Kaiser put upon the Czar to make peace was actuated by the Kaiser's fear lest the revolutionary spirit spread from Russia to Germany, and by his hope, yet lingering, of saving something from the wreckage of Russian power to use against England—not, emphatically, by his desire to co-operate with Roosevelt or to defend the territorial integrity of China. France was brought momentarily into line with her enemy by financial considerations. She had sunk enough money in Manchuria and St. Petersburg: she, too, favored peace. So did England. The British and American bankers who had financed Japan were unwilling to lend her more.

The fundamental reason for the termination of the war was the mutual exhaustion of the two belligerents themselves. The condition of Russia was obvious. It is now known that Japan also was exhausted, and that the first *bona fide* request for mediation came from her, not Russia. The Japanese army and navy, though triumphant, had shot their bolts, and their leaders knew it. The country had bled itself white. It had incurred prodigious war debts. It could borrow no more. To have continued hostilities another year would almost certainly have caused an economic collapse. Japanese armies held Korea, Manchuria and Sakhalin. Their front was dangerously distended. To strike Russia further blows would be like hitting a pillow. Mindful of Napoleon's experience, Japanese military and naval leaders actually left their posts, in the spring and summer of 1905, to return to Tokyo and insist that the cabinet make peace.[1] These were the realities that underlay the Portsmouth Peace Conference.

While Roosevelt continued to lecture the British (in June he instructed Ambassador Reid "to find out whether the English Government really does wish for peace or not")[2] events moved swiftly to bring the war to a close. As early as February, 1905, Japan had put forth feelers for terms Russia might accept.[3] On April 5 Delcassé, harassed by the Morocco crisis, intimated to the Japanese Minister to France that Russia was ready to consider peace terms.[4] As a result of this overture, which implied that France was exerting pacific influence on her ally, the Japanese Government turned for a mediator not to the ill-starred French Foreign Minister but to President Roosevelt. After the customary hints and preliminary soundings, during which the President imposed his condition with respect to Chinese integrity, he was formally invited by the Japanese Government to act as mediator (May 31, 1905).[5] On June 3 the Kaiser urged the Czar to accept

[1] Takeuchi, *War and Diplomacy*, etc., 149. Ishii, Viscount K., *Diplomatic Commentaries*, 65-78, esp. 69-72. According to Ishii, "the most eager advocate of peace in the whole Empire" was General Kodama, Chief of Staff of the army in Manchuria, and next to him, the Minister of Navy, Admiral Yamamoto. Cf. also, Dennett, *Roosevelt*, Chs. VIII, IX, X; Dennis, *Adventures*, Ch. XIV; Vagts, II, 1169-1256, the latter especially valuable for its economic analysis.

[2] Dennett, *Roosevelt*, 211.

[3] Dennis, *Adventures*, 397.

[4] Dennett, *Roosevelt*, 174. Toward the end of March Cassini and Takahira were discussing peace terms with the President. Roosevelt to Hay, March 30, 1905. Roosevelt papers.

[5] The official despatches are printed in *Ibid.*, 176-188, and Ch. IX. See also Roosevelt to Taft, April 20 and 27, 1905; Roosevelt to Sternburg, April 20, 1905.

the mediation of Roosevelt, notifying the President of his action the next day. The Czar agreed to a peace conference on June 6, and two days later the President issued his invitations to the belligerents.[1]

He had at last shouldered the onerous burden of compromise that more often earns for peacemakers the enduring resentment of one belligerent than it does the gratitude of both. For this very reason, though the further exhaustion of her ally was of infinitely greater concern to Great Britain than it was to the United States, Balfour adamantly refused to meddle in the peace conference. "The President would, I think, like me to urge upon the Japanese Minister the desirability of moderation in peace terms," Durand cabled Lansdowne June 13.

There seems to be feeling here that His Majesty's Government might properly use its influence with Japan in that direction. I have avoided everything of the kind, supposing that His Majesty's Government would probably be reluctant to take any step which could embarrass Japanese, and that in any case it is not my business. Would Your Lordship kindly inform me whether this is the attitude I should maintain?

Lansdowne at once approved his Ambassador's course.[2] To a similar appeal from the President on August 23 Lansdowne appended the note: "This is a suggestion that we should press the Japanese to make further concessions. Were we to do so our advice would not be taken and would be resented." [3] More light on the identity of British and American interests in the Far East.

The peace conference opened at Portsmouth August 10. Most of the Japanese terms were accepted. Japan's position in Korea was recognized in terms very similar to those of the recent Anglo-

[1] Cf. *Ibid.*, Ch. IX, esp. 215-235; Dennis, *Adventures*, 402 ff.; Lodge, *Selections*, II, 130 ff.; *Die Grosse Politik*, XIX, 2, 419-422, 606-609; *Krasnyi Arkhiv*, XXVIII, 190.

[2] *Brit. Docs.*, IV, 86.

[3] *Brit. Docs.*, IV, 105.

Japanese treaty. The rights, concessions and spheres of influence of the two countries in Manchuria were carefully defined and delimited, while the territory itself was restored to Chinese sovereignty. At the Japanese demands for a war indemnity and the cession of Sakhalin, however, the Russians balked. They were well aware of the precarious economic, military and diplomatic position of their foe. Witte, the leader of the Russian delegation, had proved to be an adroit propagandist, and had won the American press dramatically to his side. He and his colleagues threatened to go home before they would pay a cent of indemnity or cede an inch of Russian territory.[1] Once more Roosevelt intervened, summoning the Kaiser's aid in persuading the Czar to yield, and personally warning Japan against continuing the war for an indemnity. A compromise was arranged. Russia paid no indemnity and ceded only the southern half of Sakhalin. The treaty was signed September 5 and immediately heralded as a Russian victory.[2] President Roosevelt was accorded the same type of public acclaim that Hay had won with the open door notes. He was awarded the Nobel Prize. But the real winners of the Portsmouth Peace Conference were neither Russia nor the United States, but Japan and Great Britain.

The President had not forsaken Japan. If he had urged moderation on Tokyo he had done the same to St. Petersburg. "I was pro-Japanese before," he wrote Rockhill August 29, "but after my experience with the peace commissioners I am far stronger pro-Japanese than ever."[3] He admired the Japanese, but because he

[1] *Krasnyi Arkhiv*, IV, 68; VI, 40.

[2] Dennett, *Roosevelt*, 236-277; Dennis, *Adventures*, 410 ff. Russia recognized Japan's "paramount political, military and economic interests" in Korea; transferred to Japan—subject to China's approval—the lease of Port Arthur, Talienwan and adjacent territory as well as the railway between Chang Chun and Port Arthur, its branches and related mining and timber rights. Both parties agreed to negotiate a future convention further delimiting their respective railway spheres in Manchuria. For text of treaty see MacMurray, J. V. A. *Treaties and Agreements with and Concerning China*, I, 522-528.

[3] Roosevelt to Rockhill, August 29, 1905. Rockhill papers.

also feared them, he wished to save the Russians, whom he disliked, from too complete destruction. At the peace conference Russia had everything to win, Japan everything to lose. When, therefore, Russia "won" the remission of an indemnity, and the retention of the northern half of Sakhalin, the vast underlying achievement of Japan was momentarily—and quite undiscerningly—forgotten. Japan had obliterated Russian sea power, driven Russia from Korea, humbled her in Manchuria, undermined the Czar's throne, and reduced her, in the Far East, to a minor power. The Japanese had not made concessions to Roosevelt, but to their own statesmen and military leaders. They knew in advance that Russia was willing to cede half of Sakhalin, and possessed of this hole card, they held out for more to be sure of not losing it. Even so the cabinet incurred the displeasure of General Kodama and Admiral Yamamoto, anxious lest the conference fail and military triumph turn to disaster.[1]

Roosevelt had served Japan better than he knew, likewise England. In Tokyo, an uninformed populace rioted against the treaty and throughout Japan denounced the American President who had denied it an indemnity.[2] No country in history had ever collected an indemnity from Russia; the task, as Viscount Ishii has admitted, would in all probability have proved impossible for Japan. It was the Japanese Government's good fortune to have Roosevelt for a scapegoat. As for Great Britain, the announcement (September 27) of the new treaty of alliance was calculated to console the Japanese people for the Portsmouth Treaty. It notoriously failed to do so.[3] The condescending gesture on the part of the British was meager acknowledgment of what Roosevelt had done

[1] On this subject see esp. the interesting comments of Ishii, *op. cit.*, 73-75.

[2] Roosevelt's picture was turned to the wall in countless Japanese homes. In Tokyo where the outbreaks were especially violent, there were over a thousand casualties; police stations were set afire and martial law declared. Takeuchi, 155-157; *Krasnyi Arkhiv*, VII, 3.

[3] Cf. Takeuchi, *op. cit.*, 128-129.

for England. Without her assistance he had acted as mediator of a peace worth infinitely more to Britain than to the United States; and then, like a lightning rod, he had drawn the resentment of the Japanese people onto his own unpracticed shoulders.

Roosevelt's adventures in world politics had proved as great a failure as his efforts to revive, with notes and circulars, the doctrine of the territorial integrity of China. Both had fallen far short of their objectives, had petered out against the alliances and secret *ententes* stemming from Europe and excluding the United States ever more effectively from a position of influence in Eastern Asia. One may safely concede to Roosevelt all of the virtues signalized by the award of the Nobel Prize without in any way altering the fact that his efforts to promote American interests in the Far East by either of the above methods were futile. His intercourse with Spring-Rice, Sternburg, the Kaiser, and the Czar, his intervention in the Morocco Crisis and his Portsmouth peacemaking, may have risked nothing more vital than the dignity and moral influence of American foreign policy; but what had they gained? When the President once more turned his attention directly to China and Japan he found himself confronted by anti-American riots in Tokyo and the first Chinese boycott in history—against American goods. He must have realized his failure, for he now adopted still another method of promoting American interests in the Far East: direct negotiation with China and Japan.

The preoccupation of the European nations with their own problems was not the only reason why the President's diplomacy had thus far been so unsuccessful. There were two other reasons, both implicit in his desire to preserve the balance of power between Russia and Japan. The first was the Philippines, the second, Japan. The war had scarcely entered its second month when Roosevelt expressed his uneasiness over the astonishing Japanese triumphs. On March 21, 1904, he told Sternburg he thought the old "abrasion fronts" between Russia and Japan should be preserved in order to divert both from the Philippines and Kiaochow.[1] By May his alarm over the Japanese military success had assumed considerable proportions. "Aha!" noted the Kaiser with evident relish, "the first uncomfortable feelings creep in! the Philippines will be the next to pay!" [2] Instead of affording him a weapon, the Philippines preyed on the President's mind and inhibited his diplomacy. "The other day the Japanese Minister here and Baron Kaneko, a Harvard graduate, lunched with me and we had a most interesting talk," he wrote Spring-Rice (June 13, 1904). "I told them that I thought their chief danger was lest Japan might get the 'big head' and enter into a career of insolence and aggression. . . . Of course, they earnestly assured me that all talk of Japan's even thinking of the Philippines was nonsense. I told them that I was quite sure this was true." [3] The islands were becoming more of a hostage to fortune with each passing year. In 1906 the President admitted to Sternburg that he would be glad to be rid of them, and in 1907 he called them an "Achilles heel." [4] India and Tibet had impelled Great Britain to give ground to Japanese imperialism in Korea and Manchuria; the Philippines were leading the United States in the same direction.

Immigration difficulties were no less instrumental in causing Roosevelt's change of diplomatic front. So important is this subject to the whole development of the Far Eastern policy that a special

[1] Sternburg to Foreign Office, March 21, 1904. *Die Grosse Politik*, XIX, 1, 112-113.

[2] Sternburg to Bülow, May 9, 1904, with marginal notation by the Kaiser: "Aha! *die ersten Gefuhle des Unbehagens stellen sich ein! da die Philippinen daran glauben werden!*" *Die Grosse Politik*, XIX, 1, 113-114.

[3] Gwynn, *op. cit.*, I, 417. Roosevelt also interrogated Rockhill as to the possibility "of the Chinese becoming the mere followers of Japan in case of an overwhelming Japanese victory." Rockhill thought it unlikely. Rockhill to Roosevelt, July 7, 1905. Rockhill papers.

[4] Cf. p. 35, above. In discussing Taft's forthcoming mission to the Far East the President expressed his anxiety for the Philippines which, he said, should either be heavily fortified and defended, or given up. Roosevelt to Taft, May 31, 1905 Roosevelt papers. Cf. also Roosevelt to Taft, July 3, 1905. Roosevelt papers.

chapter has been devoted to it. Suffice it here to observe that from 1905 to 1908 the exclusion of oriental labor from the United States, largely on the vociferous insistence of the Pacific States, did much to harm American business in China and strained Japanese-American relations almost to the breaking point. China retaliated for the immigration laws of 1904, permanently excluding Chinese labor from the United States, with a boycott against American commerce that lasted from May to September, 1905.

Spontaneously organized, and varying in severity in different provinces, it sufficiently dislocated American trade to cause both concern and action on the part of the President. When Rockhill, now Minister to China, suggested to Roosevelt the remission of the Boxer indemnity, the latter replied that it would be greatly facilitated by the prompt cessation of the boycott. "I am very much dissatisfied with the Chinese attitude," he declared.[1] Because of her newly awakened national consciousness, not to mention her military and naval prowess, immigration troubles with Japan were of much more serious political consequence. The action of the San Francisco School Board in October, 1906, segregating oriental from white pupils, led to indignant protests from Japan and, as we shall duly observe, to one of the gravest problems of Theodore Roosevelt's two administrations. Temporarily resolved by the famous "Gentleman's Agreement" of 1907-1908, it injected a lingering poison into the hitherto cordial relations between Japan and America.

The President had long professed his fears of the Yellow Peril, and the Kaiser had shrewdly played upon them. Now they seemed factually substantiated. Together with the specter of a Japanese

[1] See Rockhill to Roosevelt, July 12, 1905, proposing the remission of the Boxer indemnity; Roosevelt to Rockhill, August 22, 1905, instructing Rockhill to report fully by cable on the "whole subject" of the boycott. On September 1 the President wished to know if there was any truth in the rumor that the Japanese were behind the boycott. Loeb to Rockhill, Sept. 1, 1905. Rockhill papers. For a review of the boycott, see Remer, C. F., *A Study of Chinese Boycotts*, 29-39. Cf. also Roosevelt to Taft, Sept. 2, 1905. Roosevelt papers.

invasion of the Philippines they dragged Roosevelt out of world politics and focused his attention on the new colossus of the Orient.

We have seen how the President's advisers had paved the way for a graceful retreat before the Japanese in Korea. Exactly when the President himself made up his mind to this course it is difficult to say, but it must have been quite early in the war. "We cannot possibly interfere for the Koreans against Japan," he wrote May, January 28, 1905. "They could not strike one blow in their own defense." [1] Six months later, almost to the day (July 29, 1905), Secretary of War Taft, ostensibly on a mission to the Philippines, negotiated in Tokyo a secret "agreed memorandum" with Prime Minister Katsura by which the United States approved Japan's "suzerainty over" Korea in return for a Japanese disavowal of any aggressive intentions toward the Philippines.[2] The memorandum planned and categorically approved by President Roosevelt,[3] though it bound only his administration and lacked the formality of a ratified treaty, was neither casual in execution nor ambiguous in intent. The sentiments it bestowed on Anglo-Japanese-American co-operation "for the maintenance of peace in the Far East" merely ornamented the material bargain it struck. Japan understood it as American assent to the protectorate over Korea, which speedily followed without protest from Washington.[4] Roosevelt accepted it as insurance against the Japanese conquest of the Philippines. To assert, as many have done, that the Taft-Katsura Agreement made the United States an "unsigned

[1] Dennett, *Roosevelt*, 110.

[2] For text of the agreement see Dennett, *Roosevelt*, 112-114. Also copy in Knox papers, 1907 file. "Prime Minister quite anxious for interview," Taft added in a postscript. The whole transaction was done without the knowledge of Griscom. Taft to Root, July 29, 1905. Knox papers.

[3] He wired Taft on July 31: "Your conversation with Count Katsura absolutely correct in every respect. Wish you would state to Katsura that I confirm every word you have said." Pringle, *Roosevelt*, 384; Roosevelt papers.

[4] The protectorate was declared December 21, 1905, and Korea was formally annexed August 29, 1910.

member" of the Anglo-Japanese Alliance is valid only in that the United States, like Great Britain, had given way before the imperialist ambitions of Japan on the Continent of Asia in order to secure its own imperial Asiatic possessions elsewhere.

In spite of the Taft-Katsura Agreement, Japanese-American relations under the pin-pricks of the immigration controversy, went from bad to worse. War talk became so constant and so alarming in the summer of 1907 that the President actually sent directions in code to General Wood, commanding American troops in the Philippines, for defending the islands from a momentarily expected Japanese attack (July 6). The Kaiser was still busy circulating through Sternburg rumors of Japanese reserve troops in Mexico; on July 23 the President gloomily confided to Root the "best information" from Germany, France and England "that we shall be beaten." Again Taft was despatched on a pacific mission from Manila to Tokyo, which resulted in a reassuring cable (October 18, 1907) stating that "the Japanese Government is most anxious to avoid war." [1] But the war talk failed to subside. Canadian anxieties grew with American until in March, 1908, Sir Edward Grey felt it necessary to reassure the Canadian government that in case of trouble with Japan, Canada would have Great Britain's support regardless of the Anglo-Japanese Alliance.[2] Lord Bryce, the British Ambassador in Washington, pointedly inquired the

[1] Pringle, *Roosevelt*, 408-409. For full text of cable see Knox papers, 1907 file. Hayashi anxiously inquired the truth of a rumor that the United States was going to sell the Philippines. Taft denied it. Hayashi thereupon renewed Katsura's statement of 1905 that Japan wished the United States to keep the islands "but would feel some concern if the United States were to sell the Islands to a European power." Taft nevertheless warned that, "Popular voice is now so strong in Japan that the Government could with difficulty resist pressure of war by the people should the immigration question be brought to a direct issue by Act of Congress violating Treaty." In the spring of 1908 the President was still calculating the chances of a Japanese victory in the naval war that he believed imminent. Roosevelt to Root, April 17, 1908. Roosevelt papers.

[2] See the interesting letter from Grey to Lord Bryce retailing this episode in Trevelyan, G. M., *Grey of Fallodon*, 230.

cause of the war scare from Ambassador Takahira, and no doubt in ways as yet unrevealed Great Britain exercised a restraining influence on all parties.[1] Aside from his heroic efforts to restrain the Californians and to frame a national immigration policy effective but at the same time not brutally affronting to Japan, President Roosevelt met the crisis in two ways. He sent the American battle-fleet on a world cruise, and at the same time gave more ground on the territorial integrity of China.

The cruise, which lasted from March 16, 1907, to February 22, 1909, was an obvious gesture. The President had, he said, "become uncomfortably conscious of a very, very slight undertone of veiled truculence" in the Japanese communications and concluding that "they thought I was afraid of them" had decided it was "time for a showdown."[2] He afterwards called the cruise "the most important service I rendered to peace."[3]

Besides advertising the fact that the United States was the second naval power in the world,[4] and was rapidly developing one of the most efficient navies afloat, the cruise was notable for less obvious reasons. It heralded, in dramatic style, the entrance of naval ratios into the complex of Pacific politics and likewise marked the beginning of the end of the Anglo-Japanese Alliance. In February, 1908, MacKenzie King, Canadian Commissioner of Labor and Immigration came to Washington and thanked Roosevelt "very earnestly for having sent our fleet to the Pacific."[5] Australians rejoiced at the advent of the United States as a great Pacific naval power and a counter-balance to the Anglo-Japanese

---

[1] Bailey, T. A., *Theodore Roosevelt and the Japanese-American Crises*, Chs. XI, XII; Pringle, *op. cit.*, Ch. X; *Brit. Docs.*, VIII, 455 ff.

[2] Pringle, *op. cit.*, 411.

[3] *Ibid.*, 409.

[4] Japan ranked fifth. Bailey, *op. cit.*, 262.

[5] *Ibid.*, 270-271. Four members of the British Columbia parliament in Washington at the same time also thanked the President for sending the fleet. Cf. Bryce to Grey, February 14, 1908. *Brit. Docs.*, VIII, 455.

Alliance.[1] A real identity of British and American interests in the Far East based on the common immigration policy of the United States and Great Britain's Pacific Dominions, was beginning to emerge.

Whether the cruise assisted the President in smoothing out relations with Japan or not is a moot point. "The Japanese Government are fully impressed with the seriousness of the emigration question," wrote the British Ambassador in Tokyo to Sir Edward Grey, "and sooner than imperil friendly relations with America they would, I know, themselves prohibit emigration; but a menace such as the sending of a fleet, leaves them absolutely cold." [2] The Ambassador's final judgment, however, was that the "visit of the American fleet has been an unqualified success and has produced a marked and favorable impression on both officers and men of the fleet—in fact it has had the effect our allies wanted it to and has put an end to all nonsensical war talk." [3]

While the President wielded the "big stick" of the world cruise, he "spoke softly" in Washington for another understanding further pursuing the lines laid down by Taft and Katsura three years earlier. On May 5, 1908, he signed a five-year arbitration convention with Japan which, circumscribed as it was, was a calculated gesture of peace.[4] Then, through an exchange of notes between

[1] Bailey, 284. Canada was officially chary of joint action with the United States on the immigration issue, fearing such action would antagonize Japan and so make matters worse than they were. This was also the official British attitude. See MacDonald to Grey, March 6, 1908, with Foreign Office notation. *Brit. Docs.* VIII, 456-457.

[2] MacDonald to Grey, March 17, 1908. *Brit. Docs.*, VIII, 458. Bailey, 273.

[3] MacDonald to Grey, Oct. 26, 1908. *Brit. Docs.*, VIII, 459.

[4] The convention was ratified by the Senate and proclaimed Sept. 1. It was limited in scope to differences "of a legal nature, or relating to the interpretation of treaties existing between the two contracting parties" which could not be settled by diplomacy. These were to be referred to the Hague Permanent Court of Arbitration "provided . . . that they do not affect the vital interests, the independence, or the honor of the two contracting states, and do not concern the interests of third parties." *For. Rel.*, 1908, 503-505. The convention was welcomed by England. Cf. Bailey, 292 n.; *Brit. Docs.*, VIII, 458.

Secretary of State Root and Ambassador Takahira (November 30, 1908) Roosevelt took his farthest step toward liquidating the conflict of Japanese and American interests in the Far East and easing the tension between the two countries.

The Root-Takahira Agreement was as important for what it left unsaid as for what it definitely stipulated. In the first place it applied not to Eastern Asia alone, but to "the region of the Pacific Ocean," in which both countries "firmly resolved reciprocally to respect the territorial possessions belonging to each other." They mutually disclaimed "any aggressive tendencies" in this region, declared for the "existing *status quo*," the open door in China, and in favor of "supporting by all pacific means at their disposal the independence and integrity of China." Should "the *status quo* as above described or the principle of equal opportunity as above defined" be threatened, the two Governments would "communicate with each other in order to arrive at an understanding as to what measures they may consider it useful to take."[1] There are two ways of interpreting these terms, and each has had its exponents. One is that Theodore Roosevelt had secured from Japan a new promise to support the open door and the territorial integrity of China, *in addition to* a fresh disavowal of aggressive intentions toward the Philippines. The other is that in return for a Japanese pledge to respect the security of the Philippines, the United States had given Japan a free hand in Manchuria. Only a strict, legalistic construction of the agreement makes the former interpretation plausible. The history of the events leading up to it, as well as those that followed it, argues for the latter.

With Japan inflamed over the immigration crisis and confronted by new exclusion laws, it is fantastic to suppose that she would have handed over to the United States two such munificent concessions as a pledge to keep hands off the Philippines and to respect the open door and the territorial integrity of China. She had given the first concession. What had she received in return? Care-

[1] *For. Rel.*, 1908, 511-512.

ful scrutiny of the agreement reveals that it failed to prefix the phrase "integrity of China" with the word "territorial," and that the phrase "existing *status quo*" covered a great many things not mentioned at all, many of which were somewhat prejudicial to Chinese integrity, and all of which constituted paramount Japanese political and economic influence in southern Manchuria. For the "existing *status quo*" included not only the important railway and mining rights, leaseholds and privileges in Manchuria transferred from Russia to Japan by the Portsmouth Treaty, but also Chinese recognition of that transfer by a special Sino-Japanese Treaty of 1905,[1] further recognition of Japan's special interests in Manchuria by the Franco-Japanese and Russo-Japanese treaties of 1907, and last but not least, the principle that propinquity creates special interests, so firmly established by the Anglo-Japanese Alliance Treaty of 1905. So China, as well as Japan, interpreted the agreement. At the very moment it was signed a Chinese diplomat was on his way to Washington in the forlorn hope of negotiating a German-Chinese-American treaty guaranteeing the territorial integrity of China; the Root-Takahira Agreement nipped his project in the bud. Sir Edward Grey congratulated both Japan and the United States on what he considered a most realistic understanding, ideally articulated with the Anglo-Japanese Alliance, and both China and Japan considered it American acquiescence in the latter's position in Manchuria.[2]

Was Roosevelt tricked or coerced into this bargain, or did he

---

[1] MacMurray, I, 549-574. For discussion see p. 147, below.

[2] For analysis and criticism of the Root-Takahira Agreement, see esp. Reid, J. G., *The Manchu Abdication and the Powers*, 16-35; Price, E. B., *The Russo-Japanese Treaties of 1907-1916 Concerning Manchuria and Mongolia*, 39-48, two thoroughgoing studies based on the diplomatic documents of the Western powers, the latter printing in facsimile the texts of the various treaties with which it deals. Also: Ichihashi, Y., *The Washington Conference and After*, 139; Croly, H., *Willard Straight*, 275; Bailey, *op. cit.*, 292-293; Young, C. W., *Japan's Special Position in Manchuria*, 125-126, 131 n., 147, 171; Gérard, A., *Ma Mission au Japon*, 99-100; Jessup, Philip C., *Elihu Root*, II, 34-43.

make it intentionally? The Root-Takahira Agreement, like the Taft-Katsura, was never ratified by the Senate, and according to American practice, bound only the Administration that negotiated it. The Japanese Government realized this, and worried about it, but was reassured when Takahira explained that Taft would almost certainly continue Roosevelt's policy.[1] As we shall see, Taft did precisely the opposite: he revived with vigor the co-operative policy and the doctrine of Chinese territorial integrity. In so doing he elicited the most convincing proof of all that by the Root-Takahira Agreement Roosevelt had intentionally qualified his allegiance to these doctrines, exactly as Hay had done in 1903. On December 22, 1910, at President Taft's request, Roosevelt submitted to him his mature and reasoned judgment on the Far Eastern policy of the United States.[2] The ex-President had traveled a long road since he and Lodge and Mahan had planned the annexation of the Philippines. No one could speak from experience more authentically than he. This is what he wrote:

Our vital interest is to keep the Japanese out of our country and at the same time to preserve the good will of Japan. The vital interest of the Japanese, on the other hand, is in Manchuria and Korea. It is therefore peculiarly our interest not to take any steps as regards Manchuria which will give the Japanese cause to feel, with or without reason, that we are hostile to them, or a menace—in however slight a degree—to their interests. Alliance with China, in view of China's

[1] Reid, *Manchu Abdication*, 21.

[2] On February 8, 1909, Roosevelt had written Knox a long letter on Japanese-American relations which the outgoing President said he considered the most critical problem in American foreign policy. Foreshadowing the policy recommended in the letter to Knox quoted in the text, Roosevelt stressed the importance of the immigration question. Japanese labor must be excluded, he said, but tactfully and in a way calculated to avoid the risk of war. "Our task therefore is on the one hand to meet the demands which our own people make and which cannot permanently be resisted and on the other to treat Japan so courteously that she will not be offended more than is necessary; and at the same time to prepare our fleet in such shape that she will feel very cautious about attacking us." Roosevelt to Knox, February 8, 1909. Knox papers.

absolute military helplessness, means of course not an additional strength
to us, but an additional obligation which we assume; and as I utterly
disbelieve in the policy of bluff, in national and international no less
than in private affairs, or in any violation of the old frontier maxim,
"Never draw unless you mean to shoot!" I do not believe in our taking
any position anywhere unless we can make good; and as regards Manchuria, if the Japanese choose to follow a course of conduct to which
we are adverse, we cannot stop it unless we are prepared to go to war,
and a successful war about Manchuria would require a fleet as good
as that of England, plus an army as good as that of Germany. The
Open Door policy in China was an excellent thing, and I hope it will
be a good thing in the future, so far as it can be maintained by general
diplomatic agreement; but, as has been proved by the whole history
of Manchuria, alike under Russia and under Japan, the "Open Door"
policy, as a matter of fact, completely disappears as soon as a powerful
nation determines to disregard it, and is willing to run the risk of war
rather than forego its intention.

How vital Manchuria is to Japan, and how impossible that she
should submit to much outside interference therein, may be gathered
from the fact—which I learned from Lord Kitchener in England last
year—that she is laying down triple lines of track from her coast bases
to Mukden, as an answer to the double tracking of the Siberian Railway by the Russians. However friendly the superficial relations of
Russia and Japan may at any given time become, both nations are ac-
customed to measure their foreign policy in sections of centuries; and
Japan knows perfectly well that sometime in the future, if a good
occasion offers, Russia will wish to play a return game of bowls for the
prize she lost in their last contest.[1]

With the end of Theodore Roosevelt's second administration
the Far Eastern policy of the United States had completed
another cycle of advance and retrenchment on the principle of
the territorial integrity of China.

[1] Roosevelt to Taft, December 22, 1910. Knox papers. Roosevelt papers. The
passages quoted above comprise about one-fourth of the letter, the rest of which
deals with immigration and the anti-Japanese agitation in California.

# IV. Dollar Diplomacy

SINCE Daniel Webster's era American diplomatists concentrating on the Far East had been predicting that the commerce of the United States with that region would exceed its commerce with Europe. The prophecy was especially popular among the expansionists of 1898.[1] Mahan had promised them millions of Chinese customers, and they filled in the gaps with visions of great opportunities for capital investment and a second Eldorado of mineral wealth awaiting American exploitation in China. It mattered little that the Chinese people lacked the money to buy or the credit to borrow. Doctrine and prophecy endowed them with both. Theodore Roosevelt had been roused from these dreams—so long the economic foundation of America's Far Eastern policy—by the harsh realities of world politics; but he could not prevent others from dreaming them. Though a self-styled "agnostic" in economics, his own political efforts had been frustrated in no small degree by the economic entrenchment, fortified by exclusive political understandings, of competitors for the Chinese market. He had tried unsuccessfully to achieve a commanding position among these nations by tampering with the European balance of power. Now his successors, ignoring his subsequent change of policy, would attempt to buy their way to the same elusive goal, and they, too, would fail.

President Taft came to office just at the beginning of one of the greatest expansions of American foreign investment in history.[2]

[1] Cf. Chs. I, II, above.

[2] It was the second of the three greatest expansions of direct investments abroad which took place from 1898 to 1902, 1908 to 1915 and 1920 to 1929 respectively. U. S. Department of Commerce, Bureau of Foreign and Domestic

Foreign trade was likewise steadily expanding. It became the task of the new Republican President to reaffirm his party's authorship of the circumstances to which it owed much of its power. "The diplomacy of the present administration has sought to respond to modern ideas of commercial intercourse," he declared in 1912, reviewing his accomplishments of the past four years.

This policy has been characterized as substituting dollars for bullets. It is one that appeals alike to idealistic humanitarian sentiments, to the dictates of sound policy and strategy, and to legitimate commercial aims. It is an effort frankly directed to the increase of American trade upon the axiomatic principle that the Government of the United States shall extend all proper support to every legitimate and beneficial American enterprise abroad.[1]

The genius of dollar diplomacy was no more complicated than this. Only in emphasis is it distinguishable from the foreign policy of every other nation on earth and every other American administration. Whereas Roosevelt had made a game of world politics, Taft made platitudes of foreign trade. Whereas Roosevelt had associated himself with kings and emperors, Taft presided over a systematic promotional undertaking in the less glamorous realm of commerce and investment. One of the incidental, and as it turned out, least fruitful provinces of this undertaking was the Far East.

Taft and his Secretary of State Philander C. Knox personified the close relationship of business and diplomacy that characterized their administration. The President himself actually had a better acquaintance with the Far East than his more colorful predecessor. As Governor of the Philippines and Secretary of War he had given it his close official attention. Twice, as we have seen, he had served Roosevelt as special emissary to Japan. With this diplomatic experience he combined the mental habits of a constitutional

Commerce, Trade Information Bulletin No. 731, *American Direct Investments in Foreign Countries*, Washington, 1930, 40-41.

[1] Annual Message to Congress, December 3, 1912. *For. Rel.*, 1912, vii-xxvii

lawyer and a conservative political philosophy. Knox was a lesser image of his chief. He had risen to political prominence in the Pennsylvania of Matt Quay and Boise Penrose, serving both Mc-Kinley and Roosevelt as Attorney General and succeeding Quay in the Senate on the latter's death in 1904. He was mentioned for President in 1908. His grasp of national politics was invaluable to Taft in forming a cabinet, which Knox entered more as pilot and second lieutenant than as foreign minister. Knox was also of a legalistic turn of mind, sympathetic to big business and eager to promote its interests abroad.[1] These were the inheritors of Roosevelt's latter-day policy (which one of them had shared in making) of purchasing security for the Philippines with concessions to Japanese ambitions in Manchuria, a policy they might logically have been expected to continue. Instead they scrapped it.

Knox immediately set out to reorganize his Department in the interests of business and finance. On March 20, 1908, the first of the modern geographical divisions of the State Department had been founded, the Division of Far Eastern Affairs. Knox followed Root's lead with the creation of the Latin American, Near Eastern and Western European Divisions.[2] He renovated and enlarged the Department's commercial machinery, the Bureau of Trade Relations and the Division of Information. To meet the complex needs of modern diplomacy, the geographical divisions were conceived as policy-making agencies staffed by permanent bodies of experts. Since their founding they have exerted an influence on American foreign policy that has varied with the personalities of their chiefs and the importance of the affairs within their respective jurisdictions. Probably because of the esoteric character of its business the Far Eastern Division appears to have enjoyed from the outset a peculiarly independent position within the Department. It is to this Division that we must first look for the explana-

---

[1] See the biographical sketch of Knox by Herbert F. Wright in Bemis, *American Secretaries of State*, IX, 303-357.

[2] Stuart, Graham H. *American Diplomatic and Consular Practice*, 89-104.

tion of President's Taft *volte face* on the Far Eastern policy of his predecessor.

The first Chief of the Far Eastern Division was William Phillips who had served briefly as Second Secretary of the Peking Legation. In 1907 he was appointed special assistant to Huntington Wilson, Third Assistant Secretary of State in charge of Far Eastern affairs, and from March, 1908, to January, 1909 (when he was premoted to Third Assistant Secretary of State), he himself was Chief of the new Division.[1] He was then succeeded by Willard Straight who served as Acting Chief of the Division from November, 1908, to June, 1909.[2] It was during these months, and largely under the influence of these individuals, that the United States became involved in a new effort to uphold the territorial integrity of China.

On the development of America's Far Eastern policy the imprint of Willard Straight's personality is no less vivid than Hay's or Rockhill's. Straight was a less successful American Cecil Rhodes. He dreamed of empire and he tried to build it. Graduating from Cornell in 1901 he immediately began a three-year term of duty in the Imperial Chinese Maritime Customs Service under Sir Robert Hart. The Russo-Japanese War lured him into journalism. He went to Korea as a war correspondent. There he met the future American Minister to Korea, who subsequently took him to Seoul as private secretary and Vice-Consul. He became a close and indignant observer of the Japanese absorption of Korea. When the American Legation was removed from Seoul (as he said "like the stampede of rats from a sinking ship"), he followed his chief to Havana and a few months later (June, 1906) was appointed Consul General of the first American consulate in Mukden, Manchuria. Meanwhile he had made both Roosevelt

---

[1] Stuart, *op. cit.*, 89; *State Department Register*, 1924, 176; *Who's Who*, Vol. VI, 1514.

[2] Croly, H., *Willard Straight*, Ch. VIII; *Who's Who*, Vol. VI, 1855; *State Department Register*, 1909.

and E. H. Harriman, the railroad magnate, his admirers. Taft entered his charmed circle in 1907, on the occasion of the latter's second good-will mission to Japan. When, at the age of 28, he returned from Mukden to become Acting Chief of the Far Eastern Division, he brought with him plans that coincided nicely with the broad aims of dollar diplomacy.[1]

While still at Seoul Straight had come to the conclusion that the United States owed its lack of power in the Far East to the small amount of American capital invested in China. Trade and commerce, transactions "over the counter," did not carry with them the proprietary rights that constituted the entering wedge for political influence. Even if they had, by 1908 American trade with Japan had more than doubled that with China, and the disparity was growing.[2] Investment statistics for these years are highly conjectural, but, what with the Japanese war loans held by American citizens, it is probable that the American financial stake in Japan in 1908 was at least double, and perhaps triple that in China.[3] Not only was the whole Far East attracting an infi-

[1] Biographical details from Croly, *Straight*, Chs. IV-IX.

[2] According to the figures for 1908 supplied to Knox by the Bureau of Trade Relations, the United States had the largest share, 24.5 per cent of Japan's foreign commerce as compared with the third largest share, 9.7 per cent of China's. The two shares were valued at $99,417,305 and $41,969,997 respectively. J. B. Osborn, *Memorandum Relative to American Trade Possibilities in the Far East*, September 15, 1909. Knox papers.

[3] Precise figures are not available. C. F. Remer, *Foreign Investments in China*, 249-265, estimates the total American financial stake in China, including real estate and mission property, at $19,700,000 in 1900 and $49,300,000 in 1914. Of the Japanese war loans of 1904, 1905 and 1907, Americans are known to have taken $45,000,000. Department of Commerce, Bureau of Foreign and Domestic Commerce, Trade Information Bulletin No. 731, *American Direct Investments in Foreign Countries*, 37-38. It seems reasonable to assume that a) American business investments and mission property in Japan were in the aggregate at least equal to those in China, and b) that the Chinese estimate for 1908 should be considerably lower than that for 1914. This would make the Japanese estimate for 1908 proportionately greater or, as suggested, at least double and perhaps triple the Chinese. Cf. also Field, F. V. (ed.), *Economic Handbook of the Pacific Area*, 355, and *Far Eastern Survey*, Vol. V, No. 17, August 12, 1936, 182.

nitely smaller proportion of American capital than Europe, Canada, Central and South America, but within the Far Eastern region Japan had become of much greater economic importance than China to the United States. The prophecies of 1898 had gone sadly awry. Though he had been one of the most confident of the prophets, Theodore Roosevelt had recognized these trends and had tried to re-orient American policy in accordance with them. Straight would lead the Taft Administration in an attempt to re-shape the trends to the policy, to bring American capital to the rescue of China's territorial integrity.

From 1906 to 1908 Straight made his Mukden consulate a high-pressure sales agency for American commerce in Manchuria. With Harriman, he schemed of building the Manchurian link of a round-the-world American railway system.[1] He encouraged the establishment of a Chinese-American publicity bureau which distributed its literature with such effect that the Japanese Ambassador protested to Secretary Root and the State Department took steps to liquidate the bureau.[2] Straight's campaign against Japanese expansion in Manchuria, coinciding as it did with immigration troubles, Roosevelt's anxieties over the Philippines and the resultant Root-Takahira exchange, ultimately led to his withdrawal from Mukden, but by no means to his disgrace. He was granted a furlough and then ordered home by the State Department. To Rockhill, who as Minister to Peking had disapproved

[1] Harriman had had this project in view when, in the summer of 1905 he had negotiated an abortive understanding with Ito and Katsura by which he was to have furnished the capital for reconstructing the South Manchuria Railway. Japan was still at war with Russia and might well have preferred American to Russian ownership of the railway. The conclusion of peace, the renewal of the Anglo-Japanese Alliance, and the hostility toward the United States stirred up by the Portsmouth peace terms all contributed to induce the Japanese to kill the project, and obtain their funds in London. Straight outlined the scheme to Taft and urged Harriman to revive it in 1907, but the latter was deterred by the panic of that year. Cf. Croly, *op. cit.*, 239-250; Kennan, George, *E. H. Harriman,* Ch. XVIII.

[2] Croly, 252 ff.

of Straight's over-zealous methods, the Chief of the Far Eastern Division disclosed the real reason for the latter's departure.

"I want to explain to you very privately," he wrote, "the reason of the Department's telegram to you the other day granting Straight leave of absence with instructions to report in Washington.

"The telegram was purposely made as blind as possible so that if questioned by the Japanese and Russians you would not be put in an embarrassing position.

"The reason is as follows: 'Wall Street' is feeling confident again and is looking for the investment of capital in foreign lands. It has turned to Manchuria and wants the latest advice on the situation up there, probably, I assume, in the nature of Railways, or the exploitation of the country through the central Manchurian Bank Scheme.

"Accordingly, the Secretary, who is absent from Washington, sent word that he wanted Straight recalled for the purpose of furnishing information to the interested parties." [1]

Straight reached Washington early in the fall, only to find Roosevelt launched on an opposite course, that of the Root-Takahira Agreement.[2] Dollar diplomacy in Manchuria received a momentary setback. The Root-Takahira Agreement, Straight observed in his diary, "like the Korean withdrawal, was a terrible diplomatic blunder to be laid to the door of T. R." [3]

For a month or two the wind of American policy blew against the tide, but the tide shortly prevailed. While the President and

[1] Phillips to Rockhill, July 16, 1908. Rockhill papers.

[2] Straight brought with him the draft of an agreement he had negotiated with T'ang Shao-Yi, special Chinese Envoy, who arrived in Washington in November hoping to form an alliance with Germany and the United States, and to negotiate industrial, railway and currency-reform loans for China and Manchuria. Straight's draft called for the establishment of a central Manchurian bank capitalized at $20,000,000 to finance railway construction and the development of timber and mining concessions in Manchuria. Croly, Chs. VII, VIII; Reid, *Manchu Abdication*, Ch. II; Field, *American Participation in the China Consortiums*, Ch. I; Price, *Russo-Japanese Treaties*, 39-48; Cf. p. 73, above.

[3] Croly, 276. Another indication of Roosevelt's intentional compromise with Japan.

the Secretary of State were busy with Takahira, the Chief of the Far Eastern Division was lamenting the postponement of the American financial invasion of Manchuria.[1] If Roosevelt intended the Root-Takahira Agreement as a permanent re-orientation of policy, there were influential members of the State Department who considered it merely a temporary expedient. Their chance came with the inauguration of Taft and Knox. The Far Eastern policy of the United States, wrote Assistant Secretary Phillips in a long memorandum charting the course of the new Administration, was to defend the open door and the territorial integrity of China.

The Department has in view the general extension of American influence in China so that when the commercial interests and exporters of the United States turn their attention more vigorously toward securing the markets of the Orient, they will find those of China open to their products and the Chinese public favorably disposed toward American enterprise. . . . The one great drawback to the really successful development of such intercourse is the attitude of our own manufacturers and exporters who are not sufficiently alive to the importance of sending their own representatives to China to report to them directly the needs of the Chinese people. Our bankers show the same spirit although they are undoubtedly anxious to provide some of the great loans which China is now placing in England, Germany and France.[2]

Presumably these ideas were in the back of Phillips's mind during

[1] Phillips to Rockhill, September 19, 1908: "It really looks as if American interests in the Far East were going to assume a pretty definite shape." Same to same, January 9, 1909: "T'ang leaves Washington tomorrow for good, and we are all very sorry, for he was making satisfactory headway in interesting certain influential people in this country, regarding a loan to China. . . . Of course, it is almost unnecessary to say that there are suspicions here of Japanese activity in high quarters at Peking. . . . The feeling in the Department is that it is wise for the present [to] go slow until we know more fully the course of recent events, in order that we may reserve our guns, should the occasion develop the call for their use." Rockhill papers.

[2] Memorandum of Assistant Secretary of State William Phillips, May 10, 1909. Knox papers.

the Root-Takahira negotiations and he was only waiting for a favorable opportunity to put them into effect. In any case, neither he nor Straight was more than delayed by the Agreement; they were definitely not converted.

From November, 1908, until the following June, Straight formed the link between the Department of State and the bankers who were to become the official instruments of its policy in Eastern Asia. He used each to whet the ambitions of the other. As Acting Chief of the Far Eastern Division he worked for Harriman, and as Harriman's representative, he worked for the Department of State. The railroad builder still cherished his dream of encircling the globe, a dream that Straight had done much to keep alive. Now the two dynamic personalities were fused in a common undertaking. In spite of the discouraging attitude of the out-going Roosevelt Administration, Straight continued to press his plan for financing the railways of Manchuria on both Harriman and Kuhn, Loeb and Company, to whom the latter had introduced him. He tried to help the Chinese Envoy, T'ang Shao-Yi, to raise funds from the same sources for a Chinese Currency Reform loan—anything to get American capital into China. An intimation from Russia that she might be willing to sell the Chinese Eastern Railroad spurred him on. But Japanese opposition, Roosevelt's spirit of compromise, and the general indifference of the American financial community combined to frustrate his labors. March 4 came and went and nothing definite had been accomplished.[1]

The change of Administrations brought a change in Straight's fortunes. The failure of T'ang Shao-Yi's mission to Washington [2] convinced Harriman, and his Wall Street associates that they must

[1] Croly, Ch. VIII.
[2] Due, in addition to the factors cited above, to the fall from office of his chief, Yuan Shih-k'ai. The most T'ang had been able to accomplish was to arrange the terms for the remission of the Boxer Indemnity. His mission was in other respects a failure. Cf. Reid, Ch. II.

transact their business directly with the Chinese Government. They invited Straight to become their Peking representative. He at first refused. Then, at the direct and specific instance of the Department of State, the American financial group was expanded to include J. P. Morgan and Company, the First National Bank and the National City Bank, in addition to Harriman and Kuhn, Loeb and Company. The new combination, headed by Morgan, was designated by the Department of State as the official agent of American railway financing in China. The Department indicated it as such to the Chinese Government and demanded that it be accorded the same status as the similarly designated official banking groups of England, France and Germany.[1] When this group invited Straight to become its Peking representative, he accepted. The Taft Administration had thus drafted into public service the most powerful private financial organizations in the country.

Before he left Washington, Straight played his final card as a member of the Department of State. In many ways, it was his trump. Hitherto he and Harriman had been concentrating their energies on breaking into Japan's Manchurian stronghold. In May, 1909, their interest suddenly shifted to Central and Southern China when a consortium of British, French and German bankers signed a contract with the Chinese Government for the construction of a system of railways stretching southward and westward from Hankow, in the province of Hupeh, into the provinces of Kwangtung and Szechuan. The proposed system was known as the Hukuang Railways. In 1898 the American-China Development Company, for ten years the only American firm active in Chinese railway financing, had obtained a Chinese Government contract to construct a railroad from Hankow to Canton. So languid had American interest in the enterprise proved, however, that the ownership of the firm had gone by default to a Belgian syndicate. It was repurchased by J. P. Morgan in 1905, who promptly sold out to the Chinese Government. There mat-

[1] Field, *Consortiums*, 34-36; Croly, 280-285; *For. Rel.*, 1916, 134.

ters had stood until 1909. Left to its own devices, American capital had shown little or no inclination to compete with European in this field.[1] Now, under Straight's influence, and with the approval of the new Administration, the State Department boldly assumed the initiative. At the eleventh hour Rockhill was instructed to demand American admission to a share in the loan for which the three-power consortium was negotiating with the Chinese Government. "Telegram sent to Peking which started the row about the Chinese loan," reads Straight's diary for May 24. "Bill tried to ask a question merely, but with H. W. approving, my telegram went, telling Rockhill, if press reports were true, to take immediate action." [2] Not only had Straight paved the way for an American challenge to Japanese financial supremacy in Manchuria; he had actually committed the United States to a contest over the European financial monopolies in China proper. He was now free to become dollar diplomacy's most powerful private agent, as he had been its most solicitous public servant. Taft and Knox remained to preside over the diplomatic program that he, more than any other single individual, had helped to inaugurate.

Further examination of the sources of Taft's Far Eastern policy reveals the same factors that had influenced Hay and Roosevelt. Precedent alone played an important part. Knox's advisers argued that American participation in the railway loans was but "a new

[1] Both the Chinese and the French and British Governments in 1904 and 1905 had admitted the right of American capital to a share in the Hankow-Chentu railway loan, but, in spite of State Department publicity, "as yet no American financial interests had expressed a desire to participate." Phillips to Knox, June 10, 1909. Knox papers.

[2] Croly, 282. Presumably "Bill" and "H. W." refer to Assistant Secretaries Phillips and Huntington Wilson. The American demands were based on promises given by China to Mr. Conger in 1903 and 1904 that any foreign concession for railway construction in the area should first be offered to British and American companies. For detailed account, see Field, *Consortiums*, Ch. II; Croly, 281-292; Reid, 33-35; *For. Rel.*, 1909, 144 ff. MacMurray, J. V. A., *Treaties and Agreements with and Concerning China*, I, 885 ff.

phase of the traditional policy of the United States in China and
with special reference to Manchuria. As is well known, the essential principles of the Hay policy of the open door are the preservation of the territorial and jurisdictional integrity of the Chinese Empire and equal commercial opportunity in China for all
nations." [1] "This administration inherited from its predecessors
the policy of the open door and maintenance of Chinese territorial
integrity," the Secretary once penciled on the back of a letter
from his Minister to China.[2]

Besides tradition, and the commercial factors already cited,
political considerations motivated Knox. "If China is to develop
industrially as an independent political unit," ran a lengthy State
Department memorandum of September 30, 1909, "the aid it re-
ceives from other countries must be distributed in a manner to
prevent any partisan domination at the capital.

The nations that finance the great Chinese railways and other enterprises will be foremost in the affairs of China and the participation of
American capital in these investments will give the voice of the U. S.
more authority in political controversies in that country which will go
far toward guaranteeing the preservation of the administrative entity
of China."

China's integrity would be safer if responsibility for it were shared
by a disinterested commercial nation like the United States. The
development of American commercial enterprise in China would
"constitute a far greater and more effective bar to any possible
Japanese menace in the Far East than would almost any other
line of procedure." Even the Philippines were rung in.

"So long as the U. S. holds the Philippines," the memorandum continued, "the domination of China by other nations to our exclusion
would be fraught with danger and it is unthinkable that this country

[1] State Department Memorandum, January 6, 1910. Knox papers.
[2] Actually a penciled note in Knox's handwriting pinned to a letter from Calhoun, dated October 17, 1910. Knox papers.

should be squeezed out of any combination exercising an influence at Peking. The balancing of power in China is essential to peace in the Orient just as it has been necessary in Turkey to keep Europe quiet. Our interests in Asiatic waters require the prevention of the establishment of predominant interests and influences at Peking on the part of other powers and that American prestige in China be undiminished." [1]

The Philippines had been annexed on the theory that they would provide the means of promoting American interests in China. Instead, American policy in China was being shaped to provide security for the Philippines.

There were moral arguments, also. The old missionary zeal for saving China was still strong, and still of political significance. It was, perhaps, fairly represented by the Rev. J. W. Bashford, Bishop of the Methodist Episcopal Church at Peking, whom Taft personally requested to outline his ideas as to what American policy in the Far East should be. Mr. Bashford was especially interested in Manchuria, abounding in natural resources and commercial opportunities, and now, unfortunately, the object of Japanese encroachment. Should Japan be allowed to appropriate Manchuria, he felt, France, Germany, Russia and Great Britain would speedily partition China. The United States could not tolerate this. "Posterity will not hold guiltless an administration which sits idly by and permits events to shape themselves in such a manner as to deprive her [the United States] of her vast possibilities of growth in the Pacific basin for all time to come." Mr. Bashford rejoiced that the United States had a traditional Far Eastern policy. It should insist that China and Japan take their next quarrel to the Hague Court. The Chinese, a "stronger race, commercially and industrially, than the Japanese," were fast becoming more patriotic and enlightened. The United States should aid their progress, defend the open door and the integrity of the Empire. So long as Japan believed American motives unselfish

[1] State Department Memorandum, *The Chinese Loan,* September 30, 1909 Knox papers.

there would be no war between the two nations. "Moreover, if the worst comes, a nation which is unwilling to stand for righteousness has no claim upon the Almighty for continued existence." [1]

From such old, and constant, sources as these came moral support for the imperial schemes of Straight, and the commercial program of Knox and Taft. Reduced to its simplest terms, the resulting policy was an attempt to force American capital by diplomatic pressure into a region of the world where it would not go of its own accord. The political power thus theoretically to be gained was, in turn, to be used to improve the general economic interests of the United States in the Far East. The policy tended to ignore the growing economic importance of Japan to the United States, contemplating, rather, the pot of gold at the end of the Chinese rainbow. Japanese-American diplomatic relations were still strained. The immigration problem still simmered; the security of the Philippines was still to be considered. Under these circumstances a deliberate challenge to Japanese ambitions, in a section of the world that held much the same significance to Japan as did the Caribbean to the United States, was especially bold. International politics in China and Manchuria made it still more so.

Japan had emerged from the war with Russia in straitened financial circumstances, her people feeling that they had been cheated of an indemnity. The two facts combined to heighten the determination of her statesmen to hold what they had won, and to exploit it to the fullest. Korea was safely within Japan's grasp. In 1905 it had become a Japanese protectorate, and on August 29, 1910, it was formally annexed with scarcely a murmur from any Western power.[2] By the Treaty of Portsmouth Japan had also

[1] Bashford to Taft, May 15, enclosing memorandum of May 8, 1911. Knox papers.

[2] Cf. pp. 96-97, above. In 1907 the King of Korea had sent a mission to the Hague Court to protest the Japanese annexation. A striking parallel to the Chinese appeal to the League of Nations in 1931, the action merely hastened the very

achieved the continental position from which she had been ousted by Russia, France and Germany in 1896. Russia had ceded to Japan—subject to Chinese approval—her Liaotung leasehold, the South Manchuria (Port Arthur-Changchun) Railway, and the various economic privileges and concessions related thereto. Japan had lost no time in obtaining the Chinese Government's assent to these terms. On December 22, 1905, Baron Komura had concluded a treaty with the Peking Government whereby China acquiesced in the Portsmouth transfers, in return for Japan's agreement to fulfill "as far as circumstances permit" the same conditions that had obtained under Russian tenure. The circumstantial loophole was wide. In addition, China extended to Japan new privileges in the form of special Japanese-administered residential areas in important Manchurian cities; permission to rebuild and operate (until 1924) the railroad from Antung to Mukden; timber concessions on the Yalu River. Conversations were recorded (which the Japanese afterwards claimed to be secret protocols having the force of a binding commitment) in which the Chinese Government engaged not to construct any railway parallel, or if a branch line, prejudicial to, the South Manchuria. Definite in large part, with sufficient loopholes and overtones of ambiguity to accommodate the purposes of Tokyo, the Komura Treaty became the legal basis of Japan's rapidly expanding claims to special rights and interests in Manchuria, including the right to veto the construction of any railways conflicting with the best interests of her own.[1]

thing it sought to prevent. Price, 59-60, 68, 141-142; Takeuchi, 163. Sir Edward Grey told the British Ambassador to Japan that it would be inconsistent with the terms of the Anglo-Japanese Alliance to oppose the annexation. *Brit. Docs.*, VIII, 500 ff.

[1] MacMurray, I, 549-574; League of Nations, *Appeal by the Chinese Government, Report of the Commission of Inquiry* (the Lytton Report), 44, finding the alleged commitment existent only in the minutes of the Peking Conference for December 4, 1905; Young, C. W., *Japan's Special Position in Manchuria*, 87-105, minimizing the validity of the Japanese claim, but admitting that the Chinese probably made some commitment not to build parallel railroads. Cf. also Willoughby, W. W., *Foreign Rights and Interests in China*, Ch. XI; Clyde, P. H.,

Japan next proceeded to reinforce her legal claims with political *ententes*. She already enjoyed the strong moral support of the alliance with England, with its recognition of the principle that propinquity creates special rights, and the precedent of that principle's application to both Korea and Tibet.[1] True, it had been stipulated by both parties to the Portsmouth Treaty that all of Manchuria excepting the Kwantung Leased Territory and the Port Arthur-Changchun Railway zone, should be restored "entirely and completely to the exclusive administration of China."[2] But the stipulation had been somewhat undermined by the Komura Treaty, and still further by a provision of the Portsmouth Treaty itself whereby Japan and Russia agreed to conclude "as soon as possible . . . a separate convention for the regulation of their connecting railway services in Manchuria."[3] This provision signified the intention of Japan to extend her railway privileges beyond the limits fixed at Portsmouth; and, as experience had proved, with railway rights went political "rights" and "special interests." Moderate statesmen in both nations impelled Japan and Russia toward a definition of their respective interests in Manchuria, although Russia balked at sharing any more with her late enemy after having lost so much to her at Portsmouth.[4]

European influences eventually brought them together. By virtue of her alliance with England, Japan was already part of the anti-German ring, in which France occupied the position of honest broker between her Russian ally and her British friend. In 1907 the ring was tightened by the negotiation of the Anglo-Russian *entente*,[5] the Franco-Japanese treaty of June 10, and the Russo-Japanese treaties of July 30. This wholesale and systematic liqui-

*International Rivalries in Manchuria*, 104 ff., the former questioning, the latter affirming, the validity of the alleged commitment.

[1] Cf. pp. 114-116, above.
[2] In Article III. MacMurray, I, 523; Price, 24.
[3] Article VIII. MacMurray, II, 524.
[4] Price, Ch. III.
[5] Similar in character to the *Entente Cordiale* with France of 1904.

dation of issues among the nations on whose aid Great Britain was counting in case of trouble with Germany was another outstanding achievement in the history of British diplomacy. Its significance to the Far East (and hence to the Far Eastern policy of the United States) was that it greatly strengthened Japan's—and Russia's—claims to special rights in Manchuria.

France, who, by her conquest of Indo-China and exploitation of China's southern provinces had set a striking example for Japan to follow in Korea and Manchuria, now joined with Japan in subscribing to the principle that propinquity creates special rights. She recognized Japan's "rights of propinquity and influence" in Fukien, Manchuria and Mongolia in return for Japanese recognition of her analogous rights in Kwangtung, Kwangsi and Yunnan.[1] A month later Russia and Japan exchanged public pledges to respect each other's territorial integrity and such rights as sprang from the treaties of each with China, the Portsmouth Treaty and "the special conventions concluded between Japan and Russia." At the same time they secretly partitioned Manchuria and Mongolia into Japanese and Russian spheres of influence. Japan was given a free hand to do with Korea whatever she liked. A line of demarcation was drawn across Manchuria behind which each agreed to confine its activities and which, incidentally, added substantially to the Japanese sphere. Japan recognized Outer Mongolia as a Russian preserve, tacitly retaining Inner Mongolia for herself. That economic rights were intended to carry with them political rights seems clear from the subsequent actions of both parties as well as from the language of Article I of the Secret Convention, beginning "Having in view the natural gravitation of interests and of political and economic activity in Manchuria . . ."[2]

---

[1] The treaty itself merely recognized the principle which was then specifically applied to the above regions, at Japanese request, in an exchange of notes. Price, Ch. III; MacMurray, I, 640; Gérard, A., *Ma Mission au Japon*, 7-18.

[2] Price, 34-38, 107-108, giving text of the convention.

If, by these means, Japan had not established an infallible legal claim to exclusive rights in Manchuria, she had at least built up a political claim as valid as that of Great Britain to a special position in Tibet. If she had not been able to cajole China into honoring all of this claim in the precise common-law phrases of the Occident, she had obtained for it the recognition of the great European powers whose word was much more effective than law. Morally Japan had no more right to Manchuria than France had to Indo-China, or Great Britain to Hongkong, but the moral issue is beside the point. The point is that by the time of Knox's arrival upon the scene Japan had given general notice of her determination to dominate as much of Manchuria as she could, and that, with the currency of *Realpolitik* she had purchased the consent thereto of the essential powers. In the world of fact it would be difficult to dislodge any nation from such a position, no matter what the moral or legal flaws in its armor. Yet that is precisely what Straight and Knox had set out to do.

Knox was not taken unawares by Japan. Although the secret treaty of 1907 was not made public until the opening of the Russian archives ten years later, the Japanese Government had communicated the substance of the Komura Treaty to the United States less than a month after its conclusion.[1] The Portsmouth Treaty itself, not to mention the public Russo- and Franco-Japanese conventions of 1907, were straws in the wind. Moreover, before Knox took office (while Straight was at Mukden) the United States had been afforded an unmistakable object lesson as to the political strength of these engagements. In November, 1907, a British firm had secured from the Chinese Government, in the face of strong Japanese opposition, a contract to build a

[1] Through Chargé d'Affaires Huntington Wilson, who promptly reported it to the Secretary of State, including the existence of secret protocols "containing further arrangements of no small importance." Wilson to Secretary of State, January 12, 1906. *For. Rel.*, 1906, II, 995-996. This does not prove the existence of the protocols, but it does prove that in trying to endow them with reality, Japan had given the United States advance notice of her intentions toward Manchuria.

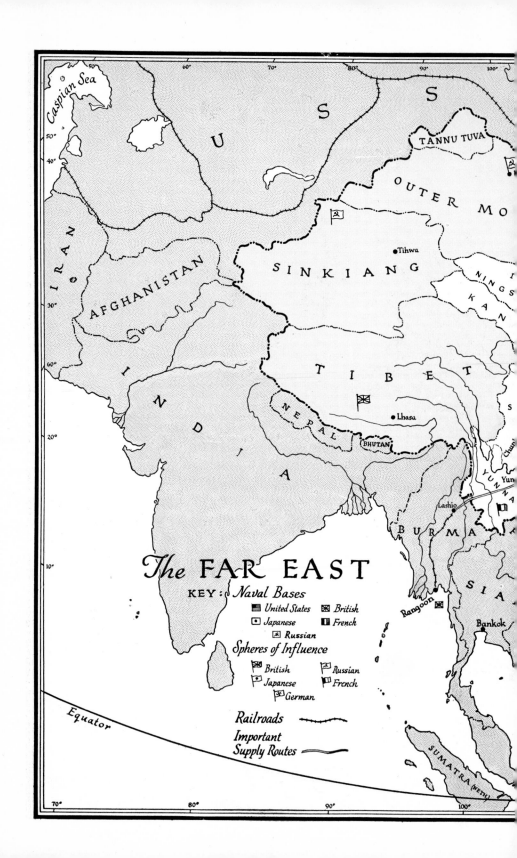

The FAR EAST

KEY: *Naval Bases*

United States    British
Japanese    French
Russian

*Spheres of Influence*

British    Russian
Japanese    French
German

*Railroads*

*Important Supply Routes*

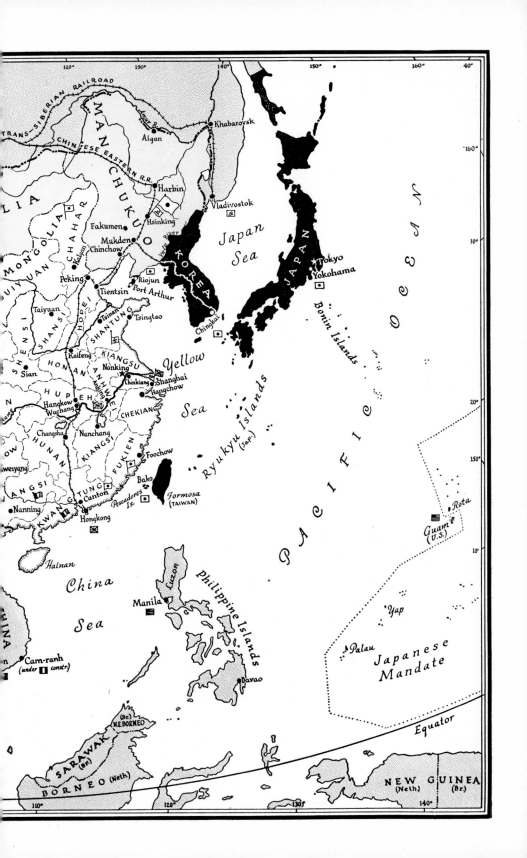

railroad between the Manchurian cities of Hsinmintun and Faku-
men. For the next two years Japanese pressure on the Chinese
Government to void the contract, and on the British Government
to withhold its diplomatic support from it, was unremitting. Invoking the Komura Treaty and its alleged protocols, Japan maintained that the proposed railroad was inimical to the best interests
of the South Manchuria. Notwithstanding the dubious legality of
the contention, it was upheld by the British Government against a
British firm, Sir Edward Grey informing the House of Commons
(March 3, 1908) that it was up to the contractors "to prove, if
they can do so, to the satisfaction of Japan that the proposed railway would not prejudice the South Manchuria line. . . ." [1] Sir
Edward gave as his pretext the railway agreement with Russia of
1899,[2] and the Komura protocols, thus recognizing the latter's
validity. It was transparently obvious that the real reason for his
action was the Anglo-Japanese Alliance. Once more Great Britain
had subsidized her interests in more important spheres at China's
(and in this case, at a British contractor's) expense. In a sense,
politics had made law: the alliance had validated the protocols.

Whatever the abstract justice of her claims to special economic
and political influence in Manchuria, Japan had made them well-
nigh impregnable by the time Knox launched his program. The
very fact of the European financial monopoly in China proper
tended further to strengthen them. On the one hand, Japan did
not have the money to break into this monopoly and so was all
the more determined to control Manchuria; on the other hand,
Great Britain and France favored giving Japanese imperialism the
utmost latitude in Manchuria in order to divert it from their own
political and economic enclaves in China, Indo-China, India and
Tibet. Governing these tendencies, in turn, was the remorseless
Anglo-German rivalry which steadily weakened the barriers to
Japanese expansion as it intensified Great Britain's concern for her

[1] Young, 106-123; Price, 46-58; Clyde, 129 ff.
[2] Cf. p. 50, above.

security in Europe. Russia profited by the same circumstances to secure her position in northern Manchuria. Both England and France needed her support against Germany and paid for it by countenancing her expansion in Mongolia and Manchuria. The path to Knox's goal was obstructed by an impenetrable political thicket of which he discerned only the merest outline. His final handicap was the Root-Takahira Agreement. Its recognition of the "existing *status quo*" meant, to Japan at least, the acquiescence of the United States Government in the political dispensations completed prior to the conclusion of the Agreement (November 30, 1908).[1] Knox was to find it difficult to convince Tokyo that such was not the case, especially since ex-President Roosevelt's construction of the Agreement tended to conform with the Japanese.

With the cards thus stacked against them, Knox and Taft opened their campaign. Their strategy never varied. For four years they tried to pump American capital into China and Manchuria. Their tactics were to demand the admission of the American banking group, on terms of equal participation, into every foreign loan floated by China and, where the demand for funds was lacking, to inspire it artificially. They were entering one of the most intricate mazes in the history of international finance. The projects that developed were so closely interrelated, and so nearly identical in design, that it is difficult to separate one from the other, and to say on which the whole precarious structure depended. The details of American efforts to participate in each were monotonously similar.

The summer of 1909 found Straight and Harriman in Europe dickering with the Russians for the sale of the Chinese Eastern Railway. Harriman's real object was the purchase of the South Manchuria Railway, but he had found the Japanese unwilling to sell. He had therefore resorted to the means by which he had built up his railway empire in the United States. He determined to force the Japanese to sell by purchasing from Russia the Chi-

[1] Cf. p. 129 ff., above.

nese Eastern Railway (which connected with the South Manchuria at Changchun, linking it to the Trans-Siberian) and by obtaining from China the right to build a railway, parallel to the South Manchuria, straight across Manchuria from Chinchow in the south to Aigun on the Siberian border. In case the threat of building the new road was not sufficient to persuade the Japanese to sell out, Harriman planned its actual construction and operation. He would smash competitors in Manchuria exactly as he had smashed them at home.

Harriman's death (September 10, 1909) deprived the scheme of its principal support. For a moment Straight was left virtually its sole protagonist. On October 2, 1909, he negotiated a preliminary agreement with the Manchurian Provincial Government for the financing and construction of the Chinchow-Aigun line by the American Consortium Group and the British contractors, Pauling and Company, the very firm to which the British Government had already denied its support.[1] But the American bankers, although not appreciating the political significance of the project, grew cautious without Harriman to lead them. Straight complained of their inertia.[2] He was finding it difficult to do business with the Russians.

At this juncture the Department of State came to his assistance. On November 6, expecting first to obtain British endorsement with which he would then confront Japan and Russia, Knox made two striking proposals to Sir Edward Grey. The first was that Great Britain join the United States in effecting the complete

[1] The American group to finance the road, Pauling and Co. to construct it. Details of the Chinchow-Aigun negotiations and the "neutralization scheme," from Croly, 296-299, 301-339; Price, 46-58; Reid, *passim;* Young, 125-168; *For. Rel.,* 1910, 231-269; *Brit. Docs.* VIII, 467-487; *Die Grosse Politik,* XXXII, 68-166; von Siebert, B., *Graf Benckendorff's Diplomatischer Schriftwechsel,* 3 vols., *passim;* Gérard, Book III, Ch. III; De Siebert and Schreiner, *Entente Diplomacy and the World,* 8-43; and manuscript sources cited below.

[2] "No one in New York knew precisely what Mr. Harriman had in mind," Straight noted in a memorandum. "No one was capable of carrying through his scheme. The directing genius had gone." Croly, 309.

neutralization of all the railways in Manchuria; and the second, that in case neutralization proved impracticable, Great Britain and the United States should together support the Chinchow-Aigun project, "inviting the interested powers friendly to complete commercial neutralization of Manchuria to participate. . . ."[1] In view of Knox's subsequent claims, the language of Sir Edward's response (November 25) is significant:

The general principle involved in the first of your excellency's two suggestions entirely commends itself to His Majesty's Government, so far as the preservation of the open-door policy and equal commercial opportunity are concerned, and would in their opinion be well adapted to securing to China full control in Manchuria. I am, however, of opinion, that until the pending negotiations for the Hukung loan have been completed, it would seem undesirable to consider the question of another international loan for China's railway undertakings, and I would suggest, therefore, that, for the present at any rate, it would be wiser to postpone consideration of the first scheme. As regards the alternative proposal contained in your excellency's note, I observe with satisfaction that the co-operation of interested powers forms part of the scheme, and I have the honor to suggest, for your excellency's consideration, that as a preliminary step toward obtaining this desirable end the two Governments should unite in endeavoring to persuade the Chinese Government to admit the Japanese to participation in the Chinchow-Aigun line, as being the parties most interested. The question of supplying funds for the purchase by China of existing lines to be connected with the Chinchow-Aigun line could be considered subsequently.[2]

Knox treated this unmistakable rebuff exactly as Hay had treated the unfavorable replies to the open door notes. Following Hay's tactics so closely as to suggest conscious imitation, he presented his twofold plan to the Japanese, Chinese, French, German and

[1] For text of proposals see *For. Rel.*, 1910, 234-235. The railroads were to be controlled by an international consortium representing the six powers most interested in China, viz.: The United States, Great Britain, France, Germany, Russia and Japan. China was to be the nominal proprietor.

[2] Grey to Reid, November 25, 1909. *For. Rel.*, 1910, 235-236.

Russian Governments (December 14), blandly announcing that he had obtained Great Britain's approval in principle, and asking for "a like favorable consideration" on the part of the other powers. Simultaneously he informed Great Britain of his action, and requested her co-operation in securing the general acceptance of his proposals.[1]

Great Britain was the first to reply (December 29, 1909). She would do nothing until she had ascertained the views of the other governments concerned, and in particular "what measure of participation would satisfy the Japanese Government in regard to this undertaking."[2] Knox tried some more bluff. On January 6 he gave a long, optimistic statement to the press, expounding the principles of the co-operative policy in phrases reminiscent of the Hay notes and once more claimed Great Britain's support.[3] The ruse did not succeed. After consulting each other, and submitting their course of action to the approval of Great Britain, Japan and Russia summarily rejected the neutralization scheme in almost identic notes presented the same day (January 21, 1910).[4] Their recep-

[1] *For. Rel.*, 1910, 236-237. Knox had previously sounded the Russian Government on the neutralization scheme. On November 10, 1909, he instructed Ambassador Rockhill to make "shrewd and discreet use, as if the ideas originated with yourself, of the fundamental ideas put before the Embassy in previous telegrams and notably in that of November sixth which quotes confidentially the memorandum to be handed to the British Government. You will find yourself free to foster the idea of Russian co-operation in neutralizing the railroads of Manchuria by joining with us, Great Britain and other interested governments supporting the open door." Knox to Rockhill, November 10, 1909. The response of the Russian minister was evasive. Rockhill to Knox, November 13. Knox and Huntington Wilson kept up a steady barrage of arguments on St. Petersburg, to no avail. Cf. despatches to and from Rockhill and State Department, November 10, 1909-January 4, 1910, including copies of neutralization and Chinchow-Aigun proposals, covering the whole transaction in detail. Rockhill papers.

[2] Foreign Office to Reid, December 29, 1909. *For. Rel.*, 1910, 242.

[3] Text of press release, *Ibid.*, 243-245. Again Knox consciously invoked precedent, declaring that his plan "was but the first step in a new phase of the traditional policy of the United States in China and with special reference to Manchuria." *Ibid.*, 244.

[4] The Japanese and Russian Governments entered into communication almost immediately after receiving the Knox proposals. Japan gave warning that she

tion of the Chinchow-Aigun proposal was scarcely more cordial. Although Japan did not specifically reject it herself, she allowed Russia to take the initiative in doing so, and, since the two powers were acting in concert, Russia's rejection (February 24, 1910) dealt the project its *coup de grâce*.[1] Both Japan and Great Britain advised Peking not to sanction the Chinchow-Aigun project without Japanese consent,[2] which all three knew would never be forthcoming. To cap the climax Russia and Japan then concluded a new treaty (July 4, 1910) drawing the lines still tighter about their respective spheres, concessions and political rights in Manchuria. This, too, had the blessing of Sir Edward Grey, who was shown the preliminary drafts of the treaty and pronounced his satisfaction at the *rapprochement* between his valuable allies.[3] "Whatever the Japanese may say there can be little doubt that the policy adopted by the U.S.A. in China hastened if it did not bring about this arrangement," he observed.[4] Both Russia and Japan publicly thanked Great Britain for her assistance against the American intrusion.[5]

would reject the neutralization scheme, January 8, 1910. By January 13 both had prepared draft replies to Knox and the Russian draft was submitted to Sir Edward Grey with the assurance that Russia was "acting in agreement with Japan." Price, 52; De Siebert and Schreiner, 12.

[1] The Chinchow-Aigun contract which Straight had obtained from the Manchurian Government the previous October, was formally ratified by the Chinese Government January 21, 1910. Although the project was not abandoned until Straight had journeyed to St. Petersburg in June, 1910, and learned from interviews with the Russian cabinet ministers that they would never consent to it, the initial Russian rejection had sealed its doom. Japan meanwhile warned Peking to undertake nothing in Manchuria without Japanese consent. See authorities cited above, p. 153. Note especially Price, 53 and 139-140. Reid, 104; *Die Grosse Politik*, XXXII, 99 n.

[2] Price, 53, 139-140; Reid, 104; *Die Grosse Politik*, XXXII, 99; Gérard, 124; Far Eastern Division Memorandum, Sept. 9, 1910. Knox papers.

[3] Price, 54; Reid, 128-131. The draft treaty also received the preliminary approval of France, Gérard, 128.

[4] Minute by Grey on MacDonald to Grey, July 2, 1910. *Brit. Docs.*, VIII, 485. Cf. Reid, 142. For text of treaty, Price, 113 ff. It was part public, part secret, like that of 1907.

[5] Reid, 105, 113; *Brit. Docs.*, VIII, 476-479.

The State Department, still euphemistically inclined, was "happy to find in the new convention . . . an additional pledge of the stability of general peace in the Far East." [1] But the Secretary of State could not disguise the abysmal failure of his diplomacy. Instead of dividing Russia and Japan, and opening the door to American participation in the financial exploitation of Manchuria, he had, as it were, nailed that door closed with himself on the outside. He had converted Russo-Japanese rivalry into a solidarity most welcome to France and England. Instead of strengthening Chinese suzerainty over Manchuria, he had weakened it. Of the European nations on whose co-operation he had counted, only Germany gave him any moral support, and that not out of deference to American principles but because Germany, too, was something of an outsider in China and because, as the Kaiser said, it suited her purposes to foster "the dilemma for England, between the yellow ally and the white brother." [2] France stood by England and Russia, while to China the American plans were a forlorn hope that the Chinese Government was powerless to help fulfill. Most ironical of all, Straight and the American financial group—supposedly the principal beneficiaries of dollar diplomacy—accused the State Department of ruining their plans by affronting the Russians, and threatened to withdraw from the field entirely unless the Department ceased to make them the instruments of such an aggressive Far Eastern policy.[3]

[1] Wilson to Rosen, July 30, 1910. *For. Rel.*, 1910, 837; Reid, 142.

[2] Reid, 78; *Die Grosse Politik*, XXXII, 72. The German Ambassador to Tokyo derided the Knox proposals as a typical bit of "naïve Washington impudence," and thought the Japanese would have "drunk ink" should they have accepted them. Mumm to Hollweg, January 2, 1910. *Ibid.*, 84; Reid, 79.

[3] Straight believed that the Russians had not been sufficiently courted by the American financiers before Knox blundered in and affronted them. On September 3, 1910, after several members of the American group had threatened to retire, Davison, Schiff and Straight had a long interview with Knox, in which they argued for a more moderate Far Eastern policy and made the threat of retirement. Knox was reduced to pleading with them to continue to support the government, a commentary on the political elements in dollar diplomacy. Cf. Croly, Ch. IX and Ch. X, 339-344.

When the inevitable recriminations began, Straight heaped most of the blame on Great Britain, as did the State Department. Straight told his friend, J. O. P. Bland, that he could not "see much use in playing very hard with you Britishers. You're all right as individuals, but my Lord! what a government you've got." The "greatest surprise" to him was, he said, "the cold-footed trimming policy exhibited by the English. . . . The saddest part of it all is that if Great Britain had played the game, the whole trouble could have been avoided." [1] Ambassador O'Brien in Tokyo was "bitterly" critical of "British unreliability," [2] and as Schuyler had reported to Rockhill, Reid was instructed to complain to the Foreign Office at "Great Britain's recent failure to co-operate with the U. S." [3] But Grey had been anything if not consistent in his refusal to support the American schemes without first securing the consent of his two Far Eastern allies. The meaning of his responses was so plain that whatever Knox pretended to think of them he must instantly have recognized their hostility. He had done so, in any case, by January 21, when both he and Taft admitted Grey's first reply to have been a rejection, and the President remarked, rather wistfully, to the German Ambassador that he wondered "what England expects to get from Japan for helping them." [4] Indeed, as already suggested, it is difficult to resist the conclusion that Knox deliberately misinterpreted Grey's replies, a well-known diplomatic practice to which Hay had also had recourse. [5] Grey did not mislead the Americans; they misled

---

[1] Straight to Blane, January 10, 1910; to Huntington Wilson, March 3, 1910. Croly, 323-324.

[2] Reid, 104; *Die Grosse Politik*, XXXII, 102-104.

[3] Above, p. 37.

[4] Reid, 93; Bernstorff to Foreign Office, January 21, 1910. *Die Grosse Politik*, XXXII, 83. Knox's instructions to Reid to remonstrate at London were further proof that he realized Great Britain was not supporting him.

[5] Grey continued to uphold the Anglo-Russian agreement of 1899, the Portsmouth and Komura Treaties, and to deny that the principle of spheres of influence in China had ever been formally repudiated. Cf. Young, 151-157; Reid, 126-127; *For. Rel.*, 1910, 267-269.

themselves in expecting anything from the British but what they got.

Once more American diplomacy had sadly miscalculated the European factors in Far Eastern politics. Straight himself had at one time contemplated the very neutralization scheme proposed by Knox.[1] If he had any legitimate complaint against Knox it was that the Secretary had pressed his plan not wisely but too well. They had both counted on Japanese and Russian opposition. They had even had timely warning that their policy might result in a new Russo-Japanese *rapprochement*, the antithesis of their aims.[2] Still, despite the abundant and clearly visible portents of the past five years, they had persisted in the belief that they could realize American commercial ambitions, win British co-operation and exorcise all political obstructions with a mere appeal to principles. The United States had neither the power to coerce Japan and Russia, nor the means of purchasing their support. At the very moment that Great Britain was anxiously working to bring Russia and Japan together, the United States made its cavalier request for British aid in driving them apart. Knox's indirect approach to Manchuria, *via* London instead of *via* St. Petersburg and Tokyo, prejudiced his chances of success. Japan and Russia considered themselves, rightly or wrongly, the arbiters of Manchuria. If Knox could not accomplish his purpose by dealing with them directly it was a fair indication that he could not do so by consorting with Great Britain, their friend and ally. Both

[1] Straight noted in his diary, January 10, 1910: "I must say I consume a certain amount of satisfaction in this project (the plan of neutralization), for it's mine, after all's said and done, and was started when I lunched with Mr. Schiff one day at the Lawyers' Club in New York." Croly, 320.

[2] As early as November 2, 1909, before the neutralization scheme was first broached to Grey, the Russian Minister to Peking had warned George Fletcher that "the continued opposition of the foreign powers to Russian policy in Manchuria might drive them to make common cause with Japan." Fletcher had replied that the United States would stick to its principles no matter who opposed them. Fletcher to Knox, November 2, 1909. Rockhill papers. A week later, Straight had relayed the same warning to J. P. Morgan. Croly, 321.

Russia and Japan had things to offer England, things that England desperately needed: security for India, assistance against Germany, a rear guard in Eastern Asia. What had the United States to offer England in comparison? For Knox to have thought that he could persuade Grey to gamble such priceless diplomatic assets on an American promotional scheme directed against Grey's own allies, and in competition with the British banking consortium group,[1] was a naïve assumption, to say the least.

Scarcely less difficulty was encountered in the attempt to open the door to American capital investment in China proper.

Straight's telegram instructing Rockhill to demand the admission of the American banking group to an equal share with the British, French and German groups in the projected Hukuang railways loan had fallen far short of its mark. On June 6, 1909, the Chinese Foreign Office, paying no attention to the belated American importunity, proceeded to initial the agreement with the European groups. The State Department thereupon protested to London, Paris, and Berlin, and intimated to Peking that unless the Chinese Government changed its attitude, the United States might reconsider the remission of the Boxer indemnity. Meanwhile Straight, representing the American group, had gone to London where, on July 7, he formally presented the American demand for equal participation in the loan to a conference of the French, German and British groups. The combined diplomatic and financial pressure of the United States made Peking waver, but not London. The British had admitted the Germans to the Hukuang loan only because they had been unable to keep them out. Now, despite the much-touted identity of British and American interests in the Far East, they were in no mood to welcome the Americans. While admitting the academic justice of the American

[1] It will be remembered that Pauling and Co., the British firm that was to share in the Chinchow-Aigun contract was not a member of the British consortium group and had previously been denied diplomatic support.

claim the Foreign Office argued that in 1905 it had inquired if the United States wished to share part of the concession with Great Britain; that "notwithstanding the publicity given to the matter, no intimation had been received at the State Department as to any intention on the part of American capitalists to take the matter up"; and that consequently "His Majesty's Government would scarcely feel justified in interfering with the arrangements concluded." [1]

Thwarted at London, the United States turned its attention to Peking, where it sought to prevent the Chinese Government from signing the contract until the American terms were met. President Taft resorted to what has been called an "unprecedented *tour de force*," [2] personally telegraphing Prince Chun, the Regent of China and insisting on "equal participation by American capital in the present railway loan." It was, indeed, an extraordinary thing for the President of the United States to address the sovereign of another nation in the interests of private American financial interests. But he did not think of them as such. "I have an intense personal interest in making the use of American capital in the development of China an instrument for the promotion of the welfare of China," he explained, "and an increase in her material prosperity without entanglements or creating embarrassments affecting the growth of her independent political power and the preservation of her territorial integrity." [3] Whatever the original sources

[1] Memorandum from the British Foreign Office, June 7, 1909. *For. Rel.*, 1909, 149-150.

[2] Croly, *op. cit.*, 295.

[3] Taft to Prince Chun, July 15, 1909. *For. Rel.*, 1909, 178. Knox simultaneously wired the Chinese Foreign Office deploring "a situation in which it seems that individuals in China or elsewhere are able to defeat the practical operations of the policy of the open door and equal opportunity, and if the objections of bankers of other countries to equal American participation are so insistent as not to be overcome by the wishes of China and of their own governments, the time has arrived when China should exercise its right to determine the matter by confining her dealings to those who are willing to respect her highest interests." *Ibid.*, 179.

of Taft's policy, it had by now flowed out onto the plane of international prestige and abstract legalism which engrossed the two
constitutional lawyers that administered it. Although Straight
favored a compromise with the Europeans, and Morgan himself
became cautious, the State Department made its demand for equal
participation a matter of principle on which it refused to yield in
the slightest.[1]

For two years the altercation over the Hukuang railways
dragged on, the British contesting the American claims at every
turn. "Negotiations are, I believe, still going on between the
British & German groups as to who should provide the American
slice of this wonderful cake," wrote Sir Valentine Chirol to Rockhill in November, 1909.[2] Two months earlier Rockhill (who had
been appointed Ambassador to Russia the previous May) had
stopped in London on his way to St. Petersburg, and had a long
conversation with Sir Edward Grey on the subject of the loan.[3]
The British Foreign Secretary apparently gave Rockhill the impression that his Government was on the whole sympathetic to
the Knox policy.[4] But the State Department felt otherwise. In
October, 1909, the loan agreement had been all but concluded
when the British suddenly refused to sign. Ambassador Reid was
instructed to convey to Sir Edward the Department's "impression"
that Great Britain alone was obstructing the negotiations, and to
ask for closer co-operation.[5] Early the next winter Montgomery
Schuyler, who had been keeping a close watch of affairs in the

[1] Cf. Wilson to Reid, July 9, 1909. *For. Rel.*, 1909, 169-171.

[2] Chirol to Rockhill, November 1, 1909. Rockhill papers. Chirol was Foreign
Editor of the London *Times* and a proponent of Anglo-American co-operation.

[3] Fletcher to Knox, October 5, 1909. *For. Rel.*, 1909, 205. The conference
was attended by Chirol who urged Sir Edward to concede to the American
demands.

[4] "It seems a long time, and a far cry, since the day, last September, when Sir
Edward Grey told you and friend Chirol that the Brit. Govt. desired nothing
better than to work with the U. S. in Manchuria!" Blane to Rockhill, May 2,
1910. Rockhill papers.

[5] Wilson to Reid, October 17, 1909. *For. Rel.*, 1909, 206-207.

Far Eastern Division, sent Rockhill the "very confidential" information that "The Dep't. is much dissatisfied with Great Britain's recent failure to co-operate with the U. S. in all important moves both in the Orient and elsewhere and Mr. Whitelaw Reid was orally instructed to tell the British F. O. so on his recent visit to Washington." [1]

A preliminary agreement was at length reached on May 23, 1910, only to be rejected, this time, by the Chinese Government. China was on the verge of the civil upheaval that was shortly to bring about the collapse of the Manchu Dynasty. Great opposition to the Hukuang loan had developed throughout the country, especially among the provincial governments, which feared it as a device of Peking for strengthening its powers with foreign aid, and as a new manifestation of foreign imperialism. Local disorders broke out, and Peking hesitated before setting its hand to the unpopular agreement. [2] Whereupon the United States united with Great Britain, France and Germany in forcing the Chinese to sign. [3] This action hastened the revolutionary *débâcle* of the government to the head of which President Taft had professed only the most disinterested concern for China's welfare.

American admission to the Hukuang railways loan, to which the European powers had assented in the agreement of May 23, carried with it American membership in the three-power—now four-power—banking consortium. The scope of this consortium was

[1] Schuyler to Rockhill, February 15, 1910. Rockhill papers. Schuyler was just about to leave Washington to become Chargé d'Affaires in Tokyo. He also reported that, "In conversation at the Department I gathered that the President is himself the great exponent at Washington of our 'vigorous Far Eastern policy' and that the Dep't. was only carrying out his wishes. Everything considerate of other foreign policy is to be subordinated to the Orient."

[2] As early as November, 1909, Chirol reported that "local opposition to the whole scheme has become loud and vigorous. . . ." Chirol to Rockhill, November 1, 1909. Rockhill papers.

[3] Minister Calhoun was instructed not to take the lead in coercing China but to act in concert with the other powers. See Adee to Calhoun, October 7, 1910. *For. Rel.*, 1910, 291.

formally defined in a quadruple agreement of November 10, 1910, in which the French, British, German and American banking groups agreed to share equally in all Chinese railway loans.[1] Despite this understanding, the powers remained deadlocked over the Hukuang loan until May 20, 1911, when a final agreement was at last concluded. The loan was floated the next month, but the Chinese Revolution intervened to delay any actual railway construction until 1913. The United States had gained admission to the four-power consortium as well as to the Hukuang railways loan on terms of technical equality with France, Germany and Great Britain. It disposed of its share of the loan with such fitful interest, however, that by 1927 no work had yet been done on the American section of the railways.[2] As for achieving the international influence sought by Knox and Taft for use in defense of China's integrity, Straight himself admitted that "the mere mention of Hukuang is like a red flag to a bull to these European Foreign Offices. . . . 'Dollar' diplomacy made no friends in the Hukuang matter." [3] That it did not give the United States the power to coerce its rivals in its own, or China's, interest, is proved by the fate of Knox's Manchurian program.

Notwithstanding his conspicuous lack of success so far, Secretary Knox made one more effort to force American capital into Manchuria. On September 22, 1910, the Chinese Government requested a loan from exclusively American sources for the double purpose of currency reform in China proper and industrial development in Manchuria. Peking was seeking to circumvent the all-

[1] The agreement also stipulated the rules of procedure for future negotiations between the consortium and the Chinese Government, as well as among the members of the consortium. Field, 44 ff. For text of agreement, MacMurray, *Treaties and Agreements*, I, 828-832.

[2] For the Hukuang negotiations, see Field, Ch. II; Croly, 296-300; Reid, 34-46, 56-61, 133; Remer, 268-272; Willoughby, W. W., *Foreign Rights and Interests in China*, 1927 ed., II, 1077 ff.; *For. Rel.*, 1909, 144-215; 1910, 269-292; MacMurray, I, 866-899.

[3] Straight to Dorothy Whitney, February 19, and Straight to Davison, February 21, 1911. Croly, 392-393.

too-effective Japanese railway monopoly in Manchuria by investing its borrowed funds in industrial projects other than railroads.
To Knox, the proposal offered another chance to bolster the sinking Chinese Government, restore its authority over Manchuria,
and stimulate the flow of American capital into the contested
province. He accepted it, and invited England, France and Germany to participate. Instantly Japan and Russia revived their
opposition.[1] In close consultation with each other, and with their
respective European allies, they brought the same forces into play
that had killed the neutralization scheme, with the same result.
Although the loan agreement was signed (April 15, 1911) the
loan itself was never floated.[2] Again Straight, alternately criticizing
Russian duplicity and the clumsiness of the State Department,
played a leading role.[3]

An opportunity now presented itself for the United States to
clear away all of its misapprehensions as to Great Britain's position
in the Far East. This was the renewal of the Anglo-Japanese
Alliance. Since it was first concluded, and more particularly since
its last renewal, the alliance had very largely governed the policies
of the two allies in the region to which it applied. In 1909 Lord
Kitchener had visited the Orient and according to the British Ambassador in Tokyo, had become "more than ever convinced of the
great practical value and utility of the Anglo-Japanese Alliance."

He considered that our policy in the Far East should be to foster
the closest relations with the Japanese Government and people, for

[1] Japan and Russia were not impressed by the circumvention of railway construction, showing that their claims to special rights in Manchuria went far beyond railways. In this position they were sustained by France and England.

[2] The currency reform loan was never issued; part of the industrial development loan was issued and recalled.

[3] So aroused were Japan and Russia at what they considered a new foreign invasion of their legitimate spheres of interest, that they seriously debated partitioning and annexing Manchuria outright. For details of this loan see Croly, 366-
403; Field, 55-56; Reid, 162-167, 188-211, 229-249, 252; Price, 60 ff.; For.
Rel., 1912, 88-94; 1913, 192-198; De Siebert and Schreiner, 28-43.

which purpose the Anglo-Japanese Alliance was a sheet-anchor; in all her legitimate aspirations we should stand by Japan through thick and thin. Personally he thought that Manchuria at any rate as far as Mukden, would, and indeed should, be Japanese, if the peace of the Far East was to be maintained in the future; the Chinese system of Government he looked upon as hopeless . . . the Japanese on the other hand were consistent in their policy, knew what they wanted, and usually got it. He was much struck by their activity and push in the matter of Railways in Manchuria; once the Antung-Mukden line was built their position would be secure, but Mukden must be Japanese. At the present moment the Japanese position was very insecure; once they held the two railways up to Mukden there would be no fear for the future. These remarks, which were of course very confidential, on the part of a man in Lord Kitchener's position, are, I venture to think, interesting.[1]

It was Grey's all-too-literal adherence to Kitchener's "interesting" views that had, more than anything else, perhaps, frustrated Knox in the Far East. The renewal of the alliance called for a show of hands all around. If either ally wished to revise its policy to accommodate the United States, now, surely, was the time to do so, especially since the cue for revising the alliance appears to have come, not from London, or Tokyo, but from Washington.

In addition to the alliance's obviously harmful moral effect on Knox's policy, two further circumstances rendered it an object of American concern in 1910. The first was President Taft's interest in promoting law and order among the nations through the medium of unlimited arbitration treaties. To the champion of such a cause the alliance was not only a material barrier, but a symbol of the very type of exclusive *Machtpolitik* he was most anxious to dispel. Secondly, Japanese-American relations had been strained by Knox's Manchurian program and by the perennial immigration problem [2] to a point that made war talk both constant and plausible. In the event of that war, Great Britain would be obliged by

[1] MacDonald to Grey, December 10, 1909. *Brit. Docs.*, VIII, 472-473.
[2] Discussed in Chapter IX.

the terms of the alliance to join with Japan against the United States. It was an alarming nightmare. Besides championing the cause of world peace, therefore, President Taft had a very practical reason for desiring to negotiate an arbitration treaty with Great Britain: he wished to banish the possibility of an Anglo-Japanese war against the United States. Thus emerged the idea of an Anglo-American treaty of unlimited arbitration which, in turn, inspired the revision and renewal for another decade of the Anglo-Japanese Alliance in advance of its legal date expiration.

Who first formulated the idea in terms of practical diplomacy is not yet certain. From such documents as are now available the honor appears to belong to Andrew Carnegie. On July 11, 1910, the crusading philanthropist wrote a letter to Sir Edward Grey quoting a speech of President Taft's in favor of arbitration treaties, and asked Sir Edward what he would think of such a treaty with the United States. Carnegie received an encouraging reply which he promptly relayed to Washington.[1] A few days later (August 5) President Taft took Ambassador Bryce for a cruise on the *Mayflower* and told him he would like to conclude an unlimited arbitration convention with Great Britain.[2] The ball had beeen put in play.

To Great Britain the proposed treaty likewise offered significant advantages. It would mitigate the unfriendly impression created by her Far Eastern policy and help Grey to restore himself to the good graces of Washington. It would insure her against embroilment with the United States and hence leave her more free to deal with Germany. And it would allay the fears of a large

[1] *Brit. Docs.*, VIII, 542.

[2] Bryce to Grey, August 9, 1910, *Brit. Docs.*, VIII, 541. The movement for peace by general arbitration appears to have been inaugurated at a dinner given by Theodore Marburg, a Baltimore publicist, on February 6, 1910, on which occasion the American Society for the Judicial Settlement of International Disputes was organized. See the illuminating review of Taft's part in the peace movement, especially valuable for the light it throws on the relations between Taft and Roosevelt, in Pringle, Henry F., *Taft*, Ch. XXXVIII.

portion of the British public that the alliance with Japan might lead them into "fratricidal" war with the United States. The great difficulty was how to articulate the treaty with the alliance. In the latter's present form it would be impossible. Grey could not, independently, agree to ignore his obligations under the alliance in case Japan became involved in hostilities with the United States, especially in view of the clash of Japanese and American policies in Manchuria. He would have to secure Japan's permission; he would have to revise the existing alliance so as to make room for the arbitration treaty with America.

Grey at once sounded Tokyo on the subject of an arbitration treaty, plainly hinting at the desired changes in the alliance. After considerable beating around the bush the Japanese took the hint and proposed revision. Parallel negotiations over the alliance with Japan and the arbitration treaty with the United States ensued, culminating in the renewal of the alliance July 13, and the signing of the arbitration treaty August 3, 1911.[1] Article IV of the new alliance treaty provided that,

Should either High Contracting Party conclude a treaty of general arbitration with a third power, it is agreed that nothing in the agreement shall entail upon such Contracting Party an obligation to go to war with the power with whom such treaty of arbitration is in force.[2]

With the signing of the arbitration treaty the United States appeared to have obtained a legal shield against joint attack by England and Japan. But the refusal of the Senate to ratify the treaty soon set things back to where they were in the beginning. Great Britain had signified her unwillingness to carry her Far Eastern policy to the point of actual war with the United States.

---

[1] For texts of each see *Brit. Docs.*, VIII, 532-533 and 590-593. For negotiations, *Ibid.*, 503-540 and 540-605. Also, Reid, *passim;* Chang, Chung-Fu, *The Anglo-Japanese Alliance,* 145-174; Dennis, *The Anglo-Japanese Alliance,* Ch. III; Reid to Knox, April 21, 1911. Knox papers; Holt, *Treaties Defeated by the Senate,* 230-235; Ishii, 54-59.

[2] *Brit. Docs., loc. cit.*

That was all. No other important changes were made in the alliance, except that Korea was recognized as part of Japan.[1] The same principles by which England connived at Japanese expansion in northeastern Asia in order to gain security for India and a makeweight against Germany, were given a new lease on life. England had had the chance to revise her Far Eastern policy to accommodate Knox and Willard Straight; emphatically she had not done so. Her attitude toward American dollar diplomacy's remaining projects was not changed.

All of the loan negotiations described so far had been carried on against the background of an impending Chinese revolution. The dissolution of the Manchu Government was the real "open door" by which outside nations made their way to positions of power and special privilege in China. This had been true in John Hay's time and the situation had not changed. It was a vicious circle. The weakness of China invited foreign exploitation and foreign exploitation, in spite of its professions of altruism, helped to keep China weak. We have mentioned the unpopularity of the Hukuang loan, and its acceleration of the oncoming revolution. The currency reform loan negotiations had a like effect. The principal issue between the Chinese and American Governments throughout had been the latter's insistence on the appointment of an American financial adviser with wide supervisory powers. Peking viewed this as an impairment of sovereignty which, under the circumstances, it could by no means afford to risk. The State Department at length yielded the point, but it was symptomatic of the type of foreign control then exercised in Chinese public affairs. The revolution, when it did come, was more anti-Manchu than anti-foreign in spirit, and yet the Manchus were to a certain extent scapegoats for the foreign money-lenders and concession-

[1] By deleting the article recognizing Japan's paramount interest there. The article referring to the security of the Indian frontier was also removed, out of deference to the Anglo-Russian *entente* of 1907, though a general statement committing Japan to the defense of peace and order in India was included, as before.

aires. The fighting began in Szechuan Province with a popular uprising against the Hukuang railway program. Thence it spread, in
the fall of 1911, until it engulfed the Manchus and resulted in
the establishment of the Chinese Republic (February 12, 1912).[1]

The revolution provided more business for the four-power consortium, and provoked a new diplomatic showdown among the
rival nations. In November, 1911, Yuan Shih-k'ai, soon to become President of the Republic, and then obviously the strongest
political leader in China, appealed to the four-power consortium
for a loan with which to pay his troops, maintain order and
reorganize the Chinese Government. Granting his request would
have implied recognition of his Government, and this the consortium powers were at first unwilling to do. Russia instantly
seized the opportunity of the revolution (for which she alone appears to have planned in advance) to extort China's assent to an
independent Mongolia under Russian tutelage. Japan likewise
gave early warning of her intention independently to support the
Manchu Government, which she found ideally impotent. Presumably she would make the price for this support an independent,
or Japanese, Manchuria. To gain a free hand in Mongolia, Russia
had given a free hand to the British in Tibet, who speedily made
use of it to detach that province from the sovereignty of China
and cement their control over its internal affairs. To Knox, the
times called for a new invocation of the co-operative policy, and
money for China to preserve her territorial integrity.

Not until December, 1911, was he able to bring a semblance
of united action out of the chaos. The most that was forthcoming
then was identic notes from the United States, France, Germany,
Great Britain, Japan and Russia urging moderation on both factions in the revolution. Apprehensive for the British stake in the
Yangtse Valley, and uncertain as to which way the wind was

---

[1] The date of the Manchu abdication. Two days later Yuan Shih-k'ai was
elected provisional President. He was formally elected President, October 6, 1913,
and inaugurated October 10.

blowing, Grey did not dare depart from a strict neutrality. Knox
therefore redoubled his efforts in behalf of Yuan Shih-k'ai and
collective action. He argued for the admission to the four-power
consortium of Japan and Russia, convinced at last that they were
more dangerous outside of it, and that inside they might be
restrained by their partners. This Grey was reluctant to concede,
preferring to barter away China's border provinces rather than
to admit more competitors to China proper. But Russia and Japan
brought such pressure to bear on their French and British allies,
that, whether Knox had favored their admission or not, they
probably would have achieved it. On June 20, 1912, they entered
the consortium.

Meanwhile negotiations for the reorganization loan had gone
forward between Yuan's government and the four-power group.
A few cash advances were made, enabling the impecunious President to keep one step ahead of insolvency. But no basic terms had
been agreed upon because the consortium governments once more
insisted on such stringent supervisory powers that Yuan considered
them incompatible with Chinese administrative integrity. In des-
peration he turned for more favorable terms to independent Belgian, German, and British syndicates, only to be thwarted by the
co-operative action of the consortium governments. The Japanese
and Russian conditions of entrance to the consortium were such as
to obtain further international sanction for their special interests
in Manchuria and Mongolia.[1] Although the conditions were made,
and accepted, with the characteristic ambiguity of diplomacy (which

[1] Price, *op. cit.*, 72, thinks that the United States was placed on record, intentionally or unintentionally, by Acting Secretary of State Huntington Wilson as
adhering to the principle that a foreign government might use "such protective
measures" within its sphere of interest in China "as may be forced by necessity"
provided that the rights and interests claimed within the sphere were protected
by treaty or convention with China. This, in other words, was a reversion to the
principle of the first Hay notes of 1899, which admitted the existence of spheres
and asked only for most-favored-nation treatment within them. See Wilson to
German Ambassador, May 9, 1912, and Memorandum of conversation between
same and Japanese Ambassador, May 16, 1912. *For. Rel.*, 1912, 79.

leaves each party free to interpret an agreement according to its own interests) American acceptance of them was a long step backward from the neutralization scheme and the Chinchow-Aigun project.[1] It was another *de facto* recognition of Japan's supremacy in Manchuria. On July 8, 1912, the two new consortium members signed a third secret treaty consolidating their respective spheres in Manchuria and Mongolia,[2] further impairing Chinese sovereignty and barring the door to dollar diplomacy yet more firmly. "Everything indicates a readjustment of relations of England, France and Russia on lines of triple *entente*" cabled Minister Calhoun from Peking. "To my mind it is no longer a question of friendly international co-operation to help China but a combination of big powers with common interests to accomplish their own selfish political aims."[3]

Before the competing powers could secure the adherence of China to their terms President Wilson withdrew American support from the reorganization loan (March 18, 1913) because he found it "to touch very nearly the administrative independence of China itself."[4] The circumstances of the withdrawal are interesting. It has commonly been supposed that the initiative came from the White House, an early manifestation of that idealism for which the new President was to become famous.[5] Actually the consortium group made the first move itself, exactly as it had after the *débâcle* of the neutralization scheme. The Chief of the Far Eastern Division described the affair vividly to Rockhill.

"The question of Far Eastern policy was raised by the bankers the day after Inauguration, and raised in categorical form," he wrote. "Three representatives of the American group (Davison, Straight and Warburg) asked immediately for a conference with the Secretary and

[1] For imposition of terms, see Price, 74; *For. Rel.*, 1912, 114 ff., 124.
[2] For text of agreement, see Price, 117.
[3] Calhoun to Knox, February 21, 1913. *For. Rel.*, 1913, 163-164; Field, 93.
[4] Field, 93; MacMurray, II, 1025.
[5] Cf. Field, 110-113; also Notter, H., *The Origins of the Foreign Policy of Woodrow Wilson*, 231-233.

the President in regard to the attitude which the Government would hereafter assume towards their activities in China. There is dissension in the group itself to begin with: the tedium of fruitless negotiations has almost worn out their patience; the Schiff crowd . . . are particularly disgruntled that they are not yet in a position to make any profit out of their endeavors. So with more than a mere semblance of lukewarmness, the group has put it up to the Administration in a way which seems to amount to about this:—They cannot be satisfied with a mere approval by the Department, but, as a condition to their staying in the business with China, they must be asked to do so by the American government."

MacMurray did not think the invitation would be forthcoming, and he was right. Two years ago, he said, he would have considered Wilson's decision "a great and quixotic renunciation of our opportunities." But the way the bankers had "led our Government around like a trick dog" persuaded him to approve the President's course.[1] MacMurray had placed the shoe on the wrong foot: the initiative in dollar diplomacy had come from Washington, not Wall Street. To the bankers went the distinction of first admitting its failure.

Wilson's judgment was vindicated by the storm of protest from all factions in Chinese politics brought down on Yuan's head by the loan agreement when it eventually was announced. On May 2, 1913, the United States alone of the great powers recognized the Chinese Republic. America's Far Eastern policy had passed through another cycle of hope, vigor, frustration and retrenchment.

[1] MacMurray to Rockhill, March 18, 1913. Rockhill papers. Rockhill agreed with him that, under the circumstances, Wilson's move was "well advised," although he felt it was "a bit hasty," and strongly disapproved of recognizing the Chinese Republic. Rockhill's own opinion was that the United States should either exert a strong control over Chinese politics, or clear out altogether. Of the two alternatives he himself appears to have preferred the former. Rockhill to MacMurray, April 11, 1913. After his departure from St. Petersburg Rockhill became special adviser to the Chinese Government, in which capacity he did much to persuade the American bankers to revive their interest in Chinese finance. Rockhill to Admiral Ts'ai Ting Kau, June 10, 23, 29; July 10, 31, 1914. Rockhill papers.

Dollar diplomacy had come to a close under the stigma of impairing rather than strengthening the territorial integrity of China.[1] It had fallen far short of its announced objectives. It had not stimulated international co-operation, but rather international competition. It certainly had not saved Manchuria either for China or for American capitalists. Financially it was unprofitable, the total American investments attributable to it in 1914 being $7,299,000, the American share of the Hukuang railways loan.[2] The American stake in Japanese trade continued to exceed that in Chinese by even greater proportions in 1912 than had existed in 1908, notwithstanding the manifest unfriendliness of American diplomacy toward Japan.[3] The only available figures for American investments during the era of dollar diplomacy indicate an appreciable decline in 1912 from 1908.[4] If these figures are too indefinite to warrant such a conclusion, the least they suggest is a profound disappointment of the hopes of the dollar diplomatists. The Far East remained, in spite of the efforts of Knox and Taft, a singularly unimportant market for American investment.

When things began to go against him in the Far East, Knox

[1] Details of reorganization loan, Chinese revolution and American withdrawal from the consortium from: Price, Ch. V; Field, Chs. VI, VII, VIII; Reid, Chs. XII, XIII, XIV; For. Rel., 1912, 46-159, 161-171; 1913, 87-202; Gérard, 108 ff.; De Siebert and Schreiner, 27-43; Die Grosse Politik, XXXII, 240-277; Graf Benckendorff's Diplomatischer Schriftwechsel, II, passim and III, esp. 265-268, describing Russo-British negotiations re: Tibet and Mongolia.

[2] Remer, 272.

[3] The average annual American import and export trade with Japan for 1910 to 1914 was $129,700,000; with China, $51,000,000. Field, ed., Economic Handbook of the Pacific Area, 470-471.

[4] Remer, 249-265, 338, gives $49,300,000 for 1914. The Department of Commerce accepts, with considerable reservations and misgivings, $175,000,000 as the total American foreign investments in the Far East and Asia in 1909 and $60,000,000 in 1912. Department of Commerce, Bureau of Foreign and Domestic Commerce, A New Estimate of American Investments Abroad, as does William W. Lockwood, Jr., in "America's Stake in the Far East, II, Investments." American Council, Institute of Pacific Relations, Far Eastern Survey, V, No. 17, August 12, 1936, 182.

declared that his policy had a higher purpose than the mere promotion of American business, or even the defense of Chinese territorial integrity. In reply to Roosevelt's critical letter (quoted in
the last chapter) he argued that the principle of respect for treaties
was at stake:

Why the Japanese should think that we ought to accept the observance by them of one treaty right due from them to us as an offset
for the disregard by them of another treaty right due from them to us
I cannot understand.

Whether the American people would ever fight in support of his
policy or not was, he thought, "academic." The United States
should stand uncompromisingly on its principles.[1] Had dollar
diplomacy originated in the same high-principled realm as Knox's
reply to Roosevelt, the latter might have been more convincing.
Coming from the diplomatic agent of Straight and Harriman, who
once told the German Ambassador that his neutralization scheme
would "smoke Japan out," [2] it sounded like a rationalization. In
any case, it did not convince Roosevelt. "Unfortunately, after I
left office," wrote the ex-President in 1913, "a most mistaken and
ill-advised policy was pursued towards Japan, combining irritation
and inefficiency. . . ." [3]

[1] Knox to Roosevelt, December, 1910. Dennett, *Roosevelt and the Russo-
Japanese War*, 321-323.
[2] Bernstorff to Foreign Office, December 30, 1909. *Die Grosse Politik*, XXXII,
71; Reid, 75.
[3] Roosevelt, *Autobiography*, 414; Dennett, *Roosevelt*, 323; Pringle, *Taft*, Ch.
XXXV.

# V. War in Europe

TO the Far Eastern policy of the United States the World War bore almost as incongruous a relation, in origin, as had the circumstances that led to the annexation of the Philippines. Both the underlying and immediate causes of the war were European, affecting the Far East but incidentally, according to the political, economic and territorial interests of the warring powers in that region. The United States became involved in the war for reasons which, by no stretch of the imagination, could be identified with its actual or supposed interests in Eastern Asia. Yet in the end, the war imposed on the United States more serious military and political responsibilities in the Far East than in Europe. It launched the Far Eastern policy on the most ambitious and sustained of all its cycles. It destroyed the Far Eastern balance of power that had existed until 1914, and substituted in its place a Japanese-American antagonism. While Britain and her allies fought to restrain Germany's expansionist tendencies in Europe, the United States, through moral suasion, diplomatic pressure, and political and military intervention resisted Japanese expansionist tendencies in the Far East.

Forces set in motion by the war combined with tradition and precedent to bring about this unlooked-for development. The United States had been challenging Japanese ambitions in China, though irresolutely and with frequent backslidings, for the better part of two decades. During this period Japan had nevertheless been making steady progress toward an imperialist goal, the sudden achievement of which the war seemed to promise her. With all her great European rivals distracted, only the United States remained potentially able to deny her the opportunity she had anticipated and instantly attempted to seize, an unobstructed path to the hegemony of China. Should the United States offer resistance it would have to do so single-handed, a fact that would impair the effectiveness of that resistance if it did not deter Wilson from making it at all. What, then, led him to make it? Three basic reasons suggest themselves: First, the precedents established by Wilson's predecessors; second, new conceptions of American foreign policy, the war-inspired gospel of the American President himself, which exalted and applied universally the doctrine that the United States must help to preserve the territorial integrity not only of China but of all independent states; third, the influence exerted on American diplomacy by foreign nations, especially China and Great Britain. The three factors are isolated for convenience. Seldom did one come into play without the other two. Together they fused the resources of American diplomacy in an effort to uphold China's territorial integrity which was to last until 1932, and which more than any of the efforts that preceded it was to bely the claim that American interests in the Far East had remained purely commercial.

The American detachment from Far Eastern politics occasioned by Wilson's withdrawal from the consortium was brought to an early end by an overture from China on the outbreak of war in Europe. Largely on account of what Japan might make of it, China feared the extension of hostilities to the Far East. So insecure was the government of Yuan Shih-k'ai that it could not command order within China, let alone withstand stress from abroad. Yuan had already deserted the revolutionary leaders on whose shoulders he had risen to the presidency and had set up a virtual dictatorship with himself in supreme power. In so doing he had aroused the open hostility of the champions of parliamentary government, led by Sun Yat-sen, and precipitated a civil conflict between them and the northern military leaders that was to bedevil Chinese diplomacy throughout the war.[1] The extension of European hostilities to the Far East would disrupt China's foreign trade and with it the customs receipts that were the government's sole independent source of revenue. This would force Yuan to seek foreign loans and further weaken his power of resistance to Japanese encroachments. Accordingly, as soon as war was declared in Europe, China turned to the United States (August 3, 1914) with the proposal that it "endeavor to obtain the consent of the belligerent European nations to an undertaking not to engage in hostilities either in Chinese territory and marginal waters or in adjacent leased territories."[2] This was but the first of a series of not wholly unsuccessful Chinese attempts to convert long-standing American sympathies for China into instruments of her own national policy.

The expansive terms of the Chinese proposal afforded a glimpse of its true purpose. Guaranteeing the neutrality of leased territories would have meant leaving Kiaochow in German possession until the termination of hostilities. For Germany to have remained ensconced in the Shantung Peninsula might have thwarted the Japanese plan of expansion that Peking unquestionably had wind of and was trying to forestall. This was a large order. But the United States had repeatedly taken the lead in projects aiming at the preservation of China's territorial integrity. Was there not every reason to believe that it might do so again? On August 7 Secretary Bryan authorized American participation in the scheme to neutralize foreign settlements in China but not leased territories. The more comprehensive aspect of the Chinese proposal,

[1] For a thoroughgoing treatment of the effects of China's internal political situation on her diplomacy during the war, see LaFargue, T. F., *China and the World War, passim.* Yuan died in 1916 after having tried to make himself emperor, but the civil strife that he had accelerated continued after his death.

[2] MacMurray to Bryan, August 3, 1914. *For. Rel.,* 1914, Supplement, 162; LaFargue, 5-6. The proposal was made by the Chinese Foreign Office to American Chargé d'Affaires MacMurray and directly, through the Chinese Minister to Washington, to the Department of State. MacMurray to Bryan, August 6. Bryan to MacMurray, August 7. *For. Rel., loc. cit.,* 162 ff.

he wired, was receiving "careful consideration." [1] Within four days' time the State Department was sounding the powers interested in China, including Germany, on their willingness to observe the neutrality of the Pacific Ocean as well as the *status quo* of the entire Far East.[2] Nothing came of the proposal because no general agreement was possible. Germany alone accepted it, though too late.[3] On August 14 Japan despatched an ultimatum to Berlin, following it August 23 with a declaration of war.

The failure of the Chinese-American venture has been generally ascribed, and with justice, to Japan's determination to force the issue, seize the German leasehold and use it as the entering wedge with which to extend her sway over as much of the rest of China as possible. But that is not the whole truth. Great Britain must share some of the onus, as well as France. Both nations obviously wished to deal their enemy a commercial blow by wiping out his business in China. Yet, in the summer of 1914, this desire was overshadowed by their fear of Japan. England approved the plan of observing the *status quo* in China,[4] but because of her designs on Germany's Pacific colonies and shipping, rejected the neutralization of the Pacific Ocean. Having thus defeated one-half of the proposal, she gave Japan precedent for defeating the other

[1] Bryan to MacMurray, 1 P.M. and 5 P.M., August 7. *For. Rel.*, 1914, Supplement, 163; LaFargue, 6.

[2] *For. Rel.*, 1914, Supplement, 164-170.

[3] On August 13 Ambassador Gerard cabled Germany's terms to Bryan. According to these, Germany "did not seek war with Japan." "If Japan, on account of the treaty with England, asks that Germany do nothing against English colonies, warships, or commerce in the East, Germany will assent in return for corresponding promise from England." Germany then proposed either the withdrawal or enforced inactivity of all British and German warships in Far Eastern waters, together with an agreement among Japan, England and Germany "that none of these three shall attack warships, colonies, territory or commerce of any of the others in the East"; the East to be defined as "all land and seas between parallels London 90 east and all Pacific to Cape Horn"; smaller limits being acceptable, if these should be considered too large. Gerard to Bryan, August 13, 1914. *Ibid.*, 169-170.

[4] Page to Bryan, August 11, 2 A.M. and 2 P.M. *Ibid.*, 165, 167; LaFargue, 8.

half. This need not imply that had Great Britain accepted the proposal *in toto* Japan would have followed suit. It does show that now, as in the past, Great Britain's European interests stood in the way of close Anglo-American co-operation in the Far East.

While Bryan was sounding the powers on the neutralization of the Pacific, London and Tokyo were engaged in the most delicate negotiations having to do with the application to the European conflict of the Anglo-Japanese Alliance, the scope of Japanese military operations, and the general disposal of war spoils in China and the Pacific. Promptly on the outbreak of war Japan had offered her services to England under the alliance. At first Sir Edward Grey declined the offer, disingenuously explaining to the Japanese Ambassador in London that because of Japan's "fine attitude of good faith and restraint" in not calling on England for assistance during the Russo-Japanese War, "now we in turn should avoid, if we could, drawing Japan into any trouble." [1] The fact is that, for much the same reasons as China, Great Britain wished to keep Japan out of the war altogether and for several days tried hard to do so.[2] Two factors defeated her purpose. The first was, obviously, Japan's determination not to be kept out. The second was Great Britain's formulation of strategy that accompanied her declaration of war on Germany (August 4).

The original British plan called for the destruction of Germany's Asiatic squadron, a task for which the combined strength of the British Asiatic squadron and the Australian navy was considered adequate. This plan was quickly expanded, however, to include the seizure of the German islands in the Pacific.[3] On

[1] Grey to Sir C. Greene, August 4, 1914. *Brit. Docs.*, XI, 329.

[2] Grey to Sir C. Greene, August 1. *Ibid.*, 256; Greene to Grey, August 2. *Ibid.*, 279; Minute by Sir William Tyrrell, August 3. *Ibid.*, 292; Grey to Greene, August 3. *Ibid.*, 298; Greene to Grey, August 3. *Ibid.*, 305; same to same, August 4. *Ibid.*, 327; Grey to Greene, August 4. *Ibid.*, 329.

[3] Of immediate value to England because of their strategic position and wireless stations, also for bargaining purposes at the end of the war. See the careful discussion of this point by Spinks, Charles N., "Japan in the World War," *Pacific Historical Review*, V, 297-311, esp. 299-300. The seizure of the islands

August 6 Australia was asked to commence operations against three of these islands, which she refused to do until the German fleet had first been disposed of.[1] This appears to have convinced London that Japanese naval assistance would be needed, for the next day (August 7) the British Ambassador to Tokyo presented a formal memorandum to the Japanese Foreign Office, specifically requesting it. The request was only "that the Japanese fleet should, if possible, hunt out and destroy the armed German merchant cruisers who are now attacking our commerce. . . . This, of course, means an act of war against Germany but this is, in our opinion, unavoidable."[2]

Still fearing that Japan would prove a Frankenstein monster if turned loose in China, Grey spent a fruitless week attempting to limit her belligerent action to a naval campaign against German vessels in the China Seas, i.e., to keep Japan out of Kiaochow and out of the German islands. Rightly or wrongly the Japanese cabinet considered this insufficient grounds—or inducement—for entering the war on England's side, insisting on the necessity of attacking Kiaochow and of enjoying an unrestricted military zone. Deadlock ensued. On August 11 Grey made a gesture of withdrawing his request, but he finally had to back down. The Japanese ultimatum to Germany went forth with no British strings attached.[3] Grey put up a bluff in the form of a statement to the

was ultimately part of the comprehensive British strategy pursued in Africa as well as in the Pacific, of destroying Germany as a colonial and naval power.

[1] *Ibid.*, 301; Colonial Office to Governor-General of Australia, August 6, 1914, British Parliamentary Papers, 1914-1916, XLV, *Correspondence Respecting Military Operations Against German Possessions in the Western Pacific*, No. 1, 1.

[2] Spinks, 303; LaFargue, 11-12. *British Documents on the Origin of the World War* are silent on the Anglo-Japanese negotiations after August 4, principal source for which is the documentary evidence contained in Ito's biographical memoir of Count Kato, Foreign Minister in the Okuma Cabinet then in power.

[3] Invoking the Anglo-Japanese alliance, the ultimatum called upon Germany to withdraw immediately (or disarm) all her armed vessels in Japanese and Chinese waters and to surrender to Japan "on a date not later than September 15, 1914 . . . without condition or compensation the entire leased territory of Kiao-

press that it was "understood that the action of Japan will not extend to the Pacific Ocean beyond the China Seas, except in so far as it may be necessary to protect Japanese shipping lines in the Pacific, nor beyond Asiatic waters westward of the China Seas, nor to any foreign territory except territory in German occupation on the Continent of Eastern Asia." [1]

Foreign Minister Kato protested Grey's statement and denied that his Government had ever made any such commitment.[2] Whether it had or not, Grey doubtless suspected that Japan did not intend to abide by it. He had been forced to consent to a Japanese attack on Kiaochow in which, more in the hope of keeping them straight than helping them fight, British forces were to co-operate with Japanese. The most he had obtained from Japan was the insertion in the demand for the unconditional surrender of Kiaochow of the clause "with a view to eventual restoration of the same to China." [3] The German Chargé d'Affaires at Peking made a frantic eleventh-hour attempt to retrocede the territory to China, retaining the right to recover it, or receive an equivalent leasehold, at the end of the war.[4] Japan promptly warned China against the deal, and Great Britain informed Peking that she could not recognize the transfer. Whereupon China turned in

chow, with a view to eventual restoration of the same to China." Germany was given until August 23 to comply. *For. Rel.*, 1914, Supplement, 170.

[1] Spinks, 309, London *Times*, August 18, 1914. Grey also assured Ambassador Page that Japan considered herself bound by the Anglo-Japanese Alliance to respect the territorial integrity of China. Page to Bryan, August 11. *For. Rel.*, 1914, Supplement, 167. Kato strove to give Washington the same impression. Cf. Guthrie to Bryan, August 15. *Ibid.*, 170-171.

[2] LaFargue, 15. On December 10, 1914, Kato informed the Japanese Diet that the ultimatum had been independently despatched, that no promise had been given England to return Kiaochow to China, and that Japan had not agreed to any limitation of her military operations whatsoever. Summaries (paraphrase) of replies by the Minister of Foreign Affairs to interpellations in the Diet, December 10, 1914. Enclosure in Guthrie to Bryan, December 31. *For. Rel.*, 1914, Supplement, 210-211.

[3] Spinks, 304-311; LaFargue, 14-15.

[4] LaFargue, 16; *For. Rel.*, 1914, Supplement, 172.

despair to Washington with a plea that the United States "under-take to bring about the immediate retrocession of the leased ter-ritory" itself taking over the German rights and handing them to China. "The Department feels sure that such a course would do more to provoke than to avert war," responded the nonplussed Secretary of State.[1] War had come to the Far East, and with it the latest menace to the open door and the territorial integrity of China.

Had Germany complied with the Japanese ultimatum it is pos-sible that Japan might have refrained from war, at least for the moment. The fact that Berlin was given a week rather than the customary one or two days to reply, together with the admittedly pro-German sympathies of part of the Japanese cabinet suggest that there was some hope in Tokyo that this might happen.[2] On the other hand the severity of the ultimatum, the character of the attack on Tsingtao, not to mention the Twenty-One Demands and what followed them, argue that Japan was merely awaiting a suitable occasion to do exactly what she did. Had the alliance with England not afforded her the pretext, something else would have—her secret ententes with Russia, perhaps, or the importuni-ties of France. If Britain had met Germany halfway, and agreed to the withdrawal or disarming of both their armed forces in the Pacific, the Far East might have been defaulted to Japan just as definitely as it was. The point is not that England must be con-demned or excused for calling on Japan for assistance. It is, rather, that in the very first days of the war the exigencies of European politics, this time dictating aggression on Germany's islands in the Pacific, had once more frustrated American hopes of enlisting the full support of England in upholding the territorial integrity of China. Neither difference of opinion as to the merits of Great Britain's cause in the World War, nor the British reluctance to

[1] MacMurray to Bryan, August 19 and 20; Bryan to MacMurray, August 20. *For. Rel.*, 1914, Supplement, 172-174.
[2] LaFargue, 11, 13.

have Japan enter it, should obscure this fundamental fact. By August 7, 1914, before the war had emerged from the low estate of *Machtpolitik*, Great Britain in spite of herself was already in retreat before Japan on certain principles on which the future of the League of Nations would depend, a retreat that would make it impossible for Lloyd George to co-operate with Wilson at Versailles, when the war had entered a nobler sphere, and the hope of the civilized world seemed to depend on Anglo-American co-operation.

Once Germany had rejected Japan's ultimatum, the latter's sweep of German possessions in the Far East was swift and thorough. On August 27 Tsingtao was invested by a Japanese fleet. Less than a week later (September 2) the first of some 30,000 Japanese troops were landed at Lungkow, in northern Shantung, commencing a long overland march to attack Kiaochow from the rear. In the conquest of Kiaochow (which fell November 7) both Germany and Japan violated China's neutrality, although the Japanese violations were the more flagrant.[1] While restricting the action of her own small contingent of troops (about 1,500) to the actual area of the German leasehold, Great Britain nevertheless condoned her ally's encroachments on neutral Chinese territory.[2] Abandoned by England, China again implored the United States to intervene, but Acting Secretary Lansing replied, prophetically, that "it would be quixotic in the extreme to allow the question of China's territorial integrity to entangle the United States in international difficulties." [3] By December, 1914, Japan, still assuring the world that she was not in the war for selfish purposes, had the entire province of Shantung and most of the

[1] Comprising, for example, the seizure and retention of the Tsingtao-Tsinan Railroad, reaching 240 miles inland from the German concession. Cf. *For. Rel.*, 1914, Supplement, 177-182; LaFargue, 17-27.

[2] In spite of the urgent plea of the British Legation in Peking to London to restrain Japan. Reinsch to Bryan, September 30. *For. Rel.*, 182.

[3] Lansing to Reinsch, November 4. *Ibid.*, 189-190; LaFargue, 23.

German islands north of the equator safely within her grasp.[1]

Japan now proceeded to use her conquest of the German sphere in Shantung as the springboard to what she hoped would be the hegemony of all China. While Peking and Tokyo wrangled over the latter's trespasses on neutral Chinese territory, the Japanese Government had been quietly preparing the most ambitious *démarche* in the history of its diplomatic relations with China. With Europe preoccupied in a war that might, conceivably, end at any moment, Japan worked fast. As early as August 26, 1914, the Japanese Minister to Peking urged Foreign Minister Kato to show his hand. Kato deferred action, however, until December 3, when he forwarded to Minister Hioki (at Peking) a number of proposals with instructions to submit them to the Chinese Government as soon as a favorable opportunity presented itself. On January 18, 1915, the proposals were handed to Yuan Shih-k'ai under the strictest injunctions of secrecy. The Chinese Dictator-President, realizing that his only hope of extricating his country from the desperate situation thus created lay in enlisting the intervention of England or the United States, and that publicity was his only available weapon, let the news leak out. The American Minister to Peking, Paul Reinsch, received a garbled version of it, through clandestine channels, on January 21, and the Japanese strategy of swift, undercover negotiations culminating in a *fait accompli* was spoiled. Gradually the world became informed of that smothering blanket of exclusive political and economic privi-

---

[1] Australian and New Zealand forces had captured the German islands south of the equator and penetrated into a few to the north, thus precipitating another delicate issue between Japan and England. *For. Rel.*, 1914, Supplement, 183-206. Japanese historians have readily admitted the war motives of eliminating a powerful European rival, from the Far East and taking revenge on Germany for the latter's part in the Triple Intervention at the close of the Sino-Japanese War. Also Kato himself had, on his own initiative, intimated to Grey that Japan would seize the opportunity of the war to consolidate her position in Manchuria and the Kwantung Peninsula, Grey expressing the opinion that these were matters to be settled between China and Japan without the intervention of a third party. *Takeuchi, War and Diplomacy*, 184-186; LaFargue, 49-50.

leges known as the Twenty-One Demands which Japan had tried to cast over China and which, had she been entirely successful, would have reduced the Celestial Empire to a state of vassalage. From February to May China fought the Demands with the meager resources at her command, publicity, temporization, artful dodging. A Japanese ultimatum (May 7) at last forced her to accept the Demands, though by no means in their original stringency, and on May 25 the acceptance was formalized in a group of Sino-Japanese treaties and exchanges of notes.[1]

As originally presented, the famous Demands were arranged in five groups, collectively aimed at the establishment of Japanese economic and political supremacy in China. Group One, subsequently the most important to the United States, called for China's "full assent" to whatever disposition of the German rights in Shantung Japan should make at the end of the war; for a Chinese promise not to cede or lease any portion of Shantung to any "third power"; and for the granting to Japan of widespread railway and commercial privileges throughout the province. Group Two perpetuated and strongly consolidated Japan's special position in Manchuria and Eastern Inner Mongolia, and evoked China's specific acquiescence therein. Group Three demanded exclusive mining and industrial privileges in the Yangtse Valley, including joint Sino-Japanese ownership of the rich iron and steel mills, smelters, collieries and mineral deposits around Hankow, the industrial capital of China. Group Four, likewise to become of special importance to American diplomacy, pledged China not to cede or lease "to any power any harbor or bay or

[1] For the most up-to-date and carefully documented analysis of the Sino-Japanese negotiations over the Twenty-One Demands, including their complete text, see LaFargue, Ch. III and appendix. Cf. also Carnegie Endowment for International Peace, Division of International Law, Pamphlet 45, *The Sino-Japanese Negotiations of 1915, passim; For. Rel.,* 1915, 79-206; MacMurray, II, 1216-1237 (all containing texts of the Demands); also Reinsch, P. W., *An American Diplomat in China,* Ch. XII; Takeuchi, 187-195; Price, *op. cit.,* 78-82; Young, *op. cit.,* 183-192.

any island" along the Chinese coast, a demand calculated to obtain international recognition of the maritime province of Fukien (opposite Formosa) as a Japanese sphere of interest. Group Five (differentiated from the preceding four groups in that the Japanese Government classified the latter as "wishes" or "desires," the former as demands requiring immediate compliance)[1] asked for widespread political rights throughout China proper which, if granted, would give the Japanese Government supervisory control over Chinese social and political institutions from schools and churches to the Chinese Government itself.

Because the Twenty-One Demands were presented to the American public as an astounding example of the treachery and aggressiveness of Japanese diplomacy, and because one of them—that relating to Shantung—was to become such a bitter issue in Japanese-American relations, it is perhaps not amiss to bear in mind the basic conflict of policies to which they were incidental. The factors impelling the United States to shatter a new lance in behalf of China's territorial integrity have been suggested. To the Japanese Government and people the Twenty-One Demands appeared, not as a bombshell of treacherous aggression, but as high statesmanship. It is unnecessary to accept the arguments of economic exigency subsequently advanced by Japan in her own defense in order to appreciate the fact that Japan herself believed in them. Not to recognize the force of that belief in Far Eastern international relations is as unrealistic as to plead for sympathy for it.

As we have seen in the previous chapters, Japan had been making great strides toward wealth and power since her war with Russia. But she had by no means reached the objectives the attainment of which she believed her geographical situation made im-

[1] A distinction consistently maintained by the Japanese Government, as proved by Kato's frank admission that he did not wish to include them, refused to do so until they had been reduced to "wishes," and expected them to be withdrawn, as they were. LaFargue, 46-47, 73-74; *For. Rel.*, 1915, 113-115.

perative. The position in Korea, southern Manchuria and eastern Inner Mongolia that she had wrested from Russia and fortified with the sundry political instruments already discussed had enhanced her sense of security, yet left it far from complete. Russia herself, though bound to Japan by various treaties, was still a menace to the north. England and the United States caused her further uneasiness. The Knox neutralization scheme and the Chinchow-Aigun project had threatened the foundations of her special position north of the Great Wall. South of it, in China proper, she had experienced the same difficulty in forcing her way into the thicket of European rights and privileges as had the United States. She had not the financial resources to compete on equal terms with Germany, France, England and the United States. When these formed the Four-Power Consortium in 1911, and began to make plans for investments in Manchuria, Japan had had to unite with Russia and apply much diplomatic pressure to gain admission. In China proper lay the raw materials and natural resources which, for Europe, were profitable speculations, but for Japan were the lifeblood of existence. The European spheres of economic interest all carried with them political influence at Peking. So did the loans of the consortium, which Woodrow Wilson had found "to touch very nearly the administrative independence of China itself." Yet Japan had not been able to make any loans or build any railways south of the Great Wall. Her position there was inferior to that of any of the Great Powers, and what is more, dependent on their whims. She had not attained her goal; she was fearful of losing what she had, and this because of the competitive imperialism of Western nations, thousands of miles away, to which China was of infinitely less political and economic significance than to Japan. Now that these Western nations were preoccupied with the war, Japan would adjust the situation. Since 1895, when France, Russia and Germany had forced her to return the Liaotung Peninsula to China, Western interventionists had repeatedly thwarted Japan in her pursuit of what, to her, was not only a just but vitally essential policy. This time she would profit by experience. She would strengthen her foothold in Manchuria and Mongolia, and make that in Shantung secure enough to withstand another Triple Intervention. She would establish access to China's raw materials, to the financial, industrial and commercial privileges which she considered indispensable to her existence as a modern industrialized state, and for which she had been too poor, financially, to compete with Europe. Because she had not been able to accomplish these ends by economic means, she would do so by political. Finally, she would make the contract so binding that it could not be broken on European council tables once the war freed Europe's attention. Such, briefly, was the origin of the Twenty-One Demands.[1]

To them China showed unexpectedly effective resistance. Before she signed the Treaties of May 25, 1915, she had succeeded, with the aid of scarcely more than the moral support of Great Britain and the United States, in appreciably modifying the Demands as originally presented. Except for one article pledging China to consult Japan first in case foreign capital should be needed for railway or harbor construction in Fukien, Group Five was withdrawn entirely, shelved "for future discussion." [2] The Chinese promise in Group One not to cede or lease any territory in Shantung to "any third power" was revised to apply to "any foreign power," a phrase that might be construed to mean Japan and so limit the scope of the concessions that accompanied it. Various Chinese reservations and loopholes appeared in the other Groups. Japan had gained valuable political and economic concessions in Shantung, southern Manchuria and Mongolia as well

[1] Cf. LaFargue, Ch. II, who stresses the Japanese sense of insecurity in Manchuria and the situation in Japanese domestic politics, particularly the demand for "something to show" for the troops lost and money spent in the conquest of Kiaochow.

[2] This article was incorporated with the single demand of Group Four in an exchange of notes relating to Fukien. Cf. MacMurray, II, 1228; For. Rel., 1915, 195-196.

as industrial and financial privileges in China proper. China had agreed by treaty to turn over the German leasehold and treaty rights in Shantung to Japan who undertook to restore to China at the end of the war, merely "the leased territory of Kiaochow Bay," and that only after China had fulfilled certain specified conditions which would, in effect, make all Shantung a Japanese sphere of influence.[1] From the Japanese point of view the success of the Twenty-One Demands had been notable. At one fell swoop they had brought Japan to a commanding position in China to which she might never have been able to buy her way in competition with Europe. But they had fallen considerably short of their most extreme objectives. The treaties and notes left China many legal straws to cling to; they failed conspicuously to reduce her to a Japanese protectorate.

The most effective opposition to the Twenty-One Demands came from the Chinese people themselves rather than from any of Japan's Western competitors; from London rather than from Washington, and from the unofficial ministrations of the American Minister to China rather than from the formal protests of the Department of State. The presentation of the Twenty-One Demands aroused large portions of the Chinese people against Japan, and accelerated their faltering progress toward national unity.[2] The activities of the American Minister to China were more subtle. Like Mr. Page in London, Paul Reinsch stood far in advance of his government in the desire to serve the nation to which

[1] In addition to turning over the German leasehold and treaty rights, China extended to Japan special financial, commercial and railway privileges throughout the province. The treaty and exchanges of notes concerning Manchuria and Mongolia renewed for 99 years the lease of Port Arthur and Dalny and the Manchurian railways, scheduled to expire in 1923; and extended Japanese special rights and privileges in both provinces along the lines of the Komura Treaty, and with the same effect, i.e., of further impairing Chinese sovereignty over the provinces. Cf. texts of treaties and notes, *For. Rel.*, 1915, 171-177; MacMurray, II, 1216 ff.

[2] Anti-Japanese defense funds and boycotts were inaugurated; factional strife abated and the Chinese press mirrored the beginning of a true sense of nationalism.

he was accredited. Throughout the Sino-Japanese negotiations he played two roles, one as the official representative of the State Department, the other as unofficial friend and adviser of the Chinese Government. He assailed the Department of State with cables predicting the direst consequences to American interests in China and advocating vigorous defense of the territorial and political integrity of China. And at the same time he was in constant communication with the Chinese Foreign Office, advising it in advance on ways of circumventing the broad strategy and individual demands of Tokyo.[1]

For the aid and comfort it gave to the Chinese rather than for the official American protest it encouraged, Reinsch's diplomacy seems worth recording. "I have had the feeling that any direct advice to China, or direct intervention on her behalf in the present negotiations, would really do her more harm than good, inasmuch as it would very likely provoke the jealousy and excite the hostility of Japan, which would first be manifested against China herself," wrote Wilson in reply to a telegram from Reinsch inviting the President's "personal attention" to the Twenty-One Demands.[2] In the winter and spring of 1915 Wilson had his hands full with the Mexican situation, the British blockade, submarine warfare and the sinking of the *Lusitania;* his thoughts were far

[1] Reinsch, *American Diplomat,* 134. Admitting that he could not under the circumstances offer them the full support of his government, Reinsch thought that the least he "owed the Chinese was to give a sympathetic hearing to whatever they wished to discuss with me, and to give them my carefully weighed opinion. . . . While not taking the responsibility of giving advice to the Chinese, I could give them an idea as to how the tactical situation, as it developed from week to week, impressed me. Dr. Wellington Koo all through this time acted as liaison officer between the Minister for Foreign Affairs and myself, although I also saw many other members of the Ministry. In discussing the consecutive phases of the negotiations, as they developed, Doctor Koo and I had many interesting hours over diplomatic tactics and analyses, in which I admired his keenness of perception. Some objection was hinted by the Japanese Legation to Doctor Koo's frequent visits to my office and house, but his coming and going continued, as was proper." *Ibid.,* 144.

[2] Reinsch, 137.

removed from any such vigorous course of action in the Far East as that urged by Mr. Reinsch.

It is true that the Department of State, as well as the American public in general, were indignant at Japan's maladroit attempts to conceal the nature of her business in Peking.[1] But when Bryan was at last possessed of a full text of the Demands, the judgment he pronounced on them was cautious. Following the line of the Taft-Katsura and Root-Takahira Agreements, he did not cavil at the Japanese contention that contiguity creates special rights and privileges. The Secretary's lengthy note (March 13, 1915) reviewed in detail the treaties, agreements and formal statements on which American policy had been based, concluding somewhat ambiguously that, "While on principle and under the treaties of 1844, 1858, 1868, and 1903 with China the United States has ground on which to base objections to the Japanese 'demands' relative to Shantung, South Manchuria, and East Mongolia, nevertheless the United States frankly recognizes that territorial contiguity creates special relations between Japan and these districts."[2] Such a concession, from the nation that had hitherto expended the greatest energy in opposing Japanese expansion in Manchuria, gave Japan good reason to believe that the United States was shaping a new course in the Far East, more consistent

---

[1] While Kato and Baron Chinda, the Japanese Foreign Minister and Ambassador to Washington, continued to emphasize the distinction between the Demands and the "requests" of Group Five, Minister Hioki at Peking kept insisting that there was no difference, and that Group Five must be accepted. First news of the Demands came to Washington in the form of truncated despatches from Reinsch and garbled press reports. At first Japan denied these (at which Bryan expressed his gratification) then admitted part of them. Only after China had furnished the Department of State with a complete, though inaccurate, text of the Demands did Japan grudgingly admit their existence in full, including Group Five. Cf. *For. Rel.*, 1915, 79-159; LaFargue, Ch. III. See also Notter, *Origins of the Foreign Policy of Woodrow Wilson*, 385-386, 410-412.

[2] Bryan to the Japanese Ambassador, March 13, 1915. *For. Rel.*, 1915, 105-111.

with that adumbrated by the Root-Takahira Agreement. Bryan concentrated his fire on Group Five and the related proposals for Japanese political control over Chinese institutions, withholding objection to the expansion of Japanese interests in Manchuria and the northern provinces, or even to the retention of German rights in Shantung.

As Japanese-American negotiations progressed, Tokyo displayed a spirit of compromise. Kato made it known that the more stringent demands concerning Fukien had been occasioned by a rumor that the Bethlehem Steel Company had signed a contract with the Chinese Government for the construction of a naval dockyard and coaling station near Foochow. The Japanese Minister reminded Ambassador Guthrie that when Secretary Hay had entertained a similar project in 1900, Japan had protested and the project had been abandoned.[1] Bryan promptly denied the existence of the alleged Bethlehem contract and disclaimed any intentions of questioning the Japanese sphere of interest in Fukien; whereupon the Japanese demands for political control in the province were relaxed in accordance with American wishes.[2] Here again, however, Bryan put the United States on record as recognizing a significant Japanese sphere of influence within China.[3]

As the probability of an ultimatum or the use of force increased, American resistance to the "requests" of Group Five stiffened. Bryan could not have been expected to swallow the bland assurances of Kato and Chinda that the obnoxious measures would not be insisted on, especially in view of the reports coming

[1] Cf. p. 83, above.

[2] Guthrie to Bryan, March 21; Bryan to Guthrie, March 26. *For. Rel.*, 1915, 113-115, 116-117; LaFargue, 63.

[3] "You are, therefore, authorized to inform the Government that this Government will view without the slightest objection any arrangement which Japan may make with China looking toward the withholding of any concession to any foreign Power which contemplates the improvement of any harbor on the coast of Fukien or the establishment of a coaling station or naval base along said coast by any foreign Power." Bryan to Guthrie, March 26. *For. Rel.*, 1915, 116-117.

from Peking. While he continued to urge moderation on Tokyo, he informally proffered the good offices of the United States in assisting with the negotiations, and invited France, Russia and England to join the United States in a warning against the imposition of Group Five.[1] Tokyo declined the offer of good offices, and the overtures to the Allies went unanswered.[2] When at length the news reached Washington that China had accepted the modified demands of the Japanese ultimatum Bryan, now preoccupied with the *Lusitania* crisis, filed the following significantly-phrased *caveat* in both Tokyo and Peking:

In view of the circumstances of the negotiations which have taken place and which are now pending between the Government of Japan and the Government of China, and of the agreements which have been reached as a result thereof, the Government of the United States has the honor to notify the Imperial Japanese Government that it cannot recognize any agreement or undertaking which has been entered into or which may be entered into between the Governments of Japan and

[1] The substance of these overtures, not published in *Foreign Relations*, is revealed in the official Russian world war archives for 1915. On May 8 the Russian Ambassador to Tokyo, Malevski, reported to St. Petersburg that the American Chargé d'Affaires had presented him a telegram from Washington suggesting that the United States, France, Russia and England join in urging patience and an amicable settlement on Tokyo and Peking. Since the wire was not received until after the despatch of the Japanese ultimatum, the American Chargé could not act on it. On May 10 Sazonov, the Russian Foreign Minister, wired Malevski that the American Ambassador at St. Petersburg had asked him "to uphold the steps which the United States plans to take to convince the Japanese Government of the necessity of peace with China. I did not assent to this plan, pointing to our treaty of alliance with Japan." Malevski to Foreign Office, May 8; Sazonov to Malevski, May 10, 1915. *Mezhdunarodnye Otnosheniia v epoku imperializma*, VII, 2, 388, 401.

[2] LaFargue, 74. For an extraordinarily interesting Japanese comment on these overtures, revealing that Russia received Japan's thanks for her moral support in ignoring them, see the despatch of the Russian Envoy in Tokyo, Malevski, to the Russian Foreign Office, May 18, 1915, retailing a long conversation with Kato. The despatch begins: "Received thanks from Kato of moral support against American attempts at interference." *Mezhdunarodnye Otnosheniia*, VII, 2, 178-479.

China, impairing the treaty rights of the United States and its citizens in China, the political or territorial integrity of the Republic of China, or the international policy relative to China commonly known as the Open Door policy.[1]

According to Mr. Lansing (who, as Counselor of the Department of State, drafted this note and advised Bryan to send it) the Department realized that both the Allies and the United States were too distracted by the war "to oppose vigorously, if at all, Japan's intentions as to China." He therefore intended the note, not to dissuade Japan from coercing China, but as a reservation "so that any agreement forced upon China at the present time could properly become the subject of discussion in the future when the conditions are more propitious." [2] The note proved everything that Lansing hoped of it. Its immediate effects were to cast doubt on Bryan's statement of policy of March 13, and to convince Tokyo that some more definite understanding with the United States was necessary. This, in turn, led to the Lansing-Ishii negotiations of 1917. The note was to gain greater fame, however, when it was discovered by Secretary Stimson and turned into the famous nonrecognition doctrine of 1932.

Meanwhile, as the Sino-Japanese negotiations moved toward their conclusion, Great Britain had not remained an indifferent spectator. The British community in China had been thoroughly alarmed by the Twenty-One Demands, which struck at the heart of the rich British commercial sphere in the Yangtse Valley. Its apprehensiveness was communicated to London, where, as early as March, embarrassing questions were asked in Parliament concerning the Government's Far Eastern policy.[3] On May 7, the

[1] Bryan to Guthrie and Reinsch (identic note), May 11, 1915. *For. Rel.*, 1915, 146.

[2] Lansing, *War Memoirs*, 284.

[3] On March 11 a Government spokesman replied to one of these that since England had respected Japanese sphere in south Manchuria, "We naturally expect that Japan should show us reciprocity and not apply for any concessions which would affect British interests." LaFargue, 67; *Parliamentary Debates*, Commons, Fifth Series, 1915, Vol. 70, 1722. March 11, 1915.

day the Japanese ultimatum was presented, Grey showed Ambassador Page a memorandum that he had submitted to the Japanese Ambassador on the sixth, and informed Page that Japan had withdrawn Group Five of the Demands. The language of the memorandum [1] was such as to suggest that the British Government had played an influential role in securing the withdrawal of Group Five.

There is further evidence to that effect. Kato himself has admitted that toward the end of April and early in May he received several warnings from London to the effect that if the imposition of Group Five caused a break with China, the Anglo-Japanese Alliance might suffer, and that if force were to be used, England must first be consulted. These warnings, according to the Japanese Foreign Minister, strengthened his hand in enforcing moderation.[2] While refusing to co-operate with the United States, Great Britain, when finally touched on her nerve center in the Yangtse Valley, had probably exerted far more influence in restraining Japan than had the United States. "Japan does not need American approval of her agreement with China," Kato told the Russian Ambassador to Tokyo, after referring to the Lansing-Bryan *caveat* as "impudent." "On the whole Kato spoke of American diplomacy not without irony." [3] The official efforts of the Wilson Administration to modify the Twenty-One Demands accomplished little, save to set the stage for more determined efforts in the future. Even so they left a question as to which way American

[1] "His Majesty's Government are very much concerned at the prospect of a war between China and Japan. They feel this may imperil the independence and integrity of China which is one of the main objects of the Anglo-Japanese Alliance. In view of Article 1 of the Alliance, we trust that the Japanese Government will not finally shut the door upon the possibility of agreements with China without consulting with us and giving us an opportunity of promoting a friendly settlement." Enclosure in Page to Bryan, May 7. *For. Rel.*, 1915, 144.

[2] LaFargue, 74-77.

[3] Malevski to Foreign Office, May 18, 1915. *Mezhdunarodnye Otnosheniiâ*, VII, 2, 478-479.

diplomacy would move, in the direction of the Bryan note of March 13, or of the *caveat* of May 11.

This uncertainty was heightened by the part played by American diplomacy in bringing China into the war. The impression is sometimes given that China entered the World War in response to Wilson's call for a crusade for democracy, and so obligated the President to champion her claims at the peace conference. The impression is not founded in fact. China declared war on Germany for reasons more intimately related to Chinese politics and Allied diplomacy than to the desires of Washington; while Wilson's sense of obligation to defend the Chinese peace claims derived from his loyalty to the League and its principles rather than from his specific interest in the Far East. If the American attitude toward China's entrance into the war had any conclusive effect, it was to determine Japan to strengthen her grip on China and to secure American acquiescence therein.

Japan followed the presentation of the Twenty-One Demands with a carefully-executed stratagem devised to obtain international sanction for the gains she had won by the Demands and for the leadership she was fast assuming in Far Eastern politics. On October 19, 1915, she adhered to the Declaration of London of September 5, 1914, by which England, France and Russia—and now Japan—agreed not to make separate peace, nor to discuss peace terms except in common.[1] This assured her of membership in the peace conference, a tactical objective essential to self-defense in case European intervention threatened at the end of the war. Next, by a series of secret bilateral treaties between Japan and each of the Allies, as well as by the Lansing-Ishii Agreement and two additional treaties with China, Japan secured advance international recognition for the claims she expected to defend at Ver-

[1] The decision met with considerable opposition in the Diet, a large portion of which wished to keep the way open to a separate peace. This opposition was overridden by the cabinet, intent upon securing for Japan acceptance as a great power and admission to the peace conference. Cf. Ishii, 101-104; Takeuchi, 196-198.

sailles. Finally, by financial and political intrigue, she brought the Peking Government into line with her policies, so that by the time China entered the war and likewise gained admission to the peace conference, her possibilities of using it to attack Japan had been reduced to a minimum.

In China, meanwhile, the Treaties of May 25, 1915, had touched off fresh outbursts of civil strife, in which Japan played off one faction against the other and stunted the growth of Chinese national unity. Already France and Russia were bargaining with Yuan Shih-k'ai for recognition of the empire he was trying to establish in return for a declaration of war on Germany. Both England and France wished to harry the last remnants of the German commercial community out of China, and to procure Chinese coolie labor to relieve the drain on their own depleted manpower. But Japan had important Allied concessions yet to gain before she would be ready to give her consent. On October 27, 1915, she prevailed on England, France and Russia to join her in warning China against Yuan's monarchical movement and later (December 6) bluntly informed the Allies that she could not approve China's entrance into the war. This scotched the project for two years.[1] Yuan died (June 6, 1916) without either realizing his imperial ambitions or obtaining from the consortium powers the loans essential to maintenance of the existing regime.

An acrimonious struggle for power ensued between Yuan's successors, President Li Yuan-hung and Prime Minister Tuan Chi-jui, in which the declaration of war on Germany was subordinated to the personal and factional ambitions of the two politicians and their respective camps.[2] Li, representing the liberal, par-

[1] The United States abstained from the warning to China on the grounds that it was of purely domestic Chinese concern. LaFargue, 81-89; For. Rel., 1915, 65-75.

[2] See especially Reinsch to Lansing, March 1, 1917, citing as prime factors in the probable declaration of war the desire of the Chinese Vice President thus to rehabilitate his reputation recently damaged by involvement in an opium purchase scandal, and Tuan's desire "of getting the upper hand over Parliament and the

liamentary elements of the south, emerged as the champion of neutrality, a course unquestionably favored by the majority of the Chinese people. They had no basic quarrel with Germany, with whom their country remained on the most friendly relations.[1] Tuan, on the other hand, supported by the military leaders of the north, saw in joining the Allies a chance to obtain the loans needed to strengthen his faction and overcome the opposition of the south.[2] After a bitter fight culminating in Li's fall from office, the dissolution of parliament, an abortive restoration of the Manchus and a two-day bombardment of Peking, Tuan forced the declaration of war (August 14, 1917) over the prostrate body of democratic government in China. The parliamentarians fled to Canton where they set up an insurgent government in defiance of Peking. Mr. Reinsch had early foreseen that the declaration of war "if carried through, would be entirely reactionary in character, as far as Chinese political institutions and practices are concerned." [3] His worst fears were confirmed—a cold *douche* to the idea that China entered the war in the interests of democracy.

Still less was her entrance a response to the promptings of Washington. When President Wilson broke off diplomatic rela-

President." *For. Rel.*, 1917, Supplement 1, 424-425. Three months later Mr. Reinsch ventured "to state conviction that it will be impossible to count even upon the moral support of China as a nation unless the Allies dissociate China's interests from those of the military clique and make it evident that participation in the war in their behalf is not to be used as a pawn in Chinese domestic politics." Reinsch to Lansing, June 6, 1917. *For. Rel.*, 1917, 54-55.

[1] As LaFargue points out, the German trading methods and democratic attitude toward Orientals had evoked this feeling, which the German Minister cultivated with propaganda subsidized by Boxer Indemnity payments. *Op. cit.*, IV, esp. 96-104.

[2] Reinsch to Lansing, May 10, 1917. *For. Rel.*, Supplement 1, 448. LaFargue, 105-110. Another motive often suggested, but of dubious strength, was the chance to abolish Germany's extraterritorial rights and use this as precedent for general abolition of the same.

[3] Reinsch to Lansing, March 1, 1917. *For. Rel.*, 1917, Supplement 1, 424.

tions with Germany (February 3, 1917) he notified all the neutral countries in the world in a circular telegram that he believed it would "make for the peace of the world if the other neutral powers can find it possible to take similar action to that taken by this Government."[1] This carefully guarded invitation was not designed to fit the precise circumstances in China or in any other single nation, but rather to give universal moral status to America's issue with Germany over neutral rights. It was, however, interpreted by Mr. Reinsch as instructions to persuade China to break with Germany forthwith, a task he eagerly set out to perform. The President had already cautioned Reinsch lest American intervention do China "more harm than good, inasmuch as it would very likely provoke the jealousy and excite the hostility of Japan,"[2] but neither this nor the passing of time had altered the American Minister's convictions. No sooner had he decoded Wilson's message than he was closeted with the President and Prime Minister of China (February 4), representing to them the "just cause" of the United States and urging them to enlist in it. But Li was full of "doubts and objections" and Tuan "far from accepting the proposal at first sight."[3] They wanted to know what there was in it for China—and for themselves. They were not so much impressed by talk of a crusade as of a *quid pro quo*. Mr. Reinsch was in a great hurry, which he has since ascribed to the fear that "adverse influences from without" might defeat his purpose.[4] By adverse influences presumably he meant those that might be expected to emanate from Tokyo. In any event, his haste in pressing the Chinese Government for a decision, coinciding with the brief absence from Peking of the Japanese Minister,[5] suggests that he

[1] *For. Rel.*, 1917, Supplement 1, 108. In his memoirs Mr. Reinsch states that he considered the President's message as "more than a pious wish" and that it was his "plain duty to prevail upon China to associate herself with the American action as proposed by my government." Reinsch, 241-242.

[2] Cf. p. 191, above.                   [4] *Ibid.*, 242, 247-248.
[3] Reinsch, 242-244.                     [5] *Ibid.*, 250.

was attempting to steal a march on the country that had up to the moment barred China's road to war.

Doubtless the Chinese suspected as much, for they at once raised the bogey of Japanese influence and used it for all it was worth. Not only did they wish to be assured of full control of their own military supplies and forces and full admission to the peace conference, as conditions to accepting Reinsch's proposal; they even demanded that the United States lend China $10,000,-000 for military purposes, fund its share of the Boxer indemnity in long-term bonds and urge the Allies to do likewise.[1] A broken cable prevented Reinsch from communicating these terms to Washington, but he continued to act on his own initiative.[2] Without official instructions, a *sine qua non* in matters of any such importance, and before the Chinese cabinet had passed judgment on his original proposal, Reinsch tentatively agreed to the Prime Minister's terms (February 7) hoping thus to induce favorable action on the part of the cabinet.[3] Two days later, the Chinese

[1] Reinsch to Lansing, February 6, 1 P.M. and 11 P.M. *For. Rel.*, 1917, Supplement 1, 401-402; also Reinsch to Lansing, February 7, 1917. *Ibid.*, 403; La-Fargue, 88.

[2] Reinsch explains his haste as follows: "If all the influences unfavorable to the action proposed were given time to assert themselves, the American proposal would be obstructed and probably defeated. The Chinese Government would act only on such assurances as I could feel justified in giving to them at this time; if I gave them none, no action would be taken. It seemed almost a matter of course, should China follow the lead of the American Government, *that the latter would not allow China to suffer through lack of all possible support in aiding China to bear the responsibility she assumed, and in preventing action from any quarter which would impose on China new burdens because of her break with Germany.* Unable to interpret my instructions otherwise than that a joint protest of the neutrals had actually been planned by the American Government, and feeling that the effect upon Germany of the American protest depended on the early concurrence of the important neutral powers, I considered prompt action essential. *I was sure that all sorts of unfavorable and obstructive influences would presently get to work in Peking.*" Reinsch, 247-248. Italics inserted. Cf. also Reinsch to Lansing, February 9. *For. Rel.*, 1917, Supplement 1, 407.

[3] For text of Reinsch's note to the Chinese Foreign Minister, see *For. Rel.*, 1917, Supplement 1, 403-404. Reinsch was careful to make all specific commit-

Foreign Office despatched a cautious note to Germany protesting the submarine blockade and threatening to sever diplomatic relations in case the note proved ineffectual. At the same time the Foreign Office confidentially assured Reinsch that, "In case an act should be performed by the German Government which should be considered by the American Government a sufficient cause for declaration of war between the United States and Germany, the Chinese Government should [at] least break its diplomatic relations with Germany." [1] The action of the American Minister had played nicely into the hands of China's leaders, supplying them the pretext lacking which they might never have dared to sound off against Germany without Japanese permission.

These results were the more ironic in that Mr. Reinsch's arbitrary procedure was speedily repudiated by the Department of State. When the cable was repaired and Washington was at last let in on what had been transpiring in Peking, Lansing curtly ordered Reinsch to "avoid giving any promises or assurances and take no other action" until further instructed.

"The American Government highly appreciates disposition of China," wired the Secretary of State, "but does not wish to lead it into danger. It regrets practical inability to give any present assurances. Unwillingness of any other important neutral to follow American example ought to be considered very gravely by China, who should in prudence avoid isolated action. The Chinese Government, therefore, would do well to consult its representatives in the Allied countries. . . ." [2]

ments subject to the approval of Washington; but he stated that he had recommended the Chinese terms to his government, indicated his "personal conviction" that they would be liberally met and concluded significantly, "I do, however, feel warranted in assuming the responsibility of assuring you in behalf of my Government that by the methods you have suggested, or otherwise, adequate means will be devolved to enable China to fulfill the responsibilities consequent upon associating itself with the action of the United States, *without any impairment of her control of her military establishment and general administration.*"

[1] Reinsch to Lansing, February 9. *For. Rel.,* 1917, Supplement 1, 407-408.

[2] Lansing to Reinsch, 1 P.M. and 4 P.M., February 10. *For. Rel.,* 1917, Supplement 1, 408.

The circular appeal to neutrals of February 3 "did not contemplate the offer to any neutral power of special inducements to take action similar to that of the United States in regard to Germany," Lansing cabled in reply to remonstrances from Reinsch. The Department was now giving "the assurances mentioned in your telegram of February 7" careful consideration.[1] On February 26 the Department categorically defined its position. It was "deeply concerned for the continued preservation of China's territorial integrity and administrative entity and the maintenance of the open door for trade and equality of opportunity for all nations in the commerce of China." It therefore favored such share of representation for China "in any conference of the present belligerents as the hostilities conducted by them within the boundaries of China entitle it to receive." But it was not at present disposed, "in the event of hostilities between the United States and Germany, to urge China to declare war also on Germany," because "the United States would not be able to give China the assistance proposed in your telegrams . . . if serious opposition should be offered to such assistance. Attempt to override that opposition," concluded Mr. Lansing, "might precipitate the very aggression which China fears." [2]

Throughout the spring and early summer, the United States continued to back water. When China broke off diplomatic relations with Germany (March 14) Lansing expressed appreciation, but again cautioned Reinsch against a Chinese declaration of war.[3] Chinese attempts to frighten the United States with the prospect that should "the American Government now abandon interest in China, the Chinese Government would be driven into the arms of Japan" [4] did not change Lansing's mind. At length, when it

[1] Lansing to Reinsch, February 17. *Ibid.*, 410.
[2] Lansing to Reinsch, February 26. *Ibid.*, 411.
[3] Same to same, March 13. *Ibid.*, 419-420.
[4] Reinsch to Lansing, March 18. *Ibid.*, 420-421. China was now trying to gain American support in an effort to bargain with the Allies for terms similar to those accepted by Reinsch. Lansing merely agreed not to allow American treaty

became evident that a declaration of war would plunge China into civil strife and signal the downfall of the democratic elements in the Chinese Government, Lansing took the extreme steps of informing the Chinese Government that,

The entry of China into the war with Germany, or the continuance of the *status quo* of her relations with that Government, are matters of secondary consideration. The principal necessity for China is to resume and continue her political entity and to proceed along the road of national development on which she had made such marked progress.

At the same time he proposed to England, France and Japan that they join the United States in identic representations to China to the same effect.[1] Compared to the energy he was subsequently to expend in her behalf Woodrow Wilson owed China less than nothing for her declaration of war on Germany. Indeed, by June, 1917, the wheel had come full circle, with Japan urging and the United States opposing China's entrance.[2]

Coincident with the faltering and contradictory diplomacy of the United States and its Minister to Peking, the international bargains were being made which, together with the exigencies of Chinese domestic politics, were the decisive factors in bringing China into the war. On July 3, 1916, Japan had concluded with Russia another treaty along the same lines as those of 1907, 1910 and 1912.[3] Part public, part secret, this one carried the two nations beyond *rapprochement*, beyond even a more definitive partition of

rights to stand in the way of such concessions as China might win from the Allies, and he qualified this agreement. See Lansing to Reinsch, March 26. *Ibid.*, 423. The Chinese Foreign Office had been less than candid with Reinsch, dickering with both the Allies and Japan behind his back. Cf. LaFargue, 93-94; Lansing to Reinsch, March 2. *For. Rel.*, 1917, Supplement 1, 412.

[1] Lansing to Reinsch, June 4, 1917. *For. Rel.*, 1917, 48-49; LaFargue, 110.

[2] England, France and Japan all took rather indignant exception, in their replies to Lansing's note, to the latter's statement that the declaration of war was of secondary importance to China's domestic unity and progress. *For. Rel.*, 1917, 71-76.

[3] Cf. Ch. IV, above.

influence in Manchuria and Mongolia, into a defensive alliance to assure "that China should not fall under the political domination of any third Power hostile to Russia or Japan." Although the past history of American relations with the two contracting parties rendered the phrase "third Power" peculiarly applicable to the United States, it could have referred either to a victorious Germany or a resurgent England. In any event, it effectively tied Russia's hands from possible interference with the position Japan had won by virtue of her conquest of Kiaochow and the Twenty-One Demands.[1]

The urgent desire of the Allies to enlist China on their side now provided Japan the lever with which to pry from them the final concessions that she had sought. On January 27, 1917 (four days before Germany made known her intention of resuming unrestricted submarine warfare, and a full week before the American rupture of diplomatic relations with Germany and Wilson's appeal to neutrals to follow suit), Japan entered negotiations with Great Britain for an agreement whereby the latter should promise to support at the peace conference Japan's claims to retention of the German rights in Shantung and the German islands north of the equator, in return for a Japanese undertaking to support England's claims to the German islands south of the equator. Great Britain agreed to the bargain February 16,[2] and the whole

[1] The public section of the treaty was the cue for an American attempt to pin down both nations to a new declaration of respect for the open door and the territorial integrity of China, which both gave in prompt and perfunctory manner. The secret convention of alliance was suspected by the United States but not published until the Bolsheviks made public the rest of the famous secret treaties, in December, 1917. The Bolshevik organ *Izvestia* labeled the convention "Secret Treaty between Japan and Russia for Joint Armed Demonstration against America and Great Britain in the Far East," which has passed for evidence indicating the anti-American character of the instrument. However, the Bolshevik caption was of journalistic rather than official diplomatic origin. Price, *Russo-Japanese Treaties*, 77-90, 144-146. Text of Treaty, *Ibid.*, 121-123. See also, *For. Rel.*, 1916, 433-446; MacMurray, II, 1220 ff.

[2] British Ambassador to Japanese Foreign Minister, February 16, 1917. MacMurray, II, 1167; Temperley, H. W. V., *History of the Peace Conference*, VI,

was kept secret until the Bolsheviks opened the Russian archives the following December. There is good reason to believe that the promise to support the British claims to the German islands south of the equator was not the only *quid pro quo* received by England. Lloyd George explained the treaty to Wilson (from whom he concealed it as long as he could) on the grounds that it was the price demanded by Japan for supplying much needed naval-convoys for Allied ships in the Mediterranean.[1] When Japan approached France and Russia with the same proposition, the *quid pro quo* was more specific. On February 20 and March 1, respectively, Russia and France secretly accepted the same Japanese terms as had the British, drawing from Japan the explicit promise not only to permit, but to encourage, China to break with Germany.[2]

In view of the provisions of the Declaration of London of September 5, 1914, which pledged its signatories not to discuss peace terms except in common, it is difficult not to conclude that London had knowledge of, and approved, the French and Russian terms. The retreat that England had begun before Japan in 1914 was thus completed. The Allies had secretly sold out Shantung to Japan in return for Chinese participation in the war and Japanese recognition of territorial conquests of their own. They had

634 ff.; Cocks, F. Seymour, *The Secret Treaties and Understandings*, 84-88; LaFargue, 95-96. Cf. also Chang, *Anglo-Japanese Alliance*, 179-186; Dennis, *Anglo-Japanese Alliance*, 49.

[1] Baker, R. S., *Woodrow Wilson and World Settlement*, I, 59-62.

[2] LaFargue, 97; MacMurray, II, 1168-1169; Cocks, *loc. cit.*; Temperley, *loc. cit.* Reinsch's activities, by raising the possibility that China might enter the war under American auspices, may have spurred Japan to make these terms with France and Russia. On the other hand, Japan had already approached England with a similar deal before Reinsch had received Wilson's message, and Allied pressure on China to enter the war—and, presumably, on Japan to permit her to do so—had been unremitting—facts which suggest that Japan considered China's ultimate participation inevitable and hastened to make terms before it was too late.

left the United States stranded in its own idealism, which they themselves had so sedulously cultivated with propaganda.

Japan now set forth to gain American assent to the program to which she had just committed the Allies. The invitation to join in reminding Peking that fighting Germany was of secondary importance to China's domestic welfare provided Japan the occasion to take the first step in this direction. In its reply to the invitation the Japanese Government called Lansing's attention to the contradiction between the professions of the Bryan note of March 13, 1915, and the unneutral activities of Reinsch, contrasting the latter's involvement "in the present political crisis in China" with Bryan's statement that "the activity of Americans in China had never been political." Bryan had given Japan to understand that the United States recognized her "special and close relations, political as well as economic, with China"; but the latest American pronouncement on China's participation in the war appeared to refute this recognition.

"In such circumstance," concluded the Japanese memorandum, "the Japanese Government believes that if the United States Government sees its way by some appropriate means to confirming the statement made by Mr. Bryan and clearly reasserting its friendly attitude toward Japan in respect of Chinese problems, it would leave a good impression on the minds of the Japanese public and would certainly contribute in no small measure to the friendly relations between our two nations. . . ." [1]

The American declaration of war on Germany (April 6, 1917) had created a situation seemingly auspicious for Japan's purposes. It had not only focused American interest on the western front, but also had made the United States and Japan technical allies. Nor is it surprising that Japan sought official clarification of America's Far Eastern policy. Quite apart from the clash of Japanese ambitions with the shifting American policy already noted,

[1] Japanese Ambassador to Lansing, June 15, 1917. *For. Rel.*, 1917, Supplement 1, 259.

the war had plunged Japan and the United States into a severe economic conflict. As in the heyday of dollar diplomacy, the United States appeared to be preparing a frontal attack on Japan's commercial and financial strongholds in Eastern Asia.

The war had obviously compelled the Allies to default any active interest in Chinese finance to Japan and the United States. Although they continued, even while hard-pressed in Europe, to defend the stakes they had carved out in China, they themselves were unable to spare funds for the loans of which China was in constant need. No Chinese government could keep its head above water without foreign financial assistance, and the relatively disinterested policy of the United States made it the favored object of Chinese borrowers. The United States had the money, but preferred to invest it in munitions and Allied war loans. As Japan proceeded to take advantage of this golden opportunity, Great Britain and France became alarmed at the possibility of Japanese economic as well as political domination of China. Powerless to prevent this themselves, both because of their lack of financial resources and their compromising political deals with their Far Eastern ally, they encouraged the United States to resist Japan's economic advance. America's own diplomatic traditions were conducive to the same end.[1] Dollar diplomacy had been contrived more as a political instrument than as the answer to the express needs of American business. It was the servant of a theory, not the supply to a demand. So now, although Wilson had withdrawn from the consortium, he had by no means abandoned the doctrine that the United States should enlist its economic, as well

---

[1] Both Reinsch and Guthrie (American Ambassador to Japan) were inheritors of this tradition. Guthrie proved himself almost as enthusiastic an exponent of American commercial expansion in Manchuria as had Willard Straight. *Vide* his despatches in connection with the controversy over Japanese discrimination in Manchurian freight rates, *For. Rel.*, 1915, 594-625; 1916, 446-450. Reinsch has revealed himself in his own memoirs as an ardent promoter of American railway construction in China for the salutary effect it would have on China's political unity and independence. Cf. Reinsch, 60-63.

as diplomatic, resources in defense of the open door and the territorial integrity of China.

With the United States out of the consortium, American bankers had attempted but few loans to China since 1913. The chief reason for this was, as it always had been, that the American investing public was simply not interested in China, and though the State Department had done its best, the interest could not be created artificially. The United States had left the consortium committed, as we have seen, to the Hukuang Loan Agreement, a one-fourth share in the currency reform loan advance, and a one-sixth share in the reorganization loan advance.[1] Aside from such specific commitments, various factors continued to hold the consortium together, despite its inactivity. Among these were the rights and options granted in the loan agreements already made as well as the terms of the six-power agreement obligating its signatories to seek no independent loans of an administrative character.[2] On the other hand, the war, the Chinese domestic whirlpool and the conflicting political aims of the consortium powers proved disintegrating forces too strong for it to withstand. As observed in the previous chapter, sheer necessity drove China to seek loans from independent, outside sources. The first American loan to be negotiated since 1913 was one of this character. In April, 1916, Lee, Higginson and Company agreed to sell $5,000,000 of Chinese treasury notes over a period of three years at six per cent interest. So unattractive did the notes prove to American investors, however, that they were never issued.[3] A month later the Chinese Government, in desperate straits, appealed directly to the Department of State, which promptly asked the American consortium group to advance China four or five million dollars for immediate administrative necessities. The group demurred, arguing that it was still bound by the consortium agreement of 1912 to

[1] Field, *Consortiums*, 116-117; *For. Rel.*, 1913, 171-176.
[2] Field, 118-121.
[3] *Ibid.*, 129; MacMurray, II, 1279 ff.

make no independent administrative loans,[1] and that world conditions made China a precarious risk. It finally refused to undertake the loan unless the State Department would guarantee China's fulfillment of obligations. At this the Department balked. It appealed to the patriotism of the bankers; they again refused, and the project was dropped [2]—another commentary on the theory that international political commitments are invariably forced by economic pressure groups.

Three industrial loans were also negotiated during 1916, two of which (eventually combined) contracted for American financing of drainage and irrigation work on the Huai River and a portion of the Grand Canal, and the third for American construction of a network of railways in China.[3] They were instantly protested, not only by Japan but also by the other consortium powers, especially France and England. Japan objected to American participation in conservancy work on the part of the Grand Canal that ran through Shantung Province, basing her objection on an old German treaty right which she claimed had reverted to her.[4] Mr. Lansing countered (January 25, 1917) with a denial that the United States had ever recognized Germany's claims to special interests in Shantung, much less Japan's accession to them, a contradiction of the Bryan note of March 13, 1915.[5] As for the railway construction project, Russia protested the portion of it extending into Mongolia; England that in Hupeh, Hunan and Szechuan; France that in Kwangsi. China needed the railways; an

[1] That is, loans without the participation of the other national banking groups.

[2] Field, 129-132; *For. Rel.*, 1916, 134-138.

[3] The first two were contracted for by the American International Corporation, the third by the Siems and Carey Corporation. Field, 129; MacMurray, II, 1304, 1313.

[4] An agreement of March 6, 1898, whereby Germany had gained from China the right of prior consultation on internal improvements in Shantung. LaFargue, 120-121; *For. Rel.*, 1916, 110-127.

[5] LaFargue, 122; *For. Rel.*, 1917, 117. The American International Corporation was sufficiently impressed with the Japanese protest to invite Japanese interests to share in the loan. *Ibid.*, 205, 207.

American firm stood ready to build them, but the three European nations, though fighting with their backs to the wall against Germany, and unable to spend a cent in China themselves, blocked the path with their empty claims and literally forced the workmen to put down their tools. Indeed they went farther than merely defeating the specific enterprise at hand. When, on August 24, 1917, Lansing protested the British attitude as "at variance with the policy of the 'open door' and equality of commercial opportunity to which the British Government has subscribed," [1] Balfour replied that a transition had taken place in China "whereunder specific areas are earmarked for the enterprise of specific countries" and that this had "gradually taken the place of a regime of free railway construction." Balfour cited as examples "the special position of Japan in Manchuria . . . as well as the position of Germany in Shantung, the French declaration regarding Hainan and the provinces bordering on Tongking, the Japanese declaration concerning Fukien, the prior rights of Russia north of the Great Wall, etc." [2] Independent American loans to China were running afoul of the same vested European interests that had thwarted the efforts of Knox and Straight.

Japan, meanwhile, had been systematically tying the dominant Chinese military clique to her leading-strings with secret loans. [3] To combat this process, the Allies had begun as early as December, 1916, to urge the United States to return to the consortium. All

[1] Memorandum, Lansing to British Ambassador, August 24. *For. Rel.*, 1917, 191-192.

[2] Memorandum presented by Spring-Rice to Lansing, September 8, 1917. *Ibid.*, 195-196. This may have been an ingenious British attempt to prepare opinion in Washington for disclosure of the secret Anglo-Japanese treaty of the previous February. Balfour came to Washington the following April, and in all probability disclosed the existence of the treaty to President Wilson. Japan was about to negotiate an executive agreement with the United States seeking recognition of the very "transition" of which Balfour spoke. The British Foreign Secretary's memorandum of September 8 could have been designed as a connecting link between the two instruments.

[3] Field, 134; LaFargue, 142; *For. Rel.*, 1918, 167-168.

through 1917 they labored to overcome Wilson's scruples. Even Japan invited the United States to rejoin, and to co-operate with Japanese banks in the matter of loans to China.[1] In the fall of 1917 Wilson yielded, convinced at last that no amount of State Department promotion could produce independent loans adequate to the Department's purposes. On November 9, Lansing announced that the American Government was considering the formation of a new four-power consortium of increased scope and greatly expanded banking groups of British, French, Japanese and American designation.[2] In pressing this decision on the United States, Great Britain and France had not concealed their motives. They did not mean to admit American capital any more hospitably to their own preserves, as witness Balfour's communication to Lansing on the subject of the "transition" in China. The very day following that communication, in the face of an imminent Japanese loan to China of major proportions, the British Foreign

[1] Field, 132; *For. Rel.*, 1916, 148-149; 1917, 117-118, 126-128. Reinsch attributed the superficially surprising Japanese attitude to Japan's realization that a formal stand with the United States on China's unity and independence would help to cover her secret dealings with the militarists. *Ibid.*, 135. LaFargue, 126-128, ascribes it to Japan's desire to avoid the competition of independent American loans. The full explanation seems at once more subtle and more obvious. The official Japanese invitation was extended to Washington January 25, 1917, *just two days before the known date of Japan's request to England for the secret treaty.* Indeed, the Japanese Ambassador in introducing the subject to Lansing, referred to a previous conversation with the British Ambassador in which the latter had plainly hinted at Japanese-American financial co-operation. See Memorandum, January 25, 1917. *For Rel.*, 1917, 117. This suggests that in connection with negotiating the secret treaties, the Allies brought pressure on Japan to make the gesture to the United States. Moreover, Japan may well have considered the same an inexpensive way of earning the American good will that she hoped to convert into recognition of her Chinese program.

[2] The final agreement organizing the new consortium was not signed until October 15, 1920. From November 9, 1917, to that date the consortium powers were engaged in the same disputes as to their respective shares and special spheres as had characterized the activities of the earlier consortiums. Cf. Field, Chs. X, XI; *For. Rel.*, 1917-1920.

Secretary had implored Lansing to demand a share in the loan.[1] Balfour was afraid, as he later explained, that "a degree of undivided control over the finances of China would be obtained by Japan were they . . . to be the sole subscribers to the loan." [2] In short, the preoccupation of the Allies in the war combined with the general lack of American interest in Chinese investments (the real reason for American withdrawal from the consortium) had removed Western capital from China and forced that country, in spite of itself, to borrow from Japan. When Wilson found that he could not combat the resultant Japanese financial monopoly if he permitted American bankers to follow their own inclinations, he determined, under British and French promptings, to re-enter the consortium and once more enlist the bankers as agents of American diplomacy. It was this actual, and threatening, Japanese-American economic warfare that gave substance to the political factors already noted, and led Japan to ask the United States for a more definite statement of its attitude toward Japan's aims and interests in China.

Secretary Lansing briefly acknowledged the Japanese request with an expression of "accord with the deep sense of the memorandum." [3] A few weeks later he replied to it in detail. Conceding that Bryan's note of March 13, 1915, had "recognized that territorial contiguity created special relations between Japan and the districts of Shantung, Southern Manchuria and East Mongolia" he denied that the phrase "special relations" thus geographically limited was intended to mean "special and close relations, political as well as economic, with China as a whole." In justification of his view he cited the Bryan-Lansing *caveat* of May 11, 1915, which had declined to recognize "any agreement or

[1] British Ambassador to Lansing, September 9, 1917. *For. Rel.*, 1917, 139.
[2] British Embassy to Lansing, October 3, 1917. *Ibid.*, 144-145. See also Jusserand to Lansing, November 19, 1917. *Ibid.*, 154-155.
[3] Wheeler to Lansing, June 18. *Ibid.*, 259.

understanding entered into then or thereafter between Japan and China impairing the treaty rights of the United States, the political or territorial integrity of China, or the international policy of the open door." Nowhere had either he or Mr. Bryan recognized Japan's interests in China as "paramount." [1] The riddle of American policy that had bothered Japan since 1915 remained unsolved. American assent to Japan's war claims had yet to be added to that of the Allies.

The difficult task now devolved on Viscount Kikujiro Ishii, who arrived in Washington September 1 at the head of a Japanese war mission similar to the French and British missions that had preceded it. The principal business of the European missions was to establish efficient means of military and political co-operation with the United States against Germany. This was of secondary consideration to Ishii. In a series of discussions lasting from September 6 to November 2, the Secretary of State and the Japanese Special Envoy fought a verbal duel over the conflicting policies of their two countries. Ishii did his best to win from Lansing recognition of Japan's "paramount interest" in China in the same sense of the phrase as that applied by previous Secretaries of State to American interests in Mexico. [2] Lansing adamantly refused to discuss the phrase, countering with the suggestion of a joint Japanese-American declaration of respect for the open door and the territorial integrity of China. Ishii argued that such a declaration was not only superfluous, but would cast doubt on Japan's honorable intentions.

The maneuver had put the Japanese diplomat on the defensive, and Lansing pressed home his advantage. He would, he said, trade a recognition of Japan's "special interests" in the non-political, geographically restricted sense of the Bryan note in return for Japanese adherence to the following declaration:

[1] Lansing to Japanese Ambassador, July 6, 1917. *For. Rel.*, 1917, 260-262.
[2] Ishii, *Diplomatic Commentaries*, 120; Lansing, 294 ff.

The Governments of the United States and Japan deny that they have any purpose to infringe in any way the independence or territorial integrity of China and they declare furthermore that they always adhere to the principle of the so-called Open Door or equal opportunity for commerce and industry in China, *and that they will not take advantage of present conditions to seek special rights or privileges in China which would abridge the rights of the citizens or subjects of other friendly states.* Moreover they mutually declare that they are opposed to the acquisition by any *other* government of any special rights or privileges that would affect the independence or territorial integrity of China or that would deny to the subjects or citizens of any country the full enjoyment of equal opportunity in the commerce and industry of China.[1]

Again Ishii demurred, and no wonder. A more categorical and binding abstinence pledge, a more emphatic iteration of the classic tenets of the Far Eastern policy of the United States than that comprised by Lansing's formula would have been difficult to imagine. Japan could not possibly accept it since by the conquest of Kiaochow, the Twenty-One Demands and the secret treaties with the Allies she was already forsworn. Nor could Lansing insist on its acceptance without vitiating his own concession to Japanese "special interests" in China. The negotiations had precipitated a dilemma, requiring the use of diplomatic ambiguity. Lansing and Ishii rose to the occasion. In a secret protocol, withheld from publication in deference to Japanese sensibilities (and

[1] Lansing, 298. The italics are Lansing's. LaFargue, 136, who bases his account of the negotiations almost exclusively on Ishii's, and who does not mention the secret protocol, offers the statement of E. T. Williams (then chief of the Far Eastern Division) that Lansing forgot to include in the final drafts of the notes the paragraphs reaffirming the open door and integrity of China policy, and that Williams noticed the oversight and inserted the paragraphs, as evidence that these were an "afterthought" and not the reason for the agreement. The secret protocol tends to invalidate the assertion that the paragraphs were an afterthought, though the conclusion that they were not the main reason for the agreement seems irrefutable. Lansing was using the declaration re the open door and China's integrity to parry Ishii's thrust for political *carte blanche* in China.

doubtless as an added concession to the purposes of the Tokyo Foreign Office, which could thus deny, or at least suppress knowledge of, its existence) Ishii agreed in so many words to the portion of Lansing's proposal pertaining to use of the war to upset the *status quo* in China.[1] Two days later (November 2, 1917) Secretary Lansing and Viscount Ishii affixed their signatures to the famous agreement which bears their name, and which incorporated the rest of Lansing's bargain. The United States recognized that "territorial propinquity creates special relations between countries, and consequently, the Government of the United States recognizes that Japan has special interests in China, particularly in the part to which her possessions are contiguous"; while Japan went on record in a long declaration of respect for the open door and the independence and territorial integrity of China.[2]

The Lansing-Ishii Agreement is still one of the most controversial subjects in American diplomatic history. Its studied ambiguity invited each signatory to construe it to suit its own purposes. And each has since made the most extreme claims of it: Japan, that it was American recognition of her paramount political influence as well as economic interest in Shantung, Manchuria and Mongolia; the United States, that it was a self-denying ordinance pledging Japan to the most meticulous respect for the open door and the integrity and independence of China.[3]

[1] The agreement was made in the form of a joint memorandum signed by the two negotiators and concluded October 31, two days before, and obviously as a condition to, the published portions of the Lansing-Ishii Agreement. The italicized clause in Lansing's proposal quoted above was incorporated in the final text of the secret protocol verbatim except for two inconsequential verbal changes. For text see *For. Rel.*, 1922, II, 595. In Lansing's date book, for November 2, 1917, the following entry appears: "Viscount Ishii—exchanged notes on China and signed confidential protocol. Arranged for publication P.M. Nov. 6." Lansing papers.

[2] The Lansing-Ishii Agreement lasted until April 14, 1923, when it was superseded by the Washington Treaties. Cf. below, Chapter VIII, p. 331 n.

[3] On November 4, two days before the agreed date of publication, Japan revealed the Agreement to the Chinese Government, construing the phrase "special

These claims are neither realistic nor sincere. The framers of the agreement knew what they were about. They understood the meaning of the words they employed. Each had recourse to ambiguity as an offensive as well as a defensive weapon. Unlike the Taft-Katsura Agreement, or the Root-Takahira Agreement, with which it is so often compared, the Lansing-Ishii Agreement was not an intentional reversal, or modification of the American Far Eastern policy. Theodore Roosevelt had acted out of conviction; Lansing out of expediency. Roosevelt followed his executive agreements with Japan with mature expositions of American policy consistent with those agreements. Lansing complained of the circumstances that made necessary his concession to Japan's "special interests"; resorted to legal quibbling to limit their scope and, at Paris, did his best to undo them altogether. In 1917, American diplomacy was preparing, not retreating from, the greatest of all its offensives against Japanese expansion. Whatever comfort Japanese diplomats may have derived from the letter of the agreement, they were soon to discover that its spirit was not one of compromise. It was a stop-gap measure, a temporization, a grudging concession to the gnat of Japanese imperialism when the United States was girding itself to destroy the dragon of German autocracy.[1]

interests" in the sense that Lansing had rejected, i.e., "paramount interest" and "special influence." Lansing, 302. Ishii, 124-132, argues that a) the two phrases, when rendered in Japanese ideograms, are indistinguishable; b) that the phrase accepted by Lansing has always admitted of political as well as economic interpretation, as witness its use in the Anglo-Japanese Alliance treaties, and construction by those parties, and c) that Lansing realized this but refused to admit it for obvious reasons.

[1] The most complete and authentic accounts of the Lansing-Ishii negotiations are those contained in the memoirs of the two principles themselves: Lansing, *War Memoirs*, Ch. XX; Ishii, *Diplomatic Commentaries*, Ch. VI. For a Japanese analysis of the negotiations, see the review of Lansing's *Memoirs* by Dr. Kiroku Hayashi in Gaiko Jiho (*Revue Diplomatique*) October 15, 1936, subsequently published in translation in *Contemporary Opinions*, October 15 and 22, 1936, for copies of which the author is indebted to Ambassador Joseph C. Grew and the staff of the American embassy in Tokyo. A legalistic defense of Lansing is to be

Such considerations cannot alter the fact that Lansing had made a political commitment to Japan, the extent of which, especially in view of what happened at Paris, invites examination. In the first place, established diplomatic usage had endowed the phrase "special interests" with political as well as economic connotations, whatever Lansing intended it to mean. In the eyes not only of the Japanese Government and people, but of China and the rest of the world, once the Lansing-Ishii Agreement was published, the burden of proof in this respect fell on America rather than Japan. Moreover, the situation in world politics at the time the agreement was being negotiated was such as to suggest that Lansing realized the political character of his concession and concealed it for much the same reasons that Japan exaggerated it. The fact is, Lansing knew of the existence of the secret treaties, with which his phrase was pale in comparison and which rendered fantastic the expectations implicit in the rest of the agreement. Ishii himself informed him that in 1915 England had "practically consented" to Japan's retention of the German islands north of the equator in return for Japanese assent to British retention of those to the south—facts of which Lansing had already been apprised by Spring-Rice in 1916.[1] Lansing later testified before the Senate Foreign Relations Committee that Ishii had led him to understand that Japan intended to return Kiaochow to China, and that no mention was made of the secret treaties affecting Shantung.[2] It is now known, however, that both Lansing and Wilson had been informed of the European secret treaties by Balfour during the latter's mission to Washington in May, 1917. Whether or not the arrangements relating to Shantung were among Bal-

found in C. W. Young, *Japan's Special Position in Manchuria*, 193-238. La-Fargue, *op. cit.*, 129-139, concludes that the agreement was "neither a Japanese victory nor an American defeat. It was simply unsatisfactory." Cf. also, Takeuchi, 201 ff. Text of agreement, except for secret protocol, is printed in *For. Rel.*, 1917, 264-265.

[1] Lansing, 291-293; United States Senate Foreign Relations Committee, *Hearings on the Treaty of Peace with Germany*, Senate Document No. 106, 66th Congress, 1st Session, 216-218. Quite possibly the arrangement had been a condition to Japan's adherence to the Declaration of London.     [2] *Ibid.*

four's revelations, Lansing at least had good cause to suspect their existence.[1] Given his knowledge and suspicion of Allied commitments to Japan, even the phrase "special interests" implied tentative recognition of them, reducing the rest of the agreement to the same status as the Bryan-Lansing *caveat* of May 11, 1915, viz., an American reservation of rights. Perhaps that is one reason why both the President and the Secretary of State denied all knowledge of the secret treaties until after the peace conference had assembled. They both had plans for the Far East, and for the rest of the

[1] For proof of Lansing's and Wilson's knowledge of the secret treaties in 1917, see the following: Dugdale, *Balfour*, II, 145-146; Lloyd George, *War Memoirs*, 1916-1917, 549-550; Seymour, *Intimate Papers of Colonel House*, III, Ch. II, esp. 61-63; Frear, Mary R., *Current History*, XXX, June, 1929, 435 ff.; testimony of members of the Senate Munitions Investigation Committee referring to a confidential document, furnished the Committee by the State Department, "which clearly indicates that before he departed from this country Balfour left with Lansing, Secretary of State, a statement which he had made on foreign policy to the British Imperial War Council. This statement referred at length to the terms of peace to which Britain was committed and the secret treaties." *Congressional Record*, 74th Cong., 2nd Sess., Jan. 17, 1936, Vol. 80, Part I, 563; Baker, R. S., *Woodrow Wilson, Life and Letters*, Vol. VII, 74-75, mentioned in Balfour's statement to Wilson and noting the omission of those pertaining to the German Islands and Shantung. Baker itemizes the contents of a letter from Balfour to Wilson, May 18, 1917, in which Balfour disclosed the terms of some but not all of the secret treaties. Those relating to Germany's islands in the Pacific and to Shantung were not mentioned in the letter. Wilson later conferred with Balfour, *ibid.*, 80. Whether he was then apprised of the omissions, or whether Balfour informed Lansing of them in a separate statement is not certain. It is certain, however, that Lansing by his own admission already knew of the treaty relating to the German islands (cf. p. 218, above). That he at least had cause to suspect the existence of some similar engagement relating to Shantung may reasonably be inferred from a telegram to Lansing from Post Wheeler, American Charge d'Affaires in Tokyo, June 27, 1917. Describing a session of the Diet at which both the Japanese Premier and Foreign Minister delivered addresses, Wheeler stated of the latter: "In reply to a question whether any pledge had been secured looking to retention by Japan of Tsingtao and the islands taken from Germany, he stated that the Japanese Government has taken properly effective measures to protect Japan's rights and interests in Shantung and the Southern Islands and concluded: 'Am very confident that upon restoration of peace the Allied powers will not object to such arrangements as Japan will deem necessary in order to ensure peace in the Orient.' "—*Foreign Relations*, 1917, Supplement 1, 452; Baker, 129-130.

world, to which an admission of such knowledge would have been prejudicial.

With the conclusion of the Lansing-Ishii Agreement, the Wilson Administration turned its back on the Far East for the better part of a year, devoting its thoughts almost entirely to the war on the western front and leaving Japan and the Allies free to take the lead in Chinese affairs.[1] These, with the United States a rather inactive, and not always willing, partner, strove to induce China to serve their war aims in ways that belied the sincerity of their allegiance to the cause of democracy. In China's civil conflict they (with the exception of Japan) played a neutral part until the supremacy of the northern militarists was assured. Then, under Japanese leadership, they threw their support to Tuan's regime and persuaded the United States to follow suit.[2] They next dangled before Tuan the bait of loans, Boxer indemnity remissions and other concessions, in the effort to secure his co-operation in such measures as confiscating German property in China, including banks, ships and real estate; deporting the entire German community from China—a measure actually carried out in 1919, after the armistice; sending Chinese coolies to labor behind the Allied trenches.[3] The objective of France and England was not Chinese military co-operation, which they knew would be impossible and useless, but the complete elimination of German commercial competition in China. The achievement of this objective gave British merchants in China peculiar satisfaction. "The majority of German residents in China are now on the high seas," exulted the

---

[1] Returning to Washington in the summer of 1918, Reinsch observed that, "After many, many departments and boards were consulted I found they were not thinking of China. Their chief problem was to train the American army and transport it to the western front." Reinsch, 356.

[2] Great Britain took the lead in appealing to Lansing to adopt this course. See *For. Rel.*, 1917, 102-104, esp. Spring-Rice to Lansing, September 3, 1917.

[3] Approximately 190,000 Chinese coolies served behind the Franco-British lines during the war. Numerous others were hired by Russian contractors in Siberia. LaFargue, 151-152.

British Chamber of Commerce of Shanghai at its annual meeting in 1919, adding that "just as the Chamber has been largely instrumental in driving them out of this country, so too it has been instrumental in destroying their trade." [1]

Tuan, on his part, appears to have been more interested in devoting such moral, political or financial support as he could secure from the Allies to the overthrow of the parliamentarians at Canton than in persecuting the German traders, a fact that deterred the Allies from lending him money. Not until October 15, 1920, were they able to agree on the terms of the consortium loan for which they had discerned such pressing need in 1917. Moreover, Allied proposals for the confiscation of German property were carefully worded to prevent reversion of ownership, or control, to China.[2] The truth is that neither the Government of China nor the Allies themselves were as much interested in China's prosecution of the war, much less China's contribution to the crusade for democracy, as they were in ulterior and purely selfish objectives within China's own borders. This situation played nicely into the hands of Japan, the only power on the scene with a consistent policy and the power to enforce it. Nor were Japan's aims very different in kind from the Allies'. France, Great Britain and Japan were all looking to an extension of their economic interests in China at the end of the war as well as to the continued enjoyment of the special rights and privileges that they had exacted from China over the past half century. They had no intention of sacrificing any of these either to Wilson's ideals or to the exigencies of the war, and they shaped their policies accordingly. The Peking Government complied with their wishes only

[1] LaFargue, 157.

[2] Italy, for example, would not agree to the original advantages proffered China by the Allies unless she could accede to part of the Austrian concession in Tientsin. For a more detailed review of China's diplomatic relations with the Allies, see LaFargue, Ch. VI; *For. Rel.*, 1917, Supplement 2, I, *The Far East in Relation to the War*, 682-703.

under pressure and in the hope of playing them off against each other at the peace conference. In the matter of Chinese participation in the war, as in that of China's entrance, the United States played a negative role—one that incurred no such moral responsibility for China's fortunes at the peace conference as Wilson was shortly to assume.

# VI. Wilson Challenges Japan

WE have said that in 1917 American diplomacy was preparing for the greatest offensive against Japanese expansion in its history. Not until the armistice lessened Wilson's preoccupation with Germany was he free to devote much energy to that offensive, which, when finally launched, took four principal forms: first, the effort to bind Japanese capital investment in China to the cooperative ordinances of the new four-power consortium; second, participation in the Allied military intervention in Siberia in order to prevent Japan from detaching the maritime provinces from Russian rule; third, insistence on the restoration of Shantung to China, and fourth, codification in treaty form of the principles of the Far Eastern policy of the United States together with the Wilsonian principles of non-aggression and collective security as applied to the Pacific Ocean and the region of Eastern Asia. The major parts of this progressively expanding program were accomplished at the peace conference and its sequel, the Washington Conference of 1921-1922. Organizing the consortium and the Siberian expedition began shortly after the conclusion of the Lansing-Ishii Agreement. The two were not unrelated, so far as the United States was concerned, for each constituted an American challenge to Japan's right to extend her political and economic influence onto the continent of Asia.

Wilson's decision in November, 1917, to permit the organization of a new four-power consortium was merely the curtain-raiser to an immensely complicated wrangle that lasted until October, 1920. Neither the President nor Lansing was finally reconciled to the impracticability of independent American loans until June, 1918. When they at last summoned the bankers to Washington, they found the latter in a recalcitrant mood. The greatly enlarged American banking group would accept Lansing's proposition only on two conditions: first, that it be assured of pooling its interests with the French, British and Japanese groups, in loans of a broadly international character, and second, that the United States Government announce that the loans were being made at its suggestion, a condition essential to their successful flotation on the American market. The government accepted these conditions. In so doing it assumed grave responsibilities toward the American investing public as well as toward the banking community. It virtually committed each to involvement in an international political contest the possible consequences of which, if it did not conceal, it certainly took no particular pains to explain.[1] The cardinal principles insisted on by the United States for the new consortium were that each national group should receive the active and exclusive support of its government; that all preferences and options in China held by the member banks should be pooled, and that the administrative integrity and independence of China should be respected. These principles collided sharply with Japan's well-known China program, as no doubt they were intended to do.

Prolonged Japanese-American negotiations ensued, in which Japan attempted to obtain the exclusion of Manchuria and Mongolia from the application of the consortium. To the Japanese way of thinking, the pooling of options and internationalization of

[1] The political character of the American consortium plans is illustrated by the way they were used during the peace conference to counteract Japan's penetration of Shantung. On July 3, 1919, one of the experts attached to the American peace commission advised Lansing to bolster the resistance of the Chinese delegates by informing them that the United States was seeking a Japanese declaration of intention to restore Shantung, in complete sovereignty, to China and that "the American Government bases much hope on the consortium as an instrument for the protection of China's interests as well as those of the United States." Hornbeck to Lansing, July 3, 1919. Lansing papers.

loans in these regions were one and the same thing as the Knox neutralization scheme. And they were. The United States was once more clearly attempting by economic means to undermine Japan's economic monopolies in northeastern Asia, monopolies that rested on old and elaborate treaty structures involving French, British and Russian, as well as Chinese assent, and which, during 1918, Japan had expanded and strengthened through the medium of independent loans to the government of Tuan Chi-jui. Irrespective of the moral rights implicit in these treaties, they were, as we have repeatedly observed, effective political instruments. Japan was not inclined to throw them over at America's behest. A compromise was finally reached by which the United States assured Japan of its "good faith" that it and the other two consortium powers (France and England) would "refuse their countenance to any operation inimical to the vital interests of Japan." Japan thereupon submitted a bill of particulars, many of which were unacceptable to Great Britain and the United States. Only when the latter agreed to accept the South Manchuria Railway zone and a number of other specified railway projects and their related mining and industrial privileges in Manchuria and Mongolia as outside the scope of the consortium would Japan consent to join.[1] This long economic contest, coinciding with the Siberian expedition and the peace conference contributed an acrimonious note to the more purely political questions at issue in the latter.

[1] Field, 142-166; *For. Rel.*, 1918, 169-199; 1919, I, 420-556; 1920, I, 497-605. Throughout the consortium negotiations the United States took the initiative, not only in drafting the general rules of the new agreement, but specifically in resisting Japanese attempts to exclude Manchuria and Mongolia. See the correspondence on this subject in the Lansing papers, esp. Lansing to Wilson, May 26, 1919; Marshall to Lansing, June 30; Memorandum of conversation between Ogadiri and Marshall at the Hotel Crillon in Paris, July 1, in which the Japanese arguing for the exclusion of Manchuria and Mongolia, pointed out that Tibet was part of China and "wondered if" Great Britain would consent to pooling her industrial loans there. Marshall found himself "unable to answer." Also Hornbeck to Lansing, July 12. Lansing papers.

Military intervention in Siberia was the concluding, and for the United States perhaps the most serious, episode of the World War in the Far East. The background of this extraordinary venture was partly European, partly Far Eastern. In March and November, 1917, two great revolutionary spasms dislodged Russia from active participation in the war against Germany. Kerensky, the leader of the first revolution, tried to continue to co-operate with the Allies. With his downfall at the hands of the Bolsheviks, in the second revolution, the danger of a separate Russo-German peace became imminent. To forestall this, rally the White Russians to renew the fight against Germany, and prevent the latter from seizing Allied military stores in Russia, France and Great Britain early began to consider sending expeditionary forces into the Murmansk region of European Russia, and westward from Vladivostok into Siberia. When these projects materialized the United States participated in them with reluctance. It did not object to the Murmansk expedition as much as it did to the Siberian, however, as indicated by the fact that Wilson agreed to take part in the first over six weeks before he did in the second.[1] Moreover, in the operations around Archangel, the United States did not adhere to any such rigid neutrality toward the Russian civil war as it did in Siberia. Since the announced purpose of both expeditions was the same, these discrepancies are enough to show that the American motives for taking part in each were different. In European Russia the United States was at first genuinely concerned with the protection of Allied military supplies and assisting the Russian elements that gave any evidence of wishing to fight Germany to do so. In the Far East its purpose

[1] "We understand from your reports that intervention at Archangel and Murmansk is regarded by the United States as a different question from that of intervention in the Far East." Balfour to Lord Reading, enclosed in Reading to Lansing, May 29, 1918. *For. Rel.*, 1918, *Russia*, II, 476. Lansing announced Wilson's assent to the Murmansk expedition June 1, 1918; to the Siberian expedition, July 17. *Ibid.*, 484-485, 287-290.

first and last was to resist the Japanese penetration of northern Manchuria and Siberia.[1]

The Russian Revolution instantly upset the *status quo* in the Far East and opened another field besides China and the German islands to Japanese expansion. Its immediate effect was to cause the breakdown of Russian control in northern Manchuria. This was an invitation to China as well as Japan, presenting the former an opportunity to reassert her sovereignty over the region. When the Bolsheviks seemed about to conquer it, the czarist Minister to Peking, though he represented a government that had long ignored China's sovereign rights in both Manchuria and Mongolia, suddenly remembered that "Russia had no territorial possessions in Manchuria" and urged the Chinese Government to send troops to co-operate with the local White Russian commander, General Horvat, against the Bolsheviks. The Allied Ministers to Peking did likewise, with the result that in December, 1917, Chinese troops intervened in the Russian civil war (albeit on nominally Chinese soil) on the side of the Whites.[2] But China was not encouraged to carry her activities to the point of re-establishing her control over northern Manchuria. The Allies had no desire to see White Russia's rights there revert to China, nor to sponsor any further Chinese intervention in the Russian civil war. Great Britain warned the Chinese Government to this effect and the United States, while recognizing "that China is entirely within her right in employing means to protect her sovereignty and territorial integrity," cautioned Peking against taking steps that might lead to armed conflict.[3] Early in January, 1918, most

---

[1] Although the original instructions to the commanders of the Murmansk and Siberian expeditions were identical, the former was placed under the superior command of the British Major General Frederick C. Poole (cf. Francis to Lansing, September 10 and Lansing to Francis, September 12, 1918. Lansing papers, 532-534) whereas in Siberia, General Graves exercised an independent command, under direct control of the War Department in Washington.

[2] LaFargue, 158-162; *For. Rel.*, 1918, *Russia*, II, 2-8.

[3] Lansing to Spring-Rice, December 29, 1917. *Ibid.*, 15.

of the Chinese troops were withdrawn and White Russian authority, in the person of General Horvat, was restored. From then
on Chinese influence in Manchuria was a minus quantity. The
province rapidly developed into a base for reactionary plots and
military campaigns, financed and instigated by England, France
and Japan, against the Bolsheviks over the border.[1] This unneutral use of Chinese territory made it liable to invasion by the
Soviet, and the possibility of Soviet attack served Japan as a convenient pretext for occupying it.

Japan had soon disclosed this intention. On January 17, 1918,
Ambassador Morris reported from Tokyo that the Japanese Government had intimated its desire to undertake independently the
occupation of Vladivostok and the operation of the Chinese Eastern and Amur Railways, should circumstances make these steps
necessary.[2] A few weeks later the British Government (which had
been urging Wilson to consent to a Siberian expedition since the
previous December) suggested to Washington that Japan be invited as the mandatory of the Allies to occupy the Trans-Siberian
and Chinese Eastern Railways.[3] Lansing promptly rejected the

[1] Such as those of the notorious cossack Semenov who with British and French,
and later Japanese, assistance organized in Manchuria the troops with which he
brutally harassed the Siberian peasantry. For a matter-of-fact account of Semenov's exploits see Graves, William S., *America's Siberian Adventure*, the memoirs
of the commanding general of the American expeditionary force. The British
Government notified Washington that it intended to support Semenov "with
money, and also with arms and ammunition," February 6, 1918. It urged the
United States to follow suit, which it pointedly refused to do. *For. Rel.*, 1918,
*Russia*, II, 38. On February 15 and March 8 Lansing received advice from Peking
that the British were carrying out their intentions with French co-operation. *Ibid.*,
46, 73. For further evidence of Japanese, British and French aid to Semenov see
*Ibid.*, 163, 169, 180, 189, 191, 444-449, 454-462; *For. Rel.*, 1919, *Russia*, 195-
604; Graves, *passim*.

[2] Morris to Lansing, January 17, 1918. *For. Rel.*, 1918, *Russia*, II, 30. The
Chinese Eastern Railroad, it will be remembered, was the part of the Trans-
Siberian that crossed Manchuria.

[3] British Embassy to Department of State, January 28 and February 6, 1918.
*Ibid.*, 35-36, 38.

scheme, denying that intervention in Russia's affairs was warranted and maintaining that should it become necessary in the future, it should "be undertaken by international co-operation and not by any one power acting as the mandatory of the others." [1] From this position the United States refused to budge. More than that, it insisted on placing the control and operation of the Chinese Eastern Railway (that is, the part of the Trans-Siberian that ran through Manchuria) in the hands of its own railway corps that had been despatched to the Far East at the behest of Kerensky to manage the Trans-Siberian.[2] Japan was not to be thwarted. In her secret treaty with Russia in 1916 she had arranged to take over a portion of the Chinese Eastern Railway in return for supplying Russia with war materials. To make sure that China would give her no trouble in this, she concluded two treaties with Peking (May 16 and 19, 1918) providing for Sino-Japanese military and naval co-operation in the event that their territories or "the general peace and tranquillity in the extreme Orient" should be menaced by the enemy.[3]

The very month after the conclusion of these treaties, Japan was furnished the excuse for invoking them. Semenov, a cossack raider subsidized by England, France and Japan to prey on the Bolsheviks, was decisively defeated and retreated into Manchuria, his original base. His defeat was excitedly ascribed by his sup-

[1] Department of State to British Embassy, February 8, 1918. The substance of this memorandum was transmitted to the French and Italian Embassies, February 14 and the Chinese and Belgian Legations, February 18, showing that it was considered by the Department of State an important statement of policy. *Ibid.*, 41-42.

[2] Headed by John F. Stevens and a group of experts, this corps, about 300 strong had been sent to Vladivostok from San Francisco in November, 1917. Its purpose was avowedly to serve the Russian people by keeping open their line of communications to Vladivostok and the Pacific, vital to their food supply. Cf. LaFargue, 166-167.

[3] For text see *For. Rel.*, 1918, 222-226. These two treaties were followed by two more (September 8, 1918, and February 5, 1919) providing for Japanese control of Chinese troops operating in Siberia and fixing the duration of the series of treaties.

porters to large numbers of freed German prisoners alleged to be swelling the ranks of the Red army.[1] Late in July Japan, citing the danger of Bolshevik and German reprisals against the fugitive Semenov, invoked her military pacts with China and marched her troops into northern Manchuria. The eleventh-hour admonishment of Washington "that the American Government trusts that the Imperial Japanese Government shares its opinion that a military occupation of Manchuria would arouse deep resentment in Russia" and so "defeat the desire of the United States and Japan to aid in the rehabilitation of Russia and to re-enlist her people in the war against our common enemy"[2] was ignored. Against the Franco-British support for Japan, and the influence Japan herself commanded over China, the United States could not prevail. For the time being all Manchuria was in Japanese hands. Washington therefore redoubled its efforts to prevent Japan from assuming independent control of the Chinese Eastern Railway. In this, though opposed as much by the British as by the Japanese, it finally scored a minor success. On January 9, 1919, an agreement was reached whereby the operation of the road was entrusted to an inter-Allied commission to be advised by a technical board headed by John F. Stevens,[3] leader of the American railway corps in Siberia. The United States had not been able to prevent Japan from independently occupying Russian Manchuria, the realization of which failure may well have helped to reconcile Wilson to military intervention in Siberia.

Whether Japan, Great Britain or France first suggested an expedition to Siberia, it is certain that all three ardently espoused

---

[1] These reports were accredited by Mr. Stevens and the American consul at Harbin. Cf. Stevens to Lansing, May 30 and Moser to Lansing, June 19. For. Rel., 1918, Russia, II, 181-182, 216-217.

[2] Polk to Morris, July 19, 1918. Ibid., 297. Cf. LaFargue, 164-172.

[3] LaFargue, 171-172; For. Rel., 1918, Russia, II, 273, 278, 292; III, 239-249; 1919, I, 590-615; Graves, 176-178. The specific designation of Stevens's prerogatives was made in a collateral agreement with Japan. See Morris to Polk, January 9, 1919. For. Rel., 1919, I, 590 ff.

the idea and for six months brought every conceivable kind of pressure to bear on Wilson before they could obtain his consent to it. Not only that, but both England and France did their best to turn the whole expedition over to Japan as their mandatory, making it a co-operative enterprise only in deference to American policy. As early as December 1, 1917, Clemenceau was trying to convince Colonel House of the desirability of sending a Japanese expeditionary force into Siberia.[1] On December 14, as Morris later reported to Washington, the British Ambassador in Tokyo, under specific instructions from London, broached the subject to the Japanese Foreign Office, leading Morris to conclude that "the initiative in the Siberian situation was taken by Great Britain and that prior to December 14 the Japanese Government had not seriously considered the question of intervention."[2] On January 8 Lord Robert Cecil, Balfour's lieutenant in the Foreign Office, wrote his chief that,

> The Japanese will not tell us what they intend to do, and are very angry if anyone else proposes to do anything. If they were not too unreasonable, the proper plan would undoubtedly be to land a force at Vladivostok to protect our stores there, *the force being in substance Japanese, with a few French, Americans and British added for the sake of appearances.*[3]

A few days later, as already noted, the Japanese Government cautiously intimated to Morris its desire to undertake such an enterprise (January 17) and Balfour sounded the State Department on it (January 28). The first impulse of both House and Wilson was to oppose Japanese intervention in any form. House was

[1] Seymour, *Intimate Papers of Colonel House*, III, 387-389.

[2] Morris to Lansing, March 22, 1918. *For. Rel.*, 1918, *Russia*, II, 84-88. That intervention became a subject of discussion between Japan and the United States about this time is indicated by an entry in Lansing's date book for December 27: "Japanese Ambassador saying his gov't agreed with us unwise to send troops to Vladivostok." Lansing papers.

[3] Dugdale, II, 186-187. Italics inserted.

convinced that it would drive Russia into the arms of Germany and, as he wrote Wilson early in March, that it would damage "that fine moral position you have given the Entente cause." He could not understand "the . . . determination of the British and French to urge the Japanese to take such a step." [1] Implicit in House's recommendations, as in the President's notes, was the fear of the Department of State that Japan would turn the intervention into a permanent conquest of Siberia's maritime provinces. [2] They could not well maintain their opposition on such impolitic grounds so, on House's advice, the President expressed his confidence in Japan but objected to the whole principle of intervention. [3]

From this position the President refused to be moved by the combined importunities of the French and British. The device contrived by the latter, of an international expedition with the United States a prominent member, proved no more acceptable to him than had independent Japanese action. But circumstances were fast undermining his resolve. As the military situation in France grew more desperate in the spring of 1918 a greater measure of force attached itself to the French arguments that the eastern front must be reconstituted in some form in order to relieve the terrific German pressure on the western. [4] From all sides, including American consular and diplomatic representatives in Russia and the Far East, came alarming reports of escaped Ger-

[1] House to Wilson, March 3, 1918. Seymour, III, 393-394. About February 28 Wilson had drafted a note to the Allied Ambassadors yielding to them on the invitation to Japan, but not joining them in it. *Ibid.*, 419. After receiving a long memorandum from House accompanied by the letter quoted above, Wilson, who had not circulated his note of February 28, withdrew it and substituted for it the note of March 5 cited below. The State Department appears to have given the substance of the first memorandum to the Japanese and Allied Ambassadors, but whatever impression it conveyed was speedily corrected by the substitution of the second note. *Ibid.*, 396, 419-420.

[2] Cf. House to Balfour, March 4, 1918. *Ibid.*, 394-395.

[3] Wilson to Allied Ambassadors, March 5, 1918. *Ibid.*, 419-420.

[4] Cf. *Ibid.*, 396-422; Bunyan, James, *Intervention, Civil War and Communism*, 63-68. There are numerous entries in Lansing's date book from January

man prisoners joining with Bolsheviks in the suppression of White efforts to renew allegiance to the Allied cause. A force of some fifty thousand Czechoslovakians, themselves liberated prisoners of war, and deserters from the Austrian army, had set out on a transcontinental journey to Vladivostok, whence they intended to return by sea to join the Allies on the western front. By June the progress of the Czechs was alleged to have been seriously impeded by Germans and Bolsheviks. Relief of the Czechs was now added to the arguments for intervention.

As General Graves, commander of the American expeditionary force in Siberia has convincingly pointed out, the Czechs never were in serious danger; German activities in that part of the world had been fantastically—or deliberately—exaggerated, and by the end of May the Allies had apparently given up any idea of sending the Czechs to the western front. The Czechs marched under orders to capture the towns they passed through, which they had little difficulty in doing. No sooner had they penetrated into eastern Siberia than they opened a widespread military campaign against the troops of the government that had permitted them to cross its territories.[1] They remained in Siberia warring against Soviet Russia—not Germany—until finally repatriated at Allied expense in the summer of 1920[2]—two and a half years after the reason for reconstituting the eastern front had ceased to exist, and three years after their advance guard had reached Vladivostok in safety. In one way or another the wandering Czechs served the interventionists, not excluding the United States, as a convenient pretext and a camouflage.

to July, 1918, showing that intervention in Siberia was receiving his constant attention. On April 6 he noted, amusingly, "Dined with Mrs. L. at British Embassy. Col. Wedgewood [British Army] just back from Siberia, only other guest. He was strongly against intervention which I think was a little disconcerting to Lord Reading." Lansing papers.

[1] See Graves, Ch. II, esp. 42-49, and *passim*; Bunyan, Ch. II.

[2] *For. Rel.*, 1920, III, 561-580.

Because, rather than in spite of this fact, they sharpened the exigencies before which Wilson at last gave way, agreeing to the Siberian expedition July 17, 1918.[1] He did so, however, only after it became evident that intervention would take place regardless of his permission, and probably with Japan in the leading role. He joined it not because he believed in it, or wished to join it, but because, as in the case of the consortium, he thought he could impose greater restraint on Japan within rather than outside of it. On July 17 the President in a personally drafted *aide-mémoire* to the Allied Ambassadors (which likewise became General Graves's confidential instructions),[2] submitted his conditions. The United States was acting in deference to the wisdom of the Supreme War Council of the Allied governments. It would tolerate no interference in Russia's domestic politics. It conceived that the sole duties of the combined expeditionary forces were to assist the Czechs, help steady genuine Russian efforts at self-government and self-defense, and guard Allied military stores. It would co-operate in the discharge of these duties "with a small military force like its own from Japan, and if necessary from the other Allies"[3] and it requested

[1] According to Lansing's date book, intervention was accepted by the President in principle July 6, the entry for which date reads: "Conference on Siberian situation at W[hite] H[ouse]—Adopted a program subject to Jap. gov't approval." Lansing papers.

[2] "President Wilson personally wrote the so-called *aide-mémoire* which General Graves sets out on page five of his story, a copy of which I personally delivered to the General. . . ." Newton D. Baker, in his foreword to Graves, *op. cit.*, x. For text see *Ibid.*, 5-10; *For. Rel.*, 1918, *Russia*, II, 287 ff.

[3] Lansing himself regretted the "insistence of Great Britain and France in taking part in this movement." "The participation of those two Governments," he declared, "will give the enterprise the character of interference with the domestic affairs of Russia and create the impression that the underlying purpose is to set up a new pro-Ally Government in Siberia, if not in Russia. It is unfortunate that London and Paris do not see this and let the United States and Japan handle the situation without seeking to interfere." Lansing to Polk, August 3, 1918. Lansing papers.

all associated in this course of action to unite in assuring the people of Russia in the most public and solemn manner that none of the governments uniting in the action either in Siberia or in northern Russia contemplates any interference of any kind with the political sovereignty of Russia, any intervention in her internal affairs, or any impairment of her territorial integrity either now or hereafter, but that each of the associated powers has the single object of affording such aid as shall be acceptable, and only such aid as shall be acceptable, to the Russian people in their endeavor to regain control of their own affairs, their own territory, and their own destiny.[1]

To this impressive adjuration the Allies—somewhat hypocritically, in view of the support they had already given Semenov—pledged their assent. In an exchange of notes followed by simultaneous public statements on August 3, Japan reaffirmed her "avowed policy of respecting the territorial integrity of Russia and of abstaining from all interference in her internal politics," [2] but did not, as is commonly stated, agree to any numerical limitation of her forces.[3] The same day a British contingent landed at Vladivostok, followed a week later by a battalion of Annamese under French command, then by the Japanese, and on August 15 and 16 two regiments of American infantry from the Philippines. The latter were joined by General Graves with additional detachments from San Francisco, September 1. The total strength of the American expeditionary force was 9,014 officers and men while Japan's ultimately exceeded 72,000.[4]

[1] *For. Rel.*, 1918, *Russia*, II, 289-290.        [2] *Ibid.*, 324-326, 328-329.

[3] The Japanese Ambassador "said his Government still felt a larger force than that proposed was essential, but in view of the necessity for immediate action, and in view of the attitude of this Government, his Government authorized him to say that they accepted our proposals, reserving the question as to the sending of additional troops to Vladivostok or elsewhere until circumstances should arise which might make it necessary." Polk to Wilson, August 3. *Ibid.*, 325. On August 8 the British made a similar declaration. *Ibid.*, 333-334.

[4] Lansing to Ishii, August 15, 1918. *Ibid.*, 346; Graves, 64. Lansing "always believed that in the end Japan would have to have a superiority in numbers but that at the outset an equal number of Americans and Japanese should be landed in order not to excite Russian opposition." Lansing to Polk, August 3, 1918. Lansing papers.

The situation that confronted the combined forces was one that permitted each to make out of it what its leaders wished. Four White Russian war lords, Kolchak, Semenov, Kalmikov and Rozanov, held sway over different parts of Siberia. The last three were cossack gangsters who terrorized the peasantry and quarreled with each other with fine impartiality. Kolchak, an admiral in the Czar's fleet, strove for nobler ends but fell a victim of his own administrative ineptitude and of circumstances beyond his control. From November, 1918, until January, 1920, he maintained a precarious rule over most of Siberia. None of the four was truly representative of the Russian people, who overthrew them all as soon as a sufficient quantity of the rifles and supplies the Allies had been furnishing Kolchak had filtered into their hands. France at first devoted what little energy she could spare the expedition to faint-hearted attempts to re-constitute the eastern front; then swung into the wake of Great Britain. Her original interest gave way to concern for the investments of French *petits rentiers* in Siberian railways which, even before the Russo-Japanese War, had been large. Great Britain seemed chiefly apprehensive of the spread of Bolshevism to India *via* China. Despite promises to the Russian people not to intervene in their domestic politics, she fought the Bolsheviks with money, arms and intrigue. Japan, on her part, was not averse to playing Semenov against Kolchak; or to fomenting by the most opportune methods at hand the disorder that she hoped would justify, or conceal, Japanese absorption of the maritime provinces.[1]

The United States fought a long diplomatic duel with Japan, trying without success to stem the tide of Japanese reinforcements and, on the fall of Kolchak, to persuade Tokyo to withdraw its forces. Far from co-operating with the United States, Great Britain egged on the Japanese against the Bolsheviks and winked

[1] See the illuminating documents revealing the motives of the various powers intervening in Russia in Lloyd George, D., *Memoirs of the Peace Conference*, I, 116, and Ch. VII, esp. pp. 242-251.

at the consequences. General Knox, the commander of the British expeditionary force, frequently caused General Graves more difficulty in observing a neutral course *vis-à-vis* the Russian civil war than did the frankly opportunistic tactics and all too obvious intrigues of Japan. By the same inter-Allied railway agreement of 1919 that had forestalled independent Japanese control of the Chinese Eastern,[1] the nations participating in the Siberian expedition assumed the responsibility of managing and operating the Trans-Siberian Railway in the interests of the Russian people. To the British, this meant in the interests of Kolchak. They thought that the Bolsheviks should be denied access to the road, and when General Graves refused to depart from his neutral course and take steps in this direction, they went so far as to bring pressure to bear in Washington for his removal.[2]

Although Stevens, various consular officials and intelligence officers, and virtually the entire State Department including Lansing himself favored actively supporting Kolchak and recognizing his government, Graves held rigidly to his instructions. In his interpretation, these did not permit him to take action for or against Kolchak or his enemies save insofar as each side might benefit from the protection of the railway sectors and military stores assigned to Graves's command. Graves realized that Kolchak did not represent the wishes of the people he pretended to govern, and that his regime could not possibly survive the removal of its various foreign props. Upheld to the last by the War Department and by the President himself, the General's conduct was an object lesson in neutrality, and perhaps the only thing that prevented some kind of Franco-British deal with Japan, paying her with Russian territory for an anti-Bolshevik crusade.

[1] Cf. p. 230, above.
[2] Cf. Graves, Ch. VI, esp. 195. When, in October, 1919, on the eve of Kolchak's collapse a new British High Commissioner to Siberia agreed with Graves's views on Kolchak and so advised the British Foreign Office, he received a telegram in reply summarily removing him from office. Graves, 269; *For. Rel.*, 1919, *Russia*, 442-443.

In any event, the American force stayed on, long after the armistice, until the complete collapse of the Kolchak regime and the diversion of Allied interest to other spheres made any such deal unlikely.[1]

Early in January the American Government announced its intention to withdraw its troops, and pointedly intimated that it would welcome a similar move on the part of Japan.[2] On April 1, 1920, the last American contingent sailed out of Vladivostok harbor. General Oi, the Japanese commander with whom General Graves had had many a hot altercation, "sent a band to the dock to furnish music" Graves recalls, ". . . and as the boat backed away from the dock the Japanese band began playing the good old American tune, 'Hard Times Come Again No More.' Some looked upon this tune as amusing, others as indicative of past official relations."[3] Japan refused to withdraw her troops from Siberia until November, 1922, and she did not evacuate northern Sakhalin, seized as indemnity for losses at the hands of Soviet troops, until 1925. She had overrun northern Manchuria, and extended her privileges and influence there. She had fought pitched battles

[1] The United States did not formally recognize the Kolchak government, though it did agree, in a joint note to Kolchak of May 26, 1919 (signed by Wilson, Lloyd George, Clemenceau, Orlando and Saionji), to support him "with munitions, supplies and food" on certain carefully stipulated conditions, chief among which was Kolchak's assurance that he would establish a constitutional democracy throughout Russia. On June 4 Kolchak accepted these conditions and on June 12 the Allies (and Wilson) pronounced his acceptance satisfactory. From June until the following November Wilson was under constant pressure to go beyond merely helping to supply Kolchak with arms and food, recognize his regime and send sufficient money and reinforcements to make it a success. Among the outstanding American advocates of this course were Consul General E. L. Harris at Irkutsk, DeWitt C. Poole, American Chargé d'Affaires at Archangel, Ambassador Morris, Stevens, Acting Secretary Polk and Lansing. Cf. *For. Rel.*, 1919, *Russia*, 322-453; Graves, Ch. VIII; *Krasnyi Arkhiv*, XXXI, 50-80.

[2] The announcement was made on January 9, 1920, following a thorough discussion of the Russian situation by Ambassador Shidehara and Secretary Lansing *For. Rel.*, 1920, III, 486-494.

[3] See Graves, 328.

against the Bolsheviks. But she had detached no Russian territory.[1]

The Siberian expedition was the second phase of the unfolding American offensive against Japanese expansion. In it, the United States had been forced to play a lone hand, not only receiving no co-operation from Great Britain or France, but often finding itself the dupe of Anglo-Japanese intrigue. Wilson had applied to Russia the same principles that the United States had long applied to China. Since public opinion in the United States after the war was almost hysterically anti-communistic, and since Washington would have no dealings with the Soviet, the world at large derived the impression that the chief aim of American diplomacy in the Far East was to resist Japanese aggression. This was a far cry from the policy of equal commercial opportunity that had once governed American relations with the Orient. And the war had merely paved the way for greater efforts yet to come.

At the peace conference, meanwhile, the American campaign against Japanese expansion had advanced far along other lines. While the new consortium groups jockeyed for position, and while the associated expeditionary forces trod on each other's toes in Siberia, Wilson and his advisers faced Japan's emissaries across the council tables at Paris. There from January 12, 1919 (the day the conference opened), until June 28, 1919 (the day the Versailles Treaty was signed), the United States fought a losing battle to defend China from the encroachments of Japan. This failing, and with Japanese-American relations moving rapidly from bad to worse, the fight was resumed at Washington two years later, with greater success.

The failure of the President to achieve the restoration of

[1] Cf. In addition to Graves, *op. cit.*, Bunyan, Ch. VI; *For. Rel.*, 1918, *Russia*, II, 1-462; III, 183-307; 1919, I, 566-615; 1919, *Russia*, 195-604; 1920, III, 481-571; also the numerous despatches and telegrams dealing with Siberia in the Lansing papers, esp. Hornbeck to Whitehouse, July 11, 1919, on Japanese instigation of Semenov, and those dated October 18-31, 1919, describing Kolchak's retreat. Miller, D. H., prints some interesting memoranda on Siberia in his *My Diary at the Conference of Paris*, IV, 375-377; XVII, 244-248.

Shantung was incidental to a greater tragedy, already recorded by many of its participants and written large in the history of the post-war world. The President's own temperament, his decision to attend the conference in person, his uncompromising attitude toward Congress and the Republicans; the aggressive partisanship of the "irreconcilables"; the secret treaties; the chasm that separated Wilson from Lloyd George and Clemenceau; procedural blunders; party politics in England and France; frayed tempers, overheated rooms and cartoons in the Paris press—all conspired to make the Versailles Treaty what it was, instead of what Wilson hoped it would be. Basically, Wilson's failure epitomized the failure of the entire European world to rise above the accumulated national hatreds and jealousies of past centuries and create the parliament of man that philosophers had envisioned. The League did not collapse under the impact of Japanese and Italian imperialism in after years; neither was it stifled by American isolationism. It was stillborn. The primary aim of France and England was never a League of Nations—they wanted a League of defense against their former enemies, a concert of power, a *pax Franco-Britannica*; and by the time Clemenceau and Lloyd George had finished with the Versailles Treaty, that is exactly what they got. With all the moral support of the warweary millions that Wilson indubitably commanded, it seems idle to suppose that he, or any other mortal, could have prevailed against such a fortress of *Machtpolitik*.

The record of the Shantung negotiations reinforces this conclusion. The Japanese delegates came to Paris armed not only with *faits accomplis*, but also with the Anglo-Japanese Alliance, the secret treaties with the Allies, as well as those with Russia and China, discussed in the previous chapter, and the ambiguous American concession entailed in the Lansing-Ishii Agreement. Nor had Japan rested content with the force of the treaties to which she had bound China in 1915. In the summer and early autumn of 1918, on the very eve of the armistice, she had secretly secured fresh Chinese commitments to certain of the Twenty-One Demands. The Chinese Government categorically agreed to the transfer to Japan of Kiaochow and the German rights in Shantung, on the understanding that while Japan was to restore to China the Kiaochow leasehold, she would retain and even expand the former German economic privileges in the province. The contract was bound (seriously damaging China's case at Paris) by the Chinese Government's acceptance of advance payment on large Japanese railway loans.[1] With such political armor Japan was prepared to withstand all the moral forces that Wilson, or anyone else, could muster to compel her to give back Shantung to China without lien or encumbrance. Great Britain and France were not disposed to compel her to do so. Indeed, they had both promised to support her claims, as had Italy. Intent themselves on such aggressive projects as stripping Germany of her colonies, partitioning the Turkish Empire and "redeeming" *Italia irridenta*, the victorious Allies could not afford to look askance at the compensation Japan was seeking in China.[2] Their own peace plans required that they make good their promises to Japan who was encouraged by their very example to defy Wilson.

Japan herself was determined to press to a conclusion the program of expansion and the quest for recognition as a great power inaugurated by the Twenty-One Demands. She still remembered the Triple Intervention that had forced her to disgorge the Liaotung Peninsula after her war with China in 1895, and the American mediation that her people rightly or wrongly held to

[1] These agreements, concluded September 24 and 28, 1918, followed a military loan agreement (July 31) and were accompanied by a war participation loan agreement, and a preliminary Manchurian and Mongolian railway loan agreement (both of September 28), all binding China ever more closely to the will of Tokyo. See LaFargue, 177; *For. Rel.*, 1919, I, 342-343, 571-572, 574-578; MacMurray, II, 1414-1415.

[2] On December 30 Clemenceau told the Chinese Minister to France "that he would like to help China but could not because of a secret treaty with Japan." Wilson to Lansing, February 4, 1919, with enclosures. Lansing papers.

blame for the dissatisfying Peace of Portsmouth. She had no intention of allowing history to repeat itself. Her delegates were bound by instructions from which they never wavered. There was no fundamental conflict between Japan and the Allies at Paris. Although Great Britain and France were each many times more deeply and more precariously involved in the Far East than was the United States, they had struck their bargains with Tokyo and were content. They were quite free of any sense of indebtedness to China since, in their estimation, her contribution to their victory had been less than satisfactory. Neither was there any fundamental conflict between Japan and the actual (Japanese-subsidized) rulers of China, the military clique that had long drawn on Tokyo for support against its factional adversaries of the south. The dividing line fell rather between Japan on the one hand, and the United States and the Chinese delegates on the other. Whatever the tactical errors for which Wilson was partially or wholly responsible, they were symptoms rather than causes of these basic conflicts of policy.

China was represented at Paris by a delegation of somewhat doubtful responsibility. For almost a year prior to the armistice the southern Chinese provinces had been in open rebellion against Peking. Not until late in November, under external pressure from the United States, the Allies, and Japan, was a truce effectuated. A domestic peace conference was then arranged, which assembled at Shanghai in February (its sessions paralleling those at Paris) and at which the warring factions renewed with unabated vigor their struggle for control of the central government. Meanwhile a peace delegation had been sent to Paris which represented a theoretical compromise between these factions, but which was quickly dominated by its two youngest members, Wellington Koo and C. T. Wang. Western-educated, intensely patriotic, enemies of the northern clique and its Japanese mentors, imbued with the idealism of Woodrow Wilson, they took the initiative in their own hands and committed their colleagues to a most ambitious program. They determined to use the peace conference as the occasion not only to undo the Sino-Japanese treaties of 1915 and 1918, but also to procure the release of China from as many as possible of the unequal treaties that kept her in a position of inferiority to the treaty powers. While this program embodied the desires of the increasingly vociferous anti-Japanese elements in China—perhaps of a majority of literate Chinese—it did not embody those of the group that remained in power at Peking and continued to do business privately with Tokyo. Whether the latter placed partisan ambition ahead of the national welfare, whether they were driven to the extremity by their country's imperative need for foreign loans, whether they were bribed, intimidated or sincerely convinced, the fact remains that the Chinese Government itself did not give undivided allegiance to Wilson's cause at Paris.[1] This reduced the President's effective allies against Japan to Messrs. Koo and Wang of the Chinese delegation and the dissident Chinese idealists—mostly students and journalists—for whom they spoke.

No sooner had the Chinese delegates arrived in Paris than they set out systematically to cultivate the sympathies and enlist the support of their American colleagues. To the expert advisers of the American commission they privately divulged their plans for converting the gospel of the Fourteen Points into a charter of liberty for China. Specifically, they sought American assistance in securing the abrogation of all Chinese treaties with Germany and Austria, and the recovery of all treaty rights held by these

---

[1] For a careful study of the way in which China's fortunes at the peace conference were affected by the situation in Chinese domestic politics, see LaFargue, Chs. VII and VIII; also *For. Rel.*, 1919, I, 270-358. It is LaFargue's opinion (*op. cit.*, 175) that the Chinese delegates were "permitted to advance claims which had little chance of ever being realized but which appealed to the very vocal 'Young China' elements in order to provide a smoke screen for the realistic maneuvering which was taking place at the Shanghai conference." This work is especially valuable for its extensive publication of the official Minutes of the Council of Ten, the Council of Five and the Council of Four at Paris.

powers, including the right of extraterritoriality, the Kiaochow leasehold and the German economic privileges throughout Shantung.[1] The Chinese based their claims on the well-chosen grounds that these treaty rights were contrary to the spirit of the open door notes.[2] The Americans needed no persuasion. They freely consulted the Chinese, helping to plot their course of action, encouraging them to ignore the agreement their government had just made with Tokyo, and to resist Japan by every means at their disposal. When the Japanese demands were ready for presentation, Wilson forced through an exception to the rule that denied China representation at meetings of the Council of Ten, brought the Chinese delegates to the meeting and gave them a chance to reply to Japan on equal terms.

The Japanese, according to schedule, demanded the direct, unconditional cession to Japan of the German islands north of the equator, and the leased territory of Kiaochow "together with the railways and other rights possessed by Germany in respect of Shantung province." Next day (January 28) Wellington Koo delivered an impassioned address as "the spokesman of one-quarter of the human race" and as the defender of Shantung, "the Holy Land of the Chinese, the Home of Confucius," and presented his country's counterclaim "for the restoration to China of the leased territory of Kiauchau, the railway in Shantung and all other rights Germany possessed in that province before the war." [3] The Chinese plea went forth to the world in a burst of

[1] The Chinese first approached members of the American delegation for confidential advice in December, before the conference opened. By January 22 they had made known their plans to the Americans and discussed them in detail. See Hunter Miller's record of a consultation with Wellington Koo on December 27, 1918, and of a luncheon meeting of January 22, 1919, together with text of Chinese aims presented at this meeting. Miller, *My Diary at the Conference of Paris*, I, 60, 88; III, 527. LaFargue, 182-184.

[2] Miller, III, 527.

[3] Secret Minutes, Council of Ten, January 27 and 28. Baker, *op. cit.*, II, 230-231; LaFargue, 196-200.

publicity, eliciting the applause of the Chinese nationalists and precipitating a dilemma that lay like a log across Wilson's path for the next three months. During this time the rival Chinese and Japanese delegations fenced for advantage, with the Americans embarrassed, and far from neutral, umpires. While thus engaged at Paris, Japanese diplomats brought constant pressure to bear at Peking to prevent the Chinese Government from following the lead of its peace delegates. Intelligence despatches kept Wilson informed of these undercover activities, and induced the President and his advisers to start backfires at both Peking and Tokyo. Reinsch was instructed to urge the Chinese Government to stand firm, and Morris to disclose to the Japanese Foreign Minister "our knowledge of what is taking place in Peking" and to "express our distress that such indications are given of Japan's unwillingness to trust the fairness and justness of the Peace Conference." [1]

In the hope of redeeming the worst sins of the peacemakers, Wilson had succeeded in making acceptance of the League of Nations Covenant, with its new code of international justice, a condition to signing the treaty of peace. Pursuing this strategy he countered each Japanese move with an appeal to the higher morality of the Covenant. Thus he parried the Japanese thrust for Kiaochow and the German islands with the mandate principle, according to which the conquered German territories would become an international trust. But to no avail. Australia and New Zealand insisted on outright annexation of German New Guinea and the German islands south of the equator, as did South Africa of German West Africa. France wanted Togoland and the Cameroons. Italy and even Belgium had similar aspirations. One by one the British, French and Italian claims based on the secret

[1] Draft of telegram to the Secretary of State, Washington, enclosed in Wilson to Lansing, February 7, 1919 (giving same instructions). See also two despatches, Robbins to Churchill, February 3, reporting Japanese activities in Peking, and Wilson to Lansing, February 4, expressing apprehension that the Japanese would force the Chinese Government to disown its Paris delegates. Lansing papers.

treaties were brought to light, each claimant demurring at any form of international control for its territorial conquests. Prime Ministers Hughes of Australia and Massey of New Zealand were particularly intransigent in the matter, refusing to hear of anything but direct annexation. The Allies themselves were Japan's most powerful defense attorneys. Only with the greatest difficulty was Wilson able to achieve a modified mandate system, from which Kiaochow was excluded, and which permitted each mandatory (except those in the class of A mandates) sovereignty over its mandated territories that could easily, and soon did, become practically absolute.[1] Wilson particularly deplored the award of the north Pacific islands to Japan and the obstructive tactics of Hughes and Massey that he held primarily to blame for it. In this the President revealed the same apprehensions for the Philippines that had caused Theodore Roosevelt so much uneasiness, showing the constant influence of the Philippines in determining American policy in the Far East. The Japanese mandate, he confided to one of his closest advisers, lay athwart the path from Hawaii to the Philippines. The mandated islands were nearer Hawaii than was the California coast. They could easily be fortified; in fact he could conceive of no use for them except as naval bases. And he did not trust the Japanese because of their actions in Siberia.[2]

Unable either to prevent the German islands from becoming a Japanese mandate, or to place Kiaochow in the mandate category, Wilson was next confronted by a Japanese demand for international recognition of the principle of racial equality. The fate of this demand reflects still more vividly the absence of co-

[1] Baker, I, 261-275; Miller, *The Drafting of the Covenant*, I, 114 ff.; II, 220-226; Seymour, *House*, IV, 283 ff., 293-300.

[2] Wilson to Hunter Miller, January 30, 1919. Memorandum of a conversation. Miller, *Diary*, I, 100. The President said that the Japanese had broken their promise to send the same number of troops to Siberia as the United States. He was mistaken in thinking that Japan had made such a promise. See above, p. 235.

operation on Far Eastern problems between the Allies and the United States, particularly between Great Britain and the United States. It also brings into the limelight one of the sharpest contradictions within the American Far Eastern policy itself. With the approval of Colonel House who, with Wilson, helped the Japanese to prepare their resolution, the latter proposed an amendment to the League Covenant providing that,

> The equality of nations being a basic principle of the League of Nations, the High Contracting Parties agree to accord, as soon as possible, to all alien nationals of States members of the League equal and just treatment in every respect, making no distinction, either in law or in fact, on account of their race or nationality.[1]

As will appear in the next chapter, this amendment was aimed at just such discriminatory legislation as the alien land laws recently enacted by the State of California. It was even more palpably a challenge to the theory of the superiority of the white race on which rested so many of Great Britain's imperial pretensions. The facts seem to be that while thoughts of California may have given Wilson cold feet when the amendment came to a final vote, both he and his advisers up to that moment actively supported it against the adamant opposition of their British colleagues.

From February 4, when the Japanese first sought House's counsel, until April 11, when the racial equality amendment was finally rejected, the Americans and British were wholly at odds on the issue (the only one, parenthetically, on which the Chinese and Japanese were united). Again Hughes of Australia emerged as the chief obstructionist, though he never lacked support from Balfour and Lord Robert Cecil.[2] Together they did all that they could to denature the amendment and keep it from coming to a vote. Balfour abruptly told House that the principle that all men

---

[1] Miller, *Covenant*, I, 183. The drafts were first submitted to the approval of House and Wilson, February 5, the amendment proposed a week later. Cf. Seymour, IV, 308-311.

[2] British Foreign Secretary and Under-Secretary.

are created equal "was an eighteenth century proposition which he did not believe was true." House replied that "he did not see how the policy toward the Japanese could be continued. The world said that they could not go to Africa; they could not go to any white country; they could not go to China, and they could not go to Siberia; and yet they were a growing nation, having a country where all the land was tilled; but they had to go somewhere." [1] Balfour sympathized with these views; [2] but, though he did not say so, the record of his country's diplomatic relations with Japan showed that Britain preferred to use portions of Chinese and Russian territory as outlets for Japanese expansion.

When the amendment came to its first parliamentary test Lord Robert Cecil, unmoved by the eloquence and logic of the Japanese arguments and acting under the instructions of his government, registered his opposition. [3] By the end of March, Hughes was threatening to make speeches rousing Dominion and American sentiment if the adoption of any racial equality amendment whatsoever, "no matter how mild and inoffensive" should be attempted. [4] Nor did Hughes stop at threats. He made statements to the Japanese press denying his responsibility for impeding the progress of the amendment, and implying that the United States was chiefly to blame, so that House felt obliged to summon Makino and Chinda, and to send secret despatches giving Ambassador Morris the "true facts," in order to counteract Hughes's

[1] Miller, *Diary*, I, 116.

[2] *Ibid.*

[3] "The presentation of the Japanese amendment by Baron Makino and by Viscount Chinda was admirably done," Miller records, "and it seemed to me that they had the support of the entire room. Cecil acted as though he were in a very difficult position, and after making his statement sat silent with eyes fixed on the table." *Diary*, I, 244-245. House, who had by this time earned Chinda's thanks for his "considerate sympathy" (Seymour, IV, 313-314) understood that "all the British Delegation were willing to accept the form the President, Makino and Chinda agreed on, excepting Hughes of Australia. He has been the stumbling block." *Ibid.*, 314.

[4] Seymour, IV, 415; Miller, *Diary*, I, 257-258.

impression and stop the anti-American press campaign it had started in Japan.[1]

It was, then, chiefly though not entirely the fault of Great Britain that the Japanese—and Chinese—hopes for the end of racial discrimination were shattered. France and Italy, as proved by their votes, favored the amendment. We have already taken note of American sympathies for it. And we have suggested that it brought to light not only the impossibility of a "co-operative" policy, but also a sharp contradiction within America's Far Eastern policy itself. This was the contradiction implicit in seeking Japan's co-operation in China and her assurances of non-aggression toward the Philippines, and at the same time arousing her antagonism by discriminating against her nationals in the United States on the presumption of their racial inferiority to Americans. The dichotomy was clearly perceived by the American delegates at Paris. On the one hand Wilson was attempting to restore Shantung to China, to obtain certain cable rights on the island of Yap, strategically situated in the Japanese mandated islands, and to guard against the use of these islands as naval bases threatening the security of neighboring American possessions. He was also engaged in trying to prevent Japan from detaching portions of Siberia, and to combat Japanese financial monopolies with the new consortium. A concession to Japan's pride of race that was anything if not consistent with the principles of the Covenant might well have facilitated his efforts to gain the co-operation he sought from Japan in other matters. Was it ever within his power to secure this concession?

In a memorandum of March 19, 1919, the Chief of the Far Eastern Division of the State Department specifically called the attention of the American delegates to the relationship between the two objectives. He hoped the delegates would support the

---

[1] *Ibid.* Also Polk to Morris, April 21, 1919, and C. A. H. to Lansing, November 28, 1919, with enclosures, outlining in detail the negotiations concerning the racial equality amendment. Lansing papers.

racial equality amendment. He reminded them of "the claims of the United States to the position of mandatory in the Pacific Islands north of the equator."

"If now we surrender to Japan our claims in those islands," the memorandum continued, "and further grant Japan our approval of the proposed amendment, a concession to her pride of race which she will highly appreciate, we are entitled to ask Japan to be equally conciliatory and to do justice to China in Shantung." [1]

Colonel House and the President himself shared this view.[2] And yet, when the amendment, much softened and revised, was at last brought to a vote and passed by the score of eleven to six, Wilson who was presiding over the meeting (April 11) and who with House had abstained from voting, ruled against adopting it because it had failed to pass unanimously.[3] Japan's "poignant regret" at this failure to realize what her delegates called "a deep-rooted national conviction" [4] embittered Japanese-American relations afresh and unquestionably increased Japan's determination not to compromise on Shantung. Why, then, did the President surrender on the very amendment that he himself had helped to phrase, that had the sympathies of his advisers, and the political implications of which were recognized by the entire American delegation?

British critics have maintained that he did so because he realized no treaty honoring the principle of racial equality would be sus-

[1] Peace Commission Memorandum initialed "E. T. W." [Williams], March 19, 1919. Lansing papers.

[2] As did Hunter Miller, who considered the amendment in its final form "just and harmless." Miller, Diary, XX, 444-452, 477.

[3] In its final form the amendment was a mere clause to be inserted in the Preamble reading "by the endorsement of the principle of equality of nations and just treatment of their nationals." In addition to Japan, France, Italy, Brazil, Greece, Yugoslavia, Czechoslovakia and China all voted in favor of adoption. Miller, Covenant, I, 461-466; Diary, VIII, 277-279; Seymour, IV, 428.

[4] Makino's words in an address on the racial equality demand, April 28, 1919. Miller, Diary, XX, 111-114.

tained by an American Senate, and that hence Hughes "rescued" Wilson from an awkward situation.[1] This theory is not well substantiated by the record of Hughes's statements to the Japanese press. House, on the other hand, passed the buck to Hughes.

"The President was for accepting it [the amendment]," House wrote, "but Cecil, under instructions from his Government, could not; and since I knew that Hughes would fight it and make an inflammatory speech in the Plenary Session, I urged the President to stay with the British, which he did." [2]

The question that next arises is, Why were House and Wilson afraid of Hughes? In the answer to this question lies the clue to Wilson's surrender. The fact is that while the President and his peace commissioners favored the adoption of the Japanese amendment, they knew it was dynamite and handled it accordingly. So long as they could confine debate over it to the inner sanctums of the peace conference they could, after the manner of the Gentlemen's Agreement, meet Japan halfway. But should the debate once break into the open, it would merely add fresh fuel to the fires already blazing in California and stimulate still worse discrimination than that which Japan was seeking to remedy. Hughes saw this flaw in Wilson's armor and aimed straight at it, with telling effect. Perhaps it is too much to say that had he not done so the President might have secured the adoption of the Japanese amendment. In the mood that they were in, the British might have held out against it to the end. Or, had it been included in the Covenant, innocuous as it was, it would have provided the American foes of the Versailles Treaty another argument for rejecting it. But the corollary to these conclusions is that had Hughes in particular and the British delegation in general not opposed the amendment and threatened to mobilize the yellow press against it, the American delegation

[1] Cf. Nicolson, Harold, *Peacemaking*, 145.
[2] Seymour, IV, 428.

might have followed its original inclinations at least to the point of voting in favor of it; and the very record of such a vote might have assisted them to dispose of Shantung according to American wishes. Such a course, moreover, would have forced Great Britain to share the onus of flouting Japan's "deep-rooted national conviction" more equally, and more openly, with the United States.[1]

A few days after the defeat of the racial equality amendment, the Japanese delegates brought up their claim to Shantung with very evident determination to see it honored or to withdraw from the conference. Since January, when the claim had first been presented and attacked by the Chinese, possibilities of a compromise between the two sides had been steadily diminishing. The stand of the Chinese delegates at Paris was rapidly crystallizing Chinese public opinion in their favor, shaking the foundations of the Sino-Japanese treaties of 1915 and 1918, threatening the downfall of the pro-Japanese elements in the Peking Government. Wang and Koo, sensing their success, soon extended their demands to embrace the complete abrogation of the offensive treaties with Japan, in addition to those with Germany, thus challenging Japan's

[1] On November 21, 1919, Senator Phelan of California wrote Lansing expressing concern over a California newspaper report that the American delegates had favored the Japanese amendment and inquiring if they had actually voted for it. Lansing at once consulted the State Department as to what reply he should make to Phelan. He was advised that "certain facts exist which make the drafting of this letter a very delicate and difficult task." The facts, then enumerated, were those cited in the text above, including the secret despatches to Morris inspired by Hughes's dealings with the Japanese press, as well as a memorandum presented by Ishii to the State Department, March 4, 1919, conveying the formal thanks of the Japanese Government for the support given by the American delegates to the racial equality proposals. Lansing was advised that the minutes of the peace conference "show that the United States at the formal meetings in no way supported the Japanese claims and that it was President Wilson's ruling at the meeting of April 11, 1919, which caused the final rejection of the Japanese proposals," and that Lansing should show Phelan "only such facts as are recorded in the minutes of the L. of N. Commission and allow him to draw his own conclusions from these." C. A. H. to Lansing, November 28; Phelan to Lansing, November 21; Polk to Morris, April 21; Lansing to Phelan, November 26, 1919. Lansing papers.

treaty rights in Manchuria and Mongolia as well as her claims to the German rights in Shantung. In vain Wilson and Lansing endeavored to forestall the inevitable. They proposed that all German possessions outside of Europe be ceded to the Allied and Associated Powers, leaving them, as trustees, to effect a just disposition; that all spheres of influence in China, European as well as Japanese, be abolished. But Japan, supported by England and France, held doggedly to her position, and the ironic situation developed in which Balfour, whose delegation had proved the nemesis of the racial equality amendment, assumed the role of mediator between Japan and the United States. Wilson's hands were tied in a dozen ways: by the secret treaties, by the rapidly growing American opposition that had forced him to seek special recognition of the Monroe Doctrine, by the departure of the Italians from the conference as a result of his appeal to the people of Italy to give up their claim to Fiume.[1] The President at last resigned himself to the choice of rejecting Japan's claim and seeing her delegates quit the conference,[2] or accepting it and having his acceptance become a target for his American enemies.

In despair he took the latter course. The Chinese were offered the alternatives of consenting to the direct cession by Germany to Japan of Kiaochow and the German rights in Shantung or of fulfilling the terms of the treaties of 1915 and 1918 which transferred these rights to Japan in amplified form. For the Chinese it was the frying pan or the fire. They refused to choose, arguing that China's participation in the war had automatically canceled both the German rights and the Sino-Japanese treaties governing

[1] Orlando withdrew from the conference April 24, and the Japanese threatened to follow suit unless they received Shantung. The Italian crisis impelled Wilson to compromise with Japan. Cf. Baker, II, 171 ff.

[2] In this Wilson's Far Eastern experts E. T. Williams and S. K. Hornbeck, as well as Secretary Lansing, differed with him. They believed the Japanese were bluffing and would have signed the Treaty on Wilson's terms. Cf. Baker, II, 258, and Lansing's testimony in the Hearings on the Treaty of Peace with Germany, U. S. Senate Document No. 106, 182.

their disposition. As for the Japanese, they would not hear of any proposal that cast doubt on the validity of these treaties. In particular, they did not wish to relinquish the rights, conferred by the Sino-Japanese Treaty of 1918, of maintaining a military garrison at Tsinan and policing the Kiaochow-Tsinan Railway. They argued that these would be temporary measures, designed merely to ensure law and order during the period of transfer and that they would respect the terms of the Sino-Japanese treaties expressly providing for the restoration of Kiaochow to China. Wilson, mindful of what was happening in Siberia, did not accept the Japanese assurances in good faith. He was fearful that Japan would use Shantung as the springboard for a conquest of all northern China, as both the Chinese delegates and his own advisers insisted that she would. He was equally troubled at having to countenance the subversion of the cardinal principle on which the League was built. The thought that China and Japan would both be members of the League and, in its forum, could ultimately adjust their mutual grievances, gave him small comfort. But the whole world, including his own country, seemed to be turning against the President, and he was beaten.

On April 30 he accepted the Japanese terms, exactly as they were stipulated by the principal Japanese delegates and exactly as they were incorporated in the Versailles Treaty. In view of the claims subsequently raised by the United States, the interchange between the President and the Japanese delegates is of peculiar importance. The terms governing the disposition of Shantung were as follows:

The policy of Japan is to hand back the Shantung Peninsula in full sovereignty to China, retaining only the economic privileges granted to Germany and the right to establish a settlement under the usual conditions at Tsingtao.

The owners of the railway will use special police only to ensure security for traffic. They will be used for no other purpose.

The police force will be composed of Chinese, and such Japanese instructors as the directors of the railway may select will be appointed by the Chinese Government.

If, explained the Japanese delegates, "China failed to carry out the agreements—if, for example, she would not assist in the formation of the police force or the employment of Japanese instructors, the Japanese Government reserved the right to fall back on the Agreements of 1915 and 1918." At this juncture Wilson made his point that in the future China and Japan would both be members of the League of Nations, and consequently, should China not fulfill her obligations Japan might "voluntarily apply for the mediation of the Council of the League of Nations." The difficulty was, Baron Chinda replied, "that President Wilson on his side did not admit the validity of these Agreements, but Japan did." The Japanese delegate "only mentioned the fact so as not to be morally bound not to invoke these Agreements."

President Wilson said that frankly he must insist that nothing he said should be construed as any admission of the recognition of the notes exchanged between Japan and China.[1]

Once more, as in the case of the Lansing-Ishii Agreement, the United States had recoiled from a head-on collision with Japan to take refuge in ambiguity and legal quibbling. Wilson had acknowledged Japan's appropriation of Shantung by accepting the Versailles Treaty but he would not recognize the legality of the appropriation on the basis of the Sino-Japanese treaties of 1915 and 1918. The President drew this fine distinction in the hope of driving into the bilateral negotiations between Tokyo and Peking a wedge for the co-operative policy of Washington and Geneva.

---

[1] Secret Minutes, Council of Four, April 30 meeting. Baker, II, 263-264. See also, *Ibid.*, II, 311-316, Ch. XXXV; LaFargue, Ch. VIII; Miller, *Diary*, VI, 77-251; XVI, 27-28, 55-56; XIX, 171-201; Seymour, IV, 450 ff.; Palmer, Frederick, *Bliss, Peacemaker*, 391, 393-396, 397. Makino had previously cited China's acceptance of a loan of twenty million yen under the terms of the 1918 treaty as grounds for upholding that agreement's validity. Cf. Miller, *Diary*, XIX, 178-179.

He had a poor legal case at best. Every other signatory of the Versailles Treaty had accepted without cavil Japan's *de facto* position in Shantung, as well as the Sino-Japanese agreements that covered it. Wilson's principal collaborators, the British and French, had been openly sympathetic toward it. On May 8, Balfour had written Curzon:

They [the Chinese delegation] could never be got to understand that, whatever might be said of the Treaty of 1915, the Treaty of 1918 between China and Japan was a voluntary transaction between sovereign states, and a transaction which gave important pecuniary benefits to China; nor did they ever adequately realise that by the efforts of Japan and her Allies, China, without the expenditure of a single shilling, or the loss of a single life, had restored to her rights which she could never have recovered for herself.[1]

It is not necessary to recite again the long list of political instruments by which Japan had obtained—in payment for services rendered—British and French sanction for her imperial ambitions. The Anglo-Japanese Alliance was still very much in force. The Japanese delegates had taken care to keep their record clear of even the appearance of accepting Wilson's reservations respecting the Sino-Japanese treaties; and Wilson had compromised his own reservations by himself signing the Versailles Treaty. The moment his decision was made he was thrown back on moral suasion as the only weapon short of force by which he might compel Japan to do that which he had been unable to compel her to do by law: return Shantung to China promptly, and with no strings attached.

News of the Shantung decision was greeted in China with rioting and anti-Japanese boycotts—followed shortly by a resumption of civil war. Wilson's mental anguish was great. Ray Stannard

[1] Balfour to Curzon, May 8, 1919. Dugdale, II, 245. Clemenceau was if anything more unsympathetic toward the complaining Chinese delegates, informing them bluntly "that they must either sign the Treaty with the intention of abiding by it or not sign." Miller, *Diary*, XVI, 458.

Baker saw him a few hours after the fateful meeting on April 30 and together they held a gloomy *post-mortem*. The President "said he had been unable to sleep the night before for thinking of it," Baker recorded.

Anything he might do was wrong. He said the settlement was the best that could be had out of a dirty past. . . . The only hope was to keep the world together, get the League of Nations with Japan in it and then try to secure justice for the Chinese not only as regarding Japan but England, France, Russia, all of whom had concessions in China. . . . He knew his decision would be unpopular in America, that the Chinese would be bitterly disappointed, that the Japanese would feel triumphant, that he would be accused of violating his own principles, but, nevertheless, he *must* work for world order and organization against anarchy and a return to the old militarism.[1]

The President laid much public emphasis on Japan's promise to restore Shantung "in full sovereignty" to China, and took care to point out that Japan would retain "only such rights as an economic concessionaire as are possessed by one or two other great powers and are only too common in China, and the whole future relationship between the two countries falls at once under the guarantee of the League of Nations of territorial integrity and political independence." [2]

In the United States, as Wilson had foreseen, the "irreconcilables" seized on the Shantung award as one of the chief reasons for rejecting the League and the Versailles Treaty.[3] "Indignation, discouragement and despair are expressed throughout China," cabled Reinsch from Peking, "anti-Japanese boycotts are being started in many places. . . . Japanese, triumphant, assert predominance in China recognized, Great Britain and France submis-

[1] Baker, II, 266.
[2] Baker, III, 315-316.
[3] Cf. Fleming, D. F., *The United States and the League of Nations*, esp. 201-203, 266, 288, 299, 326-328, 426, 445.

sive, United States must admit opposition futile." [1] The Japanese were mistaken. Their predominance in China had not been recognized, as events were speedily to prove. For although England and France were submissive, the very attitude of the "irreconcilables" showed that the United States was far from admitting "opposition futile."

To Secretary Lansing the Shantung award was "a complete surrender to Japan . . . a calamity and an abandonment of principle." [2] "Baron Makino came to see me at my request," he noted on the day the Versailles Treaty was signed, "& I spent ¾ hr. trying to persuade him to make a public statement in re Shantung, as I was fearful unless he did China would refuse to sign the treaty.—Treaty of Peace signed at 3 P.M. Chinese delegates not present." [3] Here was the clue to American strategy for the next three years. The old technique of John Hay had been revived. The United States would attempt by the use of bluff, exhortation and publicity to compel Japan to make good her promise to restore Shantung to China. Lansing had initiated a campaign that was to last until 1922. Before leaving Paris, with anti-Japanese boycotts spreading throughout China, and in the face of a seething Japanese press that depicted the United States as the champion of racial discrimination and the dog in the Shantung manger, the American delegates gave their Chinese colleagues what encouragement they could. They sent word to Peking and Tokyo that they were trying hard to induce Makino and Chinda to make a "formal open declaration defining their position" on Shantung.[4] They advised the Chinese to have no

[1] Reinsch to Acting Secretary of State, May 16, 1919. *For. Rel.*, 1919, I, 691.

[2] Lansing date book, April 30, 1919. Lansing papers.

[3] *Ibid.*, June 28, 1919. China did not sign the Versailles Treaty. She gained membership in the League by signing the Treaty of St. Germain with Austria, September 10, 1919.

[4] Hornbeck to Secretary of State, Washington, July 3, 1919. Lansing papers. For vivid descriptions of the attitude toward the United States of the Japanese press and people, see *For. Rel.*, 1919, I, 689-724.

independent dealings with Japan, and they stressed their reliance on the consortium "as an instrument for the protection of China's interests as well as those of the United States." [1]

Whatever the abstract justice of the situation, the Japanese people were correct in viewing the United States as their government's principal and most effective opponent in China, in Siberia, in the entire Pacific region. Everywhere the lines were being drawn more rigidly. Immigration troubles were increasing in severity. The Siberian expeditionary forces were at loggerheads. Naval rivalry loomed menacingly ahead. Wilson had lodged claims to special rights on the island of Yap. The Department of State was marshaling the consortium groups against independent Japanese loans. There was no prospect of compromise. On July 25 Lansing (now returned to Washington) summoned the Japanese Chargé d'Affaires to the State Department and delivered an ultimatum to him. "Told him Pres. felt compelled to make public Japanese promises in re Shantung unless Jap. Govt. did it," was the Secretary's terse notation. "He asked how soon. Told him no later than Tues." [2] Two days later, on Wilson's orders, he warned the Japanese Chargé that "negotiations on basis of agreements of 1915 & 1918 would not be tolerated." [3] On August 2 the Japanese Foreign Minister made a public statement of Japan's intentions, renewing the promise made at Paris to restore Shantung in full sovereignty to China as soon as Japan had ratified the Versailles Treaty, and to withdraw all Japanese troops from the province as soon as arrangements for the transfer had been completed. [4] But Lansing took exception to two seemingly innocuous references in the statement to the Sino-Japanese

---

[1] Hornbeck to Lansing, July 3, 1919. Lansing papers.

[2] Lansing date book, July 25, 1919. Lansing papers. This controverts the statement of Assistant Secretary of State Long that "there was no time limit set within which any action should be taken." See his memorandum of August 3, 1919, *For. Rel.*, 1919, I, 717. Also that of July 29, *Ibid.*, 716-717.

[3] Lansing date book, July 27, 1919.

[4] Text of statement, which Lansing received August 3, is printed in *For. Rel.*, 1919, I, 718.

treaty of 1915.[1] He felt obliged to remind the Japanese Foreign Minister "that nothing I agreed to must be construed as an acquiescence on the part of the Government of the United States in the policy of the notes exchanged between China and Japan in 1915 and 1918" and that the Japanese had themselves promised that "only in case China failed to co-operate fully in carrying out the policy outlined in the statement of Baron Makino and Viscount Chinda" were the agreements to be invoked.[2]

In reply the Japanese Government reaffirmed its entire willingness to restore the disputed province as soon as the three interested parties—China, Japan and Germany—had ratified the Versailles Treaty. But it categorically refused to subscribe to Lansing's interpretation of the 1915 and 1918 treaties. It was from these very contracts that the legal obligation to return Shantung to China originated, the Japanese Government argued.

The question now raised by the Secretary of State seems further to rest on the presumption that it was admitted by the Japanese delegation in Paris that the validity of the Sino-Japanese arrangements of 1915 and 1918 was at least questioned. Careful research of the reports so far received in Tokio on the proceedings of the Paris Conference has failed to disclose anything which indicates such an admission on the part of the Japanese delegation. On the contrary, Viscount Chinda at the close of the discussion on the Shantung clauses on the 30th of April defined the position of Japan in the matter "to remove any moral obligation on behalf of Japan not to invoke the agreements in question." [3]

---

[1] These were: "At the same time abiding faithfully by pledge which she gave China in 1915," a clause prefacing the renewed Japanese promise to restore Shantung as soon as the Versailles Treaty had been ratified, and the concluding sentence of the statement, which read, "Japanese Government has moreover under contemplation proposals for establishment at Tsingtau of general foreign settlement instead of exclusive Japanese settlement which by agreement of 1915 with China they are entitled to claim." *For. Rel.*, 1919, I, *loc. cit.*

[2] Lansing to Morris, August 6, 1919. *Ibid.*, 719.

[3] Memorandum first read aloud and then presented to Lansing by Japanese Chargé Debuchi, August 22, 1919. *For. Rel.*, 1919, I, 877-878. Copy in Lansing papers.

Lansing's rebuttal repeated all the arguments that China and the United States had used against Japan at Paris:

The Government of the United States had no doubt that the representatives of the Japanese Government at Paris clearly understood that a condition precedent to the assent of the President to Articles 156, 157 and 158 of the Treaty of Versailles was that the Japanese Government should agree that the Sino-Japanese Agreements of 1915 and 1918 should not be relied upon or referred to in the negotiations for the return to China of Kiao-chau and the German rights as dealt with in the Japanese statement to the Council of the Allied and Associated Governments at Paris.

The President, after careful consideration of the Japanese memorandum, directs the Secretary of State to say that he is deeply concerned that the Japanese Government have without doubt unintentionally declared a policy contrary to the understanding reached with the Japanese delegates at Paris; that during the conferences of the Council of the Principal Allied and Associated Governments Baron Makino and Viscount Chinda showed their willingness to accept the condition precedent by stating that their Government would not appeal to the Agreements of 1915 and 1918 in negotiating with China *unless the latter refused to negotiate under Articles 156, 157 and 158 of the Treaty;* and that the assent of the President to those Articles was given because he believed that the Japanese Government acting through their accredited delegates understood and agreed to disregard the Agreements of 1915 and 1918 in their negotiations with the Chinese Government relative to Kiao-chau in carrying out the agreement reached at Paris.[1]

The deadlock of April 30 remained unbroken. Not with all the ingenious syllogisms they propounded could Lansing and Wilson prevail on Japan to resign her right to settle the Shantung affair independently with China. They had not been able to undermine the legality of that right at Paris, and now, indeed, they admitted as much. In Lansing's own words the President had understood that Japan would not appeal to the treaties of 1915 and 1918 with

[1] Memorandum, Secretary of State to Japanese Chargé, August 27, 1919. *For. Rel.*, 1919, I, 720-722. Copy in Lansing papers. Italics inserted.

China "unless the latter refused to negotiate under Articles 156, 157 and 158 of the Treaty." Not only was China refusing to negotiate under the specified articles, but she had refused to ratify the Versailles Treaty at all, and was accompanying her refusal with anti-Japanese boycotts.[1] Hence, on President Wilson's own admission, the condition on which Japan could invoke the controverted treaties had become a fact. It was a vicious circle. The more strenuously Wilson assailed Japan's position, the more China was encouraged to take the very steps that rendered that position legally unassailable. Great Britain and France had accepted it as such from the beginning. Japan was not impressed by Wilson's threats to withdraw his support from the Shantung articles of the Versailles Treaty, to take the matter up at Paris, to question the validity of the 1915 and 1918 treaties.[2] The most the President and the Secretary of State could do was to keep on asking Japan to give them an assurance which Japan had not given and consistently refused to give, under all the moral pressure that they could bring to bear.

Manifestly it was part of Japan's program to exact from China —preferably through bilateral negotiations—the most extensive rights and privileges possible before relinquishing her hold on Shantung. By the same token China, realizing the danger of being left alone to the tender mercies of Japan, was doing everything in her power to make the United States her lawyer. Wilson was eager to assume this role, but could not even obtain a hearing, let alone

[1] It would be more accurate to say that the ruling faction at Peking was restrained from dealing directly with Japan because of the extreme popular opposition to this course, of which opposition the boycotts were a conspicuous manifestation. Cf. Tenney to Colby, June 1, 1920. *For. Rel.*, 1920, I, 816. On May 22, 1920, the Chinese Foreign Minister informed the Japanese Foreign Minister that China "has not been in a position to enter into direct negotiations with your Excellency's Government concerning Tsingtau in accordance with the terms of the German treaty" because 1) China had not signed the Versailles Treaty and 2) China was apprehensive "of the great popular excitement on the part of the people of this nation in reference to this question." *Ibid.*, 816-818.

[2] *For. Rel.*, 1919, I, 721.

fill a jury. So the three litigants stalled and dodged. By October Minister Reinsch, always in the vanguard of China's defenders, was contending that because they "are not economic rights but have political character and conflict with equal opportunity" the United States should prevent Japan from retaining the "railway, harbor and mining preference" formerly enjoyed by Germany in Shantung.[1] Reinsch had gone beyond demanding fulfillment of the obligation to restore Shantung to the political sovereignty of China, asking in effect that Japan be made the first object of a crusade for the abolition of spheres of influence in China—the very thing that France and Great Britain had refused so much as to consider at Paris.

"The Chinese are in a panic realizing that direct negotiations will lead to the strengthening of Japan's hold on Shantung," wired the American Chargé at Peking in January. "They would like to refer the matter to the League of Nations but hesitate to do so unless the United States Government is to be represented in the League of Nations. As soon as the ratification of the treaty by the Senate is accomplished I advise that the United States Government insist upon the reference of the Shantung question to the League of Nations.[2]

Here was another obstacle to the achievement of Wilson's Far Eastern objectives. The Senate had already voted down the Versailles Treaty (November 19, 1919) and would finally reject it on March 19, 1920. With the most influential League members committed by treaty, and openly sympathetic, to Japan, and with the world astounded by America's apostasy from the League, the chances of using that body as an instrument of American policy in the Far East were reduced to the vanishing point. To confound this confusion, the Shantung affair was being used by the American opponents of the League as a good reason for keeping the United States out of it. Japan repeatedly professed her readiness to enter

[1] Reinsch to Lansing, October 10, 1919. Lansing papers.
[2] Tenney to Lansing, January 22, 1920. *For. Rel.*, 1920, I, 814.

negotiations with China as soon as the latter should constitute a police force to replace the Japanese troops guarding the Kiaochow-Tsinan Railway. China demanded the withdrawal of these troops as a condition precedent to negotiation. The American community in China carried its agitations against Japan to a point embarrassing to the State Department.[1] But Japanese troops remained in Shantung, as they did in Manchuria, Siberia and Sakhalin. The diplomatic offensive against Japanese expansion appeared to be making little progress.

To prejudice further its chances of success, the United States now added to, instead of lessened, the desiderata it was seeking from Japan. On May 7, 1919, the Council of Four, with Wilson participating, had mandated to Japan the German islands in the Pacific north of the equator. Among these, lying athwart the path from the Hawaiians to the Philippines *via* Wake and Guam, was the island of Yap. Until his attention was drawn to it by his naval and communications experts at Paris, President Wilson, like most of his countrymen, had never heard of the island.[2] The representations of his experts led him to consider its strategic and com-

[1] The protests against the Japanese in Shantung of such groups as the American Chamber of Commerce of China, the American University Club of China, the Anglo-American Association of Peking and various missionary societies became, during 1919, a serious issue in Japanese-American relations. "The Department has observed with some feeling of embarrassment the fact that Americans in China are being accused of interfering in political questions in that country," wired the Secretary of State to the American Chargé at Peking (December 26, 1919). "While the Department believes that Americans have, as a general rule, been fairly careful as to their conduct under the rather trying circumstances which have occasionally existed, some little color has been given to such reports through facts which have come to the attention of the Department recently, relative to the circulation of requests for resolutions by American organizations in China dealing with questions of a political nature which concern only the Chinese Government and the Government of the United States." *For. Rel.*, 1919, I, 723. Cf. *Ibid.*, 686-723.

[2] So the President admitted to the Senate Committee on Foreign Relations, August 19, 1919. U. S. Senate Document No. 106, 66th Congress, 1st Sess., *Hearings on the Treaty of Peace with Germany*, Vol. 10, 505-506.

mercial value to the United States. The entire mandate of which
Yap was a part would, in the hands of a naval rival, menace the
security of the Philippines. This made the internationalization of
any particular portion of the mandate an object of American strategic interest. As an important center for telegraph cable distribution Yap would provide whoever held it the economic and
political influence ensuing from possession of ultimate powers of
censorship over news destined for, or emanating from, China, the
Philippines and the Dutch East Indies.[1] On three recorded occasions prior to the decision of May 7, therefore, Wilson and Lansing had expressed the opinion that the control of Yap should be
international.[2] Their expressions had taken the form of indefinite,
oral reservations, which none of the other parties to the decision
awarding the German islands to Japan had accepted as conditions
precedent to the award. Wilson had then concurred in the award
and signed the Versailles Treaty; and the United States had thereupon rejected membership in the League of Nations, the body
to which the supervision of mandates had been entrusted.[3] In
other words, the United States found itself in the same position
with respect to Yap as that which it had been forced into with
respect to Shantung. On August 19, 1919, Wilson told the Senate
Committee on Foreign Relations that he had "made the point that
the disposition, or rather the control, of that island should be
reserved" for a future conference on international electrical com-

[1] *Ibid.*

[2] On April 21, reporting a conversation with the Japanese delegates of that
morning, Wilson stated that "it had been understood that Japan was to have a
mandate for the islands in the North Pacific although he had made a reserve in
the case of the island of Yap which he himself considered should be international." At a meeting of the Foreign Ministers of April 30, Lansing expressed
the same view. Wilson reiterated it on May 1 and he may have done so again
on May 6. According to the minutes of the meeting, Yap was not discussed in
connection with the decision of May 7. Baker, II, 247; *For. Rel.*, 1921, II, 265-
268.

[3] See the careful review of evidence in the despatches relating to the Yap
Island Controversy, *For. Rel.*, 1921, II, 263-287.

munications, provision for which had been made at Paris and in which the United States was scheduled to take part.[1]

No more was heard of the matter until the spring of 1920, when the State Department started to organize the projected conference. Then Yap was mentioned with particular solicitude by the Dutch Government, apprehensive of Japanese control of the important cable line from San Francisco, *via* Yap, to the Netherlands Indies.[2] The Chinese Government was likewise apprehensive, urging the Department of State that it "would be quite satisfied to see the Yap-Shanghai cable allocated to the American Government but that it would be a great disappointment to China if the Japanese were to obtain this cable inasmuch as it would be another link in the efforts of Japan to entirely control the communication service into and out of China."[3] Yap had also become a pawn in the international struggle for cable monopolies in which Great Britain and the United States were acrimonious competitors, and the theater of which was world wide.[4]

[1] U. S. Senate Doc. No. 106, 66th Cong., 1st Sess., Vol. 10, 506 ff.; *For. Rel.*, 1921, II, 267.

[2] "The Netherlands Minister wishes to emphasize how vitally important it is, especially in view of the rapidly growing trade between the United States and the Netherlands East Indies, that the above-mentioned direct cable connection between these countries is only controlled by the two countries and that the mandate of Yap will not be given to a third nation." Netherlands Legation to Department of State, March 25, 1920. See also Netherlands Chargé to Secretary of State with enclosed memorandum, October 11, 1920. *For. Rel.*, 1920, I, 115-116, 132-134.

[3] Memorandum of Conversation with Chinese Counselor of Legation by Assistant Chief of Far Eastern Division, August 9, 1920. *For. Rel.*, 1920, I, 126-127. Cf. other despatches relating to International Conference on Electrical Communications. *Ibid.*, 107-168.

[4] "It is a matter of common knowledge that the highly efficient cable system of Great Britain is so closely co-ordinated with the diplomatic and commercial interests of that country that no message which might be of value either to the British foreign office or to the British Board of Trade is assured of secrecy if at any point in its journey it passed over a British line." State Department Memorandum for use of American delegates to Communications Conference, by Elihu Root, Jr., U. S. Senate, Committee on Interstate Commerce. Cable-landing licenses; hearings before a sub-committee on Senate bill 4301 (December 15, 1920-Janu-

A preliminary conference on international electrical communications was held at Washington, October 8 to December 14, 1920.[1] The preparation of the agenda as well as the opening sessions of the conference reawakened American interest in Yap and led the Department of State to revive the claims that Wilson had raised at Paris. This it did November 9, 1920, a year and a half after the Council of Four had mandated the German islands to Japan.[2]

The British Government promptly rejected the Department's contentions, pointing out that the minutes of the Council of Four contained no record that Yap had been excluded from the Japanese mandate, and that the Council of the League of Nations had formally approved that mandate. The Foreign Office saw no reason for questioning Japan's right to control the island as sole mandatory.[3] Similar replies were received from France and Japan. Italy was non-committal. Secretary Colby, who succeeded Lansing in the closing year of the Wilson Administration, and Secretary Hughes who took office with Harding in 1921 exhausted their abundant supply of legal talents in a protracted but vain effort to rehabilitate Wilson's reservations. They held that knowledge of the President's desires enjoined on the other parties to the controverted decision the same responsibilities as a condition precedent; that the award of the German islands to Japan had not expressly included Yap; that its rejection of the Versailles Treaty and de-

ary 11, 1921), 66th Congress, 3rd Session, 87; Tribolet, L. B., *The International Aspects of Electrical Communications in the Pacific Area,* 5. Tribolet suggests that Great Britain's unwillingness to support the American claims respecting Yap was due to her desire to prevent American inroads on her cable monopoly in the Pacific and the Far East, and that therefore she followed the divide and rule tactics of supporting the claims of Japan. Cf. *Ibid.,* esp. 265 ff.

[1] *For. Rel.,* 1920, I, 132-168.

[2] Ambassador Davis was instructed to remind the British Government that the United States clearly understood that Yap had not been included in the Japanese mandate on May 7, 1919, and hence reserved the right to share in the final disposition of the island. Colby to Davis, November 9, 1920. *For. Rel.,* 1921, II, 263.

[3] Davis to Colby, November 17, 1920. *Ibid.,* 263-264.

faulted membership in the League did not preclude the right of the United States to share in disposing of the spoils of a war that it had played such a decisive part in winning. But Japan was not swayed. The most France would concede was the right of the United States to raise and settle the issue directly with Japan. Great Britain merely fell back on her secret wartime treaty with Japan and offered nothing.[1]

Thus was a controversy over the status of a remote island in the western Pacific added to the unfinished business of the peace conference and the many issues—including immigration and an impending naval race—that hung fire between the United States and Japan. Under the impact of the war the United States had embarked on an ambitious attempt to stem the tide of Japanese empire. Expectations that had governed the American commitment to that program had failed to materialize. The international order, co-operation, security that Wilson had counted on had proved illusory. The balance of power that had existed in the Far East since the nineteenth century had collapsed. Political circumstances in Europe and America had left the United States to confront Japan—alone. Would the program undertaken by Wilson be revised or would another attempt be made to realize the international conditions he had envisaged when he undertook it?

[1] *For. Rel.*, 1921, II, 263-287. See also I, esp. 14-15, 52, 88, 90-93, 95, 923, 966-967.

# VII. From Paris to Washington

TO the partisans of Woodrow Wilson in 1920 it seemed as though isolationism had destroyed the last faint hopes of peace and enlightenment that had been salvaged from the Paris Conference. On March 19 the Senate had for the second time, and finally, rejected the Versailles Treaty. The President's determination to make the election of 1920 a "solemn referendum" on American membership in the League of Nations brought further disappointment. His party was routed by an opposition that beclouded the issue with the rhetorical mirage of "normalcy." Wilson's final attempt to enlist the United States in the League cost him his life. Never was the personal defeat of a statesman more overwhelming.

For the nation as a whole, however, the triumph of isolationism was more apparent than real. It is true that the election of Harding confirmed American abstention from the international government created at Paris. Once again, in the tradition of the Farewell Address and the Monroe Doctrine, the United States had shown its reluctance to take part in political affairs pertaining strictly to Europe proper. But this did not mean the end of American participation in European politics in other regions, or in world politics in general. Just as in 1898 Mahan had believed abstention from Europe compatible with co-operation in the Far East, so the very individuals who had led the attack on the Versailles Treaty, and repudiated Wilson's labors at Paris, now proceeded to steal his thunder and use it in Eastern Asia. The principles that Wilson had applied to Europe and the world at large they continued to apply, with redoubled energy, to China and Japan. Once again the United States did not hesitate to enter by the back door political provinces it refused to enter by the front door.

269

It was the Harding Administration that accomplished the international codification of America's Far Eastern policy in treaties sanctioned not by the use of force to be sure, but by the good faith of the signatories reinforced by the watchful moral guardianship of the United States. As we have suggested, the Washington Conference of 1921-1922 was the fourth move in the diplomatic campaign to arrest Japanese expansion, the other three being participation in the Siberian expedition, organization of the new banking consortium and the restoration of Shantung to China. If, by dividing its responsibilities with the co-signatories of the Washington Treaties, the United States can be said to have lightened its share of an onerous burden, and perhaps even paved the way for a strategic retreat from political involvement in the Far East, that does not seem to have been the spirit in which the treaties were written. Neither was it the spirit in which they were to be defended when put to the test.

Like the Monroe Doctrine and the open door notes, the Treaties of Washington were as much British as American in origin. Great Britain had lost much of her life blood in the World War. Her recuperation would be slow. Meantime her vast imperial interests, augmented by her conquest of the German colonies, lay exposed not only to the dangers of a fresh upheaval in Europe, but also to the possible designs of two great military and naval powers that had been invigorated rather than exhausted by the war. One of these was England's ally, Japan. The other was the United States.

Japan had far overreached the metes and bounds prescribed by the Anglo-Japanese Alliance. While the war tied her ally's hands, she had not scrupled to attack Britain's favored economic position in China or to exact high prices for meager contributions to the Allied cause. Supported by the third largest naval force in the world, Japan's expansionist policies collided sharply with British interests throughout Eastern Asia and the Pacific. As for the United States, the war had called into being an American navy that threatened to eclipse Great Britain's. In the straitened financial circumstances in which the war had left her, England could ill afford to hold up her end in an Anglo-American naval race. Naval supremacy had become such a fetish to her that she would not have relinquished it without a struggle to any power, unless first assured of an adequate substitute. Clearly, eliminating the possibility of a naval race with America and erecting new political barriers to Japanese imperialism were two of the most exigent tasks confronting British diplomacy.

By a not unusual coincidence, the United States faced the same problems. We have already observed the extent to which it was involved with Japan over Siberia, Shantung, Yap and the consortium. The immigration issue was growing daily more serious. War talk was in the air. At every point Washington and Tokyo were deadlocked. Moreover, the war had proved a powerful stimulus to the construction of an American navy "second to none." In 1914 the Panama Canal had been opened to navigation. Strategists had advocated the digging of the canal as a substitute for the maintenance of two large fleets separated by the Isthmus. The quick access from coast to coast, they had argued, would enable one fleet to do the work of two. No sooner was it completed, however, than this argument had given place to one in favor of a larger navy to protect the canal.

If the canal helped to make the United States more acutely conscious of its naval destinies, the British blockade and German submarines completed the lesson. President Wilson's demand for "incomparably the most adequate navy in the world" found ready response in the passage of the Naval Appropriation Act of 1916. If the construction schedules fixed by this act had been completed the American navy would at least have equaled, and probably outstripped, the British by 1924.[1]

[1] Buell, R. L., *The Washington Conference*, 139-144. See also Bywater, H., *Sea Power in the Pacific*, 10 ff.

The United States had emerged from the war the foremost economic power in the world. Had it wished to make itself the foremost naval power as well it could certainly have done so. But the forces impelling it toward that goal were balanced, in fact canceled, by other considerations. Though better able to bear it than any other nation, the United States had already incurred a war debt of such vast dimensions that the thought of adding to it the costs of an armaments race gave pause to the leaders of both political parties. American defection from the League did not mean the complete subversion of the ideas for which the American people believed they had been fighting. Whatever their attitude toward membership in the League, the desire to contribute to the prevention of another world war cut across all party lines. Only as to the means of making that contribution were there irreconcilable differences of opinion. Even here, there was surprising unanimity on one of Woodrow Wilson's major principles. Many of President Harding's most influential supporters including Charles E. Hughes, his future Secretary of State, agreed with their Democratic opponents that competition in armaments had been one of the chief causes of the World War, and that the United States should now take the lead in promoting universal disarmament.[1]

The Republican platform of 1920 included a plank (drafted by Elihu Root) repudiating the League and all its works, but espousing the principle of "agreement among nations to preserve the peace of the world." This was somewhat more explicitly defined as "an international association . . . based upon justice . . . and methods which shall maintain the rule of public right by development of law and the decision of impartial courts, and which shall secure instant and general conference whenever peace shall be

[1] Republican elder statesmen such as Taft, Hughes, Root, Stimson, and Wickersham had, in one way or another, opposed the "irreconcilables" (for whom Harding had been a spokesman) and favored American membership in the League under a revised covenant. So had Herbert Hoover. For the compromise between these and the Lodge group effected at the Republican Convention, see Fleming, D. F., *The United States and the League of Nations*, Chs. XII and XVIII.

threatened by political action, so that the nations pledged to do and insist upon what is just and fair may exercise their influence and power for the prevention of war." [1]

After a campaign memorable for its straddling and evasiveness, President Harding, who as a senator had identified himself with the "irreconcilables," proclaimed in his inaugural address "the wisdom of the inherited policy of non-involvement in Old World affairs." The United States, he declared, could have "no part in directing the destinies of the Old World," could "enter into no political commitments, nor assume any economic obligations or subject our decisions to any other than our own authority." Yet the United States wished to do its part "in making offensive warfare so hateful that Governments and peoples who resort to it must prove the righteousness of their cause or stand as outlaws before the bar of civilization." [2] We shall see in a moment how these thoughts led to the conception of an international conference on the limitation of armaments, to which the Root plank's suggestion of "instant and general conference whenever peace shall be threatened" may have been one of the earliest references. Suffice it here to observe that the obvious economic arguments against a naval race had been supplemented, in the United States, by a belief in international co-operation that proved strong enough to survive the partisan conflict over membership in the League of Nations.

World politics furnished perhaps the decisive argument against attempting to outbuild the British navy. The Anglo-Japanese Alliance was still in effect. Should the American building program drive these two powers to make common cause against the United States before the program could be completed, or should it merely conduce to Anglo-Japanese political solidarity in the Far East, it would be defeating its purpose. In short, the United States, like Great Britain, was groping for diplomatic means of restraining

[1] Fleming, 453.
[2] Harding, Inaugural Address, New York *Times*, March 5, 1921.

Japan, promoting a universal reduction of naval armaments and preserving the peace of the world. As in the case of the open door notes (and likewise the Monroe Doctrine) the two powers were proceeding along parallel paths that were to end in what seemed a common policy.

The United States was first led toward this diplomatic *rendez-vous* by its dislike of the Anglo-Japanese Alliance. The alliance had long been obnoxious to Washington not only because of the aid and comfort it gave to Japanese imperialists, but also because it legally bound Great Britain to go to war against the United States in the event that Japan should do so. It is true that in the renewal treaty of 1911, Great Britain had stripped the alliance of its belligerent obligations *vis-à-vis* a third power with which either ally might conclude a treaty of general arbitration. But as we have seen, the Anglo-American arbitration treaty for which special provision had thus been made was rejected by the United States Senate.[1] The legal exemption of the United States from the applicability of the alliance was short-lived.

In 1914 Great Britain and the United States concluded a treaty which was ratified by the Senate. This was one of the Bryan Peace Commission Treaties, establishing a permanent international commission to which all disputes that could not be settled by diplomacy should be "referred for investigation and report." The commission was to be given a year to complete its investigation and make its report, during which time the two signatories agreed "not to declare war or begin hostilities." Each, however, reserved the right of independent action once the report was rendered.[2] The Peace Commission Treaty was not a general arbitration agreement of the type provided for in the revised terms of the Anglo-

[1] Cf. above, Ch. IV, p. 168.

[2] The treaty was negotiated and signed by Secretary Bryan and Ambassador Spring-Rice in Washington, September 15, ratified by the Senate ten days later and proclaimed November 11, 1914. In addition to those cited above the treaty contained provisions for appointing members of the international commission, defining the commission's powers, allowing for existing bilateral arbitration

Japanese Alliance. "Investigation and report," circumscribed by the ultimate reservation of the right of independent action, was not arbitration. England's legal obligations to Japan remained a dubious quantity to Washington.

The American involvement with Japan at the end of the war rendered them still more dubious. The experience with the British in Siberia and at Paris strengthened the conviction that the alliance afforded Japan an effective political shield for her designs on the continent of Asia. When, therefore, the first rumors of negotiations for the renewal of the alliance reached Washington, the Department of State showed immediate interest, instructing Ambassador Davis in London to keep it "fully advised . . . in regard to the actual course of negotiations and in regard to the general feeling of the country on that subject.

The Department desires particularly to learn whether there is on the part of Great Britain a tendency to broaden or restrict the recognition of Japan's special interests in eastern Asia or otherwise to modify the scope or purport of the Treaty of Alliance as signed in 1911.

Is there in your opinion any ground for the supposition that Great Britain proposes to avail itself of the negotiations on this subject in order to urge upon Japan the relinquishment of claims to such special interests in China as would warrant the exclusion of Manchuria and Mongolia from the operation of the proposed consortium? [1]

It would appear from this early inquiry on the subject that Washington was more perturbed over the effects of the alliance on the Far Eastern policy of the United States than over the possibility that it might lead to embroilment with England.

Early in the spring of 1920 Anglo-Japanese negotiations were again rumored, causing the State Department to make further in-

agreements between and among the United States and the British Dominions. Its duration was fixed at five years. For full text see *For. Rel.*, 1914, 304-307. The arbitration agreement between the United States and Japan concluded in 1908 (cf. p. 128, above) was renewed for five years in 1913. *Ibid.*, 424-426.

[1] Phillips to Davis, October 2, 1919. *For. Rel.*, 1920, II, 679.

quiries in London.[1] By May the Department believed the renewal of the alliance likely, but was hopeful "that in making this renewal Great Britain will insist upon including in the terms of the Alliance such provisions as shall safeguard the principle of equal opportunity in China and the rights of China more effectively." The Department also hoped "that it will be indicated that the Alliance is not aimed at America." Ambassador Davis was instructed to watch for an opportunity to bring to the attention of the British Foreign Office two suggested modifications of the alliance "which would be a great aid to Anglo-American coöperation in the Far East and be very pleasing to American public opinion." These were:

A. To place in the preamble which states the respective interests of Great Britain and Japan in the Far East a clause including the substance of the final paragraph of the notes exchanged between Secretary Lansing and Ambassador Ishii which is as follows:
"They mutually declare that they are opposed to the acquisition by any Government of any special rights or privileges that would affect the independence or territorial integrity of China or that would deny to any subjects or citizens of any country the full enjoyment of equal opportunity in the commerce and industry of China."

B. To enlarge the exception found in article IV of the Anglo-Japanese Alliance so that it will include the Treaty for the Advancement of Peace, known as the Bryan Treaty, which was concluded between the United States and Great Britain on September 15, 1914.

Mr. Davis's instructions are vividly revealing of the American motives behind the convocation of the Washington Conference. The inclusion of Article IV[2] in the existing alliance, they went on to explain, had been "due to the fact that the negotiation of the Knox Treaty of General Arbitration was pending at the time, and it was intended by the provisions of article IV to remove the

[1] *For. Rel.*, 1920, II, 679-680.
[2] Removing the belligerent obligations of the alliance toward any third power with which either ally might conclude a general arbitration agreement.

United States from the application of the Alliance. The Knox Treaty having failed of ratification, due to the action of the United States Senate, the purpose for which the exception was made would be fulfilled if its provisions were so extended as to include the treaty of September 15, 1914.

"The suggestion might also be made, although in a less positive way, that since the orientation of Japan's foreign policy is seemingly unstable, a limitation of five years upon the duration of the agreement might well be made again, instead of ten years, so that the British Government might have a less remote chance to influence the course of Japan's actions in the Far East.

"The consortium negotiations have revealed, it is felt, a common purpose held by America and Great Britain to resist the trend toward extending to China policies of special interests which tend to infringe upon Chinese rights and upon the Open Door policy. We hope that sentiment in Great Britain will respond to the proposal that in the Anglo-Japanese Alliance the principles which form the basis of the existing sympathetic Anglo-American co-operation should be more explicitly recognized." [1]

The tone of this despatch again suggests that the American mistrust of the alliance centered on its relation to Japanese imperialism rather than on the possibility that it might involve the United States in war with England.

The impression is heightened by the British response to these early American overtures. By June 7 Ambassador Davis had found an opportunity to submit the State Department's suggestions to the Foreign Office, which assured him that they would receive full consideration and that "in any redrafting of the Anglo-Japanese Treaty of Alliance it will be made quite clear that the Alliance is not aimed at the United States." [2] In spite of persistent rumors, it

[1] Polk to Davis, May 10, 1920. *For. Rel.*, 1920, II, 680-681. The above despatch is quoted verbatim with the exception of the few introductory and explanatory sentences inserted, and the omission of a few non-essential phrases of the despatch of similar character.

[2] Davis to Secretary of State, June 7, 1920. *Ibid.*, 682.

was impossible to determine how far Anglo-Japanese negotiations had yet proceeded, or even if they had begun at all. On July 8 Prime Minister Bonar Law replied rather evasively to parliamentary questions on the subject, stating first that negotiations were "not in progress" and then that they were "not being continued." [1] It is probable that *pourparlers* had been held but had been discontinued at least partially in deference to American opinion. For on July 8 Foreign Minister Curzon and Japanese Ambassador Chinda signed and communicated to the League of Nations the following agreement:

> The Governments of Japan and Great Britain have come to the conclusion that the Anglo-Japanese Agreement of July 13th, 1911, now existing between their two countries, though in harmony with the spirit of the Covenant of the League of Nations, is not entirely consistent with the letter of that Covenant, which both Governments earnestly desire to respect. They accordingly have the honor jointly to inform the League that they recognize the principle that if the said agreement be continued after July, 1921, it must be in a form not inconsistent with that Covenant. [2]

Since the League Covenant embodied all of the principles of the American Far Eastern policy, and since it prohibited exclusive pacts involving military obligations, the Curzon-Chinda agreement may reasonably be considered a step toward meeting the expressed American objections to the alliance.

It was followed, during 1920 and 1921, by further steps in the same direction. Presumably in response to continued pressure from Washington, both British and Japanese statesmen came forward with reassuring interpretations of the extent of Great Britain's obligations in case of a Japanese-American war. The London *Times*, quasi-official mouthpiece of the British Government, Lord

---

[1] Skinner to Secretary of State, July 10, 1920. *For. Rel.*, 1920, II, 685.

[2] Bell to Secretary of State, July 26, 1920. *Ibid.*, 685-686. Text of agreement, Carnegie Endowment for International Peace, Division of International Law, *Treaties and Agreements with and Concerning China*, 1919-1929, 29.

Grey, former British Foreign Minister, Baron Uchida, Japanese
Foreign Minister, and the Japanese Ambassadors to both London
and Washington all made statements on the subject.  The *Times*
asserted categorically that shortly after its negotiation, Great Britain had notified Japan that she considered the Bryan Peace Commission Treaty a general arbitration agreement within the meaning
of article IV of the alliance.[1] Baron Uchida intimated the same
thing to the Japanese Diet on February 4, 1921, as did Lord
Grey in a public address on February 22.[2]

On June 30 the Japanese Ambassador in Washington read a
carefully prepared statement to Secretary Hughes pointing out
that the revision of the Alliance in 1911 "was conceived primarily
with the object of facilitating the negotiations which were known
to be then in progress between London and Washington for the
conclusion of a general arbitration treaty." Despite the failure of
the Senate to ratify the arbitration treaty of 1911, it was not "practically necessary to carry on the legal analysis of the question as
to whether the Peace Commission Treaty, signed and ratified by
the United States and Great Britain in 1914, should be construed
as a general arbitration treaty within the meaning of Article IV
of the Anglo-Japanese Agreement. For, apart from that question,
it was already well understood at the time of negotiating the
existing Agreement that the Alliance should in no case be directed
against the United States." [3] Whether or not Great Britain had
specifically notified Japan of her construction of the Peace Commission Treaty, she had by the very facts and circumstances of
the revision of the alliance in 1911, made it clear to her ally

[1] London *Times*, December 5, 30, 31, 1920; May 3, 1921; Dennis, A. L. P.,
*The Anglo-Japanese Alliance*, University of California Publications in International Relations, I, 60; Buell, *Washington Conference*, 128.

[2] Dennis, *Alliance*, 59, 61; Buell, 128; London *Times*, Feb. 23; Japan *Advertiser*, Feb. 5.

[3] Statement of Ambassador Shidehara read to Secretary of State Hughes June
30, 1921, and published in the New York *Times*, July 4. *For. Rel.*, 1921, II,
216-218.

that she would not permit the instrument to involve her in war with the United States.[1] Baron Kato himself, on the eve of his assumption of the Foreign Office portfolio in 1913, expressed the belief that England would break the alliance rather than tolerate such an eventuality.[2]

On the other hand, as proved by the queries of the State Department in the spring of 1920, Great Britain had taken no such stand in public, nor had she informed the United States of her attitude in private. So far as Washington knew, the legal obligations to which it objected remained intact. These in themselves do not appear to have been the crux of the matter. Rather does it seem that they were used as good talking points against the perpetuation of a political instrument that the Department of State considered harmful to its policies in Eastern Asia. In any event, neither past nor present assurances on the score of England's belligerent obligations satisfied the United States. It remained unalterably opposed to renewal.

On June 23, 1921, Secretary Hughes learned from the British Ambassador that the alliance (which was to expire July 13) would probably be renewed for another year. Mr. Hughes received the news without even mentioning the controverted military obligations. Looking "into the future" and reviewing the historic principles of America's Far Eastern policy—which he said "now in view of existing conditions also embraced the integrity of Russia" —the Secretary saw "only one serious source of difficulty in the Far East." Every issue between the United States and Japan could be settled amicably. But

if the Secretary could speak freely and in an informal and confidential way, he felt that if Great Britain and Japan had any arrangement by which Great Britain was to support the special interests of Japan, the latter might be likely, at the instance of the militaristic party, to be led to take positions which would call forth protests from this Govern-

---

[1] Cf. Ch. IV, above.
[2] Takeuchi, *War and Diplomacy*, 185.

ment, and that in making such representations this Government might find itself virtually alone; that the making of such representations might be called for by American opinion and yet might be met with considerable opposition in Japan, leading to a state of irritation among the people in both countries; that such a condition of affairs would be fraught with mischief; that if it were true that the policies of Great Britain in the Far East were like our own there should be co-operation between Great Britain and the United States, and it should be possible for the United States to find complete support on the part of Great Britain in their maintenance and execution; that this was not an attitude antagonistic to Japan, but would be in the interests of the peace of the world.[1]

The British Ambassador replied "that he was particularly struck with the statement that co-operation would not be antagonistic to Japan and he wondered if it would be possible to have co-operation with Japan,—that is, on the part of the three nations." Mr. Hughes explained that by co-operation he had not meant any form of alliance but simply "the having and maintaining of common policies." He then concluded his remarks with a mild threat. He had been advised, he said,

that a resolution for the recognition of the Irish Republic would be introduced in Congress; that the resolution in the Secretary's opinion would not pass but that it would be debated; that undoubtedly in the debate any relation between Great Britain and Japan could be seized upon by the enemies of Great Britain as indicating an attitude of disregard of what were believed to be the interests of this country, and would be made the most of, while action on the part of Great Britain indicating a desire to support the policy in the Far East to which this Government was committed, would give great aid and comfort to those who were opposing such a resolution.[2]

Here is a penetrating insight into Anglo-American diplomacy on the eve of the Washington Conference. The American Secre-

[1] Memorandum of a conversation between the Secretary of State and the British Ambassador (Geddes), June 23, 1921. *For. Rel.*, 1921, II, 314-316.
[2] *Ibid.*

tary of State was availing himself of the moss-grown Irish issue in order to bring the British into line with American policy in Eastern Asia. Great Britain stood revealed in the words of her Ambassador as reluctant to forswear her allegiance to Japan, no less so than in the days of Knox and Straight. The principal difference between the two situations was that whereas Knox had taken for granted the identity of British and American interests in the Far East, to the point of believing that he could win Britain away from Japan with the *fait accompli* of the neutralization scheme, Hughes understood that British co-operation would have to be bought and paid for in the currency of national interest. The omission of any reference by either party to the higher principles of the League Covenant does not escape notice. Neither does the British preference for alliance with a power whose policies were subversive of those laws, as compared with closer association with the United States, whose lip service to them in the region in question was constant.

As the date of the legal expiration of the Anglo-Japanese Alliance drew nearer, political forces originating within the British Empire came to the assistance of the United States. Before considering these, however, let us turn back and trace the development of negotiations over the second great American objective at the time, namely, disarmament. We have taken note of the convictions, even among Wilson's partisan enemies, that the United States should make some definite contribution toward the prevention of another war; and we have asserted that the contemplated means to this end was disarmament. We have also taken note of the factors in both British and American diplomacy militating against a naval race. Now let us see how their mutual interest in disarmament drew the two powers together and helped to foster an agreement on Far Eastern affairs.

A little over a month after the election of Harding Senator Borah introduced a resolution calling on the President to invite Great Britain and Japan "to send representatives to a conference, which shall be charged with the duty of promptly entering into an understanding or agreement by which the naval building programs of each of said Governments, to wit, the United States, Great Britain, and Japan, shall be substantially reduced annually during the next five years. . . ." [1] Whether or not the honor of first putting the idea of a disarmament conference into practical diplomacy belongs to Senator Borah, his resolution establishes him as one of the first to have done so. A few months after its introduction, President Harding endorsed the plan. "We are ready," he declared in his inaugural address, "to associate ourselves with the nations of the world, great and small, for conference, for counsel, to seek the expressed views of world opinion, to recommend a way to approximate disarmament and relieve the crushing burden of military and naval establishment. . . . America is ready to encourage, eager to initiate, anxious to participate in any seemly program likely to lessen the probability of war. . . ." [2]

These proposals fell on no such fallow ground in England as had those concerning the Anglo-Japanese Alliance. Lord Lee of Fareham, newly inducted First Lord of the Admiralty, was already seeking a means of forestalling a naval race with the United States. He subsequently acknowledged that Harding's inaugural remarks furnished him a welcome hint.

On March 16 he "created a great deal of stir" with a speech before the Institute of Naval Architects proposing a naval understanding with the United States based on the principle of parity.[3]

[1] Borah first introduced his resolution on December 14, 1920. On February 24, 1921, it was incorporated as an amendment in the Naval Appropriation Act, in which form it passed both houses of Congress with a total of only four negative votes (in the House) and was approved by the President July 12, 1921. Passage quoted above is from amendment as finally passed. For text, see *For. Rel.*, 1921, I, 27. Cf. also Buell, 147 ff.; Ichihashi, Y., *The Washington Conference and After*, 5 ff.; *Congressional Record*, 66th Cong., 3rd Sess., LX, Part 1, 310; LX, Part 4, 3740; 67th Cong., 1st Sess., LXI, Part 2, 1758; Part 4, 3226-7.

[2] Harding, Inaugural Address, New York *Times*, March 5, 1921.

[3] Young, E. J., *Powerful America*, 47, 53-54. Lee's acknowledgment of his debt to Harding was made to Charles Gelden, London correspondent of the New York *Times*, in 1933, and quoted by Young, 54.

A month later, Lord Lee took Adolph Ochs, publisher of the New York *Times* into his confidence. Mr. Ochs was invited to breakfast with Prime Minister Lloyd George within the hallowed portals of 10 Downing Street. There followed a conference between Lord Lee and Mr. Ochs. After complimenting the American publisher on "the well-known attitude of the New York *Times* toward the cause of friendly relations between the United States and Great Britain" which he said "had pleased all Englishmen greatly and was regarded as most helpful," Lord Lee declared that "the English government would wish to have it unofficially communicated to Washington that they were prepared to abandon their traditional policy and enter into an agreement with the United States for equality." [1]

Lord Lee elaborated his proposition. He deprecated the talk of war with Japan.

He thought the fear of such a conflict was a needless alarm, but as long as public opinion in the United States was that way, under such an arrangement as he proposed, the United States could, if it thought necessary, concentrate its navy in the Pacific Ocean and the English navy could be relied on for protection in the Atlantic Ocean. [2]

From a British point of view the Admiralty Lord's geographical distribution of naval strength would kill more than two birds with one stone.

By removing the American fleet from contact with the British it would lessen the chances of rivalry between the two and leave Britain actually supreme in the Atlantic. At the same time it would provide her the counterbalance to Japan in the Pacific of which she was badly in need. The United States would thus exert a restraining influence on Japan while England continued to reap the benefits of the Anglo-Japanese Alliance. Insofar as it dimin-

[1] Ochs Memorandum, Young, *op. cit.*, 49-50. The breakfast with Lloyd George took place on April 22, the conference with Lord Lee presumably on the same day, although this is not made clear by Ochs himself or Young.
[2] *Ibid.*

ished inducements to naval rivalry with England, the scheme conferred like advantages on the United States. It also permitted the concentration of the American fleet where it was deemed to be most urgently required. Lord Lee's proposals seemed "epoch-making" to Mr. Ochs, who departed the conference "in a high state of elation." [1]

The London correspondent of the *Times* was at once entrusted with the mission of carrying the highly confidential proposals to Secretary of the Navy Denby. The latter was favorably impressed and consented to have the fact communicated to Lord Lee. At this juncture Mr. Ochs and his lieutenant detached themselves from the proceedings, which rapidly passed from the preliminary to the conclusive stage.[2] To consider that, while still the ally of Japan and still planning to renew the alliance, Great Britain had proposed American naval concentration in the Pacific is to appreciate the delicacy of the business in which the publisher of the New York *Times* had shared. It is eloquent testimony to the confidence he and his paper had earned in official British circles.

With the completion of the Ochs mission, the threads of disarmament and the Anglo-Japanese Alliance became so tangled with each other that it is difficult either to separate them or to determine the precise degree of initiative displayed by the powers they bound together. This much is clear. By June 1, 1921, the British Government knew that the United States favored an international disarmament conference, opposed renewal of the Anglo-Japanese Alliance and desired, if the alliance should be renewed, that it would be in a form more consistent with the Far Eastern

[1] *Ibid.*

[2] See the Ochs, Marshall and Lee memoranda published by Young, 50-55. In his interview with the *Times* correspondent in 1933, Lord Lee stated that he had considered his *tête-à-tête* with Mr. Ochs in 1921 "an invitation for an invitation" and that he had suggested a naval conference to be sponsored by the United States and held at Washington. *Ibid.*, 54. On the strength of these memoranda, Young concludes that the initiative in summoning the Washington Conference was principally, if not entirely, British.

policy of the United States and provide specific legal exemption from military obligations for the United States. The American Government, on its part, knew that Great Britain had accepted the principle of naval parity with the United States, was willing to revise the Anglo-Japanese Alliance so as to establish the desired legal exemption, but was determined to renew the alliance in some form for at least a year. It remained for the diplomats of the two countries to work out a compromise.

In so doing they were greatly assisted by the Prime Minister of Canada, who now assumed and played with decisive effect the role of honest broker between them. We have observed how, in 1908, immigration troubles in British Columbia had paralleled those in California; how this had united Canada and the United States against Japan; how the Canadian Commissioner of Labor and Immigration, MacKenzie King, had gone to Washington and thanked President Roosevelt for sending the American fleet to the Pacific.[1] From that moment on Canadian apprehensions of the Anglo-Japanese Alliance had varied directly with American. The principal link in this bond of sympathy in addition to the geographical situation of the two countries, was a common immigration policy. But whereas the United States disliked the alliance chiefly for its harmful effect on American policy in the Far East, Canada genuinely feared the belligerent obligations it imposed on England. The more likely a Japanese-American war, the more likely Canada, as part of the British Empire, would be compelled to take up arms against the United States. This, of all members of the Empire, Canada was most loath to contemplate, not only because of her close economic and social relationship with her southern neighbor, but also because Canadian territory would form a very likely battleground in such a war.

The poor estate of Japanese-American relations in 1921 together with a resurgence in Canadian politics of the "North American" as opposed to the imperial point of view, stirred these appre-

[1] Cf. above, p. 127.

hensions afresh, and gave rise to a national demand that the alliance be terminated. As early as February, Canadian Prime Minister Arthur Meighen was urging on Lloyd George the plan of a four-power conference on Pacific affairs among the United States, Great Britain, China and Japan.[1] Late the following spring Mr. Meighen journeyed to London to take part in one of the imperial conferences periodically convoked in England for the discussion of affairs of state of concern to the entire Empire.[2] The principal item on the agenda, which included foreign affairs and imperial defense, was the constitutional status of the British Dominions as affected by their membership in the League of Nations.

The Conference opened June 20. Within a fortnight it had resolved itself into a hot debate over renewal of the Anglo-Japanese Alliance. Meighen, who had arrived in London a determined opponent of renewal, found himself alone in his convictions. Lloyd George himself, seconded by Curzon, Balfour and Lee, had decided to keep the alliance. The cabinet had not been swayed by the importunities of Washington. It was true that the defeat of Germany and the Russian revolution had invalidated two of the principal reasons for which the alliance had originally been concluded. But factors other than loyalty and a traditional dislike of change counseled renewal. India, the great treasure cave of the British Empire, and the vast British territorial and economic stakes in Eastern Asia and the Pacific, required protection if not from the old German and Russian menaces, from the menace of Japan herself. Experience had shown that the alliance's principle that propinquity created special rights and interests worked both ways,

[1] Brebner, J. B., "Canada, the Anglo-Japanese Alliance and the Washington Conference," *Political Science Quarterly*, L, March, 1935, 53.

[2] The first of these conferences was held in 1887. The official title of this one was "Conference of the Prime Ministers and Representatives of the United Kingdom, the Dominions, and India." It was notable in that for the first time the Dominions were permitted to share in the formulation of British foreign policy.

that Japanese respect for British possessions and spheres could be bought with Chinese territory of relatively slight value to Britain. Moreover, as revealed by the Siberian expedition, England considered Japan a bulwark against the spread of communism to China and India. There were the final arguments that Japan herself was eager for renewal, that it was often more expedient to take potential enemies into camp than to ostracize them, and that the opponents of renewal had as yet proposed no effective substitute.

For the most part the Dominions needed no convincing. Influenced partly by the financial and military dependence of his country on London (for which he considered American friendship a poor counterfeit) partly by his fear of an ostracized, hence vengeful, Japan, Australia's Prime Minister Hughes was vociferous in his insistence on renewal. Massey of New Zealand agreed with him. So did India's spokesman, fearful of Japan's economic imperialism and potential leadership of a Pan-Asiatic movement. Only Smuts of South Africa differed with his colleagues, and he favored revision rather than abrogation. Meighen stood alone against the field.[1]

That he was able to prevail against such powerful odds testifies as much to the force of the Canadian Prime Minister's personality as to the weight of his opinions. Doubtless he was aided by the coincident representations of Washington already mentioned. At all events, he succeeded virtually single-handed in bringing the conference to accept the idea of relinquishing the Anglo-Japanese Alliance in favor of a general understanding to be effected at a conference on Pacific affairs between the United States, Great Britain, China and Japan. On July 1, Lloyd George asked Curzon to instruct the conference in the procedure of putting Meighen's idea into practice. Renewal of the alliance was shelved. So com-

[1] Brebner, op. cit., passim; Dennis, Alliance, 64-93. For Japanese attitude toward renewal, Bell to Secretary of State, June 11, 1920, For. Rel., 1920, II, 682-684. Cf. also Whyte, Sir F., China and Foreign Powers, 24; Buell, 122-127; 130-135; Chang, 185-195.

plete was Meighen's victory that it appeared doubtful if the alliance would ever be renewed, even should the four-power Pacific conference fail to materialize.[1]

Lloyd George now found himself in a tight place. He could not afford arbitrarily to shut Britain's ally of twenty years out in the cold. He would have to approach that sensitive nation with plausible excuses and attractive compensation. At the moment he had nothing tangible to offer. He did not even know whether the United States and Japan would agree to take part in a conference on Pacific affairs, much less what could be gained from such an undertaking. News was leaking out of the imperial conference at an alarming rate. Parliament was becoming hourly more insistent on being apprised of the trend of events. The air was heavily surcharged with rumor.

At this juncture, just as Mr. Meighen had served Washington as a *deus ex machina,* the American desire for a disarmament conference helped the British Prime Minister out of his predicament. On July 5, Curzon requested Mr. Harvey, who had recently succeeded Davis as American Ambassador to London, to propose to his government "that the President invite powers directly concerned to take part in conference to be held to consider all essential matters bearing on Far East and Pacific Ocean with a view to arriving at a common understanding designed to assure settlement by peaceful means, the elimination of naval warfare, consequent elimination of arms, etc. This was official by Cabinet's direction." [2] Mr. Harvey at once inquired if the Foreign Secretary "regarded the question as pressing, requiring an immediate answer," or whether he might convey it by mail instead of telegraph and thus enable himself "to present simultaneously a more comprehensive survey of the whole situation." Curzon replied that "the latter method seemed entirely satisfactory since the Japanese Ambassador had notified that several days at least would be re-

[1] Hughes of Australia held out for renewal until the end. Brebner, 55-56.
[2] Harvey to Secretary of State, July 8, 1921. *For. Rel.,* 1921, I, 19-21.

quired interpreting views from his Government upon same subject." [1] From this interchange we learn that by July 5 the British Government had broached the idea of a conference on Pacific affairs to both the Japanese and American Ambassadors to London. The time scheme is important.

Since Earl Curzon had said there was no great hurry, Ambassador Harvey allowed two days to elapse before communicating with Washington. On July 7 he was in the act of writing his despatch when the Foreign Secretary told him "that a new element had entered the situation which seemed to require attention immediately.

This was that Lloyd George had informed him that he could no longer withstand importunate inquiries in House of Commons regarding the alliance and cognate subjects and felt that he must respond yesterday, July 7, to the effect that his Government had inquired of the United States, Japan and China and was waiting for an expression of their views. Curzon informed me that he had demurred to this program if it involved anything definite until I had an opportunity to communicate his official proposal to Washington. In view of Curzon's statement to me that the matter was not imminent the Prime Minister consented to make a general statement last evening, coupled however with a virtual pledge that on Monday [July 11] he would speak more specifically." [2]

Lloyd George had made his statement to the Commons, hoping he could say something definite on the eleventh and basing his hope on the receipt of favorable replies from the United States of America, Japan and China.[3] "In view of this situation," wired Harvey, "Curzon asked that I immediately communicate his pro-

---

[1] *For. Rel.*, 1921, I, 19-21.

[2] *For. Rel.*, 1921, I, 19.

[3] The same day—July 7—in a joint declaration similar to that of a year ago, Great Britain and Japan notified the League that should any situation arise while the alliance remained in force in which the procedure prescribed by the alliance was inconsistent with that prescribed by the League Covenant, the procedure of the Covenant should prevail. *For. Rel.*, 1921, II, 319.

posal to my Government and make every effort to obtain a reply not later than Monday morning in order to enable the Prime Minister to incorporate it in his formal statement to House of Commons." [1]

Harvey proceeded to read the Secretary of State a lesson in strategy.

"It is true," he conceded, "that the Prime Minister is being pressed for reply but I suppose he is not averse to acquiring credit for initiating a movement which may prove to be the most far-reaching and effective ever known for world peace. It is clear that if you reply favorably to proposal of British Government and the Prime Minister so announces in Parliament he will achieve that distinction whether purposely or not. The President would then be in a position, which I consider harmful and distasteful, of acting at the instigation of Lloyd George, thereby depriving himself of his rightful credit and antagonizing all anti-British elements in United States. For your and the President's consideration I suggest that this be forestalled by the President issuing statement for publication Sunday, if possible, but if not then on Monday morning, to this effect: Having ourselves conceived as a result of inquiries that nations vitally or intimately concerned in questions relating to Pacific Ocean and Far East would favorably respond to invitations to meet in conference to try to effect an understanding which would tend to insure peaceful relations through safeguarding equitably and fairly the interests of all and thus make possible suitable limitation of armaments, the President has decided to issue such invitations as soon as time, place and other necessary preliminaries could be arranged. Then the Prime Minister's reply on Monday would necessarily consist of the initiatory statement of the President and an expression of the British Government's acquiescence as it should be." [2]

[1] Harvey to Secretary of State, July 8, 1921. *For. Rel.*, 1921, I, 19-21.

[2] Mr. Harvey did not fail to add, by way of inducement, that feeling was growing stronger against the alliance; that Curzon "unhesitatingly stated that any such special arrangement would necessarily be extinguished by an understanding such as contemplated"; that the latter had had "several interviews with the Japanese Ambassador" on the basis of which "he felt sure Japan would acquiesce"; that the Chinese Minister was enthusiastic; and that "Curzon assures me that his

It is significant that the American Ambassador's eagerness to carry off the honors of the initiative sprang from a desire to enhance the prestige of President Harding with the American electorate rather than from a study of its probable effects on American interests in Eastern Asia. Harvey's long cable of July 8 was received by the State Department at 10:34 P.M. Interestingly enough, it had been crossed by a cable to Harvey himself despatched by Secretary Hughes at 4 that afternoon and reading as follows:

Ascertain informally whether it would be agreeable to the British Government to be invited by this Government to participate in a conference on limitation of armaments, the conference to be held in Washington at a mutually convenient time. Similar suggestions will be made to the French, Italian, and Japanese Governments.[1]

American interest in disarmament had led Secretary Hughes more than halfway to acceptance of the Curzon proposals in advance of their receipt.

It was a comparatively simple matter to incorporate the interests of the two powers. On July 9 Hughes replied to Harvey that the inquiry as to the British attitude toward a disarmament conference would have to stand as similar inquiries had been sent to Paris, Rome and Tokyo. "However," he continued, "this fact may help in maintaining the President's initiative which is important.

Limitation of armament question is vital here and is not confined to the Pacific. It was considered best that the group heretofore known as the five Principal Allied and Associated Powers should first be approached on this subject. If they consider it advisable an invitation can later be extended to others or program can be formulated and submitted to others as seems best. The problem of limitation of armament, how-

Government would accept any suggestions the United States might make upon all such questions which would later arise and he believes he could induce Japan to do likewise." Harvey to Secretary of State, July 8, 1921. *Ibid.*, 20-21.

[1] Hughes to Harvey, July 8, 1921. *For. Rel.*, 1921, I, 18. The "suggestions" were made to France, Italy and Japan the same day. See Hughes to Harding, July 9, 1921. *Ibid.*, 21-22.

ever, does relate to Pacific and Far Eastern questions and all the five
powers except perhaps Italy have an interest in the latter. In view of
your message, it would seem appropriate for this Government to send a
supplemental cable to the other powers to the effect that the proposed
conference on limitation of armament would be extended to include
discussion of all Far Eastern problems by powers interested and that
China would be asked to take part in that discussion. The conference
should be held in Washington at a time to be later agreed upon. Ascertain and cable immediately if this is agreeable to the British Government. If so, will send cables enlarging suggestion regarding conference
as above, and also to China regarding participation in Far Eastern discussion, and the President will announce in Monday morning [July
11] papers that on his own initiative he has asked powers whether they
would welcome such an invitation and that as soon as details have been
arranged formal invitations accordingly will be sent." [1]

An hour later Hughes submitted to the approval of the British
Government a draft of the President's proposed statement to the
press.[2] At 5:18 the next afternoon he had Lloyd George's word
that the statement was "admirable." At 6 cables went forth to
Tokyo, Paris and Rome advancing the "view of this Government
that the question of limitation of armament has relation to Pacific
and Far Eastern problems and therefore it would seem appropriate that proposed conference should also embrace discussion by
interested Powers of all Far Eastern questions and that China
should be invited to participate in that discussion." It was also
stated that injunctions of confidence were now withdrawn and
"that President will make announcement on Monday morning
July 11th that he has directed these inquiries to be made and that
this Government will issue invitation for conference in due course
if proposal acceptable." [3] The President's press release followed
according to schedule, and on July 11, 1921, the world learned
of the elaborately prearranged inspiration of Warren G. Harding.

[1] Hughes to Harvey, July 9, 1921. *Ibid.*, 23.
[2] Same to same, July 9, 7 P.M. *Ibid.*, 24.
[3] *Ibid.*, 24-25. Invitation to China was despatched at same time as above.

The United States had now taken upon itself the responsibility of persuading the other powers to accept its invitation and of arranging the time, place and agenda of the conference. Lloyd George and Curzon were not yet ready to yield the initiative entirely to Secretary Hughes. The imperial conference was still in session, and the Dominion premiers, especially those who had most urgently favored renewal of the alliance, were anxious to have a hand in shaping an acceptable substitute. Hughes and Massey would have to be back in Australia and New Zealand for the opening of their parliaments in October. Would it not therefore be possible to hold a preliminary conference on Pacific and Far Eastern affairs in London during the first part of August so as to allow these two statesmen plenty of time to attend? The disarmament conference could follow later, at Washington. This procedure Curzon suggested to Harvey July 11, after it had been "very earnestly" urged in the imperial conference by "the visiting Prime Ministers," who also urged it directly on the American Ambassador himself.[1]

Secretary Hughes did not like the idea. He made it plain in his reply that the United States was primarily interested in the limitation of armament, not the Far East, and that he did not wish to see the disarmament conference sidetracked. Neither did he care to run the risk of failure in the preliminary conference which would surely militate against success in the final, and, to the United States, the more important one. Both should be held at the same time, as planned, and in Washington, not in London. On the latter point the Harding Administration felt "so strongly . . . that it regards as essential this feature of the plan." In view of existing relations between Great Britain and Japan and since Washington had already been designated in the invitations, changing the locale of the conference to London would excite suspicion in the United States.[2] It is possible to read between the lines of

[1] Harvey to Hughes, July 11, 1921. *For. Rel.*, 1921, I, 25-27.
[2] Hughes to Harvey, July 13, 1921. *Ibid.*, 28-29.

Secretary Hughes's reply the mistrust of European diplomacy with which the experience at Paris had filled American statesmen. This factor underlay the isolationist reaction in the United States, manifest in its defection from the League and its consistent refusal to participate in any of the numerous conferences sponsored by the League during the past two years. The exigencies of American politics demanded that if the United States was to take part in any international conference whatsoever it must be one of its own calling, held under American auspices, on soil untainted by the old diplomacy.

For two weeks more Curzon continued to press for a preliminary conference. He was, Harvey explained, "duly impressed by immediate consequence of the situation in United States but frankly does not consider it as difficult or trying as his own problem, especially respecting the Dominion Premiers." [1] He proposed the alternative of "quiet consultation in London during the next few weeks" as "a plan . . . which would appease the Dominion Premiers." [2] Hughes replied that he had no objection to "consultations to facilitate preparation for the conference," but to anything approaching an advance agreement on the Far East, he remained adamantly opposed.[3]

In concurrent representations to the United States and Japan he stressed the importance the British Government attached to a preliminary meeting of the three powers to prepare the agenda on Pacific and Far Eastern affairs. If Washington would issue the invitation and Japan would accept, Curzon himself, Lloyd George, Meighen, Hughes and Massey were ready to sail from England for Bar Harbor, Maine, on August 12. They would arrive at Bar Harbor on the eighteenth, spend a week in conference there and sail back to England on the twenty-fifth. "This proposal goes

[1] Harvey to Secretary of State, July 15, 1921. *Ibid.*, 32-33.
[2] Same to same, July 19. *Ibid.*, 36-37.
[3] Hughes to Harvey, July 20. *Ibid.*, 37-39.

today to Japan," wired Harvey, "but clearly Curzon expects a favorable response." [1]

He did not get it. In a long cable of the twenty-eighth, in which his talents as a litigant were again prominently displayed, Secretary Hughes repeated that he "had not the slightest objection to all consultations that could prove helpful" but ruled out "a meeting which would partake of the nature of a preliminary conference" once and for all. [2]

The result was that on August 2 the British Ambassador in Washington "said his Government, in view of our recent conversations, would not further pursue question of preliminary conference . . . and desired the United States to take full responsibility for arrangements in order to avoid possibility of further misunderstanding." [3] From now on the initiative in organizing the Washington Conference was almost exclusively American.

It had been largely so since July 10, the day Hughes had supplemented his original invitations to a disarmament conference with those incorporating the British proposals for a conference on Far Eastern affairs. While Curzon had been dickering for a preliminary meeting, the Department of State had been soliciting favorable replies from the other powers. China, to whom the Anglo-Japanese Alliance was an instrument of oppression and any conference—especially one sponsored by the United States— offered hopes of salvation, needed no persuasion. [4] Though uncertain as to whether his country had been invited to a disarmament as well as a Far Eastern conference, the Chinese Foreign Minister readily expressed his willingness to take part in both (July 13). [5] In a few days he was proposing that Great Britain be asked to denounce her alliance with Japan as a condition prec-

[1] Harvey to Secretary of State, July 27. *For. Rel.*, 1921, I, 46-47. Foreign Office to Geddes, July 27, 45-46.

[2] Hughes to Harvey, July 28. *Ibid.*, 47-50.

[3] Same to same, August 2. *Ibid.*, 50-51.

[4] For attitude of China toward alliance see *For. Rel.*, 1920, II, 679, 684, 685.

[5] *For. Rel.*, 1921, I, 29.

edent to negotiation. "He thinks that Great Britain is suggesting Pacific conference to find possible exit from the alliance dilemma and if conference fails will fall back on the alliance," elucidated the American Chargé at Peking. "To prevent this and to assure the success of the conference Yen wants Great Britain to commit herself on the alliance before the conference." [1]

France and Italy, less concerned with the Far East than with disarmament and its possible European political implications, signified their readiness to accept the Hughes invitation July 12.[2] The next day Belgium protested at not having been included in the invitation.[3] On July 21 Russia (as yet unrecognized by any of the powers concerned) assailed the United States, Great Britain, France, Italy, Japan and China with a diatribe on the same score.[4]

With Japan, meanwhile, the United States was having difficulties. It was obvious on the face of it that the Japanese Government would not relish being asked to take part in an attempt to curb its own major policies. The incompatibility of Japan's activities in China and Siberia with the announced purposes of the conference was self-evident. Japan had not wished to give up the alliance with England. On the contrary, so anxious had she been to pre-

[1] Ruddock to Secretary of State, July 18, 1921. *Ibid.*, 33-36.

[2] *Ibid.*, 27-28.

[3] The Belgian Foreign Minister admitted his country's slight interest in the Far East, but claimed to be vitally concerned with the question of "terrestrial disarmament." He would not like it said that the United States had caused Belgium to lose the prestige she had gained with such difficulty in securing admission to the Supreme Council at the Peace Conference; and he thought Belgium could exercise influence on her allies "especially in the matter of disarmament." Whitlock to Secretary of State. *Ibid.*, 30.

[4] The protest was forwarded by Chicherin, Commissar for Foreign Affairs, to Hughes *via* the Soviet Representative and the American Chargé in Sweden. It cited Russia's undeniable interests in the Far East, protested "against its exclusion from a conference which touches it directly, and against any intention of any power whatsoever to adopt decisions touching the Pacific without consulting Russia" and refused to recognize "any decision taken by the above-mentioned conference." The protest was dated July 19. Crosby to Secretary of State, and enclosure, July 22, 1921. *Ibid.*, 40-43.

serve it that in March, 1921, she had broken a tradition of twenty-five centuries and sent her crown prince on a diplomatic visit to London. To Japan the alliance had been a badge of prestige, insurance against aggression, a protective shield for her schemes on the continent.[1] Dissenters in Tokyo there were, and anti-British feeling sometimes ran high, but the dominant industrial, military and political cliques had favored renewal. Moreover, Japan's Asiatic policies required a larger, not a smaller, army and navy.

It is true that the Japanese, like every other government concerned, was aware of the economic arguments in favor of disarmament. These, in Japan's case, were rendered the more poignant by the projected naval parity of England and America, with the political solidarity and strategic disposition of fleets that it implied. There was also some genuine dissatisfaction in Tokyo with the results of the Siberian expedition, as well as some genuine support for the cause of disarmament and collective security. Nevertheless, from start to finish Japan was an unwilling participant in the Washington Conference. Hence to have assumed the initiative in persuading her to attend the conference, quite apart from inducing her to accept its dispensations, cast Secretary Hughes in the familiar role (that Hay, Roosevelt, Knox, Lansing and Wilson had all played before him) of disciplinarian of the Far East.[2]

This becomes increasingly apparent as the record of the preliminary negotiations between Washington and Tokyo unfolds. The Japanese Government readily agreed to take part in an arms limitation conference (July 13) but hesitated to accept the invi-

[1] It was Ishii's opinion that "owing no doubt to the political needs of the moment, they [the British] now looked upon the Alliance as a nuisance and finally, by means of a clause in the Four-Power Pacific Treaty, terminated it. . . . It is believed that if a man of Sir Edward Grey's type had been directing British foreign policy at that time, an act so lacking in chivalry would not have been committed." Ishii, 59.

[2] For Japan's attitude toward renewal of the alliance, see *For. Rel.*, 1920, II, 682-684; Dennis, *Alliance*, 64-68, 91-93. For attitude toward Washington Conference, *For. Rel.*, 1921, I, 52-53; Takeuchi, Ch. XX; Buell, 149 ff., and circumstantial evidence cited in this chapter.

tation to confer on Pacific and Far Eastern problems until "precisely informed of the nature and scope of these problems." It would "be glad to hear the views which may be entertained by the United States Government in this respect." [1] Secretary Hughes at once forwarded the Japanese response to Harvey with instructions to inform Curzon of the situation and find out "through discreet inquiry . . . what subjects, if any, have been suggested by Great Britain to Japan for consideration at such a conference.

Our view is that in addition to limitation of armaments conference should cover all such Pacific and Far Eastern problems as are of international concern. For example, it would embrace open door, equality of commercial opportunity, integrity of China, integrity of Russia and practical application of these principles, also status of former German possessions in Pacific, cable and radio communication, narcotic traffic and other international Far Eastern questions. This, of course, would exclude purely domestic matters such as immigration, a point which must be frankly stated if necessary.

Would prefer not to answer Japan's inquiry until I have report of your interview with Foreign Secretary, if you can arrange to send promptly." [2]

Unlike Knox, Mr. Hughes sought advance assurance of British co-operation before committing himself to a definite program.

Curzon would give no answer until he, in turn, had sounded the Japanese Ambassador in London. When the latter refused to suggest desirable agenda Curzon would not do so. He merely used the large number of topics mentioned by Hughes as arguments for a preliminary conference.[3] After a lapse of four days (during which the Japanese Ambassador may or may not have had some more definite thoughts on the subject) the British Foreign Secretary tentatively defined his position. He felt that the conference on Pacific questions should be limited to consideration

[1] Bell to Secretary of State, July 13, 1921. *For. Rel.*, 1921, I, 31.
[2] Hughes to Harvey, July 13, 1921. *Ibid.*, 31-32.
[3] Harvey to Secretary of State, July 15, 1921. *Ibid.*, 32-33.

of the open door, the territorial integrity of China, "Shantung
and questions relating to it" and "leased territory in and around
the Pacific Ocean."

Questions which in Curzon's opinion "this conference should
ignore but leave for later determination and action" were opium
traffic, immigration, "possessions of Germany in the Pacific" and
the integrity of Russia.[1] In view of the controversy raging over
Yap, and that not yet subsiding over Siberia, it was not strange
that Curzon wished to avoid giving Japan offense by including
"possessions of Germany in the Pacific" and the integrity of Russia
in the agenda. So deeply was Britain herself involved in both
controversies that the Foreign Secretary's desire to avoid discussing them need not imply collusion with Japan.

Hughes would not compromise. Only the day before (July 18)
he had been advised by the American Chargé in Tokyo that "according to all indications" Japan would "unquestionably accept
the invitation to attend the conference" on Pacific and Far Eastern affairs.[2] He agreed with Curzon on the advisability of omitting the opium traffic and immigration. But he was firm in the
belief that Siberia and Yap should be included. Though he approved it, Curzon's proposal to discuss "leased territory in and
around the Pacific" puzzled him. "Would it be possible for you
to find out what is back of it?" he asked Harvey.[3]

With the agenda slowly taking shape in this manner, Hughes
talked over "the nature and the scope of the Pacific and Far
Eastern questions to be discussed at the proposed conference" informally with the Japanese Ambassador in Washington. In the
course of their conversations the Secretary of State "expressed the
hope" that the Japanese Government "would not press its inquiry
in this matter because of the desirability of complete acceptance
of this Government's invitation, leaving open to later determina-

[1] Same to same, July 19, 1921. *For. Rel.*, 1921, I, 36-37.
[2] Bell to Secretary of State, July 18, 1921. *Ibid.*, 35.
[3] Hughes to Harvey, July 20, 1921. *Ibid.*, 37-39.

tion the exact agenda." On July 21 he communicated this hope, officially, to Tokyo.[1] Obviously if Japan were allowed to fix the scope of the agenda as a condition to accepting the invitation to the conference, the chances of the latter's success from an American point of view would be limited. The representatives of both powers understood this clearly. So did the British. Hughes's effort to obtain British support for his agenda, as a means of inducing Japan to accept it, shows the degree to which the United States was now exercising the initiative.

Still Japan kept stalling, trying to find in Hughes's willingness to discuss the agenda (as he was now doing) the possibility of adjusting it more closely to her own interests. Not until July 26— nearly two weeks after all the other original invitations had been accepted—did she agree to attend a conference on Far Eastern affairs. Even then, her reply was conspicuously lacking in enthusiasm:

It has been brought to the knowledge of the Japanese Government that the Government of the United States is willing to proceed with exchanges of opinion regarding the agenda prior to the meeting of the conference and that it considers it advisable to adjust in that agenda the nature and scope of the Pacific and Far Eastern questions to be discussed at the proposed conference. The Japanese Government, on that understanding, are happy to be able to inform the American Government that it is their intention gladly to accept an invitation for a conference which shall embrace the discussion of the Pacific and Far Eastern questions.

The Japanese Government have been made aware through the communications and the published statement of the American Government and the conversations between the Secretary of State and Baron Shidehara that the proposition of the American Government to discuss the Pacific and Far Eastern problems is based on the close bearing they have on the question of the limitation of armaments which is the original and principal aim of the conference, and that therefore the

[1] Hughes to Bell, July 21. *Ibid.*, 39-40.

main object of discussing these problems is to reach a common under-standing in regard to general principles and policies in the Pacific and the Far East. Desiring, as they [do], to contribute to the establish-ment of an enduring peace and to the advancement of human welfare, the Japanese Government earnestly hope that the proposed conference may attain the expected results and their ideals may thereby be brought nearer to realization.

In order to ensure the success of the conference, the Japanese Gov-ernment deem it advisable that the agenda thereof should be arranged in accordance with the main object of the discussions as above defined, and that introduction therein of problems such as are of sole concern to certain particular powers or such matters that may be regarded accomplished facts should be scrupulously avoided.[1]

The interpretation of advance consultations as not excluding the possibility of a preliminary agreement is obvious.[2] So is the at-tempt to bury the whole complex of Far Eastern issues in the subject of disarmament. The recommendation that "problems such as are of sole concern to certain particular powers or such matters that may be regarded accomplished facts should be scrupulously avoided" meant nothing more nor less than that the Twenty-One Demands, Shantung, Siberia and Yap should all be omitted from the agenda. Japan's acceptance of the invitation to confer on Far Eastern affairs was in truth an invitation to the conference not to trespass on her political preserves in Eastern Asia.

Hughes treated it exactly as Hay had treated the Russian re-buff to the open door notes. He immediately published the news that all the interested powers had accepted his conference pro-posals.[3] On August 11 formal invitations to a conference on the limitation of armament and problems of the Pacific and the Far East, to convene in Washington on Armistice Day (November 11), 1921, were issued to Great Britain, France, Italy, Japan and

[1] Bell to Hughes, July 26. *For. Rel.*, 1921, I, 43-45.

[2] This, incidentally, reveals a source of Curzon's anxiety on the same score other than the demands of the Dominion premiers.

[3] Hughes to Bell, July 27. *Ibid.*, 45.

China.[1] Some additional negotiation over the agenda was required, in the process of which each power continued to show concern for its own particular interests. Japan still attached as much significance as possible to "a free exchange of views prior to the assembly of the conference." [2] France questioned the plan to draft "rules for control of new agencies of warfare," thinking, doubtless, of her submarines and the desire of the British to curb their use.[3] China wished to place the Anglo-Japanese Alliance on the agenda, but was deterred by Hughes's warning that the move might defeat its own purpose.[4] The British were anxious to dispose of all Far Eastern problems before approaching the subject of disarmament, a procedure that would expedite their search for a substitute for the Anglo-Japanese Alliance, and preserve the bargaining power of their naval superiority until it was found. They even suggested adding to the agenda the long-controverted subject of Panama Canal tolls, leading Hughes to remark to the British Ambassador that "the time had come when the constant sentiments and cordial expressions which were made at dinners and on various occasions with respect to the friendly co-operation of the two Governments should be translated into something definite." [5]

In the end the agenda, both in scope and in procedure, conformed to Secretary Hughes's wishes almost to the letter. When the Conference opened on November 12 (Armistice Day having been devoted to ceremony) it was to find limitation of armaments its first order of business. Under this broad title were listed limi-

---

[1] *Ibid.*, 56-58. Participation in the conference on disarmament was limited to the United States, Great Britain, France, Italy and Japan, the five principal allied and associated powers. In addition to these, China, Belgium, Holland and Portugal were invited to confer on the Pacific and the Far East, the last three at their own request.

[2] Uchida to Bell in Bell to Hughes, August 23. *Ibid.*, 61.

[3] Bearn to Hughes, September 16, 1921. *Ibid.*, 69.

[4] Memorandum by the Secretary of State of a conversation with the Chinese Minister, November 5, 1921. *Ibid.*, 82-84.

[5] Memorandum by the Secretary of State of a conversation with the British Ambassador, September 20, 1921. *Ibid.*, 71-74.

tation of naval armament, rules for control of new agencies of warfare and limitation of land armament, in that order. The second broad title was "Pacific and Far Eastern Questions." This covered, first, questions relating to China, including territorial integrity, administrative integrity, the open door and equality of commercial and industrial opportunity, concessions, monopolies or preferential economic privileges, development of railways, including plans relating to the Chinese Eastern Railway, preferential railway rates and the status of existing commitments. The next topic under Pacific and Far Eastern Questions was Siberia, to be discussed under "similar headings." Finally came "Mandated Islands: Subject, Electrical Communications in the Pacific." [1] The agenda read like a prospectus of America's Far Eastern policy.

[1] See agenda included in Hughes to Harvey, September 10 and Hughes to Phillips, October 4, 1921. *For. Rel.*, 1921, I, 67, 76. Also, Conference on the Limitation of Armament, Report of the American Delegation, Senate Document No. 126, 67th Congress, 2nd Session, 789-790.

# VIII. Freezing the Pacific

FROM November 12, 1921, to February 6, 1922, the delegates of the United States, Great Britain, France, Italy, and Japan applied themselves to the limitation of armament and, together with their Belgian Dutch, Portuguese and Chinese colleagues, to the problems of the Pacific and the Far East. The five-power conference on disarmament and the nine-power conference on the Pacific and the Far East, held parallel sessions. The business of the twin conferences was sifted through corps of experts and innumerable committees and sub-committees before it was acted on in the plenary sessions of the conference as a whole. The minutes and proceedings of these various meetings offer little more than a hint of the diplomatic arts required to produce the seven treaties and twelve resolutions (not to mention a Sino-Japanese and a Japanese-American treaty concluded while it was in progress) that were the handiwork of the conference. Headed by Secretary Hughes, the American delegation was composed of Elihu Root, former Secretary of State and co-author of the Root-Takahira Agreement; Henry Cabot Lodge, Chairman of the Senate's Foreign Relations Committee, and Oscar W. Underwood, ranking Democratic member of that committee. Each of these men, especially Root, made some distinctive contribution to the achievements of the conference. The real control of its infinitely complex machinery was exercised in private. Hughes of the United States, Balfour of England, Kato of Japan were the "Big Three" at Washington as Wilson, Lloyd George and Clemenceau had been at Paris. Their secret negotiations governed the transactions of their colleagues and determined very largely the outcome of their enterprise.[1]

Hughes's introductory address to the conference (November 12) was an apparent exception to this rule. The Secretary of State had scored the tactical success of placing arms limitation first on the agenda. To mobilize public opinion (on which he placed considerable reliance as a diplomatic instrument) behind disarmament, he cut short the trite amenities of a welcoming speech and presented forthwith a concrete plan for reducing the number of ships and tonnage of the American, British and Japanese navies. The plan called for an immediate halt in the construction programs of the three powers, the scrapping of ships already built or partially completed, the limitation by treaty of capital ship replacements on the basis of 500,000 tons each for Great Britain and the United States and 300,000 tons for Japan, and the application of corresponding ratios to aircraft carriers, submarines, destroyers and cruisers.[2]

Eyewitnesses have testified to the surprise of the conference at Secretary Hughes's dramatic *tour de force*.[3] Balfour paid him elaborate compliments on his strategy.[4] Whoever shared the secret, it had been closely guarded, and the conference had been compelled to put first things first as Washington saw them. In itself, the Hughes plan was less novel than its presentation. It

[1] The British delegates were Balfour, Lord Lee of Fareham, First Lord of the Admiralty, and Sir Auchland Geddes, Ambassador to the United States. The Japanese delegates were Admiral Baron Kato, Minister of the Navy; Baron Shidehara, Ambassador to the United States; Prince Tokugawa, President of the House of Peers, and Hanihara, Vice-Minister for Foreign Affairs.

[2] *Conference on the Limitation of Armament*, U. S. Senate Document No. 126, 67th Congress, 2nd Session, Proceedings of Plenary Sessions, 41-63. This document, containing in addition to the proceedings cited the minutes of the committees on the limitation of armaments and Pacific and Far Eastern questions, the official report of the American delegation and the texts of the treaties and resolutions concluded by the conference, will be referred to hereafter as *Conference*.

[3] Cf. Buell, 151 ff.; Ichihashi, Ch. III.

[4] *Conference*, 65-70.

had been carefully matured. Great Britain had, as we have seen, already accepted the principle of naval parity with the United States. With this ace in the hole, Hughes's risk in playing his hand as boldly as he did, at the very opening session of the conference, was not so great as it may have seemed.

The task of winning Japanese assent to the Hughes plan at once brought the business and procedure of the two conferences—the universal problem of disarmament and the regional problem of the balance of power in Eastern Asia—into close relationship. "The Navy seems to be sincerely in favor of a reduction of armaments," the British Ambassador in Tokyo wrote Balfour two days before the conference opened.

The Army are as a whole opposed to any reduction. The general public do not agree with this, they feel the burden of taxation, and would like to see troops withdrawn from Siberia, ex-Saghalin, but still they believe Japan has a mission on the mainland of Asia, and if they were made to feel they were abandoning that mission by any policy of retrenchment, patriotic sentiment would probably get the better of prudence and financial considerations.[1]

Naval limitation was but one of the many concessions the United States and Great Britain desired of Japan. Plainly, there would have to be compromise and bargaining at every turn.

No one realized this more clearly than Balfour. As one who had played a vital role both in concluding and renewing the Anglo-Japanese Alliance, he was peculiarly sensitive of the forces compelling his country to devise a substitute for it. He knew, and so did Hughes, that the Japanese were talking of expanding the alliance—if it had to be changed—so as to include the United States.[2] Indeed, as proved by its efforts to bring about a preliminary conference, the British Government believed the fate of the entire Washington Conference depended on some such move.

[1] Sir Charles Eliot to Balfour, November 10, 1921. Dugdale, II, 237-238.
[2] Cf. Bell to Hughes, June 11, 1920. *For. Rel.*, 1920, II, 682-684.

"When the proposal to hold a Conference about Far Eastern questions as well as disarmament was first announced last July," the British Ambassador in Tokyo commented in his letter of November 10, already quoted, "the Japanese Government saw at once that they must participate, but the official and popular attitude was hardly disguised hostility.

The whole business was regarded as an attempt to arraign Japan before an Anglo-American tribunal. . . . Things grew better when it was announced that Lloyd George had said we would either maintain the Anglo-Japanese Alliance, or substitute something better for it. . . . I do not doubt they are most anxious to continue the Anglo-Japanese Alliance. They do not believe there can be any lasting friendship with the United States, and they fear that if their alliance with us is terminated, they will be isolated. But though they prefer a simple Anglo-Japanese Alliance I think that they will consent to a tri-partite agreement with America." [1]

Balfour thought so, too, and had come to Washington with exactly that scheme in mind.[2] On November 11 he discussed the alliance privately with Hughes, reminding the latter of several good reasons for retaining it: Japan's *amour propre;* the control it gave England over Japan's actions; the security of the Dominions. He showed Hughes the drafts of two "arrangements" which he proposed to substitute for the alliance. One of these formed the nucleus of the Nine-Power Treaty relating to China.[3] The other amounted to little more than the old alliance re-written so as to include the United States. Applying to the "regions of Eastern Asia" and to the "existing territorial rights of the High Contracting Parties in islands of Pacific Ocean and the territories bordering thereon," it bound the three powers to mutual pledges of respect and consultation. If threatened "by any other Power or combination of Powers, any two of the High Contracting Parties shall be at liberty to protect themselves by entering into a mili-

[1] Dugdale, II, 241-242.
[2] *Ibid.,* 234-236, 242-243.
[3] Discussed below, p. 321 ff.

tary arrangement provided (a) this arrangement is purely defensive in character and (b) that it is communicated to the other High Contracting Party." [1] Balfour was proposing, in other words, that the United States join the Anglo-Japanese Alliance, with its recognition of Japan's and Britain's imperial stakes in the Far East, and its military obligations still intact.

Hughes considered any such "arrangement" out of the question. He took a much more unyielding stand on Japanese imperialism than did Balfour, insisting that Shantung be restored, that there was "misapprehension as to Japan's need of expansion," that Japan's railroad claims in Manchuria (which Balfour regarded as established) were inadmissible. To supersede the alliance he wanted a definitive statement resembling the Root-Takahira Agreement, which he termed a "coin to be reissued." [2] But he was facing a solid Anglo-Japanese front. Balfour made no secret of his frequent consultation with the Japanese delegates.[3] It was evident that the British Government was torn between Canada and the United States on the one hand and Japan and Australia on the other. On November 26 the Japanese approved Balfour's proposal, extending it to cover the "territorial rights *or vital interests* of any of the High Contracting Parties in the regions of the Pacific Ocean and of the Far East." [4] Hughes found himself a minority of one on the very issue the outcome of

[1] In the last clause Balfour had originally used the word "alliance," changing it to "arrangement" because he wanted a word "deliberately vague." See Hughes's memorandum of conversation with Balfour, November 11, 1921, including draft of three-power agreement. *For. Rel.*, 1922, I, 1-3.

[2] *Ibid.*, 1-3.

[3] *Ibid.*, 1-2.

[4] The Japanese draft, presented by Shidehara, also provided for the invocation of the agreement in case any of the stipulated rights and interests should be threatened by a third power or combination of powers "or by a turn of events which may occur in those regions," and for a joint conference between all three signatories in case a controversy should develop between any two of them. Memorandum of conversation between Secretary of State and Counselor of Japanese Embassy, November 26, 1921. *Ibid.*, 3-4. Italics inserted.

which would determine the success or failure of the conference.

Encouraged, doubtless, by Meighen's example at London and by the knowledge that Canada had stacked the cards in his favor, Hughes rejected the British and Japanese drafts, substituted his own and in a series of secret meetings with Shidehara and Balfour induced them to accept it. On December 2 he asked, and the next day received, Japan's consent to include France in the agreement.[1] This in itself was no mean accomplishment. "The Treaty as I originally conceived it, was of course tri-partite," Balfour wrote.

It was Hughes' idea to bring in the French in order to soothe their somewhat ruffled pride. The difficulty was to let them in without seriously offending the other Powers who were kept out. This exclusion was necessary, as the Japanese had given us to understand that the Treaty would lose much of its sentimental value if it was made the common property of all the Powers, great and small.[2]

The French had been resisting the naval ratio that Hughes had allotted them; inviting them to join the Pacific pact was a means of winning them around on this point. But that was not Hughes's only motive. He was undoubtedly pursuing a deliberate policy of generalizing the responsibilities of an undertaking that might otherwise have seemed to infringe the traditional American rule against entangling alliances. Mild as were its obligations when he had finished with them, they would certainly have been too strong for the United States had not Germany and Russia been eliminated as potential naval aggressors. With France included in the treaty there remained literally no power on earth at once

[1] *For. Rel.*, 1922, I, 5, 7.
[2] Balfour to Sir Charles Eliot, December 19, 1921. Dugdale, II, 243. Italy applied for admission to the four-power pact, but was refused on the grounds that it was limited to territorial interests of which Italy had none in the Far East. See Hughes's memorandum of conversation with Schanzer, December 3, 1921. *For. Rel.*, 1922, I, 5-7.

interested in the Pacific and possessed of a sufficient navy to menace the islands covered by the treaty.[1]

As soon as word had come from Tokyo consenting to the inclusion of France, Hughes presented his own draft of an agreement limited in application to "insular possessions and Dominions in the Pacific Ocean."[2] This draft survived a week of discussion to become, after a few slight verbal revisions, the Four-Power Pacific Treaty agreed to December 10 and signed December 13, 1921.[3] Balfour and Shidehara accepted it with little argument, save as to its precise geographical limitations.

When the relation of the treaty to the mandated islands came up for discussion Hughes, ever the astute lawyer, made an important reservation of rights. As we have seen, the United States was withholding recognition of the League's Pacific mandates as a means of pressing Britain and Japan for tariff concessions and especially for the adjustment of certain claims with respect to the island of Yap. Hughes admitted that the mandated islands were within the meaning of the phrase "insular possessions" but covered the admission by refusing to sign the treaty until an agreement on Yap, then in negotiation between Japan and the United States, should be concluded. Because Shidehara could not announce its conclusion before the signing of the Four-Power Treaty, Hughes added to the treaty the proviso that it "shall apply to the Mandated Islands in the Pacific Ocean; provided, however, that the making of the Treaty shall not be deemed to be an assent on the

[1] After the treaty was signed Hughes, at the instance of the Dutch delegate, notified Holland and Portugal in identic notes that the United States considered their Pacific possessions covered by the treaty's non-aggression pledge, and persuaded the other signatories of the treaty to follow suit. *Ibid.*, 41, 45.

[2] *Ibid.*, 7-8.

[3] For texts of Hughes's drafts and Four-Power Treaty see *Ibid.*, 7-8, 21-23, 28-29, 33-36. *Conference*, 889-893. The treaty was to supersede the Anglo-Japanese Alliance on ratification. It was to last for 10 years and indefinitely thereafter, subject to the right of any of its signatories to terminate it upon a year's notice.

part of the United States of America to the mandates and shall not preclude agreements between the United States of America and the Mandatory Powers respectively in relation to the Mandated Islands." [1]

The terms of the Four-Power Treaty were peculiarly American. In Article I, the United States, France, Great Britain and Japan undertook "as between themselves to respect their rights in relation to their insular possessions and insular dominions in the region of the Pacific Ocean.

> If there should develop between any of the High Contracting Parties a controversy arising out of any Pacific question and involving their said rights which is not satisfactorily settled by diplomacy and is likely to affect the harmonious accord now happily subsisting between them, they shall invite the other High Contracting Parties to a joint conference to which the whole subject will be referred for consideration and adjustment."

The Taft-Katsura and Root-Takahira Agreements had contained similar non-aggression pledges. With Japan ensconced in the Marshalls and Carolines, the Philippines were now more than ever hostages to fortune. Guam, Samoa, Wake, Midway, the Aleutians and Hawaii were similarly to be considered, but not so apprehensively as the Philippines. Here, manifestly, was another attempt to insure their territorial integrity.

In line with the arbitration agreements of the Taft and Wilson Administrations, the second clause of Article I might have been taken wholesale from the Bryan Peace Commission Treaty of 1914.[2] Like that, it was no arbitration treaty. It called merely for consultation, not arbitration, and even this was limited by a supplementary proviso that "the controversies to which the second paragraph of Article I refers shall not be taken to embrace questions which according to principles of international law lie exclu-

[1] *For. Rel.*, 1922, I, 8-12, 13-16, 30-31, 36-37; *Conference*, 823, 892.
[2] Cf. p. 274, above.

sively within the domestic jurisdiction of the respective Powers." [1]
Denatured as it was, however, the agreement to refer disputes to
consultation met American objections to the Anglo-Japanese Alliance. It substituted a four-power agreement to talk for a two-
power agreement to fight.

Article II of the Four-Power Treaty was a paraphrase of
Article V of the Root-Takahira Agreement.[2] "If the said rights
are threatened by the aggressive action of any other Power," it
read, "the High Contracting Parties shall communicate with one
another fully and frankly in order to arrive at an understanding
as to the most efficient measures to be taken, jointly or separately,
to meet the exigencies of the particular situation." The "coin" had
indeed been reissued.

The treaty had no sooner been signed than Shidehara began
to press for a supplementary understanding excluding from its
application the Japanese homeland, which had been included
against his wishes. The Japanese did not wish it to apply to their
main islands, in spite of the fact that these would theoretically
benefit by its non-aggression pledges. They argued that the pact
did not apply to the mainland of any of the other signatories, and
made it a point of pride that theirs should not be the only one
to profit by pledges customarily extended to weaker nations. Both
Hughes and Balfour argued for the inclusion of the Japanese
homeland, though the latter was far more insistent on the point
than Hughes. He contended that Australia and New Zealand
could not be designated as in any way inferior to the British Isles;
that they must therefore be considered part of the British main-

[1] Proviso cited above is from a declaration accompanying the treaty. *Conference*, 892.
[2] Article V of the Root-Takahira Agreement reads as follows: "Should any
event occur threatening the *status quo* as above described or the principle of equal
opportunity as above defined, it remains for the two Governments to communicate
with each other in order to arrive at an understanding as to what measures they
may consider it useful to take." The *"status quo* as above defined" applied to the
islands of the Pacific, exactly as did the Four-Power Treaty.

land, and that since they were included in the pact the Japanese mainland should be included also. Balfour was as touchy on the slight to the two Dominions implied in the exclusion of the Japanese homeland as Shidehara was on its inclusion. However, the latter eventually acquiesced and the treaty was signed on the definite understanding that it applied to the main islands of Japan.[1]

Shidehara now revived the issue. He hopefully pointed out to Hughes that various senators were objecting to the treaty on the same score. Hughes, who still thought the Japanese homeland should be included, said he would consult Lodge and Underwood about it.[2] There was so much uncertainty on the point that President Harding himself did not know whether or not the treaty applied to Japan's main islands. On December 20 he told a White House press conference that it did not, was hastily corrected by the State Department and as hastily issued another statement contradicting his first and approving the inclusion of the islands.[3] But Shidehara kept up his agitation, in which he was greatly assisted by American extremists who claimed that a pledge of non-aggression *vis-à-vis* the Japanese homeland "would obligate the United States to defend Japanese imperialism."[4] Hughes was at length compelled to agree to the exclusion of the Japanese homeland (January 14) and to sign an amendment to the Four-Power Treaty (February 6) specifically defining its application to Japan so as to include "only Karafuto (or the Southern portion of the island of Sakhalin), Formosa and the Pescadores, and the islands under the mandate of Japan."[5]

In its final form the Four-Power Treaty amounted to a composite of the Bryan Peace Commission Treaty and Article V of

[1] See the memoranda of meetings attended by Hughes, Balfour, Kato, Shidehara, Viviani and Jusserand, December 8 and 9. *For. Rel.*, 1922, I, 13-27.

[2] Hughes memorandum of conversation with Shidehara, December 19. *Ibid.*, 37-38.

[3] *Ibid.*, 38-39.

[4] Cf. Buell, 179 ff.

[5] *For. Rel.*, 1922, I, 42-44, 46-47; *Conference*, 824-825.

the Root-Takahira Agreement.[1] The mild, broadly generalized consultative obligations imposed by it were a cheap price to pay for the abrogation of the Anglo-Japanese Alliance and a new pledge of respect for the integrity of the Philippines. It was hardly enough to purchase Japanese assent to the Hughes naval program. As applied to the myriad islands covered by the Four-Power Treaty foreign policy was synonymous with naval strategy. Non-aggression pledges, however well meant, would rest on a precarious foundation if the area to which they applied were permitted to become a heavily fortified frontier, bristling with naval bases and ominous with maneuvers. This was a truism to Hughes and Balfour as much as it was to Kato.

It carried particular weight with the Japanese admiral. The geographical situation of his country necessarily rendered the disposition of naval forces in the western Pacific of more vital concern to him than to either of his colleagues. Whatever construction Balfour and Hughes might place upon it, the mission of British and American warships in the Far East could never be made to appear wholly defensive to a Japanese. Kato therefore refused to adhere to the Hughes naval treaty until he could obtain some more reliable insurance of Japan's security in her own waters than that afforded by the Four-Power Treaty.

Early in December, having first secured Balfour's approval, he suggested that Japan might consent to the 10:6 ratio if the United States and England would agree to maintain the *status quo* with respect to fortifications in their Pacific possessions. He also stipulated that Japan be allowed to retain the highly prized and all-but-completed battleship *Mutsu*, which Hughes had earmarked for the scrap-heap, and substitute in its place the *Settsu*, an older vessel.[2] On December 12 Kato made the fortification proposition

[1] Cf. *For. Rel.*, 1922, I, 51-53.
[2] The non-fortification agreement was discussed by Balfour and Hughes, December 1, and by Balfour, Hughes and Kato, December 2. See the memoranda of conversations of those dates by Sir Maurice Hankey. *For. Rel.*, 1922, I, 74-75,

definite. Hughes accepted it readily enough—provided it should
not apply to Hawaii—but he strenuously opposed the exemption
of the *Mutsu*. Fortified with the statistics of his naval experts, he
contended that this would force Britain and the United States to
retain, and even to build, vessels in compensation, and so defeat
the purpose of the naval treaty. In the end he was forced to concede the point or lose the treaty. The record of the meetings at
which it was debated shows, significantly, that it gave him far
more concern than did the non-fortification proposal.[1]

He never lost sight of his main objective, naval disarmament,
compared to which the Far Eastern dispensations, the non-
fortification agreement among them, were of secondary importance.

Extended discussion of the size and shape of the zone to be
affected finally resulted in a carefully defined non-fortification
agreement, announced December 15, 1921, and incorporated (as
Article XIX) in the Five-Power Naval Treaty signed February
5, 1922.[2] According to this article, the United States, Great
Britain and Japan agreed "that the *status quo* at the time of the
signing of the present Treaty, with regard to fortifications and
naval bases, shall be maintained" in certain of their territories and
possessions. These were specified as follows:

75-83. Hughes had been keeping in close touch with the American Embassy in
Tokyo and through it, maintaining constant pressure on the Japanese Government to accept his ratio. Cf. *Ibid.*, 61, 64-69, 88-90.

[1] See especially Hankey memorandum of meeting of December 12. *For. Rel.*,
1922, I, 90-99.

[2] This treaty, as finally signed and ratified, applied only to capital ships. It
provided for a ten year construction holiday and for the scrapping of specified
ships, built or building. Aside from prescribing qualitative tonnage limitations of
35,000 and 27,000 for capital ships and aircraft carriers, and gun caliber limitations for these two types of vessels of 16 and 8 inches respectively, the treaty was
designed to bring its five signatories, the United States, England, Japan, France
and Italy into an ultimate capital ship ratio of 5:5:3:1.75:1.75. The Treaty was
to remain in force until December 31, 1936, and thereafter subject to two years'
notice of termination by any signatory. For complete text of treaty, including
non-fortification agreement, *Conference*, 871-885; *For. Rel.*, 1922, I, 247-267.
For negotiation of, including preliminary drafts, *Ibid.*, 53-267.

(1) The insular possessions which the United States now holds or may hereafter acquire in the Pacific Ocean, except (a) those adjacent to the coast of the United States, Alaska and the Panama Canal Zone, not including the Aleutian Islands, and (b) the Hawaiian Islands;

(2) Hongkong and the insular possessions which the British Empire now holds or may hereafter acquire in the Pacific Ocean, east of the meridian of 110° east longitude, except (a) those adjacent to the coast of Canada, (b) the Commonwealth of Australia and its Territories, and (c) New Zealand;

(3) The following insular territories and possessions of Japan in the Pacific Ocean, to wit: the Kurile Islands, the Bonin Islands, Amami-Oshima, the Loochoo Islands, Formosa and the Pescadores, and any insular territories or possessions in the Pacific Ocean which Japan may hereafter acquire.

Maintenance of the *status quo* under these provisions was defined to mean "that no new fortifications or naval bases shall be established in the territories and possessions specified; that no measures shall be taken to increase the existing naval facilities for the repair and maintenance of naval forces, and that no increase shall be made in the coast defenses of the territories and possessions above specified." [1]

By promising not to fortify Guam, Pago-Pago, the Philippines and the Aleutians, the United States virtually ruled out the possibility of conducting offensive naval operations against Japan in her own waters. The same was true of the British promise regarding Hongkong. Under these circumstances Kato was willing to accept the inferior capital ship ratio allotted him by the naval treaty. He could do so in the comforting knowledge that the inferiority would tend to disappear should either the United States or Great Britain, or both, attempt to attack Japan from California, Hawaii or Singapore, their nearest bases.

Viewed through the prism of national interest, the non-

---

[1] The restriction did not, however, "preclude such repair and replacement of worn-out weapons and equipment as is customary in naval and military establishments in time of peace."

fortification agreement assumed a different shape to each of its signatories. Insofar as it constituted a practical application of the non-aggression pledges of the Four-Power Treaty, and provided the key to concurrence on the 5-5-3 ratio, it benefited all three alike. It appeared to confer the greatest immediate advantages on Japan. While the United States and Great Britain had strengthened the security of outlying possessions, Japan had strengthened the security of her homeland. Though prohibited as mandatory from fortifying the German islands now within her grasp, and obliged by the non-fortification agreement to fall back, as it were, some thousand miles from British and American possessions in the Pacific, she remained better able to strike at those possessions than their owners were to defend them. Fortified or not, Japan's island empire formed a protective screen of immense strategic value, as well as a multitude of potentially offensive submarine and air bases. Kato had removed the sword of Damocles that had hung over Japan; Balfour and Hughes had merely sheathed those hanging over Hongkong and the Philippines. Moreover, the enhanced security of her homeland could not fail to mean greater freedom of action for Japan on the mainland of Asia.

In that she had less to gain and infinitely more to lose, England's profits were commensurate with Japan's. The Far East had always occupied a subordinate position in the British scheme of things. First came Europe, then India, then Eastern Asia. No one understood the ratio better than Balfour. Witness his memorandum on British policy during the Russo-Japanese War,[1] his application of the Anglo-Japanese Alliance to the Indian frontier. The non-fortification agreement permitted Great Britain to fortify Australia, New Zealand and Singapore as much as she liked, and at the same time prohibited the creation of offensive Japanese bases within easy striking distance of these territories. Thus it vastly improved the defensive position of Britain's Pacific Dominions as well as of her Gibraltar of the Indian Ocean and all that depended

[1] Cf. Ch. III, p. 98, above.

on it. In exchange therefor Balfour had had only to disavow intentions his government did not entertain, to abandon plans for fortifications and naval expansion that it could not afford to carry out.

What of the United States? Like the Four-Power Treaty, the non-fortification agreement has been called many things by many critics. At first glance Hughes appeared to have given up more than he received in compensation. Japan had no island outposts from which to menace the American homeland. The economic superiority of the United States condemned Japan to *de facto* naval inferiority whether she chose to accept it *de jure* or not. Added security for America's far-flung Pacific islands seemed, to some, the very least that could be expected in return for acquiescence in Japan's naval supremacy in the western Pacific and consequent freedom of action in China.

Underlying much, perhaps most, of the American criticism of the Four-Power Treaty and its complement, the non-fortification agreement, were two basic assumptions. The first was that the naval bases and capital ships sacrificed by Hughes were existing, tangible assets. The second was that this sacrifice opened the floodgates for a Japanese inundation of America's supposed interests in China. The logical conclusion to which these assumptions lead is that Hughes traded a great deal for very little. It is true that, as Hughes himself knew only too well, a great expansion of fortification and capital ship construction would be the minimum prerequisite to a policy contemplating the use, or even the threat, of force to defend the open door and the territorial integrity of China. But criticism is less than valid that neglects to test the results of a policy against its stated objectives.

The decision not to use the Pacific islands as offensive naval outposts from which to promote American economic and political interests in China had been made, not at the Washington Conference, but shortly after the annexation of the Philippines, when Roosevelt first discovered the latter to be an Achilles' heel. Conceivably Hughes might have reversed the decision, but he would have had to move mountains to do so. The very fact of his insistence on the prior importance of disarmament over a Far Eastern settlement shows the extent to which the forces opposed to unlimited naval expansion had prevailed in American politics. At one of the earliest preliminary meetings of the American delegates to the Washington Conference, Root methodically canvassed Lodge and Underwood, respectively Chairman and ranking Democratic member of the Senate Foreign Relations Committee, as to whether there was any chance that Congress might appropriate the funds necessary for the expansive Far Eastern and concomitant naval policies. As co-author of the "large policy" of 1898, Lodge might have been expected to look for that chance. Instead he agreed with Underwood that it did not exist. Both delegates were emphatic in the opinion that Congress would not make the appropriation.[1]

The American delegation shaped its course accordingly. Its fundamental assumption was not that the expansion of fortifications and increase in capital ships were assets to be sacrificed, but that they were liabilities to be avoided. "It was obvious," Hughes wrote in his official report, "that no agreement for limitation was possible if the three Powers were not content to take as a basis their actual existing naval strength.

General considerations of national need, aspirations and expectations, policy and program, could be brought forward by each Power in justification of some hypothetical relation of naval strength with no result but profitless and interminable discussion. The solution was to take what the Powers actually had, as it was manifest that neither could better its relative position unless it won in the race which it was the object of the Conference to end. It was impossible to terminate competition in naval armament if the Powers were to condition their agreement upon the advantages they hoped to gain in the competition itself." [2]

[1] Cf. Jessup, Philip C., *Elihu Root*, Ch. XLVII.
[2] *Conference*, 798-799.

On this basis, none of the three powers surrendered any tangible assets in the non-fortification agreement; and such as they surrendered in the naval treaty—the capital ships, built or building, consigned by that treaty to the scrap-heap—were apportioned fairly evenly among them. The forts, the ships given up by Mr. Hughes, were the merest potentialities. The reinforcement of the four-power non-aggression pledges by a mutual abandonment of offensive fortification in the western Pacific was a tremendous boon to the owner of the Philippines. If Japan's gains seemed relatively greater it was because her geographical situation made them inevitably so, not because Hughes gave away more than he received. Hughes had given away nothing but a few blueprints which the most competent authorities of both parties had advised him stood no chance of Congressional approval.

Signing the Four-Power Treaty and the non-fortification agreement did not mean that the Harding Administration had decided to abandon American interests in China. It meant, rather, that Hughes had decided to employ a traditional as opposed to a radical method of defending those interests. Hay and Roosevelt had come eventually to the conclusion that the American people would neither fight for the open door and the territorial integrity of China nor support a Far Eastern policy based on the use of force. The reason for this attitude was, as we have several times pointed out, that the Far East was a relatively unimportant market for American commerce and investment and an area in which no vital American interests of any kind were at stake. Hughes had evidently reached the same conclusion as his predecessors. That did not prevent him, however, from making the most vigorous effort to defend China's integrity and the open door—in the traditional manner—yet on record.

Balfour had handed Hughes the drafts of two "arrangements" on November 11, one the triple entente which Hughes discarded, the other a five-power treaty relating to China.[1] The second "ar-

[1] *For. Rel.*, 1922, I, 1-2; text of draft, 271-272.

rangement," in which the United States, England, France, China and Japan were invited to participate, was dedicated to four major principles: the general peace of Eastern Asia, preservation of the territorial integrity and independence of China, equal commercial opportunity in China and international co-operation *vis-à-vis* China. To uphold these principles the contracting parties were bound by six specific articles to consult each other whenever any one of the four principles was thought to be in jeopardy; to undertake no independent military or naval action without mutual consultation; to communicate to each other all financial contracts with China and finally, to agree to no independent arrangements in any way prejudicial to these rules and principles. Hughes's defense of the integrity of China was traditional even to the point of being prompted by an Englishman. For just as the open door notes grew out of the Hippisley memoranda, the Balfour draft of November 11 became the Nine-Power Treaty of February 6, 1922.

Once Balfour had outlined his policy (as was also true in 1899) he yielded to his American colleague the initiative in implementing it. This Hughes accepted and exercised in such a way as to make the Nine-Power Treaty the most categorical and aggressive affirmation of the Far Eastern policy of the United States yet on record. He assumed that the maintenance of China's integrity was the "corollary" to the preservation of the open door and that the two principles had been ineffective in the past because they "were never a matter of binding international obligation among all the powers concerned." He stated it as his purpose "to give new vigor and reality to the co-ordinated principles of territorial and administrative integrity of China and of the 'open door' or equality of opportunity for all nations in China." [1] To this task, and to the prosecution of his cases against Japan in Shantung, Yap and Siberia, he addressed himself with as much energy as he had devoted to the Pacific and naval settlements.

Just as at Paris, the Chinese delegates made the first meeting

[1] Official report, *Conference*, 820.

of the Committee on Pacific and Far Eastern Questions the occasion for promulgating another bill of rights for the new Chinese Republic. They demanded the release of their country from the unequal treaties which the Paris Peace Conference had notoriously failed to disturb. In particular they renewed their pressure for tariff autonomy, the abolition of extraterritoriality, the restoration of Shantung, cancellation of the Twenty-One Demands and with them "all special rights, privileges, immunities or commitments, whatever their character or contractual basis, claimed by any of the powers in or relating to China." [1]

The American delegation prepared to carry out as much of this program as possible. The stage was set for a new series of open door notes, a new effort to resuscitate the co-operative policy. In the negotiations that followed Root played an influential part. It was he who revised (in phraseology rather than in purpose) the four Balfour principles, on which negotiations were to be based. These were adopted by the Far Eastern committee November 21 and by the conference as a whole December 10—the same day the conclusion of the Four-Power Treaty was announced. They bound each power:

(1) To respect the sovereignty, the independence, and the territorial and administrative integrity of China;

(2) To provide the fullest and most unembarrassed opportunity to China to develop and maintain for herself an effective and stable government;

(3) To use their influence for the purpose of effectually establishing and maintaining the principle of equal opportunity for the commerce and industry of all nations throughout the territory of China;

(4) To refrain from taking advantage of conditions in China in order to seek special rights or privileges which would abridge the rights of subjects or citizens of friendly States, and from countenancing action inimical to the security of such States. [2]

[1] *Ibid.*, 444-445; *For. Rel.*, 1922, I, 272-274. The Chinese demands were presented November 16, 1921.

[2] *Conference*, 895. Full text of Nine-Power Treaty, *Ibid.*, 893-897; *For. Rel.*, 1922, I, 276-282.

The Japanese delegates readily gave their assent to the Balfour-Root principles, but stubbornly contested their practical application to the situation at hand.

It required all of Hughes's powers of persuasion, Root's experience and moderation, and Balfour's shrewd services as mediator to bring the recalcitrant Japanese into line. And no wonder. For the principles comprised the most stringent abstinence pledge the United States had yet sought from its competitors in China.[1] In the opinion of the American delegates, the adoption of the principles "reaffirmed the postulates of American policy which were no longer to be left to the exchanges of diplomatic notes, but were to receive the sanction of the most solemn undertaking of the Powers." [2] The Far Eastern policy of the United States was being written into international law. Nor did the American delegates content themselves with a mere declaration of principles. Throughout December and January they strove to tie the Japanese down to the most definite commitments they dared hope from them. They renewed with energy the campaign to restore Shantung to China, obtain the sought-for rights on the island of Yap and secure the withdrawal of Japanese troops from Siberia. The principal fruit of their efforts was the Nine-Power Treaty, signed February 6, 1922.[3]

In the first article of this treaty the signatories endorsed the four Balfour-Root principles. In Article II they agreed "not to enter into any treaty, agreement, arrangement, or understanding, either with one another, or, individually or collectively, with any

[1] Root's fourth point incorporated almost verbation the secret protocol of the Lansing-Ishii Agreement, cf. above, Ch. V, p. 215. The injunction against "action inimical to the security of such States" looked like a concession to Japan, since it was the latter's habitual pretension that her rights and privileges in China were vital to her national security.

[2] Official report, *Conference*, 829.

[3] The signatories of the treaty were the United States, Great Britain, Japan, France, Italy, the Netherlands, Belgium, Portugal, and China.

Power or Powers, which would infringe or impair the principles stated in Article I." Article III was even more explicit:

With a view to applying more effectually the principles of the Open Door or equality of opportunity in China for the trade and industry of all nations, the Contracting Powers, other than China agree that they will not seek, nor support their respective nationals in seeking:

(a) any arrangement which might purport to establish in favor of their interests any general superiority of rights with respect to commercial or economic development in any designated region of China;

(b) any such monopoly or preference as would deprive the nationals of any other Power of the right of undertaking any legitimate trade or industry in China, or of participating with the Chinese Government, or with any local authority, in any category of public enterprise, or which by reason of its scope, duration or geographical extent is calculated to frustrate the practical application of the principle of equal opportunity.[1]

The remaining articles of the treaty bound the signatories not to support their nationals in seeking spheres of influence or "mutually exclusive opportunities in designated parts of Chinese territory"; to respect China's neutrality in case of war to which she was not a party; to communicate fully and frankly among themselves whenever circumstances seemed to require the application of the treaty. China agreed not to countenance any form of railway rate discrimination (one of the chief points of the original Hay notes), and all non-signatories having regulations with China were invited to adhere to the treaty.

The language of international law admitted of no more explicit pledge of respect for the open door and the territorial integrity

---

[1] These stipulations were "not to be so construed as to prohibit the acquisition of such properties or rights as may be necessary to the conduct of a particular commercial, industrial, or financial undertaking or to the encouragement of invention and research"; and China undertook to be guided by the principles stipulated above "in dealing with applications for economic rights and privileges from governments and nationals of all foreign countries, whether parties to the present Treaty or not."

of China. That was as far as the Nine-Power Treaty went. It did not legally bind the United States to defend the open door and the territorial integrity of China from any other nation, but merely to respect them itself. It was a self-denying ordinance rather than a collective security pact. The only sanction behind it was the good faith of its signatories. Here again Hughes had employed traditional rather than radical methods. Whatever the *moral* commitment implicit in its periodic efforts in behalf of China's integrity and the open door, the United States had never *legally* bound itself to defend those objectives against all comers. But within these traditional limitations, the self-denying ordinance was assuredly the most stringent yet applied to the competing exploiters of China.

In attempting to bring about the restoration of Shantung, a *cause célèbre* to the American delegation at Washington as it had been at Paris, Hughes found the old stalemate unbroken.[1] The Japanese were willing to restore the province, but only according to the terms of the 1915 and 1918 treaties and on the basis of independent negotiations with China. The Chinese opposed any compromise, demanding unqualified restitution with no political or economic strings attached. The exertion of all sorts of subtle pressure on both litigants was required to bring them to conference on the subject. At length Balfour and Hughes persuaded them to agree to a series of joint meetings, beginning December 1, to be attended by two British and two American "observers" to see fair play.[2]

[1] Cf. p. 252 ff., above.

[2] Balfour and Hughes had to make joint representations to the Chinese Government, through the British and American Embassies at Peking, before it would consent to discuss Shantung with the Japanese. Even then, it insisted on the face-saving tactics of having Japan take the initiative. Cf. Hughes to Schurman, November 25; Schurman to Hughes, November 27; Hughes to Warren (and Schurman) November 30, 1921. *For. Rel.*, 1922, I, 934-937. As an inducement to Japan, Balfour agreed on December 3 to return Weihaiwei to China on condition that Japan return Shantung. This was no great sacrifice for England since with the elimination of Russia and Germany from the scene the base had outlived

No less than thirty-six meetings were necessary before a settlement was made. The most favorable terms Japan would offer were immediate restitution of the province with the exception of the Tsinan-Tsingtao Railway. This Japan would sell to China for money obtained from Japanese bankers in the form of a fifteen-year loan secured by a lien on the road, Japanese technicians and accountants to share in its operation until the loan was fully repaid. The Chinese stubbornly refused to accept these terms. Twice the meetings were broken off, to be resumed only after considerable Anglo-American exhortation in Peking (not to mention the continued independent suasion of Japan on that capital). On one of these occasions Secretary Hughes even took the Chinese Minister to see President Harding who told him "it would be a colossal blunder in statecraft if China were not to take advantage of the opportunity now afforded her for the settlement of the Shantung question as the alternative might involve a risk of losing the Province." [1]

Under such influence the Chinese at last gave way. On February 4, 1922, they signed a treaty with the Japanese which restored Shantung in full sovereignty to China but which, by virtue of the terms of the Japanese railway loan, did not greatly disturb Japan's economic supremacy (and concomitant political influence) in the province. Even so, the reassertion of Chinese sovereignty was, under the circumstances, a considerable victory for China and was generally accepted as such by her partisans. It was more than a nominal success for the persistent American diplomacy that had

its usefulness and the new naval and Pacific treaties rendered it strategically untenable.

[1] Hughes to Schurman, January 25, 1922. *Ibid.*, 945. Hughes had previously instructed the American Minister in Peking to advise the Chinese Government "that a policy of insisting obstinately upon impractical points of view may defeat the hopes of China and of China's friends that the conference may help in ameliorating some at least of the existing unfortunate conditions." Same to same, December 7. *Ibid.*, 274-275. Cf. also despatches in *Ibid.*, 940-967, esp. Hughes to Schurman, January 22, 941-943, and same to same, February 15, 1922, 960-967.

begun with Lansing's invocation of the non-recognition doctrine in 1915.[1]

The remaining Chinese demands were likewise supported by Secretary Hughes, with varying but on the whole substantial success. A nine-power customs tariff treaty (signed February 6, 1922) provided for a rise in Chinese duties which, if less than the Chinese desired, would net them a substantial increase in revenue. It also set up a commission to effect widespread reforms in the Chinese tariff administration. This was not tariff autonomy, but it was a step in that direction. By a resolution adopted December 10, 1921, a similar commission was established to study, and if possible, prepare the way for the abolition of extraterritoriality. Further resolutions provided for the abolition of foreign-owned postoffices in China (except in leased territory) on condition that China provide an efficient service of her own and imposed restrictions, however mild, on foreign ownership and operation of radio stations in China.[2]

In their attack on the Twenty-One Demands, now the basis of Japan's most expansive Manchurian claims, the Chinese found Hughes an equally sympathetic though somewhat less effective ally. The Japanese summarily rejected the contention that the Sino-Japanese treaties of 1915 were invalid because forced on China against her will. They knew that they stood on solid ground in so doing since general acceptance of the Chinese contention would undermine the Versailles Treaty, to the defense of which France and England were irrevocably committed. Except for Weihaiwei, these two powers were no more willing to relinquish their Chinese spheres and leaseholds than was Japan. Without

[1] Text of treaty, *For. Rel.*, 1922, I, 948-957. Cf. also *Conference*, 125-132, 137-140, 231, 526-527, 585, 825-828; Buell, 255-264; Ichihashi, 267-287; *Conversations between the Chinese and Japanese Representatives in Regard to the Shantung Question*, prepared by the Japanese delegation, and same title, prepared by the Chinese delegation.

[2] *Conference*, 441-783, 832-844; Buell, Chs. VIII, IX; Ichihashi, Chs. XIII, XV, XVI.

their co-operation, Hughes's chances of ousting Japan from Manchuria were no better than Knox's or Lansing's had been, to say nothing of the disastrous effects such an attempt would have on the yet unsigned naval treaty. The structure of special rights and privileges that Japan had erected in Manchuria during the war was consequently left standing, and the failure of the powers seriously to contest its legality once more reinforced its political foundations.

The only satisfaction that Hughes could obtain from the Japanese with respect to Manchuria was an offer by Shidehara (February 2) of three purely nominal concessions. Japan would throw open to the consortium her railway loan options in southern Manchuria and Inner Mongolia—subject, however, to the identical conditions stipulated in the consortium agreement of October, 1920; she disavowed the intention to use Japanese military, financial, or political advisers in southern Manchuria, a region so completely under the domination of her nationals as to render such advisers superfluous; and she withdrew Group V of the Twenty-One Demands, to the realization of which she had already discovered insuperable obstacles.[1] Perceiving that Shidehara would go no further, Hughes resorted to the time-honored American tactics of ambiguity and bluff. At the next meeting of the Far Eastern Committee (February 3) he made an ominous reservation of rights. He defined American policy toward Manchuria and the Twenty-One Demands by reading the Lansing non-recognition note of May 13, 1915.[2] He warned that the United States would claim from China under the most-favored-nation clause whatever

[1] The "concession" to the consortium was based on the proviso, "it being understood that nothing in the present declaration shall be held to imply any modification or annulment of the understanding recorded in the officially announced notes and memoranda which were exchanged among the Governments of the countries represented in the Consortium and also among the national financial groups composing the Consortium, in relation to the scope of the joint activity of that organization." *Conference*, 847. Also *For. Rel.*, 1922, I, 761 ff.

[2] Cf. above, Ch. V, p. 194.

benefits accrued to Japan by virtue of the treaties of 1915. And to make perfectly sure that this claim in no way implied recognition of the contested treaties, he explained that "the question of the validity of the treaties as between Japan and China is distinct from the question of the treaty rights of the United States under its treaties with China," rights that had been "emphasized and consistently asserted by the United States."[1] These conflicting opinions were written into the minutes of the conference, as one might photograph a stalemated and abandoned chessboard. Hughes had fought China's battle in Manchuria to a standstill.

A greater measure of success crowned his efforts to achieve the more purely American objectives left on the agenda. On January 23 he had drawn from Baron Shidehara a fresh disclaimer of designs on Russian territory and a statement that Japanese troops would soon be withdrawn from Siberia and northern Sakhalin. Hughes himself and the French delegate, M. Sarraut, followed Shidehara's declaration with expressions of confidence in its sincerity, and the whole was ostentatiously spread upon the minutes of the conference.[2] To what extent Japan's subsequent evacuation of Siberia (October, 1922) and northern Sakhalin (1925) was due to American pressure is extremely uncertain. She did not withdraw from either territory until she had obtained valuable coal, oil and fisheries concessions from the Soviet Government, and until it became evident that the continued occupation of them was costing her so much that it threatened to become a major government scandal.[3] Nevertheless, Hughes had boldly taken up a matter which Japan had refused to permit the conference to discuss, and with the customary weapons of moral suasion and publicity had at least kept her on the defensive. He did so, furthermore, without European assistance, bearing the entire brunt of the responsibility for Russia's territorial integrity that

[1] *Conference,* 779 ff., 850-852.
[2] *Conference,* 698-707, 853-862.
[3] See the interesting comments on this subject in Takeuchi, Ch. XVIII.

Wilson had assumed. Finally, with regard to Yap a definite treaty between Japan and the United States was signed (February 11, 1922) a few days after the conference adjourned. American citizens were granted equal cable, radio and residential rights and facilities on the island with Japanese, in return for which the United States consented to Japan's mandate over the Pacific islands north of the equator.[1] Thus was terminated the effort to curb Japanese imperialism in the Far East that Lansing and Wilson had inaugurated in the closing year of the war.[2]

The Treaties of Washington were the apotheosis of the traditional Far Eastern policy of the United States. As we have pointed out, no power gained or lost much by them, save in the nebulous categories of ultimate goals and logical conclusions. They were primarily a recognition of existing, if brutal, facts, a consolidation of the *status quo*. By them the Pacific suffered no peaceful change; it was only partially frozen. The same was true of China. Admitting these limitations, the treaties constituted the most dynamic and the most comprehensive attempt on the part of the United States to uphold the territorial integrity of China and all that it believed to depend on it; to make the open door in China an enduring principle of international law; to obtain security for its Philippine hostages to fortune, and to confine within barriers manufactured in Washington the hungry expansionism of Japan. The treaties went as far as pen and ink could go to preserve a peace founded on such antithetical elements as those inherent in the *status quo* in the Far East.

That they were not intended as a strategic retreat for the United

---

[1] *Conference*, 863-865; *For. Rel.*, 1922, I, 599-604.

[2] On December 27, 1922, Japan agreed to cancel the Lansing-Ishii Agreement after Hughes gave her the choice of so doing or of consenting to the publication of the secret article containing pledges respecting China (cf. p. 215, above). *For. Rel.*, 1922, II, 591-599. Both Japan's desire to retain the agreement and Hughes's desire to be rid of it would seem to indicate that, whatever construction Lansing had placed upon it, usage had made it seem an American concession to Japanese imperialism in China.

States seems implicit in these facts. It seems further evident in the initiative displayed by Secretary Hughes in convoking the conference in the first place, in defining its agenda in the second and in supporting the Chinese demands in the third. It is wrong, perhaps, to say that Hughes stole Wilson's thunder, for Wilson himself had stolen Hay's. Whether the Hughes treaties would bring to American interests in the Far East any greater prosperity than had the Hay notes remained to be seen.

# IX. Immigration

THE signatures were scarcely dry on the Washington Treaties before the peace underwritten by them was disturbed by an issue they had failed to resolve. On November 13, 1922, the United States Supreme Court ruled that Japanese immigrants were ineligible to American citizenship. A year and a half later (May 26, 1924) Congress enacted laws applying rigid quotas to immigrants of all nationalities and totally excluding those ineligible to citizenship. This was the culmination of a policy that had led the United States successively to deny citizenship to Chinese immigrants, to exclude Chinese labor, to restrict Japanese immigration by executive agreement with Japan, and finally, by means of the famous statute of 1924, to close the door to all oriental immigrants whatsoever. All this while, the germs of race prejudice had polluted American relations with both China and Japan, and had profoundly influenced the development of the Far Eastern policy of the United States. Brief mention of immigration restriction has been made in the foregoing chapters. It is now time to turn back and observe how this became a primary concern of American diplomacy in the Far East, rivaling in importance the security of the Philippines.

The first oriental immigrants to enter the United States were Chinese, lured to California by the gold rush of 1848. These were followed by a steady stream of farmers, shop-keepers, contract laborers, and coolies imported to serve the needs of the gold-seekers and the settlers and railroad builders that had followed them to the Pacific Coast. By 1853 there were some 25,000 Chinese in California, a number that grew to 132,000 in thirty years.[1]

[1] Coolidge, Mary R., *Chinese Immigration*, Ch. I and appendix, 498-499.

In 1868, Secretary Seward negotiated a treaty with China recognizing the right of free immigration of Chinese subjects "for purposes of curiosity, or trade, or as permanent residents," but expressly reserving the right of naturalization.[1] Coolie labor was in demand for Central Pacific railway gangs. Seward's party, committed as it was to industrial expansion, free land and cheap labor, had much at stake in the rapid completion of the transcontinental railways. The free immigration treaty of 1868 reflected national rather than local interests.

The shortage of labor made the first Chinese immigrants welcome in California. But it was not long before their tidy farms and shops had begun to excite native resentment. The inevitable boom and collapse that followed the gold rush turned the labor shortage into a surplus, and unemployed Californians took alarm at the competition of coolie and contract laborers from China. The rapid growth of the Chinese population accentuated its racial and cultural peculiarities, infusing economic competition with race antipathy. Industrious and law-abiding though they were, the Chinese soon found themselves victims of discriminatory legislation. As early as 1855 the California legislature imposed a large head tax on Chinese immigrants. Three years later it passed an act prohibiting Chinese and Mongolian immigrants from entering the state. These and other laws of the same character were invalidated by the California supreme court, by the Federal Circuit Court in California and by a United States Supreme Court ruling that immigration fell in the category of foreign commerce, the regulation of which was exclusively the right of Congress.[2] Theoretically, the Seward treaty of 1868 placed the right of free immigration beyond the attack of state legislatures.

As the influence of California and neighboring states grew in

[1] The treaty was negotiated by Seward and Anson Burlingame, former American Minister to Peking serving in the capacity of special envoy of the Chinese Government. Dennett, *Americans in Eastern Asia,* 539 ff.; Garis, Roy L., *Immigration Restriction,* 288-289.

[2] Garis, 287 ff.; Coolidge, Ch. V.

national politics, however, the move to restrict Chinese immigration gained headway. Finding their path blocked by the federal courts and by the treaty of 1868, the Californians determined to force Congress to write new immigration laws and the Department of State to abrogate the treaty. So effective was their agitation to these ends that in 1876 a Congressional committee was appointed to investigate conditions in California. After eighteen days of hearings in San Francisco, the committee issued a sensational report. It found the white population of California in danger of being outnumbered by the Chinese, a people incapable of assimilation, and recommended Congressional legislation "to restrain the great influx of Asiatics to this country." [1]

In the Presidential election of 1876 the platforms of both parties contained anti-Chinese immigration planks. Two years later the California practice of denying Chinese the right of naturalization was sustained by a circuit court ruling that a Chinese was not a "white person" within the meaning of the United States naturalization laws.[2] In 1879, despite the opposition of the State Department, Congress took up the report of the committee of 1876, flouted the Seward treaty, and passed a bill limiting to fifteen the number of Chinese immigrants that could be landed in California by any one vessel. Though President Hayes vetoed the bill, he was forced to yield to the pressure behind it. He sent special commissioners to China to obtain the consent of the Chinese Government to the modification of the treaty of 1868.[3]

After some negotiation President Hayes's commissioners signed a treaty with the Chinese Government (November 17, 1880) that recognized the right of the United States to "regulate, limit, or suspend . . . but . . . not absolutely prohibit" the immigration of Chinese laborers. "The limitation or suspension shall be reasonable," it was stipulated, "and shall apply only to Chinese who

[1] Coolidge, Ch. VII; Garis, 288-292.
[2] In re: Ah Yup, 1 Federal Cases 223; Van Dyne on Naturalization, 42.
[3] Coolidge, Ch. IX; Garis, 292; Dennett, 542.

may go to the United States as laborers, other classes not being included in the limitations." [1] With the Seward-Burlingame treaty out of its way, Congress proceeded to enact a law suspending Chinese labor immigration for twenty years. President Arthur vetoed the law (April 4, 1882) on the grounds that twenty years was an unreasonably long period of suspension. But the restraining influence of the chief executive was waning. In his veto message, Arthur admitted the necessity of some such legislation and expressed sympathy with its objectives. The bill was thereupon repassed with a ten-year suspension, and approved by the President May 6, 1882. Skilled as well as unskilled laborers and miners were included in the suspension, and a special article provided that "hereafter no state court or court of the United States shall admit Chinese to citizenship." [2]

From 1882 to 1905 a succession of state and federal laws, judicial decisions and treaties closed the door to Chinese immigration even more firmly. Scarcely a year went by without the tightening of old restrictions or the imposition of new ones. The Chinese were attacked by Western labor unions; their morals were impeached; they were harassed in the courts and murdered in riots. Not without justice did the Chinese Foreign Office complain to the American Minister to Peking, in 1887, that American citizens in China were accorded a greater measure of protection and justice than were Chinese in the United States. The Chinese Government undertook to remedy the situation by prohibiting the emigration of laborers to the United States. The Cleveland Administration readily fell in with the plan, and on March 12, 1888, signed another treaty with China absolutely prohibiting all labor immigration to the United States for twenty years. The terms of the treaty were not drastic enough to suit the Senate, however, which added amendments forbidding Chinese laborers who had

[1] *For. Rel.*, 1881, 168-203; Coolidge, Ch. X; Dennett, 542-543; Garis, 292-293.

[2] Van Dyne, 42 ff.; Coolidge, Ch. XI; Garis, 294-295.

left the United States to return even though they held certificates
entitling them to do so. When the Chinese Government hesitated
to ratify the treaty as thus amended, Congress resorted to the novel
procedure of voting into effect the provisions of the treaty, ratified
or not, and by an act of October 1, 1888, further increasing their
severity.

In vain did China protest these high-handed measures. They
were approved by President Cleveland and sustained by court
decisions. Even the State Department turned a deaf ear to Chinese requests for their repeal. It promised merely "careful consideration" of the complaint that the laws conflicted with existing
treaty rights and were subversive of the principle of reciprocity.
In 1892 and 1893 Congress extended for another ten years, and
substantially increased in stringency, all legislation relating to the
exclusion of Chinese immigrants. China's recognition of this extension—specifically of the total exclusion of laborers for ten years
—was obtained by a new treaty (signed March 17, 1894). In
1902 Congress extended the application of the exclusion laws to
Hawaii, the Philippines and all other American possessions, and
two years later, on the expiration of the treaty of 1894, re-enacted
without term all Chinese immigration statutes on the books.
Chinese laborers were thus permanently excluded from the United
States and its possessions. No Chinese could become a citizen of
the United States by naturalization. The definition of a laborer
had been stretched so as to admit only teachers, students, merchants, travelers and government officials.[1]

China met the action of Congress in 1904 with the first systematic, large-scale boycott in her history—against American goods.
This was the boycott that "displeased" President Roosevelt and
complicated Rockhill's efforts to secure a remission of the Boxer
indemnity.[2] It was of doubtful effectiveness. Certainly it did not
induce the United States to alter its immigration policy. But it

[1] Coolidge, Chs. XII-XVII; Garis, 297-307.
[2] Cf. above, Ch. III, p. 124.

did focus American attention on the abuses of treaty rights and inhuman practices prevalent in the enforcement of the immigration laws, of which the Chinese Government had complained in vain to the State Department. Whether because of the boycott or, as seems more probable, because of a guilty conscience, the United States administered its Chinese immigration laws more efficiently, more justly, though no less rigorously after 1905.[1]

The Chinese boycott epitomized the conflict of policy growing out of the immigration issue. Since 1900, the United States had stood in the van of China's protectors, striving by moral suasion to defend the open door and the territorial integrity of the helpless empire. American traders, missionaries and diplomats had created a tradition of friendship with China that bordered on the quixotic. The State Department had done its best to promote American commercial interests in China. Yet the gratitude and profit thus earned were momentarily dissipated by the treatment meted out to Chinese immigrants in the United States. The Chinese were goaded into closing the door to American commerce. If the American immigration policy could so alienate the affections of China, to whom the friendship of the United States was not only traditional, but vital, what would be the effect of the policy on a nation that aspired to equality with the United States, possessed the power to support its pretensions and believed itself already the victim of unfriendly American diplomacy in other spheres?

As it happened, China was too weak, too preoccupied with her European exploiters to make her protests felt through the ordinary channels of diplomacy. For this reason the experience with Chinese immigrants was of comparatively slight diplomatic significance. The United States could, and did, ignore China's wishes with impunity. It violated existing treaties and dictated others in an overbearing manner. When China balked at the harsh terms demanded by the State Department, Congress dispensed with treaty sanctions altogether, and enacted laws that were even

[1] Cf. Remer, *A Study of Chinese Boycotts*, 29-39.

harsher. Scant allowance was made, either in California or in Washington, for the sensibilities of a proud and friendly people. The persecution of Chinese subjects in the United States was winked at by the courts and, in effect, condoned by the federal government. It was a less excusable counterpart of the anti-foreign riots that sometimes took American lives in China. This freedom from diplomatic restraint during the period when the United States first came to grips with the problem of oriental immigration set a precedent that proved difficult to follow. What made it so was the emergence of Japan, already a great power and self-constituted champion of the principle of racial equality, as the next and greatest source of oriental immigration to the United States. With such a nation as Japan the United States could afford to employ no such arbitrary methods of exclusion as it could with China. Diplomacy was bound to play a more important role in the Japanese immigration problem than it had in the Chinese.

Indeed, it was in the realm of foreign rather than domestic affairs that Japanese immigrants first became of concern to the United States. The first foreign country to which Japan permitted her laboring classes to emigrate was Hawaii, in which, when the permission was granted (1884) the United States had important vested interests. In search of cheap plantation labor and desiring to offset the preponderance of Chinese immigrants, Hawaiian sugar growers signed an immigration convention with Japan in 1886. There were at the time about a hundred Japanese in the Hawaiian Islands. By 1900 some 80,000 public and private contract laborers had been imported from Japan and resident Japanese numbered 61,111, or 39.7 per cent of the total population. They constituted much the largest foreign group in Hawaii, outnumbering both Chinese and native Hawaiians by over two to one, Americans by nearly nine to one.[1] The steady influx of Japanese, though origi-

[1] See tables in Ichihashi, Y., *Japanese in the United States*, 31-33. For Japanese-American diplomacy in re: the annexation of Hawaii see *Ibid.*, Chs. I-III; Bailey, T. A., "Japan's Protest Against the Annexation of Hawaii," *Journal of Modern*

nally invited by the American-dominated Hawaiian Government, soon became one of the chief talking points of the American annexationists. It led even the staunch anti-imperialist Senator Hoar to warn his colleagues that the Hawaiians would fall, "if we do not prevent it, a prey to Japan, not by conquest but by immigration. This result all parties agree that we must prevent. . . . The danger is . . . that there will be an infusion of Japanese and then an attempted annexation to Japan." [1]

Since early in the century, when American missionaries first settled there, and American traders and whalers first made them a port of call, the United States had displayed a proprietary interest in the Hawaiians. A treaty of annexation had been negotiated in 1854 only to be rejected by President Pierce on the strong protest of England. Thereafter the tide had set steadily in the direction of annexation. By a treaty of 1875 the United States had secured from the Hawaiian Government exclusive commercial privileges as well as a promise to alienate none of its territory by lease or otherwise to any other nation. The treaty was renewed in 1884, conferring on the United States the additional right to construct a naval base at Pearl Harbor. A revolution and abortive treaty of annexation followed in 1893, a *bona fide* annexation treaty in 1897, and on August 12, 1898, the islands passed under the American flag. Throughout this period Hawaiian politics had been dominated and the annexationist movement carefully nursed by an entrenched minority of American planters. [2]

Had the issue been decided by numbers of settlers alone, the islands might well have gone to Japan. Nor did the Japanese Government observe with indifference the trend toward American annexation. It had voiced no objection when Secretary Gresham deferentially sounded it on the prospect in 1893. [3] But circumstances

*History*, III, 46-61; Pratt, *Expansionists*, 125, 216 ff. and individual sources cited below.

[1] Dennett, *Americans in Eastern Asia*, 552-553.
[2] Pratt, *Expansionists*, *passim*.
[3] *Ibid.*, 125.

had shortly changed its mind. As early as 1887 the Hawaiian Government had been trying irresolutely to check the flow of Japanese immigrants into the islands. Ten years later it took drastic action. In March, 1897, just three months before the signing of the treaty of annexation with the United States, it refused admission to and sent back to Japan over a thousand Japanese immigrants.[1] The Japanese Government at once entered an indignant protest at Honolulu and backed it up by despatching thither the cruiser *Naniwa* with government officials, newspapermen and immigration company representatives on board. From May 5 until September 7, 1897, the *Naniwa* lay at anchor in Honolulu Harbor—under the watchful surveillance of three American warships—while the Japanese Government sought indemnification for the losses sustained by its immigrants and the steamship companies that had transported them to Hawaii.[2]

The situation had all the makings of an international melodrama. While the American and Japanese ships of war swung at their moorings the "Hawaiian" Government (consisting of American empire-builders) frantically negotiated for annexation to the United States, withholding reply to Japan's demands in the hope of dumping them in the lap of Washington. The effect of Japan's actions on the annexationists was electric. "If I had my way," Roosevelt wrote Mahan just before the *Naniwa* arrived at Honolulu, "we would annex those islands tomorrow.

If that is impossible, I would establish a protectorate. . . . I have been getting things in shape on the Pacific Coast just as fast as I have been allowed. My own belief is that we should act instantly before the two new Japanese warships leave England. I would . . . hoist our flag over the islands leaving all details for after action. . . . I am fully alive to the danger from Japan."[3]

---

[1] Bailey, *Japan's Protest*, 46. The exact number sent back was 1,174.
[2] *Ibid.*, 47-49.
[3] Roosevelt to Mahan, May 3, 1897. Pringle, *Roosevelt*, 171.

When the Japanese Minister to Hawaii made a statement to the press that was construed in both Honolulu and Washington as a threat of coercion, American apprehensions mounted. "Watch situation carefully," cabled Secretary of State Sherman to the American Minister at Honolulu.

If Japan should openly resort to force, such as military occupation or seizure of public property, you will confer with local authorities and Admiral, land suitable force, and announce provisional assumption of protectorate by United States over Hawaii pending consummation of annexation treaty, declaring at same time that all rights established in favor of third parties will be respected. This contingency is, however, not expected and you will be exceedingly cautious to do nothing that might tend to precipitate it, nor act except in face of overt act of hostility by Japan. Your action should be conspicuously friendly, aiming to bring about amicable results. . . .[1]

Though no "overt act of hostility" was precipitated, Japan unquestionably hastened American annexation. The Japanese Minister to Washington lost no time in protesting the treaty of annexation, which was signed June 16 and rushed to the Senate for ratification. He wished to know what provision had been made "for the preservation and maintenance of the rights acquired by Japan in her intercourse with Hawaii under the solemn sanctions of law and treaty." [2] Secretary Sherman told him that while the United States would not take upon itself any of the Hawaiian Government's obligations toward other governments, the treaty was not prejudicial to Japan's rights.[3] This did not satisfy Tokyo, which now came forward with a formal, detailed protest against the entire project of annexation:

First. The maintenance of the *status quo* of Hawaii is essential to the good understanding of the Powers which have interests in the Pacific. Second. The annexation of Hawaii would tend to endanger

[1] Sherman to Sewall, July 10, 1897. Bailey, *op. cit.*, 50.
[2] Hoshi to Sherman, June 15, 1897. *Ibid.*, 51.
[3] Sherman to Hoshi, June 16, *Ibid.*, 51-52.

the residential, commercial and industrial rights of Japanese subjects in Hawaii secured to them by Treaty and by the constitution and laws of that country. Third. Such annexation might lead to the postponement by Hawaii of the settlement of claims and liabilities already existing in favor of Japan under treaty stipulations.[1]

In his rebuttal Secretary Sherman was constrained to renew his previous assurance that the already established rights of Japanese subjects in the islands would not be disturbed by the transfer of sovereignty.[2]

To the annexationists, as one of them remarked, the Japanese protest was "one of those Providential developments which must help the treaty through the Senate." [3] Throughout the summer and fall of 1897 Japan kept up her opposition to American annexation. She did so not so much in the hope of preventing what was generally conceded even by Japanese statesmen to be a foregone conclusion, as of obtaining the indemnity she sought from Hawaii together with some kind of assurance that her rights would be respected under American sovereignty. Through the Japanese Minister to Washington she voiced her fear of the extension to Hawaii of American customs, immigration and navigation laws, continuing, meanwhile, to press her indemnity claim on the Hawaiian Government. On June 28 the latter proposed to arbitrate. The proposal was accepted, but neither party would agree to the other's conditions. With the United States in the awkward position of maintaining a virtual protectorate over Hawaii and yet refusing to assume the latter's international obligations, the State Department concluded that it would be wise to settle with Japan. The United States therefore entered the litigation as mediator, persuading Japan to withdraw her objection to annexation (December 22, 1897) in return for a promise to assume her claims if they were

---

[1] Hoshi to Sherman, June 19. *Ibid.*, 52.
[2] Sherman to Hoshi, June 25. *Ibid.*, 52.
[3] Hatch to Cooper, June 18, 1897. Hatch had advance news of the protest. *Ibid.*, 53.

not settled prior to the transfer of sovereignty. Secretary Day then prevailed on Hawaii to settle the claims before annexation by paying Japan $75,000 indemnity (July 27, 1898).[1]

Thus by 1898 the United States had learned to expect from Japan a far more zealous (and effective) defense of immigration rights than it had from China. While China registered vain protests with the State Department, Japan did not hesitate to carry that defense to the point of challenging the American annexation of the Hawaiian Islands. In so doing she played into the hands of the annexationists. Yet it is worth noting that she also received an indemnity and the recognition of principles therein implied.

Japanese immigration did not become a serious problem in the continental United States until after 1900. In 1880, two years before the Chinese population of the United States reached its peak of 132,000, there were only 148 Japanese in the entire country. It was not lawful for laborers to leave Japan until 1884. By 1900 Japanese in the United States numbered 24,326 as compared with 89,963 Chinese. Thenceforward the Japanese population increased while the Chinese declined until, at the census of 1930, the former stood at 138,834, the latter at 74,954. In Hawaii from 1900 to 1930 the Chinese population increased from 25,767 to 27,179, the Japanese from 61,111 to 139,631.[2]

The American solution of the Chinese immigration problem had been an object lesson to Japan. From the outset she endeavored to avert the discriminatory legislation by keeping emigration to the United States in conformance with American law. In 1892, when American immigration authorities objected to the recruiting of shiploads of Japanese coolies destined for California and Oregon, the Japanese Foreign Minister instructed prefectural gover-

[1] Bailey, *op. cit.*, 53-61.

[2] Census figures from Ichihashi, Chs. III, IV; Coolidge, 498, 500; *Statistical Abstract of the United States*, 1936, 11, 40. The highest census figure for Chinese in the continental United States was 107,488 in 1890. The figure for 1882 given above is an estimate based on Pacific Coast customs house figures minus deaths at 2 per cent per year.

nors to discourage the departure of contract laborers for the United States.[1] But although Japan was willing to avoid trouble abroad by self-imposed restraints at home, she was loath to recognize, by treaty, the right of the United States arbitrarily to regulate Japanese immigration according to its own national laws.

This she had been compelled to do, however, in a commercial treaty with the United States in 1894. The treaty granted each signatory reciprocal rights of entrance, travel and residence "in any part of the territories of the other," as well as free access to the courts, full protection of the laws, and complete liberty of conscience. It explicitly provided that,

In whatever relates to rights of residence and travel; to the possession of goods and effects of any kind; to the succession to personal estate, by will or otherwise, and the disposal of property of any sort and in any manner whatsoever which they may lawfully acquire, the citizens or subjects of each Contracting Party shall enjoy in the territories of the other the same privileges, liberties, and rights, and shall be subject to no higher imposts or charges in these respects than native citizens or subjects or citizens or subjects of the most favored nation.[2]

On the insistence of the United States a supplementary clause was inserted stipulating that these rights should in no way "affect the laws, ordinances and regulations with regard to trade, *the immigration of laborers*, police and public security which are in force or *which may hereafter be enacted* in either of the two countries."[3]

[1] Treat, *Diplomatic Relations*, II, 383-385, 387; Dennett, *Americans*, 549 ff.
[2] For complete text of treaty see Malloy, William M., *Treaties, Conventions, etc., between the United States and Other Powers*, I, 1028-1036.
[3] Malloy, 1030. Italics inserted. According to Hayashi Japan agreed to the clause against her will because the United States refused to sign the treaty without it and because the treaty was invaluable to Japan as a precedent for general revision of the unequal treaties from which she was seeking release. See Pooley, *Secret Memoirs of Count Hayashi*, 248; Dennett, *Americans*, 551. It seems clear that Japan was in a relatively unfavorable bargaining position on account of her own exclusionist policies toward foreigners, her refusal to permit them to own real estate, and her impelling anxiety to shake off extraterritoriality, for the eventual end of which the treaty of 1894 provided. The United States therefore had

The clause substantially modified the reciprocal and most-favored-nation privileges that preceded it, leaving the United States almost a free hand in restricting Japanese immigration.

After signing the treaty of 1894 Japan followed the same discreet policy of discouraging emigration not in conformance with American law. When anti-Japanese agitation broke out in California in 1900, the Japanese Government discontinued the issuance of passports to laborers bound for the United States.[1] But the stream of Japanese immigration into Hawaii, and via the Hawaiian, Canadian and Mexican "vestibules," into the United States continued unabated.[2] California became alarmed, and with a memorial to Congress from the state legislature in 1901 launched a drive for national restriction of Japanese immigration. Exactly as in the case of Chinese immigration restriction, the state found the federal government out of sympathy with its demands. President Roosevelt openly expressed his disapproval of discriminatory anti-Japanese legislation and privately wrote his friend Lodge that he was "utterly disgusted at the manifestations which have begun to appear on the Pacific slope in favor of excluding the Japanese exactly as the Chinese are excluded."[3] But, as had also been true of the experience with Chinese immigration, support for the demands of the Pacific Coast increased in strength until the federal government was forced to conform.

Exclusionist activities in California remained sporadic and ineffectual until 1905. Then, under the stimulus of the Russo-Japanese War, they flared up with climactic vigor. The heightened

little difficulty in securing her assent to the clause. Cf. esp. the despatches between Dun and Gresham in Treat, II, 425-427, 428. See also the interpretation of the treaty in Morris to Acting Secretary of State, *For. Rel.*, 1921, II, 323 ff.

[1] Buell, R. L., "Japanese Immigration," *World Peace Foundation Pamphlets*, VII, 287; Bailey, T. A., *Theodore Roosevelt and the Japanese-American Crises*, 2.

[2] From 1900 to 1908 inclusive the numbers of Japanese immigrants admitted to the United States each year were: 12,635; 5,249; 14,455; 20,041; 14,382; 11,021; 14,243; 30,824; 16,418. Ichihashi, 55, 57.

[3] Roosevelt to Lodge, May 15, 1905. Lodge, *Selections*, II, 122.

sense of national rivalry between Japan and the United States engendered by the war combined with the Japanese ill will earned by Roosevelt at Portsmouth to produce reaction in California. Labor unions, newspapers and politicians were encouraged to indulge their resentment of the steady influx of Japanese laborers and the constantly increasing Japanese population. Again the California legislature adopted resolutions and petitioned Congress to curtail the immigration of Japanese laborers. Similar appeals were sent to Congress by the legislatures of Idaho, Montana and Nevada. On April 1, 1905, the San Francisco Board of Education submitted to the Board of Supervisors a plan for segregating Japanese public school children, as had long been done with Chinese, in quarters apart from the regular school buildings.

The Japanese Government, with a premonition of what was coming, tried to appease the United States by restricting emigration to Hawaii, and then (in April, 1905) temporarily suspending it altogether. It was too late. Forces had been set in motion that could not so easily be checked. In a resolution of May 6, 1905, the Board of Education announced its determination "to effect the establishment of separate schools for Chinese and Japanese pupils, not only for relieving the congestion at present prevailing in our schools, but also for the higher end that our children should not be placed in any position where their youthful impression may be affected by association with pupils of the Mongolian race." [1]

The very next day a mass meeting in San Francisco started the Japanese and Korean Exclusion League on its career. The purpose of the League was to influence Congress, by propaganda and agitation, to extend the Chinese exclusion laws to Japanese immigration. It forthwith endorsed the Board of Education's segregation plan and prompted the introduction of Congressional resolutions

[1] Bailey, *Roosevelt*, 14. Details of school order and development of agitation of 1905 from *Ibid.*, Ch. I; Buell, *Japanese Immigration*, 287; Tupper, E. and McReynolds, G. E., *Japan in American Public Opinion*, 19-25; Ichihashi, 232-235.

embodying its objectives. Roosevelt, who thought that in spite of the arrogance with which their triumph over Russia supposedly had filled them, the Japanese "cannot behave worse than the State of California, through its Legislature, is now behaving toward the Japanese," [1] so strongly denounced discriminatory legislation in his annual message to Congress, and to the California Congressmen themselves, that the proposed resolutions fell flat.[2] "The feeling on the Pacific slope, taking it from several different standpoints, is as foolish as if conceived by the mind of a Hottentot," confided the President to Lodge.

These Pacific Coast people wish grossly to insult the Japanese and to keep out the Japanese immigrants on the ground that they are an immoral, degraded and worthless race; and at the same time that they desire to do this for the Japanese and are already doing it for the Chinese they expect to be given advantages in Oriental markets; and with besotted folly are indifferent to building up the navy while provoking this formidable new power—a power jealous, sensitive and warlike, and which if irritated could at once take both the Philippines and Hawaii from us if she obtained the upper hand on the seas. . . . I hope that we can persuade our people on the one hand to act in a spirit of generous justice and genuine courtesy toward Japan, and on the other hand to keep the navy respectable in numbers and more than respectable in the efficiency of its units.[3]

Roosevelt accurately discerned the conflict that was growing within America's Far Eastern policy. We have already observed how he discovered the Philippines to be an Achilles' heel and how, by means of the Taft-Katsura Agreement in 1905 he readjusted his policy on the continent of Asia in the interests of Philippine security. His communication to Lodge shows that at the same time he perceived the anomaly of seeking most-favored-commercial treatment from countries whose nationals were faced with dis-

[1] Roosevelt to Lodge, June 3, 1905. Lodge, H. C., *Selections*, II, 134.
[2] Bailey, *Roosevelt*, 17.
[3] Roosevelt to Lodge, June 3, 1905. Lodge, II, 135.

crimination in the United States. He also realized the strategic contradiction of an immigration policy provocative to the very nation on whose good will both the open door in China and the security of the Philippines most depended. The Philippines made the immigration policy dangerous; the immigration policy jeopardized the Philippines. The open door policy—especially its corollary, the territorial integrity of China—intensified the dilemma. Compromise was unavoidable; and, as we have seen, Roosevelt chose to make it by retreating on the principle of the territorial integrity of China. After considerable experimentation he rated peace, amicable trade relations, the security of American territory in the Pacific and the effective restriction of oriental immigration all ahead of the territorial integrity of China in the category of American national interests.

The President's opposition merely strengthened the determination of the California exclusionists. Even the unparalleled outpouring of Japanese sympathy during the San Francisco earthquake and fire in April, 1906, did not deter them. While the Japanese Red Cross contributed to the victims of the disaster more generously than all of the other nations of the world combined, visiting Japanese scientists were stoned in the streets, Japanese restaurants were boycotted and the Exclusion League, boasting a membership of 78,500, remorselessly pursued its goal.[1] On October 11, 1906, the Board of Education passed its fateful resolution, requiring all Chinese, Japanese and Korean children to be segregated in an oriental public school.

A variety of charges were made against the Japanese in attempted justification of the order. They were alleged to be overcrowding the schools, to be vicious, immoral, of an age and maturity too advanced for safe association with the younger American children. All of these accusations were found, on close investigation, to have been greatly (and no doubt deliberately) exaggerated. There were only ninety-three Japanese pupils in all of

[1] Bailey, *Roosevelt*, 16-27.

San Francisco's public schools when the segregation order was issued. Twenty-five of them were American citizens; twenty-eight were girls; only thirty-three were over fifteen, the two oldest, twenty. Teachers' testimony as to the exemplary conduct and general desirability of Japanese pupils completely vitiated charges of immorality. The school board seems to have acted more in response to a desire to humble the Japanese than on the merits of the case it presented. The segregation order was one with the anti-Japanese riots, boycotts and Congressional resolutions that marked the progress of the exclusionist movement.[1]

Repercussions of the segregation order reached Washington *via* Tokyo, and precipitated what Roosevelt considered the gravest diplomatic crisis of his presidency. After energetic representations on the part of the Japanese Consul in San Francisco had come to naught, and with the Japanese press aflame with indignation, the Japanese Ambassador appeared at the State Department (October 25) with instructions "to call the serious attention of the Secretary of State to the condition of affairs in San Francisco." He lodged a formal protest against the segregation of Japanese school children, as well as against the restaurant boycotts and other outrages. The protest was based on the treaty of 1894 by which, it was maintained, "Japanese subjects are . . . not only entitled to full and perfect protection in their persons and property, but are assured, in matters connected with the rights of residence, both national and most-favored-nation treatment. It is sufficient to observe that the equal right of education is one of the highest and most valuable rights connected with residence.

The Imperial Government is not aware whether the special schools, which the authorities of San Francisco propose to provide for the accommodation of Japanese children of school age, are equally good as the schools established and maintained for the instruction of the children generally of that city; but even if they were equally good, the fact

[1] Bailey, *Roosevelt*, Ch. II; Metcalf, Victor H., *Japanese in the City of San Francisco*, U. S. Senate Doc. No. 147, 59th Cong., 2nd Sess., 4 ff.

that Japanese children, because of their nationality, are segregated in special schools and not permitted to attend the ordinary public schools, constitutes an act of discrimination carrying with it a stigma and odium which it is impossible to overlook." [1]

The protest closed with an appeal to the historic friendship, and sense of justice, of the United States.

Roosevelt instantly responded. On October 26 he announced that Secretary of Commerce and Labor Victor H. Metcalf would make a special trip to California to investigate the situation. At the same time (evidence of his anxiety) he asked the acting Secretary of the Navy for an exact, ship-for-ship comparison of the American and Japanese fleets. [2] "Probably Root will have to communicate formally with the Governor of California," he wrote Senator Hale, Chairman of the Senate Committee on Naval Affairs. "Exactly how much further I shall go I do not know. It is possible I may have to use the army in connection with boycotting or the suppression of mob violence.

If these troubles merely affected our internal arrangements, I should not bother you with them; but of course they may possibly bring about war with Japan. I do not think that they will bring it about at this moment, but even as to this I am not certain, for the Japanese are proud, sensitive, war-like, are flushed with the glory of their recent triumph, and are in my opinion bent upon establishing themselves as the leading power in the Pacific." [3]

To his son the President was more emphatic. "I am being horribly bothered about the Japanese business," he declared. "The infernal fools in California, and especially in San Francisco, insult the Japanese recklessly and in the event of war it will be the Nation as a whole which will pay the consequences." [4]

[1] Instructions of Japanese Government to Ambassador Aoki, October 25, 1906. Bailey, *Roosevelt*, 64.
[2] *Ibid.*, 81.
[3] Roosevelt to Hale, October 27, 1906. *Ibid.*, 81-82.
[4] Roosevelt to Kermit Roosevelt, October 27, 1906. *Ibid.*, 83.

Roosevelt's immediate task was to persuade the Japanese Government to have patience and trust in him while he dealt with the San Franciscans. Accordingly, he took the Japanese Ambassador into his confidence, told him he would deal with the issue in his forthcoming message to Congress, and submitted to his approval an advance draft of the pertinent passage. On December 4, 1906, after learning the results of Metcalf's investigation, he delivered the message. He reminded Congress of Japan's remarkable progress toward modern civilization, of her generosity to the San Francisco earthquake victims, of the traditional friendship, the economic and cultural ties between the two nations. He termed the segregation order a "wicked absurdity," advocated legislation conferring on Japanese the right of naturalization, and bluntly warned that he would use the United States Army, if necessary, to protect the Japanese in California from further violence.

The message more than served its purpose: it was lavishly praised in Japan and by Japanese in the United States. Roosevelt's friend Baron Kaneko thought it "the greatest utterance by an American President since Washington's farewell address." But while it produced calm in Tokyo, it called forth storm in San Francisco. To the press of that city it was a "tin-soldier yawp," "an outburst of august and Jovian wrath." "Our feeling is not against Japan," declared the *Chronicle*, "but against an unpatriotic President who united with aliens to break down the civilization of his own countrymen." Roosevelt's strong-arm tactics were antagonizing the Californians proportionately as they mollified the Japanese.[1]

To straighten the tangled relations between Tokyo, Washington and San Francisco required finesse as well as bluster. Roosevelt soon realized the need for compromise. On December 18, 1906, he submitted the Metcalf report to Congress, convincing proof that the case against the Japanese school children had been

[1] Bailey, *Roosevelt*, Ch. IV; text of message to Congress, *For. Rel.*, 1906, I, vii ff.; cf. also Tupper and McReynolds, 19-37.

grossly exaggerated. Yet he accompanied it with the suggestion that a maximum age limit might be placed on attendance at the public schools. "Whether we like it or not," he admitted privately in January, 1907, "I think we have to face the fact that the people of the Pacific slope . . . will become steadily more and more hostile to the Japanese if their laborers come here, and I am doing my best to bring about an agreement with Japan by which the laborers of each country shall be kept out of the other country." [1] He considered the school order the surface manifestation of a basic conflict arising from the continued immigration of Japanese laborers *via* Hawaii, and he was determined to deal with the trouble at its source.

Since November, 1906, he and Root had been trying to induce Tokyo to agree to a treaty by which the United States and Japan agreed reciprocally to exclude each other's laborers. But the Japanese contended that, since no American laborers emigrated to Japan, the restriction would not be truly reciprocal. Nor were they disposed to come to any terms so long as the school order stood. Roosevelt was forced to drive a delicate bargain. With the co-operation of the California delegation in Congress, he "invited" the mayor and the entire Board of Education of San Francisco to the White House. There he prevailed on them (February 15) to agree to rescind the segregation order in return for his promise to put an end to the immigration of Japanese laborers and to abandon legal proceedings against the board in which the federal government was representing the Japanese.

The President now had to make good his promise to the school board. The Japanese Government had conceded that, although it was unwilling to prohibit the emigration of laborers to Hawaii, it could not object if the United States prohibited their immigration thence. An amendment was therefore added to the immigration law of 1907 (signed February 20) empowering the President to

[1] Roosevelt to Lyman Abbott, January 2, 1907. Bailey, *Roosevelt*, 124-125.

exclude from the United States immigrants holding passports "to any country other than the United States or to any insular possession of the United States or to the Canal Zone" and attempting to use them to enter the United States "to the detriment of labor conditions therein." [1] Having thus secured the means of arresting the flow of Japanese laborers from Hawaii, Roosevelt and Root turned their attention to those coming directly from Japan to the United States. They offered to rescind the segregation order as the *quid pro quo* for a reciprocal labor exclusion treaty. Japan would accept if the United States included therein naturalization rights for Japanese immigrants above the laboring class. This Root was unwilling even to discuss. He pointed to the undeniable right of the United States, sanctioned by the treaty of 1894, to exclude immigrant laborers by legislation and predicted that it would surely exercise the right if Japan refused to co-operate. Failing a reciprocity treaty, Root suggested that Japan herself impose the desired restriction.

On February 24, 1907, Foreign Minister Hayashi responded with a note that formed the basis of the celebrated Gentlemen's Agreement:

The Imperial Government . . . beg to state that they have no intention of canceling or modifying the order now in force under which no passports are granted to either skilled or unskilled Japanese laborers for the mainland of the United States other than settled agriculturalists, farmers owning or having an interest or share in their produce or crops. The Imperial Government confidently believe that a strict adhesion on their part to the foregoing order coupled with the continuation of the existing practice of inserting in all labor passports the destination of the laborers will be sufficient to make the new legislation of the United States more satisfactory and obviate the necessity of adopting additional measures.[2]

[1] Text of amendment, *Congressional Record*, 59th Congress, 2nd Sess., 2809; Bailey, *Roosevelt*, 145.
[2] Wright to Root, February 24, 1907. *Ibid.*, 165-166.

From March 9 to 14 Roosevelt had to intervene with vigorous telegrams and letters to the Governor of California to prevent the passage of a new batch of anti-Japanese bills by the state legislature. On March 13 the school order was formally rescinded. The next day an executive order of the President put the new passport ruling into effect, and by his direction the test case against the Board of Education was dismissed. Whether won by his diplomacy, or swayed by the fear of the exclusion laws that would almost certainly have followed, Japan had agreed to continue her policy of the past decade of prohibiting the direct emigration of laborers to the United States. The prohibition now assumed the character and force of a pledge, formally delivered for value received. The crisis precipitated by the San Francisco school board was past.[1]

It remained for the United States and Japan to work out the details of operation of the Gentlemen's Agreement. Their efforts to do so were complicated by a fresh series of anti-Japanese riots and disorders in San Francisco. The city was in the throes of serious labor troubles, of which to a certain extent the Japanese were victims. But there could be no doubt that the tendency to discriminate against Japanese immigrants had more than an economic origin. While laboring to make the Gentlemen's Agreement effective and at the same time to maintain friendly relations with Japan, Secretary Root had to answer more than one protest at the brutal treatment of Japanese in San Francisco. Had American citizens been subjected to the same treatment in Tokyo the United States might not have shown as much restraint as Japan was showing—at all events it had not done so under similar circumstances in the past. It was directly out of these immigration troubles on the Pacific Coast in 1907 that grew Roosevelt's war scare, his anxiety for the Philippines, his decision to send the battle fleet on its world

[1] Details of school board crisis from *Ibid.*, Chs. IV-VIII, a painstaking analysis based on Roosevelt and Root papers, Department of State Archives and California newspapers, all of which are liberally quoted.

cruise, and once more to re-shape his Far Eastern policy in the Root-Takahira Agreement—circumstances and events already discussed in Chapter III. If the California press could accuse Roosevent of disregarding the sacred precepts of states' rights, he could accuse the single municipality of San Francisco of willfully jeopardizing the interests of the entire nation.

To make matters worse, he discovered that more Japanese immigrants had entered the United States during May and June, 1907, than during the same two months of 1906. He felt that "we shall have to urge most strongly upon the Japanese Government the need of restricting the total number of passports if we are not to have trouble.

If there is not a falling off in the number of Japanese arrivals, I think we can safely count upon at least a very dangerous agitation in Congress next year for their total exclusion by a law modeled after our Chinese exclusion law." [1]

Not until the end of February, 1908, did the two governments come to a precise understanding as to the details of enforcing the Gentlemen's Agreement.[2] The memorandum reveals that considerable further negotiation was required to pin Japan down to the categorical restrictions sought by the United States. Though the total Japanese immigration for the following May was 900 as compared with 2,300 for the same month of the year before, so many laborers were still coming in that Roosevelt advised Root to notify the Japanese Government "in the plainest manner that they have nothing to expect but a Japanese exclusion law unless the figures soon begin to show a totally different complexion." [3]

As soon as the Gentlemen's Agreement had taken effect, however, immigration figures began to decline until by October de-

[1] Roosevelt to Root, July 13, 1907. Bailey, *Roosevelt*, 234.

[2] See memorandum, "The Present Arrangement Covering Immigration Between Japan and the United States," in Knox to Cullom, January 10, 1911. Knox papers. See also Jessup, *Root*, II, 18-31.

[3] Roosevelt to Root, June 18, 1908. Bailey, *Roosevelt*, 279.

partures were exceeding arrivals. The cruise of the battle fleet and
the Root-Takahira Agreement further helped to clear the air. But
the President's troubles with California were not over. In January,
1909, he learned that a bill was about to be passed by the state
legislature limiting Japanese ownership of land to five years. Once
more Roosevelt took up the cudgels with the Governor of California, wiring him that "passage of proposed legislation would be
of incalculable damage to State of California as well as to whole
Union." [1] He followed up his telegram with a letter expressing
entire satisfaction with the Gentlemen's Agreement, now "in first
class working order," and imploring the governor not to allow it to
be jeopardized by the projected land law.[2] At Roosevelt's earnest
behest, the governor and the speaker of the assembly brought
about the defeat of this and other even more offensive measures
(including a new anti-Japanese school bill) then before the legislature.

When Roosevelt left the White House that March it was with
the uneasy feeling that he had scotched the snake but not killed it.
At any moment California might precipitate a new immigration
crisis, as the constant introduction of anti-Japanese resolutions in
the legislature augured. He protested to the last that "the troubles I have with Congress don't count at all when compared with
the trouble I am having with California over Japan." [3] For five
years he had energetically held the lid down on local prejudice
while adopting his immigration policy to the needs of the nation
as a whole as well as of the Pacific Coast. The experience convinced
him that there was "no more important continuing feature of our
foreign policy" than the exclusion of Japanese laborers.[4]

The formula that he bequeathed to his successors was "to insist
on keeping out Japanese immigration; but at the same time to be-

[1] Roosevelt to Gillett, January 16, 1909. *Ibid.*, 305.
[2] Same to same, January 16, 1909. *Ibid.*, 305-306.
[3] Roosevelt to Theodore Roosevelt, Jr., February 6, 1909. *Ibid.*, 310.
[4] Roosevelt to Knox, February 8, 1909. *Ibid.*, 321.

have with scrupulous courtesy to Japan as a nation and to the Japanese who are here; and also to continue to build up and maintain at the highest point of efficiency our navy." [1] What this meant to the Far Eastern policy of the United States was recognizing, as Roosevelt advised Knox to do in 1910, that,

> Our vital interest is to keep the Japanese out of our country, and at the same time preserve the good will of Japan. The vital interest of the Japanese, on the other hand, is in Manchuria and Korea. It is therefore peculiarly our interest not to take any steps as regards Manchuria which will give the Japanese cause to feel, with or without reason, that we are hostile to them, or a menace—in however slight degree —to their interests. [2]

Roosevelt had approached the Far East by two paths, that of world politics and that of the domestic welfare of the United States. Each had led him to the same conclusion.

The problem of Roosevelt's successors was chiefly that of enforcing the measures and carrying out the policy that he had perfected. By the proclamation of March 14, 1907, the immigration of Japanese laborers from Hawaii, Canada, Mexico and other erstwhile "vestibules" had been prohibited. [3] As defined by the United States Commissioner-General of Immigration in 1908, the Gentlemen's Agreement

> contemplates that the Japanese Government shall issue passports to continental United States only to such of its subjects as are non-laborers or are laborers who, in coming to the continent, seek to resume a formerly acquired domicile, to join a parent, wife, or children residing

[1] Roosevelt to Kent, February 5, 1909. Bailey, *Roosevelt*, 319.

[2] Roosevelt to Taft, December 22, 1910. Cf. above, p. 131.

[3] The proclamation was specifically applied to "every Japanese or Korean laborer, skilled or unskilled, applying for admission at a seaport or at a land border port of the United States, and having in his possession a passport issued by the Government of Japan, entitling him to proceed only to Mexico, Canada, or Hawaii. . . ." It provided for the admission of Japanese or Koreans holding passports to the United States if the holders were not in the excluded classes Cf. Ichihashi, 244-245.

there, or to assume active control of an already possessed interest in a farming enterprise in this country; so that the three classes of laborers entitled to receive passports have come to be designated "former residents," "parents, wives, or children of residents," and "settled agriculturalists." With respect to Hawaii, the Japanese Government, of its own volition, stated that . . . the issuance of passports to members of the laboring classes proceeding thence would be limited to "former residents," and "parents, wives, or children of residents." The said government has also been exercising a careful supervision over the subject of the emigration of its laboring class to foreign contiguous territory.[1]

It was an extremely delicate balance, resting on mutual understanding and close co-operation. The slightest tremors of race prejudice, mob violence or anti-Japanese legislation in the western states could upset it. And much more depended on the success of the Gentlemen's Agreement than the mere exclusion of Japanese laborers. In Roosevelt's view, at least, it was a cornerstone of the entire Far Eastern policy of the United States.

[1] *Annual Report of the United States Commissioner of Immigration*, 1908, 125-126. Ichihashi, 245-246. In a subsequent memorandum of the State Department, it was defined as follows:

"After negotiations extending over some months, the Japanese Government finally acceded to what is generally known as the 'The Gentlemen's Agreement' by which it voluntarily undertook:

(1) To exercise great care in issuing passports and to warn the applicants therefor of the consequences of making false representation and the fraudulent use of passports.

(2) Not to issue passports to laborers, skilled or unskilled, except to those who have been domiciled in the United States, or to the families of such persons.

(3) Temporarily to suspend all further emigration to Hawaii (new emigration).

(4) To refuse further applications made by parties who had evaded the limitations placed upon the issuance of passports, such refusal to apply also to the families of the parties mentioned.

(5) To undertake the establishment of a system of registration (consular registration in the United States); failure to register, however, not to involve the forfeiture of residential rights.

An arrangement was also made for exchange of emigration statistics."—Morris to Acting Secretary of State, January 25, 1921. *For. Rel.*, 1921, II, 329.

From 1907 to 1924 the Agreement was maintained, though with difficulty. It was constantly shaken by exclusionist activities on the Pacific Coast, and by the pursuit, on the continent of Asia, of a policy precisely the opposite of that which Roosevelt had counseled. Anti-Japanese bills and resolutions kept piling up not only in the California legislature but also in those of Nevada, Oregon and Washington. In 1910 the California legislature ordered a thorough investigation of Japanese in the state by its own commissioner of labor. When he found them to constitute an indispensable source of cheap yet intelligent farm labor and in their own right "land owners . . . of the best class," the state senate censured him for having "misrepresented the wishes of the people of this commonwealth," and disapproved his report.[1] Discriminatory tendencies could not be checked by statistics, by dwindling immigration figures or by official expressions of satisfaction with the Gentlemen's Agreement on the part of the federal government.

Nor was Japan wholly content with it. In 1910, two years before it was scheduled to expire, she opened negotiations for a renewal of the treaty of commerce and navigation of 1894. Her major objective from the outset was to amend the old treaty clause reserving to the United States the right to exclude immigrant laborers by legislation.[2] The Japanese Government argued that "no attempt had been made through actual statute by either party to prohibit absolutely the immigration of laborers under that reservation . . . that the measures which it had

enforced for the past two and a half years in regulation of the question of the emigration of laborers to the United States had, it was believed, proved entirely satisfactory and far more effective than any prohibition of immigration by law would have been . . . that in view of the actual situation, the reservation of the treaty was not only not necessary, but was an engagement which, if continued, was more liable to give

[1] Tupper and McReynolds, 52-53; Ichihashi, 253-254.
[2] Cf. p. 345, above.

rise to misunderstandings than to remove difficulties, and that in any case it was a stipulation which was not unnaturally distasteful to national sensibilities." [1]

In return for omitting the "distasteful" reservation from the new treaty, Japan would continue to enforce the restrictions imposed under the Gentlemen's Agreement.

The State Department was sympathetic to the Japanese proposal. Secretary Knox believed that the right to control immigration was "an inherent right of sovereignty, whether expressed in terms of the treaty or not, and that, in the absence of an express provision to the contrary in the treaty, the United States will be at liberty to enact restrictive legislation at any time." The United States, he thought, was further protected in its enjoyment of this right in that it could "terminate the treaty under the 6 months' notice clause, or . . . at any time, without waiting for such termination, enact restrictive legislation leaving it for the Japanese Government to determine whether or not to give notice of its election to terminate the treaty under the 6 months clause."

We have, therefore, in actual operation a system for the effective control of Japanese immigration which has worked satisfactorily for over two years and which it is now proposed shall be continued in place of the unexercised reserved right in the old treaty. The latter merely reserves the right to regulate immigration. It is the stipulation of a potentiality reserved only as a means to prevent labor immigration. The new treaty will be predicated upon an existing scheme of regulation which not only recognizes the principle of regulation but is an application of that principle. Incontrovertible statistics show that under the arrangement in operation during two years and a half Japanese labor immigration has not only not increased, but has actually very materially decreased, the number of such laborers in this country. This arrangement, tried and found satisfactory, would seem preferable to the reser-

[1] Knox to Cullom, January 10, 1911. Cf. also Far Eastern Division memoranda of April 25, May 12 and 27, October 9 and 26, December 2 and 3, and Japanese Embassy memorandum, October 19, 1910. Knox papers.

vation in terms of a right the exercise of which could not be more effective or so convenient.[1]

Despite some opposition from California, the compromise favored by Knox was effected. The new treaty (signed February 21, 1911) omitted the reservation of 1894. In a special declaration attached to the treaty as a condition to signing, the Japanese Government agreed "to maintain with equal effectiveness the limitation and control which they have for the past three years exercised in regulation of the emigration of laborers to the United States."[2] The treaty was ratified by the Senate subject to the additional understanding that it should "not be deemed to repeal or affect any of the provisions" of the immigration law of 1907.[3] The Gentlemen's Agreement thus passed into its third, and final, stage of development. It had originated as an expeditious Japanese practice during the early immigration troubles of the 'nineties. In 1907 it had been elevated to the status of a formal understanding, resting on an exchange of notes. In 1911 it was recognized in a specific declaration as the condition precedent to a treaty. Such it remained until the enactment of the immigration law of 1924.

So far as checking the inflow of Japanese laborers in particular and Japanese immigration in general was concerned, the Gentlemen's Agreement was a success. During its fifteen years of operation the total admissions of Japanese to Hawaii and the United States were 171,584, the total departures 155,488—a net increase of 16,096, or 7,415 for Hawaii and 8,681 for the United States.[4] The Department of State consistently pronounced its satisfaction with these results. But the Gentlemen's Agreement did not succeed in preventing the growth of the resident Japanese population of Hawaii and the United States. A significant feature of the net

[1] Knox to Cullom, January 10, 1911. Knox papers.
[2] Buell, 290; Ichihashi, 259. Text of treaty and declaration, *For. Rel.*, 1913, 625-627.
[3] Buell, 290.
[4] *Ibid.*, 291.

immigration increase of 16,096 was that it consisted entirely of women. From 1909 to 1924 departures of Japanese males actually exceeded arrivals so as to leave a net decrease of 22,833. This decrease was more than made up by an excess of arrivals over departures of females of 38,833, the difference between the two figures accounting exactly for the net increase of 16,096. The ratio of women to men in the resident Japanese population of both Hawaii and the United States was thus greatly advanced, and with it the birth-rate. While the net increase of the resident Japanese population of the United States by immigration during the fifteen years of the Gentlemen's Agreement was only 8,681, native-born Japanese in the United States increased from 4,502 in 1910 to 29,672 in 1920. The total Japanese population of Hawaii grew during this decade from 79,675 to 109,274; that of the United States from 72,157 to 111,010.[1]

Neither did the Gentlemen's Agreement put a stop to discrimination against Japanese in the western states, and agitation for their total exclusion. Japanese women entering the United States and Hawaii did so strictly in accordance with the terms of the agreement, which permitted the immigration of non-laborers and relatives of laborers already legally settled on American soil. To either of these classes women could readily claim membership. There were so few Japanese women in the United States, however, that the men widely resorted to the device of marrying by proxy in Japan. Just as in the old country, "go-betweens" conducted the negotiations between the two families, the choice of a bride often being made from a selection of photographs. These so-called "picture brides" were then admitted to the United States under the Gentlemen's Agreement.

So strenuously did the Californians object to the practice, which they claimed to be a deliberate circumvention of the Gentlemen's Agreement, that the State Department was obliged in 1917 to negotiate with Japan in an attempt to curb it. A great deal of argu-

[1] See tables in Buell, 291; Ichihashi, 32, 64.

ment as to the validity of the marriages ensued.[1] At length, when the relations of the two countries were most embittered by wartime developments already recounted, and popular feelings were running high in each, the Wilson Administration obtained a promise from the Japanese Government (December 13, 1919) to cease the issuance of passports to picture brides after February, 1920. The Japanese Government was at pains to explain that its action was motivated by a desire to promote friendly relations with the United States and was not to be thought of as deference to the demands of the exclusionists. The Japanese Ambassador wished it particularly understood "that the settlement of the 'Picture Bride' question had no relation whatever to the stopping of anti-Japanese activity." [2]

Meantime, while constantly pressing Congress for a national exclusion law, the Californians did what they could to discourage Japanese immigration into their own state. In 1913 the legislature enacted a law prohibiting Japanese from owning land and limiting their tenure of it to leases of three years' duration. Exercising the Initiative in 1920 the people of California voted 668,483 to 222,-086 to remove even the right to lease land.[3] In each case California defied the most urgent remonstrances of the federal government. President Wilson considered the issue of such moment that he sent Secretary Bryan to California in an attempt to head off the law of 1913, but to no avail. It passed the state senate by

[1] *For. Rel.*, 1917, 848-876; 1919, II, 415-420.

[2] Memorandum of the Third Assistant Secretary, December 23, 1919. *For. Rel.*, 1919, II, 419.

[3] The laws did not mention the Japanese by name but were applied to aliens ineligible to citizenship. Cautiously worded, they provided that the right to own or lease land must conform with existing treaty rights, *viz.*, those of the treaty of commerce and navigation of 1911, which did not convey either right. For pertinent articles of 1911 treaty and land law of 1913 see *For. Rel.*, 1913, 625-628; for substance of 1920 land law, *Ibid.*, 1920, III, 1-2. For an exhaustive legal analysis of both laws and their relation to 1911 treaty, Morris to Acting Secretary of State, January 25, 1921. *Ibid.*, 1921, 323-349. Cf. also *Ibid.*, 1914, 426-434; 1920, III, 1-21.

25 to 2, the assembly by 73 to 3, leaving the governor no choice but to sign it. "The fundamental basis of all legislation upon this subject," declared the attorney general of the state, himself one of the framers of the law, ". . . has been, and is, race undesirability." Its purpose was to limit the presence of Japanese in the state by curtailing the "privileges which they may enjoy here; for they will not come in large numbers and long abide with us if they may not acquire land." [1]

Needless to say both laws drew impassioned protests from Tokyo and gave the already preoccupied State Department fresh cause for worry. "I have given the subject my most serious consideration," telegraphed the Japanese Foreign Minister to his Ambassador in Washington in 1914, "and am consequently well satisfied that the enactment in question is not only in disregard of the letter and spirit of the existing treaty between Japan and the United States of America, but is essentially unfair and invidiously discriminatory against my countrymen and inconsistent as well with the sentiment of amity and good neighborhood which has always presided over the relations between the two countries.

Nor can I escape the conviction that the said enactment which was intended to have international effect is also in excess of the authority of the State of California for the reason that the separate States of the United States are, internationally speaking, wholly unknown and entirely without responsibility. In any case, the Imperial Government are confident that such action as complained of stands without historical parallel, and they are happy to believe that the legislation in question forms no part of the general policy of the Federal Government, but is the outcome of unfortunate local conditions." [2]

[1] Ichihashi, 275. There were about 50,000 Japanese in California in 1913, out of a total population of 2,500,000. Of California's 27,000,000 acres of land suitable for agriculture, 12,726 acres were owned by Japanese. See Bailey, T. A., "California, Japan, and the Alien Land Legislation of 1913," *Pacific Historical Review*, March, 1932, 38.

[2] Japanese Minister for Foreign Affairs to the Japanese Ambassador, June 9, 1914. *For. Rel.*, 1914, 426.

The contention that the alien land laws violated the treaty of 1911 was not well founded. In the long negotiations that followed the enactment of both measures, the State Department presented a solid legal case in their defense. It pointed out that the treaty provided only for the right "to own or lease and occupy houses, manufactories, warehouses and shops" and to "lease land for residential and commercial purposes." "It will be observed," Bryan had argued concerning these clauses, that "there is no reference to the ownership of land," and further, "that the reciprocal right to lease land was confined to 'residential and commercial purposes,' and that the phrases 'industrial' and 'other lawful purposes,' which would have included the leasing of agricultural lands, [and which had been included in the original Japanese draft] were omitted." At Japan's own request, the right of each country to regulate land ownership according to its national—and in the case of the United States, state—laws had been explicitly recognized in a separate exchange of notes, in which the Japanese Ambassador had declared:

In return for the rights of landownership which are granted Japanese by the laws of the various states of the United States the Imperial Government will by liberal interpretation of the law be prepared to grant landownership to American citizens from all the States, reserving for the future, however, the right of maintaining the condition of reciprocity with respect to the separate States.

These facts convinced Bryan that the land laws did not violate the treaty of 1911, a position in which the Department was thereafter sustained by the best legal opinion at its disposal.[1]

The Department did not, however, deny the justice of Japan's complaint against the discriminatory features of the laws. Bryan tried hard to convince the Japanese Foreign Office that they were purely local, "wholly economic," in significance, and had no part in the national policy of the United States toward Japan.

[1] Bryan to Japanese Ambassador, July 16, 1913. *For. Rel.*, 1913, 641-645. In his careful review of the evidence eight years later, Morris upheld Bryan's position. *Ibid.*, 1921, II, 338-339.

". . . the President and I very earnestly attempted to induce the legislative authorities of California to reconsider or to modify their plans in the matter," he pleaded, "urging that the State should not act as a separate unit in this case but, rather, in co-operation with the Federal Government. Under the constitutional arrangement of the United States we could do no more than that."[1]

In 1921 Ambassador Morris, who resolutely defended the legality of the laws, recalled that "The Executive Department of our Government has consistently maintained that such State legislation is unwise, impolitic and dangerous."

"It appears to me," he concluded, "that there can be no reasonable doubt of the deep feeling of resentment which has been roused among the people of Japan by the California legislation. It touches both their racial feeling and their national pride. It would in my judgment be a serious mistake to treat this feeling lightly or to attribute its existence to political propaganda or diplomatic agitation. It is far deeper than that and carries with it an angry sense of injustice and humiliation. . . . I also think that by ignoring larger considerations of public policy, racial discrimination will seriously threaten our country's best interests on the Pacific and in the Far East. It is not within my province to dwell upon these interests. You are in a better position to appreciate and value them. But of one thing I am convinced. If we would conserve these interests and exercise the influence in the Orient which our position and resources justify, we must as far as is compatible with our national safety avoid actions which are certain to create among the people of Japan feelings of deep resentment and antagonism—feelings which may easily spread to other Asiatic peoples having commercial relations with us. This can only be done as I view it, by keeping clearly in mind the distinction between the prohibition of further Japanese immigration and discriminatory legislation against those Japanese aliens who are already lawfully resident in the United States."[2]

[1] Bryan to Japanese Ambassador, May 19, 1913. *For. Rel.*, 1913, 631-632.
[2] Morris to Acting Secretary of State, January 25, 1921. *For. Rel.*, 1921, II, 340, 342-343.

The solution proposed by Morris, after a long series of discussions with Ambassador Shidehara, was a comprehensive revision of the Gentlemen's Agreement. Morris believed that the agreement had failed to accomplish its purpose because it "allowed far too many exceptions" and, yet more fundamentally, because it "provides no method by which the Government of the United States can exercise any effective control at the ports of entry." [1] He favored "a prohibition of Japanese immigration in effect as drastic as the present Chinese exclusion law" accompanied by a guarantee of most-favored-nation treatment to Japanese aliens resident in the United States. An exclusion law was still as repugnant as ever to Japan. Accordingly, Morris and Shidehara drafted a treaty revising the Gentlemen's Agreement so as to prohibit further immigration of wives, children or parents of resident Japanese laborers, and specifically providing for the joint enforcement of the agreement by recognizing the right of the United States to deport immigrants not complying with its measures. In return the United States was to exchange with Japan reciprocal guarantees to the citizens or subjects of each residing in the territories of the other of "the same rights without discrimination as are accorded to the citizens or subjects of other countries," with the exception of the right of naturalization,[2]—a provision that would abrogate the alien land and other discriminatory laws, and prevent similar state legislation in the future.

This eleventh-hour attempt of the Federal Government to grasp the initiative and formulate a national, treaty-sanctioned

[1] *For. Rel.*, 1921, II, 335. In 1920 the Commissioner-General of Immigration reported that Japanese immigrants were being smuggled into the country in considerable numbers. Buell, *Japanese Immigration*, 293. Morris was convinced that many were entering the country surreptitiously.

[2] Morris himself believed that no permanent solution could be effected until Japanese were granted the right of naturalization. In submitting the treaty draft to the approval of the Secretary of State, he expressed his personal wish "that the Congress might feel justified in taking such action." But he rejected Shidehara's proposal to include the right in the treaty. *For. Rel.*, 1921, II, 343-349.

Japanese immigration policy was doomed to failure. The Morris-Shidehara drafts were snowed under by a storm of opposition from the Pacific Coast.[1] Indeed, the exclusionist movement was rapidly assuming national proportions. From 1921 to 1925 Arizona, Arkansas, Delaware, Idaho, Kansas, Louisiana, Missouri, Montana, Nebraska, Nevada, New Mexico, Oregon, Texas and Washington all enacted alien land laws similar in purpose to California's. In 1922 the United States Supreme Court finally ruled that Japanese were ineligible to citizenship by naturalization. The next year it extended the ruling to all orientals, and at the same time upheld the legality of the Washington and California alien land laws.[2]

Japanese immigrants were not the only foreigners affected by the xenophobia that possessed the country after the war. Jews, Catholics, and Negroes, as well as aliens suspected of communism or other "un-American" beliefs, became victims of a national witch-hunt. Fearing a deluge of immigration from war-depressed Europe, Congress in 1921 enacted a law limiting the number of aliens of any particular nationality to be granted admission to the United States in any one year to 3 per cent "of the number of foreign-born persons of such nationality resident in the United

[1] "I think I voice the sentiments of California when I say that in every legitimate and legal fashion the consummation of such a plan will be resisted," declared Senator Hiram Johnson. Tupper and McReynolds, 176. At its national convention in 1920 the American Legion adopted a resolution demanding the cancellation of the Gentlemen's Agreement. Labor unions on the Pacific Coast were militantly opposed to the agreement. *Ibid.*, 170-182.

[2] For state alien land laws see Japan, Consulate General, San Francisco, *Documental History of Law Cases Affecting Japanese in the United States*, II, 1014-1039. Japanese were ruled ineligible to naturalization in Ozawa *v.* U. S., Nov. 13, 1922 (260 U. S. 178), *Ibid.*, I, 1-120. The Washington and California laws were sustained as constitutional and not in violation of the Japanese-American treaty of 1911 in Terrace *v.* Thompson, Nov. 12, 1923, and O'Brien *v.* Webb, Nov. 19, 1923, *Ibid.*, II, 1-111, 111-180. In U. S. *v.* Thind, Feb. 19, 1923 (261 U. S. 204), the Ozawa ruling was sustained, amplified and rendered more explicit so as to deny the right of naturalization to any but free white persons as generally designated by the term Caucasian.

States" in the year 1910.[1] A few months before the expiration of
this act, a new one was framed reducing annual admissions of any
particular nationality to 2 per cent of the foreign-born population
of that nationality resident in the United States in 1890.[2] The
acknowledged purpose of both laws, especially of the second, was
to change the proportions of European immigration in favor of
the northern and western as opposed to the southern and eastern
countries. The method employed was a selective limitation based
on the census of 1890, when British, Scandinavian and German
stocks dominated America's alien population. In other words, by
1921 the principle of discriminating against immigrants of certain nationalities on the presumption of their inferiority to others
—the very principle to which Japan had so consistently and so
strenuously objected—was being applied by Congress to Europeans
as well as to Asiatics, and written into the national immigration
laws of the United States.

In this congenial atmosphere the plan in favor of which the
California legislature had passed so many resolutions at last
reached the floor of Congress. Early in December, 1923, bills
were introduced in both House and Senate prohibiting the admission to the United States of aliens ineligible to citizenship—legal
phraseology designed to exclude the Japanese without naming
them. Immediately the Japanese Ambassador, Mr. Hanihara,
voiced his apprehensions to Secretary Hughes.[3] The latter kept

[1] The Emergency Quota Act of May 19, 1921. The Act was renewed, in 1922,
for two more years. United States Department of Labor, *Immigration Rules and
Regulations of January 1, 1930, as amended up to and including December 31,
1936.* (*Washington*, G.P.O., 1937), 37 ff.

[2] *Ibid.*, 43 ff.

[3] According to evidence supplied by the Japanese Foreign Ministry and the
Japanese Consulate General of New York, Hanihara made oral protest to Hughes,
December 13, 1923, and followed it up with a written memorandum on January
15, 1924. Ichihashi, 300; Paul, Rodman W., *The Abrogation of the Gentlemen's Agreement* (Cambridge, 1936), 58. In a letter of February 8, Hughes
mentioned the fact that Japan had "already brought the matter to the attention
of the Department." Cf. Hughes to Johnson, Feb. 8, 1924. Buell, 353-356.

a close watch of developments in Congress and when, on February 7, 1924, Chairman Albert Johnson of the House Committee on Immigration presented another bill containing the same provision, he decided to intervene.

He wrote Johnson the next day, recapitulating at length all the arguments against statutory exclusion. Though "in favor of suitable restrictions upon immigration," he strongly disapproved of the method contemplated by the bill. In his opinion it was inconsistent with the treaty of 1911. But the question was one of policy rather than of law. The practical effects of a bill that singled out Japanese immigrants for exclusion would be unprofitable to the United States.

The Japanese are a sensitive people, and unquestionably would regard such a legislative enactment as fixing a stigma upon them. I regret to be compelled to say that I believe such legislative action would largely undo the work of the Washington Conference on Limitation of Armament, which so greatly improved our relations with Japan. The manifestation of American interest and generosity in providing relief to the sufferers of the recent earthquake disaster in Japan would not avail to diminish the resentment which would follow the enactment of such a measure, as this enactment would be regarded as an insult not to be palliated by any act of charity. It is useless to argue whether or not such a feeling would be justified; it is quite sufficient to say that it would exist. . . . The question is thus presented whether it is worth while thus to affront a friendly nation with whom we have established the most cordial relations and what gain there would be from such action.

Hughes thought the measure particularly ill-advised since it was "quite unnecessary even for the purpose for which it is devised." By applying to Japan the same quota system as that established by the act for the European nations, Japanese immigration could be cut down to not more than 250 per year, the amount equal to 2 per cent of the remarkably small Japanese population of 1890. Rigorous enforcement of the Gentlemen's Agreement—along the lines laid down by Morris and Shidehara—would prove an additional advantage. It would secure the co-operation of Japan in the difficult task of preventing smuggling, and at the same time provide a means of carefully scrutinizing and regulating the character of Japanese travelers not affected by the quota. Hughes therefore recommended that the bill be so amended as to recognize the Gentlemen's Agreement and to make no exception from the quota system of Japanese immigration.[1]

There was no action in Congress for a month. On March 11 Hughes again stated his position to the Chairman of the Senate Committee on Immigration.[2] Then, in a report of March 24, the House Committee delivered a sweeping condemnation of the Gentlemen's Agreement and called for legislation excluding aliens ineligible to citizenship.[3] On April 12 the House adopted by a vote of 323 to 71 an immigration bill containing the exclusionist provision. Meanwhile, at the latter's request, the State Department had furnished the Japanese Embassy with a critical memorandum on the Gentlemen's Agreement, and on April 10 Ambassador Hanihara and Secretary Hughes had exchanged some correspondence on the subject.

The Ambassador reminded Hughes that during the negotiation of the treaty of 1911 the United States had more than hinted at its willingness to desist from statutory exclusion in return for Japan's promise to continue to enforce the Gentlemen's Agreement. He reviewed in detail the operation of the agreement, emphasizing the progressive tightening of its restrictions, citing immigration statistics to prove its efficacy. He pointed to Japan's forbearance, to her sincere desire to live up to the agreement and even, should the United States desire it, to render it yet more stringent. His government had no intention of questioning "the

[1] Hughes to Johnson, February 8, 1924. Buell, 353-356.
[2] Hughes to Colt, March 11, 1924. *Ibid.*, 357.
[3] House Report No. 350, 68th Congress, 1st Sess.; Buell, 294-297.

sovereign right of any country to regulate immigration to its own territories."

To Japan the question is not one of expediency, but of principle. To her the mere fact that a few hundreds or thousands of her nationals will or will not be admitted into the domains of other countries is immaterial, so long as no question of national susceptibilities is involved. The important question is whether Japan as a nation is or is not entitled to the proper respect and consideration of other nations. In other words the Japanese Government ask of the United States Government simply that proper consideration ordinarily given by one nation to the self-respect of another, which after all forms the basis of amicable international intercourse throughout the civilized world. . . .

It is indeed difficult to believe that it can be the intention of the people of your great country, who always stand for high principles of justice and fair-play in the intercourse of nations, to resort . . . to a measure which would not only seriously offend the just pride of a friendly nation, that has been always earnest and diligent in its efforts to preserve the friendship of your people, but would also seem to involve the question of the good faith and therefore of the honor of their government, or at least of its executive branch.

Relying upon the confidence you have been good enough to show me at all times, I have stated, or rather repeated, all this to you very candidly and in a most friendly spirit, for I realize, as I believe you do, the grave consequences which the enactment of the measure retaining that particular provision would inevitably bring upon the otherwise happy and mutually advantageous relations between our two countries.[1]

In reply, Hughes expressed his concurrence with Hanihara's interpretation of the Gentlemen's Agreement; and to clear away "any possible misapprehension as to the nature and purpose" of the latter he communicated both letters to Congress.[2] The Secretary of State undoubtedly believed that the Japanese Ambassador's eloquent argument, together with his own sympathetic reception of it, might help to stay the hands of the exclusionists. In this he

---

[1] Hanihara to Hughes, April 10, 1924. *Ibid.*, 358-362.
[2] Hughes to Hanihara, April 10, 1924. *Ibid.*, 363.

was mistaken. Without regard to the two letters, the House passed the exclusionist measure on April 12, by the impressive majority already noted. Two days later Senator Lodge seized on the closing sentences of Hanihara's letter, particularly the phrase "grave consequences," declared they constituted a "veiled threat" to the United States and advised rejection of the amendment recognizing the Gentlemen's Agreement advocated by Secretary Hughes. The Senate followed his advice by a vote of 76 to 2. On the sixteenth it adopted by an equally large majority (71-4) a new amendment providing for total exclusion of aliens ineligible to citizenship.

In dismay Hanihara wrote Hughes denying the remotest intention of a threat, an assurance that Hughes accepted with alacrity and forwarded to Congress.[1] But the *coup de grâce* had been administered to the Gentlemen's Agreement, and Hughes was forced to resort to different tactics. While the bill (now passed by both houses) was in conference, President Coolidge himself intervened with the suggestion that the application of the exclusionist clause be postponed until 1926. During this interval a treaty would be negotiated with Japan so effectively restricting Japanese immigration as to obviate the necessity of invoking the clause. The suggestion was rejected. Coolidge reduced the requested term of postponement to one year. Again he was rebuffed. Members of the House Committee on Immigration warned their colleagues that, "After the United States has agreed to consult the wishes and interests of Asia as to immigration it could not consistently refuse to consult the wishes of Europe and the rest of the world in the same manner.

To pass the control of our immigration policy to the treaty-making power [i.e., the President] will completely silence the voice of the House of Representatives therein. It would surrender a sovereign right

[1] Hanihara to Hughes, April 17, 1924; Hughes to Hanihara same date. Buell, 364-366.

and give to foreign countries a power which the country has never conceded." [1]

These arguments were effective. On May 15 both House and Senate passed the bill containing the exclusionist clause—to become effective July 1, 1924—by votes of 308 to 62 and 69 to 9 respectively. Coolidge signed it May 26, explaining as he did so that he would have vetoed the anti-Japanese measure had that stood alone. He approved it regretfully because it formed part of a comprehensive immigration law of which the country was imperatively in need. It would have been "much better," he declared, ". . . and more effective in the actual control of immigration, if we had continued to invite that co-operation which Japan was ready to give and had thus avoided creating any ground for misapprehension by an unnecessary statutory enactment.

That course would not have derogated from the authority of the Congress to deal with the question in any exigency requiring its action. There is scarcely any ground for disagreement as to the result we want, but this method of securing it is unnecessary and deplorable at this time." [2]

The exclusion law that the Japanese and United States Governments had tried for thirty years to avoid had at last become a fact.

With a final interchange of protest and apologia between Ambassador Hanihara and Secretary Hughes,[3] the fact became history

---

[1] *Ibid.*, 310.

[2] Coolidge's statement accompanying signature of immigration act of 1924. Buell, 371. In its final form, revised and amended up to and including December 31, 1936, the exclusion clause provides that, "No alien ineligible to citizenship shall be admitted to the United States" unless the said alien belonged to certain stipulated categories. These included: immigrants previously admitted to the United States and returning from a temporary visit abroad; ministers and professors, their wives and children under 18; *bona fide* students at least 15 years of age; government officials, their families, servants and employees; tourists and business travelers, seamen, aliens in continuous transit, etc.; Chinese wives of American citizens married prior to May 26, 1924. Cf. *Immigration Laws*, 55.

[3] Hanihara to Hughes, May 31, 1924; Hughes to Hanihara, June 16, 1924. Buell, 372-380. For detailed reviews of the enactment of the immigration law

—but in no academic sense. ". . . the Japanese Government consider it their duty to maintain and to place on record their solemn protest against the discriminatory clause . . . of the Immigration Act of 1924," concluded Hanihara's final memorandum, "and to request the American Government to take all possible and suitable measures for the removal of such discrimination." [1] The thorn did not cease to rankle in Japan's flesh, nor Japan her efforts to pluck it out. It seems safe to say that the American people have never resented any policy pursued by Japan in China or elsewhere as deeply, as unanimously and with as poignant a sense of injustice as the Japanese have resented the statutory exclusion of 1924.

The action of Congress has been ascribed to unbridled sectionalism, political opportunism, the "veiled threat" of Hanihara, the efforts of the Chief Executive to circumscribe the sovereign powers of Congress with the treaty-making authority, and to a combination of all of these factors. Undeniably, each of them played its part. But the fact that the experience with Chinese immigration was recapitulated in such close detail by that with Japanese, not to mention the sweeping Congressional majorities behind the act, is sufficient to show that it had more than a political, or even a sectional, origin. In both cases the western states had not scrupled to place their local interests before those of the country as a whole. Yet every one of the Presidents and Secretaries of State who tried to restrain the exclusionists was to a greater or lesser degree converted by them. All were compelled to recognize the fact that orientals were, if not impossible of assimilation, at least more difficult than any other immigrants; and all employed the same means of dealing with the problem. The restrictions imposed under the Gentlemen's Agreement had become more and more rigorous until, as provided in the abortive Morris-Shidehara treaty, they amounted virtually to total exclusion.

of 1924 see, in addition to Buell, Ichihashi, Ch. XIX; Paul, *op. cit.*, *passim*; Tupper and McReynolds, 182-198.

[1] Buell, 375.

Japan had never contested the right of the United States to enact an exclusion law, nor did she do so in 1924. What she did object to was the singling out of Japanese immigrants for restrictions not applied to any but Chinese and other non-Caucasian Asiatic immigrants. She objected to this both as champion of the oriental races (it was the only issue on which she and China were united at Paris) and out of a sense of superiority to the other nations with which it classed her. If, from an American point of view, it mitigated the principle of discrimination to invoke it with respect to Europeans as well as Asiatics, the principle became the more invidious to the Japanese when it forced them into a position less favorable than the least favored Europeans. Perhaps the only way for Americans to sense the indignation Japan felt concerning this treatment is to reverse the situation, substituting England for Japan. Japanese exclusion of Americans is not analogous; too few Americans would be affected, economically or psychologically. It is hard for Americans, themselves a nation of immigrants, to conceive of an emigration problem—just as it is for a creditor to share with sympathy the burdens of a debtor. But suppose England, whose political and cultural influence on the United States has been greater only in degree than that of the United States on Japan, had enacted an immigration law admitting all other nationalities but totally excluding Americans. American feelings might then have duplicated Japanese.

The method of restricting oriental immigration adopted in 1924 proved no exception to the law of diminishing returns. It ran up high costs in pride and irritation that a different method, achieving the same end, might have avoided. Realizing this, or at all events impressed with the essential injustice of a device so inconsistent with the principles of foreign policy to which the United States was seeking Japan's adherence, advocates of the plan favored by Hughes of placing Japanese—and Chinese—immigration under the quota system slowly gained support. Except for the south, mindful of its own race problem, the other sections of the country had been less than sympathetic with the exclusionists from the beginning.[1] In March, 1929, the quota system was revised so as to limit the total of annual admissions to 150,000, and annual admissions of any particular nationality to "a number which bears the same ratio to 150,000 as the number of inhabitants in continental United States in 1920 having that national origin . . . bears to the number of inhabitants in continental United States in 1920, but the minimum quota of any nationality shall be 100." [2]

It was soon discovered that Japanese admissions under the revised, national origins quota would amount to no more than 185 a year—fewer, in fact, than were admitted under the exemptions of the existing law. Prominent educators, journalists, and clergymen all over the country who had opposed statutory exclusion from the outset, were now joined by west coast business organizations in advocating the quota system for China and Japan. In 1930 the National Foreign Trade Convention at Los Angeles, after deploring the effects of the law of 1924 on American exports, adopted a resolution favoring revision. Not long afterwards one of the authors of that law, Chairman Johnson of the House Committee on Immigration, announced that he would shortly introduce an amendment giving Japan her proportionate quota. The Immigration Committee of the United States Chamber of Commerce reported strongly in favor of a quota in 1931. The same year saw the founding of the California Council on Oriental Relations, an organization composed of the most prominent business and educational leaders of the state and committed to the quota system.[3]

In short, with the State Department quietly fostering it, the move for revision of the law of 1924 had made considerable prog-

[1] Only 5 per cent of the eastern newspapers favored the exclusion measure of 1924, as compared with 40-50 per cent of the midwestern, 50 per cent of the southern and 80 per cent of the western. Tupper and McReynolds, 193. Cf. Buell, Chs. II, VI, VII.

[2] *Immigration Laws*, 51.

[3] Cf. Ichihashi, Ch. XXIII; Tupper and McReynolds, Ch. VII.

ress by 1931. On the eve of his departure for Japan in September of that year the Japanese Ambassador, Mr. Debuchi, called to pay his respects to Secretary Stimson. Together they reviewed the "tranquil" state of Japanese-American relations—so tranquil that Stimson told the Ambassador that he hoped, before leaving office, to "be able to take up for successful solution the long standing source of irritation arising out of our immigration laws of nearly ten years before, and to put them upon a basis which, while conforming to our own requirements, might be not offensive to the sensibilities of the Japanese people." [1] Before Mr. Stimson could accomplish this purpose political events of which he himself was a prominent author blocked his path. To the background of these events we must now return in a final consideration of the Far Eastern policy of the United States.

[1] Stimson, Henry L., *The Far Eastern Crisis*, 3.

# X. The Quest for Collective Security

INTERNATIONAL politics are often as susceptible to doctrinal influences as are national politics. An imperialist impulse of 1898 overturned the traditions of a century and led to the annexation of the Philippine Islands. The impact of this imperialism on the Far Eastern policy of the United States caused a change of emphasis that placed political interests on a par with commercial. Thereafter, the principle of the territorial integrity of China, introduced by Hay as the means to equal opportunity for American commerce in that country, became to all intents and purposes an end in itself. The impact of the Wilsonian doctrine of collective security had a similar effect. It universalized the territorial integrity principle. By his participation in the Siberian intervention, Wilson first extended this from China to Russia; then, at the peace conference, he endeavored to apply it to every independent nation in the world. Had the United States joined the League of Nations its obligation to uphold the principle would have known no geographical bounds.

As we have observed, American apostasy from the League carried with it no such clean-cut repudiation of Wilson's leadership as the election of 1920 seemed to imply. The Washington Treaties preserved a substantial residue of Wilson's doctrines, just as the Covenant of the League had preserved (and sublimated) some of Hay's. In the decade following the conclusion of the treaties the influence of these concepts on American diplomacy in the Far East, instead of diminishing, increased. Like the imperialism of 1898, the doctrine of collective security greatly enhanced the concern of the Department of State for national interests of essentially minor significance, and for a time transformed its

Far Eastern policy into a seeming pivot of American destiny.

If the quest for universal collective security was a significant factor in the Far Eastern policy of the United States during these years, China, Russia and Japan furnished the factual substance with which that policy was obliged to deal. The rise of Chinese nationalism, the revival of Russian power and the advance of Japanese imperialism created practical problems demanding practical solutions. These were the conflicting elements artificially frozen into the *status quo* of the Washington Treaties. When they began, as it were, to thaw, to pass once more into change and motion, they presented a pragmatic challenge to all principles and doctrines. How the United States met this challenge constitutes the final chapter in the history of the diplomatic cycle inaugurated by Wilson and Lansing in 1917.

China, in 1922, had scarcely begun to emerge from the civil war and factional strife that had dominated her national politics since the abdication of the Manchus ten years earlier. An insurgent government continued to function at Canton in defiance of that at Peking. Each of these governments was subdivided into warring cliques, and neither was able to extend any effective control over the provinces, for the most part under the supreme rule of local warlords. Peking enjoyed the dubious advantage of foreign recognition as the legitimate Chinese Government. Canton was the beneficiary of the ideals and inspiration of Sun Yat-sen, an ideological force of growing potency. The source of political power throughout China, whether provincial or national, was the personal army of him who aspired to power. The loyalty and efficacy of the innumerable armies of this type depended, in turn, on the ingenuity of their freebooting leaders in raising (generally by extortion) the funds to pay them. Every successful warlord was the potential dictator of all China.

For several years both Canton and Peking were so weakened by bankruptcy and internal struggles that neither was able to pursue very far its aim of uniting the entire country under its rule. Each faced the dilemma of attempting to whittle down the unequal treaty rights which the Chinese delegates at Paris and Washington had tried so hard to abolish, and at the same time, of attempting to enlist the support of the powers that enjoyed those rights against its factional enemies in China. At length, in 1923, Sun Yat-sen turned to Soviet Russia for the material assistance the other powers had refused him. Russian military experts and political advisers helped Sun organize his cohorts of the Kuomintang (Nationalist Party) into an effective machine. This remained more or less under Russian tutelage until 1927, when Chiang Kai-shek expelled the communists—on whose shoulders he had risen to power—and converted it into a fascist dictatorship. Under Chiang's aggressive leadership Peking and Canton were at last united. Chiang made Nanking his capital and gradually extended his rule over most of China, with the notable exceptions of Manchuria and the provincial strongholds of the Chinese communist armies.

The Nationalist movement propelled China into three successive collisions: first, with the Western treaty powers, second, with Russia, third, with Japan. The quarrel with the treaty powers centered on their refusal to relinquish the rights and privileges stemming from the unequal treaties, the complete abrogation of which was a major objective of Chinese nationalism. Russia, so friendly to China from 1923 to 1927, was alienated partly by Chiang's *coup d'état* of 1927 and subsequent anti-communist policies, partly by his efforts to re-establish Chinese control over Manchuria, where the Soviet entertained ambitions not dissimilar to those of the Czars. Finally the growth of a united China touched Japan's imperial interests at innumerable points, but especially in Manchuria and the northern provinces. Each of these three collisions brought into play particular elements in the Far Eastern policy of the United States. The first, the attack on the unequal treaties, caused emphasis to be placed on those aspects of the policy having to do with the defense and protection of

American nationals, property and legal rights in China. The clashes with Russia and Japan aroused Washington's fears for the peace of the world, and led it to invoke the more purely political principles of the Far Eastern policy, those tinctured by the doctrine of collective security.

The signatories of the Washington Treaties were in no hurry to hand back to China the rights, concessions and privileges that they had obtained from her—some by the bayonet, others by the most-favored-nation clause—during the past half century. Japan took the first important step toward meeting China's demands in this respect by withdrawing her troops from Shantung. By the early winter of 1923 Japan had fulfilled the promise made at Washington, though her economic influence in Shantung remained paramount. Nor would she consent to any real modification of the privileges she claimed in other provinces on the basis of the Sino-Japanese treaties of 1915.[1] In May, 1923, Great Britain concluded an agreement with the Peking Government providing for the restoration of Weihaiwei. The port was not actually turned over to China until 1930, and even then Great Britain retained special privileges in the vicinity, such as the right to maintain a sanatorium and summer resort for the use of the British navy.[2]

The record of the individual dealings of each power with China is strikingly similar. In 1917 the Allies had granted China a five-year moratorium on her Boxer indemnity payments. When these again fell due, France wished her portion of them to be used in paying off the creditors of the Banque Industrielle de Chine, an important French institution which had recently failed. China agreed to the arrangement, proposing to make payments in her own currency at the current rate of exchange, as she had been

[1] Pollard, R. T., *China's Foreign Relations*, 252-254; Carnegie Endowment for International Peace, Division of International Law, *Treaties and Agreements with and Concerning China, 1919-1929*, 100-101, 114-129.

[2] Pollard, 254 ff., 386-387. By 1930 Great Britain had surrendered her residential concessions at Hankow, Kiukiang, Chingkiang and Amoy, and Belgium had given up her concession in Tientsin. *Ibid.*, 382 ff.

doing since 1905. But the franc had depreciated so much in the post-war French inflation that the French Government demanded payments in gold francs at the pre-war exchange rate. China would not agree to this condition; whereat France, encouraged by Italy and Belgium, refused to participate in the extraterritoriality commission, and withheld her signature from the Chinese Tariff and Nine-Power Treaties of Washington until China was forced to compromise, in February, 1925.[1]

In a treaty formally recognizing Soviet Russia in 1924, Peking achieved the apparent success of securing from Moscow a renunciation of the special rights and privileges formally enjoyed in China by the Czarist Government, including Russia's share of the Boxer indemnity and the right of extraterritoriality. In addition Russia recognized Chinese sovereignty over Mongolia and signed a provisional agreement for joint management of the Chinese Eastern Railway.[2] On the face of it this so-called Peking agreement looked like a new departure in Russo-Chinese relations, an object lesson to the other treaty powers. Yet it was accompanied by a type of interference in Chinese politics hardly less aggressive than that symbolized by the special privileges the Soviet was renouncing. While Soviet agents were treaty-making in Peking they were preparing the Kuomintang for its northward march from Canton; and, as it turned out, the recognition of Chinese sovereignty over Mongolia and the Manchurian railway agreement meant no cessation of Russian efforts to dominate these regions.

Toward tariff autonomy and the abolition of extraterritoriality, two major nationalist goals, China made slow progress. The commissions created by the Washington Treaties to study these prob-

---

[1] Pollard, 259-266.

[2] *Ibid.*, 190-194; *Treaties and Agreements, 1919-1929*, 133-144. The United States and Japan both protested at this agreement because it failed to recognize the railway's indebtedness to them for the money and materials they had advanced it during the war. France also protested on similar grounds. Cf. Blakeslee, G. H., "The Pacific Area," World Peace Foundation Pamphlets, Vol. XII, No. 3, 94-95.

lems met in 1925-1926. They were unable to arrive at a conclusive agreement on the first and reported unfavorably on the second. In 1928, however, the United States concluded a treaty with China recognizing as of January 1, 1929, the latter's complete autonomy in regard to the levying and collection of tariffs. The only condition attached to the agreement was a clause providing for reciprocal most-favored-nation treatment. The other powers fell into line behind the United States, as Washington hoped they would, so that by 1931 China enjoyed complete tariff autonomy for the first time in nearly a century.[1]

The liquidation of German, Austrian and Hungarian extra-territorial rights in China during the war, the subsequent Russian renunciation of them, and the recent success of Turkey and Siam in shaking them off—all gave impetus to China's campaign for abolition of extraterritoriality. But the extraterritoriality commission (in 1926) found conditions in China still too turbulent to acquiesce in the latter's demands. Thereafter, while the powers were willing to approve abolition in principle, and some of them specifically agreed to renounce their individual rights as soon as a sufficient number of the others should do so, none was ready to follow Russia's lead. In 1938 China still chafed at the consular jurisdiction that the United States no less than France, Great Britain, Japan and numerous smaller powers continued to exercise.[2]

Chinese nationalism drew no fine distinctions between these treaty powers who were reluctant to part with their special rights and privileges. One and all were considered obnoxious imperialists, whether the imperialism stopped at consular jurisdiction or whether, as in the case of Japan, it contemplated the alienation of

[1] Cf. *Treaties and Agreements, 1919-1929*, 230-233, 237-270; Pollard, 270-281, 347-356, 363 ff.; Blakeslee, 4-19.
[2] *Treaties and Agreements, 1919-1929*, 181-185, 279-282; Pollard, 282-287, 351-353, 370-381; Department of State, *Press Releases*, November 15, 1930; Blakeslee, *op. cit.*, 19-33.

substantial portions of Chinese territory. The partisans of both Peking and Canton could unite in ascribing many of China's ills to the hated foreigners—just as their forefathers had done in the days of the Boxer Rebellion. The campaign against the unequal treaties was marked by periodic outbursts of violence in the treaty ports, by riots, bloodshed, anti-British and anti-Japanese boycotts.

There were serious clashes between Chinese mobs and foreign police at Shanghai and Canton in 1925, and riotous incidents in numerous other localities during that year and the next.[1] Early in January, 1927, native mobs overran the British concessions at Hankow and Kiukiang. Fearful of a general anti-foreign uprising throughout the Yangtse Valley, Great Britain and the United States made formal statements proclaiming their determination to uphold the principles of the Washington Treaties, and their willingness to negotiate with whatever truly representative national government the Chinese people should establish.[2] Slight attention was paid to the conciliatory gesture by the contending forces of Peking and the Kuomintang, whose struggle for mastery of China was nearing a climax. On March 24 victorious Kuomintang troops entered the city of Nanking and proceeded to carry out a systematic attack on the foreign community. British, French, Italian, Japanese and American nationals were killed and wounded, the American, British and Japanese consulates were raided, and much foreign property was looted and destroyed. Foreign refugees hastily sought shelter in the buildings of the University of Nanking, at the British consulate and on the grounds of the Standard Oil Company. To protect the last group from the onslaughts of Kuomintang soldiers, British and American gun-

[1] Cf. Pollard, 266; Toynbee, A. J., *Survey of International Affairs*, 1925, II, 381-392; 1926, 307-317, 344-360.

[2] Japan made a similar, though more guarded, statement. Pollard, 299 ff.; text of American statement, *Treaties and Agreements, 1919-1929*, 193-197. Cf. also Bryn-Jones, David, *Frank B. Kellogg*, 215-218.

boats anchored in the Yangtse River dropped a barrage between the Standard Oil compound and its attackers. This action put a stop to further violence.[1]

The United States followed up its vigorous defense of American nationals in Nanking by participating with the other offended powers in joint diplomatic representations to the Kuomintang. On April 11 the United States, England, France, Italy and Japan presented identic notes to the Chinese Nationalists demanding punishment of troop commanders responsible for the Nanking outrages, and of all persons found to be implicated; written apology from the Commander-in-Chief of the Nationalist army "including an express written undertaking to refrain from all forms of violence and agitation against foreign lives and property," and "complete reparation for personal injuries and material damage done." [2] By this time a schism had developed in the Kuomintang between the leftists, established at Hankow, and the rightists at Nanking. Partly as a result of this confusion the protesting powers received individual and far from satisfactory replies to their notes.[3] It is said that Great Britain, France and Italy proposed some form of sanctions to enforce compliance with their demands, and that Japan would have followed their lead, but that all were restrained by the refusal of the United States to co-operate with them. Whether this was the determining factor, or whether, as Sir Austen Chamberlain intimated to the House of Commons, their moderation was actuated by the wish to help the Nanking conservatives encompass the downfall of the Hankow radicals, it is

[1] Toynbee, *Survey of International Affairs,* 1927, 382-391, a carefully documented account; Pollard, 304-305.

[2] Text of note, *Treaties and Agreements,* 1919-1929, 216; Toynbee, *Survey,* 1927, 392.

[3] Text of Chinese replies to Great Britain, the United States and Japan, *Treaties and Agreements,* 1919-1929, 216-223. The reply to Japan (who had refrained from participating in the bombardment of March 24) was noticeably more conciliatory than those to the United States and Great Britain.

a fact that the co-operative policy went no further than the identic notes of April 11.[1]

It is also a fact that after the receipt of the dissatisfying Chinese replies to these notes, the United States took the lead in conciliating the newly established Nationalist Government at Nanking. It was shortly after the Nanking incident that Chiang Kai-shek staged his *coup d'état,* purging the Kuomintang of its radical elements and orienting its policy along lines more friendly to the Western powers. On February 26, 1928, the United States opened negotiations with Chiang's government for settlement of the Nanking incident. By an exchange of notes on March 30 the Nanking Government apologized and promised full satisfaction for material damages sustained by Americans on March 24, 1927; the United States deplored the "circumstances beyond its control" that had necessitated the bombardment of Socony Hill, and each side made cautious allusions to the revision of the unequal treaties.[2] On the twenty-fifth of the following July the United States signed the treaty with China recognizing the latter's tariff autonomy.[3] The United States had thus pursued a co-operative policy, but only insofar as it concerned the protection of American nationals, property and legal rights. When the policy threatened to transcend these objectives the United States turned from coercive to propitiatory measures, and from co-operation to independent action.

In the summer of 1928 Chiang Kai-shek won for his Nanking Government the foreign recognition hitherto enjoyed by Peking. Chiang's forces entered the former capital in June, putting to rout the last opposition to his rule in that quarter. He had yet to subdue the communists and to re-establish Chinese sovereignty over the lost provinces of Manchuria.

[1] Cf. Pollard, 305-307; Toynbee, *Survey,* 1927, 393-394; Bryn-Jones, 218-219.

[2] Text of notes exchanged, *Treaties and Agreements, 1919-1929,* 223-226. The negotiations were conducted by the American Minister to China, J. V. A. MacMurray and General Huang Fu, Chiang's Foreign Minister.

[3] Pollard, 338-341; Toynbee, *Survey,* 1928, 413-418; Blakeslee, 61-65.

As Chiang proceeded toward these objectives, the United States added to its foreign policy another theoretical device for which Chiang was actually preparing the testing ground. On August 27, 1928, it became a party to the Pact of Paris, renouncing war as an instrument of national policy and promising to use only pacific means in the settlement of all disputes arising between the signatories.[1] The Kellogg Pact (as it came to be known in the United States) rested on much the same premises as the League Covenant and the Washington Treaties. It differed from the first in that it provided for no political organization or sanctions, and from the second in that it was of world-wide rather than regional application. In purpose it was the same—another self-denying ordinance, another attempt to induce the nations of the earth to subordinate their individual interests to world peace, supposedly the common interest of all.[2]

The Kellogg Pact was less than a year old when it was submitted to its first acid test, in Manchuria. In the summer of 1929 China and Soviet Russia severed diplomatic relations, fought pitched battles and came close to a formal declaration of war over the Chinese Eastern Railway. The dispute was the culmination of a series of incidents that had strained Russo-Chinese relations since Chiang Kai-shek's expulsion of communists and Soviet agents in 1927. Until that year Russia had been the friend and mentor of the Kuomintang and, at the same time, had enjoyed the benefits of the 1924 treaty with Peking providing for joint management of the Chinese Eastern Railway. She had also been able to reach a working agreement with the semi-autonomous Manchurian government along the same lines as the Peking Treaty.

As the tide of Chinese Nationalism swept northward, how-

---

[1] For text of pact see Department of State, *Treaty for the Renunciation of War*, 1-6; Stimson, Henry L., *The Far Eastern Crisis*, 271-272; also below, p. 391 n.

[2] For a succinct yet comprehensive review of the origins of the Kellogg Pact, the personalities, nations and political factors behind it, see Bryn-Jones, Chs. XVIII and XIX.

ever, it undermined Russian influence both in China proper and in Manchuria. Parting company with Moscow was one of the steps—possibly the most important—by which Chiang Kai-shek made himself dictator of China. Chang Tso-lin, the Manchurian warlord who periodically dominated the Peking Government from 1922 to 1928, was even more hostile to Russia than his southern rival. When Chang was killed in a mysterious bomb explosion after his defeat by Nanking troops in 1928, he was succeeded as ruler of Manchuria by his son, Chang Hsueh-liang. The latter inherited his father's hostility to Russia but not to the Kuomintang. He quickly recognized the authority of Chiang Kai-shek's Government, thus for the first time bringing to bear against Russia in Manchuria the full strength of the Nationalist movement.

Under the stimulus of these accumulated forces a concerted attack on the rights and privileges accorded Russia in 1924 was made. During his last period of ascendancy at Peking Chang Tso-lin had forced the withdrawal of the Russian Ambassador and raided the Russian embassy because he suspected it of intriguing against him and spreading illicit communist propaganda. On May 27, 1929, Chinese police descended on the Soviet consulates in four Manchurian cities, all situated along the line of the Chinese Eastern Railway. A number of Russian consular officials and communist agents were arrested, and documents were seized which allegedly proved that Russia was disseminating communist propaganda in contravention of the treaty of 1924. Six weeks later (July 10) Chinese authorities at Harbin seized the entire telegraph and telephone system of the Chinese Eastern Railway, replaced its Russian officials with Chinese and arrested, interned or deported over two hundred of its Russian employees.

The Soviet's defense of its rights and interests in Manchuria was prompt and energetic. On July 13 it presented to the local Manchurian government as well as to the Chinese national government at Nanking an ultimatum demanding an immediate conference to settle all questions regarding the railway, cancellation

THE QUEST FOR COLLECTIVE SECURITY 391

of all arbitrary Chinese orders affecting it and the release and reinstatement of its Soviet employees. When China failed to comply with these terms the Soviet broke off diplomatic relations (July 17). China followed suit July 20, and though both nations had just signed the Kellogg Pact, each massed troops on its borders and made ready to settle the dispute by force.[1]

According to the letter of the Kellogg Pact, it imposed only unilateral obligations on its signatories. It contained no provision for consultation, no stipulation that any one signatory or combination of signatories should attempt to enforce it in any way as against possible violators.[2] During the negotiations that preceded ratification it was explicitly understood by all parties that the Pact in no way impaired the right of self-defense, a right "inherent in every sovereign state and . . . implicit in every treaty."[3] Great Britain adhered to the pact on the equally clear understanding that this right extended to "certain regions of the world the wel-

[1] Background of Sino-Russian dispute from Pollard, 387-395; Toynbee, *Survey*, 1929, 344-351; Cooper, Russell M., *American Consultation in World Affairs*, 86-88; Blakeslee, 88-100; Kingman, Henry L., *Effects of Chinese Nationalism upon Manchurian Railway Developments*, Berkeley, 1932, 61-78; Fischer, L., *The Soviets in World Affairs*, II, Ch. 30.

[2] The two essential articles of the pact read as follows:

I. The High Contracting Parties solemnly declare in the names of their respective peoples that they condemn recourse to war for the solution of international controversies, and renounce it as an instrument of national policy in their relations with one another.

II. The High Contracting Parties agree that the settlement or solution of all disputes or conflicts of whatever nature or of whatever origin they may be, which may arise among them, shall never be sought except by pacific means.

Article III provided for ratification and duration without limit. The only reference to any form of sanction was contained by inference in a clause of paragraph 2 of the preamble stating it to be the conviction of the signatories "that any signatory power which shall hereafter seek to promote its national interests by resort to war should be denied the benefits furnished by this Treaty."

[3] Note of United States Government to Governments of Belgium, Czechoslovakia, France, Germany, Great Britain, Irish Free State, Italy, Japan, and Poland, June 23, 1928. Department of State, *Treaty for the Renunciation of War*, Washington, 1933, 56-61.

fare and integrity of which constitute a special and vital interest for our peace and safety.

His Majesty's Government have been at pains to make it clear in the past that interference with these regions cannot be suffered. Their protection against attack is to the British Empire a measure of self-defense. It must be clearly understood that His Majesty's Government in Great Britain accept the new treaty upon the distinct understanding that it does not prejudice their freedom of action in this respect." [1]

China's own adherence was tempered by misgivings, as was Russia's. The Chinese Foreign Minister observed that to make war "really impossible, it is necessary to eliminate all causes which are likely to give rise to any international dispute, and to rigidly uphold the principle of equality and mutual respect for territorial sovereignty among all nations.

My Government, therefore, firmly believes that the signatory powers will abide by the spirit of the present treaty and remove, at the earliest opportunity, all of China's unequal treaties and encroachments upon her sovereignty, as, for instance, the stationing of large numbers of alien troops on her soil." [2]

The Russian Foreign Minister, Litvinoff, took particular exception to Great Britain's reservation of right with respect to regions of "special and vital interest" to the British Empire.

"Recognition of such a right for that Government," he averred, "would amount to justifying war and might be taken as a contagious example to other signatories of the pact who, on the assumption that they have the same right, would also claim the same liberty with regard to other regions, and the result would be that there would probably be no place left on earth where the pact could be put in operation." [3]

---

[1] Chamberlain to Houghton, May 19, and same to Atherton, July 18, 1923. Department of State, *Treaty for the Renunciation of War*, Washington, 1933, 43-46, 72-73.

[2] Wang to Perkins, September 13, 1928. *Ibid.*, 138-139.

[3] Litvinoff to Herbette, August 31, 1928. *Ibid.*, 266-271.

THE QUEST FOR COLLECTIVE SECURITY     393

By January, 1929, more than fifty nations had adhered to the Kellogg Pact. But the spirit in which they had done so, the reservations insisted on by the major signatories, reduced the pact to a collection of individual declarations of the intention not to fight except in defense of whatever national interests each signatory might consider vital. Litvinoff was a shrewd prophet. The British example did prove contagious—even to Russia. For just after signing the pact Russia had broken off diplomatic relations with China, and threatened more forceful measures in defense of vested interests which, to China, were a symbol of aggression.

When the break between the two nations occurred the Kellogg Pact was essentially as meaningless as an agreement not to raise umbrellas except in rainy weather. No one was legally obligated to rescue it from this plight. But Secretary Kellogg's successor, Henry L. Stimson, considered it in the interests of the United States to do so. He assumed, and maintained throughout his tenure of office, leadership in an attempt to quicken the pact's lifeless phrases into specific rules of conduct. Much as John Hay had deliberately construed the dissatisfying replies to the open door notes as a unanimous and wholehearted approval, Stimson read into the Kellogg Pact consultative obligations and the sanction of public opinion. He denied that it was "a mere group of unilateral statements made by the signatories, declaring a pious purpose on the part of each, of which purpose the signatory was to be the sole judge and executor, and for a violation of which no other signatory could call him to account." It was his conviction that the treaty conferred positive benefits to be denied to violators; that it rested "upon the sanction of public opinion, which can be made one of the most potent sanctions in the world," and that it "necessarily carries with it the implication of consultation." [1] In Stimson's hands the Kellogg Pact became a bridge to a more active

[1] Stimson, Henry L., "The Pact of Paris." Address by the Honorable Henry L. Stimson, Secretary of State, before the Council on Foreign Relations, New York City, August 8, 1932. Washington, 1932.

co-operation with the League of Nations than Wilson, in his hour of defeat, might have imagined possible.

No sooner had Russia and China severed relations than Stimson reminded both of their obligation, as signatories of the Kellogg Pact, to settle their dispute peacefully. Stimson could find in the records of his own department precedent for interceding in this controversy. The Knox neutralization scheme of 1909 and the efforts of the United States to prevent Japan from assuming independent control of the Chinese Eastern Railway during the World War were cases in point.[1] This was not the first time that an American Secretary of State had concerned himself with Russian designs on Manchuria. But it was apparently neither tradition nor an exaggerated conception of the material interests of the United States in Manchuria that prompted Stimson's actions in the summer of 1929. Rather, it would seem, it was his desire to fashion the Kellogg Pact into a practical instrument for preserving the peace.[2]

The first responses to Stimson's reminder were reassuring. China emphatically declared that she had "no intention of using force in the present controversy." [3] "Our signature of the Kellogg pact was not just a diplomatic gesture," declared the Russian Commissar of Railroads. "When we talk of peace we mean peace, and when we condemned the imperialist policy of foreign powers defending

[1] These were specifically designated as precedents by Stanley K. Hornbeck, Chief of the Far Eastern Division of the Department of State in an address read at the Williamstown Institute of Politics, August 27, 1929. The address appears under the title of "American Policy and the Chinese-Russian Dispute" in *The Chinese Social and Political Science Review*, XIV, 1930, 41-60.

[2] After mentioning the historic principles of American policy toward China, and the part played by the United States as wartime trustee of the Chinese Eastern Railway, Hornbeck had this to say: "Of special importance to the American Government, however, was and is the relation of the United States to the Treaty for the Renunciation of War, which had been signed at Paris in August, 1928, and which was to go into effect on July 24, 1929. The American Government had sponsored this treaty. The United States has a special moral concern with regard to this treaty." *Ibid.*, 57.

[3] Statement of the Chinese Minister to Washington, July 20, 1929. Cooper, 91.

their interests in China by force we were sincere." [1] Stimson had followed his initial overtures to the two disputants with an appeal to the major signatories of the Pact for their approval of his action. By July 26 Great Britain, France, Italy, Germany and Japan had given him the desired approval, and he had received formal assurances from both China and Russia that they would not resort to force—except in self-defense. [2] For the moment it looked as though the bold initiative of the American Secretary of State had confounded skeptics and infused the pact with the effectiveness its authors had hoped for it.

The impression was soon dissipated. Negotiations between representatives of the local Manchurian and Russian governments broke down late in July. The Chinese were determined to go as far as they could toward recapturing old treaty rights in Manchuria, while the Soviet had no more intention of abandoning its share of these rights than had the Czarist government before it. Neither would accept the other's terms. When discussions between Soviet and local Manchurian officials came to nothing they were taken up by the Russian Ambassador and the Chinese Minister at Berlin. These too proved futile. On July 25, Stimson proposed a solution to Great Britain, France, Germany, Italy and Japan, with no different result. [3] Either because of the unwillingness of the dis-

---

[1] *Ibid.*, 91.

[2] *Ibid.*, 88-92; Hornbeck, "American Policy and the Chinese-Russian Dispute," *loc. cit.*, 58-59; Kingman, 76-78; Toynbee, *Survey*, 1929, 353 ff.

[3] Stimson's proposal was reported to contain plans for the appointment of a neutral commission to study the conflict, mutual troop withdrawals and suspension of hostilities, and the establishment of a body of five Chinese and five Russians presided over by a neutral chairman to manage the Chinese Eastern until the dispute could be settled. It was also rumored that Stimson proposed the formation of an Anglo-American banking group to help China buy the railway. Cooper, 92-93. In his Williamstown address Hornbeck acknowledged the existence of these reports but refused either to confirm or deny them. He would only say that if any proposals had been made they were "based on no thought of any special interest or any possible advantage to the United States." Cf. Hornbeck, "American Policy and the Chinese-Russian Dispute," *loc. cit.*, 59-60.

putants, especially Russia, to accept the mediation of a third party, or the reluctance of the powers addressed by Stimson to co-operate with him—or both—his proposal fell flat.

As the deadlock continued, fighting broke out between the Russian and Chinese troops massed each side of the Manchurian border. Soviet raids into Manchuria were frequent. At length, on November 17, a well-organized Russian force invaded the province, captured several cities and administered such a severe defeat to their Chinese defenders that Chang Hsueh-liang capitulated. He asked the Soviet for preliminary peace terms November 21, received them the next day and accepted them on the twenty-sixth. Further negotiation resulted in an agreement between the Russian and Manchurian Governments (December 3) restoring the very *status quo* that China had tried to upset. This agreement was then concurred in by Nanking in a protocol of December 22. Though the Chinese Government subsequently attempted to avoid ratification of the protocol, it was forced to accept essentially the same terms from Russia as those contained in the unequal treaties it had been attacking.[1]

The Russian invasion of Manchuria led Stimson once more to invoke the Kellogg Pact. In July he had independently reminded Russia and China of their obligations under the pact, and then solicited the other signatories' approval of his action. In August he had come forward with proposals for a settlement. Now he determined to organize some form of collective action by the major signatories of the pact. On November 25, the day before Chang Hsueh-liang accepted Russia's peace terms, Stimson entered into consultation with England, France, Germany, Italy and Japan hoping to induce them to join the United States in bringing pressure to bear on China and Russia to make peace. Germany declined to participate because she had been affording China and Russia her good offices as mediator and as agent of communication since

[1] Pollard, 396-399; Cooper, 92-95; Toynbee, *Survey*, 1929, 361-369; Kingman, 79-83.

the break in their diplomatic relations. Japan would not associate herself with the enterprise in any way, preferring to maintain a scrupulous neutrality. Great Britain, France and Italy followed Stimson's lead and, together with the United States, made an identic appeal to both disputants December 2.

The appeal consisted of another, more forcefully worded reminder to China and Russia of their obligations as signatories of the Kellogg Pact. The American note called attention to Stimson's earlier reminder, and expressed the hope that the two nations would abide by their promises and settle their controversy by pacific means. "The American Government feels that the respect with which China and Russia will hereafter be held in the good opinion of the world will necessarily in great measure depend upon the way in which they carry out these most sacred promises," the note concluded.[1] In a covering statement to the press, Secretary Stimson declared that the "efficacy of the Pact of Paris depends upon the sincerity of the Governments which are party to it.

Its sole sanction lies in the power of public opinion of the countries, constituting substantially the entire civilized world, whose Governments have joined in the covenant. If the recent events in Manchuria are allowed to pass without notice or protest by any of these governments, the intelligent strength of the public opinion of the world in support of peace cannot but be impaired." [2]

To render this sanction effective Stimson invited all the signatories of the pact to make appeals similar to that which the four great powers had just despatched to Moscow and Nanking.

The Nanking Government promptly replied to the appeal of December 2, denying that it had departed from the letter or spirit of the Kellogg Pact and reaffirming its willingness to negotiate for a peaceful settlement.[3] The Russian reply was a plain-

[1] Department of State, *Press Releases*, December 7, 1929, 83-84.
[2] *Ibid.*, 83.
[3] *Ibid.*, 86-87.

spoken rebuff. The United States had not yet recognized the Soviet Government, to which Stimson had been communicating through the French Government. On December 4 he received, *via* these channels, an indignant statement from the Soviet Foreign Commissar, Maxim Litvinoff. The latter believed that if China had pursued the same course of action toward any of the powers that now addressed Russia in the name of the Kellogg Pact, that action "would be considered by their governments sufficient cause for putting into force reservations they made when signing the pact." He reproached the United States for intervening in the dispute after peace parleys had begun, an act which he considered "unjustifiable pressure on the negotiations" and unfriendly to Russia.

The Soviet Government states further that the Paris pact does not give any single State or group of States the function of protector of this pact. The Soviet, at any rate, never expressed consent that any States themselves or by mutual consent should take upon themselves such a right.

The Soviet Government declares that the Soviet-Manchurian conflict can be settled only by direct negotiations between the Soviet Union and China on the basis of conditions known to China and already accepted by the Mukden Government, and that it cannot admit interference of any other party in these negotiations or the conflict.

In conclusion, the Soviet Government cannot forbear expressing amazement that the Government of the United States, which by its own will has no official relations with the Soviet, deems it possible to apply to it with advice and counsel.[1]

Stimson countered with the explanation that he had sponsored the appeal to Moscow "not from unfriendly motives but because this Government regards the Pact of Paris as a covenant which

---

[1] Cooper, 102; for text of Soviet reply, in French, see Wheeler-Bennett, J. W. (ed.), *Documents on International Affairs*, 1929, London, 1930, 278-280. The reply was identic in wording to all the Powers. Cf. also Litvinoff's address to the Central Commissariat of the U.S.S.R., December 4, 1929. *Ibid.*, 188-216.

has profoundly modified the attitude of the world towards peace and because this Government intends to shape its own policy accordingly." [1] But, as Litvinoff made clear in a public address on the subject, the disinterested American desire for peace appeared in a different light once it had been transmitted to Moscow. There it was considered unneutral interference on China's behalf in a dispute precipitated by the latter's summary abrogation of solemn treaty rights. This impression was strengthened by the fact—which Litvinoff found particularly reprehensible—that the United States refused to recognize the Soviet and so denied it the advantage of diplomatic representation at Washington which it freely accorded to China. The latter was thus favorably situated for presenting a one-sided view of her cause. Great Britain, France and the United States had recently defended their own treaty rights from the menace of Chinese Nationalism. That they were prepared to do so again was indicated by the armed forces they still maintained in China. In Soviet eyes this made their invocation of the Kellogg Pact in a case similarly involving Russian rights hypocritical. Moreover, the initiative which Secretary Stimson had assumed from the outset gave rise to Russian suspicions that he was imitating Hay and Knox and trying to undermine Soviet domination of northern Manchuria in order to promote American interests there.[2]

One need not question the sincerity of Secretary Stimson's disavowal of such motives to perceive that his implementation of the Kellogg Pact had failed of its stated objectives. The Soviet had resorted to force as an instrument of national policy to compel China to respect vested Russian interests in the territories that Chinese nationalism was itself forcefully attempting to reclaim. Collective invocation of the "most potent sanction" of public opin-

[1] Department of State, *Press Releases*, December 7, 1929, 87-88.

[2] Report by Maxim Litvinoff, Commissar *ad interim* for Foreign Affairs, to the Central Commissariat of the U.S.S.R., December 4, 1929. Wheeler-Bennett, 188-216, esp. 196-198; Cooper, 102-105. Cf. also Fischer, *op. cit.*, Ch. XXX.

ion had not availed against a type of procedure at which Czarist and Soviet Russia appeared equally adept. It had aroused the strong resentment of Russia and, if anything, strengthened her determination to impose her will on China. Stimson had, it is true, incurred nothing more immediately harmful to the United States than the lion's share of Russian ill will for his leadership of the venture. He had submitted the Kellogg Pact to a process of interpretation that was still in an elementary stage of development. Whither this might lead in the event that a pact violation should seem a more direct transgression of American national interests than was the case in the Sino-Russian controversy remained to be seen.

The third momentous collision into which China was propelled by the Nationalist movement, that with Japanese imperialism, completed the evolution of Stimson's policy. Japan had been anxiously watching the northward march of the Kuomintang and the resurgence of Soviet Russia as a Far Eastern power. Both forces, as they gathered momentum, constituted an increasingly serious menace to the structure of special rights and privileges that Japan had built up in China and Manchuria during the past three decades. The character of these rights and privileges, as well as of Japan's attitude toward them, had not changed since they were first acquired. They were regarded by Japanese statesmen of both liberal and conservative outlook as a lifeline of empire, and by the Japanese people as a symbol of their destiny as a great power. So they had been considered on the eve of the Russo-Japanese War, when Japan determined to risk her national life for them, and in 1915, when she had flung down the gauge of the Twenty-One Demands to China and to her Western competitors.

The passing years had strengthened rather than weakened Japan's determination to defend her claim to a special position in Manchuria. When the claim was first advanced it was the theoretical conception of a primitive nation just opening its eyes to the modern world. In 1930 it was virtually the most important vested interest of a great power, encrusted with tradition, infused with patriotism, a political imperative commanding the allegiance of all factions. Japanese family shrines preserved mementoes of fathers and sons who had died for it. Japanese businessmen had invested billions of yen in it. The fantastic overcrowding of Japan's main islands, poor in natural resources yet forced to absorb an annual population increase of a million souls, contributed to it a sense of self-righteousness or manifest destiny. Japan was convinced that her salvation depended on free access to the raw materials and markets of China, not as a population outlet but as the means of intensively industrializing her teeming millions at home.

Since the signing of the Treaty of Portsmouth and the Komura Treaty of 1905,[1] on which Japan's legal claim to special rights and interests in Manchuria was originally based, her policy in this respect had never varied. She had consistently protected, exploited and, whenever opportunity offered, expanded those rights and interests. She had obtained for them, by the various political deals already described, the recognition of Great Britain, France and Russia, her three principal competitors in China. She had used the World War to eliminate Germany from the scene and to amplify and consolidate her spheres of influence by means of the Twenty-One Demands, the Treaties with China of 1915 and 1918, and the secret treaties with the Allies in 1917. At the Washington Conference, to which she came as an unwilling guest, she had resolutely refused to accept any definite revision of her claims with respect to Manchuria and Mongolia or of the treaties on which they rested.

When, in April, 1923, Secretary Hughes brought about the abrogation of the Lansing-Ishii Agreement, the Japanese co-author of the agreement declared significantly that Japan's special interests in China were inextinguishable. They were "realities deriving from nature and geography," he said, "and not benefits conferred on Japan by the United States.

[1] Cf. p. 147, above.

Mr. Lansing and the author merely performed the role of photographers, as it were, of a condition.

Even though Americans may destroy the print because it is not to their liking, the negative will remain. And even if the negative also be destroyed, does not the substance of the picture remain? . . . The Lansing-Ishii agreement may have been canceled, but Japan's special interests in China continue to live in all their vigor. Even supposing that Japan's special interests in China had not been admitted by international agreements, they are not something which can be abolished." [1]

Thus, despite Japan's adherence to the Washington Treaties, the Kellogg Pact and the London Naval Treaty of 1930,[2] and despite all seeming trends of liberalism in Japan's post-war foreign policy, she continued to possess—and to defend—the most vital economic and political interests in China of any nation on earth. The nerve-center of this unique empire, on the security of which the Japanese people believed their fate depended, was Manchuria. There Japan governed her Kwantung leasehold, as the League of Nations Commission of Inquiry reported in 1932, "with practically full rights of sovereignty." [3] She managed and operated the South Manchuria Railway and administered all contiguous railway areas including towns and large sections of the cities of Mukden and Changchun. Within these areas police, taxation, education and public utilities were under her control. She maintained railway guards along the South Manchuria itself, a large standing army in the Kwantung leasehold and consular police scattered throughout the entire region. "The summary of the long list of Japan's rights in Manchuria," concluded the Lytton report, "shows clearly the exceptional character of the political, economic and legal relations created between that country and China in Manchuria.

[1] Ishii, *Diplomatic Commentaries*, 134-135.
[2] Discussed below, p. 408.
[3] League of Nations Publications No. C. 663 M. 320. 1932, VII, *Report of the Commission of Enquiry*, 38. This document hereafter referred to as *Lytton Report*.

There is probably nowhere in the world an exact parallel to this situation, no example of a country enjoying in the territory of a neighboring State such extensive economic and administrative privileges. A situation of this kind could possibly be maintained without leading to incessant complications and disputes if it were freely desired or accepted on both sides, and if it were the sign and embodiment of a well-considered policy of close collaboration in the economic and in the political sphere. But, in the absence of those conditions, it could only lead to friction and conflict." [1]

The basic issue underlying this "friction and conflict" was comprised not of the innumerable legal technicalities into which it proved capable of rationalization, but of elementary forces springing from the not untainted wells of Far Eastern history. What to China were invasions of sovereignty that any independent nation would wish to repel, to Japan were legitimate business enterprises and treaty rights, bought and paid for, and now a bulwark of the Japanese national economy. The situation never admitted of any such simplified interpretation as that of a struggle between agression and self-defense; and it is significant that the report of the Lytton Commission (possibly the most careful and objective contemporaneous investigation of the origins of a war in history) never so interpreted it, either in its analysis of the facts or in its recommendations. At the conclusion of their report the commissioners offered this "final reflection":

It must be apparent to every reader of the preceding chapters that the issues involved in this conflict are not as simple as they are often represented to be. They are, on the contrary, exceedingly complicated, and only an intimate knowledge of all the facts, as well as of their historical background, should entitle anyone to express a definite opinion

[1] *Ibid.*, 38, and Chs. I-IV. Cf. also Stimson, Henry L., *The Far Eastern Crisis*, Ch. I; Willoughby, W. W., *Foreign Rights and Interests in China*, I, 169-227, 360-419, and *The Sino-Japanese Controversy and the League of Nations*, Ch. I; Young, C. W., *Japan's Special Position in Manchuria, The International Legal Status of the Kwantung Leased Territory* and *Japanese Jurisdiction in the South Manchuria Railway Areas, passim*; Blakeslee, 102-119.

upon them. *This is not a case in which one country has declared war on another country without previously exhausting the opportunities for conciliation provided in the Covenant of the League of Nations. Neither is it a simple case of the violation of the frontier of one country by the armed forces of a neighboring country, because in Manchuria there are many features without an exact parallel in other parts of the world.*[1]

Japan's Western competitors had just conducted a spirited defense of their own special rights and privileges in China. They had qualified their adherence to the Kellogg Pact with reservations of the right of self-defense which, as Russia had shown both by argument and by example, could apply to just such contingencies as Japan faced in Manchuria. The authors of the Lytton Report realized, and said so, that Japan stood to lose more than any other power by the lawless conditions prevalent in China and that consequently she "felt it impossible to satisfy Chinese aspirations so long as satisfactory safeguards to take the place of her Treaty rights could not be hoped for." [2] Perhaps the most convincing proof of the exceptional character of the conflict was the fact that the commissioners made recognition of Japan's interests in Manchuria one of the ten basic principles of their proposed terms of settlement. "The rights and interests of Japan in Manchuria are facts which cannot be ignored," they affirmed, in language reminiscent of Ishii's, "and any solution which failed to recognize them and to take into account also the historical associations of Japan with that country would not be satisfactory." [3]

Japan herself had left few doubts as to how she would deal with any serious attempt of the Chinese Nationalists to circumvent her special position in Manchuria, or with any hostile or even competitive designs of Soviet Russia there. It is true that Japan had become a member of the League of Nations and a party to the Washington Treaties and the Kellogg Pact, and that during two intervals following the Washington Conference she had pur-

---

[1] *Lytton Report*, 126. Italics inserted.          [3] *Ibid.*, 130.
[2] *Ibid.*, 23.

sued more conciliatory tactics in her relations with China than was her wont. But as we have seen, neither Wilson nor Hughes had been able to induce her to accept any categorical revision of her Manchurian claims, nor had the new consortium obtained more than nominal concessions from her in that respect. The so-called "friendship policy" toward China, of which Baron Shidehara, Foreign Minister from 1924 to 1927 and again from 1929 to 1931, was principal exponent, differed from tradition in means rather than in end. From 1919 to 1931 China combated Japan's high-handed diplomacy with periodic national boycotts, causing much damage to Japanese trade.[1] As the Nationalist movement grew in strength the effectiveness of the boycotts increased. Shidehara's "friendship" policy seems to have owed what strength it had to the impotence of a China divided against itself and to the demands of Japanese business for diplomatic promotion that would not stir up boycotts rather than to any national conversion to the self-denying principles of the Nine-Power Treaty and the Kellogg Pact.

Japanese history revealed little essential difference between the Shidehara policy and its more "positive" alternatives. Parliamentary government in Japan was altogether chimerical. Probably no people in the world were more thoroughly united on foreign policy than the intensely nationalistic, emperor-worshiping Japanese. Of the two policies in point the Lytton Commission found that,

The general aims for which they worked in Manchuria were to maintain and develop Japan's vested interests, to foster the expansion of Japanese enterprise, and to obtain adequate protection for Japanese lives and property. In the policies adopted for realizing these aims there was one cardinal feature which may be said to have been common to

[1] See the detailed analyses of the Chinese boycotts in *Lytton Report, Annexes,* Part III, Special Studies by the Experts of the Commission, Study No. 8, "Memorandum on Boycotts and Japanese Interests in China"; also Remer, C. F., *A Study of Chinese Boycotts,* esp. Chs. VII-XVI.

them all. This feature has been the tendency to regard Manchuria and Eastern Inner Mongolia as distinct from the rest of China. It resulted naturally from the Japanese conception of their country's "special position" in Manchuria. Whatever differences may have been observable between the specific policies advocated by the various cabinets in Japan —as, for example, between the so-called "friendship policy" of Baron Shidehara and the so-called "positive policy" of the late General Baron Tanaka—they have always had this feature in common . . . in regard to the concrete measures which should be adopted in Manchuria, these two policies differed largely on the question as to the lengths to which Japan should go to maintain peace and order in Manchuria and to protect Japanese interests.[1]

There is no better evidence to support this conclusion than Japan's reversion to "positive" measures the instant the interests Shidehara was trying to further by conciliation seemed in serious danger. No sooner had the Nationalists entered Nanking in 1927 than the cabinet in which Shidehara was Foreign Minister fell. Its successor promptly marched troops into Shantung to protect Japanese interests, incidentally delaying Chiang Kai-shek's advance on Peking. When Chiang launched his final drive on Peking the next year, Japanese forces occupied the city of Tsinan, engaged with Chiang's in severe fighting, and drove them from the vicinity.[2] At the same time Japan warned both Nanking and Peking that she would not permit the extension of hostilities into Manchuria.[3]

Japan issued a similar warning to Chang Hsueh-liang when he succeeded his father, Chang Tso-lin as ruler of Manchuria in the spring of 1928. The elder Chang had been a fairly consistent enemy of Nanking. He had several times declared the complete independence of Manchuria from China. He had not been adverse to taking Japanese "advice," had resisted the infiltration of communism and, in short, both as an end to be played against the

[1] *Lytton Report*, 40-41.          [3] *Ibid.*, 346.
[2] Cf. Pollard, 345 ff., 359-360.

middle and as a determined foe of Russia, had served Japanese interests not unwell.[1] Just before his death, however, Chang had turned against Japan, a fact that would seem to implicate the Japanese in the bomb explosion that killed him.[2] The younger Chang was an avowed Nationalist sympathizer. When his father's assassination made him supreme warlord of Manchuria, Japan pointedly admonished him against recognizing the authority of Nanking.[3] But Chang Hsueh-liang followed his own counsel, declaring his allegiance to Nanking in December, 1928, and receiving the latter's commission as Commander-in-Chief of the North-Eastern Frontier Army and head of the government of Manchuria and Jehol, a portion of Inner Mongolia.[4]

The united Nationalists forthwith launched their campaign of economic and political redemption of the northeastern provinces, the first notable result of which was the clash with Russia already described. Japan played a more or less neutral role in the controversy of 1929 because, presumably, it suited her to allow the two forces inimicable to her interests to quarrel with each other. The outcome of the dispute showed the inadequacy of these tactics. The Chinese assault on the Soviet's position in Manchuria was a miserable failure. If it had succeeded, Japan's interests would have been the next to suffer. As it was the old incubus of Russian expansion had been revived, accompanied now by the frightening aspect of communism. Despite her failure to dislodge Russia from control of the Chinese Eastern, China continued to pursue an ambitious program of independent railway and harbor construction, dissemination of anti-Japanese propaganda and wholesale colonization by Chinese settlers, the prime motive of which was to encompass the downfall of Japanese economic and political supremacy. Events were marching rapidly toward one of those frequently recurring showdowns between China, Russia and Ja-

---

[1] Cf. Lytton Report, 28 ff., 35, 41.       [3] Pollard, 347; Lytton Report, 29.
[2] Ibid., 29; Stimson, 24.                    [4] Ibid., 30; Stimson, 24-25.

pan that formed the fabric of Far Eastern history since 1895.[1]

The crisis was postponed, not averted, by the return of Shidehara to the Foreign Ministry of Japan in the summer of 1929. In the face of domestic opposition growing stronger and more violent every day, Shidehara and his chief, Prime Minister Hamaguchi, revived the "friendship policy" toward China and made Japan a party to the London Naval Conference and Treaty of 1930.[2] But the fate of each venture showed all too clearly that Shidehara was serving a lost cause. The Japanese delegates had gone to London with instructions to insist on a 10:7 ratio *vis-à-vis* the United States in heavy cruisers and all auxiliary craft. They were obliged to accept the compromise of a 10:6 ratio in heavy cruisers, with slightly higher ratios in light cruisers and destroyers and equality in submarines in compensation. The staff of the Japanese navy adamantly opposed ratification of the treaty containing this compromise. By overriding the navy's wishes Hamaguchi precipitated a constitutional crisis and a reign of violence in Japanese politics that culminated in his own assassination and the *débâcle* of his government.[3] Secretary Stimson hailed the Lon-

---

[1] For an exhaustive review of the various forms of Sino-Japanese economic and political rivalry leading to the outbreak of hostilities in 1931, see *Lytton Report*, Chs. III, IV, VII-IX, and *Annexes*, Part III, *passim*.

[2] This treaty prolonged for five years, i.e., until 1936, the holiday in capital ship construction inaugurated by the Washington Treaty. It also extended to auxiliary classes the quantitative limitations imposed by the Washington Treaty on capital ships only. The limitations thus extended were subject, however, to an "escalator clause" permitting any signatory to depart from the limitations if, in its opinion, new construction by any non-signatory should so alter the world balance of naval power as to make such a step necessary. The other signatories would thereupon be entitled to increase their own tonnages proportionately. The treaty was signed April 22, 1930, by Great Britain, Japan and the United States. France and Italy participated in the conference, but did not sign. It was to last until December 31, 1936, providing for a new conference to be held a year in advance of expiration. For a comprehensive analysis of the conference and treaty, see Toynbee, *Survey*, 1930, 31-82; text of treaty, Department of State, *Conference Series No. 2, 1930*, "The London Naval Treaty."

[3] Takeuchi, Ch. XXV; Stimson, 9, 36.

don Naval Treaty as reinforcement for the Kellogg Pact and the whole process of disarmament and outlawry of war of which he was one of the world's outstanding advocates.[1] Yet he was forced to admit that Hamaguchi's advice to the emperor to ratify the treaty against the wishes of the admiralty "caused deep resentment" in Japan "and was probably influential in producing some of the violent reactionary consequences which followed. Mr. Hamaguchi was soon afterwards assassinated by a military fanatic, and secret organizations were formed which were destined to have a baleful influence upon the course of Japanese history." [2]

Shidehara's final effort to uphold the "friendship policy" was futile. The Chinese attack on Japan's vested interests in Manchuria intensified instead of abating, and as it did so domestic opposition to the Japanese Foreign Minister's tactics increased in direct ratio. Fighting broke out between Chinese and Korean farmers and Japanese consular police in Manchuria in July, 1931. This was followed by widespread anti-Chinese riots in Korea and a revival of the anti-Japanese boycott in China. Late in June a Japanese army officer on an intelligence mission in central Manchuria (Captain Nakamura) was secretly executed by Chinese soldiers. When news of this reached Tokyo it stimulated the growing demand for immediate settlement of the whole complex Manchurian issue, by force. "Certain internal, economic and political factors had undoubtedly for some time been preparing the Japanese people for a resumption of the 'positive policy' in Manchuria," summarized the Lytton Commission.

The dissatisfaction of the army; the financial policy of the Government; the appearance of a new political force emanating from the

[1] Cf. his address to the Associated Press, broadcast from London (whither he had gone as Chairman of the American delegation to the Naval Conference) April 21, 1930. Department of State, *Press Releases*, April 26, 1930, 188 ff.

[2] Stimson, 9. "The treaty was highly unpopular with the naval authorities in Japan," he observed at another point. "But Premier Hamaguchi had carried it through to ratification in the face of tremendous opposition as a result of which he had lost his life." *Ibid.*, 36.

army, the country districts and the nationalist youth, which expressed dissatisfaction with all political parties, which despised the compromise methods of Western civilization and relied on the virtues of Old Japan and which included in its condemnation the self-seeking methods whether of financiers or politicians; the fall in commodity prices, which inclined the primary producer to look to an adventurous foreign policy for the alleviation of his lot; the trade depression, which caused the industrial and commercial community to believe that better business would result from a more vigorous foreign policy: all these factors were preparing the way for an abandonment of the Shidehara "policy of conciliation" with China which seemed to have achieved such meager results. This impatience in Japan was even greater among the Japanese in Manchuria, where the tension throughout the summer was increasing. As September wore on, this tension reached such a point *that it was apparent to all careful observers that a breaking point must soon be reached.*[1]

One final factor must be taken into account. In the late summer of 1931 the world had just begun to feel the full effects of the great depression. England and the United States especially were preoccupied with economic chaos at home and in Europe. The collapse of the Credit Anstalt, the British departure from the gold standard, President Hoover's moratorium were the subjects on which the people and governments of the Western nations were concentrating. "If anyone had planned the Manchurian outbreak with a view to freedom from interference from the rest of the world," wrote Stimson in retrospect, "his time was well chosen." [2]

Of such elements, visible to only a few Americans and intelligible to still fewer, the second great test of Stimson's policy was compounded. On September 18, 1931, Japanese troops of the Kwantung army drove out the Chinese garrisons and seized Mukden, Changchun and several other south Manchurian cities. The attack was executed, as the Lytton Commission reported from evi-

[1] *Lytton Report*, 66-67. Italics inserted.
[2] Stimson, 5-6.

dence that seems unassailable," with swiftness and precision," on the implausible pretext of self-defense, the first step of a carefully matured plan for the military occupation of all Manchuria.[1] Whether the troops acted on their own initiative or under orders from Tokyo, they received full approval from the military branch of the government, now rapidly eclipsing the other branches in power and authority. Apparently the group that had dominated Japanese politics at every similar crisis in Japan's modern history, had once more determined to force the issue with China.

News of the Japanese attack on Mukden reached Washington September 19. On the twenty-first China appealed to the League of Nations (which had just assembled) under Article XI to take cognizance of the breach of peace and use its good offices to repair it. Simultaneously China called on the United States as "sponsor of the sacred engagements contained in" the Kellogg Pact "to take such steps as will insure the preservation of peace in the Far East, and the upholding of the principle of peaceful settlement of international disputes." [2] The same day (September 21) the Secretary General of the League, Sir Eric Drummond, communicated with Stimson "evidently to sound out our attitude and views particularly as to whether we thought the Kellogg-Briand Pact was involved." [3]

Appeals to the United States for assistance to China had seldom fallen on deaf ears, nor did this one. It elicited from the Secretary of State a galvanic response. He informed Drummond that he was following developments closely and that he was mindful of the obligations not only of the Kellogg Pact but also of the Nine-Power Treaty. He assured the League Secretary of an attitude of "co-operation and frankness," and passed on to him such

[1] *Lytton Report*, 71, and Ch. IV, entire.

[2] United States Senate Document No. 55, 72nd Congress, 1st Session, "Conditions in Manchuria," 3. This document hereinafter referred to as "Conditions in Manchuria." Cf. also Cooper, 197, Willoughby, W. W., *The Sino-Japanese Controversy and the League of Nations*, Ch. III.

[3] Stimson, 41.

information as the State Department had received from Manchuria. In this he included his own impression that an issue had arisen "between the Japanese military chiefs and their Foreign Office" together with his opinion that "while preparing to uphold treaty obligations, it would be wise to avoid action which might excite nationalistic feeling in Japan in support of the military and against Shidehara." [1] From that moment forward the United States, under Stimson's leadership, integrated its diplomacy closely with the procedures of the League.

On September 22 the League urged China and Japan, in identic telegrams, to refrain from further hostilities and to withdraw their troops pending a peaceful settlement. It also considered the proposition of sending an investigating commission to Manchuria, taking care to notify Stimson of its actions and seeking his concurrence. He was asked to make parallel representations to China and Japan and sounded as to the appointment of an American to the proposed investigating commission. [2]

While the League was thus engaged Stimson summoned the Japanese Ambassador (September 22) and through him transmitted an "earnest memorandum" to Shidehara. [3] In this he reviewed the situation that had developed in Manchuria during the past four days, a situation which, he asserted, was "of concern, morally, legally, and politically to a considerable number of nations.

It is not exclusively a matter of concern to Japan and China. It brings into question at once the meaning of certain provisions of agreements, such as the nine powers treaty of February 6, 1922, and the Kellogg-Briand pact.

The American Government is confident that it has not been the intention of the Japanese Government to create or to be a party to the creation of a situation which brings the applicability of treaty provisions

[1] Stimson, 41-42.
[2] "Conditions in Manchuria," 4; Stimson, 42, 46; Cooper, 196.
[3] Stimson, 46-47.

into consideration. The American Government does not wish to be hasty in formulating its conclusions or in taking a position. However, the American Government feels that a very unfortunate situation exists, which no doubt is embarrassing to the Japanese Government. It would seem that the responsibility for determining the course of events with regard to the liquidating of this situation rests largely upon Japan, for the simple reason that Japanese armed forces have seized and are exercising de facto control in south Manchuria."

The memorandum concluded with an expression of hope that the two powers would compose their differences without further hostilities.[1]

In spite of Stimson's disavowal of haste, his memorandum was *ipso facto* proof that he had already formed conclusions and taken a position. He had concluded that the dispute between China and Japan was the concern of "a considerable number of nations," among them the United States; that the Nine-Power Treaty and the Kellogg Pact were more than potentially at stake, and that for the disturbances in Manchuria Japan was chiefly responsible. He had taken the position that it was up to Japan to remedy the situation. He would not, however, consent to the appointment of an American to the proposed investigating commission and temporarily discouraged the League from carrying out this project because he feared such unprecedented American assistance to the League might handicap Shidehara's resistance to the military.[2]

Stimson expressed great anxiety at this time lest any measure be adopted that would embarrass the hard-pressed Japanese Foreign Minister.

"The evidence in our hands," he wrote, "pointed to the wisdom of giving Shidehara and the Foreign Office an opportunity, free from anything approaching a threat or even public criticism, to get control of the situation. . . . It seemed clear to us that no steps should be taken

[1] "Conditions in Manchuria," 4-5.
[2] Stimson, 42-43; Cooper, 198, 200-201.

which would make his task more difficult because certainly our best chance of a successful solution of the situation lay in him." [1]

Yet while the League was appealing to both China and Japan in the discreet phrases of an identic telegram, he was independently communicating to Japan alone an "earnest memorandum," the admonitory tone of which was unmistakable to any professional diplomat. He would not support a League investigating commission; yet he did not hesitate to send his own investigators to conduct a minute examination of the origin and scope of hostilities. [2] Through the American Minister to Switzerland, Hugh Wilson, who attended meetings of the Council, he kept himself in the closest possible touch with the proceedings of the League. And when, on September 23, the League asked him to back up its appeal to the disputants, he readily agreed to do so. Identic notes similar to the League's went forth from Washington to Tokyo and Peking the next day, to the accompaniment of a whole-hearted endorsement of the League's actions and a grateful acknowledgment from Geneva. [3]

The immediate results of the efforts of Washington and Geneva to clear up the trouble in Manchuria were disappointing. China

---

[1] Stimson, 34, 36. On September 23 Stimson noted in his diary: "My problem is to let the Japanese know that we are watching them and at the same time to do it in a way which will help Shidehara who is on the right side, and not play into the hands of any nationalist agitators." *Ibid.*, 37.

[2] Stimson informed Shidehara of his desire to conduct this investigation at the same time that he declined to take part in the League's, hoping thus "to accomplish the real end which the League had in mind and to do it without the dangers which I had anticipated from their proposal." His request was "immediately granted" by Shidehara and the two American investigators received their instructions September 28. Stimson, 45-46.

[3] For text of American note to China and Japan and exchanges between Washington and Geneva, see "Conditions in Manchuria," 5-8. On September 23 Stimson assured the League Council that "the Government of the United States is in whole-hearted sympathy with the attitude of the League of Nations as expressed in the council's resolution and will dispatch to Japan and China notes along similar lines." *Ibid.*, 5. Cf. also Stimson, 43; Cooper, 199-200.

replied to the various appeals by accusing Japan of unprovoked aggression and placing the burden of responsibility for a settlement on the already overladen shoulders of Shidehara. The latter was caught in a vise between the disapproving Western powers and the Japanese military and their fast-growing following. He could offer only excuses of self-defense and unconvincing assurance that Japan would withdraw her troops as soon as the safety of her nationals and their rights and property permitted.[1] On September 20 the League Council adopted a resolution, in which both the Chinese and Japanese representatives concurred, summarizing the statements of each power and urging moderation on each. The Council then adjourned until October 14.[2] Japan's approval of this resolution together with Shidehara's willingness to submit his case to the scrutiny of Stimson's investigators attested to the Foreign Minister's sincerity rather than to his ability to represent, much less to control, the destiny of his country. Japanese troops in Manchuria made no move to withdraw from their positions. Their Commander-in-Chief publicly declared that Japan would no longer recognize the government of Chang Hsueh-liang. And on October 8 a squadron of Japanese airplanes bombed Chinchow, Chang's provisional capital.[3]

The activities of the Japanese army drew fresh calls for help from Peking,[4] and led Stimson into a series of increasingly ambitious attempts to reinforce, if not actually to guide, the League and induce Japan to abandon her conquest. In a telegram to Sir Eric Drummond on October 5 he defined his course:

[1] For replies of China and Japan to the League and American appeals, see "Conditions in Manchuria," 6-7, 8-11.

[2] *Ibid.*, 11-12.

[3] *Lytton Report*, 72; Stimson, 52 ff.

[4] On October 3 China urged the United States, in the name of the Kellogg Pact, to co-operate with the League in the matter of investigating affairs in Manchuria. The American Minister to China replied (October 5) that the United States had already sent its own investigators to Manchuria and so had anticipated the Chinese request. "Conditions in Manchuria," 12-14.

I believe that our co-operation in the future handling of this difficult matter should proceed along the course which has been followed ever since the first outbreak of the trouble fortunately found the Assembly and the Council of the League of Nations in session. The Council has deliberated long and earnestly on this matter and the Covenant of the League of Nations provides permanent and already tested machinery for handling such issues as between States members of the League. Both the Chinese and Japanese have presented and argued their cases before the Council and the world has been informed through published accounts with regard to the proceedings there. The Council has formulated conclusions and outlined a course of action to be followed by the disputants; and as the said disputants have made commitments to the Council, it is most desirable that the League in no way relax its vigilance and in no way fail to assert all the pressure and authority within its competence toward regulating the action of China and Japan in the premises.

On its part the American government acting independently through its diplomatic representatives will endeavor to reinforce what the League does and will make clear that it has a keen interest in the matter and is not oblivious to the obligations which the disputants have assumed to their fellow signatories in the Pact of Paris as well as in the Nine Power Pact should a time arise when it would seem advisable to bring forward those obligations. By this course we avoid any danger of embarrassing the League in the course to which it is now committed.[1]

The last sentence of this communication was something of an understatement. It would be difficult to conceive of a more powerful American endorsement of the League than one which urged it "to assert all the pressure and authority within its competence," pledged the unstinting "independent" support of the United States and even suggested the invocation of certain treaty obligations supplementary to the League's "competence."

The vigor of Stimson's efforts to bring Japan to account increased in direct ratio with his misgivings. He had at first been

[1] Stimson to Drummond, October 5, 1931. Stimson, 51-52; "Conditions in Manchuria," 14.

apprehensive of forcing Shidehara's hand. He had not only hoped, but to a certain extent assumed, that the Foreign Minister could quench the flames of Japanese nationalism, renounce conquests both past and present and rededicate Japan to the Nine-Power Treaty and the Kellogg Pact. The bombing of Chinchow on October 8 dashed some of his hopes and prompted him to take a firmer stand *vis-à-vis* Japan. In a cabinet meeting the next day he voiced the fear that "these modern treaties initiated by Western nations, and especially designed to fit the exigencies of the industrialized world of Europe and America, might not be taken very seriously in the Orient." But, as he told his colleagues, "those treaties existed; for better or worse they represented the earnest hopes of our part of the world, and if we surrendered and permitted them to be treated like scraps of paper, the hope of peaceable development in the world would receive a blow from which it would not soon recover." [1]

Accordingly Stimson began to consider means short of the actual use of armed force by which Japan might be compelled to respect "the great peace treaties which had been publicly flouted by Japan's actions." He began to talk of "some form of collective economic sanctions against Japan," of "the exercise of diplomatic pressure and the power of world public opinion, to try to get as fair play as possible for the weaker power, China . . . ," of "a vigorous judgment against Japan backed by the public opinion of the world. . . ."

"These in substance," he wrote, "were the objectives which one after another were discussed by us at the State Department during the autumn weeks while the proceedings of the League were taking their discouraging course at Geneva and Paris." [2]

The American Secretary of State was becoming impatient with the conservatism of the League. More and more he was seizing the

[1] Stimson, 56.
[2] Stimson, 57.

initiative both in direct remonstrances with Tokyo and in the introduction of proposals at Geneva.

Soon after the bombing of Chinchow he prompted the Council to broach the idea of refereed negotiations between China and Japan similar to those conducted with respect to Shantung (with Hughes and Balfour in attendance) at the Washington Conference. The Council duly passed on the suggestion, which was rejected by Japan.[1] On October 10 Stimson obtained President Hoover's approval of a plan to have the United States participate in all sessions of the League Council having to do with the enforcement of the Kellogg Pact. Two days later he telephoned Prentiss Gilbert, American Consul at Geneva, authorizing him to take part in such sessions if invited to do so.[2] He then arranged to have the invitation extended by the Council in order to avoid giving Japan the impression that the United States was "the instigator of the entire matter—of having wormed herself into League councils in order to stir up hostilty against Japan."[3] Japan was neither deceived nor mollified by the strategy, however, strongly opposing Stimson's plan and voting against it, though in vain. With Gilbert an influential advocate the Council decided (October 17) on a joint invocation of the Kellogg Pact. And on the twentieth another pair of identic notes from Washington reminded Tokyo and Peking of their obligations under the pact.[4]

While thus spurring on the League, Stimson continued independently to urge moderation on both China and Japan and to

[1] Stimson, 59.

[2] Cooper, 207. Gilbert was to represent the United States in place of Hugh Wilson, who had gone to Washington on business relating to the forthcoming disarmament conference.

[3] Stimson, 62. The invitation was issued by M. Briand, President of the Council, October 14, and publicly accepted by Stimson, October 16. Gilbert attended Council meetings until October 24, when he retired on instructions from Stimson. Ibid., 62-66. "Conditions in Manchuria," 17-20; Cooper, 207 ff.

[4] Stimson, 65; Cooper, 212; Willoughby, 104-111; "Conditions in Manchuria," 20.

register stern protests at Tokyo.[1] On October 11 he bluntly informed Shidehara that the "explanation given by the Japanese military authorities" for the bombing of Chinchow "seems quite inadequate."[2] He followed up a League resolution of October 24, directing Japan to withdraw her troops by November 16, with recommendations of a similar nature though without the stipulation of a time limit.[3] When this did not produce the desired result he appointed the American Ambassador to England, former Vice-President Dawes, to represent the United States at the next session of the Council. His new emissary to the League held conference with the British Foreign Minister Sir John Simon before leaving for Paris, where the Council convened November 16.[4] Dawes did not actually attend the meetings of the Council, as Wilson and Gilbert had done, possibly because he was afraid of the effect it might have on his political career at home. Nevertheless, he ensconced himself in a near-by Paris hotel where he held daily interviews with the statesmen of all nationalities that crowded its corridors, and kept in telephonic connection with the Secretary of State.[5]

Unimpressed by what was happening in the Western capitals, the Japanese army methodically extended its operations from southern into northern Manchuria, capturing the Nonni River bridges in the early days of November and the city of Tsitsihar November 19.[6] As it did so Stimson began to receive "dark news as to the popular excitement in Japan which was steadily rising as her troops moved forward.

[1] On October 10 he appealed to both powers to desist from violence. "Conditions in Manchuria," 15-16.

[2] Ibid., 16.

[3] These were presented to Shidehara by the American Ambassador to Japan, Cameron Forbes, on November 5. For text see "Conditions in Manchuria," 30-32. Cf. also Stimson, 67 ff.; Cooper, 215-218; Willoughby, 112-148.

[4] It met in Paris instead of Geneva so that M. Briand could simultaneously discharge his duties to the French government and the League. Cf. Cooper, 221 n.

[5] Stimson, 75; Cooper, 222-225; Willoughby, 107, 154.

[6] Lytton Report, Ch. IV; Stimson, 70.

This came to us through many channels—our embassy at Tokyo, the Japanese embassy in Washington, our observers in contact with representative Japanese in various quarters of the world. Not only was the general feeling among the people aflame with patriotic hostility to China and the outside world, but fanatical secret societies existed which were overawing the chiefs of the army itself as well as threatening violence to the heads of the civil government. Our Embassy in Japan reported that the Wakatsuki-Shidehara Cabinet was tottering and could not last long in the face of the excited populace." [1]

Shidehara was now in the very predicament that Stimson had originally apprehended might result from outside intervention in the Sino-Japanese dispute. The Wakatsuki-Shidehara Cabinet was "tottering," and as it did so Stimson made ready for its collapse. He had come to the conclusion, he afterwards explained,

that the American people were following the proceedings both here and at Geneva with great interest . . . that they were growing puzzled and angry at the silence of their own government in the face of the defiant attitude of the Japanese army towards the representations made by us and the League.[2]

He decided to meet fire with fire. On November 19 he called in the Japanese Ambassador, Mr. Debuchi, told him that he regarded the Japanese army's activities as a violation of the Kellogg Pact and the Nine-Power Treaty and threatened to publish all the communications that had passed between Washington and Tokyo. Stimson was threatening, in other words, to invoke that "most potent sanction" of publicity. Nor was that all. After a conference with Hoover the same day he sent word (through Dawes) to Briand that in case the League wished to impose the economic sanctions provided for in Article XVI of the covenant

---

[1] Stimson, 71.

[2] *Ibid.*, 72-73. This statement is not easy to reconcile with another, which Stimson makes later in the same book, to wit: "Furthermore, to a great many of our people Manchuria was an unknown part of the earth and they wondered what we had to do with any controversy there at all." *Ibid.*, 153.

the United States was "anxious not to discourage them or to put any obstacles or dangers in their path." [1] That the United States, a non-member of the League, had begun to suggest sanctions in advance of the League itself showed the degree to which Stimson's allegiance to the doctrine of collective security was influencing his Far Eastern policy.

Events now marched rapidly to a climax. As if taking up Stimson's challenge the Japanese army renewed their briefly interrupted march on Chinchow, while at Geneva, confident either that she had a good case to present, or that she was well able to defend the case she had, Japan proposed that the League carry out its much-discussed project of sending a neutral investigating commission to Manchuria. Dawes warmly acclaimed the Japanese proposal, which was carried in a League resolution, with Japan's assent, December 10. Stimson at once congratulated the League, assuring it of his full co-operation and again giving prominent mention to the Kellogg Pact and the Nine-Power Treaty. [2] Meantime, on November 24 and 27, Stimson sternly protested to Shidehara against the Japanese advance on Chinchow, asking, and receiving, Shidehara's assurance that it would be discontinued. The Foreign Minister spent his last ounce of political strength and the Manchurian march was halted (November 27). [3] Japan's assent to the League resolution of December 10 was Shidehara's final achievement. The cabinet of which he was a member fell the next day. The Japanese army was now in supreme control in Tokyo as well as in Manchuria. Unbridled by diplomacy, it rode the crest of a tidal wave of patriotism to complete the conquest of Manchuria with the capture of Chinchow, January 2, 1932. [4]

[1] *Ibid.*, 72-77.

[2] "Conditions in Manchuria," 41-47; Stimson, 78-81; Cooper, 227-232; Willoughby, 172-205.

[3] "Conditions in Manchuria," 42-43; Stimson, 78-79. Cf. also Takeuchi, Ch. XXVI, esp. 366-368.

[4] The city was occupied January 3. Severe fighting continued in northern Manchuria during the winter and spring of 1932. *Lytton Report*, 78 ff.

"Thus," Stimson acknowledged, "our attempt to solve the Manchurian problem by discussion and conciliation had failed." [1]

Stimson's policy now underwent a subtle transition. Until the fall of Chinchow he had been trying to use the Kellogg Pact as a war preventive, construing the pact broadly enough to justify, in his mind, the most intimate American collaboration with the League. His main purpose had been, or at least had seemed to be, to prove and validate the procedures of collective security. This purpose derived, in turn, from a strong sympathy for China and the Chinese, an expansive conception of the material interests of the United States in China and a highly moralistic attitude toward world politics in general. Thus, when the fall of Chinchow convinced him that "all hope for a solution of the Manchurian problem by conciliation and for a fair settlement by even-handed negotiation with China was ended for the present," he perceived three reasons why he should not discontinue his efforts to restrain Japan:

*First:* The direct material damage to our trade which would inevitably be caused; also the less certain but nevertheless quite possible jeopardy which in the future course of such a struggle between China and Japan might threaten our own people and their territorial possessions.

*Second:* The immense blow to the cause of peace and war prevention throughout the world which would inevitably be caused if without protest or condemnation Japan were permitted to violate and disregard the group of post-war treaties which she had ratified and upon which so many hopes of our race and of our part of the world had been predicated.

*Third:* The incalculable harm which would be done immediately to American prestige in China and ultimately to the material interests of America and her people in that region, if after having for many years assisted by public and private effort in the education and development of China towards the ideals of modern Christian civilization, and hav-

[1] Stimson, 82.

ing taken the lead in the movement which secured the covenant of all the great powers, including ourselves, "to respect her sovereignty, her independence and her territorial and administrative integrity," we should now cynically abandon her to her fate when this same covenant was violated.[1]

In Stimson's mind the economic dreams of the dollar diplomatists and all the prophets of a century past who had seen in China a rich commercial market of the future, blended with the idealistic visions of the missionaries through whose eyes many, perhaps most, Americans were inclined to look at China. "China is a country so vast and at present so undeveloped in the normal needs of a population of her type and intelligence," he reasoned, "that the possibilities of a commerce with her, which will supply her needs as she develops along the pathway of modern civilization, are literally enormous." And:

For several centuries Eastern Asia has owed its character mainly to the peaceful traditions of this great agricultural nation. If the character of China should be revolutionized and through exploitation become militaristic and aggressive, not only Asia but the rest of the world must tremble. The United States has made a good start in the development of China's friendship. It would have been the most short-sighted folly to turn our backs upon her at the time of her most dire need.[2]

For these reasons, Stimson turned from conciliation to coercion, casting about "to find some way of formally expressing the moral disapproval of the world against the breach of the peace in Manchuria and, if possible, to put behind that expression a sanction which would bring pressure upon the party responsible to make amends." [3]

Disappointed at the failure of the League to take more forceful action against Japan, Stimson shifted his attention to the resources offered by American diplomacy. From these he selected, as the

[1] Stimson, 88-90.          [3] *Ibid.*, 92.
[2] *Ibid.*, 90-91.

most powerful weapon of the type he desired, the Bryan-Lansing non-recognition doctrine that had been used in connection with the Twenty-One Demands in 1915.[1] On January 4, 1932, he obtained President Hoover's consent to a bold, independent move. He would step out of his role of collaborator with the League, enlist the support of England and France, and apply the non-recognition doctrine to Japan's Manchurian conquest. On January 5 he revealed his design first to the British, then to the French Ambassador, and invited their governments to take similar steps. Then on January 7, without waiting for replies from London or Paris, he despatched an identic note to China and Japan informing them that the United States

cannot admit the legality of any situation *de facto* nor does it intend to recognize any treaty or agreement entered into between those governments, or agents thereof, which may impair the treaty rights of the United States or its citizens in China, *including those which relate to the sovereignty, the independence, or the territorial and administrative integrity of the Republic of China, or to the international policy relative to China, commonly known as the open-door policy;* and that it does not intend to recognize any situation, treaty, or agreement which may be brought about by means contrary to the covenants and obligations of the Pact of Paris of August 27, 1928, to which treaty both China and Japan, as well as the United States, are parties.[2]

This non-recognition note was steeped in tradition. Not only was it a leaf from the experience of Lansing and Bryan in 1915, and an invocation of the Kellogg Pact similar to that which Stimson himself had made during the Sino-Russian dispute of 1929; it was also the latest formal, grand-scale affirmation of the doctrine of the open door and the territorial integrity of China. It was Stimson's version of the Hay circular of July 3, 1900. The technique of its delivery was wholly traditional; it was another overture to Britain (and France), based on an assumed

[1] Cf. p. 194, Ch. V, above.
[2] "Conditions in Manchuria," 53-54; Stimson, 96-97. Italics inserted.

identity of interest, to join the United States in attempting to restrain Japanese expansion in Manchuria. The foregoing chapters of this book record the many occasions on which these tactics had been tried before, and with what success. Hay, Roosevelt, Knox and Wilson had all committed themselves to the same policy—on the same assumption—and all had been disappointed. So was Stimson. The European powers to which he appealed for co-operation acted true to form. France merely waited for, and followed, England's lead. The British response was one of studied casualness—a Foreign Office *communiqué* (January 9) which credited at face value Japan's frequently professed intention of maintaining the open door in Manchuria and deprecated the necessity of addressing "any formal note to the Japanese Government on the lines of the American Government's note." The *communiqué* was accompanied by an editorial in the London *Times* characterizing China's administrative integrity as an ideal rather than an existing fact and endorsing the Foreign Office's wisdom in refusing to associate itself with Stimson's action.[1]

The Chinese reply (January 12) to Stimson's note merely reiterated that country's protestations of innocence and accusations of Japan. Japan's (January 16) was an elegantly ironic rebuff reminiscent of Soviet Russia's to Stimson in 1929—and of Czarist Russia's to Hay in 1900.[2] Stimson afterwards criticized the British Government for letting him down on this occasion, holding it responsible for encouraging Japan to maintain a defiant attitude.[3] Despite her obligations as a member of the League, a framer of the Nine-Power Treaty and a signatory (with reservations) of the Kellogg Pact, Great Britain was no more willing to interfere with Japan in Manchuria, in 1932, than she had been on the eve

---

[1] Stimson, 101-103; Cooper, 236-237; Toynbee, *Survey*, 1932, 540 ff. Just as Hay had done in the case of the July 3 circular of 1900, Stimson distributed copies of his non-recognition note to all the signatories of the Nine-Power Treaty, an obvious invitation to them to take similar action. None did.

[2] For text of Chinese and Russian replies see "Conditions in Manchuria," 54-56.

[3] Stimson, 103-109.

of the Portsmouth Conference, or when Knox launched his neutralization scheme, or when Wilson vainly sought to undo the evil wrought by the secret treaties of 1917. The Anglo-Japanese Alliance had been dissolved at Washington, but Manchuria remained, in the estimation of London, a zone of absorption for Japanese energies that might otherwise be spent in the Yangtse Valley, Australasia or the vast, delicate outworks of the Indian frontier. It was not until he had challenged this deep-seated British conviction that Stimson discovered its strength.

For the next two months the United States remained alone and unsupported in its commitment to the non-recognition doctrine, despite Stimson's constant pressure on London and Geneva to concur in it. Fighting broke out in Shanghai soon after the middle of January and the war spilled over from Manchuria into China proper. China had retaliated for the invasion of Manchuria with the most effective anti-Japanese boycott in history. To smash this economic resistance, and, quite possibly, to share the limelight hitherto monopolized by the army, the Japanese navy followed up a series of incidents and demands with an offensive against the Chinese sections of the city that opened January 28. The Japanese were held at bay by the Chinese Nineteenth Route Army until Japanese army reinforcements were landed and an encircling movement forced the Chinese to retire (March 2).[1]

With the extension of hostilities to Shanghai Stimson redoubled his efforts to secure British co-operation and to assist the League to bring judgment against Japan. On January 24 he and Hoover decided that the safety of American nationals and property in the vicinity required the presence of naval vessels at Shanghai. Stimson promptly called in the British Ambassador proposing a joint warning to Japan against using the International Settlement as a base of operations, and asking him "if we should send such vessels, would the British do likewise."[2] Stimson was thinking of

[1] *Lytton Report*, Ch. V.
[2] Stimson, 135-137.

more than the mere protection of American citizens and their possessions. "We knew that China was feeling deserted and helpless," he wrote.

"Many of her statesmen already were insisting that in relying upon the League Covenant and the other peace treaties, she had depended upon a broken reed and been deserted by the powers upon whose influence she had counted. We felt that in such a crisis it was more important than ever before to maintain the sanctity of those treaties and to make it clear to China that her interests under them were not entirely forgotten." [1]

Accordingly, in soliciting Great Britain's participation in a joint movement of naval vessels to Shanghai, Stimson pointed out to the British Ambassador "that not only would it tend to tranquilize the fears of foreigners, *but it would convince China that we were not oblivious to our responsibilities in the situation*." [2] He acknowledged, in other words, a political as well as a purely legal motive for the proposed move.

This motive seems evident in another decision made by Hoover and Stimson at about the same time. By what Stimson described as "a fortuitous concurrence of events," the winter of 1932 found the entire American fleet maneuvering in the Pacific between California and the Hawaiian Islands. The maneuvers had been scheduled the preceding summer, before Japan had launched her attack on Manchuria, though it seems unlikely that the persons responsible for planning them could have been totally oblivious to the possibility of trouble in that quarter of the world. At all events Hoover and Stimson had considered revising the plans when hostilities commenced in Manchuria, "but decided that, in view of the fact that it was so well known that they had not originated as a threat to Japan" they "should be allowed to continue.

[1] *Ibid.*, 135.
[2] *Ibid.*, 137. Italics inserted.

Thereafter, just when the Japanese were making their attack on Shanghai, the American fleet in the course of these maneuvers came to Hawaii on February 13th. After further careful consideration it was allowed to remain in that neighborhood and was not dispersed or sent back to the Atlantic on the conclusion of the maneuvers." [1]

The reason for this decision, according to Stimson, was the fear that Japan might be "inflamed to a state of fanatical excitement" and launch a sudden attack on "the possessions of European and American governments in the neighborhood.

In such a situation the presence of the entire American fleet assembled at a port which placed it on the flank of any such outbreak southward towards Hongkong, French Indo-China or the Philippines, undoubtedly exercised a steadying effect. It was a potent reminder of the ultimate military strength of peaceful America which could not be overlooked by anyone, however excited he might be." [2]

The security of the Philippines undoubtedly gave the President and his Secretary of State cause for concern, though not enough, apparently, to deter them from pursuing a policy highly aggravating to the one power best able and most likely to attack the islands. Their decision to keep the American fleet at Pearl Harbor suggests that Stimson had persuaded Hoover that the cause of world peace, as he was attempting to serve it, would benefit by a martial gesture on the part of "peaceful America." [3]

When he approached the British Ambassador with suggestions of joint action at Shanghai, Stimson calculated that the Japanese threat to Great Britain's interests in the Yangtse Valley "would probably at last startle the merchants of Great Britain into a realization of what Japanese aggression towards China ultimately

[1] Stimson, 138.

[2] *Ibid.*, 138.

[3] On January 31, Stimson and Hoover ordered the Thirty-first Infantry and the last remaining destroyers from Manila to Shanghai, concentrating in the latter port the entire American Asiatic Squadron ordinarily based at Manila. Cf. Stimson, 140.

meant to them and that we should find British co-operation with us more ready and willing now than we had found it on January 7th."[1] To a certain extent his expectation was fulfilled. On January 29 he received a reply "favorable in its tenor" to the questions he had asked the ambassador.[2] The same day the British sharply protested to Japan against the bombing of Chapei (the native quarter of Shanghai) and requested Stimson to do likewise. This he did, "in order to confirm the spirit of full co-operation."[3] On the thirty-first he learned from the American embassy in London that the British were sending two cruisers and reinforcements of marines to Shanghai; whereupon the United States Thirty-first Infantry was ordered from Manila to Shanghai and the entire American Asiatic squadron was concentrated in Shanghai harbor.[4]

At Geneva American and British diplomacy were more closely co-ordinated. China invoked Articles X and XV (January 29) obliging the League to turn from conciliation to the adjudication of responsibility and possibly the application of sanctions.[5] Sir Eric Drummond forthwith appointed a committee, consisting of the local diplomatic and consular representatives of League states, to report directly to the Council on conditions in Shanghai. At Drummond's invitation, Stimson instructed American Consul-General Edwin S. Cunningham to co-operate with the committee.[6] He likewise instructed Hugh Wilson, United States Minister to Switzerland, "to keep constantly in touch with the handling of the Shanghai situation by the League and to constitute himself a

[1] Stimson, 134.
[2] *Ibid.*, 139.
[3] *Ibid.*, 140.
[4] *Ibid.*, 140.
[5] Cooper, 241 ff.; Willoughby, 217 ff.
[6] "The subsequent reports of this committee upon the rapid sequence of events in Shanghai have become the chief source of the recorded history of those events. Mr. Cunningham assisted in their labors and concurred in general with their report." Stimson, 141.

liaison officer for the interchange of information between them and us." [1] As the Japanese offensive developed at Shanghai, the United States, through its diplomatic, consular and naval representatives, and in intimate co-operation with Great Britain, helped to guard the International Settlement, vigorously protesting the landing of Japanese troops in it. [2] The American Asiatic Squadron rode at anchor in ominous proximity to the ships of the invaders. The wires from Washington to Tokyo were hot with expostulation.

A Japanese request for the good offices of the neutral powers in making peace at Shanghai (January 31) inspired Stimson to exercise the initiative still more vigorously. He and Hoover quickly drew up peace terms, telephoned Prime Minister MacDonald and Foreign Minister Sir John Simon for their approval, and with the concurrence of France and Italy presented them to the belligerents (February 2). The terms called for an immediate armistice, "no further mobilization or preparation whatever for further hostilities between the two nations," mutual troop withdrawals, the establishment of neutral zones policed by neutrals and "negotiations to settle all outstanding controversies between the two nations in the spirit of the Pact of Paris and the resolution of the League of Nations of December 10, without prior demand or reservation and with the aid of neutral observers or participants." [3] Stimson thus tried to do what neither Wilson nor Hughes had been able to accomplish: to induce Japan to abandon the principle —that she had been so resolutely defending since 1915—of settling her issues with China independently, without outside intervention. China, not surprisingly, readily accepted Stimson's terms. But Japan would not agree to suspend her war preparations until her immediate demands on China were met, or to make a comprehensive settlement of all outstanding controversies "with the aid of neutral observers or participants." [4]

---

[1] *Ibid.*, 141.
[2] *Ibid.*, 141-146.
[3] *Ibid.*, 148.
[4] *Ibid.*, 149 ff.; Cooper, 243; Willoughby, 320-323.

In the face of this latest Japanese rebuff, Stimson proposed another Anglo-American *démarche* supplementary to the proceedings of the League. He wished to encourage the League to impose sanctions on Japan and hoped that Congress might be persuaded to do so. He felt that an embargo of Japanese goods "would have more chance of being adopted by Congress if it were recommended following the invocation of the Nine Power Treaty than if it had been recommended solely by the League of Nations." [1] He therefore invited England (February 9) to join the United States in a formal invocation of the Nine-Power Treaty "in order to clarify the thought and focus the moral support of the world upon the situation which had taken place in Shanghai." [2] Stimson repeatedly called Sir John Simon on the transatlantic telephone during the next few days, pressing the invitation on him as urgently as he could.[3] But to no avail. Simon would not step out from behind the constitutional shield that English membership in the League afforded him. He would not join the Secretary of State in the maneuver, especially conspicuous for the representative of a state that was not a member of the League, to prepare the way for the imposition of sanctions before these had been recommended or even considered at Geneva.[4]

Again Stimson was thrown upon his own resources and again he acted more boldly than Great Britain or the League. As if to confound the adjudication of responsibility or any possible disci-

[1] Stimson, 161.
[2] *Ibid.*, 162.
[3] *Ibid.*, 162-164.
[4] "The British Government are in a very special degree charged with the protection and defense of British interests," Sir John Simon told the House of Commons (February 22), "and there is no part of the world in which it can be said with more complete truth than in the Far East that British interests are summed up in the words 'Peace and Trade.' We do not seek to secure trade through the boycott of other people . . . it would be quite improper for anyone to attempt to pronounce a partial or interim judgment in a matter where everything depends on the report which will have to be made by the League of Nations." Parliamentary Debates, House of Commons, 5th Series, Vol. 262, 182.

plinary action by the League, Japan on February 18 raised the effigy of Manchurian independence. While Japanese bombers continued to rain destruction on Shanghai the sovereign state of Manchukuo was proclaimed.[1] For a moment Stimson felt "doomed to inaction, while a great tragedy was following its predestined course." But only for a moment. On February 21 a "solution" occurred to him by which he "might state our views on the Nine Power Treaty without having them nullified by an expression of the doubts and fears of others." [2]

The next evening, he and his advisers composed a long public letter to Senator Borah, Chairman of the Senate Foreign Relations Committee. Summarizing the Far Eastern policy of the United States since the promulgation of the open door notes, and reminding the powers, especially Japan and Great Britain, of what he considered to be their obligations under the Nine-Power Treaty and the Kellogg Pact, Stimson held that it was "clear beyond peradventure that a situation has developed which cannot, under any circumstances, be reconciled with the obligations of the covenants of these two treaties, and that if the treaties had been faithfully observed such a situation could not have arisen."

He accompanied this charge with a veiled threat and a challenge. He contended that the Nine-Power Treaty was but one of several "interrelated and interdependent" treaties negotiated at the Washington Conference; that the "willingness of the American Government to surrender its then commanding lead in battleship construction and to leave its positions at Guam and in the Philippines without further fortifications, was predicated upon, among other things, the self-denying covenants contained in the Nine-Power Treaty"; and he strongly implied that a violation of that treaty might release the other powers from observing the limitations of the Four-Power Pact and the Naval Treaty and nonfortification agreement. He concluded with a challenge to the rest

[1] *Lytton Report*, Ch. VI.
[2] Stimson, 165.

of the world to unite with him in applying the non-recognition principle to "any situation, treaty or agreement entered into" by Japan and China "in violation of the covenants of these treaties, which affected the rights of our Government or its citizens in China." Universal acceptance of this challenge would, he believed, place a *caveat* on such action which would "effectively bar the legality hereafter of any title or right sought to be obtained by pressure or treaty violation." [1]

Stimson declared that his famous communication to Borah

was intended as a message of encouragement to China; as an explanation of policy to the public of the United States; as a suggestion of future possible action to the nations who were to be assembled at the coming meeting of the Assembly of the League of Nations; as a gentle reminder to the Conservative party, which was now in control of the British government, that they, through Lords Salisbury and Balfour, were joint authors with us of the Open Door policy and the Nine Power Treaty, and finally, as a reminder to Japan, that if she chose to break down one of the group of treaties arrived at at the Washington Conference, other nations might feel themselves released from some of those treaties which were as important to her as the Nine Power Treaty was to us. [2]

The letter to Borah, extending the non-recognition doctrine to cover violations of the Nine-Power Treaty as well as of the Kellogg Pact, was Stimson's last notable contribution to the quest for collective security in which he had been a leader. Practically speaking, he had committed the United States not to recognize Manchukuo. To make sure of universal concurrence in this policy he did his utmost to expedite the adoption of a non-recognition resolution by the League. He put mild pressure on London, whose intentions regarding the resolution he mistrusted, by withdrawing Consul General Cunningham from the peace conferences

[1] Stimson to Borah, February 23, 1932. Stimson, 166-175. The letter was made public February 24.
[2] Stimson, 175.

then taking place at Shanghai under the aegis of the neutral powers and at the urgent desire of Great Britain. He then pointedly informed the British why he had done so.[1] Whether or not this decided them, they hastily reassurred Stimson and themselves, proposed the resolution, which was unanimously adopted by the Assembly March 12, 1932. The United States at last had company in the position of solitary opposition to Japan in which Stimson's note of January 7 had placed it. The Secretary of State applauded the resolution and the American Consul General in Shanghai resumed his place at the peace conferences.[2]

The local representatives of the neutral powers at Shanghai, working in conjunction with a League Committee at Geneva, at length drew up peace terms that were signed by Japan and China on May 5. The last of the invading Japanese troops departed May 31.[3] Japan called off her forces largely because the determined resistance of the Chinese Nineteenth Route Army had involved her in a conflict of unexpected proportions; because of the increasing pressure exerted by the neutral powers through old-fashioned channels of diplomacy; and in the last analysis, because she had bitten off in "Manchukuo" all that she could chew for the present. To the end, she was unmoved by the hesitant censures of the League, obdurate in her defiance of the Nine-Power Treaty and the Kellogg Pact. Traveling to Geneva in April, to represent the United States at the Disarmament Conference of that year,

[1] Stimson, 177-178.

[2] *Ibid.*, 179; Cooper, 252. More cautious than Stimson's note, the League's non-recognition resolution merely proclaimed "that it is incumbent upon the members of the League of Nations not to recognize any situation, treaty or agreement which may be brought about by means contrary to the Covenant of the League of Nations or to the Pact of Paris." Willoughby, 299-301.

[3] The United States, in the person of Consul General Cunningham, played an important role in supervising the fulfillment of the peace terms of May 5. A neutral commission was established for this purpose by the peace treaty, of which commission Cunningham served as Chairman. For final negotiations and terms of peace see Willoughby, Ch. XIV, esp. 352-359; Cooper, 251 ff.; Stimson, 182-183; Toynbee, *Survey*, 1932, 502-515.

Stimson found the air poisoned by the mutual mistrust of Europe and America engendered by the war debt problem and symptomatic of the great depression in which the western nations floundered.[1] He hoped against hope that the League, now sitting in judgment of Japan, would yet be able to call that nation to task. But in vain. Japan formally recognized Manchukuo in a treaty signed September 15. On October 2 the report of the Lytton Commission was published, finding many historical and not unreasonable causes for Japan's action in Manchuria, but condemning the action itself on every count and calling for the restoration of Manchuria to Chinese sovereignty.[2]

Late in November the League met to consider ways of carrying out this injunction. After a long and dramatic debate it adopted the Lytton Report (February 24, 1933); the Japanese delegation walked out of the Assembly, and Japan forthwith resigned from the League. Manchuria had gone the way of Korea. The combined efforts of Washington, London and Geneva to restrain Japan, to arrest a process of Far Eastern imperialism of which Great Britain and France were two of the principal originators, and in which they were still silent partners, had proved a total failure. The germs of a local conflict had been spread by the "most potent sanction" of public opinion into an incipient world-wide epidemic. The last ties of diplomacy that bound Japan to a world of thought yet strange to her were severed.

Stimson nevertheless held resolutely to his conviction that the world must choose between collective security and self-destruction,

[1] Stimson, 202.

[2] Major General Frank R. McCoy of the United States Army served on the Lytton Commission, with Stimson's approval, though as the official representative of the League, and not of the United States. Cf. Stimson, 81, 190 n., 207; Cooper, 232-233, 258. A "large measure of autonomy designed to meet the local conditions and special characteristics" of Manchuria was recommended, as well as a comprehensive Sino-Japanese settlement recognizing both Chinese sovereignty and Japanese rights in the contested areas, to be negotiated under the auspices and according to the principles of the League. *Lytton Report*, 126-139.

and that therefore he must not abandon his labors in the interests of the former.[1] While Japan extended her conquest into Mongolia, with the invasion of Jehol early in January, 1933, the Secretary of State did everything in his power to keep the League "steeled up to the ultimate momentous step of a formal judgment in respect to Japan."[2] On January 9 he held an all-day conference on foreign policy with President-elect Roosevelt, as a result of which the League was assured "through various unofficial channels" that "a change in American policy towards the Far Eastern controversy on the part of the new administration need not be apprehended."[3] The day after the League's adoption of the Lytton Report, and the melodramatic exit of the Japanese delegation from the Assembly, Stimson declared to the press:

In their affirmations, respectively of the principle of non-recognition and their attitude in regard thereto, the League and the United States are on common ground. The League has recommended principles of settlement. In so far as appropriate under the treaties to which it is a party, the American Government expresses its general endorsement of the principles thus recommended.[4]

On March 4 Secretary Stimson left office, and on March 27 Japan gave due notice of her decision to resign from the League.

Woodrow Wilson would have sensed the irony of a situation in

[1] Of the advantages he thought were held by members of the League as compared with those of the United States he wrote: "In short, they lived in a world purporting to be governed by law and its methods. We still lived in what was little better than a world of anarchy, governed by force or the threat of force." Stimson, 189.

[2] Stimson, 220.

[3] According to Stimson, he "quite unexpectedly" received an invitation from Roosevelt, in the latter part of December, 1932, "to visit him for a discussion of foreign policy." Stimson, 226. A few days after the conference, which was held at Roosevelt's home at Hyde Park, New York, the latter made a statement to the press in which he declared himself "wholly willing to make it clear that American foreign policies must uphold the sanctity of international treaties. That is the cornerstone on which all relations between nations must rest." Cooper, 264

[4] Stimson, 229-230.

which the Secretary of State of the party that had ground Wilson's foreign policy under foot in 1920 appeared, as champion of that policy, to pledge the President-elect of Wilson's own party to uphold and perpetuate it. The Roosevelt-Stimson conference of January 9, 1933, was a symbol of the inconsistency that is the norm of party politics. It was at the same time a manifestation of the power of tradition and precedent—periodically invigorated by such doctrinal influences as the imperialism of Theodore Roosevelt's generation, the dollar diplomacy of Knox and Taft and the collective security of Wilson and Stimson—to bind all administrations to the principle of the territorial integrity of China.

Had Stimson made use of the machinery of collective security in order to further these old American interests? Or had he subordinated the interests to the machinery? In one sense he had conducted the first of the two great international experiments (of which the second was the effort to restrain Italy from invading Ethiopia in 1935) that submitted collective security to the pragmatic test and found it wanting. He himself regretted "the misfortune it had been for the world that this first great test of the strength of the collective structure, in which the war-torn Caucasian nations were so terrifically interested, should have come to a head in an issue between other races on the opposite side of the world." [1] Unquestionably his labors, like Wilson's, reflected the ideals and the hopes of many, who, had they been realized, would have become his disciples instead of his critics.[2]

On the other hand, he had based his efforts on premises many of which were unfounded in fact or history. He had tried to achieve an old objective by certain new methods, and he had failed. He had tried, as his several predecessors had tried before him, to preserve the territorial integrity of China. To that end he had ventured as deeply into world politics as Theodore Roosevelt.

---

[1] Stimson, 201.

[2] For a convenient summary of contemporary public opinion, cf. Tupper and McReynolds, op. cit., Ch. IX.

He had all but involved himself in the domestic affairs of Japan. He had revived the non-recognition doctrine and pledged his successor to maintain it. He had employed the American Asiatic Squadron, the entire American fleet, and the press of the United States to put every possible weight into his diplomacy save the overt threat of force. His undisputed, though often unsupported, leadership of this collective effort to curb Japanese expansion left the United States to bear the brunt of a Japanese antagonism that Stimson's discreet European collaborators were altogether happy to avoid. So ended the long cycle of American attempts to prevent Japan from expanding on the continent of Asia launched by Wilson and Lansing in 1917.

# XI. The "24-Hour" Policy: Conclusion

THE continuity of principle that since 1898 had been an out-standing characteristic of the Far Eastern policy of the United States was not broken by the Democratic successors of Hoover and Stimson. President Franklin D. Roosevelt and Secretary of State Cordell Hull had no sooner taken office than they confirmed the assurances exchanged by Stimson and Roosevelt the previous January. On the same day that it adopted the Lytton Report, the League had created an Advisory Committee to follow the situation in the Far East, "to assist the Assembly in performing its duties . . . and . . . to aid the members of the League in concerting their action and their attitude among themselves and with the non-Member States." The United States was invited to co-operate in the work of this committee.[1] Secretary Hull accepted the invitation (March 13) stating that the United States was "prepared to co-operate with the Advisory Committee in such manner as may be found appropriate and feasible" and instructing Hugh Wilson, the American Minister to Switzerland, to participate in its delib-erations but without the right to vote.[2] Wilson assisted the Com-mittee in drawing up recommendations for general application of the non-recognition policy toward Manchukuo, which, when com-pleted, were approved by Washington.[3]

Besides upholding the non-recognition doctrine, the Roosevelt Administration continued to adhere to the Stimson-Hoover policy of active collaboration with the League. On May 20, 1933, the

[1] Drummond to Secretary of State, February 25, 1933, with enclosure. Depart-ment of State, *Press Releases*, March 18, 1933, 177-178.

[2] *Ibid.*, 176-177.

[3] The American approval covered all of the committee's recommendations ex-cept a few particulars. Cf. Cooper, 272-278; Willoughby, 500 ff., 520-533.

Chairman of the American delegation to the Geneva Disarmament Conference, Norman H. Davis, declared that the United States was ready not only to do its part "toward the substantive reduction of armaments but, if this is effected by general international agreement, we are also prepared to contribute in other ways to the organization of peace."

"In particular," he elaborated, "we are willing to consult the other states in case of a threat to peace, with a view to averting conflict. Further than that, in the event that the states, in conference, determine that a state has been guilty of a breach of the peace in violation of its international obligations and take measures against the violator, then, if we concur in the judgment rendered as to the responsible and guilty party, we will refrain from any action tending to defeat such collective effort which these states may thus make to restore peace." [1]

This conditional promise of American co-operation in the imposition of sanctions on aggressor states was tonic for the League after its failure in the Far East. It was fulfilled, moreover, when Italy invaded Ethiopia in 1935. Then, in a situation to which Congress reacted by passing laws calculated to reinforce the neutrality of the United States in time of foreign war, Roosevelt and Hull did everything they could, under the circumstances, to abet the process of collective security and facilitate League action against Italy.[2]

In the Far East, however, they pursued different tactics from those of their predecessors. They surrendered no principles, yet they strove to ease the severe tension that Stimson had left be-

[1] Department of State, *Press Releases*, May 27, 1933, 390.

[2] Before the outbreak of hostilities they reminded England and France as well as both disputants of their obligations to abide by the Kellogg Pact which they asserted was "no less binding now than when it was entered into by the 63 nations that are parties to it." When hostilities developed they embargoed exports of munitions to the belligerents and discouraged exportation of other war materials (oil, copper, trucks, tractors, scrap iron and scrap steel) not covered by the neutrality laws and in all of which the United States traded with Italy in considerable volume and not at all, or scarcely at all, with Ethiopia. This official instigation of an embargo of commodities over and above those specifically

tween the United States and Japan. There was a prompt abatement of contentious note writing to Tokyo. While Japan consolidated her Manchurian conquest, added Jehol to it, invaded China proper and forced on the latter (in the Tangku Truce, May 31, 1933) a demilitarized zone south of the Great Wall, Secretary Hull made no public protest other than that implicit in his endorsement of the non-recognition policy. On November 16, 1933, the United States resumed diplomatic relations with Russia after a lapse of sixteen years. The effect, if not the design, of this move was to redress appreciably the balance of power in Eastern Asia. It was in turn balanced by the withdrawal of the American fleet from the Pacific, a gesture of friendship toward Japan.[1]

The change of tactics brought an improvement in American relations with Japan. On February 21, 1934, the Japanese Foreign Minister, Koki Hirota, sent an "informal and personal message" to Secretary Hull emphasizing his country's desire for peaceful diplomatic and expanded commercial relations with the United States. Hull's response (March 3) was cordial:

You express the opinion that viewed in the light of the broad aspects of the situation and studied from all possible angles no question exists between our two countries that is fundamentally incapable of amicable solution. I fully concur with you in that opinion. Further I believe that there are in fact no questions between our two countries which if they be viewed in proper perspective in both countries can with any warrant be regarded as not readily susceptible to adjustment by pacific processes. It is the fixed intention of the American Government to rely, in prose-

designated by the neutrality laws therefore amounted to economic pressure on Italy and encouragement to the League to impose sanctions on the latter. Especially was this true of Hull's efforts to dissuade American firms from selling oil to Italy in advance of, and in spite of, the League's refusal to include this commodity in the sanctions it eventually did impose. Cf. Department of State, *Press Releases*, esp. September, October and November, 1935; Shepardson and Scroggs, *The United States in World Affairs*, 1934-1935, 243-249; 1936, Ch. II.

[1] Cf. Scroggs and Merz, *The United States in World Affairs*, 1933, Ch. XIV, and 288-296, printing text of notes exchanged between the United States and Russia and of the Tangku Truce.

cution of its national policies, upon such processes. If unhappily there should arise in the future any controversy between our two countries, the American Government will be prepared, as I believe it always has been in the past, to examine the position of Japan in a spirit of amity and of desire for peaceful and just settlement, with the confident expectation that the Japanese Government will be prepared to examine the position of the United States in the same spirit.[1]

Hull concluded with some allusions to Japan's intentions toward nations other than the United States and to "the Family of Nations," but he omitted reference to the sore point of China's territorial integrity. The Hirota-Hull notes might have formed the basis of a comprehensive liquidation of issues between the United States and Japan. But for that the time was not yet ripe.

Hirota's overture proved to be the prelude to the establishment of a Japanese oil monopoly in Manchukuo which belied Japan's professed intention of maintaining the open door in that puppet country. American, British and Dutch oil companies were frozen out of the Manchurian market, notwithstanding the protests of their respective governments to Japan. The latter at first referred the protesting powers directly to Manchukuo, then, as the monopoly tightened (April, 1935) contended that by refusing to recognize Manchukuo they had forfeited their claim to open door treatment there.[2] The United States was not satisfied with this argument. However it might revise its tactical considerations of Chinese territorial integrity, it showed no sign of abandoning its century-old objective, originally the chief end of its Far Eastern policy, of seeking for its citizens equal commercial opportunity in that quarter of the world.

It was not yet certain what position Roosevelt would take should Japan again trespass against the integrity of China on as large a

[1] Exchange of notes between the Secretary of State and the Japanese Minister for Foreign Affairs. Department of State, *Press Releases*, March 24, 1934, 160-162.

[2] Shepardson and Scroggs, *The United States in World Affairs*, 1934-1935, 151-158.

scale as she had in 1931 and 1932. When in April, 1934, a "spokesman" for the Japanese Foreign Office (Mr. Eiji Amau) proclaimed his country the political guardian and economic entrepreneur of China, and warned the powers against financial, political or commercial undertakings prejudicial to Japanese interests in China, an opportunity was presented to Hull to declare himself on that controversial subject. But although the Amau statements inspired numerous legalistic and scholarly refutations of Japan's right to any such "Asiatic Monroe Doctrine," [1] and although Great Britain took prompt and rather categorical exception to it, Hull contented himself with a statement the substance of which was considerably milder than the British. This was tendered by the American Ambassador to Japan, Mr. Joseph C. Grew, to the Japanese Foreign Minister April 29, 1934, a full week after the British and to the accompaniment of birthday felicitations from President Roosevelt to Emperor Hirohito.

The tone of the State Department's published version of the note was as significant as its content:

Recent indications of attitude on the part of the Japanese Government with regard to the rights and interests of Japan and other countries in China and in connection with China have come from sources so authoritative as to preclude their being ignored and make it necessary that the American Government, adhering to the tradition of frankness that has prevailed in relations between it and the Government of Japan, reaffirm the position of the United States with regard to questions of rights and interests involved.

The relations of the United States with China are governed, as are our relations with Japan and our relations with other countries, by the generally accepted principles of international law and the provisions of treaties to which the United States is a party. The United States has with regard to China certain rights and certain obligations. In addition, it is associated with China or with Japan or with both, together with

[1] Cf. Willoughby, *The Sino-Japanese Controversy and the League of Nations,* Ch. XXVIII.

certain other countries, in multilateral treaties relating to rights and obligations in the Far East, and in one great multilateral treaty to which practically all the countries of the world are parties.

Treaties can lawfully be modified or terminated only by processes prescribed or recognized or agreed upon by the parties to them.

In the international associations and relationships of the United States, the American Government seeks to be duly considerate of the rights, the obligations, and the legitimate interests of other countries, and it expects on the part of other governments due consideration of the rights, the obligations, and the legitimate interests of the United States. In the opinion of the American people and the American Government, no nation can, without the assent of the other nations concerned, rightfully endeavor to make conclusive its will in situations where there are involved the rights, the obligations, and the legitimate interests of other sovereign states.

The American Government has dedicated the United States to the policy of the good neighbor, and to the practical application of that policy it will continue, on its own part and in association with other governments, to devote its best efforts.[1]

The calm tenor of the note, and the fact that it was presented after the British had registered their protest, indicated that the Roosevelt Administration was taking pains to avoid the initiative (that Stimson had sought) in opposing Japanese expansion. Yet for all its deferential phrases, it reaffirmed American allegiance to the same principles and treaty rights that Stimson had tried to defend, and it refused to recognize Japan's superior right to disregard them.

During the next two years Japan continued to strengthen her grasp on Manchukuo and to push forward by smuggling and intrigue her economic and political penetration of Inner Mongolia and the northern Chinese provinces. Had the League succeeded in checking Italy in 1935 it is not improbable that Washington and Geneva might have made another concerted attempt

[1] Department of State, *Press Releases*, May 5, 1934, 244-245. Cf. Shepardson and Scroggs, *The United States in World Affairs*, 1934-1935, 164-170.

to check Japan. But it did not succeed, chiefly because, as in the case of the conquest of Manchuria, the great European powers on whom it depended for motivation refused to sacrifice, or even to risk, particular national interests for the supposedly general, international interests of the world. At all events, the Far Eastern policy of the United States as it pertained to the preservation of China's territorial integrity rested on the Stimson non-recognition note of January 7, 1932, and the Hull statement of April 29, 1934. An attempt by Japan, late in 1935, to convert the five northern provinces of Hopeh, Chahar, Suiyuan, Shansi and Shantung into an autonomous area caused no change in this attitude. Hull took public notice of Japan's activities in a statement very similar in character to that of the previous year.[1]

If Roosevelt showed less of an inclination to break lances for China than had Stimson, in another important respect he took an unyielding stand against Japan. This was in the matter of naval ratios. As she marched forward on her continental expansion, Japan had been conducting a determined campaign for naval parity with Great Britain and the United States. Her adherence to the London Naval Treaty had brought political defeat and assassination to the statesman who had counseled it. Subsequently the achievement of recognized naval equality with the two great Western sea powers became, in Japan, a national shibboleth to rank with the recognition of racial equality. On December 29, 1934, Japan gave the required advance notice of her intention to terminate her adherence to the Washington Naval Treaty after

[1] In a statement to the press (December 6, 1935) he declared that the United States was "closely observing" developments in north China, that, "The views of the American Government with regard to such matters, not alone in relation to China but in relation to the whole world, are well known" and that, according to these views it was "most important in this period of world-wide political unrest and economic instability that governments and peoples keep faith in principles and pledges." The United States had "abiding faith in the fundamental principles of its traditional policy." It respected the treaties to which it was a party and bespoke the same respect of other countries. Department of State, *Press Releases*, December 7, 1935, 487-488.

December 31, 1936, thus causing it to expire on the same date as the London Treaty of 1930.

She severed her last remaining connections with the naval limitation agreements of the Western sea powers by refusing to ratify the London Treaty as proposed for renewal by its signatories in conference at the British capital in the winter of 1935-1936. Preliminary conversations held during 1934 by British, American and Japanese diplomats and naval experts had failed to dissuade Japan from insistence on parity. Finding the British and American delegates at London deaf to all arguments in favor of parity, the Japanese delegates bolted the conference (January 15, 1936). The United States, Great Britain and France proceeded to conclude a three-power agreement (March 25, 1936) continuing among themselves qualitative limitations but no quantitative ratios. Through an exchange of notes, however, the United States and Great Britain agreed to maintain the principle of equality in the size of their respective fleets as well as in the size and type of their vessels.[1]

Japan's denunciation of the Washington and London Treaties precipitated a situation in the Pacific comparable to that which her flouting of the Nine-Power Treaty had precipitated in China. By January 1, 1937, she was technically free to attain parity with Great Britain and the United States. Her naval budgets promptly swelled to record-breaking proportions. But her path to this objective was effectively blocked by the vast programs of naval expansion forthwith inaugurated by her two economically more powerful rivals. Beginning in 1934 President Roosevelt secured

[1] The treaty of 1936 also provided for an exchange of information among the three signatories with regard to construction plans at least four months in advance of the actual commencement of construction. Japan refused to adhere even to these qualitative limitations, the treaty containing which was ratified by the United States Senate May 18, 1936. For text see Department of State, *Press Releases*, March 28, 1936, 264-278, and May 16, 1936, 486-489. Cf. also Shepardson and Scroggs, *The United States in World Affairs*, 1934-1935, Ch. X; 1936, Ch. III.

Congressional appropriations and allocations of public works and other emergency funds to build the American navy up to the existing treaty limits behind which preceding administrations had allowed it to lag. When the last hopes of persuading Japan to re-enter the naval pacts faded, Roosevelt accelerated his construction schedules with the greatest peace-time naval appropriations (for 1936-1937 and 1937-1938) in American history. Harassed by affairs in Europe as well as in Asia, Great Britain had already committed herself to unprecedented naval expenditures, the purpose of which included rapid completion of the modernized naval base at Singapore. France made proportionate increases, and, like England, looked to the defense of her Far Eastern possessions.

Thus in the complex strategy of naval construction Japan was confronted by the greater resources of her two principal competitors and by their common determination to maintain *de facto* the ratios established at Washington. Although Roosevelt's program did not contemplate the maintenance of exact parity with Great Britain, it was based on the principle of parity, and it provided for a substantially greater margin of superiority over Japan, especially in capital ships, than in the past.[1] Furthermore, the London

[1] According to figures submitted at the hearings of the House of Representative Committee on Naval Affairs, 75th Congress, 3rd Session, January 31, 1938, completion of the Roosevelt program would affect the American-British-Japanese ratios in the total number of vessels of the various classes as follows:

|  | United States | British Empire | Japan |
|---|---|---|---|
| Capital ships | 21 | 25 | 14 |
| Aircraft carriers | 6 | 11 | 10 |
| Heavy cruisers | 18 | 15 | 12 |
| Light cruisers | 23 | 69 | 31 |
| Destroyers | 260 | 227 | 155 |
| Submarines | 106 | 84 | 68 |

Cf. Shepardson and Scroggs, *The United States in World Affairs*, 1937, 270-271; also *Ibid.*, 82-87; 1936, 106 ff. For a most lucid exposition of the factors and prospects of American, British, French, Italian, German and Japanese naval strategy, see Talbot, Lieutenant-Commander Melvin F., "Navies and National Policy," *The Yale Review*, XXVII, Winter, 1938, 333-347.

agreement of 1936 supplemented by the Anglo-American understanding on parity, insured Britain, France and the United States
against competitive building among themselves, which, in turn,
lessened the pre-occupation of the United States with French and
British building plans and enabled it to concentrate more freely
on those of Japan.[1]

When Japan formally declined to adhere to the maximum gun
caliber of fourteen inches prescribed by the 1936 treaty, the three
parties to that treaty adopted an increased maximum of sixteen
inches (April 1, 1937).[2] The next year Japan would neither confirm nor deny rumors that she was planning capital ships of a
tonnage in excess of the maximum limit of 35,000 maintained by
the other powers. After a preliminary conference, the United
States, Great Britain and France made formal inquiries in Tokyo.
On February 5, 1938, Ambassador Grew presented the American
request for information, failure to divulge which by February 20,
it was stipulated, would be construed as confirmation of the
rumors.[3] Japan replied a week later, rejecting the request.[4] Whereupon the three powers exchanged notes (March 31, 1938) announcing their intention to keep pace with Japan and raise their
own capital ship tonnage limit.[5] This they did in an agreement
signed June 30, 1938, fixing the limit at 45,000 tons.[6] The United
States played an active part in bringing about these revisions,
focusing its attention as it did so on one nation: Japan. In much
the same manner as his cousin three decades earlier, Franklin D.
Roosevelt made expanding and strengthening the American navy

---

[1] The qualitative limitations of the London Treaty of 1936 were extended to
Russia and Germany through bilateral British treaties with each in July, 1937,
and to Italy through a provision of the Anglo-Italian Agreement of April 16,
1938. Germany had already agreed to limit her navy quantitatively to 35 per cent
of the total British tonnage in the Anglo-German Naval Treaty of 1935.

[2] Department of State, *Press Releases*, July 10, 1937, 25; *Ibid.*, February 5,
1938, 223-224.

[3] *Ibid.*, 223-226.

[4] *Ibid.*, February 12, 1938, 256-257.

[5] *Ibid.*, April 2, 1938, 437 ff.

[6] New York *Times*, July 1, 1938.

a counterpart of his withdrawal from political involvement in China.

There were several clues to this dual policy, so reminiscent of Theodore Roosevelt's admonition to speak softly and carry a big stick and of his latter-day faith in the frontier maxim, "Never draw unless you mean to shoot." There was, in the first place, the great domestic program of social and economic reform, long overdue in the United States, on the success of which Franklin Roosevelt had staked his political fortunes and the country as a whole had pinned its hopes. In theory, at least, this would be sufficient to deter him from any ventures into world politics not absolutely imperative for the national security. Although it did not constrain him from supporting the League during the invasion of Ethiopia, it may well have dampened his ardor for sending good money after bad in the Far East. Secondly, curtailment of political intervention in Eastern Asia was in keeping with the Good Neighbor policy dramatically emphasized by the President in his dealings with Central and South America. Still another clue was the steadily increasing body of public opinion calling for the reduction to a minimum of American involvement in foreign politics likely to eventuate in war. Manifestations of this opinion varied from the extreme isolationism inherent in the Senate's rejection (January 29, 1935) of American membership in the World Court to the revised conception of neutral rights embodied in the Neutrality Laws of 1935-1937, the product of nation-wide study of the factors that had involved the country in the World War.

Possibly the most compelling, and certainly the most immediate, reason of all for Franklin Roosevelt's Far Eastern policy was the security of American territorial possessions in the Far East—the selfsame factor that had determined Theodore Roosevelt's policy in 1905 and 1908. Once again, as it had done with such unfailing regularity in the past, the hypothetical key to commercial and political influence in China, the Philippine archipelago, underwent metaphorical transformation into an Achilles' heel. Only this time the process was complicated by a decision regarding the islands that was potentially as epochal as had been their annexation. In an act of Congress signed by the President March 24, and approved by the Filipino legislature May 1, 1934, the United States granted the Philippines their independence. This was to be achieved at the end of a ten-year probationary period during which the Philippine "commonwealth" would enjoy a wide measure of local autonomy under American supervision and protection. The commonwealth was duly inaugurated, with Manuel Quezon as president in 1936, making 1946 the year of complete independence.

The Far Eastern policy of the United States was as indirect a consideration in the liberation of the Philippines as it had been in their annexation. An independence movement, paralleled by one in the islands themselves, had been in progress almost from the moment they became an American possession. The Democratic Party, traditionally anti-imperialist, had been a consistent advocate of independence and, in the Jones Act of 1916, had gone so far as to promise it as soon as the Filipinos should establish a stable government. In 1929 an independence resolution had failed to pass the Senate by the narrow margin of five votes. No less than ten such bills were introduced in Congress during 1931 and 1932, one of which, the Hare-Hawes-Cutting Bill, was finally passed. Vetoed by Hoover (January 13, 1933) who considered the transition to self-government defined by it too abrupt, and international conditions in the Far East too chaotic, it was promptly repassed over his veto—only to be rejected by the Philippine legislature the following October.

The Filipinos wanted independence, but one of the most ambitious and resourceful of their politicians, Manuel Quezon, objected to certain provisions of the act, notably its tariff and immigration restrictions and its reservation for the future maintenance of American military and naval bases in the islands, and martialed his forces to defeat it. He then hurried to Washington in the hope of winning more favorable terms from the Roosevelt Administration. He was disappointed. The only concession made in the Tydings-Cutting Act, which was speeded through Congress with Roosevelt's approval and which Quezon was obliged to accept, was a waiver of the reservation concerning military bases and an undertaking to settle the matter of a naval base by negotiation with the Philippine Government. Otherwise it was identical to the Hare-Hawes-Cutting Act.[1]

The driving force behind all these independence bills was more economic than political, springing from the demands of American agriculture and labor rather than from calculations of foreign policy. Under the free trade conditions that had obtained between the two since 1913, the Philippines had built up a large volume of sugar, coconut oil and hemp cordage exports to the United States.[2] Sugar exports to the United States, a virtual monopoly, comprised over 60 per cent of the Philippines' total exports of all commodities, and 25 per cent of the total American sugar imports.[3] When the World War quadrupled the volume of these exports, domestic American producers of the commodities with which they competed organized to demand tariff protection against them. Sugar-cane and sugar-beet growers, dairy farmers and cottonseed oil manufacturers (for whose products coconut oil derivatives formed inexpensive substitutes) and cordage manufacturers began to agitate for Philippine independence in order that the proscribed

[1] Kirk, Grayson L., *Philippine Independence*, Chs. II-V, esp. 102-127; Scroggs and Lippmann, *The United States in World Affairs*, 1933, 25-29; 1934-1935, 142-144.

[2] The extent of Philippine dependence on the American market for their leading exports is revealed by the following figures, showing the percentage of total Philippine exports in the given commodity destined for the United States in 1932: sugar, 99.9 per cent; coconut oil, 95.8 per cent; tobacco and cigars, 50.6 per cent; copra, 59.5 per cent; desiccated coconut, 99.9 per cent; cordage, 62.3 per cent. Field, F. V., ed., *Economic Handbook of the Pacific Area*, 461.

[3] 72 per cent of the United States sugar imports came from Cuba. Figures are for 1931. *Ibid.*, 474.

commodities might be shut out by tariff walls. They were joined by American labor organizations, constitutionally opposed to imperialism and, especially on the Pacific Coast, anxious to stop the increasing influx of Filipino immigrants.[1]

It was these groups and their representatives in Congress, concerned with their own material interests at home rather than with the remote and, to them, nebulous objectives of American diplomacy in the Far East, who brought independence to the Philippines. Yet it was in the realm of foreign policy that their action would have the greatest national significance. Economically the Philippines were of far less importance to the United States and its citizens as a whole than they were politically. The 5.2 per cent of America's total annual imports of which they were the source had proved to be sufficiently competitive with domestic American products to rouse American agriculture against them. The 2.3 per cent of the United States' total exports and the 1.06 per cent of its total foreign investments absorbed by the Philippines were negligible compared to the expense of governing and protecting the islands.[2] The immediate, total destruction of these economic relationships might cause distress to the Filipinos (more particularly to the small Chinese, Japanese and American communities that exploited the native population and controlled most of the islands' wealth).[3] It might impede or complicate the economic readjustment that independence would necessitate. But it would cause scarcely a ripple in the American national economy; it would pass

[1] The immigration laws extended by the United States to the Philippines in 1902 (cf. Ch. IX, p. 337, above) applied to Chinese itinerants; they did not prevent native Filipinos from emigrating to the United States, which they had a perfect right to do. Before the war the annual average of Filipino immigration into the United States was 1,849. From 1920 to 1929 it was 4,610. Field, *Economic Handbook*, 38-40. For analysis of the various groups supporting the Philippine independence bills, see Kirk, esp. Ch. LV.

[2] Trade percentages are 1931-1935 averages, from Farley, Miriam S. "America's Stake in the Far East, I: Trade," *Far Eastern Survey*, Vol. 16, July 29, 1936, 168. Investment percentage is for 1930, from Field, *Economic Handbook*, 340.

[3] In 1934 not more than 30 per cent of the domestic trade of the islands was

unnoticed by the overwhelming majority of the American people.[1]

Politically, on the other hand, the Philippines had been undoubtedly the greatest single American diplomatic hostage to fortune in the Far East or anywhere else. As such they bore a vital relation to every single American citizen and to the entire national economy. President Roosevelt's willingness to waive the right to maintain military bases on the islands, his evasiveness with respect to a naval base, indeed his very approval of the Tydings-McDuffie Act were generally interpreted as a decision to fulfill the wish Theodore Roosevelt had expressed to Taft and Sternburg, and rid the United States of its costly hostage. It was both praised and condemned as a withdrawal from active participation in Far Eastern politics and as a renunciation of potential American economic predominance in China.

As had been true in the case of the non-fortification agreement of 1921, a great part of this criticism was wide of the mark. The function of the Philippines as the key to the markets of Asia had yet to be demonstrated. The decision not to seek economic predominance in China was taken not by Franklin D. Roosevelt and his advisers, but by generations of Americans whose lack of economic interest in that country had defied predictions for a century. It had been confirmed when the United States failed to convert Manila into another Hongkong, the type of base the authors of the large policy had envisioned, and reconfirmed in the non-

in the hands of the Filipinos themselves, the rest being controlled for the most part by Chinese, with whom Japanese were becoming increasingly active competitors. An American and foreign population amounting to only 1 per cent of the total native population paid four-fifths of the taxes collected by the government. Scarcely one-seventh of the total land area of the islands was under cultivation. Most of the export trade, industry, banking and shipping was foreign-owned and managed. Cf. Malcolm, George A., *The Commonwealth of the Philippines*, Chs. XV, XVI; Kirk, Ch. VI.

[1] The chances are that it would also pass unnoticed by large numbers of the Filipinos themselves whose extremely primitive standard of living was virtually untouched by foreign trade, commerce and investment.

fortification agreement of 1921. The Tydings-McDuffie Act was merely its latest, perhaps final, confirmation. Had the United States or any fair proportion of its citizens shared the convictions of Mahan, it would have been as difficult for a farmers' lobby to liberate the Philippines as it would have been for a similar English minority to dictate the evacuation of Singapore.

The conclusion that it presaged a withdrawal from Far Eastern politics was misleading because it took too much for granted. The islands were not yet free. They were to remain exactly as great an American hostage to fortune as they had ever been—conceivably greater—until 1946. During this period the increased measure of autonomy to be enjoyed by the Filipinos might easily produce foreign entanglements which the United States, as protector of the "commonwealth," would be obliged to liquidate. Nor was it certain that, even after 1946, the United States could resist the inevitable appeals to its humanitarian instincts that would be made if invasion threatened the islands. Possession of them made the United States almost as close a neighbor to Japan as it was to Cuba, rendering illusory the vast barrier of the Pacific. The Washington Treaties were shattered. Collective security had proved a myth. Under such circumstances as these it was not illogical to arrive at the formula of a policy in China not too offensive to Japan matched by a navy of sufficient strength to give pause to any attacker of the Philippines—to avoid actions that might provoke such an attack and to develop a fleet that might retaliate in other spheres in case it should be attempted.

The outbreak of July 7, 1937, of the undeclared war between China and Japan presented a serious challenge to Roosevelt's policy. Whatever his plans for the future, whatever the broad underlying trends and principles of his diplomacy, he was now confronted with an immediate crisis demanding immediate action. Japan had determined to press her campaign of conquest, begun in 1931, to a conclusion. The unexpectedly widespread and ferocious fighting that resulted soon took its toll of American lives and property in China. Protection of its citizens abroad was a primary obligation of the United States, just as it was of China and Japan. It was an obligation that every country in the world attempted to discharge, no matter what its form of government or how meager its resources. Yet there was imminent danger that the defense of American nationals, property and legal rights might lead to involvement in the political issues of the war and ultimately in the war itself.

This had happened in 1917. The issues were particularly liable to confusion in China. Among the more prominent factors that made them so were the long record of American attempts to help China resist Japanese penetration; the strongly pro-Chinese sentiments of the American people; the uncertain legal relationship between belligerent and neutral caused by the innovation of an undeclared war; the unusual basis of foreign legal and property rights in China; the presence of American legation guards and river gunboats directly in the path of hostilities. Any or all of these factors might create confusion in the mind of neutral, or belligerent, or both, as to where legal protection left off and political intervention began.

The situation was further complicated by the Neutrality Laws and by the precedent of co-operation with the League of Nations that Roosevelt and Hull had committed themselves to observe. These were manifestly antithetical in spirit. And each was paradoxical in itself. The Neutrality Laws, but recently extended by Congress (January 6, 1937) to apply to the Spanish Civil War, required a mandatory and impartial embargo of loans and munitions exports to belligerents, but left it to the President's discretion to find—or not to find—a state of war in existence. Thus he might invoke the laws or refuse to invoke them as he saw fit, a power which, in the changing configuration of world politics, might conceivably be used for unneutral purposes. On the other hand, collaboration with the League according to the precedent established by Stimson, sanctioned by Norman Davis and upheld by Hull and

Roosevelt *vis-à-vis* Italy in 1935 would be academic unless the League could be revived from its fainting condition.

Through this fog of uncertainties the President steered essentially the same course, during the first year of the war, that he had been steering before it began. He continued to endorse the various treaties Japan was trampling underfoot, but he declined to take the initiative in any collective effort to defend or enforce them. Since the principal League powers, in particular Great Britain, were even less disposed to assume this initiative than they had been in 1932, no such effort was made. The United States concentrated on the protection of its nationals, their property and legal rights, eschewed intervention in the political issues of the war, and proceeded with determination to build up its navy. Neutrality, preparedness and watchful waiting—familiar slogans in American history—were the keynotes of this policy which, as the President himself said of it, rested on a "24-hour basis." [1]

The policy was not immediately defined, but unfolded gradually as the war progressed, to the frequent confusion of both friendly and hostile critics. The Administration's first formal pronouncement on the war was a declaration by Secretary Hull (July 16) of the broad principles of American diplomacy. In the excitement of the first days of war, it was remarkable for its detachment. The Secretary had been "receiving from many sources inquiries and suggestions arising out of disturbed situations in various parts of the world." Armed hostilities, wherever existing, were a potential menace to the rights and interests of all nations. Therefore he felt it his duty to make "a statement of this Government's position in regard to international problems and situations with respect to which this country feels deep concern."

This country constantly and consistently advocates maintenance of peace. We advocate national and international self-restraint. We advocate abstinence by all nations from use of force in pursuit of policy and

[1] Cf. Department of State, *Press Releases*, September 18, 1937, 227.

from interference in the internal affairs of other nations. We advocate adjustment of problems in international relations by processes of peaceful negotiation and agreement. We advocate faithful observance of international agreements. Upholding the principle of the sanctity of treaties, we believe in modification of provisions of treaties, when need therefor arises, by orderly processes carried out in a spirit of mutual helpfulness and accommodation. We believe in respect by all nations for the rights of others and performance by all nations of established obligations. We stand for revitalizing and strengthening of international law. We advocate steps toward promotion of economic security and stability the world over. We advocate lowering or removing of excessive barriers in international trade. We seek effective equality of commercial opportunity and we urge upon all nations application of the principle of equality of treatment. We believe in limitation and reduction of armament. Realizing the necessity for maintaining armed forces adequate for national security, we are prepared to reduce or to increase our own armed forces in proportion to reductions or increases made by other countries. We avoid entering into alliances or entangling commitments but we believe in co-operative effort by peaceful and practicable means in support of the principles hereinbefore stated.[1]

These generalities were received with satisfaction by persons of widely divergent convictions, both at home and abroad.[2] Roosevelt had yet to define his policy by actions. Nevertheless, it was a significant fact that he had made his initial comment on the most devastating invasion of China in modern history a statement of universal rather than regional principles; and he had mentioned neither Japan nor the territorial integrity of China. As the fighting spread to Shanghai and took its first toll of American life and property, Mr. Hull became a little more explicit. "We consider applicable throughout the world, in the Pacific area as elsewhere,

[1] Department of State, *Press Releases*, July 17, 1937, 41-42.
[2] By the end of August over 60 nations had formally acknowledged and expressed their approval of the Hull statement, including Germany, Italy and Japan. Only Portugal took serious and detailed issue with it. See Department of State, *Press Releases*, July, August and September, 1937, 41-42, 87-107, 121-143, 167, 285.

the principles set forth in the statement of July 16," he declared on August 23. "That statement of principles is comprehensive and basic. It embraces the principles embodied in many treaties, including the Washington Conference treaties and the Kellogg-Briand Pact of Paris. . . . This Government is endeavoring to see kept alive, strengthened, and revitalized, in reference to the Pacific area and to all the world, these fundamental principles." [1]

A Chinese appeal to the League (September 12) further clarified Roosevelt's intentions. China had already asked the signatories of the Nine-Power Treaty to take note of Japan's aggression. Now she set in motion the machinery of collective security that had failed so conspicuously to save her in 1932. Her appeal was referred to the League's Far Eastern Advisory Committee on which the United States had been represented by a non-voting member in 1933. Again the United States was invited to participate in the work of the Committee, and again it accepted (September 20), on the same non-voting conditions. [2] The American Minister to Switzerland, Leland Harrison, maintained "informative contact" with the Committee just as Hugh Wilson had done before him; and on October 5 the Committee adopted two reports, finding Japan guilty of violating the Nine-Power Treaty and the Kellogg Pact and calling the signatories of the former, including Japan, into conference "to seek a method of putting an end to the conflict by agreement." [3]

The same day—October 5—President Roosevelt made a sensational speech at Chicago summoning the "peace-loving nations" to "make a concerted effort in opposition to those violations of treaties and those ignorings of humane instincts which today are creating a state of international anarchy and instability from which there is no escape through mere isolation or neutrality." War, he

[1] Department of State, *Press Releases*, August 28, 1937, 167.

[2] *Ibid.*, September 25, 254-255.

[3] The Committee's reports were approved and adopted by the Assembly October 6. Shepardson and Scroggs, *The United States in World Affairs*, 1937, 217 ff.

declared, must be quarantined like an epidemic disease.[1] The Chicago speech, which caused rejoicing among the champions of collective security both at home and abroad, proved to be the prelude to American concurrence in the findings of the League Advisory Committee and acceptance of an invitation to attend the conference recommended by it. On October 6, simultaneously with the Assembly's adoption of the Committee reports, Hull announced that,

> In the light of the unfolding developments in the Far East, the Government of the United States has been forced to the conclusion that the action of Japan in China is inconsistent with the principles which should govern the relationships between nations and is contrary to the provisions of the Nine Power Treaty of February 6, 1922, regarding principles and policies to be followed in matters concerning China, and to those of the Kellogg-Briand Pact of August 27, 1928. Thus the conclusions of this Government with respect to the foregoing are in general accord with those of the Assembly of the League of Nations.[2]

Stimson came out of retirement with a letter to the New York *Times* (October 7) suggesting an Anglo-American boycott of Japan. And on October 16, the United States accepted an invitation tendered by Belgium to attend the Nine-Power Conference, to convene at Brussels October 30.

For a moment Roosevelt seemed about to follow in Stimson's footsteps. But only for a moment. So reluctant were the great powers signatory to the Nine-Power Treaty to take any kind of disciplinary action toward Japan that none would sponsor the conference. They prevailed on Belgium to do so. Great Britain and France were too preoccupied with Germany, Italy and the war in Spain to bestow more than rhetorical praise on the Chicago speech. They made it clear that they expected the United States to take the lead in effectuating any such "quarantine" in the Far

---

[1] Text of speech, Department of State, *Press Releases*, October 9, 1937, 275 ff ; Shepardson and Scroggs, *The United States in World Affairs*, 1937, 278-282.

[2] *Press Releases*, October 9, 1937, 284-285.

East as the President envisioned. And this the latter showed himself as unwilling as ever to do. The American delegates went to Brussels, as the President himself was at pains to point out, "without any commitments on the part of this Government to other governments." He also emphasized the fact that the purpose of the conference was "to seek by agreement a solution of the present situation in China" rather than to coerce or bring pressure on either of the belligerents.[1]

The search for a solution proved futile. Since the beginning of the war Japan had insisted that she would tolerate no outside interference in it nor any third-party mediation for peace. It was therefore virtually a foregone conclusion that she would refuse the invitation to attend the Brussels Conference, as she did. With one of the belligerents unrepresented there could be no conciliation. After three weeks of rather academic discussions (November 3 to 24) the conference adjourned, reaffirming as it did so "the principles of the Nine-Power Treaty as being among the basic principles which are essential to world peace and orderly progressive development of national and international life." [2] Norman H. Davis, the American representative, congratulated his colleagues on having enunciated "fundamental principles which, in their relations with one another, should contribute substantially toward molding a sound and helpful world opinion and official thought." He particularly stressed the point that the conference was merely recessing, not permanently adjourning. Its failure to bring about peace negotiations, he asserted, made it "all the more important to continue earnestly and actively to seek every possible peaceful means for hastening a cessation of hostilities and bringing about a constructive settlement. For myself, I may say that with this

[1] *Press Releases*, October 23, 1937, 313.

[2] It also resolved that "a prompt suspension of hostilities in the Far East would be in the best interests not only of China and Japan, but of all nations," and provided for a resumption of its sittings "whenever its chairman or any two of its members shall have reported that they consider that its deliberations can be advantageously resumed." Cf. Text of report adopted by the Nine-Power Conference, November 24, 1937. *Press Releases*, November 27, 396-401.

end in view, I am returning home for consultation with my government." [1]

Whatever Mr. Davis may have hoped to accomplish at Brussels, his official actions there had contrasted strikingly both with Stimson's in 1932 and with the sentiments of the Chicago speech. No "quarantine" had been imposed at Brussels. The United States, under Roosevelt and Hull, had made no such effort to mobilize collective action in restraint of Japan as had their predecessors. They had taken part in a conference, the announced purpose of which was conciliation, not coercion, and the failure of which sent American policy flowing back into its necessitously neutral course.

To protect the lives of American citizens in China, their property and the whole complex structure of residential, commercial, missionary and juridical rights that the United States enjoyed by treaty with China, Roosevelt acted independently and with resolution. His primary concern from the beginning was the safety of the more than 10,000 Americans trapped in various parts of China by the outbreak of hostilities.[2] These he urged to evacuate the rapidly spreading areas of combat and provided them the necessary military and naval assistance to do so. Admiral Harry E. Yarnell, Commander-in-Chief of the Asiatic Squadron was stationed in Shanghai Harbor on his flagship, the cruiser *Augusta*, to supervise the work. Emergency appropriations were obtained from Congress to defray expenses, and reinforcements of marines were despatched to Shanghai. Marine and infantry detachments stationed at Peiping and Tientsin were kept on active duty, as were the nine river gunboats cruising in Chinese waters that formed a part of the Asiatic Squadron. The right to maintain armed forces at Peiping and Tientsin, to guard the legation and defend the line of communications between the two cities in case of a recurrence of the circumstances of 1900, rested on the Boxer Protocol of 1901.

[1] Statement of Norman Davis, United States Delegate to the Brussels Conference, November 24, 1937. Shepardson and Scroggs, *The United States in World Affairs*, 1937, 284-285, and Ch. X.

[2] Cf. *Press Releases*, October 2 and November 6, 1937, 266-267, 351.

It was enjoyed in common with the other signatories of the protocol, including Japan. The United States had contributed small marine detachments to the defense of the International Settlement at Shanghai since the Nationalist uprising of 1927. British, French and American gunboats had been patrolling Chinese rivers long before the advent of Japan to world power, their right to do so having been guaranteed by the treaties of Tientsin in 1858.

The way in which these various military and naval forces were used in 1937 formed another striking contrast to the action of Stimson in 1932. Then, the entire American Asiatic Squadron had been ostentatiously concentrated in Shanghai Harbor and the American fleet had been allowed to remain at Honolulu, with what motives we have taken note. From July, 1937, to July, 1938, the maximum military and naval establishments in China amounted to 528 marines at Peiping, 814 infantry at Tientsin, 2,555 marines at Shanghai and 13 (of which 9 were the river gunboats exclusively on duty there) of the Asiatic Squadron's total of 44 vessels. These figures included all reinforcements, the largest of which was the 1,500 marines sent to Shanghai in August, 1937. All contributed substantially to the main task before them, with the result that by November 6, 1937, 4,600 Americans had been evacuated from China and, in a war of grand scale and unsurpassed ferocity, surprisingly few had lost their lives. Moreover, Secretary Hull several times took occasion to express "the desire and intention of the American Government to remove these forces when performance of their function of protection is no longer called for. . . ." [1] The withdrawal, in February and March, 1938, of the marine reinforcements from Shanghai and of the infantry detachment from Tientsin attested to the sincerity of this intention.[2]

[1] Hull to McReynolds, December 4, 1937. *Press Releases*, December 11, 1937, 417.

[2] Figures relating to American armed forces in China from *Ibid.*, 417. Hull to Garner, January 8, 1938. *Ibid.*, January 15, 1938, 101-102. For troop withdrawals see *Ibid.*, February 5, 1938, 199-200; February 19, 266; March 5, 285.

By such means, though the circumstances were far more trying, the extreme tension that had developed between Washington and Tokyo in 1932 was averted. Conversely, the protection of American nationals and legal rights in China—by the customary procedures of diplomacy—was facilitated, the danger of involvement in more warlike procedures lessened. Proof of this was afforded when the gunboat *Panay* of the Asiatic Squadron, assisting in the evacuation of American embassy officials from Nanking, and three vessels belonging to the Standard Oil Company were attacked and sunk by Japanese bombing planes on December 12, 1937. Although Japan attempted to excuse the attack on various implausible pretexts, she apologized for it in advance of the first American representations and went to unprecedented limits to meet the vigorous demands for satisfaction when they were presented. The officer responsible for the attack was removed from his command, renewed assurances of respect for American rights and interests in China were given and a promise of indemnification made, on the strength of which Hull announced the incident closed, December 24.[1] The United States presented its bill for indemnity March 22, 1938, and Japan paid it in full on April 22.[2] No more serious incident was precipitated during the first year of the war than this unprovoked destruction of an American naval vessel. In obtaining satisfaction for it, as it did, the United States was undoubtedly assisted by the fact that it had kept free of hostile coalitions and coercive enterprises and so could approach Japan with an ironclad claim admitting of no political suspicions.

In the defense of residential, commercial, missionary and other rights in areas occupied by Japanese troops and earmarked by the Japanese Government as future spheres of influence, the results of

[1] *Press Releases*, December 18 and 25, 1937, 444-452, 497-508.

[2] The amount assessed (and collected) was $2,214,007.36. $1,945,670.01 was for property losses sustained, and $268,337.35 for death and personal injury cases resulting from the attack. No punitive damages were assessed. *Press Releases*, March 26 and April 23, 1938, 410, 504.

the Roosevelt policy, as indeed the character of that policy, were more problematical. These rights were the legal embodiment of the open door principle that the United States had upheld from the beginning in all its dealings both with China and Japan. The open door principle was, in turn, but a regional definition of equality of opportunity, whether commercial, religious, juridical or political, a universal objective of American diplomacy. As the war progressed, Hull energetically protested Japanese infringements of these rights, making due reservations with respect to the assessment and collection of damages.[1]

His purpose was not only to assist American citizens to obtain indemnification for property losses resulting from the war but also to bind Japan as securely as possible to *de jure* recognition of American treaty rights in those portions of China actually or potentially under Japanese domination. In a less restricted sense, he was attempting to stimulate Japanese respect for the universal procedures of international law, according to which the United States might some day wish to settle with Japan issues of greater consequence than the open door in China; issues, for example, such as the status of the Philippines after 1946.

"The interest and concern of the United States in the Far Eastern situation, in the European situation, and in situations on this continent are not measured by the number of American citizens residing in a particular country at a particular moment nor by the amount of investment of American citizens there nor by the volume of trade," Mr. Hull wrote in a public letter to Vice President Garner of January 6, 1938.

"There is a broader and much more fundamental interest—which is that orderly processes in international relationships be maintained. Referring expressly to the situation in the Far East, an area which contains approximately half the population of the world, the United States is deeply interested in supporting by peaceful means influences contributory to preservation and encouragement of orderly processes. This interest far transcends in importance the value of American trade with

[1] Cf. *Press Releases*, esp. January 22, 29, and February 5, 12 and 19, 1938.

China or American investments in China; it transcends even the question of safeguarding the immediate welfare of American citizens in China." [1]

Stimson had made exactly the same premise the starting point to his collaboration with the League of Nations in 1931. What "orderly processes" did the Secretary of State have in mind? The phrase could have referred with equal pertinence to the classic precepts of international law or to the processes of collective security. So far Roosevelt and Hull had, whether by choice or by necessity, laid primary emphasis on the former. Yet in the Presidential address at Chicago, in sundry utterances by Secretary Hull, in the concluding remarks of Norman Davis at Brussels, they had shown that they had not completely abandoned interest in the latter. President Roosevelt had chosen not to invoke and apply the Neutrality Laws to the Sino-Japanese War, for a variety of officially unexplained reasons. Among these, conjecture supplied the possibility that he was preparing a legislative attack on the laws in order to remove all trammels from his discretionary powers in foreign affairs and, ultimately, to organize some form of collective action against Japan. Another equally plausible possibility was that the President and his advisers had feared to invoke the laws lest they create the impression that they were abandoning the American citizens and legal rights in China to their fate, and so impair their diplomatic efforts to protect them. [2]

[1] *Press Releases*, January 15, 1938, 100-105.

[2] The decision not to invoke the Neutrality Laws was a subject of great controversy during the entire first year of the war. Its obvious inconsistency with the application of the laws to the Spanish Civil War was quickly pointed out. The President based his decision, as he had a perfect legal right to do, on the technicality that war had not been formally declared; hence he was not legally bound to find a state of war in existence. He did not, however, hesitate to concur with the League's finding that Japan had violated the Kellogg Pact. This and other inconsistencies were rationalized by Administration spokesmen in Congress, first on the ground that finding a state of war in existence would impel Japan to declare war and so confound the efforts of the peacemakers; then on the ground that the purpose of the laws was not to maintain a legally consistent neutrality,

Despite all criticisms and conjectures, all subtle hopes and possible ulterior motives, the fact remained that during the first year of the Sino-Japanese War that began in July, 1937, the Far Eastern policy of the Roosevelt Administration had rested on these foundations: protection of American nationals and legal rights in China; non-intervention in the political issues of the war; maintenance of American naval predominance in the Pacific Ocean. For the moment primary emphasis in the execution, if not in the principles, of the Far Eastern policy had been shifted from the preservation of China's territorial integrity to defense of the open door in that country—from the position of the July third circular of 1900 to that of the first Hay notes of September 6, 1899. Was the change intended to be permanent? The President did not say. A "24-hour basis" was all he would claim for his policy. The problems of Philippine independence, Japanese-American naval rivalry, the open door in China had been posed anew, not solved. On their solution depended a great many things, varying upwards in importance from the small American economic stake in China to the freedom of the American people from involvement in a war seemingly devoid of any potentialities of material or spiritual gain.

The regularity with which the United States had, during the past four decades, reverted to the position taken by Roosevelt indicated that attempting to preserve the territorial integrity of China was not and never had been a truly vital American national interest. It had been conceived in principle as the means to an

but to keep the United States out of war. Other possible reasons for the decision were to protect China's access to American loans and munitions, to obviate the declaration of a blockade and, when Japan finally declared a war blockade applicable to Chinese vessels (August 25, extended September 5), to avoid or minimize the difficulties over neutral rights that would result from formal recognition of a state of war. On September 14 the President did prohibit the shipment of munitions on government-owned vessels and warned privately owned merchant vessels that they carried such cargoes at their own risk. Cf. Shepardson and Scroggs, *The United States in World Affairs*, 1937, 198-206.

end, not an end in itself. As an end in itself, not all of the material interest and humanitarian idealism of which it was compounded had been sufficient to make it a success. From 1900 to 1932 American efforts in behalf of China's integrity had passed through a number of cycles, all ending in failure. With what consequences? Jeopardizing the security of America's own territorial integrity (by antagonizing the most likely attacker of the Philippines). Encouraging Chinese patriots to hope for, if not to count on, a type of American support that never materialized. Obstructing the most profitable trend of American commerce and investment in the Far East which, since 1900, had been toward Japan, not China. Rendering the exclusion of Japanese immigrants, in Japan's eyes, the addition of insult to injuries, the whole having a baleful effect on every phase of Japanese-American relations. Stimulating naval rivalry between the two nations. Involving the United States in European politics *via* the back door of Eastern Asia.

What of the open door itself? Missionaries had once sought the protection of American gunboats in attempting to exercise their treaty right to spread the gospel in China. By 1938 they had for the most part either renounced this protection or directed their attention to goals with which it was incompatible: disarmament, world peace. Commercially American citizens were still interested in China. An American economic mission to the Far East in 1935 devoted over forty pages of its report to the possibilities of American trade with China, as compared with seventeen pages to Japan and eight pages to the Philippines.[1] The inauguration by Pan-American Airways of passenger service across the Pacific in 1936 was further evidence that no wholesale liquidation of American commercial interests in China was in view. Yet the value of these interests was subject to considerable misapprehension.

[1] National Foreign Trade Council, *American Trade Prospects in the Orient, Report of the American Economic Mission to the Far East*, New York, 1935.

For a hundred years the United States had listened to predictions that its commercial and financial stake in the Far East would soon exceed that in Europe, predictions which had stubbornly refused to materialize. From 1931 to 1935 an annual average of 19 per cent of the total foreign trade of the United States (24 per cent of its imports, 15 per cent of its exports) was with the Far East, half its trade with Europe, no greater in export value than its trade with Canada. In round numbers, 19 per cent of the total foreign trade of the United States meant $724,500,000 out of $3,738,000,000. Of this sum, in 1935, 43 per cent represented American trade with Japan, 24 per cent with Netherlands India, British Malaya and French Indo-China, 18 per cent with the Philippines and 14 per cent with China and Hongkong.

The excess in value of American commerce with Japan over that with China was remarkable. In spite of a policy relatively hostile to the former and friendly to the latter, American trade with Japan had, since 1900, roughly doubled and at times tripled that with China. Japan's share of the total American imports and exports had risen steadily over this period from 4.3 per cent to 8.6 per cent and from 1.9 per cent to 8.4 per cent, respectively; while the corresponding Chinese percentages had risen only from 2.7 per cent to 3.2 per cent and from 2.3 per cent to 3.7 per cent. In 1936 the value of American exports to Japan and China was $204,300,000 and $55,400,000, respectively; of imports from the two countries, $171,000,000 and $82,800,000, respectively. These figures showed Japan to be the United States' third best customer, the United States Japan's best customer, China ranking well below Japan in each capacity.[1]

Investment statistics revealed similar discrepancies between for-

---

[1] Figures from Field, *Economic Handbook*, 470 ff.; Farley, Miriam S., "America's Stake in the Far East, I: Trade," *Far Eastern Survey*, V, July 29, 1926, 161-170; same author, *America's Stake in the Far East*, American Council, Institute of Pacific Relations pamphlet, New York, 1936, *passim*; Staley, Eugene, *War Losses to a Neutral*, League of Nations Association, New York, 1937, 6-10.

eign policy and economic fact. Since 1912 American direct and
portfolio investments in the Far East had risen from an estimated
$100,000,000 to approximately $758,000,000 in 1935. This sum
represented about 6 per cent of the total foreign investments of
the United States of $12,630,000,000. It was divided as follows:
Japan, $387,000,000; the Philippines, $151,000,000; China, $132,-
000,000; Netherlands India, $68,000,000; British Malaya, $20,-
000,000. Financially as well as commercially Japan exceeded
China in importance to the United States. The insignificant value
of the whole Far East to American investors and the small fraction of that value represented by China were conspicuous. In spite
of the prophecies and promotional efforts of American diplomacy
Europe, Canada, the West Indies, South and Central America all
continued to rank ahead of the Far East as American investment
markets. Americans owned a mere 6 per cent of the total foreign
investments in China in 1931, as compared with Britain's 36 per
cent ($1,189,000,000) and Japan's 35 per cent ($1,136,900,000).[1]

In view of these figures it would have been a gratuitous cal-
culation that rated the open door in China an American national
interest of vital importance. Reinforcing this conclusion was the
record of the initiative taken by the State Department in the matter
of the consortium loans. American financial interest in China had
frequently been the artificial creation, and the servant, of political
design, a fact that disproved the contention that foreign policy is
invariably the creature of economic pressure groups. We have
taken note of the uses to which Knox and Lansing put the Ameri-

[1] Remer, C. F., *Foreign Investments in China*, Ch. XV; Field, *Economic
Handbook*, 334-341, 355; Lockwood, W. W., "America's Stake in the Far East,
II: Investments," *Far Eastern Survey*, V, August 12, 1936, 175-185. The figure
for American investments in China in 1938 accepted by the Department of Commerce and by Secretary Hull was $132,000,000—practically the same as in 1933.
To this figure some estimates added $40,000,000 of Chinese obligations in de-
fault since the World War, $25,000,000 to $35,000,000 covering the properties
of American citizens permanently residing in China and $40,000,000 of properties
of American missionary and other charitable organizations. Hull to Garner,
January 8, 1938. *Press Releases*, January 15, 1938, 102. Cf. Remer, *loc. cit.*

can Consortium group. In 1922 J. P. Morgan and Company, writing on behalf of the group to Secretary Hughes, not only recognized the true nature of these uses but refused to approve them. They declined to lend money to the Chinese government as a political palliative. It was well enough, they reasoned, for British and French banking houses to do this—"large, powerful banks, generally with long-established business in the Far East, and with close political and governmental associations." But:

The American Group is in quite a different position. It is composed of approximately forty institutions and banking houses scattered throughout the country, *few if any of which have any direct or active business in the Far East*. The Group was formed at the instance of the Department of State for the purpose of endeavoring to serve [save?] the situation and to assist in maintaining the door in China open to American trade. To this end the Group is prepared to do all that it can within the limitations imposed upon it by the charters or traditions under which its members function. Its banks, for instance, cannot buy for their own account blocks of Chinese Government securities, unless they can see their way clear to an early resale of such securities to the American investing public.[1]

For the Department of State repeatedly to turn to American bankers for assistance in realizing the opportunities that lay behind the open door in China emphasized the theoretical nature of those opportunities. For the bankers to refuse this assistance showed that the American business community was not greatly interested in them.

There were other than material calculations that had shaped the Far Eastern policy of the United States, however. To strive for equal commercial opportunity in China, by one means or another, was consistent with American political philosophy as well as with the geographical and economic imperatives that had determined American relations with Eastern Asia. The desire to assist

[1] The American Group to the Secretary of State, August 4, 1922. *For. Rel.*, 1922, I, 783-785. Italics inserted.

China to become the master of her own destinies reflected an in-
nate American idealism in which Japan herself had once shared
and benefited. It was true, as the Chief of the Far Eastern Division
of the Department of State declared in 1934 that "the American
people have believed and continue to believe in principles which
are expressed in the formulae of 'sovereignty,' 'independence,' and
'equality of opportunity.'" [1] The United States had upheld the
same principles in her early dealings with Japan. It was true, as
Secretary Hull asserted in his letter to Vice President Garner in
January, 1938, and as he proved by his notes of protest at Japanese bombing of Chinese civilians, that in thinking of the Far
East, as a people and as a nation, the United States was concerned
with less tangible, less materialistic things than trade and commerce. Yet in national ideals as in national interests, history seemed
to show that the open door and the territorial integrity of China
were of secondary importance. At the very height of Stimson's
effort in their behalf, in 1932, they were eclipsed by the ideals of
domestic social and economic justice to which the depression had
given such sharp stimulus. Theodore Roosevelt had concluded,
after much reflection, that the open door and the territorial integrity of China were ideals for which the American people would
not fight. His conclusion was substantiated by the experience of
his successors. Even Stimson regarded "any suggestion of sending
armies to Asiatic ports or any other warlike action as not only
politically impossible but as a futile and wrong method of procedure. . . ." [2]

Still another factor that had shaped the course of American
diplomacy in the Far East was the influence of Europe, especially
of Great Britain. It was wholly logical that England should have
attempted, as she did, to balance the power of the United States

[1] Hornbeck, Stanley K., *Principles of American Policy in Relation to the Far
East* (an address before the Ninth Conference on the Cause and Cure of War,
Washington, January 18, 1934), 6.
[2] Stimson to editor of the *New Republic*, December 29, 1937.

against other, more hostile powers menacing her interests in the Far East. Nor were the effects of this tendency wholly inimical to American interests. Insofar as it made for the elimination of naval rivalry between the world's two greatest sea powers, and enhanced the security of their territorial possessions in the Far East it conferred like benefits on each. Yet many an American diplomatic venture had foundered on the too-casual assumption that British and American interests in that quarter of the globe were identical. It is unnecessary to recite the evidence contained in the foregoing chapters that disproved, or at least stringently qualified, that assumption. Great Britain's principal Far Eastern interests were the security of India and the Pacific Dominions. All other interests, including her vast financial stake in China and the territorial integrity of that country were subordinate to these. If, at times, the means she had pursued toward these greater ends had coincided with American procedures, at other times they had conspicuously failed to do so, disappointing the American statesmen who had taken Anglo-American co-operation for granted, as an axiom of Far Eastern diplomacy.

Complicating all of these problems, darkening the atmosphere in which they were studied, the issue of Japanese immigration hung like a cloud over the Pacific. Exigencies of race relationship and economic competition had made it necessary for the United States to curb the flow of oriental immigrants into its territories. But the methods it had employed in so doing had proved no exception to the law of diminishing returns. They had offended the one nation whose co-operation the success of American diplomacy in other spheres most urgently required. Thus they, too, had impaired the security of the Philippines, the defense of the open door and, for that matter, the preservation of China's territorial integrity—consequences which other no less effective methods might have avoided.

Such were the complex and often conflicting elements of the policy that Franklin D. Roosevelt had placed upon a "24-hour basis." The policy had originated in a mood of imperialist expansion that had long since passed. It had outlived this mood, assured of longevity by the precedents it had established while it lasted, and periodically rejuvenated by fresh doctrines. What would become of it in the future? History supplied no certain answer. The Far East was still, relatively, as remote from the United States in 1938 as it had been in the era of sail. China was still so huge, so amorphous and now so tense with martial energy that her complete domination by Japan or by any other single nation seemed unlikely. There were slight grounds for believing that the open door in all China would be entirely closed. Nor was it a foregone conclusion that the constantly tilting scales of world power would never again reach equilibrium in the Far East. A wholesale "withdrawal" of Americans from residence, commerce, philanthropy, navigation, religious missions and travel in the Far East seemed as unreal a contemplation as a comparable withdrawal from Europe or South America. History offered no reason to believe that the United States was running away from its Far Eastern destinies, or that it should do so. It offered many reasons for believing that the United States should understand those destinies, in their true proportions.

# APPENDIX

## Hippisley Memorandum

### MEMORANDUM ON THE "OPEN DOOR" IN CHINA

The mercantile communities of the United States and Gt. Britain, realising the important field for their enterprise which under existing conditions is afforded by China, and the vastly extended field for it which they might legitimately look forward to under improved conditions in the future, earnestly desire the maintenance of the "open door," *i.e.*, of the rights possessed under the existing treaties of Tientsin. In other words, they ask that they be assured the equality of opportunity which all nations alike have hitherto enjoyed under those treaties for (a) commerce, (b) navigation, and (c) exploitation of mines and railroads.

## Rockhill Memorandum

### MEMORANDUM

No one person has done more within the last few months to influence public opinion in the United States on the Chinese question than Lord Charles Beresford, by his book "The Break-Up of China," and by the speeches he has made in the United States. By these means he has sought to prove the identity of interests of our two countries and the necessity of an Anglo-American policy in China. It seems desirable to preface the following remarks by examining the data supplied by Lord Charles, endeavoring to control his views, and to show, if possible, the truth or fallacy of his conclusions.

For one who has devoted the better part of his life to the study of Chinese affairs, the book of Lord Beresford comes as an agreeable surprise—so far as regards foreign commercial relations with China, and is on the whole rather encouraging than dispiriting. The volume of foreign trade has steadily increased, and everywhere signs are not wanting of its further extension; the Chinese Government has not failed to fulfill any of its pecuniary obligations to foreigners, and is endeavoring, in a clumsy, uncertain way it is true —but that is not entirely its fault, to take some further steps in the direction needed for its internal development. If, on the other hand, the Empire is in a disturbed condition, and if foreign interests suffer thereby, this is entirely due to the unseemly haste of some of the Treaty Powers in their scramble for commercial advantages and acquisition of territory. This they lament but do not seek to remedy.

Lord Beresford's interviews with the various foreign mercantile organizations at the treaty ports of China bring clearly before us the fact that they have not in the last twenty years had any new ground for complaint against the Chinese Government, that they are to-day suffering, not perhaps even quite so severely as years ago, from the existence of certain restrictions, especially those resulting from internal revenue taxes, which have been the subject of endless correspondence between the diplomatic representatives in Peking and the Chinese Government for the last quarter of a century and with which every one interested in affairs in that Empire must by this time be pretty familiar.

The grievances of which the foreign mercantile class in China has to complain and a remedy to which lies with the Chinese Government, are all proper subjects for diplomatic discussion and no one can doubt that if within the last two years steady and united pressure had been brought to bear on it by the Treaty Powers, some of them would be in a fair way to settlement at the present time.

Take for example *likin*. In the rush for concessions to foreigners in China and the necessity for that country to find funds to insure the payment of interest on the loans she has been forced to contract to carry out more or less urgent public works recommended by them, the Treaty Powers have compelled her to increase her internal revenue taxes and have per-

manently fastened on the country
this very tax (*likin*) they had for
twenty-five years and more been
trying to have suppressed. Again
take the transit pass system by
which foreign goods are allowed
to be carried throughout the Empire on the payment of one-half
the import duty, and which system the British merchants claim
is an utter failure, we know by
the successful endeavors of the
French Government in enforcing
this right under the treaties for
goods imported into southwestern
China, that if failure it is in other
parts of the Empire, the fault lies
with the foreigners themselves.

Lord Beresford's opinion that it
is primarily necessary for the development of China to make a
military and naval power of that
Empire, is, I think, the weakest
part of his work, and his opinion
is at variance with that of all
those who know best China and
the Chinese. So far as the protection of foreign interests is concerned, the Chinese Government
is, and has been since the suppression of the Taiping rebellion, able
to protect them whenever and
wherever it has chosen to, as in-

numerable cases familiar to the Department can show.

In the various memoranda submitted to Lord Beresford by the British merchants of China and published in his book, the need for China to increase her armament to insure their security, is no where hinted at, but in all of them we find the cause of the present stagnation of trade attibuted, and rightly to my mind, to the vacillating policy of the home Governments, frequently brought about by apathy and lack of knowledge regarding Chinese affairs, the resulting ability of the Chinese Government to escape the performance of its treaty obligations, and to the jealousies and lack of concerted action of the Powers in treating questions of general interest.

No more representative foreign body can be found in China than the China Association at Shanghai. In its memorandum to Lord Beresford, we read: "It seems plain that such security (as foreign trade requires) can only be found in the entire reform of the present corrupt state of Chinese government. The undertaking of such a task, no doubt, bristles with difficulties, and entails responsibilities which will necessarily be complicated by international jealousies; it is, nevertheless, clear that unless the situation be boldly faced, still greater difficulties and still greater international trouble will have to be faced in the near future. . . . The establishment of a government in Peking, which is not only strong, but which is in sympathy with the wishes and feelings of the nation at large, is, we believe, a first necessity if China is to be saved from partition. . . . Weakness in Peking must inevitably mean disruption and partition of the Empire. . . . We say, then, that the one thing wanted for the development of trade, for the protection of capital, and for the extension of enterprise in China is security, which can only be effected through pressure from without. . . ."

That the task of strengthening the central government is a comparatively easy one, the history of China's progress in the last fifty years conclusively shows. The introduction of telegraphic lines throughout the Empire, the Maritime Customs service, the more recent organization of a system of imperial railways and their withal successful working, and a variety of other reforms are all operating in the same direction, so that Lord Beresford's statement (p. 231) "no reforms . . . can possibly be brought about in a country so hopelessly corrupt as China until the first and initial step is taken of giving authority to those in power which only an effective military and police can supply," is a hasty and erroneous conclusion.

That the existence of a strong and well officered and disciplined army and navy in China might assist that country to ward off the attacks of a foreign foe, is likely; that, in the absence of such a force, and with the present aggressive policy of some of the Treaty Powers, the creation of "spheres of interest" (or influence) easily reached by rail or by the sea by the interested Power from its own territory, should be held to be the only way of insuring China against complete partition, is comprehensible; but that the United States should lend a hand to the carrying out of either of these two policies seems absolutely suicidal to our vast and

Last year when the British Govt. was energetically insisting on the necessity of maintaining the "open door" in China, Mr. Balfour's speeches foreshadowed a policy which, though nominally aiming at that object, conceded to the various Powers the possession of spheres of influence or interest in which they would enjoy special rights and privileges in respect of railroad and mining enterprises: and the undertakings entered into by Gt. Britain with Germany as regards Shantung and with Russia as regards Manchuria go to show that this is the policy which the British Govt. has definitely adopted to govern its relations with other Powers in China. A policy the object of which is to maintain the "open door" and at the same time to recognise spheres of interest with special, and practically exclusive, rights as regards mines and railroads, is possibly feasible; but it certainly is feasible only on the condition that adequate steps are taken to prevent the special mining and railroad rights being so stretched as to include territorial growing interests in that part of the world.

British writers on Chinese questions, and especially Lord Beresford, have advocated in the strongest terms the "open door policy" or equality of treatment and opportunity for all comers, and denounce in the strongest terms the system of "Spheres of Influence" (or interest); but such spheres have now been recognized by Great Britain as well as by France, Germany and Russia, and *they must be accepted as existing facts.*

jurisdiction and the power to impose discriminating taxation in any form.

In any case the undertakings above referred to have already practically deprived Britishers of equality of opportunity as regards mines and railroads in certain important districts of China, and would appear to render it difficult for other nationalities to insist on the maintenance of their equality of opportunity as regards those enterprises in the districts concerned—though the importance of this curtailment of previously existing rights is much reduced by the facts that the concessions for mines and railroads already granted in China will require years to fulfil, even if they do not require a larger amount of capital than is likely to be forthcoming for investment in that country, and that these concessions are distributed among all of the wealthy nations.

But while adopting the policy of spheres of interest, which, we will admit, political reasons may have forced it to do, Great Britain has tried to maintain also the "open door" policy, the only one which meets with the approval of its business classes, for by it alone can they be guaranteed equality of treatment in the trade of China. In this attempt to minimize the evils brought about by the necessities of her foreign policy, Great Britain has been, however, unable to secure to her people perfect equality of opportunity, for she has recognized special and exclusive rights first of Germany and then of Russia in their areas of activity, more particularly those relating to railways and mines. What these rights may eventually be claimed to include, no one can at present foretell, though it would not be surprising if the exercise of territorial jurisdiction and the imposition of discriminating taxation were demanded under them—at least by France. Should such rights be conceded, our trade interests would receive a blow, from which they could not possibly recover.

To sum up then, we find to-day in China that the policy of the "open door," the untrammeled exercise of the rights insured to Treaty Powers by the treaty of Tientsin, and other treaties copied on it or under the most favored nation clause, is claimed by the mercantile classes of the United States and other powers as essential to the healthy extension of trade in China. We see, on the other hand, that the political interests and the geographical relations of Great Britain, Russia and France to China have forced those countries to divide up China proper into areas or spheres of interest (or influence) in which they enjoy special rights and privileges, the ultimate scope of which is not yet determined, and that at the same time Great Britain, in its desire not to sacrifice entirely its mercantile interests, is also endeavoring to preserve some of the undoubted benefits of the "open door" policy, but "spheres of influence" *are an accomplished fact,* this cannot be too much insisted on. This policy is outlined

Equality of opportunity as regards (c) having practically then
already gone by the board, it
would seem that the utmost that
can now be attempted is to safeguard equality of opportunity as
regards (a) and (b)—commerce
and navigation. To do this it appears essential that the nations in
favour of the "open door" policy
should bind themselves, and secure undertakings from the other
powers, to the effect that each in
its respective spheres of interest or
influence

(1) will in no way interfere
with any treaty port in such sphere
or with the interests vested in it:

(2) will promise that, unless
the ports opened to trade in it are
declared free ports, the Chinese
treaty tariff as existing or as hereafter amended shall apply to all
merchandise landed or shipped, no
matter to what nationality such
merchandise may belong; and that
the dues and duties so leviable
shall be collected by the Chinese
Govt.: and

(3) will levy no higher har-
bour dues on vessels of another
nationality frequenting any port in

by Mr. Balfour in his Manchester
speech of January 10, 1898.

Such then being the condition
of things, and in view of the
probability of complications soon
arising between the interested
powers in China, whereby it will
become difficult, if not impossible,
for the United States to retain
the rights guaranteed them by
treaties with China, what should
be our immediate policy? To this
question there can, it seems, be
but one answer, we should at once
initiate negotiations to obtain from
those Powers who have acquired
zones of interest in China formal
assurance that (1°) they will in
no way interfere within their
so-called spheres of interest with
any treaty port or with vested
rights in it of any nature; (2°)
that all ports they may open in
their respective spheres shall either
be free ports, or that the Chinese
treaty tariff at the time in force
shall apply to all merchandise
landed or shipped, no matter to
what nationality belonging, and
that the dues and duties provided
for by treaty shall be collected by
the Chinese Government; and
(3°) that they will levy no higher
harbor dues on vessels of other na-

such sphere than shall be levied on vessels of its own nationality, and no higher railroad charges on merchandise belonging to subjects of other Powers transported through such sphere than shall be levied on similar merchandise belonging to its own nationals transported over equal distances.

Such an arrangement would go far to secure an open market for merchandise in China and to remove dangerous sources of international conflict: and it is not anticipated that any serious difficulty would be experienced in attaining it. If the declarations of responsible British statesmen mean anything, they should ensure hearty support from Gt. Britain. Germany by her enlightened policy in

tionalities frequenting their ports in such spheres than shall be levied on their national vessels, and that they will also levy no higher railroad charges on merchandise belonging to or destined for subjects of other powers transported through their spheres than shall be levied on similar merchandise belonging to its own nationality.

In other words, we should insist on absolute equality of treatment in the various zones, for equality of opportunity with the citizens of the favored powers we cannot hope to have, in view of the well known methods now in vogue for securing privileges and concessions, though we should continually, by every proper means, seek to gain this also.

Such understandings with the various Powers, and it is confidently believed that they could be reached at present, would secure an open market throughout China for our trade on terms of equality with all other foreigners, and would further remove dangerous sources of irritation and possible conflict between the contending powers, greatly tend to re-establish confidence, and prepare the sanctioning the establishment of a Chinese Customs-house at Kiao-chow and in rendering it all possible assistance—in marked contrast to the narrow, unjust, and shortsighted policy of Gt. Britain in expelling the Chinese Customs-house from the Kowloon extension, inevitably to the enormous increase of smuggling—shows that little opposition is to be anticipated on her part. The doubtful Powers have hitherto been Russia and France, but the Ukase issued by the Czar on the 15th inst. declaring "Talien-wan a free port during the whole period of the treaty for the merchant ships of all nations" removes all doubt as to Russia's attitude and justifies the expectation that she would co-operate in such an undertaking as that proposed; and it is little likely that France would refuse to listen to Russia's advice—opposed though it is to her traditional policy in China of insisting that, whenever in any degree possible, territorial jurisdiction is included in any rights conceded—and so stand out in opposition alone.

way for concerted action by the Powers to bring about the reforms in Chinese administration and the strengthening of the Imperial Government recognized on all sides as essential to the maintenance of peace.

Great stress has been laid by British writers on the role of Russia in China which they contend is a "purely political and military conquest" and who, "though she may mean to eventually build up a commerce, only wants for the present the Chinese seaboard and ports for strategic purposes." (Colquhom. *"China in Transformation."* 326.) Lord Beresford says (32) that he was told at Niuchuang by the British residents that "they regarded Manchuria as really a Russian province . . . that though the Russians might not impose a tariff on goods just at present, they were placing themselves in such a powerful military position that they would be able to do so in the near future, . . . and the merchants considered their trade threatened by such exhibition of military power." In the face of these apprehensions of the British merchants at Niuchuang, who were but feeling in their persons the discomforts and restrictions which all foreigners may sooner or later have to experience when settled in the sphere of influence of some rival power, it is agreeable to have to record the opening of the port of Ta-lien-wan (near Port Arthur and an infinitely better port than Niuchuang, being below the line of winter and ice), to the merchant ships of all nations during the whole of the lease under which it is held by the Emperor of Russia's ukase of August 15th of this year. This I conceive will greatly help to allay fears and doubts as to Russia's attitude in China, and justifies the belief entertained that she would co-operate in bringing about such international understanding as is here outlined. The recent statement of a Russian writer inspired by a personage enjoying for years the friendship of the Emperor of Russia, that "the independence and integrity of China is a fundamental principle of Russia's policy in Asia" (*N. A. Rev.*, July, '99, p. 16), may or may not be absolutely correct; at all events, it may well be taken as indicating the present trend of

Russia's policy, and seems to insure the friendly consideration at St. Petersburg of the arrangement here suggested. Whatever the ulterior object of Russia may be, its present one is unquestionably conciliation, for any haste might prove the spark which would cause the explosion by which the Chinese Empire would be shattered.

Nor does the assent of Germany to the proposed agreement seem very doubtful; she has declared Kiaochao a free port and allowed a Chinese custom house to be established there, in pleasing contrast by the way with the illiberal and shortsighted policy of Great Britain which has expelled the Chinese custom house from the Kowloon extension in front of Hongkong, and while she has insisted on certain exclusive mining and railroad rights in her sphere of interest, it seems highly probable that as German capital flows slower and slower into these enterprises, as it undoubtedly will as the vast requirements for long years to come of the already granted concessions are more exactly determined, she will find it greatly to her advantage to encourage and foster the enterprises of other nations.

No reference has been made to the way in which the Japanese Government would consider the propositions here suggested, because these measures are so clearly advantageous to Japan and so much in line with its own policy in China, that it must meet with its hearty approval.

It is particularly important for obvious reasons of both domestic and foreign policy that the initiative for these negotiations should be taken by the United States. Such a policy cannot be construed as favorable to any power in particular, but is eminently useful and desirable for the commerce of all nations. It furthermore has the advantage of insuring to the United States the appreciation of Chinese Government, who would see in it a strong desire to arrest the disintegration of the Empire and would greatly add to our prestige and influence at Peking.

France is the only doubtful country from whom some opposition might be anticipated, it being her well known policy in China to claim all implied jurisdictional rights wherever possible, but it is

The issue of the Czar's ukase just referred to opens the door for *pourparlers* on this subject and renders the present a specially opportune moment for entering on them.

A. E. H.
17-viii-99

little likely that in this question, as in others, she would decline to listen to Russia's advice and stand out in opposition alone.

The prospect seems bright therefore *at the present moment* of bringing to a successful conclusion the negotiations needed to attain the ends here indicated and which will, it is thought, relieve our commercial world from the just apprehension and perturbation in which recent events have thrown it, giving it equal treatment so far as commerce and navigation go, with the subjects of any other Power.

Respectfully submitted,
W. W. Rockhill

Washington, 28th of August, 1899.

The sources for the above memoranda are the Rockhill papers.

## ADEE MEMORANDUM OF SEPT. 6, 1899, REVIEWING RUSSIAN AND GERMAN ASSURANCES IN RE: AMERICAN TRADE IN KIAOCHOW, PORT ARTHUR AND TALIENWAN

The complete text of the memorandum reads as follows:

"I find no such notice; indeed there is no communication on the subject of Kiao-Chow from the German Embassy. Dr. von Holleben however seems to have orally expressed his 'personal' opinion that the port would be opened to foreign trade, for the conversation, or rather conversations, were related to Amb. White in Instruction No. 347 of Feb. 11, 1898, by which he was directed to ascertain informally the views of the German Government in the matter and at the same time to express the interest of the U. S. therein. The reply to this Instruction (Despatch No. 318 of Feb. 28, 1898) brought back Mr. von Bulow's (oral) assurance that 'there was no intention to close the port to foreign trade and commerce' . . . and 'that it had not entered into the plans of the Government to exclude other powers from the advantages of commerce with China or with any part of it.' Yet, a few days before, on Feb. 5, the same Mr. von Bulow, in a speech delivered at the Reichstag declared that in his opinion Kiaochow should be kept as an open port but that he did not feel at liberty to make any promise to Europe especially as England had preserved her liberty of action in this respect at Hong Kong (Desp. No. 283 of Feb. 11, 1898).

"The only report of this description was received from Russia in Desp. No. 25 of Jan. 19, 1898, in which Mr. Hitchcock lays before the Dept. the substance of conversations he had with the Russian Minister for Foreign Affairs, the British Ambassador, the Japanese Minister, and the German Ambassador in regard to the occupation of Kiao Chow by Germany. The German representative said that 'the harbor

492

of Kiao Chow will be open to the vessels and commerce of all nations—upon equal terms and conditions.' This despatch was sent to Berlin in the Instruction above mentioned No. 347.

"The Russian Chargé here, Mr. de Wollant, in his note of March 28, 1898, announcing the lease of Port Arthur and Talienwan says: 'I must add that the port of Talienwan will be opened to foreign commerce and that the broadest hospitality will be extended there to vessels of friendly nations.'

"See note on page 3 of the Instructions to Amb. White: It would seem that on the contrary, our Ambassador at *St. Petersburg* had received assurances from the *German* Emperor's Ambassador to Russia in regard to Kiao Chow.

"The Russian Minister for Foreign Affairs however told Ambassador Hitchcock (Confidential Despatch No. 9 of March 19) that while Russia needed Port Arthur for a military harbor and Talienwan for a commercial port, she had 'no desire, either to occupy Chinese Territory, other than the ports named nor to interfere in any way with the trade of other nations with China.'

"The Russian Chargé announced in the same note (March 28, '98) the lease of the two ports, and the opening of one of them (Talienwan) to foreign commerce.

"See note on page 1 of Instruction to Germany."

Of the despatches referred to in the memorandum, copies of Nos. 347, 318 and 25 are in the Rockhill papers. The substance of the Chargé's communication of March 28 is retailed in a despatch from Sherman to Denby, March 31. *For. Rel.*, 1898, 182.

## Rockhill Draft

D of S
Wash. Sept. 1899
The Sec. of State to Mr Choate
London.

Sir:

The Government of H.B.M. [having] has [repeatedly] declared that its policy and its very traditions precluded it from using any privileges which might be granted it in China as a weapon for excluding commercial rivals [from China], and that freedom of trade for Great Britain in that Empire meant freedom of trade for all the world alike. While [recognizing] conceding by [convention] formal agreements first with Germany then with Russia the possession of spheres of influence or interest in China in which they are to enjoy special rights and privileges, most especially in respect [to] of railroads and mining enterprises, H.B.M. Government has *therefore* sought to maintain at the same time what

## Final Draft

Department of State,
Washington, September 6, 1899.

Sir:

The Government of Her Britannic Majesty has declared that its policy and its very traditions precluded it from using any privileges which might be granted it in China as a weapon for excluding commercial rivals, and that freedom of trade for Great Britain in that Empire meant freedom of trade for all the world alike. While conceding by formal agreements, first with Germany and then with Russia, the possession of "spheres of influence or interest" in China in which they are to enjoy special rights and privileges, more especially in respect of railroads and mining enterprises, Her Britannic Majesty's Government has therefore sought to maintain at the same time what is called the "open-door" policy, to insure to

494

is called the "open door" policy, [or] to insure to the commerce of the world in China equality of treatment within said spheres for their commerce and navigation. This latter policy is *alike* urgently demanded [not only] by the British mercantile [classes] communities [but also] *and* by those of the United States, as it is held by them to be the only one which will improve existing conditions, enable them [can] to maintain their positions in the markets of China and [allow them to extend their] and extend their [oppor] operations in the future. While the Government of the United States [is in] will in no way commit[ted] itself to a recognition of exclusive rights [or control] of any power within or control over [the limits of the Chinese Empire and] any portion of the Chinese Empire under such agreements as have within the last year been made, it cannot conceal its apprehension that under existing conditions there is a possibility, even a probability, of complications [soon] arising between the Treaty Powers [in China] which may imperil the rights insured to the United States under our treaties with China. This Government

the commerce of the world in China equality of treatment within said "spheres" for commerce and navigation. This latter policy is alike urgently demanded by the British mercantile communities and by those of the United States, as it is justly held by them to be the only one which will improve existing conditions, enable them to maintain their positions in the markets of China, and extend their operations in the future. While the Government of the United States will in no way commit itself to a recognition of exclusive rights of any power within or control over any portion of the Chinese Empire under such agreements as have within the last year been made, it can not conceal its apprehension that under existing conditions there is a possibility, even a probability, of complications arising between the treaty powers which may imperil the rights insured to the United States under our treaties with China.

This Government is animated

is Animated by a sincere desire that the interests of our citizens may not be prejudiced through [any] exclusive treatment by any of the controlling Powers within their so-called "spheres of interest", [and in the hope that] in China, and hope[ing] also to [receive] *retain* there an open market for the [merchandise] *commerce* of the world, [in China and to] remove dangerous sources of international irritation *and* [to] *hasten thereby united or concerted action of the Powers at Peking in favor of the administrative reforms so urgently needed for strengthening the Imperial Government* [by which alone] *and maintaining the integrity of China in which the whole western world is alike concerned, can be brought about.* [and] It believes[ing] that such a result may be greatly assisted by a declaration [by the of intentions] by the various Powers claiming "spheres of interest" in China of their intentions as regards [for] treatment of foreign trade therein. [this] The present moment seems a particularly opportune one for [calling submitting to] *informing* H.B.M. Government *of* the sincere desire of

by a sincere desire that the interests of our citizens may not be prejudiced through exclusive treatment by any of the controlling powers within their so-called "spheres of interest" in China, and hopes also to retain there an open market for the commerce of the world, remove dangerous sources of international irritation, and hasten thereby united or concerted action of the powers at Pekin in favor of the administrative reforms so urgently needed for strengthening the Imperial Government and maintaining the integrity of China in which the whole western world is alike concerned. It believes that such a result may be greatly assisted by a declaration by the various powers claiming "spheres of interest" in China of their intentions as regards treatment of foreign trade therein. The present moment seems a particularly opportune one for informing Her Britannic Majesty's Government of the desire of the United States to see it make a formal declaration and to lend its support in obtaining similar declarations from the various powers claiming "spheres of influence" in China, to the effect that each in the United States to see it [give its support lend its support to obtaining bind itself] *make* [give] *a formal* [assur] *declaration* and to lend its its support in obtaining similar [assu formal assurances] *declarations* from the various Powers claiming "spheres of influence" in China to the effect that each in its respective spheres of interest or influence

1. Will in no way interfere with any treaty port or any vested [rights] interest within any so-called "sphere of interest" or leased territory it may have in China.

2. That the Chinese treaty tariff of the time being shall apply to all merchandise landed or shipped to all such ports as are within said "sphere of interest" (unless they be "free ports"), no matter to which nationality it may belong, and that duties so leviable shall be collected by the Chinese Government.

3. That it will levy no higher harbor dues on vessels of another nationality frequenting any port in such "sphere" than shall be levied on vessels of its own nationality, and no higher railroad charges over lines built, controlled or operated within its "sphere" on mer-

its respective spheres of interest or influence—

First. Will in no wise interfere with any treaty port or any vested interest within any so-called "sphere of interest" or leased territory it may have in China.

Second. That the Chinese treaty tariff of the time being shall apply to all merchandise landed or shipped to all such ports as are within said "sphere of interest" (unless they be "free ports"), no matter to what nationality it may belong, and that duties so leviable shall be collected by the Chinese Government.

Third. That it will levy no higher harbor dues on vessels of another nationality frequenting any port in such "sphere" than shall be levied on vessels of its own nationality, and no higher railroad charges over lines built, controlled, or operated within its "sphere" on chandise belonging to citizens or subjects of other nationalities transported through such "sphere" than shall be levied on similar merchandise belonging to its own nationals transported over equal distances.

The recent ukase of His Majesty the Emperor of Russia declaring the port of Ta-lien-wan open to the [commerce] merchant ships of [the world] all nations during the whole of the lease under which it is *to be* held by Russia, removing as it does all uncertainty as to the liberal and conciliatory policy of that Power together with the assurances given this Government by Russia, justifies the expectation [H.M. Russia]—will cooperate in such an understanding as is here proposed, and our Ambassador at the Court of St. Petersburg has been instructed accordingly to submit the proposition above detailed to H.I.M. and ask their early consideration. Copy of my instructions to Mr Tower is herewith enclosed for your *confidential* information.

The action of Germany in declaring the port of Kiao-chao [is] a "free port" and the aid [to] the Imperial Government has given

merchandise belonging to citizens or subjects of other nationalities transported through such "sphere" than shall be levied on similar merchandise belonging to its own nationals transported over equal distances.

The recent ukase of His Majesty the Emperor of Russia, declaring the port of Ta-lien-wan open to the merchant ships of all nations during the whole of the lease under which it is to be held by Russia, removing as it does all uncertainty as to the liberal and conciliatory policy of that power, together with the assurances given this Government by Russia, justifies the expectation that His Majesty will cooperate in such an understanding as is here proposed, and our ambassador at the court of St. Petersburg has been instructed accordingly to submit the propositions above detailed to His Imperial Majesty, and ask their early consideration. Copy of my instruction to Mr. Tower is herewith inclosed for your confidential information.

The action of Germany in declaring the port of Kiaochao a "free port," and the aid the Imperial Government has given

[the] China in the establish-
[ment] there of a Chinese Customs-house [indic] coupled with
the *oral* assurances [given] *conveyed* the United States by Germany that our interests within its
"sphere" would in no wise be affected by its occupation of this portion of the Province of Shan-tung,
tend to show that little opposition
[is to] may be anticipated from
that Power to the desired declaration—

The interests of Japan, the next
most interested Power in the trade
of China, will be so clearly served
by the proposed arrangement, and
the declarations of its statesmen
within the last year are so entirely
in line with the views [entertained
by this Government] here expressed, that its hearty co-operation
is confidently counted on.

[Another argument in favor of
the policy here outlined may be
found in the]

You will at as early a date as
practicable submit the above [sug-
gestions] considerations to H.B.M.
Principal Secretary of State for
Foreign Affairs and request their
immediate consideration.

I enclose herewith a copy of the
instructions sent to our Ambassa-

China in the establishment there
of a Chinese custom-house, coupled with the oral assurance conveyed the United States by Germany that our interests within its
"sphere" would in no wise be affected by its occupation of this portion of the province of Shantung, tend to show that little opposition may be anticipated from
that power to the desired declaration.

The interests of Japan, the next
most interested power in the trade
of China, will be so clearly served
by the proposed arrangement, and
the declaration of its statesmen
within the last year are so entirely
in line with the views here expressed, that its hearty cooperation
is confidently counted on.

You will, at as early date as
practicable, submit the considerations to Her Britannic Majesty's
principal secretary of state for foreign affairs and request their immediate consideration.

I inclose herewith a copy of the
instruction sent to our ambassador

dor at Berlin bearing on the above subject.—

I am, etc.,

Rockhill papers. The above is written entirely in Rockhill's handwriting including revisions. Brackets denote deletions, italics insertions.

at Berlin bearing on the above subject.

I have the honor to be, etc.,

JOHN HAY

*For. Rel.* 1899, 131-133.

# THE JULY THIRD CIRCULAR

Department of State,
Washington, July 3, 1900.

In this critical posture of affairs in China it is deemed appropriate to define the attitude of the United States as far as present circumstances permit this to be done. We adhere to the policy initiated by us in 1857, of peace with the Chinese nation, of furtherance of lawful commerce, and of protection of lives and property of our citizens by all means guaranteed under extraterritorial treaty rights and by the law of nations. If wrong be done to our citizens we propose to hold the responsible authors to the uttermost accountability. We regard the condition at Pekin as one of virtual anarchy, whereby power and responsibility are practically devolved upon the local provincial authorities. So long as they are not in overt collusion with rebellion and use their power to protect foreign life and property we regard them as representing the Chinese people, with whom we seek to remain in peace and friendship. The purpose of the President is, as it has been heretofore, to act concurrently with the other powers, first, in opening up communication with Pekin and rescuing the American officials, missionaries, and other Americans who are in danger; secondly, in affording all possible protection everywhere in China to American life and property; thirdly, in guarding and protecting all legitimate American interests; and fourthly, in aiding to prevent a spread of the disorders to the other provinces of the Empire and a recurrence of such disasters. It is, of course, too early to forecast the means of attaining this last result; but the policy of the Government of the United States is to seek a solution which may bring about permanent safety and peace to China, preserve Chinese territorial and administrative entity, protect all rights guaranteed to friendly powers by treaty and international law, and safeguard for the world the principle of equal and impartial trade with all parts of the Chinese Empire.

You will communicate the purport of this instruction to the minister for foreign affairs.

HAY.

*For. Rel.* 1900, 299.

# BIBLIOGRAPHY

## I. MANUSCRIPT SOURCES: OFFICIAL AND PRIVATE PAPERS

### OFFICIAL

Department of State Archives, 1898-1906

### PRIVATE

Hippisley, Alfred E.: papers supplied the author by Mr. Hippisley

Rockhill, W. W.: private collection

Bryan, William Jennings: Collection in Division of Manuscripts, Library of Congress

Knox, Philander C.: Collection in Division of Manuscripts, Library of Congress

Lansing, Robert: Collection in Division of Manuscripts, Library of Congress

McKinley, William: Collection in Division of Manuscripts, Library of Congress

Roosevelt, Theodore: Collection in Division of Manuscripts, Library of Congress

Root, Elihu: Collection in Division of Manuscripts, Library of Congress

## II. PRINTED SOURCES: OFFICIAL DOCUMENTS, ETC.

a. THE UNITED STATES

Department of State:

*Papers Relating to the Foreign Relations of the United States,* 1896-1922.

*Commercial Relations of the United States with Foreign Countries,* 1898-1902.

*Press Releases,* 1929-1938.

*The London Naval Treaty, 1930.* Conference Series No. 2, Washington, 1930.

*Treaty for the Renunciation of War, Text of the Treaty, Notes Exchanged, Instruments of Ratification and of Adherence and other Papers,* 1930.

Department of Commerce:

*American Direct Investments in Foreign Countries,* Trade Information Bulletin No. 731, Washington, 1930.

*A New Estimate of American Investments Abroad,* Washington, 1931.

Department of Labor:

*Immigration Rules and Regulations,* Washington, 1937.

Commissioner General of Immigration:

*Annual Report,* Washington, 1908.

Senate Documents:

56th Cong., 2nd sess., No. 148. *Papers Relating to the Treaty with Spain,* Washington, 1901.

59th Cong., 2nd sess., No. 147. *Japanese in the City of San Francisco, California,* Washington, 1906.

66th Cong., 1st sess., No. 106. *Treaty of Peace with Germany, Hearings,* Washington, 1919.

67th Cong., 2nd sess., No. 126. *Conference on the Limitation of Armaments,* Washington, 1922.

72nd Cong., 1st sess., No. 55. *Conditions in Manchuria,* Washington, 1932.

*The Congressional Record:*

55th Cong., 3rd sess.

59th Cong., 2nd sess.

66th Cong., 3rd sess.

67th Cong., 1st sess.

74th Cong., 1st sess.

Hearings Before the Subcommittee on Senate Bill 4301, December

15, 1920-January 11, 1921. 66th Cong., 3rd sess., Washington, 1921.

b. GREAT BRITAIN

Gooch, G. P., and Temperley, H. W. V. (eds.), *British Documents on the Origins of the World War, 1898-1914,* London, 1926-1938.

British Parliamentary Papers, 1914-1916, XLV, *Correspondence Respecting Military Operations against German Possessions in the Western Pacific,* London, 1915.

Parliamentary Debates, *House of Commons,* Fifth Series, 1915; Vol. 70; 1932, Vols. 262, 263.

c. GERMANY

*Die Grosse Politik der Europäischen Kabinette, 1871-1914,* Berlin, 1921-1927.

d. FRANCE

*Documents Diplomatiques Français, 1871-1914,* 3 series, Paris, 1929-1937.

e. RUSSIA

*Mezhdunarodnye Otnosheniia v epoku imperializma,* Series III, Vols. 1-4, 6-8, Moscow, 1931-1935.

*Krasnyi Arkhiv,* Vols. 1-85, Moscow, 1922-1937.

f. JAPAN

Consulate General, San Francisco, *Documented History of Law Cases Affecting Japan in the United States,* 2 vols., San Francisco, 1925.

g. LEAGUE OF NATIONS

*Report of the Commission of Enquiry* (with annexes). Document C. 663. M. 320, 1932, VII, Geneva, 1932.

h. MISCELLANEOUS

Malloy, William M. (ed.), *Treaties, Conventions, International Acts, Protocols and Agreements between the United States and Other Powers,* 2 vols., Washington, 1910.

MacMurray, J. V. A. (ed.), *Treaties and Agreements with and Concerning China,* 2 vols., New York, 1921.

Carnegie Endowment for International Peace, Division of International Law, *The Sino-Japanese Negotiations of 1915*, Washington, 1921.

—— *The Consortium*, Washington, 1921.

—— *Treaties and Agreements with and Concerning, China 1919-1929*, Washington, 1929.

Royal Institute of International Affairs (J. W. Wheeler-Bennett, ed.), *Documents on International Affairs*, London, 1930.

Kautsky, Karl (ed.), *Outbreak of the World War* (German documents collected by Karl Kautsky), New York, 1924.

Varneck, E., and Fisher, H. H., *The Testimony of Kolchak*, Stanford University, 1935.

## III. LETTERS, DIARIES, MEMOIRS, ADDRESSES, ETC.

Balfour, A. J.: *Retrospect: An Unfinished Autobiography*, Boston, 1930.

Gérard, A.: *Ma Mission au Japon, 1907-1914*, Paris, 1919.

Graves, William S.: *America's Siberian Adventures*, New York, 1931.

Gwynn, Stephen: *The Letters and Friendships of Sir Cecil Spring-Rice*, 2 vols., Boston, 1929.

Hoover, Irwin: *Forty-two Years in the White House*, Boston, 1934.

Ishii, Kikujiro: *Diplomatic Commentaries* (translated and edited by W. R. Langdon), Baltimore, 1936.

Ito, Seitoku (ed.): *Kato Takaaki*, 2 vols, Tokyo, 1929.

Lansing, Robert: *War Memoirs*, Indianapolis, 1935.

Lloyd George, David: *War Memoirs, 1914-1917*, 3 vols., Boston, 1933-1934.

Lodge, Henry C. (ed.): *Selections from the Correspondence of Theodore Roosevelt and Henry Cabot Lodge, 1884-1918*, 2 vols., New York, 1925.

Miller, David Hunter: *My Diary at the Conference of Paris*, 21 vols. (privately printed), New York, 1924.

Nicolson, Harold: *Peacemaking, 1919*, Boston, 1933.

Pooley, A. M. (ed.): *The Secret Memoirs of Count Tadasu Hayashi*, New York, 1915.

Reinsch, Paul S.: *An American Diplomat in China*, New York, 1922.

Roosevelt, Theodore: *Autobiography*, New York, 1913.

Seymour, Charles (ed.): *The Intimate Papers of Colonel House*, 4 vols., Boston, 1926 and 1928.

Shotwell, James T.: *At the Peace Conference*, New York, 1937.

Siebert, B. von (ed.): *Graf Beckendorff's diplomatischer Schriftwechsel*, 3 vols., Berlin, 1928.

Stimson, Henry L.: *The Far Eastern Crisis: Recollections and Observations*, New York, 1936.

—— *The Pact of Paris*, Department of State Publication, Washington, 1932.

Vaughan, Miles: *Covering the Far East*, New York, 1936.

## IV. BIOGRAPHIES, HISTORIES, SPECIAL STUDIES, ARTICLES

Abend, Hallett, and Billingham, A. J.: *Can China Survive?*, New York, 1936.

Adachi, Kinnosuki: *Manchuria, a Survey*, New York, 1925.

Bailey, Thomas A.: *Theodore Roosevelt and the Japanese-American Crises*, Stanford, 1934.

—— "California, Japan and the Alien Land Legislation of 1913," *Pacific Historical Review*, I, March, 1932, 36-59.

—— "Japan's Protest against the Annexation of Hawaii," *Journal of Modern History*, III, 1931, 46-61.

Baker, Ray S.: *Woodrow Wilson and World Settlement*, 3 vols., Garden City, 1922.

Barnes, Joseph (and others): *Empire in the East*, New York, 1934.

Beard, Charles A.: *The Idea of National Interest*, New York, 1934.

—— *The Open Door at Home*, New York, 1934.

Bemis, Samuel F.: *A Diplomatic History of the United States*, New York, 1936.

Bemis, Samuel F. (ed.): *The American Secretaries of State and Their Diplomacy*, Vols. IX and X, New York, 1927-1929.

Bienstock, Gregory: *The Struggle for the Pacific*, London, 1937.

Blakeslee, George H.: "The Pacific Area," *World Peace Foundation Pamphlets*, XII, Boston, 1929.

Bowers, Claude G.: *Beveridge and the Progressive Era*, Boston, 1932.

Brebner, J. B.: "Canada, the Anglo-Japanese Alliance and the Washington Conference," *Political Science Quarterly*, L, March, 1935, 45-59.

Bryn-Jones, David: *Frank B. Kellogg*, New York, 1937.

Buell, Raymond L.: *The Washington Conference*, New York, 1922.

—— "Problems of the Pacific," *World Peace Foundation Pamphlets*, VIII, Boston, 1925.

—— "Japanese Immigration," *World Peace Foundation Pamphlets*, VII, Boston, 1924.

Bunyan, James: *Intervention, Civil War and Communism in Russia, April to December, 1918*, Baltimore, 1936.

Bywater, Hector C.: *Sea Power in the Pacific*, New York, 1921.

—— *The Great Pacific War*, New York, 1925.

Cameron, Meribeth E.: "American Recognition Policy toward the Republic of China, 1912-1913," *Pacific Historical Reveiw*, II, 1933, 214-230.

Chamberlin, W. H.: *Japan over Asia*, New York, 1937.

Chang, Chung-Fu: *The Anglo-Japanese Alliance*, Baltimore, 1931.

Clark, Grover: *The Great Wall Crumbles*, New York, 1935.

Clyde, R. H.: "The Open Door Policy of John Hay," *The Historical Outlook*, XXII, May, 1931, 210-214.

—— *International Rivalries in Manchuria*, Columbus, 1926.

—— "Railway Politics and the Open Door in China, 1916-1917," *American Journal of International Law*, XXV, 1931, 642-657.

—— *A History of the Modern and Contemporary Far East*, New York, 1937.

—— "The Manchurian Freight-Rate Controversy, 1914-1916," *Far Eastern Review*, XXVI, 1930, 410-412, 480-483.

Cocks, F. Seymour: *The Secret Treaties* (2nd ed.), London, 1918.

Cook, A. E., and Hagerty, J. J.: *Immigration Laws of the United States*, Chicago, 1929.

Coolidge, Mary R.: *Chinese Immigration*, New York, 1909.

Coons, A. G.: *The Foreign Public Debt of China*, Philadelphia, 1930.

Cooper, Russell M.: *American Consultation in World Affairs*, New York, 1934.

Cortissoz, Royal: *The Life of Whitelaw Reid*, 2 vols., London, 1921.

Croly, Herbert: *Willard Straight*, New York, 1924.

Curti, Merle E.: "Bryan and World Peace," *Smith College Studies in History*, XVI, April-July, 1931.

Das, Taraknath: *Foreign Policy in the Far East*, New York, 1936.

Deane, Frederick: "The Chinese Eastern Railway," *Foreign Affairs*, III, September, 1924, 147-152.

Denlinger, S., and Gary, Chas. B.: *War in the Pacific*, New York, 1936.

Dennett, Tyler: *Americans in Eastern Asia*, New York, 1922.

—— *Roosevelt and the Russo-Japanese War*, New York, 1925.

—— *John Hay*, New York, 1933.

—— "The Open Door Policy as Intervention," *American Academy of Political and Social Science Annals*, CLXVIII, 1933, 78-83.

—— "Mahan's 'The Problem of Asia,'" *Foreign Affairs*, XIII, 1935, 464-473.

—— "Seward's Far Eastern Policy," *American Historical Review*, XXVIII, 1932, 45-62.

Dennis, A. L. P.: *Adventures in American Diplomacy, 1896-1906*, New York, 1928.

—— *The Anglo-Japanese Alliance*, University of California Publications, I, Berkeley, 1923.

De Siebert, B., and Schreiner, G. A.: *Entente Diplomacy and the World, 1904-1914*, London, 1921.

Dewey, A. Gordon: *The Dominions and Diplomacy*, 2 vols., New York, 1929.

Djang, Feng Djen: *The Diplomatic Relations between China and Germany since 1898*, Shanghai, 1936.

Dugdale, Blanche E. C.: *Arthur James Balfour*, 2 vols., New York, 1936.

Dulles, F. R.: *America in the Pacific*, Boston, 1932.

—— *Forty Years of American-Japanese Relations*, New York, 1937.

Dunning, W. A.: *The British Empire and the United States*, New York, 1914.

Egerton, H. E.: *British Colonial Policy in the Twentieth Century*, London, 1922.

Etherton, Percy T.: *The Crisis in China*, Boston, 1927.

Falk, Edwin A.: *Togo and the Rise of Japanese Sea Power*, New York, 1936.

Farley, Miriam S.: "America's Stake in the Far East, I: Trade," *Far Eastern Survey*, V, July 29, 1936, 161-170.

—— "America's Stake in the Far East," American Council, Institute of Pacific Relations Pamphlet, New York, 1936.

Fay, Sidney B.: *The Origins of the World War*, 2 vols., New York, 1928.

Field, F. V.: *American Participation in the China Consortiums*, Chicago, 1931.

—— (ed.): *Economic Handbook of the Pacific Area*, Garden City, 1934.

—— "America's Stake in the Far East, III: The Cost," *Far Eastern Survey*, V, August 26, 1936, 189-193.

Finch, George A.: "American Diplomacy and the Financing of China," *American Journal of International Law*, XVI, 1922, 25-42.

Fischer, Louis: *The Soviets in World Affairs*, 2 vols., London, 1930.

Fleming, D. F.: *The United States and the League of Nations, 1918-1920*, New York, 1932.

Franke, Otto: *Die Grossmächte in Ostasien von 1894 bis 1914*, Hamburg, 1923.

Frear, Mary R.: "Did President Wilson Contradict Himself on the Secret Treaties?", *Current History*, XXX, 1929, 435-443.

Garis, Roy I.: *Immigration Restriction*, New York, 1927.

Garvin, James L.: *The Life of Joseph Chamberlain*, 3 vols., New York, 1932-1934.

Gillett, F. H.: *George Frisbie Hoar*, Boston, 1934.

Godshall, W. L.: *The International Aspects of the Shantung Question*, Philadelphia, 1923.

Greenberg, A. A.: *Public Opinion and the Acquisition of the Philippine Islands*, unpublished.

Gulick, Sidney L.: *Toward Understanding Japan*, New York, 1935.

Hall, Henry L.: *Australia and England*, London, 1934.

Hall, Luella T.: "The Abortive German-American-Chinese Entente of 1907-1908," *Journal of Modern History*, I, 1929, 219-235.

Hammond, John Hays: "American Commercial Interests in the Far East," *American Academy of Political and Social Science Annals*, XXVI, 1905, 83-88.

Harrington, F. H.: "The Anti-Imperialistic Movement in the United States, 1898-1900," *Mississippi Valley Historical Review*, XXII, 1935, 211-230.

Hayashi, Kiroku: "Dr. Hayashi Defends Japan against Lansing's 'War Memoirs,'" *Contemporary Opinions* (Tokyo), October 15 and 22, 1936.

Holt, W. Stull: *Treaties Defeated by the Senate*, Baltimore, 1933.

Hornbeck, Stanley K.: *Contemporary Politics in the Far East*, New York, 1916.

—— "China Today: Political," *World Peace Foundation Pamphlets*, X, Boston, 1927.

—— "China and American Foreign Policy," *American Academy of Political and Social Science Annals*, CXXXVIII, 1928, 31.

—— "American Policy and the Chinese-Russian Dispute," *Chinese Social and Political Science Review*, XIV, 1930, 41-60.

—— *Principles of American Policy in Relation to the Far East*. Department of State, Washington, 1934.

Howland, C. P. (ed.): *Survey of American Foreign Relations*, New Haven, 1930.

Hsu, Shuhsi: *China and Her Political Entity*, London, 1926.

—— *The Manchurian Question*, Peking, 1929.

Hubbard, G. E.: *Eastern Industrialization and Its Effect on the West, with Special Reference to Great Britain and Japan*, London, 1936.

Ichihashi, Yamato: *The Washington Conference and After*, Stanford, 1928.

—— *Japanese in the United States*, Stanford, 1932.

Ishimaru, Tota: *Japan Must Fight Britain*, New York, 1936.

Jessup, Philip C.: *Elihu Root*, 2 vols., New York, 1938.

Joseph, Philip: *Foreign Diplomacy in China*, London, 1928.

Kennan, George: *E. H. Harriman*, 2 vols., Boston, 1922.

Kent, P. H. B.: *The Twentieth Century in the Far East*, London, 1937.

Kingman, H. L.: *Effects of Chinese Nationalism upon Manchurian Railway Developments, 1925-1931*, Berkeley, 1932.

Kirk, Grayson: *Philippine Independence*, New York, 1936.

Korostovetz, Ivan I.: *Rossia na Dalnem Vostoke*, Berlin, 1926.

Kunz-Lack, Ilse: *Die Deutsche-Amerikanischen Beziehungen, 1890-1914*, Stuttgart, 1935.

LaFargue, T. E.: *China and the World War*, Stanford, 1937.

Langer, W. H.: *The Diplomacy of Imperialism, 1890-1902*, 2 vols., New York, 1935.

Latourette, K. S.: *A History of Christian Missions in China*, New York, 1932.

—— "China, the United States and the War," *League of Nations Pamphlets*, II, 1919, 168-226.

Lattimore, Owen: *Manchuria: Cradle of Conflict*, New York, 1935.

Lockwood, W. W.: "America's Stake in the Far East, II: Investments," *Far Eastern Survey*, V, 1936, 175-185.

Mahan, A. T.: *The Influence of Sea Power Upon History* (14th ed.), Boston, 1898.

Mahan, A. T.: *The Influence of Sea Power upon the French Revolution and Empire, 1793-1812*, 2 vols., Boston, 1892.

—— *The Interest of America in Sea Power, Present and Future*, Boston, 1897.

—— *Lessons of the War with Spain*, Boston, 1899.

—— *The Problem of Asia*, Boston, 1900.

Malcolm, George A.: *The Commonwealth of the Philippines*, New York, 1936.

Mar, Timothy T. G.: *Anglo-Chinese Diplomacy, 1895-1911*, unpublished.

McCordock, R. S.: *British Far Eastern Policy, 1894-1900*, New York, 1931.

Miller, David Hunter: *The Drafting of the Covenant*, 2 vols., New York, 1928.

—— *My Diary at the Conference of Paris*, 21 vols., privately printed, New York, 1924.

Millis, Walter: *The Martial Spirit*, New York, 1931.

—— *The Future of Sea Power in the Pacific*, New York, Foreign Policy Association, 1935.

Minrath, P.: *Das Englisch-japanische Bündnis von 1902*, Stuttgart, 1933.

Morley, Felix: *The Society of Nations*, Washington, 1932.

Morse, H. B., and McNair, H. F.: *Far Eastern International Relations*, Boston, 1931.

Mowat, R. B.: *The Diplomatic Relations of Great Britain and the United States*, London, 1925.

Muto, Chozo: *A Short History of Anglo-Japanese Relations*, Tokyo, 1936.

National Foreign Trade Council: *American Trade Prospects in the Orient*, New York, 1935.

Nevins, Allan, *Henry White*, New York, 1930.

Norton, H. K.: *China and the Powers*, New York, 1927.

Notter, H.: *The Origins of the Foreign Policy of Woodrow Wilson*, Baltimore, 1937.

Olcott, C. S.: *The Life of William McKinley*, 2 vols., Boston, 1916.

Palmer, Frederick: *Bliss, Peacemaker*, New York, 1934.

Parlett, Sir Harold: *A Brief Account of Diplomatic Events in Manchuria*, London, 1929.

Paul, Rodman W.: *The Abrogation of the Gentlemen's Agreement*, Cambridge, 1936.

Peffer, Nathaniel: *Must We Fight in Asia*, New York, 1935.

Pollard, R. T.: *China's Foreign Relations, 1917-1931*, New York, 1933.

Pooley, A. M.: *Japan's Foreign Policies*, New York, 1920.

Pratt, Julius W.: "The 'Large Policy' of 1898," *Mississippi Valley Historical Review*, XIX, 1932, 219-242.

—— "American Business and the Spanish-American War," *Hispanic American Historical Review*, XIV, 1934, 162-201.

—— *Expansionists of 1898*, Baltimore, 1936.

Price, Ernest B.: *The Russo-Japanese Treaties of 1907-1916 Concerning Manchuria and Mongolia*, Baltimore, 1933.

Price, Willard: *Pacific Adventure*, New York, 1936.

—— *Children of the Rising Sun*, New York, 1938.

Pringle, Henry F.: *Theodore Roosevelt*, New York, 1931.

—— *William Howard Taft* (to be published).

Puleston, W. D.: *Captain Alfred Thayer Mahan* (to be published).

Quigley, H. S.: *Chinese Politics and Foreign Powers*, New York, Carnegie Endowment for International Peace, 1927.

Reid, John G.: *The Manchu Abdication and the Powers*, Berkeley, 1935.

Remer, C. F.: *Foreign Investments in China*, New York, 1933.

—— *A Study of Chinese Boycotts*, Baltimore, 1933.

—— *The Foreign Trade of China*, Shanghai, 1926.

Reuter, Bertha A.: *Anglo-American Relations during the Spanish-American War*, New York, 1924.

Rippy, J. Fred: "The European Powers and the Spanish American War," *James Sprunt Historical Studies*, XIX, 1927, 22-52.

Roemer, Hans: "Der Stand der Philippinenfrage," *Munich Zeitschrift für Geopolitik*, V, 1934, 298-311.

Romanov, B. A.: *Rossiia v Manchzhuriia*, Leningrad, 1928.

Schuman, F. L.: *American Policy Toward Soviet Russia since 1917*, New York, 1928.

Schurmann, J. G.: *Philippine Affairs, a Retrospect and Outlook*, New York, 1902.

Scroggs, W. O. (and others): *The United States in World Affairs*, 1931-1937, New York, Council on Foreign Relations, 1932-1938.

Shiman, Russell G.: *China and the Breakdown of American Isolation*, unpublished.

Shippee, L. B.: "Germany and the Spanish-American War," *American Historical Review*, XXX, 1925, 754-777.

Sinobu, Z.: *Taisho Gaiko Jugonen-shi* (A History of Foreign Relations During the Taisho Era, 1912-1926), Tokyo, 1927.

Snow, Edgar: *Red Star over China*, New York, 1938.

Sokolsky, George E.: *The Tinder Box of Asia*, Garden City, 1932.

Spinks, C. N.: "Japan's Entrance into the World War," *Pacific Historical Review*, V, 1936, 297-311.

—— *A History of the Anglo-Japanese Alliance, 1902-1922*, Stanford University Doctoral Dissertation, unpublished.

Staley, Eugene: *War Losses to a Neutral*, New York, League of Nations Association, 1937.

Steiger, G. N.: *China and the Occident*, New Haven, 1927.

—— *A History of the Far East*, New York, 1936.

Stolberg-Wernigerode, Otto, Graf Zu: *Deutschland und die Vereinigten Staaten im Zeitalter Bismarck's*, Berlin, 1933.

Stoye, Johannes: *Japan, Gefahr oder Vorbild?*, Leipzig, 1936.

Stuart, Graham H.: *American Diplomatic and Consular Practice*, New York, 1936.

Sullivan, Mark: *The Great Adventure at Washington*, New York, 1922.

T: "Canada and the Far East," *Foreign Affairs*, XIX, 1935, 388-397.

Takeuchi, Tatsuji: *War and Diplomacy in the Japanese Empire*, New York, 1935.

Talbot, Melvin F.: "Navies and National Policy," *Yale Review*, XVII, 1938, 333-347.

Tanin, O., and Yohan E.: *When Japan Goes to War*, New York, 1936.

Taylor, C. C.: *The Life of Admiral Mahan*, London, 1920.

Temperley, H. W. V. (ed.): *A History of the Peace Conference of Paris*, 6 vols., London, 1920-1924.

Toynbee, Arnold J. (ed.): *British Commonwealth Relations*, London, 1934.

—— (and others): *Survey of International Relations, 1927-1937*, London, Royal Institute of International Studies, 1928-1938.

Treat, Payson J.: *Diplomatic Relations between the United States and Japan, 1853-1895*, 2 vols., Stanford, 1932.

—— *The Far East*, New York, 1935.

Trevelyan, G. M.: *Grey of Fallodon*, Boston, 1937.

Tribolet, L. B.: *The International Aspects of Electrical Communications in the Pacific Area*, Baltimore, 1929.

Tupper, E., and McReynolds, G. E.: *Japan in American Public Opinion*, New York, 1937.

Vagts, Alfred: *Deutschland und die Vereinigten Staaten in der Weltpolitik*, 2 vols., New York, 1935.

Van Dyne, Frederick: *A Treatise on the Law of Naturalization of the United States*, Washington, 1907.

Ware, Edith E.: *Business and Politics in the Far East*, New Haven, 1932.

Whyte, Sir Frederick: *China and Foreign Powers*, London, 1928.

Williams, E. T.: *China Yesterday and Today*, New York, 1923.

—— *Tibet and Her Neighbors*, Berkeley, 1937.

Willoughby, W. W.: *Foreign Rights and Interests in China*, 2 vols., Baltimore, 1927.

Willoughby, W. W.: *China at the Conference*, Baltimore, 1922.

—— *The Sino-Japanese Controversy and the League of Nations*, Baltimore, 1935.

Yakhontoff, Victor A.: *Russia and the Soviet Union in the Far East*, New York, 1931.

—— *Eyes on Japan*, New York, 1936.

Yen, En Tsung: *The Open Door Policy*, Boston, 1923.

Young, C. W.: *The International Relations of Manchuria*, Chicago, 1929.

—— *Japan's Special Position in Manchuria*, Baltimore, 1931.

—— *The International Legal Status of the Kwantung Leased Territory*, Baltimore, 1931.

—— *Japanese Jurisdiction in the South Manchuria Railway Areas*, Baltimore, 1931.

Young, E. J.: *Powerful America*, New York, 1936.

## V. NEWSPAPERS AND PERIODICALS

The New York *Times*, August 18, 1914; December 5, 20, 31, 1920; May 3, 1921; February 23, 1921; July 4, 1921; July 1, 1938.

The London *Times*, August 16, 1899; March 5, 1921.

The New York *Commercial*, May 13, 1898.

The Japan *Advertiser*, February 5, 1931.

The *New Republic*, March 29, 1922; December 29, 1937.

# INDEX

Adams, Henry, 3, 28
Aleutian Islands, 312, 317
Alien land laws, of California and
other states, 364 ff., 369
Anglo-German declaration in re: open
door, 1900, 81
Anglo-Japanese Alliance, 37, 88-91,
97, 99, 126-127, 130, 151, 256, 270,
284, 426; negotiated, 1902, 88-91;
renewed 1905, 115-116; renewed
1911, 165-169; application to Indian frontier, 115, 318; application
to World War, 180; American apprehensions of, 275 ff.; plans for revision of, 278 ff.
Anglo-Russian Convention of 1907,
116
Anti-imperialists, 32, 33
Arbitration conventions, Anglo-American, 39, 167-169, 274; Japanese-
American, 128
Australia, 181, 294, 318; demands of,
at Paris Conference, 245

Baker, Ray S., 256-257
Balfour, Arthur James, British Foreign
Secretary and Prime Minister, 18,
21, 111-112, 211, 218, 231, 247,
253, 305-307, 309; on British pol-
icy in the Far East, 98-99, 113-114;
urges U. S. participation in con-
sortium loans, 213; and Four-Power
Treaty, 308-310; and Nine-Power
Treaty, 308-309, 321-324
Beresford, Lord Charles, 48, 49
Beveridge, Senator Albert J., 10, 34
Björkö, Treaty of, 110
Boer War, 50, 82, 85
Bolsheviks, 226-228, 233, 236, 237,
239, 320
Borah, Senator William E., 282; pro-

poses disarmament conference, 283;
Stimson's letter to, 433 ff.
Boxer Rebellion, 61, 80, 386; U. S.
policy during, 78-80; international
co-operation during, 86; indemnity,
124, 160, 201, 220, 337, 383;
protocol, 461
Boycotts, Chinese, 122, 124, 257, 262,
338, 405, 409, 426
Briand, Aristide, French Foreign Min-
ister and Premier, 420
Bryan, William Jennings, 33, 178, 197,
210, 364; and Twenty-One De-
mands, 192, 194, 207, 213; alien
land laws, 366; Peace Commission
Treaty, 274, 279, 312-314
Bryce, Viscount James, 126, 167
Brussels Conference of 1937, 459-462
Bülow, Prince Bernhard von, German
Chancellor, 20, 96, 107, 108, 109

California, 247, 346, 348, 355; anti-
Japanese legislation, 334-335, 347,
360; Chinese immigrants in, 333,
335; alien land laws, 357, 364-367
Cambon, Jules, French Ambassador, 27
Canada, and Anglo-Japanese Alliance,
126, 127, 286 ff.
Canton, 199, 381, 384, 386
Caribbean Sea, 3, 4, 10, 34, 85, 87,
146
Carnegie, Andrew, and arbitration
treaties, 167-169
Cassini, Count, Russian Ambassador,
60, 97
Cecil, Lord Robert, 231, 247, 248, 251
Chamberlain, Joseph, 18, 19, 37, 54;
on the open door, 43-45; advocates
Anglo-American Alliance, 48, 51
Chang, Hsueh-liang, Manchurian ruler,

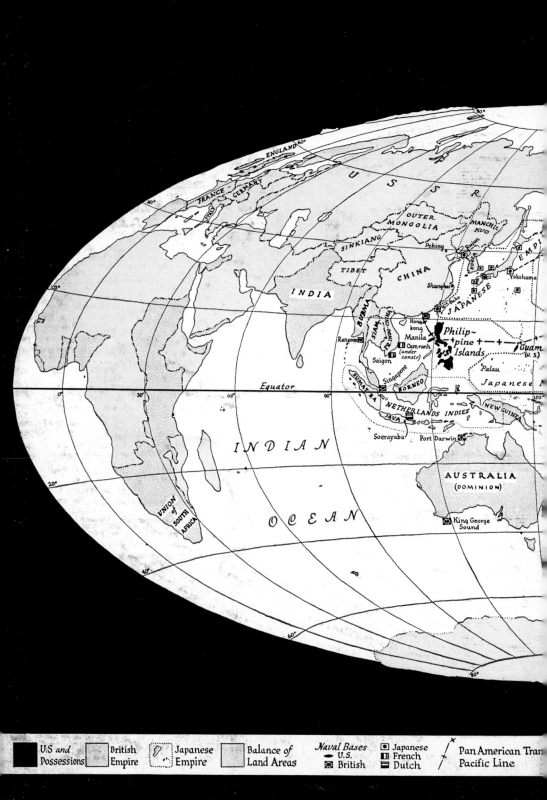

ENGLAND
FRANCE
ITALY
GERMANY
U. S. S. R.
OUTER MONGOLIA
MANCHU-KUO
SINKIANG
TIBET
CHINA
Peking
Peiping
KOREA
JAPANESE EMPIRE
Yokohama
Shanghai
INDIA
BURMA
SIAM
FRENCH-INDO-CHINA
Hong kong
Manila
Kobe
Philip~pine Islands
Guam (U.S.)
Rangoon
Cam-ranh (under constr)
Saigon
Palau
Singapore
BORNEO
Japanese M
SUMATRA
NETHERLANDS INDIES
NEW GUINEA
JAVA
Soerayaba
Port Darwin
Equator
INDIAN OCEAN
AUSTRALIA (DOMINION)
UNION of SOUTH AFRICA
King George Sound

80°
60°
40°
20°
30°
60°
90°
150°
80°
60°

Equator

U.S and Possessions    British Empire    Japanese Empire    Balance of Land Areas    *Naval Bases* U.S. · British ⊠    Japanese · French ⊡ Dutch ⊟    Pan American Trans Pacific Line ✕